QUASI-STELLAR SOURCES

SOURCES

and

GRAVITATIONAL COLLAPSE

Including the Proceedings of the First Texas Symposium on Relativistic Astrophysics . . . Edited by IVOR ROBINSON, ALFRED SCHILD, *and* E. L. SCHUCKING

THE UNIVERSITY OF CHICAGO PRESS
Chicago and London

The Symposium was supported by the Aeronautical Research Laboratory, Wright-Patterson Air Force Base, Air Force Office of Scientific Research, National Aeronautics and Space Administration, National Science Foundation, Office of Naval Research, the Southwest Center for Advanced Studies, and The University of Texas.

Library of Congress Catalog Card Number: 64-24966

THE UNIVERSITY OF CHICAGO PRESS, CHICAGO & LONDON
The University of Toronto Press, Toronto 5, Canada

PREFACE

In June, 1963, Peter Bergmann and the editors of this volume sent out invitations to a symposium which began as follows:

For more than ten years, the nature of the strong extra-galactic radio sources has been one of the most fascinating problems of modern astronomy. For a time, it was believed that such radio sources were due to collision of galaxies. But it has emerged in the course of the last few years that this explanation is untenable in most of the cases. The spectacular nature of strong radio sources becomes clear if one considers the enormous amounts of energy involved. The estimates indicate that more than 10^{60} ergs are consumed in such a process, a weight of more than five hundred thousand suns. This energy requirement has so far ruled out nearly all of the explanations and theories put forward to explain such extraordinary events.

In February, Fred Hoyle and William Fowler suggested that energies which lead to the formation of radio sources could be supplied through the gravitational collapse of a superstar. Such an object, with a mass between one hundred thousand and one hundred million solar masses, would be located in the center of the galaxy. The gravitational collapse of this supersun could supply the necessary energy if it were to shrink down close to the Schwarzschild radius.

Last March, astronomers and radio-astronomers in Australia and California identified two extragalactic radio sources with galaxies of a type never seen before. The source 3C273B seems to be a superstar, and according to Harlan Smith, has a diameter of about a light-week. It is the brightest known object in the universe, about a million million times brighter than the Sun. According to Sandage and Smith, its brightness varies by about 50 per cent.

The intriguing new discoveries and the theory put forward by Hoyle and Fowler open up the discussion of a wealth of exciting questions. Among the problems raised are the following:

a) The astronomers observed some unusual objects connected with radio sources. Are these the debris of a gravitational implosion?

b) By what machinery is gravitational energy converted into radio waves?

c) Does gravitational collapse lead, on our present assumptions, to indefinite contraction and a singularity in space time?

d) If so, how must we change our theoretical assumptions in order to avoid this catastrophe?

These are only some of the questions posed by this interesting new development in astrophysics and general relativity.

It emerges that the many-sided and basic aspects of the question of gravitational collapse make it imperative to bring experts from many fields together for a thorough discussion. After checking with some of the protagonists, we have come to the conclusion that a conference late this year at the Southwest Center for Advanced Studies in Dallas, Texas, might be well timed.

The symposium was held December 16–18, 1963. Some three hundred scientists from many countries attended.

Special thanks are due to Peter Bergmann, our colleague on the organizing committee; Lauriston C. Marshall, who played a decisive role in initiating the symposium; and

Nell deCluit, Jack Robottom, and the staff of the Southwest Center, who were of great help with all the arrangements.

The symposium was sponsored by the Southwest Center for Advanced Studies, The University of Texas, and Yeshiva University, with the support of the Aerospace Research Laboratory (Wright-Patterson Air Force Base), the Air Force Office of Scientific Research, the National Aeronautics and Space Administration, the National Science Foundation, and the Office of Naval Research. We wish to thank these institutions and agencies for making the symposium possible.

This book contains revised versions of all the invited addresses which were delivered at the symposium,* together with two invited papers by Ginzburg, who was unable to come. Most of the authors have revised their addresses rather extensively, incorporating many of the points raised in the discussions as well as subsequent findings. For this reason we have not attempted to reconstruct the discussions as they actually took place. We were, however, supplied with the remarks made by Gratton, Greyber, and Vandekerkhove. There was no time during the symposium for the delivery of contributed papers. A written version of a paper by Terletzky is included. No proofs were sent to the authors; the editors are therefore responsible for any errors that may have been overlooked.

The papers first published in other journals and reprinted here fall into two categories. Some of them are expanded versions of papers delivered at the symposium. The others are included in order to make the book a self-contained exposition on the subject. Reprinted papers are marked with asterisks in the lists of references that appear at the end of each chapter.

We thank the editors of the *Astrophysical Journal, Nature, Physics Today,* and *Reviews of Modern Physics* for permission to reproduce articles from their journals.

* The contribution of Professor John A. Wheeler and his co-workers is being published, in expanded form, as a separate volume, *Gravitation Theory and Gravitational Collapse,* by the University of Chicago Press.

CONTENTS

EDITORS' INTRODUCTION

To listen to Cristoforo Colombo, sitting in a dimly lit favorite tavern with a glass of port, recounting his adventures and describing vistas of far lands never seen before, must have made an exciting, unforgettable evening. To hear the reports of the astronauts who set foot on our Moon and the moons of Mars may be an equally rewarding experience in the future. But one might doubt if this could ever match the strange fascination of an evening with the late Walter Baade from the Mount Wilson and Palomar Observatories. For more than a quarter of a century he had worked with the biggest optical telescopes on Earth. When he told what he had seen and discovered in careful scanning of thousands of plates, the incredible grandeur of the cosmic realm, the galactic and extragalactic world, began to unfold behind numbers, pictures, and astronomical gossip. This man in his dark blue tie and gray suit, wearing brown shoes of enormous size, was absolutely fascinated by his research. Gesticulating, incessantly smoking, with carefully parted thin white hair, white somewhat bushy eyebrows, protruding hawk nose, Baade saw the mysteries of the universe as the greatest of all detective stories in which he was one of the principal sleuths. Sparkling with ideas, confident of the latest numbers and results, modest but full of ferocious criticism, independent and amiable, he told us one evening the story of Cygnus A:

"In 1951, at a seminar talk that Minkowski gave in Pasadena on the theories of radio sources, I got mad. I had just published the theory of colliding galaxies in clusters and identified the Cygnus A source with such a pair in collision. Nobody would believe that there were extragalactic radio sources. Minkowski reviewed all the other theories first; and then, at the end of the seminar, as if he were lifting a hideous bug with a pair of pincers, he presented my theory. He said something like: 'We all know this situation: people make a theory, and then, astonishingly, they find the evidence for it. Baade and Spitzer invented the collision theory; and now Baade finds the evidence for it in Cygnus A.'

"I was angry [said Baade] and I said to him 'I bet a thousand dollars that Cygnus A is a collision.' Minkowski said he could not afford that; he had just bought a house. Then I suggested a case of whiskey, but he would not agree to that either. We finally settled for a bottle, and agreed on the evidence for collision—emission lines of high excitation. I forgot about the thing until, several months later, Minkowski walked into my office and asked 'Which brand?' He showed me the spectrum of Cygnus A. It had neon-five in emission, and thirty-seven-twenty-seven, and many other emission lines. I said to Minkowski: 'I would like a bottle of Hudson Bay's Best Procurable,' that is the strong stuff the fur hunters drink in Labrador.

"But that was not everything. For me, a bottle is a quart; but what Minkowski brought was a hip flask. I did not drink it. I took the flask home as a trophy. But that's not the end of the story. Two days later, it was a Monday, Minkowski visited me in order to show me something—he saw the bottle and emptied it."

Baade chuckled: "Isn't it a shame that you get no returns when the horse you bet on is a dead-sure thing?"

That was six years ago, and the horse is dead. Most of the experts would agree now that Minkowski had a right to consume the whiskey because Baade had not won his bet. But in one thing he was right. He had put Cygnus A where it belonged, deep out in space time, some five hundred million light-years away. And with this distance determination, based on the redshift of the galaxy, the major discovery of contemporary astronomy emerged: the existence of violent events in galaxies, with tremendous release of energy, in the range of 10^{60} erg.

Cygnus A is the brightest radio source in the constellation Cygnus or Swan (hence the "A"), and the second brightest in the whole sky. Another current notation for this source is 3C 405 (No. 405 in the third *Cambridge Catalogue of Radio Sources*).

The first to "see" Cygnus A was Grote Reber, an amateur astronomer (like Sir William Herschel). With a $2000 homemade radio telescope in his back yard in Wheaton, Illinois, Reber made a radio map of the Milky Way, which was published in 1944. Several patches of high intensity appeared on his chart. One of them was Cygnus A. The resolution, however, was poor. It is given by the ratio of wavelength to aperture. Reber, observing waves about a million times as long as those of visible light, would have needed a mirror some 600 meters in diameter to attain the same accuracy as an optical astronomer using his unaided eye. In fact, his mirror was 10 meters wide; and it was not clear whether the Cygnus A radio source was many times the angular size of the full moon, or ten thousand times smaller.

The first to discover the discrete nature of the Cygnus source was the British physicist Stanley Hey, one of the co-discoverers of the Sun in the radio range. Hey and his two co-workers, S. J. Parsons and J. W. Phillips, used modified 64 MHz anti-aircraft radar sets after World War II. In the region of Cygnus they found a rapidly fluctuating radio source. This result they published in *Nature* in 1946. Their paper, entitled "Fluctuations in Cosmic Radiation at Radio Frequencies," came to the conclusion: "It appears that such marked variation could only originate from a small number of discrete sources."

Within two years the Australian radio astronomers, John G. Bolton and G. T. Stanley, succeeded in giving a much more accurate position of the Cygnus source by using an ingeniously devised interferometer. They showed that the angular diameter of the source was less than 8 minutes of arc. Their paper in *Nature* bore the title: "Variable Source of Radio Frequency Radiation in the Constellation of Cygnus."

The argument that Cygnus A was a point source (a "radio star") seemed undefeatable: the intensity fluctuations were considerable (up to 15 per cent) and noticeable within seconds. Such an object could, therefore, only have stellar dimensions, dimensions of the order of light-seconds (the Sun is about 5 light-seconds across). But the argument was completely wrong. When the Australians and their colleagues in Cambridge and Jodrell Bank recorded waves of the same frequency simultaneously at two different places, they found little correlation in their intensity fluctuations. Thus it was established that the fluctuations come about at a place many billion times nearer than expected: in the F-layer of our own ionosphere. The phenomenon is the analogue of the optical scintillation of starlight.

It might have seemed that the evidence for the discrete nature of Cygnus A was exploded. Not at all. Every schoolboy knows the simple difference between stars and planets (point- and disklike objects) on the night sky: stars twinkle, planets do not. The conclusion of the radio astronomers was unshaken. Cygnus A had to be a point source because it twinkled.

The next decisive step in the mystery story of Cygnus A came in 1951. F. Graham Smith in Cambridge got the first accurate position of this source. With a precision never before obtained in radio astronomy, he measured the location at R.A. $19^{\mathrm{h}}57^{\mathrm{m}}45.3^{\mathrm{s}} \pm 1^{\mathrm{s}}$, declination $+40°35' \pm 1'$ (coordinates for 1950). He airmailed these precious numbers at once to Walter Baade in Pasadena. Baade received the letter near the end of August, 1951.

"I really became interested," he says. "Up to then I had refused to be drawn into attempts to identify the Cygnus source. The positions had not been accurate enough. But I knew that with the Cambridge data something could be done. They are still unsurpassed." He determined to observe the position of the source during his next trip to Mount Palomar, if it could possibly be worked into the schedule.

A night on Palomar at the 200-inch telescope is always a nerve-racking experience for Baade. Although he has been observing for years, he still feels excited every time he operates the telescope. Furthermore, each night is a gamble, since seeing conditions are unpredictable. The entire night may be lost because of poor weather, and information obtained by the giant instrument is so valuable that every available second is scheduled in advance for definite observations —and every available second must be used. Baade usually spends ten to twelve consecutive nights on Mount Palomar, and he approaches the work with the tenseness of an athlete before a big game. He loses about ten pounds during every session.

Baade's next session started September 4. It turned out to be a good night. He took sets of photographs of the Andromeda galaxy and of certain bright nebulae in the Milky Way—these observations were part of continuing long-term studies—and before midnight he found time to squeeze in the extra project. He focused the 200-inch telescope on the position indicated in Smith's letter, and took two photographs of Cygnus, one in blue and one in yellow light. He developed the photographs himself the next afternoon.

"I knew something was unusual the moment I examined the negatives. There were galaxies all over the plate, more than two hundred of them, and the brightest was at the center. It showed signs of tidal distortion, gravitational pull between the two nuclei. I had never seen anything like it before. It was so much on my mind that while I was driving home for supper, I had to stop the car and think."

Baade does not remember exactly when the correct idea occurred to him, but the time was somewhere between the stopping of the car and the end of supper. He interpreted an irregular gray-black blob on a photographic plate as the mark of an event that had never been observed before in the long history of astronomy. The chances against observing this particular event are conservatively estimated at a hundred million to one. Baade decided it was a traffic accident of truly cosmic proportions. Two spiral galaxies—flattened island universes, each containing billions of stars were colliding head-on, face to face, like a pair of cymbals.

That evening, before entering the observing cage of the telescope, Baade examined the plate again briefly, "to take one last look and hold the Cygnus pictures in my mind." In the cage he spent a large part of the night trying to find flaws in his interpretation. But there was something about the appearance of the two nuclei, something that gave the feeling of two overlapping or merging disks, and the notion of colliding galaxies seemed inescapable.

It is doubtful that the idea would have occurred to any other astronomer in the world, but Baade's experience over the past decade or so had trained him specifically to recognize that image on the photographic plates. Interpreting difficult astronomical records, and difficult records in all branches of science, depends in part on what the investigator has seen in the past, and on his ingenuity in noting significant differences and similarities. It depends in a subtle way on what the investigator is ready to see. Because of his previous research, Baade was uniquely ready to understand the meaning of the evidence before him. [Reported in Pfeiffer (1956).]

Then came the famous bet. Minkowski was converted to the collision theory, and with him nearly all of the astronomers in the West. In 1954 Baade and Minkowski gave an extensive discussion of their findings in the *Astrophysical Journal*. The idea of colliding galaxies seemed to have an irresistible impact. Velikovski's modest idea of "Worlds in Collision" seemed to have attained reality on a grand scale. The flux measurements for Cygnus A indicated a total energy output in the radio frequency range of about 10^{44} erg/sec. If the collision lasted for some 3 million years (10^{14} sec) this gave a total energy output of 10^{58} erg in the form of radio-frequency radiation. The collision theory seemed to be able to provide energies of that order. According to the ideas of Baade and Spitzer, a collision of galaxies in a rich cluster would take the following form: the stars of two colliding galaxies would not collide, only the gas in their disks. Assuming a relative velocity of 1000 kilometers per second (10^8 cm/sec), a gas content of 1 per cent, a mass of 10^{11} solar masses (2×10^{44} gm) one would obtain a kinetic energy of 10^{58} erg. Assuming higher gas content, higher masses, and higher relative velocities one could perhaps push this estimate up by two or three orders of magnitude. But still there was one uncomfortable fact about the collision theory right from the beginning: the high efficiency of the conversion of kinetic energy into radio-frequency radiation. The efficiency factor seemed to be close to 100 per cent. If one assumed the highest collision energy one might get the efficiency down to 0.10 per cent, still uncomfortably high if Cygnus A was not the artifact of a superb cosmic radio engineer. There is now hardly any doubt among the experts that collisions of galaxies in rich clusters occur. The question is: Do such collisions lead to the formation of strong radio sources?

Four years later came another decisive step. It was the summer of 1958 and the scene was the Cité Universitaire of Paris. One hundred and sixty-two radio astronomers from seventeen countries came together to discuss the status of their new art. Tremendous progress had been achieved in the few years that had gone before. Observers in several countries had found convincing evidence for the spectacular theory of Vitali Lazarevich Ginzburg, of the Lebedev Physical Institute in Moscow, and Iosif Samuelovich Shklovski, of the Shternberg Astronomical Institute in Moscow. The brilliant young theoreticians, both of whom were unable to attend the conference, had independently suggested that highly relativistic electrons exist in strong non-thermal radio sources and that the radio emission was synchrotron radiation. Shklovski went further and suggested that the continuum portion of the visible light from the Crab Nebula (the supernova of 1054 in our Galaxy) had the same origin. This process occurs on a very modest terrestrial scale in the largest particle accelerators. It had already been proposed as an explanation of the radio outbursts from the Sun and possibly other stars. Shklovski and Ginzburg, however, were the first to imagine that this phenomenon might take place in clouds of particles measuring light-years or even thousands of light-years across. Their idea, published in 1953, created a revolution in astrophysics. It was confirmed immediately by the discovery of the predicted polarizations in the light of the Crab Nebula (M1) and the galaxy M87. But as Geoffrey Burbidge showed in his introductory lecture in Paris, the new breakthrough in understanding made the mystery of Cygnus A and other strong radio sources still more puzzling than before. The British astrophysicist computed from the theory of synchrotron radiation the minimum energy of Cygnus A, contained in relativistic electrons and in the magnetic field, as 2.8×10^{59} erg.

He also put forward (independently of Ginzburg) that a much larger amount of energy might still be present in relativistic protons. He thus arrived for Cygnus A at a minimum total energy contained in protons and magnetic field of 3.9×10^{60} erg, corresponding to a mass equivalent of two million times the mass of the Sun. These staggering numbers were clearly not in favor of the collision theory or any other explanation.

Among the many papers presented in Paris there was another one that proved important for the discussion of Cygnus A: Jennison from Jodrell Bank reported his measurements on the structure of this radio source. His astonishing result was that the radio emission came from two bright sources 82 seconds of arc apart, several times the diameter of the Galaxy. Such a structure, now known to be quite frequent among strong radio sources, was also no evidence to support the collision theory.

The identification of other strong radio sources reported in Paris were not favorable to Baade's idea. Multiple-centered elliptical galaxies (which usually contain no considerable amount of gas) were identified, and also field galaxies outside of clusters, where the probability of a collision was extremely small.

Thus after the Paris Symposium the enigma of the strong radio sources had begun to emerge in its true and colossal proportions: Mysterious energy sources exist in the universe able to supply more than 10^{60} erg, or perhaps even many times more than that, in the form of relativistic particles.

Viktor Amazapovich Ambartsumian had already refuted the collision theory for Cygnus A in 1958 at the Solvay Conference in Brussels. But he had not been able to propose a physically feasible mechanism for the energy sources. And so, since no workable alternatives showed up, the collision theory was not generally discarded. In 1960, when Otto Struve treated it as superseded in one of his *Sky and Telescope* articles, Rudolph Minkowski, who had himself once attacked the theory, wrote a long letter to *Sky and Telescope* correcting Struve. At that time Minkowski had just finished his beautiful work on 3C 295 identifying the most distant object in the universe (this record was broken only recently by Maarten Schmidt's measurement of the redshift of 3C 147). Minkowski's radio source 3C 295 showed up exactly where it should have been according to the collision theory: in a rich cluster of galaxies.

It was another spectacular discovery, made in 1963, that again directed the attention of astrophysicists to the mysterious, huge energy sources: the discovery of the quasi-stellar radio sources. The history of their discovery was a case of mistaken identity, strangely similar to that of Cygnus A.

A radio source like Cygnus A would be observable even at far greater distances. If the diameter of such a source could be measured it would provide a very interesting test for models of the universe. Fred Hoyle was the first to discuss this cosmological test at the Paris Symposium. He pointed out that the Einstein–de Sitter universe, for instance, would lead to a minimum diameter of radio sources in contrast to the steady-state model. Hoyle's test became a strong incentive to search for radio sources of smallest diameters.

Mainly through the work of Palmer and his collaborators at Manchester the structure of many radio sources, and especially their diameters, became measurable. Among the many sources measured was one that could not be resolved: 3C 48. A huge interferometer with a maximal base length of 61000 wavelengths, limited in size essentially by the width of England, gave the result that the radio source 3C 48 had a diameter of less than 4 seconds of arc. The Californian radio astronomers in Owens Valley used their 90-foot twin dishes for a positioning of 3C 48 that was six times better than the Cambridge measurements. With this position from Thomas A. Matthews, Allan R. Sandage of the Mount Wilson and Palomar Observatories, the world's leading cosmologist, identified 3C 48. On his plates, taken with the 200-inch optical telescope at Mount Palomar, he found at the position of 3C 48 a sixteenth-magnitude star of a strange blue color and with a faint wisp.

Sandage made his discovery known at the 107th Meeting of the American Astronomical Society, held December 28–31, 1960, in New York City. His unscheduled paper announced the discovery of the first true radio star. An account of this paper in *Sky and Telescope* says: "Since the distance of 3C 48 is unknown, there is a remote possibility that it may be a very distant galaxy of stars; but there is general agreement among the astronomers concerned that it is a relatively nearby star with most peculiar properties." And so it stayed for more than two years. Sandage found variations in brightness which seemed to give definite proof of the stellar nature of 3C 48. The mere thought that a galaxy, a system of 10^{11} stars (distributed over a huge volume of space) could vary simultaneously in brightness seemed so utterly ludicrous that it could apparently be discarded instantly. But still the spectrum of this strange radio star in the constellation Triangulum was very difficult to interpret. It was years before Sandage and Matthews finally sent the results of their observations and calculations to the *Astrophysical Journal* (see reprint in this volume). But then a note at the end of their paper reveals the dramatic changes that took place at the beginning of 1963 through the identification of 3C 273.

The British radio astronomer Cyril Hazard had found an ingenious way to obtain positions and dimensions of discrete radio sources with an unsurpassed accuracy. In observing occultations of the radio source by the Moon, he was able to find radio positions that were as good as optical ones. Together with his co-workers M. B. Mackey and A. J. Shimmins he used the 210-foot dish at Parkes in Australia to apply his method to 3C 273. This source turned out to consist of two components, called A and B, separated by 20 seconds of arc. The B-source had a radio diameter of less than a half-second of arc and coincided with the image of a thirteenth-magnitude star. Never before was the identification of a radio source achieved with the same degree of certainty (see reprint in Appendix I to this volume).

At first it seemed that another "radio star" had been found, i.e., another object of the 3C 48 class, now called "quasi-stellar radio sources," "quasi-stellar objects," or more shortly, "quasi-stellars" (the term "quasars" coined by Chiu has not found general acceptance among astronomers). The optical spectrum of 3C 273B showed bright emission lines, but it seemed impossible to identify them. They belonged apparently to forms of matter never found in the universe before. It was the Dutch astronomer, Maarten Schmidt, from California Institute of Technology, who found the correct solution: all wavelengths are shifted to the red by an amount of 16 per cent. Now the lines belonged to familiar elements like hydrogen (see reprint in Appendix I to this volume).

J. B. Oke in Pasadena checked Schmidt's interpretation by finding the redshifted Hα line in the infrared spectrum of 3C 273B with a spectrum scanner (see reprint in Appendix I to this volume).

What was the nature of the redshift? Was it a gravitational redshift of a superdense star or the Doppler shift of a distant receding galaxy? The decision was not easy. A galaxy like 3C 273B had never been seen before. It actually had to be some kind of a superstar outshining the biggest galaxies, an object about a million million times brighter than the Sun. However, the alternate hypothesis of a nearby superdense star posed even greater difficulties and had to be discarded: 3C 273 was a distant galaxy.

Greenstein and Matthews tried to reinterpret Sandage's spectrum of 3C 48, allowing for an unknown redshift (see reprint in Appendix I to this volume). This was possible and the redshift came out even larger than that of 3C 273B. As in the case of Cygnus A the radio-star hypothesis had been disproved. The distance of 3C 48 had been underestimated by a factor of a million.

Again there were now the indications of tremendous energy requirements. The A-component of 3C 273 had been identified optically with a small nebula. If both were of common origin and had separated with the velocity of light, the minimum age of 3C 273 would be a hundred thousand years. Assuming a constant output of optical energy over this time would lead to an energy estimate of about 10^{58} erg.

The fabulous nature of this energy source attained a new aspect when Allan Sandage (see reprint in this volume of his article from the *Astrophysical Journal*) and Harlan Smith and Dorrit Hoffleit discovered the variability of 3C 273B (see reprint in Appendix I to this volume). Variability of such an object was equivalent to switching on and off the light of hundred thousand millions of suns within short times.

A large energy release over a short time is called an explosion. Already in 1943 the astronomer C. K. Seyfert of Vanderbilt University had found evidence for violent events in some galaxies that made a supernova explosion of a star appear as a firecracker compared to a big bomb. The most amazing photographs of an exploding galaxy are those of the nearby system M82. The beautiful pictures in the light of the Hα line and the spectroscopic measurements published in 1963 were clear-cut proof for the existence of such super-super-explosions which are not necessarily connected with strong radio emission (see reprints of papers by Lynds and Sandage, and by the Burbidges and Sandage in this volume). The explosions seem to take place near the center of the galaxies. The frequency of these occurrences indicates that such events of gigantic violence might even happen repeatedly in many galaxies. There is now some preliminary evidence for a former explosion in the center of our own Galaxy.

When the structure of extragalactic radio sources became known in some detail, the picture of single or repeated explosions at the center of radio galaxies became very suggestive. Ambartsumian, Bolton, and Hanbury Brown stressed the point of view that the central regions of galaxies might be the seat of this mysterious activity. The double nature of many strong radio sources might then be due to the fact that the debris of the explosion, relativistic particles contained in magnetic fields and emitting synchrotron radiation, had been thrown out from the center in opposite directions along the axis of rotation.

What energy sources for these violent events could possibly tie together strong radio sources, quasi-stellars, medium-strong radio sources like M87, and Seyfert galaxies? Many "wild" ideas had been proposed, for example, matter-antimatter annihilation or a chain reaction of supernova explosions in the dense central regions of a galaxy, but none of these won general acclaim. If the number 10^{60} erg for strong radio sources had to be taken seriously, something still "wilder" was being called for. Fred Hoyle and William Fowler supplied it: gravitational collapse of a massive superstar in the center of a galaxy. A first exploration of this fascinating proposal was one of the main topics of the Dallas Symposium.

Here we shall end this sketchy, non-technical account of the events that led to the holding of the Symposium in Dallas. The reader will find additional pre-Dallas information in an article by Jesse L. Greenstein in the December, 1963, issue of *Scientific American*. A report on the Symposium can be found in chapter i of this volume. A careful reader of this volume might find a few discrepancies between Dr. Chiu's report and the original papers. But we feel that this does not detract materially from the value of this excellent article that tries to sum up what experts in many fields had to say who were united only by their diverse interests in quasi-stellar sources.

We regret that we were not able to include more reprints of relevant recent papers or some of the older ones. In many cases the reader will have no difficulty finding them through the references given in this volume.

Only some aspects of the great energy events were discussed at Dallas. The bearing of these events on high-energy astronomy and cosmology will be discussed at the second Texas Symposium on Relativistic Astrophysics at Austin, December 15–19, 1964.

REFERENCE

Pfeiffer, J. 1956, *The Changing Universe* (London: Victor Gollancz Ltd.), pp. 107–109.

PART I

REPORT ON THE

TEXAS SYMPOSIUM

chapter 1 GRAVITATIONAL COLLAPSE

With the exception of a few supernova remnants which are in our galaxy, most cosmic radio sources are "radio galaxies." Although flare stars do emit radio waves occasionally, no ordinary stars with strong, steady radio emission have been found. The typical optical power of stars is from 10^{30} ergs/sec (white dwarfs) to 10^{33} ergs/sec (super giants). For comparison, the optical power of the sun is 4×10^{33} ergs/sec. The typical radio power of supernova remnants is around 10^{36} ergs/sec. For a giant galaxy (containing approximately 10^{11}–10^{12} stars with a total mass of around $10^{11}\odot$, where $\odot$ = solar mass = 2×10^{33}g), the optical power is around 10^{44} ergs/sec. Radio emission from normal galaxies is generally weaker, the power ranging from 10^{37}–10^{39} ergs/sec. For certain peculiar galaxies, the so-called "radio galaxies," the radio emission rate ranges from 10^{41}–$10^{44.5}$ ergs/sec.

However, since 1960, another kind of strange object has been found—"quasi-stellar radio sources"; these formed the center of discussion at the symposium. Their radio power is around 10^{44} ergs/sec and their optical power is around 10^{46} ergs/sec, *which is 100 times the total energy output rate of a giant galaxy!* To date nine of these objects have been found. On photographic plates, these peculiar radio sources have star-like appearances, and one of them showed erratic light variations with a time constant of the order of one year and a long-term quasi-period of ten years. A modest estimate of the total energy content of each of these objects (in the form of the kinetic energy of electrons of 1 BeV energy) gives a minimum of 10^{60} ergs, which is the *rest energy* of about 10^6 suns.

Are "quasi-stellar radio sources" stars? Ordinary stellar-structure theory precludes stars of mass greater than $100\odot$. In such stars, radiation pressure dominates and because of the thermodynamic properties of radiation, these stars will pulsate with large amplitudes. As a result of this pulsation, mass will be ejected, thereby reducing the mass of the star. Are "quasi-stellar radio sources" galaxies? Their angular size is less than $0.5''$, while normal galaxies at corresponding distances (determined by their red shift) will have an angular size of the order of $3''$. In several cases, the light variation precludes this possibility because galaxies do not have light variations.

So far, the clumsily long name "quasi-stellar radio sources" is used to describe these objects. Because the nature of these objects is entirely unknown, it is hard to prepare a short, appropriate nomenclature for them so that their essential properties are obvious

HONG-YEE CHIU, Goddard Institute for Space Studies and Columbia University.

Reprinted and slightly abridged from *Physics Today*, **17**, 21–34, 1964.

from their name. For convenience, the abbreviated form *"quasar"* will be used through-out this paper.

The idea of having a meeting on gravitational collapse came after the discoveries of the enormous energy output of quasars and the subsequent gravitational-collapse theory of F. Hoyle of Cambridge University and W. A. Fowler of the California Institute of Technology to explain this enormous energy output. When the symposium met, the original hypothesis of Hoyle and Fowler (reviewed at the meeting by E. M. Burbidge of the University of California at La Jolla) was abandoned and was replaced by those to be reported later. Meanwhile, new observational data had been accumulated and were presented at the meeting. It seems safe to say that, at the present time, the interior structure and the physical mechanism of the energy production of quasars are still not understood.

Fusion of hydrogen into heavier elements will yield an energy of about one percent of the rest energy of matter. If the energy source of the quasars were nuclear in nature, it would be necessary that $10^8\odot$ of hydrogen be burned in around 10^6 years. It is rather unlikely that nuclear energy could be released in unison on such a large scale. Moreover, nuclear reactions usually take place in the interior of a star; the energy released gradual-ly diffuses out, and finally is radiated thermally as black-body radiation, peaked at an energy of around 2 eV. How can the energy of electrons be elevated from a few eV to a few BeV without violating the second law of thermodynamics? Using the most efficient thermodynamic cycle, a nuclear-energy source many orders of magnitude higher is needed! Therefore, there is only one energy source left for us to consider: gravitational energy. Incidentally, the gravitational field is the weakest field in nature, but it is the only one that allows us (at least theoretically) to extract up to $\frac{8}{9}$ of the rest energy of matter.

After this brief introduction to the central theme of the discussions, I shall now report the individual papers that were presented at the symposium. In order to have continuity in this report, I shall not report the talks chronologically, but in a logical manner.

Reviewing the common properties of radio sources, T. Matthews of Caltech pointed out that radio emission from normal galaxies is rather weak compared with their optical emission. Their radio power is around 10^{37-39} ergs/sec while their optical power is around 10^{44} ergs/sec. Some rare, peculiar spiral galaxies may have a radio emissive power of around 10^{40} ergs/sec. Strong radio galaxies with a radio power of 10^{41-44} ergs/sec are most frequently found among the so-called D systems. These are galaxies with elliptical-like nuclei and large envelopes. Some strong sources are also identified with elliptical galaxies. The optical emission rate of quasars is around 10^{46} ergs/sec and their radio emission rate is around 10^{44} ergs/sec.

To date, a total number of nine quasars have been identified from the contents of the revised 3C catalogue (3C stands for the *Third Cambridge Catalogue of Radio Sources*) which contains about 470 radio sources, many of them still unidentified optically. This catalogue was compiled by a group working under M. Ryle of the University of Cam-bridge. The two quasars which have been extensively studied and which were extensively discussed at the meeting have catalogue numbers 3C273 and 3C48 respectively.

Radio interferometers with a resolution of the order of 1" of arc were first used to study the shape of some of the stronger quasars. This method also enables one to locate accurate positions for these sources. This was done chiefly by the Manchester group (R. P. Allen, B. Anderson, R. G. Conway, H. P. Palmer, V. C. Reddish, and B. Rowson) and by the Caltech group (P. Maltby, T. A. Matthews, and A. T. Moffet). In the radio position of 3C48, an object resembling a 16^m star was found on the photographic plate.[1]

---

[1] Superscript m stands for the magnitude; $m = -2.5 \log_{10} F + C$ where F is the observed energy flux and C is a constant. At a distance of 32.5 light years the sun has a magnitude of $+4.85$. This is also the distance at which the absolute magnitude of an object is defined. A 6^m star is just barely visible to the eye. A difference of 5 magnitudes amounts to a difference in measured energy flux of 100.

This "star" was surrounded by a nebula measuring $5'' \times 12''$ which does not resemble any galaxy.

At the same time, lunar occultation observations of 3C273 were carried out by the Australian group (C. Hazard, M. B. Mackey, and A. J. Shimmins). This other method of observation provided an optical identification for 3C273. Because of gravitational perturbations, the orbital plane of the moon is not fixed in space but precesses with a period of around 19 years. Thus, the moon, with an angular size of 30 minutes of arc, can occult stars within a belt of $20°$ as it moves around the earth. When a radio source is occulted, one can learn from the diffraction pattern about the location, shape, and size of the radio source. In particular, it is easy to tell if a source is an extended one. It was found that 3C273 consists of two sources, A and B; their separation is $19.5''$. Component B is slightly elliptical and four times weaker than component A. Using the $200''$ Hale telescope, A. Sandage of Mt. Wilson and Palomar Observatory obtained photographs which show, at the radio position of A, a nebula shaped as a jet, pointing away from a 13^{m} star-like object which is identified as component B.

Radio spectra for both components of 3C273 and for 3C48 have been obtained. Briefly, the mechanism for radio emission and the nature of radio spectra can be described in the following way. The optical radiation of stars and nebulae is chiefly emitted by thermally excited ions. The spectra of stars and nebulae are rich in absorption or emission lines; their over-all features can be understood in terms of black-body radiation peaked around certain optical wavelengths. The radio spectra that are normally observed can be broadly classified into two categories: thermal and synchrotron emission. In the thermal spectrum, the intensity per unit frequency increases towards shorter wavelengths for emission from "optically thick" emitters. This kind of spectrum resembles that of the long-wavelength end of a black-body thermal radiation, hence its name. Most likely it is produced by electron bremsstrahlung, which occurs when electrons pass very near ions. In the synchrotron spectrum, the intensity decreases towards the shorter wavelengths, and usually the intensity per unit frequency is proportional to $\nu^{-\alpha}$, where ν is the frequency and α is a positive number usually between 0.3 and 1.2 (for most sources, α has a value of around 0.8).

The paths of electrons in a magnetic field are not straight lines but curves. Hence these electrons suffer acceleration while traveling on a curved path. These "accelerated" electrons then radiate polarized electromagnetic waves, primarily in the radio region. Such radiation from monoenergetic electrons was first observed in electron synchrotrons, hence the name synchrotron radiation. The observed cosmic-ray spectrum is usually

$$N(E)dE = E^{-k}dE$$

where $N(E)dE$ is the flux in the energy band dE and k is a positive number; $k = 1.5$ for high-energy cosmic-ray particles. We may assume that the relativistic electron component of cosmic rays also obeys this law. Then the synchrotron radiation intensity per unit frequency is proportional to $\nu^{-\alpha}$.

The radio spectrum of 3C273 is a composite of the two sources A and B, and can be resolved as indicated. This resolution was obtained from lunar occultation observations. The spectrum of A seems to belong to the synchrotron type, and that of B to the thermal type. However, this interpretation of the observed spectrum of source B would require a temperature of the order of 10^{9} ° K. Such a high temperature contradicts the lifetime estimated by present theory.

The optical spectrum of 3C48 has also been available for some time. Several emission lines were found, but no unequivocal identification with lines of known atoms or ions could be made. Moreover, J. Greenstein of Caltech found that the spectra of some fainter quasars, 3C147, 3C196, and 3C286 (also showing somewhat weaker emission lines), looked quite different from that of 3C48.

M. Schmidt studied the spectrum of the bright object, 3C273. He found four emission lines which formed a simple harmonic pattern with separation and intensity decreasing towards the ultraviolet. This series of lines looks like that of any hydrogen-like atoms. Unfortunately, they correspond to no elements found on earth. A unique interpretation can only be made by assuming a red shift ($\Delta\lambda/\lambda$) of 0.16 and that the emitting element is hydrogen. (A far greater red shift has to be assumed if the emitting element consists of other hydrogen-like atoms.) Indeed, with this interpretation, a red-shifted Hα line (shifted from 6563Å to 7590Å) was found in the infrared by J. B. Oke of Caltech. Similarly, the line spectra of all other quasars can be interpreted as red-shifted emission lines and forbidden lines. In 3C48 the emission line identified corresponds to that of [Mg II] and the forbidden lines to those of [O II], [Ne III], and [Ne IV]. In 3C48 the red shift is 0.37. The corresponding velocity (if the red shift is interpreted as the Doppler shift) is around 0.15 c and 0.3 c for 3C273 and 3C48, respectively.[2]

Another feature of quasars is that they show a strong ultraviolet excess even at a red shift of $\Delta\lambda/\lambda = 0.8$. Using filter techniques, A. R. Sandage and M. Ryle have successfully identified a few more quasars (3C9, 3C216, 3C245) from a number of objects showing strong ultraviolet excess.

Could quasars be stars in our galaxy with a high receding velocity? This is extremely unlikely. First, the gravitational field of our galaxy cannot retain stars with a velocity $<10^{-3}$ c. Second, the proper motion (apparent motion of stars with respect to background stars) would appear large compared with other stars of much smaller velocity.

W. H. Jefferys of Wesleyan University (Connecticut) studied the proper motion of 3C273. Since 3C273 is fairly bright, its image was found among many sky-patrol plates dating back to 1888. Plates from many observatories using different telescopes, accumulated over the past fifty years, were used to determine the proper motion. The inertial system used is the so-called FK3 system. This refers to a group of more than 900 stars catalogued in the *Dritter (Third) Fundamental-Katalog des Berliner Astronomischen Jahrbuchs* (Kopff, 1934) with the highest precision then available.[3] The measured proper motion of 3C273 is 0.001 $\pm$ 0.0025 seconds of arc per year. The standard deviation is from uncertainties associated with the accuracy of the absolute position of stars in the FK3 system. From the value of proper motion and the velocity derived from the differential rotation of our galaxy, the distance of 3C273 is >65000 light years, and this puts 3C273 on the border of our galaxy (the size of our galaxy is 10^5 light years). A similar result was also obtained by W. J. Luyten of the University of Minnesota, using more recent plates.

Can the red shift be gravitational in nature? The red shift of light from a self-gravitating body of radius R, mass M, is of the order of $GM/Rc^2 = 10^{-6}(M/\odot)(R/R\odot)^{-1}$. ($R\odot$ = solar radius = 7×10^{10} cm). In order to have a red shift as large as 0.1, $(M/\odot)(R/R\odot)^{-1}$ $\approx 10^5$. For a star of one solar mass and an $R \sim 10^6$ cm, a density of about 10^{15} g/cm^3 would be required. (E. E. Salpeter of Cornell University reviewed the equilibrium configuration of superdense stars. It is not possible for superdense stars of mass $\ll \odot$ to exist, nor can the red shift of light from superdense stars exceed 0.3.) The presence of spectral lines implies a surface temperature of the order of 10^4 ° K. From the radius of superdense stars, one can estimate the total radiative power, and thus deduce the distance from the observed flux. If 3C273 were a superdense star, its distance would be 0.3 light years and it would be practically inside our solar system! From the intensity of the forbidden lines J. Greenstein further concluded that the distance would be even smaller. Such stars would have been discovered by Kepler through the failure of Kepler's laws!

[2] The Doppler shift is $d\nu/\nu = (-v/c)(1 - v^2/c^2)^{-1/2}$, where v is the relative velocity of the source and the observer. For the same velocity most cosmological theories predict a shift $d\nu/\nu$ in between $(-v/c)(1 - v^2/c^2)^{-1/2}$ and $-v/c$ (linear).

[3] Recently, the FK4 Catalogue, containing more than 1200 stars, has been published.

One may also assume that quasars have bigger masses and bigger radii than super-dense stars. For example, one can assume that 3C273 is a star at a distance of 1000 light years. In order to be compatible with the energy output rate, the radius has to be 10^{13} cm. Then, in order to account for the red shift, the mass has to be $10^7 \odot$! W. A. Fowler pointed out that such stars cannot even burn hydrogen, because they would fall within their gravitational radius before the temperature would be high enough ($10^7 °$ K) to burn hydrogen!

D. Williams of the University of California at Berkeley reported the observation of interstellar absorption lines in 3C273. When radio waves of distant galaxies reach us, part of the energy at the 21-cm wavelength is absorbed by hydrogen in our galaxy. A very weak 21-cm absorption line was found in the radio spectrum of 3C273 with a line shift corresponding to a velocity of 1 km/sec $\pm$ 10 km/sec. This effect, however, is very marginal.

Since no other rational interpretation can be given to the red shift, one can only attribute it to the cosmological red shift. Using Hubble's law, the distance of 3C273 is placed at 1.8×10^9 light years. This gives an energy output rate for 3C273 of 10^{46} ergs/sec at optical frequency. Some people will question whether Hubble's law is well established. Hubble's law states that the distance of galaxies to us is linearly related to their red shift:

$$\text{Distance} = \frac{\text{Recession velocity}}{H}.$$

The proportionality constant $H (\approx 100$ km–sec^{-1}–megaparsec^{-1})[4] is known as Hubble's constant. $H^{-1}c$ is a measure for the dimension of our universe; at a distance $\approx H^{-1}c$ the red shift is total. One often hears that astronomical observations are not accurate enough to distinguish one type of cosmological theory from another, and many have expressed doubts about applying Hubble's law to obtain the distances of unknown objects from their red shift. The answer is that these two problems are somewhat different in nature. Assuming that the local density of galaxies is the same throughout the universe *at a given time* and that the curvature of the universe is everywhere constant, different cosmological theories will predict different galactic densities as a function of the distance (this galactic density is observed from a single space-time point) and the distance is obtained from the red shift by the above equation. The galactic density observed at a single space-time point would be different for different cosmological theories because of the expansion of the universe, and because the expanding rate as a function of the distance is different in different theories. Unfortunately, the various cosmological theories predict measurable differences in galactic densities only at distances much beyond the reach of the world's most powerful telescope—the 200" Hale telescope at Mt. Palomar. Hubble's law, however, is established accurately for neighboring galaxies by applying knowledge of the period-luminosity relation of Cepheid variables. (Cepheids are bright variables of luminosity $\sim 10^5 \, L\odot$, and their period is related to their luminosity by a simple law. Hence, by observing the period and the apparent brightness of Cepheid variables of other galaxies, one can obtain a distance.) Then the absolute brightness of more distant galaxies is related to the red shift through a complicated statistical analysis eliminating the difference in intrinsic luminosities of individual galaxies. The result is a law that can be trusted to within a factor of 2 in distance estimates. Hence we believe that Hubble's law may be applied to quasars to obtain their distance accurately.

H. J. Smith of McDonald Observatory took a bold look at quasars. Is there light variation in these objects? Sky-patrol plates from Harvard University Observatory are available back to 1888. Although a large number of old plates have aged and become unreliable, some of them are still in fairly good condition. In measuring light variations,

[4] 1 parsec = 3.25 light years.

one only needs to compare the image of 3C273 with neighboring stars. Smith and D. Hoffleit of Yale found a large light variation with an amplitude up to 50 percent and a quasi-cycle of fifteen years. A. R. Sandage observed 3C273, 3C48, and 3C196 more recently with a photoelectric device and found some erratic variations up to a few tenths of a magnitude. From statistical theory, if 3C273 were a galaxy with a nominal number of stars ($\sim 10^{10}$), the expected annual variation would be much less than 10^{-5} of the variation of any star. This limit is obtained by assuming that all stars in the galaxy are variables of the same period. Hence it is not possible that 3C273 and other quasars are compact galaxies. Further, in order that the light from such an object can vary with a time constant ~ 1 year (the shortest variation observed), the physical dimension of 3C273 cannot be much bigger than the time it takes light signals to go across it—namely, one light year.

Having established that quasars are neither local stars nor galaxies, the next thing to do was to study further the details of their spectra. J. Greenstein reported that these lines have been identified with the forbidden lines O^+, Ne^{++}, and Ne^{++++}. Certain atomic excited states decay through higher-order interactions, and their lifetimes are long (~ 1 second). Under ordinary laboratory discharge-tube density ($\gtrsim 10^{15}$ particles/cm³), collisional de-excitation takes place before atoms in these excited states can decay, and the corresponding lines are ordinarily unobservable in the laboratory (forbidden). The presence of forbidden lines indicates low electron density ($< 10^7/cm^3$). As the density increases, forbidden lines gradually disappear.

The observed forbidden lines are [O II], [O III], and [Ne III], but [Mg II] is not a forbidden line. Incidentally, a sizable fraction of energy radiated ($\sim 20\%$) is contained in these lines. From their observed relative strength the electron number density N_e may be established. Knowing the distance from the red shift, the absolute intensity of the strength of these lines and hence the total number of atoms emitting them may be determined. The table lists Greenstein's results.

Quasar	N_e/cm^3	Radius (parsec)	$M/\odot$ (of emitting parts)
3C273	10^7	0.6	2×10^5
3C48	10^5	5	2×10^6

If quasars were superdense stars, the differential red shift at different layers would limit the thickness of the emitting layer to that corresponding to the observed width of forbidden lines. This would limit the total number of emitting ions. From this limit and the observed intensity of forbidden lines, Greenstein concluded that quasars would have to be as close as the moon! Such large gravitational perturbations on the solar system could not have escaped the keen eye of Kepler. Hence, from the presence of forbidden lines one can argue indirectly but strongly that the red shift cannot be gravitational.

The lower limit for the masses of 3C273 and 3C48 can be estimated as follows: From the line broadening, we can estimate the kinetic velocity of emitting atoms. It turns out to be 1500 km/sec. In order that these atoms be bound gravitationally at a distance of 0.6 parsec, the center of 3C273 must contain a mass of at least $10^8 \odot$. This is the lower limit for the masses of 3C273 and 3C48.

One can also obtain the mass from energy estimates. To know the total energy radiated, one needs to know the age of quasars. The energy output rate is 3×10^{46} ergs/sec, equivalent to the nuclear energy output from the burning of one solar mass of hydrogen in one day. In 3C273, there is a jet, component A, 150000 light years away from the other component, component B. It is most likely that the jet was ejected from 3C273. If one accepts this interpretation, then the age of 3C273 must be at least 150000 years. This gives a value of 10^{59} ergs for the total energy radiated.

But this is not the whole story about the energy content of quasars. The optical emission can be interpreted as resulting from collisional excitation caused by the thermal motion of ions. From the shape of the radio spectrum, the radio emission is most likely from synchrotron radiation. Thermal radiation with such strong intensity would require a temperature of the order of 10^9 ° K and at this temperature its lifetime against neutrino loss is less than a few days. Relativistic electrons moving in a magnetic field can radiate predominantly in the radio region. To date, we do not know of any way of accelerating high-energy electrons with high efficiency, and it seems consistent with known cases (e.g., the Crab Nebula) that about 1 percent of the energy stored in all high-energy particles may be in the form of high-energy electrons. Also, magnetic fields contain energy. A minimum estimate of the total energy consistent with radio data is at least 10^{60} ergs.

The presence of a magnetic field is further supported by the discovery of polarization in the optical region. One does not expect a very large polarization, because the plane of polarization of electromagnetic waves will be rotated while passing through a plasma; the rotation angle is different for different frequencies (Faraday rotation). Hence, for a given band width, the polarization decreases as electromagnetic waves pass through a plasma. At a wavelength of 4500 angstroms, a polarization of 0.45 ($\pm$0.15) percent, based on twelve observations, has been obtained by McDonald. The angle of polarization is defined to $\pm 5°$. This indicates that there is a small component of synchrotron radiation in the optical region as well.

To summarize the discussion on the observed features of quasars, we conclude that (1) quasars are massive objects with a mass $\geq 10^8 \odot$ which are confined to a space of about one parsec; (2) they are not composed of stars but seem to be coherent masses; (3) their lifetime is at least 10^5 years; (4) they radiate radio waves strongly, but radiate most strongly in the optical region; (5) their surface is composed of very tenuous matter of a particle-number density of the order of $10^7/cm^3$; and (6) their total energy content is larger than the rest energy of $10^6 \odot$.

Now I shall report some theoretical speculations based mostly on the energy requirement of quasars. All of the 10^{60} ergs of energy ($= 10^6 \odot c^2$) are in the form of magnetic fields and high-energy particles, and a possible energy source is gravitational energy, which can be released in violent events (e.g., collapse); thus all the energy released may be in the form of high-energy particles. The prevalent theory of gravitation is general relativity. General relativity predicts some singularities, one of which, the Schwarzschild singularity, will be discussed briefly below.

Classically, if one is able to accumulate matter indefinitely and statically, the escape velocity at the surface will eventually exceed the light velocity. As an interesting historical sidelight, I remind the reader that in conjunction with the corpuscular theory of light, Laplace demonstrated in 1795 that a body of the dimension of the orbit of the earth around the sun, with a density of that of the earth, would not allow any of its rays to escape. Hence, he concluded that the most luminous object in the universe may not be visible.

The same conclusion holds in relativity theory. In fact, the mass limit calculated according to Newtonian theory is exactly the same as that predicted in general relativity theory! The light emitted at a distance R from a sphere of mass M is red-shifted by the factor $(1 - 2GM/Rc^2)^{-1/2}$ as observed by distant observers; for light emitted at the surface, defined by $R^* = 2GM/c^2$, the red shift is infinite. R^* is called the gravitational radius or the Schwarzschild radius. The time dilatation factor is also $(1 - 2GM/Rc^2)^{-1/2}$. To an outside observer, a body falling towards R^* will never reach it, since in approaching it, the time dilatation factor $(1 - 2GM/Rc^2)^{-1/2}$ diverges and the motion will slow down and eventually stop (time machine!). Signals sent out by the falling body will be more and more red-shifted to very long wavelengths. To a local observer falling towards the center, however, the time of descent is finite. In fact, from the present radius of the sun (7×10^{10} cm), the time of descent towards the center, assuming the sun is within its gravitational radius, is less than one day. For a proton, $R^* = 10^{-33}$ cm; for the sun,

$R^* = 2.6 \times 10^5$ cm; and for a massive object $M \sim 10^8 \odot$, $R^* \sim 10^{13}$ cm. For a collapsing star in which the pressure can be neglected, J. R. Oppenheimer and H. Snyder, then of the University of California at Berkeley, found in 1939 that the above conclusion was still valid.

Although no light can cross the gravitational radius, the gravitational field and the electrostatic field of the gravitational singularity (those carried by the so-called longitudinal gravitons and photons) can be felt by external observers. Thus, the Schwarzschild singularity can be detected through its gravitational field, but it cannot be seen. Also, because for a comoving observer the Schwarzschild singularity does not seem to exist, many relativists believe it is just a singularity introduced by the particular coordinate one chooses to describe the gravitational field. Various efforts have been made to find a coordinate system free of the Schwarzschild singularity, including a modification of the topology of the space-time continuum, but in all cases, singularities always reappear at other places.

In practice, the Schwarzschild singularity sets an ultimate limit on how far a body can collapse gravitationally. This limit is actually approached in the model proposed by F. Hoyle and W. A. Fowler. In a bold attempt, F. Hoyle analyzed the conditions for the formation of large coherent masses. The difficulties of forming large masses are (1) angular momentum and (2) breaking up of large masses to smaller ones prematurely. The period of rotation is proportional to R^{-2} (R is the dimension of the object), but all other time scales (the free-fall time, the time of transit of hydromagnetic waves across a body) are proportional to $R^{-3/2}$ in the nonrelativistic case. Hence, rotation will prevent matter from condensing further when the speed of rotation at the equator equals the escape velocity. As a comparison, rotation becomes important during the formation of the sun when the radius of the protosun is around 10 to 100 times the present value.

In the relativistic region, all time scales have the same dependence on R. Other physical characteristics of the body (density, mass, magnetic field, and so on) then determine which time scale becomes the most important one. In order that a large coherent mass may be formed, the gravitational time scale must be the shortest one. A comparison of the gravitational time scale [$\sim (3\pi/32G\rho)^{1/2}$] and the hydromagnetic time scale [$\sim (4\pi\rho)^{1/2} R/H$], where H is the magnetic field, shows that, for a magnetic field of 10^{-6} gauss and a density of 10^{-21} g/cm^3, the gravitational time scale is shorter than that of the hydromagnetic wave when the mass is greater than $10^6 \odot$. (As a comparison, the galactic magnetic field is in between 10^{-6} gauss and 10^{-5} gauss, the interstellar matter density is 10^{-24} g/cm^3, and the density of nebulae is 10^{-21} g/cm^3.) From a similar comparison of the rotation time scale ($\sim \omega^{-1}$) with the gravitational time scale, one finds that for $\omega = 10^{-15}$ sec^{-1} (the angular velocity of a galaxy), the condition is $\rho > 5 \times 10^{-24}$ g/cm^3. Thus one need not have a spectacular density in order to overcome the limit imposed by angular momentum.

In this simple argument, one does not consider the transfer of angular momentum from one part of the body to the other. If considerable amounts of angular momentum are transferred, the previous argument is not valid. It is not known whether angular momentum may be transmitted in large quantities. Optimistically, one hopes the inner part can fall a great way before transfer of angular momentum becomes important.

Thus, conceivably, a large mass ($\gtrsim 10^6 \odot$) can condense to a density of around 10^{-16} g/cm^3. At this density, due to rotation, the body becomes appreciably flattened (Fig. 1). Let the thickness of the disc be W, the diameter be D. Now the time scale for the vertical direction is determined by W and this gravitational time scale is much larger than the hydromagnetic time scale. Fragmentation can now take place in the outer part. The mass m in each fragmented blob is given by $m/M \sim (W/D)^2$; for $W/D = 10^{-2}$ and $M = 10^6 \odot$, we have $m = 10^2 \odot$.

The temperature of the gas can be calculated by applying the virial theorem (which equates the thermal energy of a self-gravitating sphere to its self-gravitational energy).

The calculated value for this case is around 10^4 ° K, somewhat below the ionization temperature of hydrogen at the corresponding density. Further contraction (now taking place individually in smaller blobs) will raise the temperature, and hence ionize the gas. The ionization of hydrogen requires an energy of about 10^{13} ergs/g and the thermal (and gravitational) energy is about 10^{12} ergs/g at 10^4 ° K. The gravitational energy is proportional to R^{-1}. To obtain an energy of 10^{13} ergs/g, a contraction by a factor of ten, or an increase in density by a factor of 10^3 is needed. The density suddenly increases from 10^{-16} g/cm³ to 10^{-13} g/cm³.

The gas cloud becomes opaque to radiation only until $\rho \sim 10^{-11}$ g/cm³. During the contraction phase, energy has to be supplied to the radiation field as well. Hence the contraction cannot stop until a density of 10^{-11} g/cm³ is reached. As I have mentioned earlier, stars of masses $\gtrsim 10^2 \odot$ are not stable against pulsation. A check on the thermodynamic mechanical properties of a 100 $\odot$ star shows that it is only marginally in stable equilibrium. Now a rapid contraction takes place almost like a collapse, suddenly raising the density from 10^{-16} g/cm³ to 10^{-11} g/cm³ in a time comparable to the gravitational free-fall time. Will the collapse stop? In a star of a few solar masses, we are quite sure

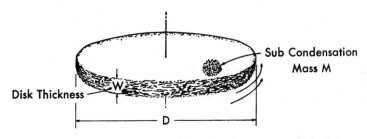

FIG. 1.—Flattened disc in Hoyle's theory

that the collapse will stop before nuclear energy generation runs wild. The kinetic energy associated with the collapse will be damped out in the subsequent oscillations. In a $10^2 \odot$ star, the collapse will probably overshoot, and the accompanied oscillation will have very large amplitude.

The most efficient damping mechanism is the electron-pair annihilation process of neutrino production. But this is important only when $T > 10^9$ ° K; at lower temperature, there is no damping. Since the temperature fluctuation of the star is very large, nuclear reactions (hydrogen burning) will proceed in a somewhat erratic manner. An estimate of the actual time scale for nuclear burning is difficult; but, in order to fit those sporadic light variations in 3C273, the time scale for nuclear burning should be around one year. This rate also fits the observed energy flux (3×10^{46} ergs/sec).

S. A. Colgate of Lawrence Radiation Laboratory and A. G. W. Cameron of Goddard Institute for Space Studies pointed out, however, that F. Hoyle's mechanism does not provide enough high-energy particles for radio emission. Shock waves generated by supernovae, traveling in the very tenuous matter in which these stars are embedded, will accelerate particles to relativistic velocities. A considerable amount of gravitational energy will be released during supernova collapse. Moreover, shock waves will generate hydromagnetic waves throughout the medium, which may explain the long-term light variations (15 years) of 3C273.

Remnants of these massive stars may be in the form of neutron stars or a Schwarzschild singularity, either of which may accelerate particles to relativistic speeds. This may be the mechanism that produced a jet in M87, a galaxy. The idea of acceleration was advanced by Ya. B. Zel'dovich of the USSR.

Another alternative suggested by Hoyle is that the inner region of the big body can collapse gravitationally to extreme density; rotation can either be crushed by gravitational force or dissipated by radiating gravitational waves, assuming a non-cylindrical shape was achieved through fission. F. Dyson of the Institute for Advanced Study remarked that the difficulty associated with a gravitational-collapse theory is that it would be over in one day (the local time it takes for a test particle to cross the Schwarzschild singularity of $10^2 \odot$). How can a state of collapse be maintained for over 10^6 years, which would be required in quasars?

T. Gold of Cornell pointed out that in supernova explosions the light output increases rapidly but declines slowly, and this is in contradiction to what is observed in quasars.

Hoyle summarized his talk with a diagram which is reproduced here as Fig. 2.

W. A. Fowler then discussed a similar mechanism for massive objects. As condensation takes place, the inner part begins to rotate rapidly, and fission can take place. When the inner part bifurcates into a nonsymmetrical form, gravitational radiation will take

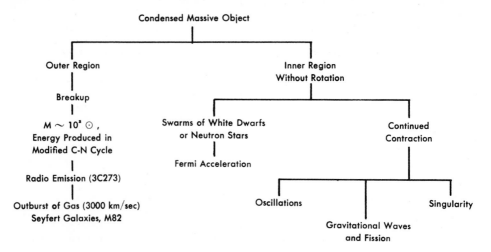

FIG. 2.—Chart summarizing possible mechanisms of gravitational collapse proposed by F. Hoyle

place, radiating away an appreciable amount of rotational energy (which is comparable to the total rest energy). This raises the potential energy outside, and part of the matter will have a positive binding energy. Mass will be ejected. The difficulty here, as pointed out by a number of others, is that one cannot avoid a coupling between inside and outside if fast nonsymmetrical rotation takes place.

T. Gold presented the idea that if stars escaping from star clusters can carry away enough angular momentum, star clusters can collapse, and collisions between stars will occur more frequently. Energy released in such collision processes is fairly large, and certain radio phenomena can be explained.

A number of other topics not related to massive objects, but relevant to gravitational collapse or to galactic structure were also discussed.

E. M. Burbidge reviewed several proposed mechanisms for strong radio sources. Originally, a radio source in Cygnus was identified with a pair of galaxies appearing to be in collision. R. Minkowski of the University of California at Berkeley postulated that collision between normal galaxies could generate high-energy particles responsible for radio emission, but this idea was later rejected because the energy thus released would be far too small. Also, the known number of radio sources is much greater than would be expected from the frequency of galactic collisions for most optically identified sources not associated with clusters of galaxies. G. R. Burbidge of the University of California at La Jolla and F. Hoyle proposed that collisions between galaxies and anti-galaxies (composed of anti-matter) might give enough energy. However, there are many inconsistencies in this proposal. For example, why should matter and anti-matter be separated until the right moment to annihilate? Another mechanism is the emission of radio waves through the interaction of a turbulent magnetic field with gases. One can perhaps explain the radio emission from M82 by this mechanism, but in an elliptical galaxy, there is practically no gas! The existence of large scale, strong magnetic fields in elliptical galaxies is also unlikely.

If one accepts supernova remnants as the only radio emitters in a galaxy, one needs a total number of 10^8 supernovae spreading over 10^6 years. I. Shklowsky of the USSR suggested that during the early stages of galactic evolution, rapid star formation can take place, and supernova activities may be stronger than at present. A. G. W. Cameron modified Shklowsky's idea, proposing that in regions rich in gas and low in magnetic field, massive stars can condense simultaneously. After going through their normal evolutionary sequence, they become supernovae—all in around 10^6 years. Remnants of these supernovae can account for the radio emission. The difficulty is the same as in the proposal of G. R. Burbidge and F. Hoyle: in elliptical radio galaxies there appears to be very little gas.

G. R. Burbidge postulated that in the center of a galaxy, if the separation between presupernova stars is around a few light days, the supernova explosion of one of them may trigger the rest of them to become supernovae. In order that his mechanism may work, a stellar density of 10^7 stars/cubic parsec is needed. Such a high density may exist and escape detection. However, one does not know of any trigger mechanism.

H.-Y. Chiu of Goddard Institute for Space Studies reported on a study of the evolution of presupernova stars in which it was found that a very dense core will develop before a star undergoes collapse. Almost all the energy released during collapse will be dissipated in the form of neutrinos, and the dense core will become neutron matter.

E. E. Salpeter reviewed the equilibrium configuration of neutron stars. At a density greater than 10^{12} g/cm^3, matter is composed predominantly of neutrons, and at an even higher density ($>10^{16}$ g/cm^3) hyperons may exist. These neutrons cannot decay because all electron states are filled up. There exists a mass limit for neutron stars, and no static equilibrium configuration is possible if the mass exceeds this limit. This limit for a perfect Fermi gas is $0.76\odot$ (Oppenheimer-Volkoff mass limit). If real gases are considered, the limit varies somewhat, but in no case does it exceed $3\odot$.

H. Bondi of King's College, London (reported by E. E. Salpeter), derived a rigorous upper limit ($\Delta\lambda/\lambda < 0.615$) for the red shift of light emitted from the surface of neutron stars. A more realistic limit is found to be around 0.3, which incidentally also excludes the possibility that the large red shift (>0.3) of some quasars is a gravitational red shift. In principle, this is the upper limit of the red shift for light emitted from any self-gravitating body.

J. A. Wheeler of Princeton discussed another kind of gravitational singularity. He assumed that one can accumulate matter *statically* until at the center, the time metric g_{00} vanishes (this corresponds to a classical situation in which the gravitational potential *at the center* of the body is equal to its rest energy). Any matter dropped through a hole to the center will give away energy equivalent to its rest energy and thus the total gravitational mass (as observed by external observers through its gravitating effect) cannot increase. Such a singularity acts as a gravitational machine, converting all matter into energy. Since the number of nucleons is conserved, Wheeler postulated the existence of a class of new massless bosons, the δ ray, which carries the nucleon number. One of the chairmen remarked that δ rays, if they exist, may be used to transport ponderable matter at the speed of light.

However, it is not known if one can really accumulate matter statically until this kind of gravitational singularity comes into existence. All neutron-star models studied so far indicate that a dynamical collapse will take place when the mass exceeds the critical mass limit (the mass limit was reviewed by Salpeter).

A spirited discussion then took place, reemphasizing some of the points discussed during the meeting. E. L. Schucking of the Southwest Center for Advanced Studies pointed out that other discussions relevant to massive objects, cosmic rays, and cosmic x and γ rays had been omitted from the discussion. P. Bergmann of Yeshiva University remarked that in the past general relativistic effects had been observed only in the weak field limit. Now new developments of astrophysics have made relativity a more physical theory. He expressed hope that a quantized version of relativity theory may play an important part in understanding massive objects. R. Minkowski expressed satisfaction that within the past ten years the technique of optically identifying radio sources had made great progress. On the other hand, a theoretical understanding of the structure of large masses is lacking. In one context, J. R. Oppenheimer, who pioneered the study of neutron stars and gravitational collapse, remarked that the present situation in interpreting quasars resembled that of quantum electrodynamics eighteen years ago, when all one had was confusion and lots of data. If the meeting taught us anything, it has taught us that those two dark clouds in the otherwise clear sky of physics (Kelvin, at the turn of the last century, was referring to natural radioactivity and x rays) are still there. But they are now to be found at the very edge of our universe.

PART II

COLLAPSE

REPORT ON THE PROPERTIES
chapter 2   # OF MASSIVE OBJECTS

F. HOYLE, F.R.S., AND WILLIAM A. FOWLER

The bigger they come, the harder they fall.—ROBERT FITZSIMMONS (1862–1917)

I. INTRODUCTION

By a massive object we mean upward of 10^6 $M\odot$ concentrated in a comparatively small volume, say, less than 1 (pc)$^3 \sim 3 \times 10^{55}$ cm^3. The object will be regarded as coherent in the sense that it possesses a common envelope, although it may possess structure in its interior—for example, it could contain subregions in which the density is locally much higher than the mean density. For the moment we ignore the question of how such an object might be formed—the observational evidence would seem to give strong support to the postulate of the existence of massive objects, and it is therefore reasonable to inquire into their properties without further ado. We turn a blind eye, a deaf ear, and a cold shoulder to written, oral, and implied criticism, respectively.

Any collection of matter will collapse under self-gravitation in a time of order $(\rho G)^{-1/2}$, ρ the initial density, G the gravitational constant, unless collapse is prevented by non-gravitational forces. It seems unlikely that magnetic forces will prevent collapse once contraction starts, because magnetic forces and gravitational forces keep step together. If gravitational forces are initially the larger, they are always the larger. Nor does it seem as if pressure forces, such as we may expect to develop through compression, can be adequate to balance gravity when the gravitational coupling constant effectively diverges under general relativistic conditions as is the case for massive condensations. The calculation of the pressure appears to be of considerable importance, however, in relation to a possible fragmentation of the object. We begin by obtaining a relation between ρ and the temperature T for a massive cloud that condenses from a diffuse state—i.e., $\rho \ll \sim 10^{-16}$ gm cm^{-3} initially, implying that an object of mass 10^6–10^8 $M\odot$ has an initial volume $\gg \sim 1$ (pc)^3.

II. THE RELATION BETWEEN DENSITY AND TEMPERATURE
FOR A MASSIVE OBJECT

We take the initial density to be so low that the object is at first optically thin to radiation in the Balmer continuum. The radiation rate is $\sim 10^{-24}$ n_e^2 erg cm^{-3} sec^{-1},

Supported in part by the Office of Naval Research and in part by the National Aeronautics and Space Administration.

F. HOYLE, F.R.S., St. John's College, Cambridge, England. WILLIAM A. FOWLER, California Institute of Technology.

17

where n_e is the electron density, and we take into account the fact that the electron temperature will not turn out to be much different from 10^4 ° K. The radiation emitted in the collapse time $(\rho G)^{-1/2}$ is therefore $\sim 10^{-24}\, G^{-1/2} \rho^{-3/2}\, n_e{}^2$ erg gm^{-1}, which may be compared with $\Re T \sim 10^{12}$ erg gm^{-1}, the work done in the compression. The comparison shows that for $n_e \sim 10^{18} \rho^{3/4} G^{1/4} \sim n^{3/4} G^{1/4}$, where n is the total density of hydrogen atoms per cm^3 and radiation removes the energy generated by compression, provided our assumption that the object is optically thin remains valid. We show next that this is the case until n increases to $\sim 10^8$ atom cm^{-3}, i.e., $\rho \sim 10^{-16}$ gm cm^{-3}.

We have $n_e/n \sim (G/n)^{1/4} \sim 10^{-4}$, for $n \sim 10^8$ cm^{-3}. In the absence of a thermodynamic radiation field the ionization is maintained by collisions. To obtain $n_e/n \sim 10^{-4}$ an electron temperature not much below 10^4 ° K is required. Now the hydrogen is very opaque to Lyman-α quanta, and collisional equilibrium involving collisions of both the "first and second kinds" is set up between the ground state and the $2s$, $2p$ states. The population of the latter is determined essentially by the Boltzmann factor, exp $-E/kT$, which for a level excitation of 10 eV and $T \sim 10^4$ ° K is $\sim 10^{-5}$ (we have not included the weight factor for the $2s$, $2p$ states because T should be a little below 10^4 ° K). Hence for a total hydrogen density of $\sim 10^8$ atom cm^{-3} the density of atoms in the $2s$, $2p$ states is $\sim 10^3$ cm^{-3}. Remembering that the cross-section for ionization into the continuum—i.e., for absorption of a quantum in the Balmer continuum by an excited atom—is $\sim 10^{-17}$ cm^2, the mean free path for such a quantum is $\sim 10^{14}$ cm. Taking the total mass as $10^7\, M\odot$ the dimension of the object is ~ 1 pc when $n \sim 10^8$ atom cm^{-3}. Hence the time required for a quantum in the Balmer continuum to escape is $\sim \frac{1}{3}(3 \times 10^4) \times (10^8) = 10^{12}$ sec, the first factor in parentheses being the ratio of the dimension of the object to the mean free path and the second factor being the time that would be required if there were no absorptions and re-emissions. Finally, we compare this result with $(\rho G)^{-1/2}$, which for $\rho \sim 10^{-16}$ gm cm^{-3} is $\sim 3 \times 10^{11}$ sec. We conclude that, for the masses in question, enclosure conditions have just about set in for the Balmer continuum at the stage where $\rho \sim 10^{-16}$ gm cm^{-3} and where the dimension of the object is ~ 1 pc. The enclosure conditions are not much different for the Paschen continuum, etc., so we conclude that enclosure of radiation occurs for a collapsing object at about this density.

It must not be supposed, however, that the thermodynamic radiation field corresponding to $T \sim 10^4$ ° K is set up immediately once radiation becomes trapped within the object. The required radiant energy density is $aT^4 \sim 10^2$ erg cm^{-3}, whereas the matter energy density $\Re \rho T$ is only $\sim 10^{-4}$ erg cm^{-3}. Evidently, compression will remain essentially isothermal until enough work has been done to build up the thermodynamic radiation field. Compression from ρ_1 to ρ_2 gives $\Re T \ln \rho_2/\rho_1$ per unit mass or $\Re T\, \rho_2 \ln \rho_2/\rho_1$ per unit volume. Writing

$$\Re T\, \rho_2 \ln \rho_2/\rho_1 \sim aT^4 \,,$$

with $\rho_1 \sim 10^{-16}$ gm cm^{-3}, $T \sim 10^4$ ° K, we obtain $\rho_2 \sim 10^{-11}$ gm cm^{-3}. We conclude that the density must rise to at least 10^{-11} gm cm^{-3} even under enclosure conditions, before the thermodynamic radiation field can be fully established. It still remains to consider the energy necessary to ionize the bulk of the hydrogen atoms. This amounts to $\sim 10^{13}$ erg gm^{-1}, so that we also require

$$\Re T \ln \rho_2/\rho_1 \sim 10^{13} \,,$$

i.e., $\ln \rho_2/\rho_1 \sim 10$. As it happens, this again leads to $\rho_2 \sim 10^{-11}$ gm cm^{-3}. It appears then that thermodynamic conditions will be set up for a density of order 10^{-11} gm cm^{-3}. Because the radiation field has an appreciably higher energy content than the matter, the ratio β of gas pressure to total pressure is appreciably less than unity. This implies that in any subsequent adiabatic compression the density varies nearly as the cube of the temperature. To sufficient accuracy

$$\rho \sim 10^{-23} T^3 \text{ gm cm}^{-3}, \ T \text{ (in } ^\circ \text{ K)} ,$$

or

$$\rho \sim 10 \ T_8{}^3 \text{ gm cm}^{-3}, \ T_8 \text{ (in units of } 10^8 \,{}^\circ \text{ K)} , \tag{1}$$

the constant of proportionality being fixed to give $\rho \sim 10^{-11}$ gm cm^{-3} for $T \sim 10^4\,^\circ$ K.

III. FRAGMENTATION

Hoyle and Fowler (1963a) obtained the following equation for the relation between ρ, T necessary for pressure forces to *balance* gravitational forces within a body of mass $M \ (\gg M\odot)$:

$$\rho \approx 1.3 \times 10^2 \left(\frac{M_\odot}{M}\right)^{1/2} T_8{}^3 \text{ gm cm}^{-3} . \tag{2}$$

This agrees with equation (1) for $M \approx 10^2 \ M\odot$. For larger masses the pressure corresponding to equation (1) is inadequate to provide support against gravity. Collapse therefore continues even after enclosure of radiation and after the establishment of the thermodynamic radiation field. We have seen that the latter occurs at $\rho \sim 10^{-11}$ gm cm^{-3}, at which stage an object of mass $10^7 \ M\odot$ has dimensions of order 10^{17} cm, and the velocity of infall ~ 1000 km sec^{-1}. If the kinetic energy corresponding to this velocity could be converted to heat, the temperature would be substantially increased. Instead of equation (1) we should have $\rho \sim 10^{-2} \ T_8{}^3$ gm cm^{-3}, and this would agree approximately with equation (2) for the total mass of the object. It follows that, if a process can be found for converting the dynamical energy of infall to heat, then pressure forces can compete with gravity. However, so long as the object remains a coherent cloud this cannot be done—all that can be achieved is the simple adiabatic compression leading to equation (1).

Should the object fragment into masses of order $10^2 \ M\odot$, two processes for generating heat can arise, one a dynamical process along the lines of the previous paragraph, the other due to nuclear reactions. We shall consider them in turn, noting that any such fragmentation either requires the magnetic intensity to be such that

$$\frac{H^2}{8\pi} < aT^4 , \tag{3}$$

or else the fragments are formed by compression parallel to the lines of force. With $T \sim 10^4\,^\circ$ K in equation (3), $H < \sim 50$ gauss. Remembering that $\rho \sim 10^{-11}$ gm cm^{-3} at the stage where the thermodynamic radiation field with $T \sim 10^4\,^\circ$ K first becomes established, and that $H \propto \rho^{2/3}$ for isotropic compression, the condition on H can be written $H < \sim 10^9 \ \rho^{2/3}$ gauss. If the object were to form with ρ initially $\sim 10^{-21}$ gm cm^{-3}, then $H < \sim 10^{-5}$ gauss, certainly a possible condition.

With the object fragmenting into some 10^5 objects, each of mass $\sim 10^2 \ M\odot$, collapse continues. The dynamical energy of collapse is now possessed by the fragments. Mutual perturbations can probably be expected to endow the fragments with sufficient angular momentum to prevent them all falling into the center. The original object is replaced by a cloud of particles moving with speeds of order 1000 km sec^{-1}. The particles possess a significant target area, however, and collisions between them must occur from time to time. The effect of collisions is to convert the dynamical energy to heat, exactly the process we are looking for.

A star of mass $10^2 \ M\odot$ has a radius $\sim 10^{12}$ cm. The total projected area of the 10^5

fragments is therefore $\sim 10^{29}$ cm^2, while the total projected area of the whole region occupied by the fragments is $\sim 10^{34}$ cm^2 for a characteristic dimension of 10^{17} cm. This
means that the chance of a particular fragment experiencing collision in a single transit
of the system is $\sim 10^{-5}$, so that with 10^5 fragments in all we expect 1 collision per transit.
The time for the latter is just the characteristic dimension divided by the speed of the
fragments, about 10^9 sec. Hence we have 1 collision per 10^9 sec; and the whole system of
fragments collides together in $\sim 10^{14}$ sec.

The total energy yield per collision is $\sim 10^{51}$ erg, so that the rate at which energy is
released is $\sim 10^{42}$ erg sec^{-1}, a value comparable with the optical emission from the nuclei
of the Seyfert galaxies.

The above values refer to an object of total mass $M = 10^7 M\odot$, radius $R \sim 10^{17}$ cm.
For other values of M, R, but keeping the fragment masses the same, the collision frequency varies as $M^{5/2}R^{-7/2}$, while the energy yield per collision varies as M/R, so that
the rate of energy release varies as $M^{7/2}R^{-9/2}$. Evidently, it would be easy to change M, R
so that the rate of energy release was increased to $\sim 10^{46}$ erg sec^{-1}, the value associated
with the quasi-stellar objects. But there would be an increase of the collision frequency
by nearly the same factor, to about 1 collision per 10^5 sec, and it would be hard to understand the light variations observed for 3C 48 and 3C 273 in terms in collisions. However,
we have described a process whereby dynamical energy can be converted to heat, permitting the pressure to increase far above the value given by equation (1).

IV. NUCLEAR REACTIONS

The lifetime for the nuclear evolution of an autonomous star of large mass is $\sim 10^6$ yr,
which is of the same order as the time scale derived in the previous section for the dynamical evolution through collisions in the case $M = 10^7 M\odot$, $R \sim 10^{17}$ cm. Hence nuclear
evolution must also be considered, especially as the energy yield exceeds 10^{18} erg gm^{-1},
compared to $\sim 10^{16}$ erg gm^{-1} in the dynamical case. This greater yield would, indeed,
go some way toward compensating a more drastic choice for M, R, e.g., $M = 10^8 M\odot$.
Moreover, there is an important distinction to be drawn between an autonomous star
and a fragment embedded inside a gaseous object.

An autonomous star of large mass is very largely convective throughout its interior.
The switch from convective transport in the interior to radiative transport, as the surface is approached, is caused by the photospheric boundary condition, by the necessity
for transmitting the outward flux into space as radiation. In fact, for large enough mass
the internal temperature, and hence the rate of nuclear evolution, is controlled by the
photospheric condition. Now for a fragment embedded in a gaseous medium convection
may well continue from the interior of the fragment out into the medium itself. There
need be no photospheric condition in the usual sense. It is possible therefore that higher
temperatures exist inside fragments than in autonomous stars and that nuclear evolution takes place much more rapidly. The limit is set only by the efficiency of convection
in the external medium.

An interesting situation arises if the internal temperature becomes high enough for
β-decays in the CNO cycle to have longer lifetimes than (p, γ) reactions. For example,
N^{13} may no longer decay to C^{13} but may form O^{14} through $N^{13}(p, \gamma)O^{14}$. At very high
temperatures—in excess of 5×10^8 ° K—the cycle leaks badly past Ne^{20}, but for temperatures less than 4×10^8 ° K there is a similar catalytic behavior of C, N, O as in the
normal cycle. However, the details are different and more complicated, as can be seen
from Figure 1.

At temperatures high enough for the cycle time to be determined by the β-decays
$(T^8 > \sim 1.5)$ the time around the cycle is about 300 sec, and the rate of hydrogen burning is given by

$$\frac{dX}{dt} \approx 10^{-3} X_{CNO},$$

with t in seconds, provided the hydrogen concentration X does not become very small compared to unity. Even for X_{CNO} as low as 10^{-3} the time scale is only $\sim 10^6$ sec. However, it will be recalled that energy production for the cycle is likely to be highly concentrated toward the center of a fragment. But even allowing for this, significant evolution can occur in a time scale of ~ 1 yr, much less than the normal value of $\sim 10^6$ yr.

The energy yield from burning $10^2 \, M\odot$ of hydrogen is $\sim 10^{54}$ erg. If the burning takes place over 1 yr the energy production rate $\sim 3 \times 10^{46}$ erg sec^{-1}, about the rate required for the quasi-stellar sources.

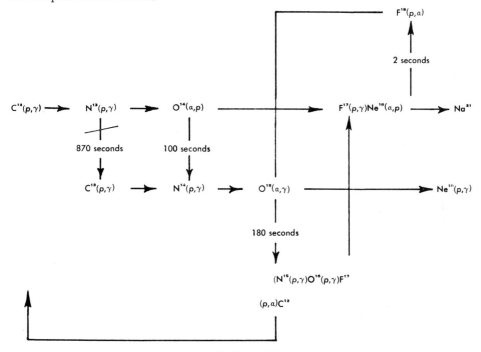

Fig. 1.—Modified CNO cycle

Consider next, what convective situation in the gaseous medium would be necessary to carry a flux of $\sim 10^{46}$ erg sec^{-1}. Take a sphere of radius r surrounding the particular fragment in which equation (3) holds, and suppose material of density ρ moves with velocity v, so that the rate at which matter crosses the sphere is $\sim 4\pi r^2 v \rho$. The energy content per unit mass is $(\frac{3}{2} P_g + aT^4/\rho)$, where P_g is the gas pressure. Now inside the fragment we expect ρ, T to be related by equation (1). Moreover, for β appreciably less than unity the adiabatic relation between ρ and T is close to $\rho \propto T^3$, so that equation (1) can be used, not only inside the fragment, but also in the external convective medium. Neglecting P_g in the energy content we have

$$\frac{aT^4}{\rho} \sim 5 \times 10^{16} \rho^{1/3},$$

and the convective energy transport is given by multiplying this expression by the mass flow $\sim 4\pi r^2 v \rho$ and by an efficiency factor, q, say. Equating this convective transport to the value 10^{46} erg sec^{-1}, we obtain

$$\rho \sim 10^{21} r^{-3/2} v^{-3/4} q^{-3/4} \, .$$

With $v \sim 10^7$ cm sec^{-1}, $r \sim 10^{16}$ cm we have $\rho \sim 10^{-8}$ gm cm^{-3}, provided q is not very small. The corresponding mass $\sim 10^8$ $M\odot$, and the time scale of the convection $r/v \sim 3 \times 10^8$ sec. The thermal energy content per gram $\sim 10^{14}$ erg is comparable to the dynamic energy, and the temperature T at $r \sim 10^{16}$ cm is $\sim 10^5$ ° K.

V. COMPARISON WITH THE OBSERVATIONS FOR 3C 273

We are indebted to our colleagues, Jesse L. Greenstein, J. Beverley Oke, Allan R. Sandage, and Maarten Schmidt for the information that the spectrum of 3C 273 is essentially due to electron-proton recombinations. It has already been noted above that the emission rate in the Balmer continuum is given by $\sim 10^{-24} n_e^2$ erg cm^{-3} sec^{-1}. The presence of the 5007 Å forbidden line of [O III] in the spectrum implies that n_e cannot be much greater than 10^7 cm^{-3}, giving $\sim 10^{-10}$ erg cm^{-3} sec^{-1}. Hence, to obtain a total radiation rate of $\sim 10^{46}$ erg sec^{-1}, an emitting volume of $\sim 10^{56}$ cm^3 is required—i.e., about 1 (pc)^3. For a mass $\sim 10^7$ $M\odot$ the density can only be $\sim 10^{-16}$ gm cm^{-3}.

According to the views developed in previous sections, the energy production of 3C 273 is not likely to come from the whole emitting volume, but from an inner region with characteristic dimensions no greater than $\sim 10^{17}$ cm. Our view is that energy is brought to the surface of this inner region by convection, the time scale for the convection being a few years. In the more extensive outer region energy is transported by radiation, however. The light variations of 3C 273 require that the time scale for escape of the radiation also be no more than a few years. This will be the case provided the optical depth of the outer region is not more than about 10. Indeed, electron scattering with $n_e \sim 10^7$ cm^{-3} gives about this optical depth.

Our picture then is that radiation from an inner region with dimension between 10^{16} and 10^{17} cm passes through a tenuous outer region of dimension $\sim 10^{18}$ cm, which might be a ring of matter rotating about a more massive interior. For a total mass of 10^8 $M\odot$ the rotary velocity of the ring would be ~ 1000 km sec^{-1}.

We suspect that the dimension of the inner region may be nearer to 10^{16} cm than to 10^{17} cm, for the reason that the effective temperature would be comparable to the Sun if the emitting surface had a radius as large as 10^{17} cm. A distinctly bluer color is needed, implying a significantly smaller radius.

As regards the origin of the light variations, dynamic collisions might make an appreciable contribution to the energy output, but the light variations can hardly arise from individual collisions, since many collisions occur in a year in that case. Rapid nuclear evolution of a particular fragment supplies significantly more energy than a single collision, and might possibly be the source of the light variations. The suggestion by Harlan Smith (1963) that the emitting surface might be in regular pulsation, after the manner of a variable star, has difficulty in arriving at a short enough period. The inner region would have to possess approximate mechanical equilibrium with pressure forces balancing gravity. The associated ratio of specific heats is then very close to $\frac{4}{3}$, a circumstance that considerably lengthens the period. Another possibility is that the inner region has a rotary period of ~ 10 yr. This is certainly possible for a mass of 10^7–10^8 $M\odot$ having characteristic dimension $\sim 10^{16}$ cm. A lack of rotational symmetry would be necessary to explain the light variations, however.

On this picture the tenuous outer region has little importance in determining the energy output. However, it does have great importance in determining the final spectrum, particularly over wavelengths accessible to observation. The differences of spectrum between one quasi-stellar source and another could very well arise from differences in the size and mass of the outer region.

VI. ROTATION

The angular velocity of a particle moving in a circular orbit of radius 1 pc about a body of mass 10^8 $M\odot$ is $\sim 2 \times 10^{-11}$ sec^{-1}, while the mean density interior to the orbit is $\sim 10^{-15}$ gm cm^{-3}. For an object condensing from a typical galactic density of $\sim 10^{-23}$ gm cm^{-3} the angular velocity increases as $\rho^{2/3}$ if angular momentum is constant. Hence an angular velocity of $\sim 2 \times 10^{-11}$ sec^{-1} at $\rho \sim 10^{-15}$ gm cm^{-3} would correspond to $\sim 10^{-16}$ sec^{-1} at $\rho = 10^{-23}$ gm cm^{-3}, if angular momentum is constant as it must be when the cloud has no connection to an external medium. Typical values of the angular velocity in spiral galaxies are of order 10^{-15} sec^{-1}. Hence we see that the picture of the structure of massive objects developed above requires less angular momentum than would usually be the case for a spiral, but not by a large factor. Angular velocities in elliptical galaxies, particularly those of small ellipticity, are likely to be less than in spirals, and this could well be the reason why extremely violent processes associated with massive objects seem to occur in the former but not in the latter.

We have considered an inner region of dimension $\sim 10^{16}$ cm surrounded by an outer region of volume ~ 1 (pc)^3. The above considerations apply to the outer region. Either the inner region would have initially to possess much less angular momentum than the outer region, or a process of transfer of angular momentum must occur. We regard the latter possibility as more likely. The process of angular momentum transfer could well arise from a clock-spring winding of a magnetic field. For transfer over a time scale of $\sim 10^5$ yr the magnetic intensity need not be very great, since many rotation periods of the system are involved. The required intensity is $\sim (Mv/t)^{1/2} R^{-1}$, where $t \sim 10^5$ yr $\sim 3 \times 10^{12}$ sec in the time scale. With $M = 10^8 \, M_\odot$, $R \sim 10^{17}$ cm, $v \sim 3 \times 10^8$ cm sec^{-1}, the required intensity is ~ 30 gauss, comparable with the permissible limit obtained from equation (3) for the case $R \sim 10^{17}$ cm. Indeed, our requirement for fragmentation was $H < \sim 10^9 \rho^{2/3}$ gauss, and $\rho \sim 5 \times 10^{40} R^{-3}$ for $M = 10^8 \, M_\odot$. Hence, for arbitrary R, the fragmentation condition on H is $H < \sim 10^{36} R^{-2}$ gauss, whereas the angular-momentum transfer requires $H > \sim 10^{23} R^{-5/4}$ gauss, the time scale again being taken as 10^5 yr. The two conditions can just be met. However, it must be emphasized that even if the simple fragmentation requirement were not satisfied some fragments could still form through condensation parallel to the magnetic lines of force. The condition for angular-momentum transfer would therefore seem the more important.

VII. THE STRONG RADIO SOURCES

It is interesting to compare gravitation as an energy source with nuclear reactions. The latter are capable of yielding $\sim 6 \times 10^{18}$ erg gm^{-1}, this being the value for conversion of H^1 to He^4. The gravitational potential energy GM/R is $\sim 10^{16}$ erg gm^{-1} for $M = 10^8 \, M_\odot$, $R = 10^{18}$ cm, so that gravitation cannot compete with nuclear reactions if the dimension of an object is of the order of the outer region of 3C 273. For a dimension $R \sim 10^{16}$ cm, comparable to what we suggest for the inner region of 3C 273, the gravitational energy is $\sim 10^{18}$ erg gm^{-1}, and gravitation then competes on about equal terms with nuclear reactions. However, for still smaller R, $R \sim 10^{14}$ cm, gravitation gives overwhelmingly the stronger contribution, $\sim 10^{20}$ erg gm^{-1}. For such R consideration of general relativity also become dominant. We have suggested previously (Hoyle and Fowler 1963b; Hoyle, Fowler, Burbidge, and Burbidge 1964; Fowler 1964) that the energy output of strong radio sources is derived from the gravitational contribution when R is comparable with the Schwarzschild radius $R \sim 2 \, GM/c^2 \sim 3 \times 10^{13}$ cm for $M = 10^8 \, M_\odot$. Only in this way does it seem possible to understand the very large energies required for the strong radio sources, upward of 10^{60} erg.

However, a critical problem arises as to the process that gets gravitational energy out of an object. Fragmentation, followed by multiple collisions between fragments might be invoked at smaller R than in Section III, e.g., for $R \sim 10^{14}$ cm. Yet the release of energy in many comparatively small-scale events does not fit the observational evidence very well. The typical radio source seems to be associated with the violent emission of one or more (often two) well-directed jets. The jets must move outward with speeds close to c, and must contain mass in excess of 10^6 $M_\odot$. These are not character-istics to be expected from a summation over many small-scale events.

Moreover, a theoretical objection can be raised to the dynamic collision hypothesis in the case where rotation is important, as it almost certainly is when R becomes as small as 10^{14} cm. The argument of Section III proceeded on the basis that fragments move in random orbits. This is not valid when rotation is important, since the fragments then tend to move along more or less parallel orbits. Collisional effects are much re-duced. The same argument strengthens the case for nuclear reactions as the source of the *optical* energy of quasi-stellar objects.

If angular-momentum transfer to an outer region of dimension $\sim 10^{18}$ cm can permit an inner region to condense to dimension $R \sim 10^{16}$ cm, as seems necessary if we are to understand the optical emission of objects such as 3C 273, then the same process can

$$\frac{dU_{gr}}{dt} \approx \frac{G}{45\,c^5} \sum_{\alpha\beta} \left(\dddot{D}_{\alpha\beta} \right)^2 \text{ Landau and Lifshitz 1962}$$

$$D_{\alpha\beta} = \int \rho \left(3 x^\alpha x^\beta - \delta_{\alpha\beta} x_\gamma^2 \right) dV \text{ [3]}$$

System radiates significantly in $\sim 10 \left(\dfrac{2GM}{R c^2} \right)^{-7/2}$ rotations.

Might promote fission through ordinary instability.

Pieces fly in opposite directions.

FIG. 2.—Gravitational waves

presumably permit a further condensation to $R \sim 10^{14}$ cm. In fact, less angular momen-tum needs to be transferred as R decreases. As the Schwarzschild critical radius is ap-proached, the inner region rotates with a speed near c. Unless the rotating inner mass pre-serves strict axial symmetry, a new process then comes into operation, the radiation of gravitational waves. The result of the first-order gravitational theory is probably correct. It requires significant radiation of the dynamical energy of rotation in $a^{-1}(2G\dot{M}/Rc^2)^{-7/2}$ revolutions, where a is a form factor that might perhaps be as large as 0.1. For $R \sim 10^{16}$ cm, $M = 10^8$ $M_\odot$, $2\,GM/Rc^2 \sim 1/300$, and $\sim 10^{10}$ orbital revolutions would be required. Since the time required per revolution would be ~ 1 yr the total time needed for evolu-tion through the emission of gravitational waves is much longer than the evolutionary time arising from other processes—e.g., angular-momentum transfer, through the agency of a magnetic field. The situation changes dramatically as R decreases. For $R \sim 10^{14}$ cm, only $\sim 10^3$ revolutions are required. Moreover, since the orbital period is now only $\sim 10^4$ sec, the total evolution time ~ 1 yr. The time shortens even more as the critical radius is approached, to ~ 1 day.

The interesting possibility arises that this rapid removal of energy may induce ordi-nary fissional instability. As Lyttleton (1953) has shown, the system breaks into two unequal pieces that recede from each other at a speed comparable to the original orbital speed. Furthermore, the relative speed of recession of the pieces can remain large throughout the separation. Such a process contains the main features demanded by observation, two jets at speed $\sim c$ moving in opposite directions. One of the jets, that corresponding to the smaller piece, would move faster so that the jets would not move outward at the same speed—a result that does not seem in contradiction to observation. A further advantage of the process is that it should be largely independent of initial conditions, unless perhaps a magnetic field is needed to induce the initial departure from axial symmetry. A considerable measure of reproducibility in the radio source phenomenon is therefore to be expected.

The fissional hypothesis and the formulae for gravitational radiation are shown in Figure 2.

VIII. COLLAPSE INSIDE THE CRITICAL SCHWARZSCHILD RADIUS

The problem of the collapse of an object of uniform density without rotation and without pressure was solved by Oppenheimer and Snyder (1939). The following is a brief résumé of the details:

Oppenheimer-Snyder Analysis

Object of uniform density, without rotation, implodes from rest.

$$\text{Initial density } \rho_0. \qquad a = \frac{8\pi G}{3}\rho_0.$$

In terms of co-moving coordinates

$$d s^2 = d t^2 - S^2(t)\left(\frac{d r^2}{1 - a r^2} + r^2 d\Omega^2\right) \qquad \text{inside,}$$

$$d s^2 = d t^2 - S^2\left(t\,\frac{r_b^{3/2}}{r^{3/2}}\right)\left(\frac{K^2 d r^2}{1 - a r_b^3/r} + r^2 d\Omega^2\right) \qquad \text{outside,}$$

$$c = 1, \qquad K = \frac{1}{S}\frac{\partial}{\partial r}(rS).$$

Inside $\chi = t$. Outside $\chi = t\, r_b^{3/2}/r^{3/2}$.

$$\left(\frac{dS}{d\chi}\right)^2 = a\,\frac{(1 - S)}{S},$$

$$a^{1/2}\chi = \frac{\pi}{2} - \sin^{-1} S^{1/2} + S^{1/2}\sqrt{1 - S}.$$

Implosion into singularity in proper time $(3\pi/32G\rho_0)^{1/2}$.

Event Horizon: So long as (1) $R > a r_b^3$, (2) $R > r_b S$, the well-known Schwarzschild metric can be used in the exterior.

$$d s^2 = d T^2\left(1 - \frac{2GM}{R}\right) - \frac{dR^2}{1 - (2GM/R)} - R^2 d\Omega^2.$$

$$R = rS.$$

Light emitted from the object can reach an external observer so long as $S > ar_b^2$.

$$R = r_b S \rightarrow 2GM \quad \text{as} \quad S \rightarrow ar_b^2 .$$

In the limiting case the light reaches the external observer as $T \rightarrow \infty$, and is infinitely redshifted.

> *Important:* This use of the Schwarzschild metric requires the energy-momentum tensor to be zero in the exterior.

It is generally agreed that the conclusions of this analysis are not critically dependent on most of the initial assumptions, on uniform density, on precise spherical symmetry, on implosion from rest, or even on the assumption of zero pressure provided the mass is large ($\gg M_\odot$). The assumption of zero rotation may be important, however. We have seen throughout that rotation probably plays a major role in the evolution of massive objects.

The effects of rotation can, however, be profoundly modified by relativistic effects. In ordinary dynamics rotational forces increase more rapidly as a system condenses than do gravitational forces. But this need not be the case as the critical Schwarzschild radius is approached. When the energy density, including rest-mass energy, increases as R^{-4} gravitational forces keep step with rotational forces. This is the case for a radiation field, for example, and the latter can make an appreciable contribution to the energy density as the critical radius is reached. Moreover, the rotary energy itself increases the gravitational force. Fission reduces rotary forces in separating fragments. The fragments could then fall inside their individual critical radii. Thereafter, rotary forces could fail to catch up with gravity, so that the situation could approximate to the analysis of Oppenheimer and Snyder.

IX. THE SINGULARITY?

The existence of a singularity as a possible development in the theory of relativity is worrying, since it implies a breakdown of the principle of equivalence—corresponding singularities do not exist in electromagnetic theory, so a co-moving observer falling into the singularity *can* distinguish between falling in a gravitational field and being pulled by a "rope"—i.e., being subject to an electromagnetic force.

A singularity also implies a contradiction in what we assume about the nature of matter. Transformation of one baryon into another apart, we assume that the world lines of particles are complete lines. From an arbitrary point on a world line we can pass to infinity in either direction along the line. This property is violated at a singularity. Instead of a complete line we have a broken line. If the Universe had a singular origin, the line has two ends. It becomes a segment of a line.

The point of view of Hoyle and Narlikar (1964) is that if world lines can be broken then a mathematical expression of the fact should be given. The procedure adopted was to require that the action of a particle be stationary, not only with respect to a slight deviation of any finite portion of the trajectory (i.e., with fixed ends), but also with respect to small variations of the position of a broken end. This procedure also makes better sense, in that the action associated with a segment of a line is finite, and the requirement that the variation of a finite quantity be zero has meaning. The action of a complete line is infinite and the meaning of its variation is obscure.

In order to give expression to the required property of the action, Hoyle and Narlikar find it necessary to introduce a coupling between the ends of broken lines. This implies the existence of a field radiated by "ends," which Hoyle and Narlikar call the C-field, the coupling used being scalar. The definition of the coupling, together with the stationary property of the action, determine all equations. When solved in the cosmological case it is found that the Universe did not have a singularity. Similarly, it is found that collapsing objects do not implode into singularities.

These results can be understood in terms of the energy density of the C-field. Negative values are permitted. As an object implodes inside the critical radius, positive energy flows out, giving a non-vanishing energy-momentum tensor *outside* the object, thereby *disturbing* the usual exterior solution. Eventually, so much energy flows out that the energy density inside the object becomes negative. The infall is then *resisted* by the gravitational field and the collapse is ultimately halted. *Oscillations* occur in which the object may emerge outside the critical radius. Hoyle, Fowler, Burbidge, and Burbidge (1964) have suggested that such oscillations may provide a long-term energy source of high-speed particles.

REFERENCES

Fowler, W. A. 1964, *Rev. Mod. Phys.*, **36**, 545.
Hoyle, F., and Fowler, W. A. 1963a, *M.N.*, **125**, 169.
———. 1963b, *Nature*, **197**, 533.*
Hoyle, F., Fowler, W. A., Burbidge, E. M., and Burbidge, G. R. 1964, *Ap. J.*, **139**, 909.*
Hoyle, F., and Narlikar, J. V. 1964, *Proc. Roy. Soc. London*, in press.
Landau, L., and Lifshitz, E. 1962, *The Classical Theory of Fields* (Reading, Mass.: Addison-Wesley Publishing Co.), p. 366.
Lyttleton, R. A. 1953, *The Stability of Rotating Liquid Masses* (Cambridge: Cambridge University Press).
Oppenheimer, J. R., and Snyder, H. 1939, *Phys. Rev.*, **56**, 455.
Smith, Harlan. 1963, private communication.

ON RELATIVISTIC
chapter 3 ASTROPHYSICS

F. Hoyle, William A. Fowler, G. R. Burbidge, and
E. Margaret Burbidge

I. THE FATE OF MASSIVE BODIES

a) Introduction

Gravitation tends to pull aggregates of matter together. A logical question evidently arises as to the ultimate outcome of this process. In astronomy it has usually been supposed that astrophysical evolution proceeds in such a way that, given sufficient time, a cold body in hydrostatic equilibrium remains a body that can maintain its equilibrium over all further time. Yet it is known that no such equilibrium state can be found for a mass appreciably greater than $M_\odot$. The Chandrasekhar limit gives 5.76 $M_\odot/\mu_e{}^2$ for the maximum mass that can be supported by degenerate electron pressure. A similar result applicable at higher densities for neutron degeneracy was obtained by Oppenheimer and Volkoff (1939)—in fact, the maximum mass was about 0.7 $M_\odot$. Even the doubtful assumption of a hard-core neutron potential, allowing the nuclear fluid at high densities to behave like an incompressible liquid, only extends the maximum mass to about 3 $M_\odot$, a result obtained immediately from the Schwarzschild interior solution, using nuclear densities. Evidently, however, it is possible for gravitation to pull together much larger masses than these. The conventional view is that in all such cases a process of mass ejection takes place, conveniently reducing the final mass below one or the other of the limits just mentioned. We wish to emphasize that this view is no more than a superstition. The existence of white dwarfs has sometimes been taken as supporting evidence, but the white dwarfs can be explained in terms of the evolution of stars whose masses have never appreciably exceeded the limits mentioned above. For massive stars (and very massive objects) there is no evidence, either from theoretical studies of stellar evolution or from observation, that mass loss plays any such role. Indeed, it would be a curious situation if astrophysical processes occurring long before the onset of the final implosion crisis were to operate always to prevent the crisis from arising. This would imply an unlikely "foreknowledge" on the part of natural processes.

In this paper we propose to accept the situation that stars with masses greater than

F. Hoyle, St. John's College, Cambridge, England, and California Institute of Technology. William A. Fowler, California Institute of Technology. G. R. Burbidge and E. Margaret Burbidge, University of California, San Diego.

Reprinted from the *Astrophysical Journal*, **139**, 909–928, 1964.

the critical mass can reach a stage of catastrophic implosion in which general relativity becomes dominant. In the following section we give a brief review of what might be called the classical implosion problem (Datt 1938; Oppenheimer and Snyder 1939). In later sections we shall consider modifications demanded by (i) non-zero internal temperature, (ii) rotation, (iii) the non-classical discussion of Hoyle and Narlikar (1963). This will conclude Section I of the paper.

b) The Classical Implosion Problem

The object is assumed uniform and spherically symmetric and the internal pressure is zero. Outside is empty space, and the line element is Galilean at infinity. The object is taken to implode from rest without rotation.

The interior solution, obtained from Einstein's equation, is found to be identical to the simple elliptic cosmology with line element

$$d s^2 = d t^2 - S^2(t)\left(\frac{d r^2}{1 - r^2} + r^2 d\Omega^2\right), \tag{1}$$

$$d\Omega^2 = d\theta^2 + \sin^2\theta\, d\varphi^2 , \qquad\qquad c = 1 . \tag{2}$$

The coordinates r, θ, φ are intrinsic—that is to say, they always have the same values for any particular particle. It is possible to choose such coordinates so that $r = 0$ for any assigned particle. These conditions arise out of the special conditions of homogeneity and isotropy treated in cosmology. The same conditions arise in the case of a finite object from uniformity and spherical symmetry and from considering implosion from rest without rotation.

Einstein's equations give

$$\frac{\dot{S}^2}{S^2} = -\frac{1}{S^2} + \frac{8\pi G\rho}{3}, \tag{3}$$

where the proper density ρ satisfies the condition $\rho S^3 = $ constant. The right-hand side of equation (3) always has a zero. In the cosmological case the zero gives the value of the scale factor S at maximum expansion of the universe, while in the case of a finite object the zero refers to the initial state of rest. If quantities at the zero are referred to by the subscript zero then

$$S_0 = \left(\frac{8\pi G\rho_0}{3}\right)^{-1/2} \tag{4}$$

It is evidently possible to redefine the r coordinates so that $S = 1$ at maximum phase. The line element then takes the form

$$d s^2 = d t^2 - S^2(t)\left(\frac{d r^2}{1 - a r^2} + r^2 d\Omega^2\right), \tag{5}$$

where

$$a = \frac{8\pi G\rho_0}{3}. \tag{6}$$

Equation (3) becomes

$$\frac{\dot{S}^2}{S^2} = a\,\frac{(1 - S)}{S^3}. \tag{7}$$

It is usual to work with equations (1) and (3) in cosmology, but equations (5) and (7) are more convenient in the implosion problem. It should be noted that, whereas in cosmology, $r = 0$ can be any assigned particle, in the implosion problem $r = 0$ refers uniquely to the center of the body.

A further difference is that an exterior solution must also be found for the implosion problem. At first sight it might be thought most convenient to use Schwarzschild coordinates for the exterior,

$$ds^2 = e^\nu \, dt^2 - e^\lambda \, dR^2 - R^2 \, d\Omega^2 \,. \tag{8}$$

(The radial coordinate is characterized by the property that the sphere through R, T has area $4\pi R^2$, independent of T.) The advantage of these coordinates is that for a non-radiating object the T coordinate can be chosen such that

$$e^\nu = e^{-\lambda} = 1 - \frac{\text{constant}}{R} \tag{9}$$

and the line element is static. An awkward problem arises, however, in matching the interior and exterior solutions at the boundary of the object. The boundary has a constant r coordinate, r_b say, but the R coordinate is not constant. For this reason it is convenient to complete the exterior solution in terms of the r, t coordinates. With the solution obtained a transformation to R, T can be found.

The exterior solution has the remarkable property that Einstein's equations, instead of being partial in r, t, become ordinary equations with $r^{-3/2} \, t$ as variable. The line element is

$$d s^2 = d t^2 - S^2 \left(\frac{t r_b^{3/2}}{r^{3/2}} \right) \left(\frac{K^2 d r^2}{1 - a r_b^3 / r} + r^2 d\Omega^2 \right), \tag{10}$$

where $K = (1/S)\partial/\partial r(rS)$, and S satisfies equation (7) but with differentiation taken with respect to $t r_b^{3/2}/r^{3/2}$. The exterior solution is, therefore, closely similar to the interior solution.

Turning now to the transformation to Schwarzschild coordinates, our aim is to determine the constant in equation (9). This is achieved most easily by noticing that Schwarzschild coordinates can also be used for the interior—subject to a proviso to be mentioned later—and that e^ν, e^λ are continuous at the boundary. In fact

$$R = rS(t) \qquad \text{and} \qquad T = \Phi \left(\int \frac{r \, dr}{1 - a r^2} + \int \frac{dt}{S \dot{S}} \right) \tag{11}$$

transform the line element from equation (5) to equation (8) with

$$e^\lambda = \frac{1}{1 - a r^2 - r^2 \dot{S}^2}, \qquad e^\nu = \frac{S^2 \dot{S}^2 (1 - a r^2)}{(1 - a r^2 - r^2 \dot{S}^2) \Phi_1^2}. \tag{12}$$

Here Φ is any differentiable function and Φ_1 is the derivative with respect to the argument. For the purpose of determining the constant in equation (9) nothing more need be known about Φ.

Inserting for $\dot{S}^2$ from equation (7) we have

$$e^{-\lambda} = 1 - \frac{a r^2}{S} = 1 - \frac{a r^3}{R}. \tag{13}$$

Applying equation (13) at the boundary $r = r_b$ we see that the constant in equation (9) is $a r_b^3$. Remembering the definition of a we can write e^{λ} in the conventional form

$$e^{-\lambda} = 1 - \frac{2GM}{R} \tag{14}$$

by defining

$$M = \frac{4\pi}{3} \rho_0 r_b^3. \tag{15}$$

For an observer in the exterior, M is the gravitational mass of the object. It remains constant throughout the implosion for a non-radiating object.

An event horizon develops at $R = 2GM$. Once the object has contracted inside the sphere with this R coordinate no further signals can cross the sphere. Writing $R = r_b S(t)$ for the boundary, we see that the boundary coincides with the event horizon when

$$S = \frac{2GM}{r_b} = a r_b^2, \qquad a = \frac{8\pi G \rho_0}{3}. \tag{16}$$

The proper time required for the object to fall inside the event horizon is

$$\int_{S=1}^{S=a r_b^2} dt = \int_1^{a r_b^2} \frac{dS}{\dot{S}} = \frac{1}{a^{1/2}} \left[\frac{\pi}{2} - \sin^{-1} a^{1/2} r_b + a^{1/2} r_b \sqrt{(1 - a r_b^2)} \right], \tag{17}$$

and implosion into a singularity occurs in a proper time

$$\int_0^1 \frac{dS}{\dot{S}} = \frac{\pi}{2 a^{1/2}}. \tag{18}$$

The square root of equation (7), choosing the negative sign, is used in the evaluation of these integrals.

Initially, we have $R = r_b$. At the event horizon $R = 2GM = a r_b^3$. Hence, if implosion occurs from a dispersed state, $a r_b^2$ must be $\ll 1$, since by a dispersed state we mean that the initial area of the boundary is large compared with the area of the event horizon.

The proper time required for implosion from the event horizon into the singularity is

$$-r_b(1 - a r_b^2)^{1/2} + a^{-1/2} \sin^{-1} a^{1/2} r_b \simeq \tfrac{2}{3} a r_b^3, \quad a r_b^2 \ll 1, \tag{19}$$

i.e., for implosion from a dispersed state. In terms of M, $2 a r_b^3/3 = 4GM/3$. So far units with $c = 1$ have been used. In conventional units the proper time for implosion from the event horizon into the singularity is

$$\frac{4GM}{3\,c^3} \simeq 6.6 \times 10^{-6}\,\frac{M}{M_\odot}\,\sec \smile 660\,\sec\ \text{for}\ M = 10^8\,M_\odot. \tag{20}$$

It was mentioned above that the transformation (11) is subject to a proviso, namely, that e^λ, e^ν must not become negative. In fact the transformation is singular for $S = ar^2$, and e^λ, e^ν are negative for $S < ar^2$. Since $S \to 0$ it is clear that the transformation to Schwarzschild coordinates fails sooner or later at all points of the interior. The transformation also fails at all exterior points within the event horizon.

The transformation can, of course, be made even when $S < ar^2$, but R, T are not the usual Schwarzschild coordinates. Because of the negative values of e^ν, e^λ the space- and timelike roles of R, T are inverted—R becomes the time coordinate and T a space coordinate. These transformation difficulties explain why Schwarzschild coordinates are unsuitable for the solution of the whole implosion problem.

c) The Effects of Internal Pressure

Even a uniform pressure is capable of modifying equation (7) for S. The equivalent equation (3) can be written as

$$\frac{\dot{S}^2}{S^2} = -\frac{1}{S^2} + \frac{8\pi GE}{3}, \tag{21}$$

since the energy density E is just ρ in the absence of internal pressure. When there is a non-zero pressure, E is not equal to ρ, however. Equation (21) holds for uniform pressure, but not when there is a pressure gradient.

Now at very high densities, $> \sim 10^{16}$ gm cm^{-3}, quantum statistics prevent $E = \rho$. Thus even for zero temperature we have $E \propto \rho^{4/3}$ at very high densities. For $\rho \propto S^{-3}$, $\dot{S}^2$ is determined by a term of order S^{-2} for small S, not by a term of order S^{-1}. This evidently only accentuates the onset of the singularity.

Pressure is also important in a discrete object because a pressure gradient is always present, on account of the necessity for the pressure to be zero at the boundary. The effect of a pressure gradient is to change the mathematical structure of Einstein's equations from ordinary equations to partial equations in the coordinates r, t. The problem is then harder to handle and less is known about its solution, except in the special case of equilibrium when the t coordinate drops out.

One might be tempted to speculate that pressure gradients will ultimately halt an imploding object, since this is the case in the Newtonian approximation whenever the ratio of specific heats is greater than $4/3$. But the same result is not true if relativity effects are sufficiently important. While a formal solution, applicable in detail to the most general case, has not yet been given, a disproof follows from a simple *reductio ad absurdum* argument. For example, consider a cold object with degeneracy pressure— that is, $P \simeq \frac{1}{3}E \propto \rho^{4/3}$. If such a pressure were able to halt an implosion the resulting motion would be oscillatory between radii R_1, R_2, say—where R is once again the Schwarzschild coordinate. An equilibrium solution for the object must then exist with a radius between R_1, R_2. But this is not possible if the total mass exceeds the limiting values mentioned in the Introduction. Hence implosion cannot be halted for sufficiently large mass, $> \sim M_\odot$.

A similar argument can be used for a non-zero temperature. Although an equilibrium solution with a radius between R_1 and R_2 may be possible, the thermal energy necessary to maintain the equilibrium state becomes impossibly large as M is increased, a result recently demonstrated by Iben (1963). The mass in question depends on the value of R

at which the equilibrium solution is sought, failure occurring when $2GM/R$ becomes of order unity.

A hot object evolves through the escape of energy. This leads to R being ultimately reduced to the stage where $2\,GM/R$ is of order unity. Hence a pressure gradient must finally fail to prevent implosion; the only exception to this statement in the spherically symmetric case being when the mass falls below one or the other of the limiting values, $\sim M_\odot$.

d) Neutrino Losses

Because of the development of the event horizon one might take the view that singularities are of no consequence to an external observer, since the observer loses contact with an imploding object after it has fallen inside the event horizon. But while this is true for electromagnetic communication the external observer still has contact with the object in the sense that he can detect a gravitational field—unless there is some way in which the object can radiate its gravitational mass. This question, with particular reference to neutrinos as the radiating agent, has recently been discussed by Michel (1963). In the present section we shall re-examine this question.

To understand the issue more clearly it is convenient to use the Schwarzschild form (8) for the line element outside the object, and to consider a situation in which the energy-momentum tensor is small at all points between the object and the observer. Over a small time interval the line element can be considered static, with e^ν and e^λ given by equation (9). However, over a long time the constant in equation (9) may change secularly. Thus the 41-component of Einstein's equation is

$$\frac{d\lambda}{dt}\frac{e^{-\lambda}}{R} = -8\pi G T_4{}^1. \tag{22}$$

If we define M by

$$e^{-\lambda} = 1 - \frac{2GM}{R}, \tag{23}$$

equation (22) gives

$$\frac{dM}{dt} = -4\pi R^2 T_4{}^1. \tag{24}$$

The right-hand side of equation (24) is just minus the energy flow through the sphere of coordinate R—for example, in the electromagnetic case $T_4{}^1$ is the radial component of the Poynting vector.

We continue by estimating the energy flow in the form of neutrinos, on the basis that an object of initial mass M_0 implodes from a comparatively dispersed state in which the density ρ and the temperature $T_9 = T/10^{9\,\circ}$ K are related by

$$\rho = 2.0 \left(\frac{a}{G}\right)^{3/4} \frac{T^3}{M_0{}^{1/2}}$$

$$= 2.8 \times 10^5 \left(\frac{M_\odot}{M_0}\right)^{1/2} T_9{}^3 \text{ gm cm}^{-3}. \tag{25}$$

This equation was obtained by Hoyle and Fowler (1963a, b) for polytropes of index 3. Iben (1963) has investigated the *matter* density-temperature relation for the equilibrium state using the adiabatic approximation and has shown that equation (25) holds quite accurately up to $M \simeq 10^5\,M_\odot$ and is only a factor of 2 too high at $M \simeq 10^9\,M_\odot$. Evidently in an imploding situation the temperature corresponding to a given density is less than it is in an equilibrium state. Hence the adoption of equation (25) must tend to exaggerate the neutrino emission, as it also does for masses above $10^5 M\odot$. Since we shall show that neutrino emission does not reduce M significantly, our conclusion applies *a fortiori*.

A sample of material moves in the ρ, T_9-plane along a track determined by the usual thermodynamic relation,

$$\frac{P}{\rho^2} d\rho - dU = \frac{dU_\nu}{dt} \cdot dt, \tag{26}$$

in which P is the pressure, U the internal energy per mass, and dU_ν/dt the neutrino loss per unit mass per unit time. Equation (26) holds for an observer who is co-moving with the material and who uses locally flat coordinates. According to Fowler and Hoyle (1964) the left-hand side of equation (26) takes the simple form

$$\frac{P}{\rho^2} d\rho - dU = \tfrac{11}{3} \frac{aT^4}{\rho} \left(\frac{d\rho}{\rho} - 3 \frac{dT}{T} \right) \tag{27}$$

at T_9 appreciably in excess of unity—the case with which we shall be concerned. The expression (27) includes contributions to pressure and internal energy both from radiation and from electron pairs. The pairs contribute 7/4 of the contributions of the radiation in both cases. We also have from Fowler and Hoyle (1964) for $T_9 > 2$

$$\frac{dU_\nu}{dt} = \frac{4.3 \times 10^{15}}{\rho} T_9{}^9 \text{ erg gm}^{-1} \text{ sec}^{-1} (T_9 > 2) \tag{28}$$

for ρ in gm cm^{-3} provided all neutrinos and antineutrinos generated by $e^- + e^+ \rightarrow \nu + \bar{\nu}$ escape, and provided the neutrinos are not seriously redshifted by the gravitational field. Below $T_9 \sim 2$ neutrino losses are much smaller than given by equation (28).

We shall find that all significant neutrino loss occurs before nuclear densities are reached. Implosion can be considered to take place in accordance with

$$\frac{\dot{S}^2}{S^2} \sim \frac{8\pi G \rho_0}{3S^3}, \tag{29}$$

where we neglect the $-S^{-2}$ term in equation (7) since we are concerned with $S \ll 1$, and where we also neglect the slowing of the implosion due to the pressure gradient, and the slight acceleration due to the contribution of pairs and of radiation to E. This last contribution is $11aT^4/4$ and becomes equal to ρc^2 when $\rho = 23T_9{}^4$ in our units. For stars with $M \leq 10^9 M\odot$ which follow equation (25) the condition $\rho = 23T_9{}^4$ is never reached before the event horizon.

From $\rho S^3 = $ constant, we have

$$3 \frac{dS}{S} + \frac{d\rho}{\rho} = 0. \tag{30}$$

Combining equations (29) and (30), and remembering that the negative sign must be taken in the square root of equation (29),

$$dt = -\left(\frac{3}{8\pi G\rho}\right)^{1/2}\frac{dS}{S} = \frac{1}{(24\pi G\rho)^{1/2}}\frac{d\rho}{\rho}. \tag{31}$$

Inserting in equation (26) leads immediately to

$$\frac{d\rho}{\rho}\left[1 - \frac{1}{(24\pi G\rho)^{1/2}}\frac{dU_\nu/dt}{11aT^4/3\rho}\right] = 3\frac{dT}{T}, \tag{32}$$

and using equation (28) this can be expressed numerically in the form

$$\frac{d\rho}{\rho}\left(1 - 7\cdot10^{-5}\frac{T_9^5}{\rho^{1/2}}\right) = 3\frac{dT_9}{T_9}. \tag{32'}$$

This can be integrated straightforwardly and the constant of integration determined with the aid of equation (25) to yield

$$\rho \simeq 2.8\times10^5\left(\frac{M\odot}{M_0}\right)^{1/2}T_9^3\left(1 - 10^{-4}\frac{T_9^5}{\rho^{1/2}}\right)^{-3/5}. \tag{33}$$

This result shows that the material continues to follow a track $\rho \propto T_9^3$ so long as the second term in the second parentheses is small compared with unity. However, with increasing temperature the second term increases in importance. In the limit for high temperature the term in the second parentheses yields

$$\rho \simeq 10^{-8}\,T_9^{10}. \tag{34}$$

The track (33) of the material in the ρ, T_9-plane is a curve with equations (25) and (34) as asymptotes. The asymptotes intersect at the point

$$\rho \simeq 1.6\times10^{11}\left(\frac{M\odot}{M_0}\right)^{5/7}\text{gm cm}^{-3}, \qquad T_9 = 83\left(\frac{M\odot}{M_0}\right)^{1/14}. \tag{35}$$

We note at this point that pressure gradients can be effectively treated as decreasing the value of G used in equation (32). However, we see that a pressure gradient which reduces G to 10 per cent of its full value will only increase the time of fall, $(24\pi G\rho)^{-1/2}$, by a factor of $10^{1/2}$. Thus the calculations made below for neutrino losses using the free-fall time cannot be seriously low in value for this reason, and in fact other approximations more than compensate for the free-fall assumption.

Subject to the assumption that all neutrinos escape without redshift effects arising, we are now in a position to estimate the total neutrino loss along the path (33). This proviso means that the integration must not be carried beyond the event horizon where the neutrinos are redshifted to zero energy. According to the work of Section II the event horizon has Schwarzschild coordinate $R = ar_b^3$, while $M_0 = 4\pi\rho_0 r_b^3/3$, $S = ar_b^2$. The proper density at the event horizon is obtained from $\rho = \rho_0 S^{-3}$, which gives $\rho = \rho_0 a^{-3}r_b^{-6}$ at the event horizon. Using the definition of a, $a = 8\pi G\rho_0/3$,

$$\rho_{\max} = \left(\frac{3}{8\pi G}\right)^3\frac{1}{\rho_0^2 r_b^6} = \frac{3}{32\pi G^3}\cdot\frac{1}{M_0^2}. \tag{36}$$

It will be recalled that units with $c = 1$ were used in the former work. To express ρ in conventional units, a factor c^6 must be introduced on the right-hand side of equation (36). Numerically, we obtain

$$\rho_{\max} = 1.85\times10^{16}\left(\frac{M\odot}{M_0}\right)^2\text{gm cm}^{-3}. \tag{37}$$

Equations (25) and (37) yield a maximum temperature

$$(T_9)_{max} = 4.1 \times 10^3 \, (M\odot/M_0)^{1/2} \, . \tag{37'}$$

Thus stars with $M > 10^7 \, M\odot$ do not reach $T_9 \sim 2$ and neutrino losses are much smaller than calculated in what follows.

The expression for the energy loss per gram of material along the path (33) from $\rho = 0$ to ρ_{max} or from $t = 0$ to $t(\rho_{max})$ is

$$E_\nu = \int_0^\infty \frac{dU_\nu}{dt'} \, dt' = \int_0^{t(\rho_{max})} \frac{dU_\nu}{dt} \, dt$$

$$= \int_0^{\rho_{max}} \frac{dU_\nu/dt}{(24\pi G\rho)^{1/2}} \frac{d\rho}{\rho} \tag{38}$$

$$= 1.92 \times 10^{18} \int_0^{\rho_{max}} \frac{T_9^9}{\rho^{5/2}} \, d\rho \text{ erg gm}^{-1},$$

where dt' is the time interval and dU_ν/dt' is the energy loss measured by an external observer. It will be clear that the redshift decrease in the energy loss is just canceled by the time dilation for such an observer. It is simpler to use the calculations of the local co-moving observer and to cut off the loss which he calculates at the time he measures, $t(\rho_{max})$, corresponding to infinite time for the external observer. Eliminating the temperature by means of equation (33) yields

$$E_\nu = 5.0 \times 10^{18} \left(\frac{M_0}{M\odot}\right)^{3/7} \int_0^{Z_{max}} \frac{Z^{2/7} dZ}{(1+Z)^{9/5}}, \tag{39}$$

where

$$Z = 8.5 \times 10^{14} \left(\frac{M_0}{M\odot}\right)^{5/6} \rho^{7/6}$$

and

$$Z_{max} = 8.1 \times 10^5 \left(\frac{M\odot}{M_0}\right)^{3/2} .$$

The integral in equation (39) is $\Gamma(9/7) \, \Gamma(18/35)/\Gamma(9/5) \sim 1.67$ for $Z_{max} = \infty$. For our purposes a sufficiently accurate integration of (39) for $Z_{max} > 1$ or $M_0 < 10^4 \, M\odot$ is

$$E_\nu = 8.3 \times 10^{18} \left(\frac{M_0}{M\odot}\right)^{3/7} \left[1 - 10^{-3} \left(\frac{M_0}{M\odot}\right)\right]^{27/35} \text{ erg gm}^{-1}, \quad \frac{M_0}{M\odot} < 10^4. \tag{40}$$

This expression has a maximum value at $(M_0/M\odot) \simeq 2 \times 10^3$ at which value $E_\nu(\text{max}) \simeq 1.37 \times 10^{20}$ erg gm^{-1} = 0.15 c^2. Thus only 15 per cent of the rest mass is lost in the maximum case. As might be expected it can be shown that $E_\nu(\text{max})$ is independent of the numerical coefficient, 4.3×10^{15}, in equation (28). Furthermore, it can be shown that $E_\nu(\text{max})$ does not depend critically on the power of T_9 in equation (28). For very large exponent $E_\nu(\text{max})$ approaches ~ 22 per cent. The point is that any mechanism of great energy loss is quenched by the large redshift which arises when collapse to the event horizon occurs.

These arguments apply to nuclear processes which customarily depend on a high power of the temperature. High temperatures are reached only near the termination of collapse when redshifts are large. On the other hand the second expression in equations (38) indicates for any dU/dt = constant, for example, that the energy release diverges on evaluation at the lower limit of integration. Thus it is not possible to rule out large losses for processes such as gravitational radiation which do not depend critically on temperatures.

For $Z_{max} < 1$ which corresponds to stars with $M_0 > 10^4 M_\odot$ one finds

$$E_\nu \simeq 1.5 \times 10^{26} \left(\frac{M_\odot}{M_0}\right)^{3/2} = 1.7 \times 10^5 \left(\frac{M_\odot}{M_0}\right)^{3/2} c^2 \text{ erg gm}^{-1}, \quad 10^4 < \frac{M_0}{M_\odot} < 10^7. \quad (41)$$

The upper limit, $10^7 \, M_\odot$, occurs because equation (28) grossly overestimates neutrino losses along the evolutionary path of such stars. Thus for $M_0 = 10^6 M_\odot$, $E_\nu = 1.5 \times 10^{17}$ erg gm^{-1} $= 1.7 \times 10^{-4} c^2$ and the fractional energy loss is very small indeed. Michel (1963) has suggested that the energy gained by the envelope if the imploding core loses *all* of its rest-mass energy and thus no longer acts gravitationally on the envelope is $2.9 \times 10^{49} \, (T_9)_{coll} \, (M/M_\odot)^{3/2}$ erg, where M is the total mass of the star and $(T_9)_{coll}$ is the temperature at which collapse of the core begins. This expression must be multiplied by E_ν/c^2 on the basis of our analysis and the mass of the collapsing core (M_0 in our notation) must be estimated. Michel (1963) used $M_0 \simeq 0.37 \, M$. The explosion energy of the envelope thus becomes

$$E_{env} \simeq 2 \times 10^{55} \, (T_9)_{coll} \text{ erg },$$

or

$$\frac{E_{env}}{M c^2} \sim 10 \left(\frac{M_\odot}{M}\right) (T_9)_{coll}, \quad 10^4 M_\odot < M < 10^7 M_\odot, \quad (42)$$

which is $\sim 10^{-3}$ at $M \sim 10^4 M_\odot$ and only 10^{-6} at $M \sim 10^7 M_\odot$ when the reasonable estimate $(T_9)_{coll} \sim 1$ is employed. Thus neutrino losses from collapsing cores cannot lead to envelope explosions with appreciable fractions of the rest-mass energy of a star.

It is worth noticing, by way of concluding the present section, that the track (33) applied to ordinary stellar masses determines the situation under which neutrino emission could produce a free-fall implosion. This track lies far below the track actually followed by evolving stellar material (Hoyle and Fowler 1963a, b). This shows that free-fall implosion is never produced in ordinary stars by neutrino emission.

e) Rotation

The implosion of a discrete body including rotational effects has not been solved in general relativity. Rotation effects have been studied in cosmology, and we are encouraged to think that what is known about the cosmological case may be adequate for a general discussion. As emphasized in Section II, the implosion of a finite body without rotation is closely similar to the cosmological case.

We have so far regarded $S(t)$ as a scale factor applicable to all three space coordinates. Now we regard S as applicable only to a coordinate taken parallel to the axis of rotation. A different scale factor $R(t)$ will be used for two coordinates taken perpendicular to the rotation axis. In Newtonian mechanics the differential equations for R, S are of the form

$$\frac{\dot{R}^2}{R^2} \simeq \frac{a}{R^3} - \frac{\Omega^2}{R^4}, \qquad a = \frac{8\pi G \rho_0}{3}, \qquad (43)$$

$$\frac{\dot{S}^2}{S^2} \simeq \frac{2a}{R^2 S}, \qquad (44)$$

where Ω is the angular velocity at $R = 1$, and terms which become small as the implosion proceeds have been omitted.

The right-hand side of equation (43) has a zero for sufficiently small R, implying that implosion is halted and reversed to explosion so far as the coordinates perpendicular to the axis of rotation are concerned. But no such effect occurs for the coordinate parallel to the rotation axis. In the cosmological case implosion continues indefinitely for this coordinate (Narlikar 1963). However, for a finite body a different situation can arise due to a pressure gradient, as will now be seen.

Suppose that at the onset of implosion from a dispersed state the body is essentially spherical in shape, with $R = S = 1$. Rotation eventually causes S/R to decrease below unity. Now the pressure gradient necessary to maintain equilibrium in a direction parallel to the rotation axis can be considerably less than would be necessary for the whole mass in the absence of rotation. In fact the problem of support is reduced to that for a mass of only $M(S/R)^2$. For sufficiently small S/R this can be reduced below the limiting value of order $M\odot$, and equilibrium is possible either through electron degeneracy or nucleon degeneracy. Hence it is in principle possible for a rotating object to maintain itself whatever the total mass M, as was pointed out by Hoyle (1947). For $M \gg M\odot$ the shape must be that of a thin disk. Although in the imploding case oscillations must occur, we expect they will eventually become damped away, perhaps by repeated bursts of neutrino emission.

At first sight one might suppose that, because of this effect, implosion to a singularity never occurs in any actual case, since presumably there is never a complete absence of rotation. This view is incorrect, however. If ρ attains nuclear densities, the energy density E cannot be taken as ρ and the Newtonian equations (43) and (44) require modification. We must have $E \propto \rho^{4/3}$, and the terms in a are changed to the proportionality R^{-4} for the $\dot{R}^2$ equation and to $R^{-8/3} S^{-4/3}$ for the $\dot{S}^2$ equation. Hence both terms on the right-hand side of the $\dot{R}^2$ equation behave in the same way as $R \to 0$, and there is no root if Ω is small enough. The gravitational field can be strong enough even to crush rotation, a result that never occurs in the Newtonian case.

The situation is further complicated, even in the case $E \simeq \rho$, by the circumstance that a rotating disk can be locally unstable. Contraction parallel to the rotation axis increases the density by R/S. A local aggregation is then unstable against contraction *perpendicular* to the rotation axis. Indeed, a spherical aggregation of mass $\sim (S/R)^2 M$ can shrink as a whole by a factor R/S before rotation again prevents contraction perpendicular to the axis. Hence the density can rise by a total of $(R/S)^4$. We may state this in the following way: If a rotating disk of mass M and radius a breaks up into more or less spherical fragments of mass $x^{-2} M$ ($x \gg 1$), the density in each fragment can increase to $\sim x^4 M/a^3$.

The important issue is whether nuclear densities are reached before or after the fragment masses become of order $M\odot$. If before, no equilibrium is possible, since rotation becomes ineffective before the fragment masses are small enough for pressure gradients to maintain equilibrium. If after, we expect the implosion to be halted, and a final state reached in which the object has divided into stable fragments with masses $\sim M\odot$ that move in nearly coplanar orbits about a common center.

Set $x^{-2} M \simeq M\odot$. The density then increases by $(M/M\odot)^2$ above the value at which rotation first impeded shrinkage perpendicular to the axis. Write ρ_1 for this density, so that the fragments have density $\rho_1 (M/M\odot)^2$. Our two cases depend on whether this value is $>$ or $< \sim 10^{16}$ gm cm^{-3}. Hence our cases are given by

$$\rho_1 \gtrless \sim 10^{16} \left(\frac{M\odot}{M}\right)^2 \text{gm cm}^{-3}. \tag{45}$$

This density is close to that which occurs at the event horizon. Hence we arrive at the conclusion that, if rotation does not become dynamically important until after an imploding object has retreated within the event horizon, singularities develop.

When the "less than" sign applies in equation (45) two cases appear to arise. If ρ_1 is sufficiently small compared with the right-hand side of equation (45) the relevant pressure can arise from electron degeneracy and the object fragments into white dwarfs. At larger values of ρ_1 nucleon degeneracy occurs, however, and the object fragments into neutron stars.

f) The Prevention of Singularities in C-Field Cosmology

Hoyle and Narlikar (1963) have shown that equation (21) is modified to

$$\frac{\dot{S}^2}{S^2} = -\frac{1}{S^2} + \frac{8\pi GE}{3} - \frac{A^2}{S^6} \tag{46}$$

by the presence of the C-field of steady-state cosmology where A is a small constant. Since E is proportional only to S^{-4} at very high densities, the right-hand side of equation (46) can have two zeros. In fact, for any physical motion there must be two roots, a larger root with the $-S^{-2}$ term essentially compensating the E term—this is just the dispersed state—and a smaller root with the $-A^2 S^{-6}$ term essentially compensating the E term. This result arises from the negative-energy density of the C-field. Although the concept of a negative-energy density is strange, several arguments can be advanced in its support:

1. A negative-energy field is gravitationally repulsive. The expansion of the universe can be taken as evidence of the existence of such an effect—otherwise we must take the unsatisfactory step of imposing special initial boundary conditions.

2. Matter must be "created" either continuously or at the "origin" of the universe. A negative-energy field appears necessary to obtain a mathematical description of the creation process.

3. A negative-energy field now seems to be necessary if singularities are to be avoided. The singularities are prevented through the gravitational repulsion of the field.

The two roots of the right-hand side of equations (46) imply that the object oscillates between a maximum S_1 and a minimum S_2 instead of imploding into a singularity. It is to be expected (Hoyle and Narlikar 1963) that the oscillations are gradually damped in the sense that S_1 decreases. Neutrino emission is probably the main damping agent, although charged particles may also be emitted. The object never attains a static state —that is, S_1 can never be reduced to S_2 because the damping ceases when the redshift cuts off the emission. The maximum S_1 then takes its value, ar_b^2, at the event horizon, whereas $S_2 \ll ar_b^2$, that is, at minimum the object lies far inside the event horizon. This is because the coefficient A^2 is very small.

According to Hoyle and Narlikar it seems unlikely that the maximum density can be less than 10^{30} gm cm^{-3}, corresponding to an interparticle separation of 10^{-18} cm, or less. Nuclear physics gives no real guidance as to what might happen under such conditions. Boson fields are to be expected with energy densities proportional to S^{-4}, individual bosons have energies proportional to S^{-1}. At $\rho \simeq 10^{16}$ gm cm^{-3} the energies are of order 1 BeV, while at $\rho \simeq 10^{30}$ gm cm^{-3} energies of order 10^5 BeV would be expected. The possibility exists that such bosons emerge from the surface of the object. At first sight it might seem as if nothing of this kind could be detected by an outside observer, since the object lies far inside the event horizon at stages where the density is very high. However, particles can be pushed outside the event horizon by the expansion of the object itself. Any massless boson that emerges radially from the surface always stays ahead of the surface. So long as the surface crosses the event horizon the particle is ultimately disgorged into the outside world. Decay could provide electrons and protons or neutrinos and neutrons if appropriate weak coupling interactions exist.

It is clear that at just this point a serious gap exists in our knowledge, a situation that has been strongly emphasized by Wheeler (cf. Wheeler, Wakano, and Harrison 1958). A filling of this gap would provide an interesting connection between high-energy physics and astronomy.

II. ASTROPHYSICAL CONSEQUENCES

In the previous sections we have described the various situations which have been envisaged as the final stages of evolution of a star which reaches the end point of thermonuclear evolution with a mass greater than the mass which can be supported either by degenerate electron pressure or degenerate neutron pressure. While it is not clear which of these theoretical possibilities is the correct one, in each case the star eventually reaches a situation in which it ceases to communicate with the outside world except through the action of its gravitational field. In the theory of Hoyle and Narlikar there is the possibility that such an object will be able to radiate some fraction of its mass energy as it pulsates, but such pulsations will eventually damp out and the remnant will disappear.

Thus we conclude that the following facts should be taken into account.

1. Invisible mass is likely to be present wherever the condensation and evolution of stars have occurred. How much mass is present will depend on the masses of the stars which condensed, and on what fraction of this mass can be ejected in the stages of evolution prior to catastrophic implosion.

2. In these circumstances star formation is a one-way process which removes uncondensed material in the universe and transforms it into a form which makes it immune to further evolution.

In modern theories concerning the evolution of stars and galaxies it has been supposed that much of the material which is condensed into a first generation of stars will be ejected and condensed into a second generation, etc. While such processes do occur, it is necessary to take into account that fraction of the mass which goes into an invisible form and no longer plays a direct role in the evolution.

3. In the theory of Hoyle and Narlikar mass energy can be radiated by the object after it has reached the collapsed state. This energy is bound to be radiated in the form of high-energy quanta. It thus provides a continuous energy input for non-thermal radio sources.

We now discuss the implication of these results for astrophysics in more detail.

a) The Presence of Invisible Mass

We first discuss the stellar mass function and the mass-to-light ratios for aggregates of stars and for galaxies.

In our Galaxy the number of stars born with masses between M and $M + dM$ is proportional to $\sim M^{-1.4}\, d \log M$ at any rate for masses up to $5\, M\odot$ (for a review of the work on clusters cf. Burbidge and Burbidge 1958). This means that, whereas most stars lie at the bottom end of the mass range, the total mass of a group of stars comes mainly from the upper end of the range. Except for a few stars in very young clusters, stars near the upper end have already evolved. Hence most of the mass originally condensed into stars has evolved, in the sense that the stars into which it was originally condensed are no longer visible. The question evidently arises as to what has happened to this material. There seem to be only two possibilities: (i) The bulk of the material was ejected from the stars in the course of their evolution and is now condensed into further stars. (ii) The stars evolved into imploding objects and the mass is now invisible. The possibility of the material being stored permanently in the interstellar medium as gas appears to be excluded, since not more than 10 per cent of the mass of the Galaxy seems to be in the form of gas.

The first of these possibilities can be tested by considering what would be expected for the mass-to-light ratio in our own Galaxy. Consider first the simple case of main-sequence stars with the mass distribution $M^{-2.4}\, dM$ extending from $M_0 \approx 0.1\, M\odot$ up to M of the order of, or greater than, $M\odot$. Write M^* for the upper limit of mass and L^*

for the upper limit of luminosity. The mass-to-light ratio is

$$\sim \int_{M_0}^{M^*} M^{-1.4} dM \div \int_{M_0}^{M^*} L M^{-2.4} dM. \tag{47}$$

With $L = L^*(M/M^*)^4$ on the main sequence, equation (47) is approximately evaluated to give $6.5(M^*/L^*) \, [(M^*/M_0)^{0.4} - 1]$. Next, we require values for M^*, L^*. In the Galaxy $M^* \simeq M\odot$ for the old star distribution, while $L^* \simeq 2L\odot$ at the so-called break point of the main sequence. Hence in solar units we have a mass-to-light ratio of $\sim 3[(M^*/M_0)^{0.4} - 1]$. Similar data do not exist for other galaxies. However, the theory of stellar evolution would not permit a significantly larger value to be taken for M^*/L^*, unless the galaxies in question were substantially older than our own.

The mass-to-light ratio calculated in the previous paragraph must be reduced to allow for young clusters and for stars that have evolved off the main sequence. Giants, in particular, contribute appreciably to the light but not to the mass. Hence the expected mass-to-light ratio cannot be much greater than ~ 3.

The mass-to-light ratio for the solar neighborhood is about 4 (Schmidt 1963a), while Burbidge, Burbidge, and Prendergast, and Page (cf. Burbidge 1961) have found values of order 3 or less for a number of spiral galaxies, mainly of type Sc. These values are consistent with a choice of $0.1 \, M\odot$ for M_0. On the other hand, the mass-to-light ratios for some spirals are $\sim$10–15 (M31, NGC 253, M81, and others; cf. Burbidge 1961) while the average value for elliptical galaxies (Page 1962) is about 30. Such values point to the existence of hidden mass, unless the mass function for stars is grossly different in other galaxies from what it is in our own. Obscuration of light might perhaps falsify the observed values in dusty spirals, but obscuration cannot be important for the ellipticals.

Hidden mass in the above sense could come from (i) faint white dwarfs, (ii) very faint main-sequence dwarfs, corresponding to a very small value for M_0, (iii) imploded evolved stars that have not lost appreciable fractions of their original masses, (iv) imploded objects of very large mass. As far as our Galaxy is concerned the number of white dwarfs in the solar neighborhood is not sufficient for (i) to make more than a modest contribution to the total mass. Nor is there any direct evidence from the solar neighborhood to support (ii). However, it seems probable that considerable numbers of red dwarfs are present in some galaxies (Spinrad 1962) and that the mass function is not the same as it is in our own Galaxy. We have pointed out elsewhere the difficulties associated with the assumption of a universal mass function (Burbidge, Burbidge, and Hoyle 1963). On the other hand, either a very low value for M_0 or a very gross difference in the mass function for main-sequence stars has to be assumed to obtain the mass-to-light ratios for ellipticals, and the observations do not indicate that such large differences as these, in fact, exist.

An upper limit for the importance of (iii) can readily be calculated. Suppose the $M^{-2.4} dM$ distribution extends at birth to an upper limit M^{**}, M^* being the upper limit to which it applies at present. Then the total mass born over the whole range from M_0 to M^{**} exceeds the range from M_0 to M^*—the latter being the present-day observed range—by the factor

$$[1 - (M_0/M^{**})^{0.4}]/[1 - (M_0/M^*)^{0.4}] \approx 1/[1 - (M_0/M^*)^{0.4}]$$

for sufficiently large M^{**}. Taking $M^* \simeq M\odot$, $M_0 \simeq 0.1 \, M\odot$, this factor is 5/3. The mass-to-light ratios, including hidden mass in the form (iii), then becomes ~ 5. Such a value is clearly compatible with the mass-to-light ratios of galaxies such as our own, and perhaps with M31, M81, NGC 253, etc. However, the much larger ratios which are found for many elliptical galaxies might indicate that very massive objects have imploded and are present in the form of invisible mass, that is, possibility (iv) may be required to explain the observational results.

It is self-evident that direct *observational* evidence for the presence of invisible mass can never be forthcoming. The arguments given above concerning the mass-to-light ratios are indirect but give some indication of phenomena which may be explained by these developments in the theory. However, we do not believe that the discussion in the first part of the paper is strongly dependent on the indirect observational arguments. We do assert that masses which arrive at the end point of evolution and implode must follow one of the paths described in that section. Another phenomenon which might suggest that some mass is present in the form of invisible matter is the presence of invisible (often called "infrared") members of binary star systems.

Another problem of some significance is that concerning the stability of clusters of galaxies (cf. the papers published in *A.J.*, **66**, 533–636, 1961). It is found by applying the virial theorem to clusters and groups of galaxies that in nearly all cases it must be supposed either that the systems are expanding, or else that a very large amount of invisible matter must be present. Probably systems of both types occur. In the case of clusters and groups which are stable by virtue of their containing a large fraction of mass in invisible form, it is quite reasonable to suppose that much of this is made up of large masses $\geq 10^5 \, M\odot$ which have imploded.

b) *The Effect of the Concept of Imploded Mass on Stellar Evolution and Nucleosynthesis*

The rate at which the material in a galaxy is enriched in the heavy elements is dependent, first, on the efficiency of the processes of nucleosynthesis in the interiors of stars and, second, on the processes which will redistribute this material into the interstellar medium. The discussion given in Section I of this paper strongly suggests that the latter process is much less efficient than has been thought up to the present, since in some proportion of the stars with masses above the critical mass we may expect that the implosion will occur and the mass will vanish. Thus some modification of the calculations of the rate of enrichment of heavy elements as a function of star formation as they have been made by Schmidt (1963*b*) is required, since he made the assumption that all of the mass in a star in excess of the white dwarf mass would be returned to the interstellar medium. In the case of massive supernovae (Burbidge, Burbidge, Fowler, and Hoyle 1957; Hoyle and Fowler 1960; Fowler and Hoyle 1964) the possibility that mass vanishes when these stars have evolved is of particular interest. It is usually supposed that there have not been more than $\sim 10^8$ supernovae in the lifetime of the Galaxy, whereas the number of stars that have been born with $M > 2M\odot$ is probably of order 10^{10}. It therefore seems necessary to argue that only a small fraction of imploding stars, about 1 per cent, become supernovae. A similar result is obtained if we simply take the known number of star deaths among A, B, and O stars in young clusters, together with an assumed present-day supernova rate of ~ 1 per 10^2 years. Rotation may supply the restraining factor. Imploding stars with too much rotation may attain stable disklike structures in accordance with the considerations of Section I(*e*) and these also have the property of hiding mass. It may well be necessary for a star to satisfy the "greater than" condition of equation (45) in order that it become a supernova. The physical reason could be that superdense conditions are needed in order that relativistic particles be generated.

It has been stressed previously (Fowler and Hoyle 1960) that, if we suppose that the *r*-process elements are made in supernovae in sufficient amount to explain the light-curves on the californium hypothesis, then taking an average rate of supernovae as 1 per 300 years far too much *r*-process material would be produced. This difficulty can be avoided if Type I supernovae are taken to have such small mass and such long evolution times that none evolved in the Galaxy before the solar system formed. However, an alternative explanation which involves the rejection of the californium hypothesis will be explored in the next section. A similar difficulty is encountered when we consider the production of iron peak elements in Type II supernovae, that is, too much iron is produced. However, it now appears possible that much of the elements synthesized in these massive stars are never ejected but are contained in the imploded mass, so that this difficulty can be surmounted.

Finally, in this section we turn briefly to the evolution of a globular cluster. In a recent analysis of the dynamics of M3, Oort and van Herk (1959) came to the conclusion that more than half the mass was originally in the form of stars with average masses of 4.4 $M\odot$. Since these stars must have evolved long ago they argued that the excess mass above the white dwarf mass, i.e., 3.8 $M\odot$ per star, must have been ejected and lost from the cluster. This assumed mass loss through stellar evolution is far greater than the mass loss due to the evaporation of stars. However, according to our earlier considerations, this mass may not have been lost to the cluster but may still be present in invisible form. While the observable dynamical effects would be small (a change in mass by a factor of 2 corresponds to a change in velocity dispersion by $\sqrt{2}$) the possible presence of such mass rather than its assumed ejection should be considered; although it could still be the case that the dynamical processes involved produced a sufficient recoil on the remnants to cause escape from the cluster.

c) The Injection of Energy into the Interstellar and Intergalactic Medium from Collapsed Stars

The imploding bodies discussed in Section I have the property that gravitation is in principle capable of yielding $\sim 9 \times 10^{20}$ erg gm^{-1}, much greater than the energy yield from any nuclear reaction (Hoyle and Fowler 1963a, b; Burbidge 1962a). But classical implosion into a singularity does not seem to provide an atomic or nuclear mechanism whereby the full dynamical energy stored in a collapsing body can be returned in an observable form to the outside world.

As pointed out by Hoyle and Fowler (1963a) it is probable that hydrogen burning can retard the implosion at a central temperature near $8 \times 10^{7\,\circ}$ K for a limited time ($\sim 10^6$ years) and supply the positive internal energy ($\sim 10^{59}$ ergs for $M \sim 10^8 M\odot$) necessary for hydrostatic equilibrium under general relativistic conditions (Iben 1963) as well as that required to match the radiated energy ($\sim 10^{60}$ ergs for $M \sim 10^8 M\odot$). In fact, radio stars may well represent the early stage of the implosion of massive objects where the luminosities predicted by Hoyle and Fowler, $L = 2 \times 10^{38} (M/M\odot) \rightarrow 2 \times 10^{46}$ ergs sec^{-1} for $M = 10^8 M\odot$, are of the order of magnitude observed for 3C48 for example (Greenstein and Matthews 1963). The radius and effective surface temperature depend critically on the structure of the star during hydrogen burning. Hoyle and Fowler (1963a) give $R \sim 10^{11} (M/M\odot)^{1/2}$ cm for polytropic index $n = 3$, but this could be low by as much as a factor of 10^2 to 10^4, since a larger index is indicated if general relativistic considerations are taken into account. Thus $R \sim 10^{14} (M/M\odot)^{1/2}$ cm with considerable uncertainty. Similarly the surface temperature $T_e \sim 7 \times 10^{4\,\circ}$ K given by Hoyle and Fowler (1963a) may be too high and a value $T_e \sim 10^{4\,\circ}$ K is probably to be preferred with an uncertainty of a factor of 3 either way.

During the hydrogen-burning period the central density is $\sim 10^{-1}$ to 10^{-2} gm cm^{-3} and the ratio of gas pressure to total pressure is $\sim 10^{-2}$ to 10^{-3}, these values holding for $M \sim 10^6 M\odot$ to $10^8 M\odot$ using equations given by Hoyle and Fowler (1963a). Setting $\gamma a = 3\gamma - 4 \sim \beta/2 \ll 1$ in equation (130.3), p. 192, of Eddington (1930), these values lead to periods of pulsation $\Pi \sim (80\pi/3G\beta\rho)^{1/2} \sim 1.2 (G\beta\langle\rho\rangle)^{1/2} \sim 10^6$ to 10^7 sec. Smith and Hoffleit (1963) have found evidence in 3C273 for light variations with periods in this range. In view of this relatively satisfactory model for radio-star behavior we must emphasize once again that somewhat less than 1 per cent of the rest-mass energies of these objects is required to account for the energy requirements discussed above. Hydrogen burning can supply this energy. However, if the light output of such an object is to be attributed to the comparatively steady luminosity of a massive star during its "main-sequence" evolution, at least one previous outburst involving the evolution and collapse of another massive star must be invoked to account for the radio flux from the source.

It is also possible that rotation prevents the development of a singularity, at any rate in some cases, and that collapse to disklike aggregations of white dwarfs or neutron stars can give rise to large energy sources. The mechanism whereby such aggregations act as sources is far from clear, however.

Another possibility is the release of energy in the form of gravitational radiation. Because of the critical dependence of this release on rotation and on the model of collapse as discussed in Hoyle and Fowler (1963b) it is difficult to make realistic estimates of the energy release and we have not attempted to do so. Our remarks in Section I(d) concerning the difficulty in abstracting energy from collapsing systems are subject to the qualification that gravitational radiation rates have not yet been determined.

The non-classical oscillations discussed in Section I(f) seem to provide a more convenient energy source. Energy can be derived through a damping of the oscillations until the redshift cutoff is reached. The yield is then about 5×10^{20} erg gm^{-1} (Hoyle and Narlikar 1963). If the fraction of all material involved in this process is f, the energy density for the whole universe is $\sim 5 \times 10^{20}$ $f \rho_c$, where ρ_c is the cosmological mass density, usually taken as $\sim 3 \times 10^{-29}$ gm cm^{-3}. This gives $\sim 10^{-8} f$ erg cm^{-3}. As stated in Section I, the main damping agent is probably neutrinos, and the present estimate can be taken as referring to the energy density of $\nu, \bar{\nu}$.

The speculations of Hoyle and Narlikar on the oscillatory problem lead to extraordinarily great densities at maximum compression, which has the advantage that very high-energy particles would surely be generated. These speculations also have the advantage of relating high-energy physics with astrophysics and cosmology. If k is the fraction of the energy released as relativistic electrons and protons, the cosmic-ray energy density for the whole universe would be $\sim 10^{-8} fk$ erg cm^{-3}.

Burbidge and Hoyle (1964) have suggested that massive objects may be the source of cosmic rays and that the energy density may be ~ 1 eV cm^{-3} everywhere in space. This would require $fk \simeq 10^{-4}$. It seems unlikely that k could be more than a few per cent, in which case Burbidge and Hoyle require f to be not much less than 1 per cent. Since matter condensed into galaxies has mean density $\sim 3 \times 10^{-31}$ gm cm^{-3}—i.e., only ~ 1 per cent of the value taken above for the total cosmological density, we evidently require an appreciable fraction of the mass of the galaxies to have evolved into imploded objects. This question has been discussed in the previous sections.

To account for the energy contained in non-thermal radio sources, if we take the point of view that this is energy released in collapse to very high-density configurations, it is therefore necessary to suppose that the model of Hoyle and Narlikar, and not the classical implosion solution, is correct. If we make this assumption, then the supernova remnants and the objects which give rise to the powerful extragalactic radio sources continuously inject high-energy particles and quanta into the surrounding medium, and the bulk of the energy injected must be in the form of neutrinos. This hypothesis leads to quite a different picture of the evolution of a supernova remnant than that previously developed.

First of all, it is possible to suppose that the interacting particles which are ejected at the earliest phase are the source of visible radiation of the supernova, either through direct synchrotron radiation or through the penetration of the particles into an expanding envelope, ejected perhaps as a consequence of a nuclear explosion in the outer parts of the star.

We now turn to the situation in the Crab Nebula, the remnant of the supernova of AD 1054 which shows evidence of its continuing activity through the moving wisps observed by Baade and the presence of high-energy electrons with synchrotron lifetimes much less than the age of the remnant.

It is remarkable that no star brighter than about 18^m appears at the present day to be associated with the Crab Nebula. This, taken together with the estimates of Oster-brock (1957) and O'Dell (1962) of no more than 0.3 $M\odot$ for the mass of the nebula, leads to the challenging question of what has happened to the original star. Since it has not been disintegrated, the major part of the mass must still exist as a compact object. It cannot be a white dwarf, since cooling could not have reduced its luminosity sufficiently in only 10^3 years. It can scarcely be a single neutron star since it is unlikely that the original mass was less than $M\odot$. The interesting possibility is that the star is now in the oscillatory state discussed in Section I(f) and that the continuing activity of the Crab Nebula is due to a steady output of high-energy particles.

The present picture allows a different point of view to be taken about the origin of the filaments of the nebula. The volume of the nebula is $\sim 10^{56}$ cm^3. The mass of inter-stellar gas normally present within such a volume, situated as it is quite near the galactic plane, would be $\sim 3 \times 10^{32}$ gm. If the filaments only have mass $\lesssim 0.3$ $M\odot$ it follows that they must be largely interstellar gas, unless the region of the Crab is extraordinarily void of gas. We take the view that the whole filamentary structure is interstellar in origin, that no significant expanding envelope was emitted, and the light of the supernova was produced by particles of high energy, perhaps by the synchrotron process. A similar supposition for all Type I supernovae explains the absence of detectable lines in the spectra of these stars.

On this point of view, the approximately exponential decay of the light-curves of Type I supernovae can then no longer be attributed to Cf^{254}, or to other very heavy nuclei subject to spontaneous fission. Damping of the oscillations of the central object may be expected to proceed quite rapidly to the stage where redshift effects become important, and exponential decay of the light-curve could arise from this damping. We urge that observational astronomers turn their attention to the question of which of the two alter-natives we have suggested for the light-curves of Type I supernovae is the correct one. Is the source of the energy radioactivity or gravitation?

The present outward speed of the filaments is ~ 1000 km sec^{-1}, the total kinetic energy being $\sim 10^{48}$ erg. It has been argued in the past that the energy of the relativistic particles associated with the Crab cannot be greater than the kinetic energy of the filaments; otherwise the nebula would expand faster than it is observed to do. This argument is only correct, however, if the relativistic particles are trapped within the filaments. This has always been assumed because in the past it was felt to be difficult to explain the origin of even 10^{47} erg in the form of high-energy electrons. The same difficulty does not arise in the present picture. The rest energy of a star of mass 1–10 $M\odot$ is 10^{54}–10^{55} erg. Even though most of this energy emerges as neutrinos, the energy available for charged particles could readily exceed 10^{50} erg. This leads us to the quite different point of view that the filaments have derived their outward motion from the *momentum* of the rela-tivistic particles, not from their energy. We suppose that the particles are emitted by the central object and that they experience deflection by the filaments—the interstellar magnetic field within the filaments forces the particles to fan out in much the shape of a comet's tail in order to get around a filament on which they are incident. The filamentary structure itself may arise from the ability of the high-energy particles to punch holes in the gas. Indeed, the ravaged appearance of the nebula could be a consequence of such violent fluting.

If the filaments take up a fraction θ of the outward momentum of the relativistic par-ticles the filamentary kinetic energy E_f will be related to the particle energy E_p by

$$E_f \simeq \theta \, \frac{V}{c} \, E_p, \qquad (48)$$

where V is the filamentary velocity. With $E_f \simeq 10^{48}$ erg, $V \simeq 10^8$ cm sec^{-1}, $E_p \simeq 3 \times 10^{50}$ θ^{-1} erg. Individual relativistic particles spend perhaps 10 years within the nebulosity—

the radius is about 3 light years while allowance for deflections and spiraling motions reasonably increases the time to 10 years. Hence in the 10^3 years of existence of the Crab we expect there to have been about 10^2 generations of relativistic particles. The energy content at any moment is then $\sim 10^{-2}\,E_p \simeq 3 \times 10^{48}\,\theta^{-1}$ erg. Oort and Walraven (1956) and Woltjer (1957) estimate the energy content, excluding protons and excluding electrons that do not emit synchrotron radiation either in the radio band or the visible spectrum, as 10^{47} to 3×10^{48} erg depending on the intensity of the magnetic field. The energy content could be as high as 10^{49} erg.

Deflection around a knot of gas arises from compression of the magnetic field. Deflection becomes appreciable when the magnetic pressure $H^2/8\pi$ increases to a value comparable with the energy density of the incident beam of particles. Taking the total resident energy as $\sim 10^{49}$ erg and the volume as 10^{56} cm^3, the latter is $\sim 10^{-7}$ erg cm^{-3}. Hence we expect compression to raise H to a value of order 10^{-3} gauss, a value that has been used in past investigations. Partly because of the compression of the field, and partly

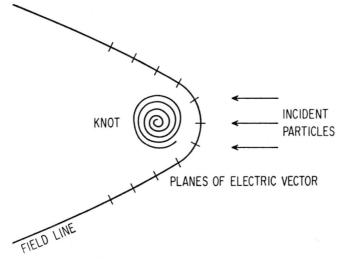

Fig. 1.—Magnetic field lines bent around a knot of gas by a beam of incident relativistic particles produce the polarization vectors shown above for an observer with line of sight perpendicular to the field lines.

because the electrons spend a comparatively long time in the region of compression, we expect synchrotron emission to occur mainly at the inside faces of knots and filaments of gas—i.e., the faces turned toward the central star.

If the central star emits particles at a steady rate, one might at first sight expect the outward motion of the gas to be decreasing, because of the increasing quantity of interstellar material swept up by the system. However, this need not be the case since θ also depends on the amount of gas in the system. In fact, so long as $\theta < 1$ we expect θ to be proportional to the total mass. Then it can easily be shown that the system accelerates. Deceleration sets in when θ increases toward unity.

It is also easy to see that interesting polarization effects can arise. For the simple case of a coplanar fluting around a knot of gas, an observer with a face-on view finds the polarization structure shown in Figure 1. This detail is mentioned because the polarization structure of the Crab contains an example of this special case (Woltjer 1957). A general discussion of polarization lies far outside the present work. The problem is complicated by the unknown three-dimensional structure of the system, by the lack of regularity in the arrangement of the knots and filaments, and by uncertainty in our knowledge of the initial run of the magnetic field lines.

In this picture of a supernova remnant tremendous fluxes of particles will escape into the disk of the Galaxy, and this picture would be inconsistent with the estimates of the relativistic electron energy density in the disk $\leq 5 \times 10^{-14}$ erg/cm^3 if the particles were contained in the Galaxy. Taking 10^{59} erg as the total production in the lifetime T of the Galaxy and taking 3×10^{66} cm^3 as the volume of the disk the requirement is that

$$10^{59} \frac{t}{T} \leq 5 \times 10^{-14} \times 3 \times 10^{66},$$

where t is the escape time. Thus $t \leq \sim 10^{-6} \, T \sim 10^4$ years. Thus the Galaxy must be entirely open as is indicated on other grounds (cf. Ginsburg and Syrovatsky 1961).

The extragalactic radio sources probably have short lifetimes $\sim 10^6$ years (Burbidge 1962b; Burbidge, Burbidge, and Sandage 1963), but in many cases much shorter time scales within these are indicated. Examples are M87 which contains optical synchrotron electrons with half-lives $\sim 10^2$–10^3 years, the nuclei of Seyfert galaxies, and the starlike extragalactic objects (Matthews and Sandage 1963; Schmidt 1963c; Hazard, Mackey, and Shimmins 1963; Oke 1963; Greenstein and Matthews 1963) which show light variations over time scales of months and years (Matthews and Sandage 1963; Sandage 1963; Smith and Hoffleit 1963; Shklovsky 1963). These characteristics all indicate that continuous activity takes place in such objects. Since the tremendous energies required to explain these objects most likely come from gravitational sources, the Hoyle-Narlikar hypothesis of continuous energy injection appears to be indicated.

We are indebted to Dr. John Gaustad for pointing out an error in the original draft of Section II(a) of this paper.

This work was supported in part by the National Science Foundation, the Office of Naval Research, and the National Aeronautics and Space Administration.

One of us (W. A. F.) wishes to acknowledge support by the John Simon Guggenheim Foundation during the period 1961–62, when this work was started.

REFERENCES

Burbidge, E. M., Burbidge, G. R., Fowler, W. A., and Hoyle, F. 1957, *Rev. Mod. Phys.*, **29**, 547.
Burbidge, E. M., Burbidge, G. R., and Hoyle, F. 1963, *Ap. J.*, **138**, 873.
Burbidge, G. R. 1961, *A.J.*, **66**, 619.
———. 1962a, *Ann. Rev. Nuclear Sci.*, **12**, 507.
———. 1962b, *Prog. Theoret. Phys. Japan*, **27**, 999.
Burbidge, G. R., and Burbidge, E. M. 1958, *Handbuch der Physik*, **51**, 134.
Burbidge, G. R., Burbidge, E. M., and Sandage, A. R. 1963, *Rev. Mod. Phys.*, **35**, 947.*
Burbidge, G. R., and Hoyle, F. 1964, in preparation.
Datt, B. 1938, *Zs. f. Ap.*, **108**, 314.
Eddington, A. 1930, *Internal Constitution of the Stars* (Cambridge: Cambridge University Press).
Fowler, W. A., and Hoyle, F. 1960, *Ann. Phys.*, **10**, 280.
———. 1964, *Ap. J. Suppl.*, in preparation. This paper gives an extensive discussion of the topics covered by W. A. Fowler in the Henry Norris Russell lecture given at the Alaska meeting of the American Astronomical Society, July, 1963.
Ginsburg, V. L. and Syrovatsky, S. I. 1961, *Suppl. to Prog. Theoret. Phys. Japan*, No. 20.
Greenstein, J. L., and Matthews, T. A. 1963, *Nature*, **197**, 1041.*
Hazard, C., Mackey, M. B., and Shimmins, A. J. 1963, *Nature*, **197**, 1037.*
Hoyle, F. 1947, *M.N.*, **107**, 231.
Hoyle, F., and Fowler, W. A. 1960, *Ap. J.*, **132**, 565.
———. 1963a, *M.N.*, **125**, 169.
———. 1963b, *Nature*, **197**, 533.*
Hoyle, F., and Narlikar, J. V. 1963, *Proc. Roy. Soc.*, in press.
Iben, I. 1963, *Ap. J.*, **138**, 1090.*
Matthews, T. A., and Sandage, A. R. 1963, *Ap. J.*, **138**, 30.*
Michel, C. 1963, *Ap. J.*, **138**, 1090.
Narlikar, J. V. 1963, *M.N.*, **126**, 203.

O'Dell, C. R. 1962, *Ap. J.*, **136**, 809.
Oke, J. B. 1963, *Nature*, **197**, 1042.*
Oort, J. H., and Herk, G. van. 1959, *B.A.N.*, **14**, 299.
Oort, J. H., and Walraven, T. 1956, *B.A.N.*, **12**, 285.
Oppenheimer, J. R., and Snyder, H. 1939, *Phys. Rev.*, **56**, 455.
Oppenheimer, J. R., and Volkoff, G. M. 1939, *Phys. Rev.*, **55**, 374.
Osterbrock, D. E. 1957, Pub. *A.S.P.*, **69**, 227.
Page, T. L. 1962, *Ap. J.*, **136**, 685.
Sandage, A. R. 1963, private communication.
Schmidt, M. 1963*a*, private communication.
———. 1963*b*, *Ap. J.*, **137**, 758.
———. 1963*c*, *Nature*, **197**, 1040.*
Shklovsky, I. S. 1963, private communication.
Smith, H. J., and Hoffleit, D. 1963, *Nature*, **198**, 650.*
Spinrad, H. 1962, *Ap. J.*, **135**, 715.
Wheeler, J. A., Wakano, M., and Harrison, K. 1958, *La Structure et l'évolution de l'univers*, ed. R. Stoops (Solvay Conf. Rept., Brussels).
Woltjer, L. 1957, *B.A.N.*, **14**, 39.

MASSIVE STARS, RELATIVISTIC POLYTROPES, AND GRAVITATIONAL RADIATION

chapter 4

William A. Fowler

I. INTRODUCTION

Twenty-five years ago Robert Oppenheimer and his students Robert Serber,[1] George Volkoff,[2] and Hartland Snyder[3] investigated the equilibrium and gravitational contraction of massive stars in the advanced stages of stellar evolution when nuclear sources of energy have been exhausted. They concluded that "when the pressure within stellar matter becomes high enough, a new phase consisting of neutrons will be formed. . . . For masses greater than $\frac{3}{4} M_\odot$ there are no static equilibrium solutions. . . . When all thermonuclear sources of energy are exhausted a sufficiently heavy star will collapse. Unless fission due to rotation, the radiation of mass, or the blowing off of mass by radiation, reduce the star's mass to the order of that of the sun, this contraction will continue indefinitely. . . . The total time of collapse for an observer comoving with the stellar matter is finite, . . . ; an external observer sees the star asymptotically shrinking to its gravitational radius." It is a tribute to Robert Oppenheimer's genius that these are the few statements about massive stars accepted as true today.

In recent times there has been a renewal of interest in massive stars kindled by the suggestion of Fred Hoyle[4] and myself that stars with mass of order $\sim 10^8\ M_\odot$ may accumulate at the center of galaxies, or in intergalactic space, and may serve as the source of the prodigious energies involved in emission or storage in the radio *galaxies* and *stars*. [At our present state of knowledge we must italicize the words *galaxies* and *stars* when used in connection with radio sources.] A general discussion of the relativistic and astrophysical aspects of the situation has been given in collaboration with our colleagues Geoffrey and Margaret Burbidge.[5]

There is no convincing evidence that the radio *stars* have lifetimes in excess of 10^5 to 10^6 years. Thus the total energy radiated is $\sim 10^{59}$ ergs, as reported for 3C273 by Schmidt[6] and for 3C48 by Greenstein and Matthews,[7] corresponding to an observed and theoretical[4] luminosity of $\sim 10^{46}$ erg sec^{-1}. It is noteworthy that this energy requirement is well within the nuclear resources of a star with $M = 10^8\ M_\odot$ since $10^8\ M_\odot c^2 \sim 10^{62}$ ergs and hydrogen burning supplies energy equivalent to $\sim 1\%$ of the rest mass energy. Con-

WILLIAM A. FOWLER, California Institute of Technology.

Reprinted from *Reviews of Modern Physics*, **36**, 545–555, 1964.

version of $\sim 10\%$ of the hydrogen into helium in a star with $M = 10^8\,M_\odot$ is adequate to meet the observed luminosity requirements of the radio *stars*. This leads to the interesting question concerning the properties of massive stars under circumstances such that the proviso mentioned in the first paragraph above "when nuclear sources of energy have been exhausted" is not applicable. Part II of this paper discusses a limited but important aspect of the properties of massive stars, namely the fact that hydrostatic equilibrium in such stars requires a positive total energy above the rest mass energy of the particle constituents or in nuclear parlance "a negative binding energy." In the discussion the internal structures of the massive stars will be approximated as relativistic polytropes.

It must be emphasized that the energy storage requirements ($\lesssim 10^{62}$ ergs) found by Maltby, Matthews, and Moffet[8] for the strong, extended radio sources associated with *galaxies* cannot be met from nuclear resources and that gravitational energy must be called upon in the ultimate collapse of the massive condensations. During the early, *stellar* stages of a radio source nuclear energy can supply the optical and radio luminosity requirements. The ultimate requirements for sources which extend far beyond the confines of the *galaxies* with which they are identified can be met only by gravitational energy transferred in some way from the collapsing core of the massive star to the envelope and eventually the external surroundings. Part III of this paper discusses a possible mechanism of this transfer. Part IV is a summary.

II. BINDING ENERGY OF A MASSIVE STAR IN HYDROSTATIC EQUILIBRIUM

Feynman[9] and Iben[10] have shown that the binding energy of a massive star must be negative when general relativistic terms in the equation for hydrostatic equilibrium are appreciable. This result applies in some cases even when the relativistic parameter $2GM/Rc^2$ is small compared to unity. Here, we will attempt to understand this result in the simplest possible way by investigating general relativistic effects in massive stars in the first-order approximation beyond the classical Newtonian terms.

The total energy E of a star exclusive of the rest mass energy when infinitely dispersed at zero temperature is equal but opposite in sign to the binding energy E_b and is given by

$$E = -E_b = (M - M_0)\,c^2\,. \tag{1}$$

In this expression M is the mass of the star given in terms of the stellar radius R and the mass M_r interior to r by

$$M = \int_0^R dM_r = \int_0^R \rho\,dV = \int_0^R 4\pi\rho\,r^2 dr\,. \tag{2}$$

Spherically symmetric coordinates have been used and r has been chosen to give the "coordinate" element of volume dV, in the usual manner. Note that $V = \frac{4}{3}\pi r^3$ is the volume interior to r. In the third equality in Eq. (2) we have used

$$dM_r/dr = 4\pi\rho\,r^2 \tag{3}$$

where

$$\rho = \rho_0 + u/c^2 \tag{4}$$

is the mass-energy density measured by a local observer and includes both the rest mass ρ_0 of the "atoms" in the star plus the mass equivalent u/c^2 of the internal energy per unit volume of the atomic constituents and of radiation. The rest mass of the star is given by

$$M_0 = \int_0^R \rho_0 \left(1 - \frac{2GM_r}{r\,c^2}\right)^{-1/2} dV \tag{5}$$

where a "proper" element of volume has now been employed.

By "atoms" in the previous paragraph we mean the nuclei plus the electrons necessary to balance the nuclear charges. The rest mass energy as well as the kinetic energies of electron–positron pairs or other particle pairs created by the radiation field must be included in the internal energy u on the assumption that the pairs will be annihilated on dispersal to infinity. In principle we calculate the binding energy of the atomic constituents in the star at a given time. This is then the energy required to disperse these constituents to infinity and zero temperature without nuclear or atomic changes. Atomic energy changes in this dispersal can certainly be neglected and in most but not all cases nuclear changes will not occur during the dispersal. Any changes which do occur must be taken into account by calculating the binding energy relative to the nuclei which result upon dispersal. This aspect of the problem will not appear explicitly in what follows.

It is convenient to eliminate ρ_0 by use of Eq. (4) so that in further calculations we will use

$$E = \int_0^R u \left(1 - \frac{2GM_r}{r\,c^2} \right)^{-1/2} dV + \int_0^R \rho\, c^2 \left[1 - \left(1 - \frac{2GM_r}{r\,c^2} \right)^{-1/2} \right] dV + E_{\mathrm{dyn}} . \quad (6)$$

We have now included the dynamical energy E_{dyn}, which arises from bulk motions throughout the star and which should properly be included in M. Classically $E_{\mathrm{dyn}} = \int \frac{1}{2} \rho \dot{r}^2 dV$. In the classical approximation one can neglect $2GM_r/rc^2$ in the first integral but not in the second. Then

$$E \approx \int_0^R u\, dV - \int_0^R \frac{GM_r}{r} \rho\, dV + E_{\mathrm{dyn}} = \int_0^R 3\epsilon p\, dV - \Omega + E_{\mathrm{dyn}} , \quad (7)$$

where Ω is the gravitational *binding* energy taken as a positive quantity. For a polytrope of index n, it is well known that Ω is given by

$$\Omega = \frac{3}{5-n} \frac{GM^2}{R} \to \frac{3}{2} \frac{GM^2}{R} \quad \text{for} \quad n = 3 . \quad (8)$$

In the first integral of the last part of Eq. (7) the ratio $\epsilon = u/3p$ is determined by the state of the matter and radiation in each shell in the star. We calculate the contributions to u and p for nuclei, ionization electrons, electron–positron pairs and radiation in the nondegenerate approximation which holds for massive stars and find that

$$\epsilon - 1 = \frac{u}{3p} - 1 = \frac{\beta}{3} \left[x - 3 - \frac{3}{2Z} \frac{n_0}{n_e} + z \left(1 - \frac{n_0}{n_e} \right) \right] \left[1 + \frac{1}{Z} \frac{n_0}{n_e} \right]^{-1} , \quad (9)$$

where β is the ratio of gas pressure to total pressure, x is the mean kinetic energy of the electrons and positrons in units of kT, n_0 is the original number of ionization electrons per cm^3 necessary to balance the nuclear charge Z, n_e is the total number of electrons and positrons per cm^3, and z equals $m_e c^2/kT$. The quantity x is tabulated by Chandrasekhar[11] as U/PV. Below $T = 10^9$ deg at sufficiently high densities, $x = \frac{3}{2}$, $n_e = n_0$, so that

$$\epsilon - 1 = -\tfrac{1}{2}\beta \leq 0 \qquad T \leq 10^9 \text{ deg} . \quad (10)$$

At higher temperature and sufficiently low densities, $n_e \gg n_0$, so that

$$\epsilon - 1 = \tfrac{1}{3}\beta\, [\, x + z - 3\,] \geq 0 . \quad (11)$$

The situation can also occur at high temperature and high density where $n_e \sim n_0$ and $x \sim 3$ so that $\epsilon - 1 \sim 0$. In general, ϵ starts at $\frac{1}{2}$ at very low temperatures, rapidly rises to unity in massive stars, reaches a maximum ~ 1.2 around $T = 2 \times 10^9$ degrees and returns to unity at higher temperature. The internal energy per unit volume, $u = 3\epsilon p$, varies throughout a star primarily because of the rapid inward rise of pressure p and not because of the variations in ϵ. In what follows we will neglect variations in ϵ and introduce its average value $\bar{\epsilon}$ for order-of-magnitude estimates.

We now turn to the classical calculation of E through Eq. (7). The integration over $3\epsilon p dV$ can be carried out by use of the expression for the pressure gradient in the star. In the classical case

$$\frac{dp}{dr} = -\rho\left(g + \frac{dv}{dt}\right) = -f\rho g = -f\rho\frac{GM_r}{r^2}, \tag{12}$$

where ρ is the density, $g = GM_r/r^2$ is the acceleration due to gravity, and dv/dt is the actual acceleration of the material measured positively in the outward direction, i.e., increasing r. In this note we will not attempt to treat dynamic effects $(dv/dt \neq 0)$ except through the use of the variable f which has been introduced in the last parts of Eq. (12). For implosion $(dv/dt < 0)$, $f < 1$; for explosion $(dv/dt > 0)$, $f > 1$. As in the case of ϵ we will introduce an average value $\bar{f}$.

The classical calculation then proceeds as follows:

$$\int_0^R 3\epsilon p dV = 3\epsilon p V \Big|_{V=0}^{p=0} - \int_0^R 3\epsilon V dp - \int_0^R 3pV d\epsilon$$

$$\approx + \int_0^R 4\pi r^3 \epsilon f \rho g dr \approx \overline{\epsilon f} \int \frac{GM_r}{r}\rho dV = \overline{\epsilon f}\Omega, \tag{13}$$

where the approximation in neglecting variations in ϵ and f are now apparent, in particular $d\epsilon \approx 0$. Thus

$$E \approx (\overline{\epsilon f} - 1)\Omega + E_{\mathrm{dyn}} \frown (\overline{\epsilon f} - 1)\Omega + E_{\mathrm{dyn}}. \tag{14}$$

Note that the product ϵf must be averaged over pdV and that the second approximation must be used with caution. In the case of hydrostatic equilibrium throughout a star, $f = 1$ everywhere, $E_{\mathrm{dyn}} = 0$, and

$$E_{\mathrm{eq}} \approx (\bar{\epsilon} - 1)\Omega \approx -\tfrac{1}{2}\bar{\beta}\Omega \qquad \text{for} \qquad T \leq 10^9 \text{ deg}. \tag{15}$$

Thus a classical star is bound by $\tfrac{1}{2}\Omega$ for $\bar{\beta} = 1$ where radiation pressure can be neglected (small stars) and has zero binding for $\bar{\beta} = 0$ where radiation pressure is dominant (very massive stars). At temperatures above 10^9 deg electron–positron pair formation can lead to stars with total positive energy or negative binding as indicated by Eq. (11). If this energy cannot be supplied after the star has passed through bound states of quasi-hydrostatic equilibrium at low temperatures then $\overline{\epsilon f}$ must remain less than unity. This means that at least part of the star must contract fairly rapidly and it can be argued that the inner regions where the temperature is highest and ϵ is the largest will be most susceptible to rapid contraction.

For the general relativistic case we replace Eq. (12) by

$$\frac{dp}{dr} = -f\rho\frac{GM_r}{r^2}\left(1 + \frac{p}{\rho c^2}\right)\left(1 + \frac{4\pi p r^3}{M_r c^2}\right)\left(1 - \frac{2GM_r}{r c^2}\right)^{-1} \equiv -f\rho\frac{\textcircled{G}M_r}{r^2}. \tag{16}$$

Note that the *effective* gravitational constant $\mathcal{G}$ diverges as $2GM_r/rc^2 \to 1$. *Gravity changes from the weakest to the strongest interaction under appropriate circumstances!* The first integrand in Eq. (6) contains $(1 - 2GM_r/rc^2)^{1/2}$ in the denominator so we divide Eq. (16) by this term and expand the two sides to obtain

$$d p \left(1 + \frac{GM_r}{r c^2}\right) \approx - f \rho \frac{GM_r}{r^2} \left(1 + \frac{p}{\rho c^2} + \frac{4 \pi p r^3}{M_r c^2} + \frac{3 G M_r}{r c^2}\right) d r . \tag{17}$$

Just as in the classical case, we use Eq. (17) to evaluate the first integral in Eq. (6). In addition the second integrand can be expanded and the final result is

$$E = (\overline{\epsilon f} - 1)\Omega + \frac{4 \pi G}{c^2} \overline{\epsilon(f+1)} \int p r M_r d r + \frac{16 \pi^2 G}{c^2} \overline{(\epsilon f - 1)} \int \rho p r^4 d r$$

$$+ \frac{12 \pi G^2}{c^2} \overline{(\epsilon f - \tfrac{1}{2})} \int \rho M_r^2 d r + E_{\text{dyn}} \tag{18}$$

where the various averages, $\overline{\epsilon f}$ and $\overline{\epsilon}$, involve different "weighting" functions but we ignore these differences.

We first investigate Eq. (18) in the case of hydrostatic equilibrium where $f = 1$, $E_{\text{dyn}} = 0$. It is also possible to make the approximation $\overline{\epsilon} = 1$ except in the first term where, when the term is important, $\epsilon - 1 = -\tfrac{1}{2}\overline{\beta}$ with $\overline{\beta}$ the appropriate average over

$$\beta \approx (\eta_n^{1/4}/\mu)(T/T_c)^{(n-3)/(n+1)} \qquad T \le 10^9 \text{ deg} . \tag{19}$$

Here μ is the mean molecular weight taken to be constant throughout the star and T_c is the central temperature. Equation (19) can be shown to hold approximately for massive stars ($M \ge 10^3 M_\odot$) at central temperatures less than 10^9 degrees. The quantity η_n is given by

$$\eta_n = \frac{3}{4\pi} (n+1)^3 \frac{\mathfrak{R}^4}{a G^3} \left(\frac{M_n}{M}\right)^2 \tag{20}$$

$$= 335 (M_\odot/M)^2 \qquad \text{for} \qquad n = 3 , \tag{21}$$

where M_n is the constant of integration for the mass scale for the second order differential equation for a polytrope of index n. For example, $M_3 = 2.018$. The second constant applies to the radius scale and will be designated by R_n in what follows. For example, $R_3 = 6.897$. For the polytrope of index 3, β is constant throughout the interior and

$$\overline{\beta} = \beta = \frac{4.3}{\mu} \left(\frac{M_\odot}{M}\right)^{1/2} \ll 1 \frown 10^{-2} , \quad M \frown 10^6 M_\odot ; \ \overline{\beta} \frown 10^{-4} , \quad M \frown 10^{10} M_\odot . \tag{22}$$

It will be found for all massive polytropes that $\overline{\beta}$ is small compared to unity.

In any case for hydrostatic equilibrium Eq. (18) becomes

$$E_{\text{eq}} = - \tfrac{1}{2}\overline{\beta}\Omega + \frac{8 \pi G}{c^2} \int p r M_r d r + \frac{6 \pi G^2}{c^2} \int \rho M_r^2 d r . \tag{23}$$

Massive stars are highly convective and with $\beta \sim 0$ this corresponds most closely to a polytropic structure with index $n = 3$. For $n = 3$, $\Omega = \tfrac{3}{2} GM^2/R$ and the integrals in

Eq. (23) can be integrated numerically using Table 6 in Eddington's *The Internal Constitution of the Stars*.[12] The result is

$$\frac{E_{eq}}{M c^2} = -\tfrac{3}{4}\beta \left(\frac{GM}{R c^2}\right) + 5.1 \left(\frac{GM}{R c^2}\right)^2 = -\tfrac{3}{8}\beta \left(\frac{R_g}{R}\right) + 1.3 \left(\frac{R_g}{R}\right)^2 \qquad \text{for} \qquad n = 3 , \quad (24)$$

where $R_g = 2GM/c^2 = 3.0 \times 10^5 \, (M/M\odot)$ cm is the limiting gravitational radius of the polytrope.

Equation (24) gives the first two terms in a general expansion in terms of the dimensionless parameter

$$\frac{R_g}{R} = \frac{2GM}{R c^2} = \left(\frac{32\pi G^3}{3 c^6} M^2 \bar\rho\right)^{1/3} = \left[\frac{\bar\rho (M/M\odot)^2}{1.8 \times 10^{16}}\right]^{1/3} . \qquad (25)$$

In general it is assumed that general relativity becomes important when this parameter is the order of unity, or

$$\bar\rho = 1.8 \times 10^{16} (M\odot/M)^2 \text{ g cm}^{-3} , \qquad (26)$$

so that for stars near one solar mass the critical mean density is the order of 10^{16} g cm^{-3} which exceeds nuclear densities ($\sim 2 \times 10^{14}$ g cm^{-3}). However, for massive stars, e.g., $M = 10^8 \, M\odot$, the critical mean density is the order of unity, the central densities are only ~ 100 g cm^{-3} and *general relativity is seen to be important even in the range where the atomic and nuclear properties of matter are fairly well understood*. Equation (24) shows in addition that the general relativistic second order term in the binding energy of a star is comparable to the nonrelativistic first order term when

$$2GM/Rc^2 \approx 0.3 \, \beta \approx (1.3/\mu)(M\odot/M)^{1/2} \approx 3 \times 10^{-4}$$
$$\text{for} \quad \mu = \tfrac{1}{2} , \qquad M = 10^8 \, M\odot , \qquad n = 3 , \qquad (27)$$

or

$$\bar\rho \approx (4.0 \times 10^{16}/\mu^3)(M\odot/M)^{1/2} \text{ g cm}^{-3} \approx 3.2 \times 10^{17}(M\odot/M)^{1/2}$$
$$\text{for} \quad \mu = \tfrac{1}{2} \approx 3.2 \times 10^{-11} \text{ g cm}^{-3} \qquad \text{for} \qquad M = 10^8 \, M\odot , \qquad \dot n = 3 . \qquad (28)$$

The minimum in E_{eq}/Mc^2 occurs at one-eighth this density or $2GM/Rc^2 = 0.15\beta$. It will be apparent that general relativistic considerations cannot be neglected even during relatively early stages of the contraction of massive stars. It will also be clear that the perturbation approximation used in evaluating the second order terms in Eq. (24) is quite accurate under these circumstances. The structure of the star is that of a classical polytrope. At the same time the classical result for massive stars supported by radiation pressure is a near-zero binding energy. Thus the relativistic second order term becomes dominant in the binding energy calculation at anomalously large radii and low densities.

For many purposes, particularly regarding the rates of nuclear processes, it is advantageous to replace the radius R in the collapse parameter by the central temperature. This can be done quite simply since the radius of a polytrope of index n is related to the central temperature T_c by

$$R = \frac{GMR_n}{(n+1) M_n} \left(\frac{\mu\beta}{\Re T}\right)_c = \left[\frac{3G}{4\pi(n+1) a}\right]^{1/4} \left(\frac{M}{M_n}\right)^{1/2} \frac{R_n}{T_c}$$
$$= \frac{5.83 \times 10^9}{(T_9)_c} \left(\frac{M}{M\odot}\right)^{1/2} \text{cm} \qquad \text{for} \qquad n = 3 . \qquad (29)$$

Using Eqs. (23) and (29) the result for E_{eq}/Mc^2 for three polytropes is

$$\frac{E_{eq}}{Mc^2} = -\frac{9}{4}\frac{\Gamma(3/2)\Gamma(5/4)}{\Gamma(11/4)}\frac{\Re}{\mu c^2}T_c + \frac{19}{35}(2\pi)^{1/2}\frac{a^{1/2}G^{3/2}M}{c^4}T_c^2 \tag{30}$$

$$= -2.1 \times 10^{-13}T_c + 5.0 \times 10^{-27}(M/M_\odot)T_c^2 \qquad \text{for} \qquad n = 0 ,$$

$$\frac{E_{eq}}{Mc^2} = -3\frac{M_3}{R_3}\frac{\Re}{\mu c^2}T_c + 3\frac{M_3}{R_3}\frac{a^{1/2}G^{3/2}M}{c^4}T_c^2 = -1.6 \times 10^{-13}T_c \tag{31}$$

$$+ 3.3 \times 10^{-27}(M/M_\odot)T_c^2 \qquad \text{for} \qquad n = 3 ,$$

$$\frac{E_{eq}}{Mc^2} = -\frac{9}{4}\frac{\Gamma(3/2)\Gamma(7/4)}{\Gamma(13/4)}\frac{\Re}{\mu c^2}T_c + \frac{2}{15}(6\pi)^{1/2}\frac{a^{1/2}G^{3/2}M}{c^4}T_c^2 \tag{32}$$

$$= -1.3 \times 10^{-13}T_c + 2.2 \times 10^{-27}(M/M_\odot)T_c^2 \qquad \text{for} \qquad n = 5 .$$

In the numerical expressions we have set $\mu = \frac{1}{2}$ since the first term is important at low temperatures before hydrogen burning sets in. Equations (30), (31), and (32) show that the ratio of the second order term to the first order term is relatively independent of the polytropic structure.

The first term in Eqs. (30), (31), or (32) shows the linear decrease with central temperature of the total energy of the star (increase in binding energy) as the star begins contraction from the dispersed stage. It corresponds to the classical case, Eq. (15). The second term arises from the first order general relativistic approximation. This term is positive and leads at high enough temperatures to positive total energies and negative binding energies as shown by Iben[10] by more exact theoretical and numerical treatment of the problem. Equations (30), (31), and (32) reproduce Iben's numerical results in good approximation. The minimum total energy is reached at

$$T_c = 2.5 \times 10^{13}\, M_\odot/M \qquad \text{for} \qquad n = 3 \tag{33}$$

and the energy returns to zero and goes positive at

$$T_c = 5 \times 10^{13}\, M_\odot/M \qquad \text{for} \qquad n = 3 . \tag{34}$$

This behavior is illustrated for $M = 10^6\, M_\odot$, $10^7\, M_\odot$, $10^8\, M_\odot$ in Fig. 1. In all three cases the energy necessary to establish hydrostatic equilibrium becomes large and positive before hydrogen burning sets in at 8×10^7 deg as determined by Hoyle and Fowler.[4] The zero energy temperatures are 5×10^7, 5×10^6, 5×10^5 degrees, respectively.

The second order terms in Eqs. (24), (30), (31), and (32) show that hydrostatic equilibrium under general relativistic conditions ($T_c > 5 \times 10^{13}\, M_\odot/M$ degrees) requires large amounts of internal energy for pressure support. Can nuclear reactions provide this energy? The conversion of hydrogen into helium releases 0.7% of the rest mass energy of that fraction of the star consumed. An upper limit is set by the fraction of the hydrogen in the central regions ($\sim 0.3\, M$) which can be burned before gravitational red shifts terminate energy release. It is of the order of 15%. Thus $10^{-3}\, Mc^2$ can be made available in hydrogen burning and consequently

$$E_{eq}/Mc^2 \approx 3.3 \times 10^{-27}(M/M_\odot)T_c^2 \leq 10^{-3} \qquad \text{for} \qquad n = 3 . \tag{35}$$

Hoyle and Fowler (1963) estimate that hydrogen burning through the CNO-cycle in massive stars where $\rho_c \sim 0.01$ to 0.1 g cm^{-3} occurs at $T_c \sim 8 \times 10^7$ deg so that

$$M/M_\odot \leq 10^8 \qquad (4^1 H \rightarrow {}^4He) . \tag{36}$$

Helium burning and subsequent exothermic reactions in the core release only 3×10^{-4} Mc^2 and occur at still higher temperatures where the equilibrium energy required is very great indeed. Equation (35) thus indicates that for $M \geq 10^8 \, M \odot$ nuclear reactions cannot supply the internal energy necessary for hydrostatic equilibrium.

There is an additional question. For $M < 10^8 \, M \odot$ is the hydrostatic equilibrium stable or unstable? The problem is a difficult one when relativistic considerations are taken into account but the customary classical argument[12] indicates that a star in equilibrium is not stable to sudden (adiabatic) contraction or expansion for radii smaller than those at the point at which E_{eq}/Mc^2 is a minimum. For a polytropic structure with index $n = 3$, the condition for stability from Eqs. (19), (24), (29), and (31) is therefore

$$R \geq (3/\pi)^{1/2}(R_3/\beta)(2GM/c^2) = (6.8/\beta)(2GM/c^2) \,,$$

which is just twice the value given by the erroneous condition $E_{eq} > 0$. This can be rewritten as

$$\beta/6 \approx \Gamma_1 - \tfrac{4}{3} \gtrsim 1.12(2GM/Rc^2) \,,$$

where $\Gamma_1 = d \ln p/d \ln \rho$. Classically, $\Gamma_1 - \tfrac{4}{3}$ averaged throughout the star must exceed zero for stability. General relativity sets an even more stringent requirement on this

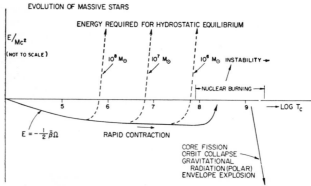

FIG. 1.—The energy required for hydrostatic equilibrium in massive stars is shown schematically (*dashed lines*) as a function of the central temperature during contraction. The possible evolution during rapid contraction before nuclear burning and collapse afterward is also shown. The instability during nuclear burning is emphasized.

quantity for stability. On sudden contraction, the adiabatic increase in pressure is not as great as that required for the new equilibrium so contraction continues. Similarly, sudden expansion is followed by further expansion.

For stars with $M > 10^6 \, M \odot$, Fig. 1 indicates that the contraction begins before the onset of nuclear burning. It is thus reasonable to assume that contraction continues during the nuclear burning although it may well be slowed somewhat by the release of nuclear energy. Under these circumstances we return to Eq. (18) and let f be less than unity. The equation then shows that the positive relativistic terms can be balanced by the first term and the total energy held constant as must be the case when the nuclear energy is small compared to that required for equilibrium. In Eq. (18) one can now set $\bar{\epsilon} \sim 1$ in all terms. Numerically it is found that

$$\frac{E}{Mc^2} = -\tfrac{3}{2}(1 - \bar{f})\left(\frac{GM}{Rc^2}\right) + (9.2\,\bar{f} - 4.1)\left(\frac{GM}{Rc^2}\right)^2 + \frac{E_{dyn}}{Mc^2} \qquad \text{for} \qquad n = 3 \qquad (37)$$

and

$$\frac{E}{Mc^2}=-3.8\times10^{-14}(1-\bar{f})\left(\frac{M}{M_\odot}\right)^{1/2}T_c+6.0\times10^{-27}(\bar{f}-0.45)\left(\frac{M}{M_\odot}\right)T_c^2+\frac{E_{\mathrm{dyn}}}{Mc^2}. \quad (38)$$

For $M = 10^8\,M_\odot$ the first and second terms cancel for $\bar{f} = 0.7$ at $T = 10^9$ degrees and for $\bar{f} = 0.6$ at $T = 2\times10^9$ degrees. Note that the general relativistic second term vanishes and becomes negative for $\bar{f} \le 0.45$.

The above results indicate that a situation intermediate between hydrostatic equilibrium ($\bar{f} = 1$) and free fall ($\bar{f} = 0$) can lead to a constant total energy. As $\bar{f}$ decreases it is only necessary that E_{dyn} increase, as indeed will be the case. Thus, as shown in Fig. 1, rapid contraction at some fraction of the free fall rate occurs for massive stars with $M \ge 10^6\,M_\odot$ early in their evolutionary history.

The characteristic free fall time for the outer layers of a star originally at radius R is given by

$$\tau_{ff} \approx \left(\frac{R^3}{2GM}\right)^{1/2} \approx 6\times10^{-14}R^{3/2}\left(\frac{M_\odot}{M}\right)^{1/2}\ \mathrm{sec}\,. \quad (39)$$

Choose R at the moment when the minimum in E_{eq}/Mc^2 is reached, namely

$$R \approx \frac{1}{0.15\beta}R_g \approx 0.8R_g\left(\frac{M}{M_\odot}\right)^{1/2} = 2.5\times10^5\left(\frac{M}{M_\odot}\right)^{3/2}\ \mathrm{cm}\,. \quad (40)$$

This radius is 2.5×10^{14} cm for $M = 10^6\,M_\odot$, 2.5×10^{17} cm for $M = 10^8\,M_\odot$, and 2.5×10^{20} cm for $M = 10^{10}\,M_\odot$. (These values are approximate for a polytropic structure with index 3 and can be somewhat larger if the index exceeds 3, e.g., $R \sim 10^{18}$ cm for $M \sim 10^8\,M_\odot$.) The free fall time for the outer radiating shell of a star is thus

$$\tau_{ff} \approx 2.5\times10^{-13}(M/M_\odot)^{1/4}\ \mathrm{yr}\,. \quad (41)$$

This time is 7.5×10^{-3} yr for $M = 10^6\,M_\odot$, 25 yr for $M = 10^8\,M_\odot$, and 7.5×10^4 yr for $M = 10^{10}\,M_\odot$, and can be somewhat increased if polytropes with index >3 are considered. In addition, from the arguments advanced in the previous paragraph, the actual time will be somewhat longer than the free fall time especially for the outer layers where f may be only slightly less than unity during the initial stage of the contraction where the greater part of the time is spent. However, even for $f = 0.99$, an increase only by a factor $(1 - f)^{-1/2} = 10$ is obtained. Taking all factors into account the collapse time for $M = 10^8\,M_\odot$, for example, could be as long as 10^3 years.

Thus, it will be clear that only for the very highest masses under consideration, namely $10^{10}\,M_\odot$, are the collapse times comparable to the 10^5 to 10^6 year lifetimes associated[6,7] with the stellar stage of radio sources. For the smaller mass range it is necessary to give up the special symmetry inherent in spherical collapse and to look to other mechanisms which will lead to a period of quasi-stability for the radio *stars*. One possibility is rotation. A large initial rotation can lead to a flattened disk configuration which can fragment into smaller stars with characteristic times of stable evolution comparable to the observed lifetimes. Somewhat smaller rotations can certainly slow contraction along the two axes normal to that of the rotation. Contraction of the outer material along the third coordinate will be impeded if turbulence is set up by the catastrophic collapse of the central regions of the star described in Part III to follow.

If it is granted that rotation, turbulence, convection, or other mechanisms set time scales for the collapse of the outer layers of massive stars comparable to those suspected for radio *stars*, then it is possible to use the original estimates of Hoyle and Fowler[4] to demonstrate that the nuclear resources of the star can meet the luminous energy requirements if not the requirements for hydrostatic equilibrium. They estimated the luminosity of a massive star to be

$$L \approx 5 \times 10^4 \frac{M}{M_\odot} L_\odot \approx 2 \times 10^{38} \left(\frac{M}{M_\odot}\right) \text{erg sec}^{-1} \approx 2 \times 10^{46} \text{ ergs sec}^{-1}$$

(42)

$$\text{for} \quad M = 10^8 \ M_\odot \ .$$

This estimate was based on a polytropic structure of index 3 but, unlike the stellar radius, is relatively independent of the index or for that matter of more complicated possibilities in internal structure. When the calculation was published,[4] optical luminosities of this great magnitude had not been reported and radio luminosities had been found only up to 10^{45} erg sec^{-1}. Subsequently[6, 7] it was shown that the radio *stars* are extragalactic and that their optical luminosities are indeed of order 10^{46} erg sec^{-1}.

Since $10^{-3} Mc^2 \approx 2 \times 10^{51} (M/M_\odot)$ ergs can be made available by hydrogen burning it will be clear from comparison with Eq. (42) that the duration is independent of mass and is given by

$$\tau(4 \ ^1\text{H} \rightarrow \ ^4\text{He}) \approx 10^{13} \text{ sec} \approx 3 \times 10^5 \text{ yr} \ .$$

(43)

This interval matches the estimated lifetimes for radio *stars* quite well. It is not necessary that the hydrogen burning in the central regions extend over this interval. The stellar dimensions are such that heat transfer by convection from the interior to the surface and by radiation to the exterior actually sets the time scale. In the model discussed in Part III the nuclear energy from hydrogen burning is released in a short interval. However, during the 3×10^5 year interval when contraction is impeded by rotation, etc., the luminosity requirements must be met *in toto* by the nuclear rather than by the gravitational resources of the star.

Another point of interest during the quasi-stable stellar stage concerns the classical pulsation period of massive stars. This period is given by

$$\Pi \sim (G\bar{\beta}\bar{\rho})^{-1/2} \sim 10 \text{ yr}$$

(44)

for $\bar{\beta} \sim 10^{-3}$ and $\bar{\rho} \sim 10^{-7}$ g cm^{-3}. This mean density occurs for $M = 10^8 \ M_\odot$ just beyond the point in the contraction where $E_{eq} = 0$. Smith and Hoffleit[13] observe periods of this order in the luminosity fluctuations of the radio *star* 3C273.

III. ENERGY RELEASE IN COLLAPSE OF THE CORE OF A MASSIVE STAR

Michel[14] has recently discussed the collapse of massive stars after the exhaustion of nuclear energy. He argues on general grounds that the central core of the star will collapse much more rapidly than the outer regions so that a separation of core from envelope will characterize the event. Moreover, if energy is transferred in some manner from core to envelope as suggested by Hoyle and Fowler,[4] then the envelope may actually explode away from the imploding core. These ideas can be clarified by reference to Fig. 2 which shows the run of certain variables: density ρ, effective temperature $T/\mu\beta$, mass M_r interior to radius r, and gravitational potential φ, all in the classical approximation. Figure 2 has been drawn for a polytrope of index $n = 3$ on the grounds that this polytrope will match the internal structure at least approximately during the quasi-static period in which contraction is impeded by rotation, turbulence, and convection, The decrease in ρ, $T/\mu\beta$, and $|\varphi|$ with increasing R is illustrated as well as the increase in M_r. The acceleration due to gravity is seen to rise linearly at small r, reach a maximum at $r = 0.22 \ R$ and decrease thereafter. Upon the failure of internal pressure support the linear region will collapse homologously ($\ddot{r} \approx g \propto r$) and it can be argued that the region within $g = g_{max}$ will collapse in an approximately similar fashion at a much greater rate than the outer regions where g is smaller. The figure shows that $M_r \sim 0.3\ M$ at g_{max} and in what follows it will be taken that the collapsing core has this mass, $M_c \sim 0.3\ M$.

Michel[14] suggested that a loss of energy by the collapsing core, as for example by neutrino emission, reduces its gravitational mass and in turn the absolute value of the gravitational potential throughout the envelope is reduced. For radiation support dominant ($\beta \ll 1$), the envelope binding energy is approximately zero before core collapse so the decrease in gravitational potential energy results in an excess energy which is dissipated in explosion of the envelope.

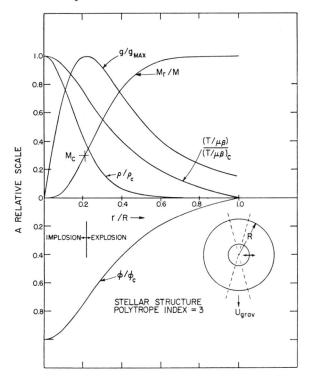

Fig. 2.—The run of the variables, ρ, $T/\mu\beta$, φ, M_r, and g vs radius in a polytrope with index $n = 3$. The mass of the core containing all the material below $g = g_{max}$ is seen to be $M_c = 0.3\ M$. The polar loss of gravitational radiation accompanying implosion of the core and explosion of the envelope is shown.

On the other hand, HFB[2] showed that the energy loss by the most effective neutrino-antineutrino production mechanism

$$e^+ + e^- \rightarrow \nu + \bar{\nu} \tag{45}$$

does not lead to a substantial decrease in the mass-energy content of the core of stars with $M > 10^6\ M_\odot$. Their calculation can be simplified somewhat for such large masses. For an observer comoving with a representative sample of the internal matter, the energy loss from reaction (45) is

$$\frac{dU_\nu}{dt} \sim \frac{4.3 \times 10^{15}}{\rho} T_9{}^9\ \text{erg g}^{-1}\ \text{sec}^{-1} \qquad \text{for} \qquad T_9 > 2. \tag{46}$$

For this same observer the density-temperature relation in the material at hand is very closely that given by the adiabatic relation (as the final result demonstrates) namely

$$\rho \sim 2.8 \times 10^5 \, (M\odot/M_c)^{1/2} T_9{}^3 \, . \tag{47}$$

The pressure gradient in the material is sufficient to balance the classical gravitational term in Eq. (16). However, during the collapse the relativistic terms become comparable to the classical terms, imbalance results and inward acceleration comparable to that in classical free fall follows. This can be seen from Eq. (12) by increasing g to $\sim 2g$, setting $dp/dr \sim -\rho g$, thus finding $dv/dt \sim -g$ just as for $dp/dr \sim 0$ classically. This permits the use of the classical free fall relation

$$dt \sim \frac{1}{(24\pi G\rho)^{1/2}} \frac{d\rho}{\rho} \, . \tag{48}$$

The total energy loss can be calculated by substituting Eq. (47) into Eq. (46) and integrating the resulting $dU\nu/dt$ over dt as given by Eq. (48). It might be argued that this loss should be calculated in the time coordinate of an external observer. However, the red shift in $dU\nu/dt$ and the time dilation in dt will compensate at least in first order. It is necessary only to set the upper limit on t equal to that finite value measured by the comoving observer when the core has reached the gravitational radius $2GM_c/c^2$. This time can be evaluated in terms of the limiting density given by Eq. (26). It should be recalled that the density throughout the core is substantially constant before collapse (0.4 < $\rho/\rho_c < 1$ from Fig. 1) and remains so during the homologous implosion. Thus the integrated energy loss is

$$E_\nu = \int_0^{t_{max}} \frac{dU_\nu}{dt} \, dt \sim \int_0^{\rho_{max}} \frac{dU_\nu/dt}{(24\pi G\rho)^{1/2}} \frac{d\rho}{\rho} \sim 90 \left(\frac{M_c}{M\odot}\right)^{3/2} \int_0^{\rho_{max}} \rho^{1/2} dp$$

$$\sim 1.5 \times 10^{26} \left(\frac{M\odot}{M_c}\right)^{3/2} \, \text{erg g}^{-1} \, . \tag{49}$$

In terms of the fractional loss per unit of rest mass energy, this becomes

$$\frac{\Delta M_c}{M_c} = \frac{E_\nu}{c_2} \sim 1.7 \times 10^5 \left(\frac{M\odot}{M_c}\right)^{3/2} \, . \tag{50}$$

For $M_c = 0.3 \, M$, $M = 10^8 \, M\odot$ the result is a fractional loss in mass by the core equal to $\sim 10^{-6}$ and even smaller for greater masses. Reaction (45) is not effective in the Michel mechanism for the "transfer" of energy from core to envelope.

Gravitational radiation was suggested as a mode of energy loss by Hoyle and Fowler[4] and by Hoyle[15] but numerical estimates were not given. Gell-Mann[16] emphasized the importance of gravitational radiation particularly in the case of a rotating star where the rotation can lead to fission of the collapsing core. The interval during which a prolate deformation of the core develops and ultimately results in fission will not be discussed in detail here and only one feature will be emphasized. It is during this interval that the nuclear energy of the core is considered to be transferred by convection and radiative transfer to the *inner* part of the envelope. Convection is rapid, temperature gradients are large and the distances are short compared to those involved in the previous problem of bringing energy to the stellar surface during the collapse interval for a spherical nonrotating star.

sive stars. Today, the strong radio sources may indicate that such massive stars exist and, if so, further study of these peculiar objects may reveal answers to difficult but interesting questions.

IV. SUMMARY

The contents of this summary pertain in particular to a star with mass equal to $10^8\ M\odot$ and in general to stars with mass in the range excess of $10^6\ M\odot$.

(1) In a nonrotating, spherically symmetric, massive star, general relativistic considerations become important and gravitational collapse sets in at radius $R \sim 10^{18}$ cm and central conditions $\rho_c \sim 4 \times 10^{-10}$ g cm^{-3}, $T_c \sim 2.5 \times 10^5$ deg. Collapse to the gravitational radius $R_g \sim 3 \times 10^{13}$ cm occurs in a local time interval $\sim 10^3$ years for the outer regions and ~ 1 year for the inner regions. Large red shift effects preclude the release of significant amounts of energy from such a rapidly collapsing system.

(2) Rotation, assisted by internal turbulence and convection, is suggested as a possibility in impeding rapid gravitational collapse in massive stars. Rotation can lead to fission of the rapidly collapsing core before collapse of the envelope has reached appreciable velocity. During the development of the prolate deformation which leads to fission, the core releases nuclear energy in amount $\sim 10^{-3}\ Mc^2 \sim 10^{59}$ ergs into the envelope. This energy is sufficient to meet the luminosity requirement of the radio *stars* for 10^5 to 10^6 years. Upon fission the binary components collapse in ~ 0.1 year to their gravitational radii. A turbulent, quasi-stable envelope of convecting, radiating material surrounds the rotating binary system. Other more complicated nonspherical internal structures could conceivably support the radiating envelope.

(3) Appropriate choices for the parameters involved can be made which lead to lifetimes for the binary system also in the range 10^5 to 10^6 years. In a relatively short interval (~ 0.1 year) at the end of this period, gravitational radiation from the rotating binary, which does have a quadrupole moment, injects energy into the envelope material in amount $\sim 10^{-2}\ Mc^2 \sim 10^{60}$ ergs. It is suggested that the resulting polar explosion may lead to the development of the strong, extended radio sources with at least two components.

(4) On the model discussed it is found that the gravitational resources of a massive star exceed the nuclear resources by only a factor of ten. Only 1% of the rest mass energy is made available for all forms of radiation. This and other problems are noted briefly at the end of Part III.

ACKNOWLEDGMENTS

The author is indebted to many of his colleagues in physics and astronomy at the California Institute of Technology and the Mt. Wilson–Palomar Observatories for discussions of the subject matter of this paper. He is especially indebted to Professor Murray Gell-Mann who reopened the question of gravitational radiation, in particular that from a rotating binary system, and who collaborated in estimating the importance of gravitational radiation in collapsing systems. To Fred Hoyle, Geoffrey Burbidge, and Margaret Burbidge, he is indebted for constant collaboration over the past year on the subject of massive stars.

REFERENCES

[1] J. R. Oppenheimer and R. Serber, *Phys. Rev.*, **54**, 540 (1938).
[2] J. R. Oppenheimer and G. M. Volkoff, *Phys. Rev.*, **55**, 374, 413 (1939).
[3] J. R. Oppenheimer and H. Snyder, *Phys. Rev.*, **56**, 455 (1939).
[4] F. Hoyle and W. A. Fowler, *Monthly Notices Roy. Astron. Soc.*, **125**, 169 (1963); *Nature*, **197**, 533 (1963).*
[5] F. Hoyle, W. A. Fowler, G. R. Burbidge, and E. M. Burbidge, *Astrophys. J.*, **139**, 909 (1964). (This reference will be referred to subsequently as HFB².)
[6] M. Schmidt, *Nature*, **197**, 1040 (1963).
[7] J. L. Greenstein and T. A. Matthews, *Nature*, **197**, 1041 (1963).*
[8] P. Maltby, T. A. Matthews, and A. T. Moffet, *Astrophys. J.*, **137**, 153 (1963).*

[9] R. P. Feynman, private communication (1963).

[10] I. Iben, Jr., *Astrophys. J.*, **138**, 1090 (1963).*

[11] S. Chandrasekhar, *An Introduction to the Study of Stellar Structure* (University of Chicago Press, Chicago, Illinois, 1938), p. 347, Table 24.

[12] A. S. Eddington, *The Internal Constitution of the Stars* (Cambridge University Press, Cambridge, England, 1930).

[13] H. S. Smith and D. Hoffleit, *Nature*, **198**, 650 (1963).*

[14] F. C. Michel, *Astrophys. J.*, **138**, 1097 (1963).*

[15] F. Hoyle, *New Scientist*, **17**, 681 (1963).

[16] M. Gell-Mann, private communication (1963).

[17] L. D. Landau and E. M. Lifshitz, *The Classical Theory of Fields* (Addison-Wesley Publishing Company, Inc., Reading, Massachusetts, 1962), p. 366.

[18] F. Hoyle and J. V. Narlikar, *Proc. Roy. Soc.* (London) **A273**, 1 (1963).

MASSIVE STARS IN QUASI-
chapter 5 ## STATIC EQUILIBRIUM

Icko Iben, Jr.

INTRODUCTION

Starlike condensations of 10^6–10^8 solar masses have been suggested recently (Hoyle and Fowler 1963*a*, *b*) as the origin of the large energies (10^{58} to 10^{61} erg) required to account for strong radio sources on the usual hypothesis of electron synchrotron radiation. Hoyle and Fowler make quantitative estimates on the supposition that a particular solution of the classical hydrostatic equations—the polytrope of index 3—provides a suitable approximation to the structure of the massive star during all phases prior to a presumed eventual implosion of central regions and explosion of outer regions.

It is the purpose of this note to point out that an understanding of the behavior of a very massive body during gravitational contraction through starlike phases requires the solution of the full dynamic equations of general relativity. Whereas the equations of classical hydrodynamics permit quasi-static solutions which are consistent with a collapse rate which decreases with time, the quasi-static solutions to the relativistic equations suggest that, if the star does not fragment, the rate of collapse must increase with time prior to nuclear burning. For stellar masses above 10^8 solar masses, it does not appear likely that nuclear fuel can be burned rapidly enough to halt the collapse.

EQUATIONS AND SOLUTION

In the case of spherical symmetry, the time-dependent metric may be written as (see, e.g., Tolman 1934)

$$(ds)^2 = e^{\nu(r,\,t)}(dt)^2 - \frac{1}{c^2}\{ e^{\lambda(r,\,t)}(dr^2) + r^2[(d\theta)^2 + \sin^2\theta(d\phi)^2]\}. \tag{1}$$

When time variations are neglected,

$$e^{-\lambda} = (1 - 2GM(r)/rc^2), \tag{2}$$

where

$$\frac{\partial M(r)}{\partial r} = 4\pi r^2 \rho, \qquad M(0) = 0 \tag{3}$$

Supported in part by the Office of Naval Research and in part by the National Aeronautics and Space Administration.

Icko Iben, Jr., California Institute of Technology.

Reprinted from the *Astrophysical Journal*, **138**, 1090–1096, 1963.

and

$$\frac{\partial P}{\partial r} = -(\rho + P)\frac{e^{\lambda}}{c^2}\left[4\pi GPr + \frac{GM(r)}{r^2}\right]. \tag{4}$$

Here Pc^2 and ρc^2 are, respectively, the pressure and energy density in a local frame of reference, c is the velocity of light, and G is the gravitational constant.

If R is defined as the position at which the matter density vanishes, then $M_s = M(R)$ represents the entire energy content of the star in mass units. Since the star radiates energy, M_s must change with time. If it is assumed that the total number of nucleons in the star remains constant, then

$$N = \int_0^{\text{surface}} q(r)\, 4\pi r^2\, e^{\lambda/2} dr = \text{constant}, \tag{5}$$

where $q(r)$ is the local nucleon density in number/cm^3 and $4\pi r^2 e^{\lambda/2} dr$ is the volume of a spherical shell in a local frame of reference. The total rest mass of the system is obtained by integrating

$$\frac{\partial M_m(r)}{\partial r} = \rho_m 4\pi r^2 e^{\lambda/2}, \tag{6}$$

where ρ_m is the local rest mass density of nuclei and associated electrons. Since they vanish when all components of the system are at rest at infinity, electron-positron pairs are not included in $M_m(r)$. The total binding energy of the system is simply $(M_0 - M_s)c^2$, where $M_0 = M_m(R)$.

Hoyle and Fowler (1963a) give arguments for assuming that the temperature gradient in a massive star is close to the adiabatic gradient. If flow is adiabatic, then

$$\frac{\partial \rho}{\partial r} = \frac{\rho + P}{\rho_m}\frac{\partial \rho_m}{\partial r}. \tag{7}$$

Table 1 gives the value of $(M_0 - M_s)/M_0$ as a function of rest mass and central temperature for pure hydrogen configurations satisfying equations (3) through (7). Electron-positron pairs are included in the equation of state, as described in the Appendix. Entries are omitted when leptons become partially degenerate near the center.

For 100 solar masses the result is as might be expected from the classical virial theorem—the binding energy is directly proportional to the thermal energy content of the system and therefore increases linearly with central temperature.

Inspection of other rows in Table 1 shows that the binding energy passes through a maximum at $T_c \sim 3.4 \times 10^{13}\ (M_\odot/M_0)°$ K, goes to zero at $T_c \sim 6.8 \times 10^{13}\ (M_\odot/M_0)°$ K, and then becomes increasingly negative with increasing central temperature. The maximum binding energy is roughly 3.6×10^{54} erg, nearly independent of rest mass. For $M_0 = (10^8 - 10^9)M_\odot$, the relative maximum in binding energy which occurs in the neighborhood of $T_c \sim 10^9°$ K is correlated with the creation of pairs near the center.

It might be argued that the occurrence of negative binding energies is due to a faulty choice of density gradient. However, by constructing an approximate analogue to the classical virial theorem, it becomes evident that the negative binding energy phenomenon is actually implicit in the relativistic equations.

At sufficiently low densities and temperatures, both electrons and nucleons may be treated as non-relativistic and non-degenerate so that, for a pure hydrogen configuration,

TABLE 1

$(M_0 - M_s)/M_0$ FOR PURE HYDROGEN STARS, ADIABATIC APPROXIMATION

Log $(M_0/M_\odot)$	Log T_c							
	6.0	6.5	7.0	7.5	8.0	8.5	9.0	9.5
2.0	$+1.67 \cdot 10^{-7}$	$+5.28 \cdot 10^{-7}$	$+1.67 \cdot 10^{-6}$	$+5.27 \cdot 10^{-6}$	$+1.68 \cdot 10^{-5}$	. . . . . .	. . . . . .	. . . . . .
3.0	$+1.65 \cdot 10^{-7}$	$+5.21 \cdot 10^{-7}$	$+1.65 \cdot 10^{-6}$	$+5.20 \cdot 10^{-6}$	$+1.64 \cdot 10^{-5}$	$+5.08 \cdot 10^{-5}$	. . . . . .	. . . . . .
4.0	$+1.63 \cdot 10^{-7}$	$+5.14 \cdot 10^{-7}$	$+1.62 \cdot 10^{-6}$	$+5.11 \cdot 10^{-6}$	$+1.58 \cdot 10^{-5}$	$+4.68 \cdot 10^{-5}$	$+9.43 \cdot 10^{-5}$	. . . . . .
5.0	$+1.61 \cdot 10^{-7}$	$+5.07 \cdot 10^{-7}$	$+1.58 \cdot 10^{-6}$	$+4.76 \cdot 10^{-6}$	$+1.27 \cdot 10^{-5}$	$+1.65 \cdot 10^{-5}$	$-3.49 \cdot 10^{-4}$	$-1.26 \cdot 10^{-2}$
6.0	$+1.58 \cdot 10^{-7}$	$+4.77 \cdot 10^{-7}$	$+1.28 \cdot 10^{-6}$	$-1.80 \cdot 10^{-6}$	$-1.71 \cdot 10^{-5}$	$-2.88 \cdot 10^{-4}$	$-4.12 \cdot 10^{-3}$	$-6.76 \cdot 10^{-2}$
7.0	$+1.29 \cdot 10^{-7}$	$+1.70 \cdot 10^{-7}$	$-1.64 \cdot 10^{-6}$	$-2.79 \cdot 10^{-5}$	$-3.20 \cdot 10^{-4}$	$-3.53 \cdot 10^{-3}$	$-4.40 \cdot 10^{-2}$	$-5.65 \cdot 10^{-2}$
8.0	$-1.66 \cdot 10^{-7}$	$-2.76 \cdot 10^{-6}$	$-3.16 \cdot 10^{-5}$	$-3.32 \cdot 10^{-4}$	$-3.56 \cdot 10^{-3}$	$-4.27 \cdot 10^{-2}$	$-8.64 \cdot 10^{-2}$	$-8.34 \cdot 10^{-2}$
9.0	$-3.13 \cdot 10^{-6}$	$-3.25 \cdot 10^{-5}$	$-3.38 \cdot 10^{-4}$	$-3.56 \cdot 10^{-3}$	$-4.50 \cdot 10^{-2}$	$-8.81 \cdot 10^{-2}$	$-7.60 \cdot 10^{-2}$	$-7.64 \cdot 10^{-2}$

$$\rho \cong \rho_m(1 + 3\theta) + \rho_r,$$

$$P \cong 2\theta\rho_m + \tfrac{1}{3}\rho_r,$$

(8)

where $\theta = kT/M_H c^2$, $\rho_r = aT^4/c^2$, $k =$ Boltzmann's constant, $M_H =$ hydrogen rest mass, and $a =$ radiation density constant.

Denoting the average of any variable γ by $\langle \gamma \rangle = \int \gamma dM_m / \int dM_m$, one finds from equations (3), (6), and (8) that

$$\frac{M_0 - M_s}{M_0} = \langle \epsilon \rangle = \langle 1 - (1 - 2\phi)^{1/2}(1 + 3\theta + \sigma) \rangle$$

(9)

$$= \langle -(3\theta + \sigma) + \phi(1 + \delta)(1 + 3\theta + \sigma) \rangle,$$

where $\phi = GM(r)/rc^2$, $\sigma = \rho_r/\rho_m$, and $\phi(1 + \delta) = 1 - (1 - 2\phi)^{1/2}$. Multiplying both sides of equation (4) by $4\pi r^3 dr$ and integrating the left-hand side by parts yields

TABLE 2

$(M_0 - M_s)/M_0$ AS A FUNCTION OF POLYTROPIC INDEX n, $T_c = 10^8 \,^{\circ}$ K

Log $(M_0/M_\odot)$	n					
	0.5	1.0	2.0	3.0	4.0	4.5
8.0......	$-5.35 \cdot 10^{-3}$	$-4.99 \cdot 10^{-3}$	$-4.27 \cdot 10^{-3}$	$-3.56 \cdot 10^{-3}$	$-2.85 \cdot 10^{-3}$	$-2.50 \cdot 10^{-3}$
7.0......	$-4.62 \cdot 10^{-4}$	$-4.31 \cdot 10^{-4}$	$-3.75 \cdot 10^{-4}$	$-3.20 \cdot 10^{-4}$	$-2.65 \cdot 10^{-4}$	$-2.37 \cdot 10^{-4}$
6.0......	$-2.80 \cdot 10^{-5}$	$-2.57 \cdot 10^{-5}$	$-2.12 \cdot 10^{-5}$	$-1.71 \cdot 10^{-5}$	$-1.38 \cdot 10^{-5}$	$-1.20 \cdot 10^{-5}$
5.0......	$+1.46 \cdot 10^{-5}$	$+1.42 \cdot 10^{-5}$	$+1.34 \cdot 10^{-5}$	$+1.27 \cdot 10^{-5}$	$+1.19 \cdot 10^{-5}$	$+1.15 \cdot 10^{-5}$
4.0......	$+1.88 \cdot 10^{-5}$	$+1.81 \cdot 10^{-5}$	$+1.69 \cdot 10^{-5}$	$+1.57 \cdot 10^{-5}$	$+1.45 \cdot 10^{-5}$	$+1.39 \cdot 10^{-5}$
3.0......	$+1.89 \cdot 10^{-5}$	$+1.83 \cdot 10^{-5}$	$+1.71 \cdot 10^{-5}$	$+1.59 \cdot 10^{-5}$	$+1.48 \cdot 10^{-5}$	$+1.42 \cdot 10^{-5}$

$$\langle (1 - 2\phi)^{1/2}(6\theta + \sigma) \rangle = \langle \phi(1 - 2\phi)^{-1/2}(1 + 5\theta + \tfrac{4}{3}\sigma)(1 + a) \rangle,$$

(10)

where $a = 4\pi P r^3/M(r)$. Elimination between equations (9) and (10) gives, after some rearrangement,

$$\langle \epsilon \rangle = \langle 3\theta - \phi(1 - 2\phi)^{-1/2}[a + (5\theta + \tfrac{4}{3}\sigma)(1 + a) + \delta + 3\theta(1 + \delta)(1 - 2\phi)^{1/2}] \rangle.$$

(11)

From equation (4) it is evident that when gas pressure is small relative to radiation pressure, as it certainly is in the massive stars under consideration, $\langle \sigma \rangle$, $\langle \phi \rangle$, $\langle a \rangle$, and $\langle \delta \rangle$ are all nearly proportional to $M_0^{1/2} T_c$. The negative term in equation (11) therefore increases quadratically with increasing central temperature and must eventually dominate the positive contribution which depends only linearly on central temperature. It is further clear that the temperature at which negative binding energies first appear decreases nearly linearly with increasing mass.

A comparison of equations (9) and (11) shows that when binding energy becomes negative, $(\langle \sigma \rangle) \sim (\langle \phi \rangle) \gg (\langle 3\theta \rangle)$. It may be inferred that the appearance of negative binding energies is to be attributed as much to the difference between the pressure relative to energy density properties of particles with rest mass and of particles with negligible rest mass as to an effect on the equilibrium conditions due to space curvature in a strong gravitational field.

The precise relationship between total energy content and central temperature of course depends on structural details. To illustrate that negative binding energies can nevertheless not be avoided in the quasi-static approximation by altering structural details, a set of models characterized by different degrees of central condensation has been constructed. For each model it has been assumed that

$$\frac{1}{\rho_m}\frac{\partial \rho_m}{\partial r} = \frac{n}{1+n}\frac{1}{P}\frac{\partial P}{\partial r},$$ (12)

n being the so-called polytropic index of the star.

Table 2 gives the binding energy relative to rest mass energy as a function of mass and polytropic index when $T_c = 10^8\,^\circ$ K. For $M_0 \geq 10^6\,M\odot$, binding energy is negative for all distributions having a finite radius ($n < 5$) but becomes slightly less negative with increasing n. For $M_0 \leq 10^5\,M\odot$, binding energy is positive but increases slightly with decreasing n.

This behavior follows from the fact that, for a given central temperature, low values of n correspond to more compact (smaller radius, higher mean density) distributions of matter and consequently to larger values of $\langle\phi\rangle$. As may be seen from equation (11), second-order terms proportional to ϕ dominate the first-order term when binding energy is negative. A more compact distribution (smaller n) thus leads to more negative binding energies. This is the case when $M_0 \geq 10^6\,M\odot$.

When binding energy is positive, second-order terms in $\langle\epsilon\rangle$ may be neglected. From equations (9) and (11) one obtains

$$\langle\epsilon\rangle = \langle 3\theta\rangle = \langle\phi - (\sigma + 3\theta)\rangle = \tfrac{1}{2}\langle\phi - \sigma\rangle.$$ (13)

Denoting the ratio of gas pressure to total pressure by β, then $\sigma = (1 - \beta)6\theta/\beta$. With the help of equation (13), $\langle\phi\rangle = \langle 6\theta/\beta\rangle = \langle 6\theta\rangle/\bar\beta$, giving finally the classical expression for binding energy

$$\langle\epsilon\rangle = \tfrac{1}{2}\bar\beta\langle\phi\rangle.$$ (14)

For given central temperature, a more diffuse distribution (larger n) now corresponds to weaker binding. This is the situation when $M_0 \leq 10^5\,M\odot$.

CONCLUDING REMARKS

It is clear that, contrary to the classical picture, a very massive star cannot continue to condense indefinitely through a sequence of quasi-static configurations. Upon approaching the maximum in the binding energy curve for such configurations, the star must either continue to condense dynamically or break up into smaller parts with a net increase in binding energy.

Assuming that collapse is more probable than fragmentation, it is probable that the rate of collapse increases with increasing condensation. When dynamic terms are included, but macroscopic velocities are small compared to c, then to first order in dynamic terms one must have that

$$\frac{M_0 - M_s}{M_0} \sim \langle\epsilon\rangle - \left\langle r\,\frac{d^2 r}{d t^2} + \tfrac{1}{2}\left(\frac{d r}{d t}\right)^2\right\rangle\frac{1}{c^2},$$ (15)

where dr/dt and d^2r/dt^2 are macroscopic velocity and acceleration, respectively.

If the distribution of matter and temperature is assumed to be roughly similar to that given by the quasi-static solution, then, beyond a critical central temperature, $\langle\epsilon\rangle$ becomes increasingly negative with increasing condensation. Since M_s must decrease with time, the quantity $\langle r(d^2r/dt^2) \rangle$ must grow large and negative to offset the decrease in $\langle \epsilon \rangle$. The rate of collapse of a major portion of the star must therefore increase with time as long as equation (15) remains approximately valid.

Schwarzschild and Härm (1959) have demonstrated that, on the basis of classical hydrodynamics, stars above 65–100 solar masses become pulsationally unstable during hydrogen burning via the CN cycle. However, if a very massive star is collapsing dynamically on reaching the hydrogen-burning phase, it is possible that nuclear fuel cannot be burned rapidly enough to stop the collapse.

If the distribution of matter during dynamic collapse is roughly the same as that given by the quasi-static solutions in the adiabatic approximation, then nuclear burning via the CN cycle does not become rapid enough to supply even the surface output until $\log T_c = 7.8$ to 7.93 for $M_0 = (10^6$ to $10^9)M\odot$. The lifetime against CN-cycle burning at these temperatures is on the order of 3×10^6 yrs. These estimates are based on the assumptions that surface luminosity is $L \sim 3.5 \times 10^4 L\odot (M_0/M\odot)$, as given by Hoyle and Fowler (1963a) and that $X_{\mathrm{CN}} = \sim 0.01$ and $X_{\mathrm{H}} \sim 1.0$.

From Table 1 it follows that at least $4.5 \times 10^{-2} \times 940 = 42$ MeV per nucleon is required to stop the collapse of a star of 10^9 solar masses if it reaches a central temperature of about $10^{8\,\circ}$ K. Since a total of only ~ 6 MeV per nucleon is available from the conversion of hydrogen to helium, hydrogen burning cannot stop the collapse, and it is likely that the star will continue to implode through all nuclear burning stages. If $M_0 = 10^8 M\odot$, collapse cannot be halted if T_c exceeds $1.1 \times 10^{8\,\circ}$ K. But the lifetime against hydrogen burning at this temperature is on the order of 10^4 years, whereas estimates based on equation (15) indicate that an upper limit to the time required for the central temperature to rise from $T_c \sim 7.8 \times 10^{7\,\circ}$ K (onset of nuclear burning) to $T_c \sim 1.1 \times 10^{8\,\circ}$ K is only 3×10^5 sec. Again, hydrogen burning cannot stop the collapse.

Similar arguments may be made for less massive stars with the result that conditions for stopping the collapse through explosive hydrogen burning become more favorable with decreasing mass. In particular, since the properties of models with $M_0 \leq 10^4 M\odot$ and $T_c < 3 \times 10^{8\,\circ}$ K are essentially identical with those obtained by means of the classical equations, the results of Schwarzschild and Härm (1959) are probably valid for $M_0 \leq 10^4 M\odot$.

In conclusion, if it is granted that an initially bound configuration of 10^8 solar masses or more can be formed with sufficiently low angular momentum that it reaches starlike phases without fragmenting, then it is likely that implosion will continue through nuclear burning stages. If the mass of the initial configuration is less than 10^4 but greater than 10^2 solar masses, then pulsational instability is likely to accompany hydrogen burning. Above 10^4 solar masses and below a critical mass M_c, hydrogen burning will reverse the collapse explosively. The value of M_c can be only determined by solving the full dynamic equations of general relativity.

The author would like to thank Professor R. P. Feynman for suggesting this problem and Professor William A. Fowler and Dr. F. C. Michel for stimulating discussions.

APPENDIX

When temperatures are low enough that nucleons may be treated non-relativistically and yet high enough that the electron-positron gas is non-degenerate, the expressions for energy and pressure in a system of H^1 and He^4 are quite straightforward. Let

$$\rho_n = \text{nucleon rest mass density} \, (\mathrm{gm/cm^3}) \, ,$$

$$q_n = \rho_n \left(\frac{X}{M_p} + \frac{Y}{M_a} \right) = \text{nuclei/cm}^3 \, , \tag{16}$$

(16)

$$q_e = \rho_n \left(\frac{X}{M_p} + \frac{2Y}{M_a} \right) = \text{electrons/cm}^3 \text{ exclusive of pairs},$$

and

$$\rho_m = \rho_n + m_e q_e = \text{rest mass/cm}^3 \text{ exclusive of pairs}.$$

Here M_p, M_a, and m_e are, respectively, the mass of the proton, the mass of the α particle, and the mass of the electron. The mass fractions of hydrogen and helium are given by X and Y. Energy density and pressure are additive quantities so that

$$\rho = \rho_n + q_n \frac{3}{2} \frac{kT}{c^2} + \rho_+ + \rho_- + \rho_r,$$

(17)

$$P = q_n \frac{kT}{c^2} + P_+ + P_- + \tfrac{1}{3}\rho_r,$$

where ρ_+ and ρ_- are the energy densities and P_+ and P_- are the pressures associated with the positrons and electrons, respectively. All other quantities are defined in the text.

At temperatures sufficiently low that electrons may be treated non-relativistically, pairs may be neglected ($\rho_+ = P_+ = 0$) and

$$\rho = \rho_m + \tfrac{3}{2} \frac{kT}{c^2} (q_n + q_e) + \rho_r$$

(18)

$$P = (q_n + q_e) \frac{kT}{c^2} + \tfrac{1}{3}\rho_r.$$

When $X = 1$, $Y = 0$, these expressions reduce to equations (8) in the text if one makes the identification $M_H = m_e + M_p$.

The non-relativistic approximation is satisfactory as long as $\langle (\text{electron velocity}/c)^2 \rangle_{av} \ll 1$ or $3kT/m_e c^2 \sim T_9/2 \ll 1$. When this condition is not met, electron-positron pairs must be included and treated relativistically.

The number density of positrons and electrons is given by

$$q_\pm = \frac{8\pi}{h^3} \int_0^\infty \frac{p^2 \, dp}{e^{\pm a + \epsilon/kT} + 1},$$

(19)

where a is the electron chemical potential, h is the Planck constant, and $\epsilon^2 = (m_e c^2)^2 + (cp)^2$. In the non-degenerate approximation (Chandrasekhar 1939),

$$q_\pm = \frac{C}{z} \sum_{n=1}^\infty (-1)^{n+1} \frac{(e^{\pm a})^n}{n} K_2(nz),$$

$$\rho_\pm = \frac{m_e C}{z} \sum_{n=1}^\infty (-1)^{n+1} \frac{(e^{\pm a})^n}{n} \left(\frac{3K_3(nz) + K_1(nz)}{4} \right),$$

(20)

and

$$P_\pm = \frac{m_e C}{z^2} \sum_{n=1}^\infty (-1)^{n+1} \frac{(e^{\pm a})^n}{n^2} K_2(nz),$$

where $C = 8\pi(m_e c/h)^3$, $z = (m_e c^2/kT) \cong 5.90/T_9$, and the K's are defined by Chandrasekhar. The degeneracy parameter a may be found by solving

$$q_e = q_- - q_+ . \tag{21}$$

In actual computations, the values of the functions K_ν may be taken from the asymptotic series

$$K_\nu(z) = \left(\frac{\pi}{2z}\right)^{1/2} e^{-z}\left[1 + \frac{4\nu^2 - 1}{1!\, 8z} + \frac{(4\nu^2 - 1^2)(4\nu^2 - 3^2)}{2!\,(8z)^2} + \cdots\right]. \tag{22}$$

For $z \geq 2$, the first four terms in the expansion for K_1 and K_2 give an accuracy to better than 1 per cent.

A first approximation to the degeneracy parameter is obtained by setting

$$q_e = \tfrac{1}{2} J(e^a - e^{-a}) ,$$

or

$$e^{\pm a} = \pm\left(\frac{q_e}{J}\right) + \left[\left(\frac{q_e}{J}\right)^2 + 1\right]^{1/2}, \tag{23}$$

where $J = 2\, CK_2(z)/z$. Better values for a may be obtained by successive iterations on equation (21); however, for all models discussed in the text, the first approximation to a is sufficient.

In performing stellar structure computations, the derivatives $d\rho_m/dP$ and dT/dP are found from the series expansions for $(\partial\rho/\partial T)_{q_e}$, $(\partial\rho/\partial q_e)_T$, $(\partial P/\partial T)_{q_e}$, and $(\partial P/\partial q_e)_T$ in conjunction with the derivative $dq_e/d\rho_m$ and either equation (7) or equation (12) in the text.

REFERENCES

Chandrasekhar, S. 1939, *An Introduction to the Study of Stellar Structure* (Chicago: University of Chicago Press), chap. x.
Hoyle, F. and Fowler, W. A. 1963a, *M.N.*, 125, 169.
————. 1963b, *Nature*, 197, 533.
Schwarzschild, M., and Härm, R. 1959, *Ap. J.*, 129, 637.
Tolman, R. C. 1934, *Relativity Thermodynamics and Cosmology* (Oxford: Clarendon Press), pp. 240, 244, 232, and 220.

chapter 6 COLLAPSE OF MASSIVE STARS

F. C. MICHEL

I. INTRODUCTION

The intense radio emission from certain galaxies observed recently (Maltby, Mat-thews, and Moffet 1963) appears to demand energy sources of 10^{60} ergs. Hoyle and Fowl-er (1963*a, b*) have examined the possibility that exceedingly massive stars, $10^6 \, M\odot$ to $10^8 \, M\odot$, are formed at or near the galactic centers. They explain that, when the central temperature of these bodies reaches the vicinity of 1 or 2×10^9 degrees K, the neutrino emission becomes an important energy-loss mechanism, and the central portion of the star will collapse. If the gravitational energy involved in the collapse could somehow be transmitted to the outer layers of this star, then a source of sufficient energy would be available to account for the observed strong radio sources. The ejection of a large mass of gas, about $6 \times 10^6 \, M\odot$, with a net energy of about 10^{56} to 10^{59} ergs from the center of M82, evidently the result of a single event about 1.5×10^6 years ago, has now been observed (C. R. Lynds and A. R. Sandage, unpublished) in confirmation of the basic idea that the energy source is initially localized in a very massive body.

II. THE MODEL

Hoyle and Fowler (1963*b*) suggested that rotation might lead to the energetic disrup-tion of massive stars. The purpose of this note is to suggest an alternative model for the collapse of such very massive bodies which leads in a natural way to the ejection of the outer shell without requiring the assumption of rotation or other asymmetrical effects.

As the neutrino loss from the center of such a massive star becomes appreciable, the pressure will start to fall, resulting in failure of hydrostatic equilibrium and, therefore, in motion toward the center. This inward motion in turn compresses the gas and pushes its temperature and pressure higher. Since the neutrino energy loss rate increases roughly as T^9 at temperatures around 10^9 degrees, this approach to a new quasi-equilibrium state in fact leads to higher temperature and an even greater rate of energy loss, until finally free fall toward the center would not be able to convert gravitational energy into neutrinos at the rate demanded by the central temperature. At this point there seems to be essentially nothing to halt the collapse until the matter becomes highly degenerate, at which time compression can increase the pressure without increasing the temperature.

Supported in part by the Office of Naval Research.

F. C. MICHEL, California Institute of Technology.

Reprinted from the *Astrophysical Journal*, **138**, 1097–1103, 1963.

The neutrino emission will then cool the center below 10^9 degrees and no longer be an important factor. At the outset it was perhaps possible, by quasi-homologous contraction of the entire star, to supply the neutrino energy; however, as the energy loss accelerates, a point is reached at which fall of the outer layers cannot keep up, and as the collapse proceeds, only the material within progressively smaller radii can keep pace. If nothing else were considered, the entire star might be expected to end up in the collapsed state with the central regions collapsing quite rapidly and eventually the outer layers falling in.

Now we come to the central point: the attraction of the outer parts to the center is given *not* by the rest mass inside but by the total mass energy, as is well known and experimentally (Eötvös 1890; Zeeman 1917) verified. The neutrinos streaming out of the central regions thereby carry away the gravitational attraction of these regions. The rapid stage of collapse must occur in about the free fall time, about 10^3 sec. Consequently in a time of this order the gravitational attraction is "turned off" almost completely. The outer shell is essentially no longer bound, and the internal energy of the gas plus radiation is suddenly released. Since the internal energy is comparable to the gravitational binding energy, and we are considering a star bound by roughly 10 per cent of its rest mass, the outer layers are obliged to explode outward until its parts would eventually be traveling at velocities near to $0.3\,c$ if all the internal energy were converted into translational motion. The energy is most probably converted into many other modes such as high-energy particles and magnetic fields. The model then is simply this: The center collapses and releases almost all of its total energy as neutrinos, thereby giving up almost all of its "gravitational mass" and releasing the internal energy initially bound in the outer shell.

III. RELATIVITY CONSIDERATIONS

We now turn to a number of obvious questions concerning this description. The most unfamiliar point is the collapse of matter to the stage where almost all of its total energy is lost. As we have noted, the collapse possibly halts when the matter becomes degenerate. For these massive stars, however, the central density is initially only 10 to 100 gm cm^{-3} while the gravitational binding energy is already 10 per cent of the rest mass, thus they are very far from degeneracy but near to gravitational binding equal to the rest mass. Furthermore, no *static* solution seems to exist (Wheeler 1962) for a degenerate neutron-gas star at zero temperature with $M > 0.7\,M\odot$. It is therefore unlikely that degeneracy can actually halt the collapse. For these large binding energies it is necessary to examine the consequences of general relativity. We see from the Schwarzschild metric for the region immediately outside the collapsing region, approximately

$$ds^2 = \frac{dr^2}{1 - 2m/r} + r^2(d\theta^2 + d\phi^2 \sin^2\theta) - \left(1 - \frac{2m}{r}\right) c^2 dt^2, \qquad (1)$$

where $m = GM_r/c^2$ and $M_r =$ mass energy within radius r, that the main effect is just a slowing down of the collapse rate which otherwise would apparently be complete in a time of order 10^3 sec. This can be seen equivalently as being due to the gravitational red shift of the neutrinos lessening the energy loss rate together with a lessened fall rate due to the reduced attraction of the parts of the collapsing body for each other. The matter therefore only *approaches* being totally bound. The collapse time from 10 per cent to, say, 90 per cent binding will still be of the order 10^3 sec, and it is unimportant to the model that the binding be complete.

It might be questioned whether such high central temperatures are possible since the classical equations give $|\Omega| \approx Mc^2$ when $T = 10^9$ degrees and $M = 7 \times 10^8\,M\odot$ and

Newtonian mechanics must fail. In the general theory (Møller 1952) the hydrostatic equilibrium equation becomes

$$\frac{dP}{dr} + (P + \epsilon c^2)\frac{1}{2b}\frac{db}{dr} = 0 , \tag{2}$$

where $b = 1 - 2\phi/c^2$, P is the proper pressure, and ϵ is the proper mass-energy density. Defining $(1 - \beta)P = aT^4/3$, the radiation pressure, gives

$$P = \frac{a}{3(1 - \beta)} T^4 , \tag{3}$$

and the mass-energy density is

$$\epsilon = \frac{a}{(1 - \beta)} T^4 + \frac{a}{3(1 - \beta)}\left(\frac{\mu\beta c^2}{\Re}\right) T^3 , \tag{4}$$

where μ is the mean molecular weight and $\Re$ is the gas constant. The second term on the right-hand side of equation (4) is just the rest-mass density, ρc^2, where $P = \rho\Re T/\mu\beta$ has been used to write ρ in terms of T. Hoyle and Fowler (1963b) give $\mu\beta \approx (180/\pi^2)^{1/2}$ $(M\odot/M)^{1/2} (1 + 180\bar{K}_2/\pi^4)^{-1/4}$ where the factor $(1 + 180\bar{K}_2/\pi^4)^{-1/4}$ corrects approximately for electron-positron pair formation. The neutrino loss rate becomes important (Hoyle and Fowler 1963a, b) before this factor differs appreciably from unity, and the correction for pairs is neglected here. The quantity $\mu\beta$ describes local conditions in the star and is related to the macroscopic parameters of the star by an appeal to the Newtonian theory. Equation (2) together with equations (3) and (4) may now be integrated to give

$$b = \left(1 - \frac{2m}{R}\right)\tau^2/(\tau + T^2) , \tag{5}$$

where $\tau = \mu\beta c^2/4\Re = 1.19 \times 10^{13} (M\odot/M)^{1/2}$ degrees, and the constant of integration was chosen to match the exterior Schwarzschild solution (eq. [1]) at the surface of the star. In the Newtonian formulation, ϕ is usually set equal to zero at the surface of the star in which case equation (5) may be expanded to first order in T to yield $\phi = 4\Re T/\mu\beta$ as required for a polytrope of index $n = 3$. We see that no limit is imposed on the temperature since $b > 0$ for all finite T. From the form of equation (5) it is apparent that deviation of $\mu\beta$ from the value adopted from Hoyle and Fowler (1963b) plays no important role in this conclusion. Having $\mu\beta = 0$ corresponds to a star, or region thereof, composed entirely of radiation. This would not give $b = 0$ as suggested by equation (5), since the constant of integration must now be redetermined. If $\mu\beta = 0$ within radius r_c and $T = T_c$, $b = b_c$ at this radius, then $b = b_c(T_c/T)^2$ for $r < r_c$ and $b_c > b > 0$. The ultimate fate of the collapsed core must rest heavily on general relativity considerations, but this is not relevant to the immediate problem.

IV. ENERGY RELEASE

Assuming then that the collapse to near total binding occurs, how much energy is actually released? The fraction of the total gravitational binding energy released is easily calculated in terms of the radius R_c within which all the material is ultimately trapped in the collapsed core, and for a polytrope of index n this is

$$f_{\text{released}} = [(5 - n)M_c/3M] (1 - RM_c/R_cM + R'u/M') \tag{6}$$

in notation of Eddington (1959). Figure 1 is a plot of this function for index $3(\gamma = \frac{4}{3})$. One sees that, for a broad range of collapse radii, over a third of the total gravitational binding energy of the star is released. The actual determination of R_c/R of course involves a rather complicated dynamic process. In this paper we will make a qualitative argument to essentially limit R_c/R within a reasonably narrow range about 0.24. At the initial stages of neutrino loss the star at first may attempt to remain in quasi-equilibrium by undergoing a homologous collapse. If the gravitational energy released in the collapse succeeds in matching the neutrino loss rate we have the situation shown in Figure 2 assuming a T^9 neutrino loss rate and a homologous collapse of a polytrope with index 3 (the index is not critical for the qualitative argument here, although 3 should not be too far from the truth). In Figure 2 the neutrino curve is proportional to $4\pi r^2 T_r^9$, and the gravitation curve is proportional to the gravitational energy density, $4\pi r^3 \rho(d\phi/dr)$, for a homologous collapse. Integration of these quantities over dr gives the rate of energy change for the entire star. Actually n should be taken slightly less than 3, otherwise the internal energy increase equals the increase in gravitational binding. From Figure 2 it may be seen that the collapse rate required to *locally* match the neutrino loss rate is far from homologous. Matter at $R_c/R \leq 0.21$ cannot keep pace and will be obliged to fall

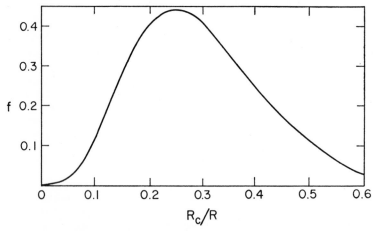

FIG. 1.—Fraction of gravitation energy released, f, from collapse of region within radius R_c

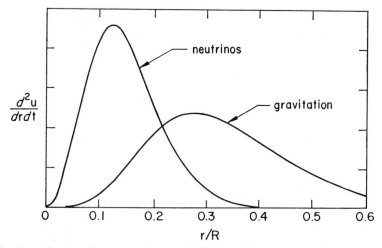

FIG. 2.—Rate of energy change per unit of radial distance. The area under the two curves is equal, corresponding to a net balance of the two rates.

relatively faster, while for $R_c/R \geq 0.29$ the production rate is much too large and the matter will move proportionately slower. Implicit here are the assumptions that $\mu\beta$ and γ are sensibly constant near the center of the star and that the specific internal energy is given by $P_{gas}/\rho(\gamma - 1)$. Since the variation in temperature expected from the standard polytropic model is relatively small (≈ 20 per cent) over the region of interest, these assumptions should be reasonably well satisfied.

The time, t_c, required for a shell of matter at radius R_c to free-fall to the center of the star, keeping constant the total energy inclosed within that shell, is given in the non-relativistic approximation by solving

$$\frac{d^2 r}{dt^2} = -\frac{GM_c}{r^2},$$

where M_c is the total mass-energy/c^2 within R_c. The square of the mean fall velocity can then be shown to be, in the notation of Eddington (1959)

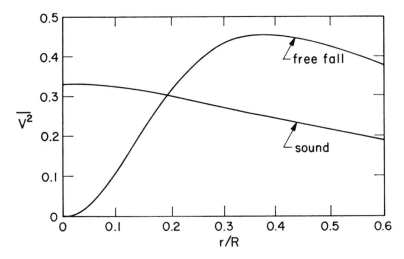

FIG. 3.—Squares of the mean free fall and sound velocities between the center and r in units of $\phi_0 = (GM\ R'/R\ M')$. A polytrope of index 3 is assumed here.

$$\langle v \rangle_f^2 = \frac{8}{\pi^2} \frac{GM_c}{R_c} = \phi_0 \left(-\frac{8}{\pi^2} z \frac{du}{dz} \right),$$

where the subscript (0) denotes quantities evaluated at the center of the star. The mean velocity of sound squared is given by

$$\langle v \rangle_s^2 = \left(\frac{\langle \gamma p \rangle}{\rho} \right) = \phi_0 \left(\frac{\langle u \rangle}{n} \right).$$

These two quantities are plotted for a polytrope of index 3, in Figure 3. From this figure we see that a shell at $R_c = 0.20\ R$ will fall to the center in the same time that sound would travel this same distance. Within this radius the sound velocity exceeds the mean fall velocity and vice versa. A shell much outside $0.20\ R$ will suffer relatively little energy loss due to neutrinos, and its inward motion will be primarily due to the changing pressure gradient resulting from the inward motion of the inner regions. If the inner regions collapse at a rate near to free-fall these pressure gradients (e.g., sound waves) are not propagated outward as rapidly as the mass motion required for this shell to keep pace with the collapse. The lag between the motion of the inner regions and shells with radii greater than 0.20 R should then lead to a separation of the star into a collapsing core and a relatively unperturbed outer shell at a radius not too much larger than 0.20 R. The limits $0.21 \leq R_c/R \leq 0.29$ are therefore roughly consistent with dynamical considerations, and from Figure 1 the gravitational energy release is estimated to be around 42 to 44 per cent.

The radius of a massive star is given by Hoyle and Fowler (1963b) to be

$$R = \frac{5.8 \times 10^{18}}{T_0} \left(\frac{M}{M_\odot} \right)^{1/2}, \tag{7}$$

neglecting a small correction for pair formation. The gravitational binding energy for a polytrope of index n is

$$|\Omega| = \frac{3}{5-n} \frac{GM^2}{R}. \tag{8}$$

Combining (7) and (8) together with an estimate of 0.43 for f gives for the total energy release

$$E_{\text{release}} = 2.9 \times 10^{40} T_0 \left(\frac{M}{M_\odot} \right)^{3/2} \text{ergs} .$$

For $T_0 = 10^9$ degrees and $M = 10^8 \, M_\odot$ the energy release is about 3×10^{61} ergs.

V. CORRECTIONS TO THE MODEL

Special discussion is required for the assumption of a hot massive star in hydrostatic equilibrium as a starting point prior to the neutrino loss processes. It has been shown (Iben 1963) that the binding energy of a massive, spherically symmetric, pure hydrogen star, assuming hydrostatic equilibrium and the adiabatic condition, has a *maximum* binding energy of about $3 \, M_\odot c^2$ at a central temperature of $3 \times 10^{13} \, (M_\odot/M)$ degrees. The net binding energy of a star is relatively small due to the tendency of the internal energy to nearly cancel the gravitational binding energy. When general relativistic corrections are included, the gravitational binding energy is itself reduced, thereby allowing the net binding energy ultimately to become negative and therefore have a maximum. For $M = 10^8 \, M_\odot$ this maximum is reached at $T_0 \approx 3 \times 10^5$ degrees. At this relatively low temperature the star is radiating thermal energy but has essentially no nuclear source to replace this loss. Consequently the internal energy, and therefore the pressure, must drop below that necessary to satisfy hydrostatic equilibrium. Since the pressure is *less* than necessary to maintain equilibrium, the star will begin to contract, with Iben's calculations serving as the initial condition for the contraction. Ultimately the central temperature will reach $T_0 \approx 10^9$ degrees, initiating the neutrino-loss process envisioned in the previous sections. The difficulty here is in arriving at a semiquantitative estimate of the energy release. A polytrope description is suspect for a star not in equilibrium, and it is imperative that an attempt be made, by electronic computer perhaps, to follow the evolution of a massive star and determine its structure when $T_0 \approx 10^9$ degrees. It is nevertheless useful perhaps to speculate on the route that might be followed. Until $T_0 \approx 3 \times 10^7$ degrees, the inner regions would be expected to fall relatively faster than the outer, since the former are in a higher gravitational potential where corrections to the gravitational binding energy are largest. Above this temperature hydrogen-burning provides a source of internal energy for the inner regions which slows the contraction there and allows the outer regions to "catch up." Although the rate of hydrogen burning proceeds very rapidly above 10^8 degrees in the CNO cycle (Burbidge, Burbidge, Fowler, and Hoyle 1957), the calculations of Iben (1963) show that for $M = 10^8 M\odot$ and $T_0 \approx 1.4 \times 10^8$ degrees the entire nuclear energy available is insufficient to supply enough internal energy to re-establish hydrostatic equilibrium. In the CNO cycle the hydrogen-burning may be complete somewhat before $T_0 \approx 10^9$ degrees is reached, while in the pp chain the burning will probably not be complete. In the latter case our assumption of an index-3 polytrope may not be too unrealistic, since the hydrogen-burning should keep the star near to equilibrium. In the former case the outer shell may have a structure relatively more diffuse than expected for an index-3 polytrope and therefore less gravitational energy to release by the neutrino mechanism. On the other hand, having the star in incomplete hydrostatic equilibrium means that the internal energy (hence T_0) is less than a polytrope having a similar density distribution; therefore, the star will be denser than previous estimates when $T_0 \approx 10^9$ degrees, which increases the energy release. The

TABLE 1*

Index	Model	f_{max}	f_1	f_2	$\Delta R/R$
0..........	Incompressible fluid	0.47	0.29	†	0.44
3..........	Standard	.44	.43	0.41	.28
5..........	Extended atmosphere	.49	0.44	.24	.28‡
∞	"Isothermal"	0.44§	‖	0.32§	0.28‡

* The maximum fraction of the gravitational energy that can be released is f_{max}. If R_c is taken at the intersection of the two curves in Fig. 2, when those curves are replotted for the corresponding index, then f_1 is the fractional release at this radius. Fig. 3 yields in the same way f_2. The relative spread in collapse radii for which $f \geq \frac{1}{2}f_{max}$ is given by $\Delta R/R$.

† The velocity of sound is infinite.

‡ The radius is infinite for this model. A radius has been defined here to be $5R_{1/2}$ where $\rho(R_{1/2}) = \frac{1}{2}\rho_0$ to provide a scale factor. For $n = 3$ this very nearly reproduces the actual radius.

§ Both M and Ω are infinite in this model so the density distribution has been arbitrarily set to zero beyond the radius defined in n. ‡.

‖ The energy loss by neutrinos is unrestricted in the isothermal model.

fractional energy release is actually not very sensitive to the density distribution if no mass point is allowed at the origin and the density is a monotonically decreasing function of radius. Table 1 gives the parameters discussed above for polytropic mass distributions other than index 3.

VI. SUMMARY

Neutrino emission at $T_0 \geq 10^9$ degrees is conjectured to lead to the collapse of the central regions of massive stars and consequent ejection of the outer shell with an estimated energy release of 3×10^{61} ergs for $M = 10^8 M\odot$. This estimate is uncertain due to the unusual evolution of such massive stars, although the figure 3×10^{61} may be within an order of magnitude. The purpose of this note is (1) to point out that gravitational effects can play an important role in the release of energy from massive stars and (2) to provide incentive for the study of the evolution of such stars since the energy release is comparable to that actually observed.

The author wishes to express appreciation to Professor William A. Fowler for many helpful suggestions and to Professor R. P. Feynman and Dr. I. Iben, Jr., for valuable discussions.

REFERENCES

Burbidge, E. M., Burbidge, G. R., Fowler, W. A., and Hoyle, F. 1957, *Rev. Mod. Phys.*, **29**, 547.
Eddington, A. E. 1959, *The Internal Constitution of the Stars* (New York: Dover Publications, Inc.),
    chap. iv.
Eötvös, R. V. 1890, *Math. u. naturw. Ber. aus Ungarn*, **8**, 65.
Hoyle, F., and Fowler, W. A. 1963a, *M.N.*, **125**, 169.
———. 1963b, *Nature*, **197**, 533.*
Iben, I., Jr. 1963, *Ap. J.*, **138**, 1090.
Maltby, P., Matthews, T. A., and Moffet, A. T. 1963, *Ap. J.*, **137**, 153.*
Møller, C. 1952, *The Theory of Relativity* (London: Oxford University Press), p. 329.
Wheeler, J. A. 1962, *Geometrodynamics* (New York: Academic Press), p. 123.
Zeeman, P. 1917, *Proc. Amsterdam*, **20**, 542.

THE INSTABILITY OF A TOROIDAL MAGNETIC GEON AGAINST

chapter 7 GRAVITATIONAL COLLAPSE

Kip S. Thorne

I. THE PROBLEM

This conference has called renewed attention to the problem of very massive, spherically symmetric bodies which, according to Einstein's theory of relativity, collapse past the gravitational radius and on into a singularity. In this paper we shall consider a similar situation: the gravitational collapse of bodies made not of matter but of electromagnetic fields—geons.

The motivation for studying collapsing geons is most certainly *not* that they might play a role in quasi-stellar radio sources; far from it. There is not the slightest reason to believe that geons exist in nature or could be constructed by man. Rather, our motivation is that the analysis of a collapsing geon is much simpler than the analysis of a collapsing sphere of matter in one important respect: The relation between pressure and energy density for the electromagnetic field is more precisely known and much easier to work with than the equation of state for nuclear matter at high densities—a mixture of heavy nuclei, electrons, neutrons, and even hyperons. Consequently, a geon permits the study of the nature of gravitational collapse as a phenomenon within Einstein's theory of relativity without entangling one in the uncertainties and complexities of the equation of state.

The Einstein-Maxwell equations for interacting electromagnetic and gravitational fields allow the existence of many types of geons (Wheeler 1955, 1962). Wheeler has emphasized that all geons are unstable against gravitational collapse, electromagnetic explosion, or leakage of electromagnetic radiation out of the active region, and that those which undergo gravitational collapse should be very useful in studying the issue of the final state of collapsed systems.[1] However, only recently has the study of geon collapse been pursued in earnest.

The initial studies of geon collapse (M. A. Melvin and J. A. Wheeler, unpublished) involved a toroidal magnetic geon (a toroidal bundle of magnetic-field lines bound together against the disruptive Maxwell-Faraday pressures by their mutual gravitational attraction). It soon became clear that the analysis would be greatly simplified by con-

---

Kip S. Thorne, Palmer Physical Laboratory, Princeton University.

[1] See his 1963 Les Houches lectures (Wheeler 1964) for a detailed exposition of this theme.

sidering the limiting case in which the major axis of the torus is infinite. Thus, Melvin and Wheeler were led to consider a cylindrically symmetric bundle of magnetic-field lines of infinite length. By using Weyl's theory of axially symmetric gravitational fields (Weyl 1919; Weyl and Bach 1922; Levi-Civita 1919), Melvin succeeded in constructing a cylindrical *static* geon of this type, in which the Maxwell-Faraday pressures are *precisely* counterbalanced by the gravitational forces (Melvin 1964*a*). This solution was at first believed to be *unstable* against *spontaneous* gravitational collapse or electromagnetic explosion.[2] However, subsequent analyses have argued for stability! (Melvin 1964*b*; Thorne 1964). No perturbation of the system, which vanishes outside a finite region around the symmetry axis, can lead to gravitational collapse or electromagnetic explosion. This surprising result appears to stem from the fact that Melvin's system is *not* a highly concentrated accumulation of electromagnetic energy as it appears at first glance; rather, it is the most *diffuse* distribution of electromagnetic and gravitational energy possible under the circumstances. Melvin's system is *not a geon;* it is a magnetic *universe.*

Melvin's magnetic universe presents many interesting problems, but since they are apparently unrelated to gravitational collapse, this is not the place to discuss them. Nevertheless, we can learn a lesson from the problems which the early misinterpretation of Melvin's solution caused: Although the *mathematics* of toroidal geons is simplified by letting the major radius become infinite and thereby obtaining cylindrical geons, the *interpretation* of the solutions so obtained becomes vastly more difficult. The Newtonian approximation, the most powerful guide we have to the interpretation of solutions of Einstein's equations, is applied easily only in an *asymptotically flat* space. For example, in order to define the mass of an object in an unambiguous manner, one must get sufficiently far away that orbits about it obey Kepler's laws to a close approximation. This occurs only in an approximately flat region of space. But one can never get so far away from a cylindrical geon that space becomes asymptotically flat. Just as an infinite line charge creates a logarithmically diverging term in the electrostatic potential of Maxwell theory, so a source of infinite length creates diverging terms in the metric of Einstein's theory. The logarithmic term causes no special problems in electrostatics because of the linearity of the theory. But in the non-linear Einstein theory the divergent terms become real impediments to the interpretation of solutions.

For these reasons it is appropriate to turn away from the study of cylindrical geons and return to a toroidal geon of the type originally considered by Wheeler and Melvin. The analysis of the full dynamical behavior of a toroidal geon would be quite difficult. Fortunately, however, it is not necessary to perform the *full* analysis in order to verify the instability of the geon and get some insight into its collapse. For the purposes of this discussion we need only examine the geon at a moment of time symmetry.

What we propose to do is to examine, at a moment of time symmetry, a sequence of toroidal magnetic geons all having the same total flux Φ and the same *proper* major circumference $2\pi b'$, but having different *proper* minor radii a'. We will determine the mass M of the geon as measured by an external observer, and the geometry of the spacelike hypersurface of time symmetry, as functions of Φ, b', and a'. From these features of the system we will infer that toroidal magnetic geons with sufficiently small minor radii are unstable against gravitational collapse. Finally, we will compare these toroidal geons with a collapsing cloud of dust and from the similarity between the two at the moment of time symmetry, we will argue that their dynamical evolution should be similar.

---

[2] The belief in its instability was strongly supported by numerical calculations of the dynamics of the system when perturbed, which were performed by the author and reported at the Symposium on Gravitational Collapse. Because these calculations have since proved irrelevant to the issue of gravitational collapse, they are reported elsewhere (Thorne 1964) rather than here.

II. THE SOLUTION

The analysis of a system at a moment of time symmetry requires the solution of the initial value equations of general relativity

$$R_\mu{}^0 - (\tfrac{1}{2})\delta_\mu{}^0 R = 8\pi G T_\mu{}^0$$

analogous to div $\mathbf{E} = 4\pi\rho$ and div $\mathbf{B} = 0$ in electromagnetism (Darmois 1927; Stellmacher 1937; Lichnerowicz 1955; Foures-Bruhat 1956). At a moment of time symmetry these four equations reduce to one:

$$^{(3)}R = 16\pi G T_0{}^0,$$

where $^{(3)}R$ is the scalar curvature of the hypersurface of time symmetry (Brill 1959). Brill has shown that when one has axial symmetry as well as time symmetry, one can put the metric on the hypersurface of time symmetry in the form

$$d\sigma^2 = \psi^4[e^{2q}(d\rho^2 + dz^2) + \rho^2 d\phi^2]$$

and that the initial value equation then becomes

$$4(\nabla^2\psi)/\psi + \nabla^2 q - (1/\rho)(\partial q/\partial\rho) = -8\pi G\psi^4 e^{2q} T_0{}^0 .$$

Here ∇^2 is the *flat-space* Laplacian operator.

Brill has found that the quantity q ("gravitational wave factor") is often associated with gravitational radiation (Brill 1959; Wheeler 1964). Because we wish to minimize the amount of gravitational radiation present, and because we want our initial value equation to be as simple as possible, we set $q = 0$.[3] In this case the metric is

$$d\sigma^2 = \psi^4 d\sigma_1{}^2 = \psi^4(d\rho^2 + dz^2 + \rho^2 d\phi^2) , \tag{1}$$

and the initial-value equation reads

$$\nabla^2\psi = -2\pi G\psi^5 T_0{}^0 . \tag{2}$$

Here $d\sigma_1{}^2$ is a Euclidean "base metric," and $d\sigma^2$, the actual metric of the problem, is conformally flat. The initial value equation is just Poisson's equation with $-2\pi G\psi^5 T_0{}^0$ as the source of the "conformal correction factor" ψ.

We now further specialize the time-symmetric and axially symmetric geometry to the case of a toroidal magnetic geon (Fig. 1). Let the magnetic field lines be entirely contained within a torus of major radius b and minor radius a, as measured in the base metric and let $b \gg a$ ("slender ring"). Let the magnetic field lines be so distributed in the torus that $2\pi G\psi^5 T_0{}^0$ is uniform throughout it.[4] Finally, let the coordinate r measure base-metric distance from the guiding center of the torus

$$r = [(\rho - b)^2 + z^2]^{1/2} .$$

[3] Setting $q = 0$ does not actually remove *all* gravitational radiation. If it did, outside the source of the gravitational field the solution to the initial-value equation would also be a static solution to the full-vacuum field equations.

[4] This condition is not necessary to the analysis. The solution in the case of a non-uniform source leads to a conformal correction factor ψ which is identical to that of eq. (3) outside the geon, if that equation is rewritten in terms of the base-metric quantities ρ, z, and b. However, *inside* the geon the more general case gives a more complicated expression for ψ. Since the added complications yield no new insights, we avoid them.

Under these conditions the form of the solution to the initial value equation for ψ (eq. [2]) can be seen directly from the electrostatics of a charged circular ring: Far away the electric potential varies as (total charge)/(distance to ring), while nearby it varies as $2 \times$ (line density of charge) $\times$ log (distance to center of wire). Similarly, the behavior of the conformal correction factor far from the geon is governed by (observed mass of geon)/(distance to geon), while near the edge of the torus it is governed by (magnetic mass-energy per unit length) $\times$ log (distance to guiding line of torus).[5] Note that the analogy is *not* a complete one. For the geon the scale of lengths changes as one moves from the near region to the far region. Consequently, the *observed mass*, which governs the gravitational pull far away, is *not* equal to the line integral of the *magnetic mass-energy per unit length*, which governs the gravitational pull nearby. What a difference from elementary electrostatics!

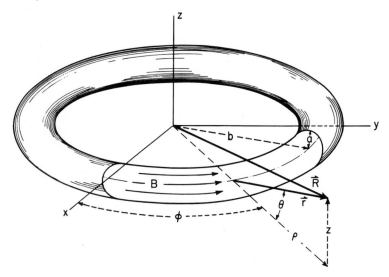

FIG. 1.—A toroidal magnetic geon at a moment of time symmetry as seen in the base metric. The magnetic-field lines thread the interior of the torus and are confined entirely within it. The electric field vanishes at the moment of time symmetry, but the time rate of change of the electric field ordinarily does not ($\dot{\boldsymbol{E}} = \operatorname{curl} \boldsymbol{B}$).

We turn now from a qualitative description of the solution to a precise statement of it. Set $c = G = 1$. The solution external to the geon can be put in the form

$$\psi(\boldsymbol{R}) = 1 + \frac{1}{\pi} \frac{M_m}{M} \frac{M_m}{[\,z'^2 + (\rho' + b')^2\,]^{1/2}} \mathrm{K} \left(\left[\frac{4\rho'b'}{z'^2 + (\rho' + b')^2} \right]^{1/2} \right)$$

$$\approx 1 + M/(2R), \quad \text{when} \quad R \equiv (\rho^2 + z^2)^{1/2} \gg b, \tag{3}$$

$$\approx 1 + \frac{M_m}{M} \frac{M_m}{2\pi b'} \log \left(\frac{8b'}{r'} \right), \quad \text{when} \quad a' < r' \ll b',$$

[5] In comparing this statement with eq. (3) one should remember that far away the appropriate coordinates are those of the background metric ρ, z, r. But nearby the appropriate coordinates are the renormalized ones ρ', z', r'. Consequently, the appropriate conformal correction factor far away is ψ, but nearby it is $\psi' = \Psi/\psi_o = (M/M_m)\psi$.

where K is the complete elliptic integral of the first kind. The masses appearing here are M, the mass measured by an external observer, and M_m, the magnetic mass obtained by integrating $(B^2/8\pi)$ over the physical volume of the torus. The terms ρ', r', and z' are renormalized values of ρ, r, and z constructed so as to make the metric flat inside the torus:

$$\rho' = \psi_o^2\rho, \qquad r' = \psi_o^2 r, \qquad z' = \psi_o^2 z,$$

where $\psi_o = \psi(r = 0)$. We have yet to write down the conformal correction factor ψ for the interior of the geon. In the case where $b' \gg a'$ ("slender ring") and $\psi^5 T_0^0 = $ (constant throughout torus), which we are considering, both the conformal correction factor ψ and the physical magnetic field B (as measured in a locally Lorentz reference frame) turn out to be essentially uniform throughout the torus.

$$\psi(\mathbf{R}) = \psi_o = M_m/M . \qquad\qquad (\mathbf{R} \text{ inside torus}) \quad (4)$$

The masses which appear in our equations can be expressed in terms of the total magnetic flux $\Phi = B\pi a'^2$, the proper minor radius $a' = a\psi_o^2$, and the proper circumference $2\pi b' = 2\pi b\psi_o^2$. The externally observed mass, M, is

$$M = M_m + M_p \qquad\qquad (5)$$

where M_m, the "magnetic mass," and M_p, the "gravitational potential mass," turn out to be

$$M_m = (\Phi^2 b')/(4\pi a'^2)$$
$$= (B^2/8\pi) \times \text{(proper volume of torus)} \qquad (6)$$

and

$$M_p = -M_m \frac{M_m}{2\pi b'} \log\left(\frac{8b'}{a'}\right).$$

It is interesting to note that, if we had calculated the mass of the geon in the Newtonian approximation (Wheeler 1964), we would have obtained precisely the same result, providing we had remembered that the magnetic pressure, $B^2/8\pi$, and energy density, $B^2/8\pi$, *both* act as sources for and feel the gravitational field. M_m is just the "mass" obtained by integrating the energy density over the torus; and M_p is just the gravitational potential energy of a Newtonian geon.

Let a particular toroidal geon (characterized by Φ, a', and b') be observed as it evolves away from its moment of time symmetry. Will it explode, or will it collapse? To get some insight into this question, consider a sequence of geons all having the same total flux Φ and major circumference $2\pi b'$, but having different minor radii, a'. Plot their masses as functions of a' (Fig. 2). For large a' where the magnetic mass dominates, the measured mass varies as $1/a'^2$. However, as a' decreases, the negative gravitational potential mass becomes more and more important, and it eventually wins out causing the measured mass to decrease as $-1/a'^4$ (second term in eq. [5] dominates over first term).

Turn now from a family of geons to the behavior of a particular geon as it evolves away from its configuration of time symmetry. If a' is sufficiently large ("dilute field configuration"), we can use ordinary Maxwell theory to solve the problem, and we will find, of course, that the geon flies apart because of the magnetic pressure. On the other hand, if a' is sufficiently small ($< 10^{-5}$ light years in the case of Fig. 2), the gravitational attraction between the magnetic field lines should dominate over the electromagnetic repulsion, and the geon should collapse. In either case, as the geon evolves away from its configuration of time symmetry, the changing magnetic field creates electric fields.

A precise description of the gravitational collapse of a toroidal geon must await the full solution of the dynamical equations. However, we can make a few general statements about collapse dynamics at this point. As has been discussed by Wheeler (1964), there are two possible modes of collapse: (1) a mode in which the magnetic field lines collapse onto the guiding center of the torus (minor radius shrinks to zero as major radius remains finite) and (2) a mode in which the field lines all contract to a point (major and minor radii simultaneously shrink to zero). Wheeler shows that mode (2) is a very reasonable mode of gravitational collapse. On the other hand, two facts suggest

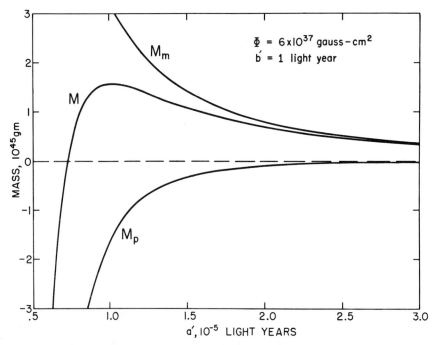

FIG. 2.—The magnetic mass, gravitational potential mass, and measured mass of a time-symmetric toroidal magnetic geon as functions of the configuration at the moment of time symmetry. Here we consider geons all having the same flux $\Phi = 6 \times 10^{37}$ gauss-cm², and the same proper circumference $2\pi b' = 2\pi$ light-years, but having different proper minor radii a'. Since $M_m =$ (constant depending on b' and Φ) $\times (b'/a')^2$ and $M_p = -$(another constant depending on b' and Φ) $(b'/a')^4 \log (8b'/a')$, these curves will have the same shape independently of Φ and b'. In particular, as a' decreases the observed mass, M, will always rise slowly, reach a maximum, then fall off rapidly toward $-\infty$.

that mode (1) might never occur: First, there are two cases on record[6] in which magnetic flux is capable of *preventing* gravitational collapse; but (to the author's knowledge) there are no known examples of the collapse of a magnetic-flux-containing-and-conserving system. Second, we shall see later that in the limit $M = 0$, Φ, b', a' finite, the time-symmetric hypersurface of a toroidal magnetic geon is curved up into a closed universe with 3-sphere topology. If the geon were to collapse onto its guiding line, one might expect the topology of a 3-torus instead.

Because the maximum in the curve for mass versus minor radius should mark the point separating exploding geons from collapsing geons, it is of interest to examine the

---

[6] The two cases are Melvin's magnetic universe (Melvin 1964a; Thorne 1964) and the Reissner-Nordstrom solution for a "wormhole" threaded by an electromagnetic field (Wheeler 1964).

"critical geons" corresponding to this maximum. We do so in Table 1. Here we have an indication of how preposterous it would be to believe geons exist in nature or could be created and studied experimentally. To be near criticality a laboratory-size geon must have field strengths corresponding to supranuclear energy densities, while a geon of more reasonable field strengths must be fantastically large.

The huge magnetic field encountered in the laboratory-size geon reminds us that the equation of state for the electromagnetic field becomes very complicated when a field strength of the order of the characteristic field of electron pair theory is reached:

$$F_{crit} = mc^2/[e(\hbar/mc)] = 4.4 \times 10^{13} \text{ gauss} = 1.3 \times 10^{18} \text{ volt/m}$$

(Euler and Kockel 1935; Heisenberg 1936). When such field strengths are reached, vacuum polarization, virtual pair production, and occasionally even real pair production occur. Then we are back in the realm of elementary particle physics and all the complica-

TABLE 1

VALUES OF PROPER CIRCUMFERENCE, PROPER MINOR RADIUS, MAGNETIC FLUX, MAGNETIC FIELD STRENGTH, MAGNETIC ENERGY DENSITY, AND MASS FOR SEVERAL "CRITICAL GEONS"*

	Laboratory-size Geon	Astrophysical-size Geon	Universe-size Geon
Proper circumference, $2\pi b'$	60 m	6 light-years	6×10^{10} light-years
Proper minor radius, a'	10^{-2} cm	10^{-5} light-years	10^5 light-years
Magnetic flux, Φ	6×10^{22} gauss cm²	6×10^{37} gauss cm²	6×10^{47} gauss cm²
Magnetic field strength, B	2×10^{26} gauss	2×10^{11} gauss	20 gauss
Magnetic energy density, $B^2/8\pi$	1.6×10^{30} gm/cm³	1.6 gm/cm³	1.6×10^{-20} gm/cm³
Magnetic mass, $M_m = (B^2/8\pi) \times$ volume.	3×10^{30} gm	3×10^{45} gm	3×10^{55} gm
Gravitational potential mass, M_p	-1.5×10^{30} gm	-1.5×10^{45} gm	1.5×10^{55} gm
Measured mass, M	1.5×10^{30} gm	1.5×10^{45} gm	1.5×10^{55} gm

* Geons which are expected to collapse if squeezed but explode if distended; or, more precisely, geons corresponding to a maximum in the M versus a' curve.

tions which it adds to the collapse phenomenon, to escape from which we turn to the study of geons. Fortunately, however, we are free to consider large geons as well as small ones, so that if, in following the collapse of a particular geon, one finds uncomfortably large field strengths developing in the center, he need only turn to a much larger geon in which a given stage of collapse is characterized by much smaller field strengths.

Return to the curve of observed mass versus minor radius for fixed flux and major radius (Fig. 2). There is one disturbing thing about this curve: the mass M goes *negative* for minor radius $a' < 0.72 \times 10^{-5}$ light-years. *This is impossible*, according to a theorem of Brill (1959) on the positive-definiteness of mass in time-symmetric, axially symmetric systems. What is wrong here? The answer is that our solution (eqs. [3]–[6]) is *not physically admissible* in those cases where the mass M is negative. Whenever M is negative the conformal correction factor ψ is *not* everywhere positive; it contains a nodal 2-surface surrounding the geon. As was pointed out by Brill, such a nodal surface in the space of the base metric is a single point of the hypersurface of time symmetry, since $d\sigma^2 = 0$ everywhere on it. The region outside the node of ψ is totally cut off from the geon, and the geometries of both the exterior and interior regions exhibit cusplike singularities at the node. Configurations of negative mass are thus ruled out.

It is still puzzling that as the minor radius a' is decreased toward a certain finite value $(0.72 \times 10^{-5}$ light-years in the case of Fig. 2), the observed mass M approaches arbitarily close to zero. To understand this phenomenon better, we examine the geometry of the hypersurface of time symmetry as a' approaches a'_o, that value for which the observed mass M vanishes. Figure 3 presents "imbedding diagrams" of the geometry of the ρ-ϕ 2-surface for geons with successively decreasing values of a'. It is seen from this figure that, as a' approaches a'_o, the throat between the exterior region and the geon closes off leaving, in the limit of $a' = a'\zeta$, (1) a geon so dense that it has closed space up around itself, and (2) a perfectly flat, empty exterior region.

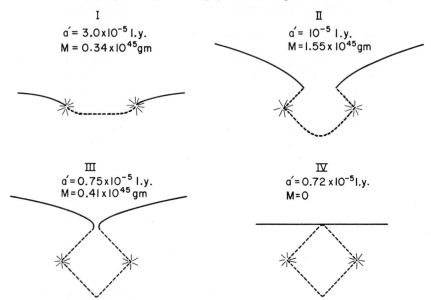

I
$a' = 3.0 \times 10^{-5}$ l.y.
$M = 0.34 \times 10^{45}$ gm

II
$a' = 10^{-5}$ l.y.
$M = 1.55 \times 10^{45}$ gm

III
$a' = 0.75 \times 10^{-5}$ l.y.
$M = 0.41 \times 10^{45}$ gm

IV
$a' = 0.72 \times 10^{-5}$ l.y.
$M = 0$

FIG. 3.—"Imbedding diagrams" of the geometry of the $\rho - \varphi$ 2-*surface* for geons all having the same flux $\Phi = 6 \times 10^{37}$ gauss-cm² and proper circumference $2\pi b' = 2\pi$ light-years, but having different proper minor radii a'. In these diagrams we plot $(\frac{1}{2}\pi)$ (proper circumference of a circle about the geon's center) $= \rho\psi^2(\rho) \equiv \Re$ horizontally against a fictitious vertical coordinate ζ. ζ is so constructed that in the region where the curve is solid the proper length of a radial line segment is $d\sigma = (d\Re^2 + d\zeta^2)^{1/2}$ but in the region where the curve is dotted $d\sigma = (d\Re^2 - d\zeta^2)^{1/2}$. (Thus, two points separated by a 45° *dotted* line are actually very close together.) In more physical terms, if one rotates the figures about the vertical axis one obtains from the solid parts of the curves the $\rho - \varphi$ 2-surface as it looks imbedded in a Euclidean 3-space, and from the dotted parts the $\rho - \varphi$ 2-surface as it looks imbedded in a Minkowski 3-space with "imaginary" vertical axis. The regions in which the magnetic field is located are indicated by radiating lines.

From the diagrams it is clear that as a' decreases toward $a'_o = 0.72 \times 10^{-5}$ light-years (the value for which the observed mass vanishes), the geon pinches off from the exterior region, leaving, in the limit $a' = a'_o$, a Lorentz-flat exterior (Diagram IV). The geon which is separated from the exterior space at $a' = a'_o$ is so dense that it curves space up around itself into a closed universe. At the point in this closed universe farthest from the geon's center the hypersurface of time symmetry is flat.

Although this figure specializes to the case $\Phi = 6 \times 10^{37}$ gauss-cm² and $b' = 1$ light-year, the imbedding diagrams would be essentially unchanged if Φ and b' were chosen differently.

This situation is strikingly similar to the one depicted in Figure 4 for a collapsing cloud of dust (Oppenheimer and Snyder 1939; Klein 1962; Beckedorff 1962; Beckedorff and Misner 1964). The topologies of the hypersurfaces of time symmetry are identical in the two cases; and in both cases the same type of pinch-off occurs as the surface area of the energy-containing region is reduced.[7] The similarity between the hypersurfaces of

[7] It is striking that in the pinch-off the entire torus, including its central "hole," separates from the external universe. One might have expected the pinch-off to occur in a canal-like region around the ring. A similar situation arises when one has two Schwarzschild solutions very close together: They share a

time symmetry in the two cases is so striking that one is led to expect that the dynamical behavior of a collapsing geon will resemble that of a collapsing dust cloud. In particular, it seems likely that, as the geon collapses, an event horizon similar to the "Schwarzschild singularity" will develop.

The detailed investigation of the dynamics of the collapse of a toroidal magnetic geon —free of all reference to any equation of state—should give still further insight into gravitational collapse in general and the issue of the final state.

The author is indebted to the U.S. Air Force Contract AF49(638)-304 for funds which made his attendance at the symposium possible, and to the Danforth Foundation for support during the period in which this research was conducted. He also wishes to thank Professor John A. Wheeler for valuable discussions, suggestions, and criticisms of this work.

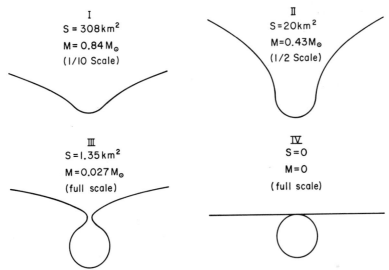

I
S = 308 km²
M = 0.84 M⊙
(1/10 Scale)

II
S = 20 km²
M = 0.43 M⊙
(1/2 Scale)

III
S = 1.35 km²
M = 0.027 M⊙
(full scale)

IV
S = 0
M = 0
(full scale)

FIG. 4.—"Imbedding diagrams" of the geometry of the hypersurface of time symmetry for collapsing clouds of dust. For each dust cloud, if one takes a two-dimensional surface of constant azimuthal angle φ at the moment of time symmetry and imbeds it in Euclidean 3-space, one obtains the surface formed by rotating the corresponding curve about its vertical axis. Four diagrams are shown corresponding to clouds of dust all containing 1 $M_\odot$ of matter ($\int T_0{}^0 dv_{\text{physical}} = M_\odot$) but having different surface areas. As the surface area shrinks from ∞ to 0, the mass of the cloud as measured from the exterior shrinks from 1 $M_\odot$ to 0. In the limit where the surface area reaches zero, the dust cloud pinches off from the exterior region and one is left with a flat, empty exterior universe and a separate closed Friedman universe viewed at the moment of time symmetry.

The dust cloud is located in the circular region of each diagram, while the parabolic region corresponds to empty space outside the cloud's surface.

REFERENCES

Beckedorff, D. L. 1962, "Terminal Configurations of Stellar Evolution" (Senior thesis, Princeton University).
Beckedorff, D. L., and Misner, C. W. 1964 (to be published).
Brill, D. R. 1959, *Ann. Phys.*, **7**, 466; (see also his "Time-Symmetric Solutions of the Einstein Equations: Initial Value Problem and Positive Definite Mass" [Ph.D. thesis, Princeton University]).
Brill, D. R., and Lindquist, R. W. 1963, *Phys. Rev.*, **131**, 471.
Darmois, G. 1927, *Les Équations de la gravitation einsteinienne* ("Mém. d. sci. math.," Vol. **25** [Paris: Gauthier-Villars]).

common throat which opens out into the universe, and it is only *below* the common throat that they separate from each other (Brill and Lindquist 1963; cf. especially their Fig. 3).

Euler, H., and Kockel, B. 1935, *Naturwiss.*, **23**, 246.
Foures-Bruhat, Y. 1956, *J. Rat. Mech. Anal.*, **5**, 951.
Heisenberg, W. 1936, *Zs. Phys.*, **98**, 714.
Klein, O. 1962, in *Werner Heisenberg und die Physik in unserer Zeit.* (Braunschweig: Vieweg).
Levi-Civita, T. 1919, *Rend. Acc. Lincei*, **28**, 3, 101.
Lichnerowicz, A. 1955, *Theories relativistes de la gravitation et de l'electromagnetisme* (Paris: Masson et Cie.).
Melvin, M. A. 1964*a*, *Phys. Letters*, **8**, 65.
———. 1964*b* (to be published).
Oppenheimer, J. R., and Snyder, H. 1939, *Phys. Rev.*, **56**, 455.
Stellmacher, K. 1937, *Math. Ann.*, **115**, 136.
Thorne, K. S. 1964 (to be published).
Weyl, H. 1919, *Ann. Phys.*, **54**, 117.
Weyl, H., and Bach, R. 1922, *Math. Zs.*, **13**, 134.
Wheeler, J. A. 1955, *Phys. Rev.*, **97**, 511.
———. 1962, *Geometrodynamics* (New York: Academic Press).
———. 1964, in B. DeWitt and C. DeWitt, *Relativity, Topology and Groups* (1963 Les Houches Summer School [New York: Gordon & Breach)].

THE STABILITY OF MULTISTAR

chapter 8 # SYSTEMS

T. Gold, W. I. Axford, and E. C. Ray

The discovery of the powerful sources of energy among distant galaxies forces one to look at the various ways whereby matter might become much more concentrated in certain systems. Hoyle has discussed the collapse of a mass of gas and pointed out the problems, to a large extent due to initial angular momentum, of arranging for the final contraction of a single object of great mass and density. He discussed there the breakup into a number of subunits and the possible later evolution of such a fragmented system. We will discuss another possible avenue for the contraction of matter to form a system of high density and great mass.

Star systems such as globular clusters have been discussed in the literature, and most authors have concluded that such systems have evolutionary time scales that are so long that no great change in the density of a cluster can be expected in the age of our Galaxy. There is no question regarding the secular stability—no multistar system is secularly stable, but all will tend to lose some stars and shrink down the volume occupied by the remainder. The only doubt concerns the speed of these processes.

Chandrasekhar's calculations concern the statistical effects of exchanges of momentum between two stars at near encounters. Through this process stars will occasionally be given the velocity of escape from the cluster and in escaping will remove energy, leaving the remainder in a more negative energy state and therefore more tightly bound. Evaporation rates for elliptic galaxies calculated on this basis are about 10^{25} years. There is doubt, however, whether the near encounter of two stars is the major process for redistributing the kinetic energy, or whether encounters between one star and the simultaneous gravitational effects of a number of others dominate in the process.

With the inverse square law of gravitation and, unlike plasma physics, in the absence of any shielding effect, one may suspect any scale of interaction to contribute to the changes of momentum of the test star. The largest possible scale is, of course, that of the cluster itself, and there is no doubt that the momentum of any one star is very significantly affected by an interaction on this scale, for any individual star performs an oscillation in the total gravitational field. What intermediate scales of interaction might be significant in the motion of any one star is not known, especially for the case where gravitation tends to make for more lumpy and less even distribution of mass than a random assembly would have been. The lumpiness considered here is a collective effect of a small set of stars in the cluster, acting on each other through their mutual gravitational fields,

T. Gold, W. I. Axford, and E. C. Ray, Cornell University.

rather than the purely statistical clumping shown by Chandrasekhar (1960) not to be important.

It is known that any dispersion in mass of the stars greatly speeds up the rate of evaporation of the lighter ones. Any tendency toward equipartition of kinetic energy will give the less massive stars a higher speed and therefore will allow them more readily to reach the velocity of escape. The effective dispersion of mass would be enhanced if there were bound subsystems in the cluster. Double, triple, and higher-numbered bound star systems will act for the purpose of distant encounters much like single stars of the combined mass. It will, therefore, be important to be able to conclude what degree of sub-clustering exists within the cluster, both so far as fully bound subsystems are concerned and also temporary nearly bound systems.

For close encounters multiple systems may be even more effective in accelerating the test star. Since the configuration of the multiple system may change significantly during the encounter, the encountering star may gain or lose energy in the process. Such gains of energy may then be statistically more important in the acceleration of the test star to the velocity of escape from the cluster than any individual encounters. On other occasions the passing star may, of course, deliver energy to the multiple system, and multiple systems therefore provide an energy reservoir which can be depleted and replenished, and which may speed up the dynamical relaxation of a cluster.

From an observational point of view one is certainly tempted to suspect that the relaxation processes are much faster than the classical calculations involving near encounters have suggested. The mere fact that there are many globular clusters whose similarity and smooth distribution of density suggest a relaxed configuration and whose mean density is so large compared with that of general galactic material makes a strong case that evolution and shrinkage of clusters has taken place within the age of the Galaxy. If globular clusters had reached their present configuration without these dynamical effects one would have to understand how a gas cloud could have contracted to this very high mean density before contracting into a multitude of stars. Why then would stars form at the very much lower densities in galaxies? Whatever the details of the star formation process, it is certainly critically dependent on mean density. It is hard to see how a discussion of the process would fit the case of the galaxies as well as that of the globular clusters.

The angular momentum possessed by any diffuse mass is usually enormously greater than the amount that gravity can overcome when the system is more condensed. Any discussion of the contraction of very large masses must therefore be concerned with this problem.

Globular clusters are, as the name implies, generally round in outline or show only a very small amount of flattening. Does this imply that they do not own much angular momentum? It is true that the shape of a cluster does not itself necessarily define its angular momentum. It is clear that the shape would in the first instance be unaffected if, for example, all stars encircling the center of mass in one sense had their motions suddenly reversed so as to encircle it in the opposite sense while those already going in that sense were left unaffected. This change would give the cluster a large amount of angular momentum but would leave the shape of orbits unchanged. Nevertheless, we must expect the shape of a cluster in fact to reveal its angular momentum if relaxation has gone far. In the example mentioned we would be transforming a relaxed cluster into one of identical shape but a lesser degree of relaxation. If, in that new condition, it were allowed to relax through star encounters we feel certain, although we are not aware of any proof, that the cluster would adopt a flattened outline.

How, then, can it come about that these highly concentrated galactic masses that represent the globular clusters have contracted so far without apparently being impeded by angular momentum? If their mass were spread out to fill a volume at a mean galactic density then it would represent a mass whose angular momentum was several orders of magnitude less than the mean of comparable galactic masses. This suggests that the contraction of multistar systems by evaporation of stars is a process in which enough angular momentum is shed so that the remaining cluster never gets substantially flattened.

We might define a quantity we call the "dynamical flattening" of a cluster as the ratio of the energy of rotation that would be possessed by an object of the same moment of inertia and the same angular momentum, to the kinetic energy of the "thermal" motions of the stars. This quantity must be much less than unity for all clusters possessing a shape of nearly spherical symmetry. Can it be that this quantity is stabilized at a small value during the evaporation of stars and the consequent shrinkage of any multistar system?

If a gas mass condenses it does so, while complying with the virial theorem, by the emission of energy in the form of nearly massless photons. A multistar system, on the other hand, can contract only by the emission of massive objects, namely, individual stars. The circumstances are therefore different in that the gas cloud could not possibly have avoided an increase of the dynamical flattening. The multistar system, however, can reject significant amounts of angular momentum in the evaporation of stars and the possibility therefore exists that the remainder maintains small dynamical flattening.

The following example will illustrate the process. If one were to shoot off space probes in random directions from the surface of the rotating Earth, one would find that they robbed the Earth of angular momentum, for it would always be easier to achieve the velocity of escape for those fired off in the forward direction in the sense of rotation than for those fired off in other directions. This would be particularly true if most objects could be accelerated only to less than the velocity of escape. Similarly, a rotating globular cluster will lose stars a little more readily in the forward direction of its sense of rotation and even a small amount of rotation may suffice to make a large difference in the probability of escape. This is so especially because of the fact that many stars spend a long time possessing energies very close to that of escape before in fact escaping.

The relaxation process in a multistar system would tend to set up a Maxwellian distribution of velocities, except for the fact that velocities above those of escape must be absent. But if the cluster has angular momentum what will be the velocity distribution set up? Clearly it cannot be a Maxwellian one, for that has no angular momentum. The actual distribution must then be a more complicated one, but it is likely to be better described by a Maxwellian distribution in a rotating frame than by one in a fixed frame. Probably the best rotating frame to choose for such a representation would again be one derived by dividing the angular momentum of the globular cluster by its moment of inertia. It is in this rotating system, then, that we might consider the probability of escape as in the example of space vehicles shot off from the Earth.

If the evaporating stars took with them only the average amount of angular momentum and not a preferentially larger amount, and if the escaping stars left with only just the energy of escape, then it can be shown that the dynamical flattening would increase with time as $R^{-3/2}$, where R is a characteristic radius of the cluster. No substantial contraction could have taken place in globular clusters and left them as round as they are unless the statistical tendency is for the evaporating stars to take away much more than the mean angular momentum.

One might, therefore, make the following conjecture. Star systems that show a large amount of flattening, as, e.g., elliptical galaxies, have done most of their contraction in the gaseous phase prior to star formation. Star systems like globular clusters that are nearly spherical have done most of their contraction as star systems.

We have discussed the evidence that the contraction of a star cluster may not lead to the continuous build-up of the dynamical flattening. If this is so, it is however also likely that in the event of the dynamical flattening being below a certain number the effect of rotation would be of little consequence in selecting the stars for evaporation and that therefore, as we have said, the dynamical flattening would increase and would, no doubt, continue to do so until the rotation becomes effective in selecting stars for evaporation. Clusters would therefore tend to be stabilized at a particular value of the dynamical flattening, and the observational indication is that this value is much smaller than unity.

There seem to be two advantages, therefore, in attempting to account for great concentrations of matter as a contraction of a star system rather than as a contraction of gas. First, the great stumbling block of angular momentum is absent there if the star system keeps throughout its contraction a balance between the angular momentum and the energy rejected, while the gas system rejects energy but is soon prevented from further contraction by the angular momentum. Second, a gas system would be expected to break up into stars when the densities became much greater than mean galactic densities. Thereafter the discussion would, in any case, have to concern itself with the contraction of a star system. The disadvantage of the explanation in terms of a star system lies in the fact that a very large proportion of the mass has to be lost before a high density can be reached.

For the case of a shrinking multistar system in which the escaping stars take away only exactly the energy of escape, the contraction would keep N^2/R constant (where N is the number of stars and R a characteristic radius of the cluster). If, in the statistics of escaping stars, they receive more than that energy, then the system will shrink more for a given loss of numbers. The absolute speed of the evaporation process is what is greatly in doubt, but it is clear that the rate of all relaxation effects will continue to increase as the cluster contracts, and as the densities and velocities increase. Multistar systems will thus go slowly through the early phases of their evolution, but progressively faster later, and must come to an almost sudden end. What will be the nature of the final phases? When densities and velocities have become very high, tidal encounters and collisions between stars must become frequent. Under these circumstances the rate of shrinkage would be accelerated even more, since such encounters represent an additional energy loss. The final state of a multistar system is then one of a high frequency of star-to-star collisions at very high relative speeds. Such an object may look as if in it a great number of supernovae explosions were occurring in rapid succession. Mass and angular momentum would continue to be rejected from the system but it would now flatten since energy losses other than the evaporation of stars would now be important. After the exhaustion of the nuclear energy the central region that possessed insufficient angular momentum to hold itself out against gravitation would slip away into that other state of matter dominated by gravitation about which we have heard so many conjectures.

REFERENCE

Chandrasekhar, S. 1960, *Principles of Stellar Dynamics* (New York: Dover).

APPENDIX

We discuss here the considerations leading to the curves shown in Figure 1.

To obtain N^2/R = constant as the evolutionary track of a cluster, together with the suggestion that actual clusters may depart from these curves above, rather than below (as plotted in Fig. 1), we begin with the virial theorem. It is (Chandrasekhar 1960)

$$2T' + \Omega = \tfrac{1}{2} \frac{d^2I}{dt^2},$$ (1)

where T' is the total kinetic energy of all the stars which were initially in the cluster, Ω is their total potential energy, and $I = \Sigma_k m_k r_k^2$ is the second moment of the system. It is reasonable to suppose that stars still bound in the cluster contribute negligibly to d^2I/dt^2. On the other hand, the stars which have so far escaped have the property that $d^2I/dt^2 = 4t$, where t is the total kinetic energy they will have when their potential energy is negligible. Let T denote the total kinetic energy of stars still bound in the cluster. Then equation (1) becomes

$$2T + \Omega = 0 .\qquad(2)$$

In addition, we have $T' + \Omega = -E$, where E is a positive constant. Using the above definitions, this becomes

$$T + \Omega = -(E + t).\qquad(3)$$

Solving equations (2) and (3) together, we obtain

$$\Omega = -2(E + t),\qquad(4)$$

$$T = E + t .\qquad(5)$$

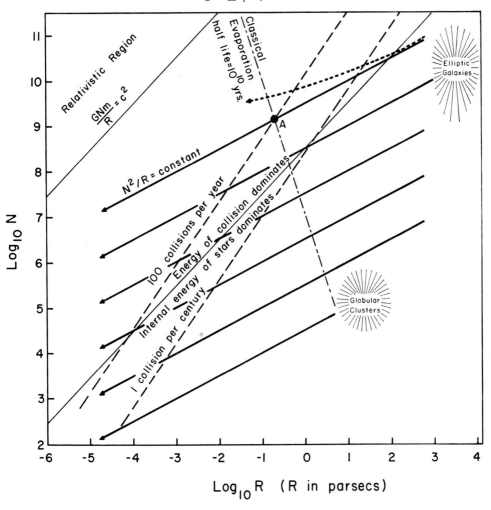

FIG. 1

Let τ denote the average kinetic energy carried away by a star, N_0 the initial number of stars in the cluster, and N the current number. Let m be the average mass of a star and define R to be such a radius that

$$\Omega = \frac{GN^2m^2}{R}. \tag{6}$$

Then, from equation (4),

$$N^2/R = 2E/(Gm^2) + 2\tau(N_0 - N)/(Gm^2). \tag{7}$$

If $\tau = 0$, then N^2/R is constant and some samples of such curves are plotted in Figure 1. If τ differs from zero, it must be positive. Then N^2/R must steadily increase. It must be noticed that τ, if non-zero, is probably dependent on N. If the cluster obeys some reasonable similarity relation as it contracts, τ must presumably increase strongly as N decreases since t does. The dotted curve in Figure 1 suggests the evolutionary curve to which this situation would lead.

The collision rate ω_c is obtained by noting that a star with velocity v moving through a region where the number density of stars is n, makes collisions at the rate $n\sigma v$ per unit time, where σ is an appropriate collision cross-section. Thus for the whole system the total collision rate must be approximately given by

$$\omega_c = \frac{3\sigma}{8\pi} \frac{N^2v}{R^3} = \frac{3\sigma}{8\pi}(Gm)^{1/2}\frac{N^{5/2}}{R^{7/2}}, \tag{8}$$

where we have taken the mean number density to be

$$\langle n \rangle = N/\tfrac{4}{3}\pi R. \tag{9}$$

In plotting the loci of constant ω_c we have assumed that n is equal to 1 solar mass and $\sigma = 4\pi r_\odot^2$, where $r_\odot$ is the radius of the Sun. In fact, this is an underestimate of the cross-section, since gravitational effects must be important wherever $Nr_\odot < R$, which is the case for most of the region in the diagram to the right of the line $\omega_c = 100$.

The lifetime of a cluster against evaporation as calculated by Chandrasekhar (1960, eqs. [111] and [115]) is given approximately by

$$\tau_e = \frac{200}{(mG)^{1/2}} \frac{N^{1/2}R^{3/2}}{\log_e N}. \tag{10}$$

Curves of constant τ_e in the diagram are essentially straight lines since the logarithm term in the denominator of equation (10) varies extremely slowly. The line for an evaporation lifetime of 10^{10} years is shown.

The curve $GNm/R = c^2$ is the locus of points where the gravitational potential energy is c^2, so that general relativity is important. The locus representing the onset of relativistic conditions lies well to the left of the locus

$$N/\omega_c = 1/H, \tag{11}$$

where H is Hubble's constant. This represents the condition that every star in the cluster should on the average suffer a collision once in the lifetime of the universe; thus it is clear that for clusters of reasonable initial size collisions become important long before a relativistic regime is reached for the cluster as a whole.

In star-to-star collisions the release of energy due to the kinetic energy of the colliding stars will dominate to the left of the line given, while the internal energy of the stars will dominate to the right. This is calculated under the assumption that no nuclear energy contributes to the event (which may often be untrue) and that the internal energy of stars is characterized by 20 million degrees. Small clusters can therefore only result in collisions of the weak kind while massive clusters would come into the strong collision regime before being completely destroyed.

The point A corresponds to an energy release by collisions of approximately 10^{45} erg/sec.

GRAVITATIONAL COLLAPSE
chapter 9 # AND ROTATION

R. P. KERR

In the past all exact solutions of collapsing gravitational systems have been spherical-ly symmetric and have been based on the exterior Schwarzschild solution. This solution may be written in a form first given by Eddington (1924):

$$d s^2 = d x^2 + d y^2 + d z^2 - d t^2 + \frac{2m}{r} (d r + d t)^2, \tag{1}$$

where $r^2 = x^2 + y^2 + z^2$, and units have been chosen so that the velocity of light $c = 1$ and the gravitational constant $G = 1$.

This metric has a true singularity at the origin $r = 0$. However, it has peculiar physical properties inside and on the Schwarzschild sphere, S,

$$r = 2m. \tag{2}$$

S is a null surface, outside ($r > 2m$) of which the metric is static, the t-axis being time-like. Inside $S(r < 2m)$ the metric is *not* static since the t-axis is spacelike.

For matter collapsing all the way to and beyond the Schwarzschild sphere we have the following behavior: matter and energy can pass from the exterior to the interior of S, but can never move out again, and so a spherically symmetric system collapsing beyond the Schwarzschild sphere can no longer radiate energy to the outside. It cannot be seen by an outside observer; only its gravitational field can be felt.

A collapsing particle will reach the Schwarzschild sphere and pass into its interior in a finite proper time, i.e., in a finite time as measured by a comoving clock. However, for a distant observer the time of collapse, measured by his clocks, is infinite. He will never observe the stage where the collapsing matter reaches the Schwarzschild sphere and passes to the inside.

This behavior causes difficulties in theories which attempt to explain the large energies emitted by quasi-stellar sources in terms of the gravitational collapse of large masses into the Schwarzschild sphere S.

In this paper we wish to show that the topological and physical properties of S may

This research has been sponsored by the Aerospace Research Laboratory, Office of Aerospace Research, and the Office of Scientific Research, U.S. Air Force.

R. P. KERR, The University of Texas.

change radically when rotation is taken into account. This suggests that it would be worthwhile to re-examine the problem of gravitational collapse for a mass whose external gravitational field is the stationary field of a rotating body.

An exact solution of Einstein's gravitational field equation for empty space is given by the metric (Kerr 1963):[1]

$$d s^2 = dx^2 + dy^2 + dz^2 - dt^2 + \frac{2 m \rho^3}{\rho^4 + a^2 z^2} (k_\mu dx^\mu)^2, \tag{3}$$

where k_μ is a null vector field given by

$$k_\mu dx^\mu = dt + \frac{z}{\rho} dz + \frac{\rho}{\rho^2 + a^2} (xdx + ydy) + \frac{a}{\rho^2 + a^2} (xdy - ydx), \tag{4}$$

m and a are arbitrary constants, and ρ is given by

$$\frac{x^2 + y^2}{\rho^2 + a^2} + \frac{z^2}{\rho^2} = 1. \tag{5}$$

The surfaces of constant ρ are confocal ellipsoids of revolution.

For large spatial distances, ρ is given asymptotically by

$$\rho = r + 0(r^{-1}). \tag{6}$$

The metric (3), expanded in powers of r^{-1} becomes

$$d s^2 = dx^2 + dy^2 + dz^2 - dt^2 + \frac{2 m}{r} (dt + dr)^2$$

$$+ \frac{4 m a}{r^3} (xdy - ydx)(dt + dr) + 0(r^{-3}). \tag{7}$$

The term of order r^{-1} shows, e.g., by comparing with equation (1), that m is the mass of the body producing the gravitational field. The term of order r^{-2} shows, by comparing with the solution of the linearized field equations, that am is the angular momentum about the z-axis of the rotating body.

The metric of equation (3) has a true singularity on the circle Γ,

$$z = 0, \qquad R \equiv (x^2 + y^2)^{1/2} = a. \tag{8}$$

This is the analogue of the true Schwarzschild singularity at $r = 0$ in equation (1).

The analogue of the Schwarzschild sphere is now the null surface S given by

$$\rho^4 + a^2 z^2 = 2m\rho^3. \tag{9}$$

In Figure 1 S is plotted in the (R, z)-plane for the two cases, $m < a$ and $m > a$. It will be observed that S has a cusp on Γ. This is not significant, since the points of Γ are singularities. For $m > a$, S splits into two disjoint parts, S_1 and S_2. As $a \to 0$, the outer surface, S_1, becomes the Schwarzschild sphere, while S_2 collapses into the origin. When $a = m$ the two components, S_1 and S_2, touch on the z-axis. For $a > m$ the surfaces are as in

---

[1] More general vacuum solutions are given by Kerr and Schild (1964).

Figure 1, a. When $m \to 0$ $(a \neq 0)$, S shrinks to the ring Γ. In most physical situations $a \gg m$, and so neither S_1 nor S_2 has the topology of a sphere.

There is a further complication of this metric, which is not present when $a = 0$. Suppose we define D as the disk bounded by Γ given by

$$R < a, \qquad z = 0 . \tag{10}$$

It is represented in Figure 1 by a solid line. We shall now show that the metric in equation (3) is not even differentiable, let alone analytic, on D. To see this we first observe that equation (3) has two distinct real roots, $\rho_+ > 0$ and $\rho_- < 0$, for all points except D. In order for the metric to be continuous, we choose the root ρ_+ for all points. From equation (5) this gives

$$\rho_+ = \frac{a\,|\,z\,|}{\sqrt{a^2 - r^2}}, \qquad \text{near } D , \tag{11}$$

and so ρ_+ is not differentiable on D. Substituting equation (11) into equation (3) we can easily see that the metric itself is not differentiable on D.

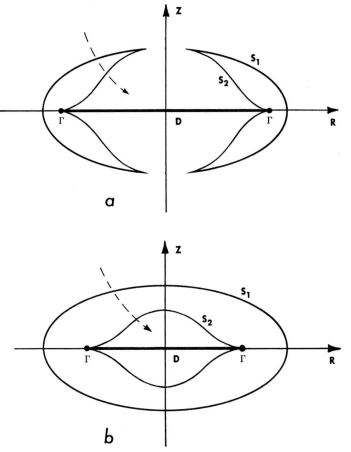

FIG. 1.—a, the "Schwarzschild surface" for $a > m > 0$. The solid disk, D, is a branch cut, bounded by the ring, Γ. b, the "Schwarzschild surface" for $m > a > 0$.

This behavior may be compared to that of $Z^{1/2}$ in the complex plane, with the branch point at the origin corresponding to the ring Γ. The function ρ^2 is real and positive at all points, except Γ, but ρ is two-valued. As with $Z^{1/2}$ it is necessary to introduce two spaces, E_1 and E_2, with the topology of the points of R^4, less the ring Γ and the disk D. The points above D in E_1 are joined onto the points below D in E_2, and vice versa. The points of D should be thought of as a branch cut. The points immediately above the disk D in E_1 are not close to those immediately below the disk D in E_1. In E_1 we take the root ρ_+, whereas in E_2 $\rho = \rho_- \leq 0$. An observer passing through the ring Γ will observe that ρ changes sign, but the metric tensor is now analytic at all points of the space.

To interpret the space with $\rho = \rho_-$ we observe that if ρ is replaced by $-\rho$ in equation (3), and the coordinate transformation $t \rightarrow -t$, $y \rightarrow -y$ is performed, then the metric of equations (3) and (4) is recovered except that the mass has the opposite sign. This means that if we take $m > 0$ in E_1 then an observer at a large distance from the origin in E_2 will consider that there is a negative mass near the origin.

It is not possible to say whether a rotating galaxy with this metric as its external field would allow much greater radiation than a non-rotating galaxy. However, all the evidence at present appears to confirm this. In particular, when $a > m$ radiation and matter will not be trapped inside S, as will be seen from the direction of the arrows in Figure 1, b. As a radiating particle collapses inside S_1 its radiation can be received by an observer outside the body, since it can cross S_2 in the indicated direction and then escape along the z-axis.

REFERENCES

Eddington, A. S. 1924, *Nature*, **113**, 192.

Kerr, R. P. 1963, *Phys. Rev. Letters*, **11**, 522.

Kerr, R. P., and Schild, A. 1964, Proceedings of the American Mathematical Society's Symposium on Applications of Partial Differential Equations in Mathematical Physics, New York City, April, 1964 (in press).

PART III

IDENTIFICATION OF GALAXIES WITH RADIO SOURCES

A DISCUSSION OF GALAXIES IDENTIFIED WITH RADIO
chapter 10 SOURCES

Thomas A. Matthews, William W. Morgan, and Maarten Schmidt

I. INTRODUCTION

In the past the galaxies identified with radio sources have been called at various times colliding spirals, ellipticals, or S0 galaxies, in addition to the normal spirals. However, to date no attempt has been made to classify the objects using only those sources for which the identifications are well established and for which a classification can be made from optical photographs. In the course of this study, certain groups of objects have emerged as being associated with radio sources. This paper presents the observational data and describes the classes into which the objects fall.

The definition of a well-identified radio source is not easy as it is based on the sum of the knowledge about identified sources. The first requisite is a reasonable positional agreement of the radio centroid with the optical object. For most of the identifications to date, this agreement is within the errors of measurement of the radio centroid. However, some identifications are felt to be certain where the optical object is displaced from the radio centroid by as much as one-half of the radio diameter (e.g., 3C 273). In these cases we must draw more heavily on the other criteria for making an identification.

The second criterion is the presence of unusual optical features on direct photographs. These include such things as: close double galaxies in a common envelope which sometimes show signs of gravitational interaction; the presence of the D-galaxy characteristics (see below); the dominant character of the galaxy in luminosity and size when in a cluster; asymmetrical faint outer extensions which seem to be related to the radio structure; the presence of an unusually blue object, particularly when in high galactic latitude; the presence of an ultraviolet excess in an object, such as Sandage has used to discover several quasi-stellar objects; the starlike appearance of some non-stellar objects; the presence of absorption unexpected in some types of galaxies; and the presence of jets, plumes, or other unusual structures. The presence of one or more of these unusual

Thomas A. Matthews, Owens Valley Radio Observatory, California Institute of Technology. William W. Morgan, Yerkes Observatory, University of Chicago. Maarten Schmidt, Mount Wilson and Palomar Observatories, Carnegie Institution of Washington and California Institute of Technology.

Reprinted from the *Astrophysical Journal*, **140**, 35–49, 1964.

features does not prove that the object is the required identification, since other similar objects are known (for at least some of the features) which do not have associated radio sources. However, the more unusual the object, the more probable is the identification.

The third, and very important, criterion is based on the optical spectra. Most of the optical objects have unusually strong emission lines which immediately set them apart as being unusual. For these reasons, the spectra that have been taken of many of the identified sources contribute a great deal to the certainty of their identification (Schmidt, in preparation).

Some radio sources fall in a region where many optical objects are found; and if the true identification is very faint, one will be tempted to misidentify the optical object. These misidentifications usually stand out when a sufficient amount of information is known about the object, and it is felt that all such misidentifications have been eliminated from the list of objects described in this paper.

Before an identification could be included in this discussion, there had to be adequate plate material available to allow the galaxy to be examined in some detail, so that an optical form classification could be given. The plate material used for this study was primarily the blue and red 48-inch Schmidt plates that were taken for the *National Geographic Society–Palomar Observatory Sky Survey*. In addition, large-scale 200-inch plates of some of the objects were available.

II. DATA FOR SOURCES

The fifty-two extragalactic radio sources listed in Table 1 have the following information given: (1) the name of the source, together with NGC numbers and other names—when they exist; (2) the distance to the source; (3) the logarithm of the total radio power emitted in ergs/sec; and (4) the optical form types.

The distances ($r = cz/H$) of the objects were determined mainly from the measured redshifts, on the assumption that the Hubble constant $H = 100$ km/sec/Mpc. The redshifts are almost all determinations by Schmidt; some were measured by Minkowski (1961a, b), with some corrections (Maltby, Matthews, and Moffet 1963); a few were determined by Greenstein (1961, 1962). The distances of the spiral and irregular galaxies were kindly estimated by Sandage, mostly from his photographs for determining the sizes of H II regions. If no redshift was available for the more concentrated galaxies a photometric distance was estimated from the apparent magnitude and an assumed $M_{pg} = -20.5$ (Maltby *et al.* 1963). Allowance was made for interstellar absorption where necessary. The photometric distances are inclosed in parentheses. The source of the redshift when not determined by Schmidt is indicated in the notes to Table 1.

The radio luminosities,[1] L, are calculated from the equation

$$L = 4\pi r^2 \int_{\nu_1}^{\nu_2} S_\nu d\nu, \tag{1a}$$

where

$$S_\nu = S_{400} \left(\frac{\nu}{4 \times 10^8} \right)^{-n} \left(1 + \frac{z}{2} \right)^2 \qquad \nu_1 \leq \nu \leq \nu_2 \tag{1b}$$

and

$$S_\nu = 0 \quad \text{when} \quad \nu < \nu_1, \quad \nu > \nu_2. \tag{1c}$$

The values of S_{400} and n were taken from the work of Kellermann (1963). The cutoff frequencies were chosen to be ν_1 (emitted) $= 10^7$ c/s and ν_2 (emitted) $= 10^{11}$ c/s, except for those sources which show curvature in a (log S_ν versus log ν) plot. The cutoff fre-

---

[1] The limits of integration and the parameters used here are not the same as those used by Maltby, Matthews, and Moffet (1963). In that paper ν_2 was assumed to be 10^{10} c/s; thus the luminosities given in Table 1 will be greater for most sources.

TABLE 1

DATA ON RADIO SOURCES

No.	Source	NGC	Other	r (Mpc)	log L	Optical Type
1.	....	224	M31	0.83	38.69	gkS5
2.	MOO–222	253	....	3.2	39.08	afS6
3.	3C 33	....	....	180	42.83	DE4
4.	3C 40	545–7	....	53	41.48	cD4
5.	3C 47	....	....	1280	44.21	Qs
6.	3C 48	....	....	1100	44.67	Qs
7.	3C 66	....	....	64	41.88	ED2
8.	3C 71	1068	M77	11	40.13	gS2p
9.	3C 75	....	....	65	41.67	db
10.	3C 78	1218	....	87	42.25	DE3
11.	3C 83.1	1265	....	54	41.55	ED3–4
12.	3C 84	1275	Per A	54	42.03	ED2
13.	MO3–31	1316	For A	17	41.77	D3–4
14.	3C 88	....	....	91	42.06	D4
15.	3C 98	....	....	92	42.19	ED3
16.	MO5–43	....	Pic A	100	43.11	ND1
17.	3C 147	....	....	1640	45.29	Qs
18.	3C 195	....	....	(320)	42.92	DE3
19.	3C 218	....	Hya A	160	43.22	cD2
20.	3C 219	....	....	520	43.60	cD5
21.	3C 227	....	....	(300)	43.06	N1
22.	3C 231	3034	M82	3.2	39.62	I
23.	3C 234	....	....	550	43.46	N1
24.	3C 264	3862	....	63	41.60	DE1
25.	....	4258	....	6.2	39.17	gS5
26.	3C 270	4261	....	11	40.33	ED3
27.	3C 272.1	4374	M84	11	40.24	E2
28.	3C 273	....	....	470	44.49	Qs
29.	3C 274	4486	Vir A, M87	11	41.67	E2
30.	....	4490	....	6.3:	38.78	I
31.	3C 278	4782–3	....	43	41.37	db
32.	M13–42	5128	Cen A	4.7	41.87	DE3
33.	....	5236	M83	7.2	39.62	fgS1
34.	....	5457	M101	3.5	38.09	fS1
35.	3C 295	....	....	1380	45.30	cD:
36.	3C 310	....	....	160	42.47	db
37.	3C 315	....	....	320	42.95	db
38.	3C 317	....	....	100	41.96	cD4
39.	3C 327	....	....	310	43.15	DE3–4
40.	3C 338	6166	....	90	41.69	cD4
41.	3C 348	....	Her A	470	44.20	cD4:
42.	3C 353	....	....	91	42.86	D2
43.	3C 382	....	CTA 80	170	42.50	D3:
44.	3C 386	....	....	(10)	40.04	DE2
45.	3C 388	....	....	270	42.94	cD3:
46.	3C 405	....	Cyg A	170	44.71	cD3
47.	3C 430	....	....	(50)	41.50	ED4:
48.	3C 433	....	....	300	43.25	D4:
49.	3C 442	7236–7	....	79	41.51	db
50.	3C 445	....	....	170	42.52	N1
51.	M23–112	....	....	250	42.32	D5
52.	3C 465	7720	....	88	41.96	c?D4

NOTES TO TABLE 1

No. 3.—DE4 in D3 envelope, with major axis of nucleus turned toward minor axis of envelope. 200-inch plate by Minkowski. Spectrogram by Schmidt with slit along major axis of nucleus shows strongly

[Notes to Table 1 continued on page 108]

inclined lines; spectrogram with slit along minor axis shows no inclination. The radio source is discussed in the text.

No. 4.—cD3 in D4 envelope. Brightest galaxy in cluster A194, richness 0. Secondary galaxy in edge of envelope. Redshift by Minkowski and Zwicky (see Maltby *et al.* 1962; Minkowski, *Pub. A.S.P.*, **70**, 143, 1958).

No. 5.—Redshift by Schmidt (Schmidt and Matthews 1964).

No. 6.—Redshift by Greenstein (Greenstein and Matthews 1963).

No. 7.—In cluster A347, richness 0. Secondary galaxy in outer envelope. 200-inch plate by Minkowski. Redshift by Minkowski (see Maltby *et al.* 1962).

No. 8.—Redshift from Humason, Mayall, and Sandage (1956).

No. 9.—ED2 + ED1 in common envelope. In cluster A400, richness 1. The radio centroid is displaced by a little less than one-half the radio diameter from the dumbbell. No other galaxies are suspected of contributing to the radio emission. Redshift by Minkowski (see Maltby *et al.* 1962).

No. 11.—In cluster A426, richness 2. Redshift from Humason *et al.* (1956).

No. 12.—Classified on 48-inch Schmidt red plate. On this plate the peculiar features discussed by Baade and Minkowski (1954*b*) and by Burbidge *et al.* (1963) are not very prominent. Brightest galaxy in cluster A426, richness 2. Redshift from Humason *et al.* (1956).

No. 13.—For A classified from a slightly enlarged positive copy of 48-inch Schmidt plate by E. Herzog. Absorption in nuclear region (Burbidge *et al.* 1963). Member of the Fornax I cluster of galaxies (Zwicky 1959), richness 1.

No. 14.—Probably in poor clustering.

No. 16.—Form classified on direct photograph from Mount Stromlo 74-inch plate taken by W. Tifft. Probably in poor clustering.

No. 17.—Redshift by Schmidt (Schmidt and Matthews 1964).

No. 18.—DE3 in D1 envelope. May be similar to 3C 33. Brightest galaxy in faint clustering. Secondary nucleus in envelope. 200-inch plate by Schmidt.

No. 19.—Double nucleus; not completely resolved. There is another galaxy in the outer envelope. In poor, faint cluster; very much brighter than any other cluster member. 200-inch plates by Sandage and Baade. The radio structure has three components: a halo of about 5′ in diameter, an elongated core shown in Figure 9, and a hot spot of 11″ diameter whose exact location is not known. Redshift by Minkowski (1961*b*).

No. 20.—cD1: in D5 envelope. At center of cluster of richness 2, of which it is by far the brightest member. A second fainter galaxy in position angle 120° is joined to the brighter one by a bridge. This second galaxy also has extensions in position angles 120° and 240°. Only the bright galaxy has emission lines. 200-inch plate by Sandage; classified from positive copy.

No. 21.—Bright. Possible nebulous wisp in direction of centroid of radio source. The radio centroid falls 30″ to the east of the galaxy in the direction of the stronger component of the double radio source. The intensity ratio of the components is 4:1, and the over-all diameter is 2.1′ in position angle 90°. 200-inch plate by Schmidt.

No. 23.—Type galaxy for class N1. On edge of grouping of around 6 faint galaxies. N1 much brighter than other galaxies in group. Almost starlike on 48-inch E plate. Brightness greatly enhanced on 48-inch O plate, and stellar in appearance. 120-inch Lick plate by E. M. Burbidge.

No. 24.—Probably outlying member of cluster A1367, richness 2. The radio source has a diameter of about 3′ and is displaced by 1.2′ to the northeast from the galaxy.

No. 26.—A member of the Virgo cluster of galaxies, richness 1. Redshift from Humason *et al.* (1965).

No. 27.—According to Sandage, there is absorption in the nucleus (Wade 1960). A member of the Virgo cluster of galaxies, richness 1. Redshift from Humason *et al.* (1956).

No. 28.—Redshift by Schmidt (1963).

No. 29.—A member of the Virgo cluster of galaxies, richness 1. Redshift from Humason *et al.* (1956).

No. 31.—DE2 + DE2 in common envelope. Redshift by Greenstein (1961).

No. 32.—From 48-inch plate by Minkowski, reduced to 4 × 5-inch positive. The distance is that determined by Sersic (1960). The radio source is discussed in the text.

No. 35.—Outstandingly brightest member of a cluster, richness 4:. There are four other galaxies in a tight group surrounding the cD galaxy. Redshift by Minkowski (1960).

No. 36.—DE2 + DE3 in common envelope. In faint, poor cluster.

No. 37.—DE2 + DE3 in common envelope. At edge of faint, elongated cluster, richness 0.

No. 38.—cD2 in D4 envelope. Three condensations in—or projected on—envelope. Outstandingly brightest galaxy in cluster A2052, richness 0.

No. 39.—Near edge of faint cluster, richness 0. Superposed on scattered light from bright star on 200-inch plate by Schmidt.

No. 40.—Three secondary components in same envelope. Outstandingly brightest member of cluster A2199, richness 2. 200-inch plate and redshift by Minkowski (1961*a*).

No. 41.—Partially obscured by star image. Her A is centrally located in very faint cluster of richness

[Notes to Table 1 continued on page 109]

2, visible on 48-inch E plate, and not on 48-inch O plate. All galaxies in this cluster are much fainter than Her A. 200-inch plate by Minkowski. Redshift by Greenstein (1962).

No. 42.—Possibly in very loose, poor clustering, of which it is not the brightest member. Inner, faint clustering on 200-inch plate. 200-inch plate by Minkowski.

No. 45.—Brightest member of faint cluster of richness 0.

No. 46.—Double nucleus. Outstandingly brightest member of a cluster of richness 2:. 200-inch plate by Baade. Redshift by Minkowski (Baade and Minkowski 1954a).

No. 47.—Western of 2 similar galaxies. 200-inch plate by Schmidt.

No. 48.—On edge of clustering. There is a smaller ED1 galaxy on the northern edge of the envelope. The D4: galaxy is the only one with emission lines in its spectrum (Schmidt). 200-inch plate by Minkowski.

No. 49.—D1 + D3 in common envelope. Brightest member of an extended cluster of richness 0. Redshift by Greenstein (1962).

No. 50.—Eccentric envelope. 200-inch plate by Minkowski.

No. 51.—D1 in D5 envelope. Probably located in A2638, richness 2. Very much brighter than any other cluster member. If member of this cluster, type would be cD1 in D5 envelope.

No. 52.—D2 in asymmetric D4 envelope. Round, bright companion in same envelope. In cluster A-2634, richness 1. The radio source is discussed in the text. 200-inch plate by Minkowski.

---

quencies were determined for each source from these plots of fluxes, corrected to the scale of Kellermann (1963), from the following sources: Mills, Slee, and Hill (1958, 1960), Heeschen (1961), Heeschen and Meredith (1961), Goldstein (1962), and Conway, Kellermann, and Long (1963). In order to eliminate any false effects with distance, all the calculations were done in terms of emitted frequencies. Cosmological corrections to the luminosity were made on the assumption that $q_0 = 0$ (Sandage 1961a, b). The form of this correction is shown in equation (1b). The main uncertainty in the calculated radio luminosities comes from the uncertainties in the upper cutoff frequencies, which may be much higher for some sources.

III. DESCRIPTION OF CLASSIFICATION OF THE OPTICAL FORMS

The general classification scheme devised by Morgan (1958) has been modified as follows:

a) Spirals.—These are classified from the single point of view of the relative brightness of the nuclear region of each galaxy to the total brightness of its main body. Since this quantity is well correlated with the integrated spectrum of the nuclear region, the "S" notation has prefixes of "a," "f," "g," or "k," corresponding to the average spectral types of successively brighter nuclear regions. A rough equivalent to the Hubble type is given in Table 2. However, there is no simple transformation between the two systems, because of the multiple criteria employed by Hubble in classifying the spirals.

An inclination class follows the form class (S) on the present system; these are numerals from 1 to 7, with 7 used for an edge-on galaxy. The inclination 0 is not used, because of possible confusion with the Hubble type S0; an S1 spiral on the present system has a circular cross-section. The complete type, then, for a galaxy like M31 would be gkS5.

b) Ellipticals.—The classification is similar to that of Hubble, except that class E0 is not used; an E1 elliptical is considered to have a circular cross-section.

c) D galaxies.—These galaxies have an elliptical-like nucleus surrounded by an extensive envelope. They are of great interest in connection with the classification of radio sources. Some of the optical forms of these sources would be classified S0 on the Hubble system; however, the class S0, as used by Hubble, applies to galaxies having a variety of superficial appearances; that is, a mental picture of a unique galaxy form could not be derived from the class S0. The S0 class was subdivided in the Hubble-Sandage atlas into subgroups which were more nearly homogeneous; however, the S0 galaxies are described in the Hubble-Sandage atlas as being flattened systems; and no D galaxies as defined here are observed to be highly flattened.

The D galaxies occur over a great range in luminosity—both optical and radio. An inspection of D galaxies in the rich clusters of Abell's catalogue (1958) shows that their range in optical luminosity is at least 10–1—and may be considerably greater. In addition, their range in size is great; the supergiant D galaxies observed near the center of a number of Abell's rich clusters have diameters 3–4 times as great as the ordinary lenticulars in the same clusters. These very large D galaxies observed in clusters are given the prefix "c," in a manner similar to the notation for supergiant stars in stellar spectroscopy.

d) The "dumbbells."—This is a group allied to the D galaxies, in which two separated, approximately equal, nuclei are observed in a common envelope. They may well be related to the galaxies which have one or more fainter companions in their envelopes, the dumbbells being the extreme cases of very close multiple galaxies when there are only two equal components.

e) The "N" galaxies.—These are galaxies having brilliant, starlike nuclei containing most of the luminosity of the system. A faint, nebulous envelope of small visible extent is observed.

These N systems may be related to the "compact" galaxies discovered by Zwicky (1963a, b).

f) The quasi-stellar sources.—Galaxies in this category look like stars on photographs taken with the great reflectors; sometimes the starlike images are accompanied by faint

TABLE 2

TYPES OF SPIRALS

Hubble	Morgan
Sc	aS–fgS
Sb	gS–gkS
Sa	kS

nebulous wisps. In the case of the quasi-stellar sources, several criteria are needed to segregate the type. In addition to the starlike appearance, they have a large ultraviolet excess and a large redshift. They can be distinguished spectroscopically from the other strong sources by the great width of the emission lines in their spectra (200-inch spectrograms by Schmidt).

The optical form types in the last column of Table 1 are, therefore, of the following seven categories:
  i) Spirals and Irregulars (S, I)
 ii) Ellipticals (E)
iii) Galaxies having form types intermediate between E and D (ED and DE, with the preceding letter describing the dominant characteristic)
 iv) The D galaxies (D)
  v) The dumbbells (db)
 vi) The N galaxies (N)
vii) The quasi-stellar sources (Qs).

IV. THE OPTICAL FORM GROUPS OF THE RADIO SOURCES

Figure 1 shows the relationship between radio luminosity and the optical form types listed in Table 1. Certain general features are apparent:

a) There is an apparent minimum in the frequency of occurrence near $L = 10^{41}$ erg/sec. The sharp cutoff at $L = 2 \times 10^{41}$ erg/sec is not real, being caused mainly by a radio selection effect (see below), which makes it difficult to observe large-diameter radio sources below a fuzzy limit occurring in this neighborhood. However, since small-diameter objects can be observed below $L = 10^{41}$ erg/sec, there must be a decline in number of D, db, N, and Qs sources below $L = 10^{41}$ erg/sec. From the above considerations there is probably a real minimum in the frequency of occurrence of radio sources near $L = 10^{40}$ erg/sec. We label the sources "strong" and "weak" as they are greater or less than this value.

b) All spiral galaxies identified as radio sources, with the exception of the Seyfert galaxy NGC 1068, are in the "weak" group. When more spirals are investigated, the tail of their distribution may well extend above $L = 10^{40}$ erg/sec.

c) All identified radio galaxies of the types D, db, N, and Qs lie among the "strong" sources.

d) The range in radio luminosity of the D-type radio sources is of the order of 10^4 to 1.

e) The quasi-stellar objects are found among the most luminous sources. The four sources of this type listed in Table 1 have radio luminosities ranging from 2×10^{44} to 2×10^{45} erg/sec. The most luminous of these, and also the most distant object known (3C 147), is rivaled in its radio luminosity only by 3C 295. The quasi-stellar sources form a much more compact group in luminosity than the D-type radio galaxies, but there may be different selection effects in discovery for members of the two groups.

f) The N radio galaxies, which most closely resemble the quasi-stellar group in their optical appearance on direct plates, are of considerably lower radio luminosity than the latter group.

g) From Table 1 it is seen that there are no greatly flattened galaxies among the strong

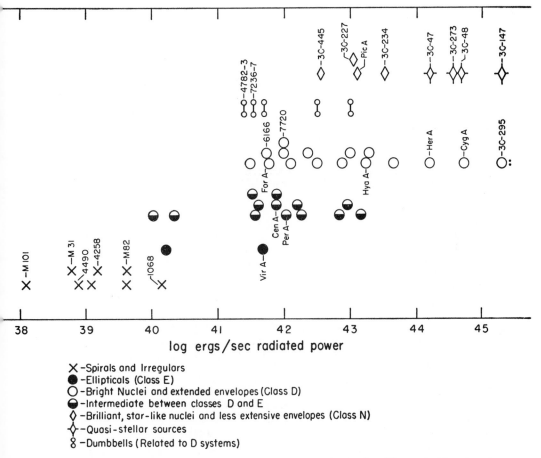

X – Spirals and Irregulars
● – Ellipticals (Class E)
○ – Bright Nuclei and extended envelopes (Class D)
◐ – Intermediate between classes D and E
◇ – Brilliant, star-like nuclei and less extensive envelopes (Class N)
✧ – Quasi-stellar sources
⧂ – Dumbbells (Related to D systems)

Fig. 1.—The relationship between optical form class and radio luminosity. The vertical location of the plotted points has no significance; the form classes have been separated vertically for clarity.

radio sources. This is quite different from the weak sources, where the majority are probably ordinary flattened spirals; this fact suggests the conclusion that the strong sources are intrinsically different from the weak sources.

Selection effects in Figure 1.—The very different factors in discovery conditions for the different groups in Figure 1 almost certainly result in differing selection effects. It seems quite possible that some new quasi-stellar sources will be discovered having luminosities lower than the group illustrated. This may also be true in the case of the N sources. However, the upper limit in radio luminosity for the spirals is probably more trustworthy, since the identified radio spirals are among the brightest optical members of their class.

The distribution of sources near $L = 10^{41}$ erg/sec is influenced by a radio selection effect. This arises because most of the radio observations have been made with two-element interferometers which do not respond to sources of low surface brightness. Thus, although small-diameter, apparently weak sources will be seen, large-diameter ones will not. The effect is roughly the same for the Cambridge 3C instrument and the Caltech interferometer. Single-dish measurements and pencil-beam arrays will be affected differently and will be able to detect sources of lower surface brightness; but they too will be limited eventually by background irregularities, confusion and instrumental baseline instabilities. This limitation means that large-diameter sources which would have values of their radio luminosity less than about 10^{41} erg/sec have not been seen. This does not mean that identifications cannot be made for $L < 10^{41}$ erg/sec for the strong radio sources, since sources of 50 kpc diameter are still easily seen at $L = 10^{40}$ erg/sec.

V. THE RADIO PROPERTIES OF THE OPTICAL FORM GROUPS

1. *Weak Sources, $L < 10^{40}$ erg/sec, "Normal" Spirals, and Irregulars*

Hazard (1963) has recently published a study of ten sources which belong to this category. His results emphasize that these radio sources belong together as a group. He feels that all their spectral indices are near $n \sim 0.5$. Only in the case of NGC 4490 are his values for S_{400} and n in disagreement with the ones used here. If his values are used, L for NGC 4490 becomes 3.9×10^{39} erg/sec, reducing the spread of L for this class of sources. These galaxies are difficult to observe with small radio telescopes because they are apparently very weak sources and tend to be confused with other nearby sources and with background irregularities. The radio structure of these sources is invariably a single source centered on the galaxy. As Hazard has pointed out, in some cases (NGC 1068, NGC 253) the source is much smaller than the galaxy, and is confined to the nuclear region in NGC 1068. In other cases (M31, IC 342), the radio source has a halo component comparable in size to the galaxy, and which contains up to 90 per cent of the flux. The remaining flux is in a small source centered in the nuclear region. None of this class of sources shows the characteristic double radio structure of the strong radio sources.[2] The relationship between the radio structure and the nuclear region of the galaxies suggests that activity in this region is responsible for the radio source, as seems to be the case for the strong radio sources. However, there seems to be clear separation between the strong and weak sources in their optical appearance and in their radio structure. Only NGC 1068 has the radio luminosity of the weakest of the strong radio sources.

2. *Strong Radio Sources, $L > 10^{40}$ erg/sec*

These radio sources cover a range of 2×10^5 in radio luminosity, and their diameters range from ≤ 1 to 500 kpc. In contrast to the weak sources, their radio structure is generally double, the majority of the radio radiation coming from two separate regions usually being symmetrically placed about the parent galaxy. The study of Maltby and

---

[2] The double structure found by Maltby and Moffet (1962) for NGC 253 is not the only model that will fit the observations. A single source having a diameter of approximately 5′, and elongated in the direction of the major axis of the galaxy, is entirely consistent with Maltby's (1962) observations (see also Mathewson and Rome 1963).

Moffet (1962) showed that for all *resolved sources*, about 73 per cent are double, 17 per cent are simple (well described by a single symmetrical Gaussian), and 10 per cent are halo-core objects (a small, bright source near the center, superimposed on a faint extended source). This percentage of simple sources is too large, since about 15 per cent of the doubles would be seen end-on, thus resembling singles. Correcting for the 15–20 per cent of the doubles which are seen end-on, the doubles comprise 80–85 per cent of all resolved radio sources; about 5–10 per cent are simple, and 10 per cent are halo-core objects. These percentages also hold for the *resolved identified sources*. However, at least 28 per cent of the identified sources are smaller than 1′. These sources have a small linear diameter—less than the size of the parent galaxy. In fact, *about 60 per cent of the identified radio sources have components which are no larger than the associated galaxy*, the remaining 40 per cent of the sources being sometimes very much larger than the galaxy. The sizes of the galaxies are discussed in Section VII.

a) D, DE, and E galaxies.—The radio structure of the weakest of the strong radio sources ($L \sim 10^{40}$ erg/sec) tends to be simple; only 3C 270 has the characteristic double structure. This tendency is further strengthened when other identified sources not included in this study are considered.

b) Dumbbell galaxies.—Although there are only five of these objects listed in Table 1, their radio structure seems to differ significantly from the rest of the strong radio sources. Three of the five sources (60 per cent) have a simple radio structure. This should be compared to the 17 per cent of all unidentified radio sources which have that radio structure.

c) N galaxies.—The radio structure of all of these objects is unusually long and narrow when compared to the other strong radio sources. In addition, they show definite signs of having a more complex structure than the simple double-source model; often small-diameter components are suggested by the observations.

d) Quasi-stellar objects.—Most of the quasi-stellar radio sources have one or more components of very small radio diameter. In addition, most of them have a low-frequency turnover in their radio spectrum (Matthews and Sandage 1963). Schmidt and Matthews (1964) show that in many respects 3C 47 has characteristics which do not resemble those of the other quasi-stellar sources. It has a large radio diameter of about 200 kpc with little or no sign of any very small-scale structure, and a steep radio spectrum with no sign of flattening at the low-frequency end; and the optical flux falls on or above an extrapolation of the ($\log S_\nu$ versus $\log \nu$) relation. The full range of characteristics of the quasi-stellar sources will not be known until more objects have been studied. However, we can already state that the radio structure of these objects includes unresolved point sources (3C 48 and 3C 196 [Matthews and Sandage 1963]), doubles (3C 147 [Rowson 1963] and 3C 273 [Hazard, Mackey, and Shimmins 1963]), and halo-core objects (3C 47 [Schmidt and Matthews 1964] and 3C 286 [Matthews and Sandage 1963]).Thus most, if not all, of the radio structures of the other strong radio sources are found in the quasi-stellar radio sources—suggesting that the difference in optical appearance may only be one of time or perhaps some other parameter.

VI. DISCUSSION OF THE RELATIONSHIP OF THE OPTICAL AND RADIO FEATURES

1. *Centaurus A, NGC 5128*

The outer radio contours of Centaurus A show the large extent of this source and its elongation in the north-south direction. On closer examination, Figure 2 suggests that each of the outer sources is composed of two sources. This splitting into several components is seen much more clearly in the Australian 210-foot dish results (Kerr 1962), where at least three components are seen in each of the outer sources. If we include the central source, it would seem that at least four separate events have occurred in the nuclear region of NGC 5128, which have ejected high-energy electrons and magnetic fields in a direction which is approximately that of the major axis of the outer envelope of the galaxy.

This galaxy is known to rotate (Burbidge and Burbidge 1959, 1962) about an axis perpendicular to the absorbing lane; that is, about an axis parallel to the major axis of the outer envelope. In addition, faintly visible on the high-contrast print (see Figs. 3 and 4), there are extensions of the envelope along this same axis which can be followed for about 33' to the northeast (45 kpc), and 28' to the southwest (38 kpc); after which this latter turns and runs about 12' to the northwest (16 kpc). These extensions have already been noted and are illustrated from different plate material by H. M. Johnson (1963). He found a greater extension to the northeast by a factor of 1.2, and in addition some structural details which are too faint to be confirmed by the 48-inch plate. These faint extensions reach out into the nearby part of the outer radio sources. The northeast extension reaches the 20-unit contour line in Figure 2, while the southwest extension reaches the 5-unit contour line before it turns to the northwest.[3] The contour map made from the observations at Parkes with the 210-foot dish[4] (see also Johnson 1963) shows that the northeast extension runs out along a ridge of maximum radio intensity to what looks like a secondary radio maximum. The southwest extension almost reaches the radio minimum, then turns and follows approximately a line of constant flux.

Such optical extensions and elongations along the axis of rotation of a galaxy are very unusual, and are probably impossible to explain as an equilibrium configuration of the gas in a rotating galaxy—and difficult to explain if they are composed of stars. They might be explained by ejection of gas by the activity in the nuclear region which has produced and ejected the radio sources.

2. Fornax A, NGC 1316

Fornax A (Figs. 5 and 6) is the radio source with the strongest known optical extensions. They are illustrated very well in Arp's photograph (Fig. 6; see Arp 1964). The hooklike feature reaches a distance of 30 kpc from the center of the galaxy; it then turns and continues for another 34 kpc, penetrating the half-intensity contour of the strongest radio source and becoming invisible just before reaching the peak of the radio emission. The radio contours are taken from the work of Wade (1961) and include a correction for the effects of antenna beam width. In the center of the galaxy there are some dust clouds, of much less importance than in NGC 5128, but which cross the nucleus of the galaxy in a similar manner. However, their structure away from the nucleus (see Burbidge, Burbidge, and Sandage 1963) is reminiscent of a barred spiral, thus suggesting that the axis of rotation of the galaxy is inclined at a fairly large angle to the plane of the sky. No rotation has been measured for the galaxy. The extensions start out perpendicular to the absorbing lane as in NGC 5128; however, in NGC 1316 the nuclear region is also elongated in this same direction. If the matter has been ejected along the axis of rotation and subsequently moves away from the axis, it would be drawn out into a spiral pattern by the rotation of the galaxy.

The western source is the strongest and has the highest polarization at 10 cm (Gardner and Whiteoak 1963). Its intrinsic polarization angle of 66° for the electric vector is perpendicular to the run of the end of the hooklike feature. In addition, the hook is the strongest of the optical extensions, thus suggesting the effects of a magnetic field. The intrinsic polarization angle of the weaker source (eastern) is 103°, which is roughly perpendicular to the sharp boundary of the fainter extension on that side, which reaches a distance of 49 kpc from the galaxy. It appears that the structure of the optical extensions is intimately related to the radio sources.

3. 3C 465, NGC 7720

This radio source has a complex radio structure (Maltby and Moffet 1962). It has an over-all size of 5'; but there is more than one smaller component, having a diameter <1', within this region. The galaxy NGC 7720 (Figs. 7 and 8) seems to be responsible for most, if not all, of the radio emission. There are other elliptical galaxies nearby which could be

---

[3] The effects of the central double source have been eliminated in this plot.

[4] The central double source is included in the contours of this plot.

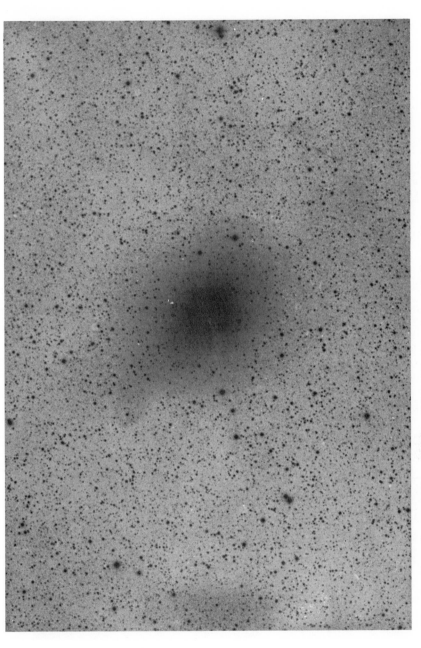

FIG. 3.—The radio source Centaurus A = NGC 5128. Print from 48-inch 103a-E plate + red Plexiglass filter by Minkowski. Note outer extensions in directions normal to equatorial absorbing band.

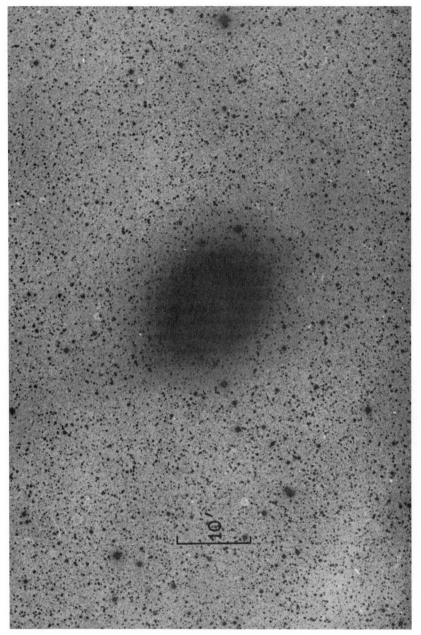

10′

FIG. 4.—The radio source Centaurus A = NGC 5128. Same data as Fig. 3

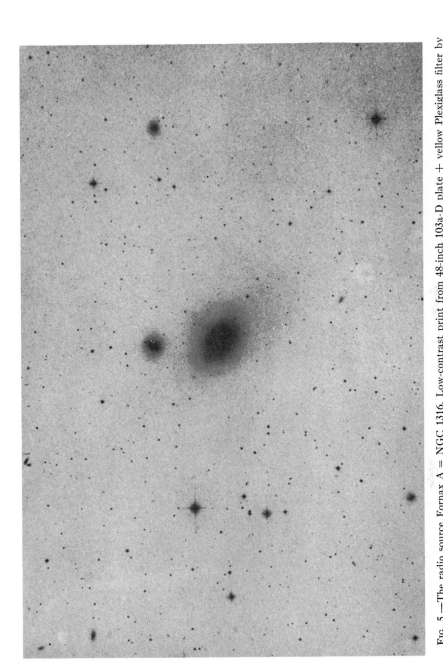

Fig. 5.—The radio source Fornax A = NGC 1316. Low-contrast print from 48-inch 103a-D plate + yellow Plexiglass filter by E. Herzog.

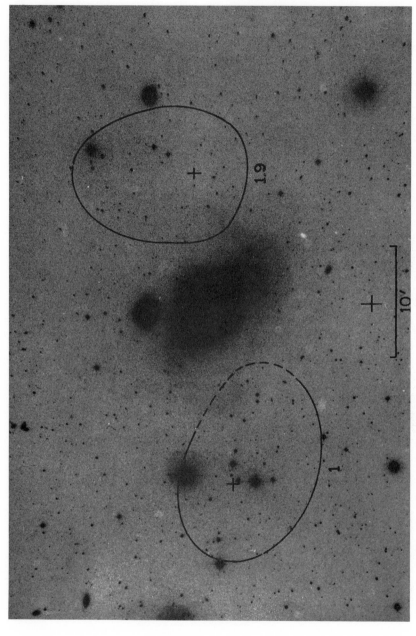

Fɪɢ. 6.—The radio source Fornax A = NGC 1316. High-contrast print from three superposed 48-inch 103a-J plates + Wratten 4 filter, by Arp (1964). Half-intensity radio contours are plotted; crosses locate positions of peak radio intensity.

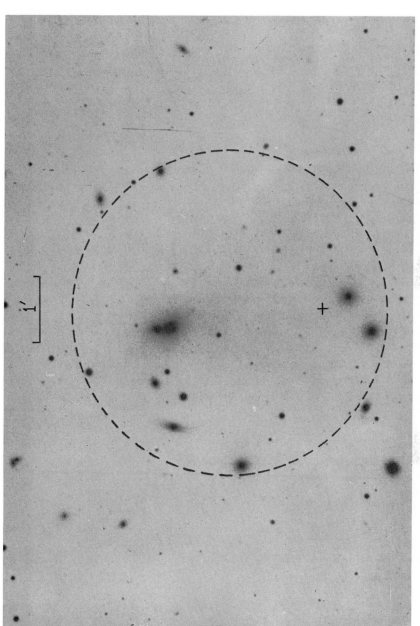

Fɪɢ. 7.—The radio source 3C 465 = NGC 7720. Print from 200-inch 103a-O plate by Minkowski. The dashed curve is the half-intensity radio contour; the cross represents the mean error in the radio position.

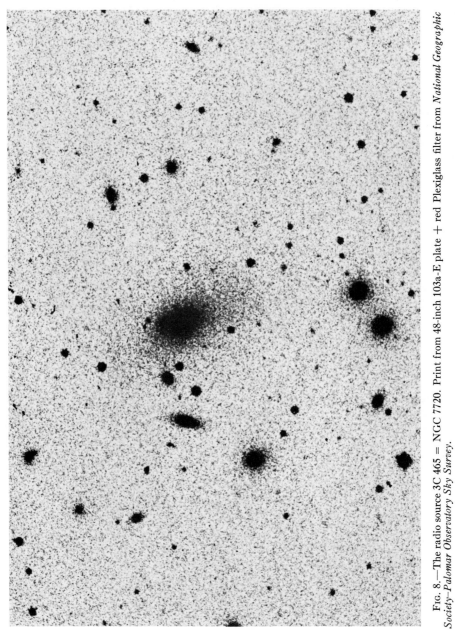

FIG. 8.—The radio source 3C 465 = NGC 7720. Print from 48-inch 103a-E plate + red Plexiglass filter from *National Geographic Society–Palomar Observatory Sky Survey.*

weak radio sources; however, none of them gives any indication of being peculiar. If one of them were like 3C 270 (NGC 4261), which is an ED galaxy, then it would only contribute about $\frac{1}{40}$ of the total flux. The object 3C 465 is very probably a displaced source, and it seems significant that the centroid of radio emission falls on the strong, asymmetrical, southern extension of NGC 7720 as shown in Figure 7.

4. *3C 33*

The galaxy has a circular nucleus (2.5″ in diameter) imbedded in an elongated structure (3.3″ × 8.4″), whose minor axis is in position angle 163°. This latter constitutes the main body of the galaxy. There is a faint outer envelope, which can be seen to a diameter of 9.4″ × 22″, and which is extended along this same "minor" axis. Spectra of the galaxy have been taken by M. Schmidt. A spectrogram orientated east-west shows inclined emission lines, while a spectrogram with the slit orientated north-south shows no inclination of the emission lines. The shape of the main body of the galaxy, and the spectral evidence, suggest that the galaxy is rotating about an axis in position angle 163°. Again we have the anomalous extension of the outer envelope along the axis of rotation. The radio source is known to be double with a separation of 3.8′ ± 0.6′ in position angle 18° ± 3° (Maltby and Moffet 1962; Lequeux 1962). Thus the outer envelope is extended in much the same direction as the line joining the radio components, the angular difference being 35°. The radio source is unusual since the diameter of the components is certainly less than 20″ (Lequeux 1962) and is probably about 4″ in diameter (Allen, Anderson, Conway, Palmer, Reddish, and Rowson 1962). The sources are comparable in size to the nuclear region of the galaxy, even though they are each at a distance of about 100 kpc from the galaxy. The cosmic-ray particles must have been tightly confined since their ejection, presumably by a magnetic field. The source has a polarization of 8 per cent at 10.6 cm (Seielstad, Morris, and Radhakrishnan 1963), which is a higher value than is found for most sources. The intrinsic polarization angle of 101° shows that the magnetic vector is intermediate between the orientation of the radio source and the outer envelope. The high degree of polarization indicates that the magnetic field is fairly well aligned.

VII. THE PROBLEM OF THE D GALAXIES

A survey of the richest clusters of galaxies listed by Abell has resulted in the discovery of a number of clusters having a single (or multiple) dominating, large, centrally located galaxy of the D type; in most cases, these are not radio sources. In appearance these supergiant galaxies seem to be no different from the cD galaxies identified as strong radio sources; both are located in clusters of galaxies, and dominate the clusters in which they occur. In addition, none of these objects is highly flattened.

Of the twenty-six clusters in Abell's catalogue having richness 2 and greater, and distance-group 4 or less, there are ten clusters of this type (which we shall label cD clusters); of these ten, only one (A2199) is a known radio source. The ten cD clusters are listed in Table 3.

Using a round figure of 15 kpc for the diameter of the main body of the larger lenticulars in clusters, we derive the approximate linear diameters of the optical envelopes of the cD galaxies, listed in the last column of Table 3. They are only intended to be rough approximations; more accurate diameters should be derivable from the redshift distances.

It can be seen that the cD galaxies as defined in Table 3 are objects of considerable interest because of their size. The explanation as to why some are strong radio sources and others are not known to be radio sources at all is an interesting problem for the future. About one-fourth of the strong radio sources plotted in Figure 1 are cD galaxies in clusters.

The diameters of the cD galaxies in Table 3 can be compared to the diameters of the galaxies associated with radio sources. Table 4 gives the results of some measurements on 48-inch and 200-inch plates for six galaxies. The major axes are visible out to diameters of 38–66 kpc and average around 50 kpc. The galaxies must have significant densities even farther out, perhaps as far as 100 kpc. Thus a large percentage of radio sources are actually still imbedded in the parent galaxy, while only the very large halo and double sources are well outside the galaxy.

VIII. ARE RADIO SOURCES COLLIDING GALAXIES?

The evidence now seems to be conclusive that extragalactic radio sources are not, as a class, colliding galaxies. The optical form families described, and illustrated in Figure 1, seem to refer to individual—rather than to colliding—galaxies.

TABLE 3

CD CLUSTERS OF GALAXIES

(Distance < 5; Richness > 1)

No.	Abell	Dis-tance	Rich-ness	Brightest Galaxy	Diameter of cD Galaxy in Units of Lenticulars	Diameter of cD Galaxy in kpc
1.	389	4	2	cD2 in D5 envelope	$2\frac{1}{2}$	38
2.	401	3	2	cD2 in D5 envelope	4	60
3.	754	3	2	cD4	3	45
4.	787	4	2	cD3 in D4 envelope	4	60
5.	1775	4	2	cD3	3	45
6.	1795	4	2	cD3	$2\frac{1}{2}$	38
7.	1904	3	2	{cD1 in D4 envelope / D1 + D1 in cD5 envelope	3 / 3	45 / 45
8.	2029	4	2	cD2 in D5 envelope	5	75
9.	2199	1	2	cD4	4	60
10.	2670	4	3	cD2	$2\frac{1}{2}$	38

NOTES TO TABLE 3

No. 2.—A401. Cluster elongation 5, in same position angle as D5 envelope. Rich and compact.

No. 4.—A787. cD3 + companion, in common D4 envelope.

No. 5.—A1775. 2 equal, circular nuclei in common envelope.

No. 6.—A1795. Second—and possibly third—condensation within same envelope.

No. 8.—A2029. Elongated nuclear region of cluster similar in orientation to D5 envelope. Standard type for cD galaxies.

No. 9.—A2199. Radio source 3C 338 (see Table 1). Several condensations in common envelope of cD4.

No. 10.—A2670. Compact cluster.

TABLE 4

OPTICAL DIAMETERS OF GALAXIES ASSOCIATED WITH RADIO SOURCES

Source	Visible Size of Galaxy (kpc)	Notes
For A.	51 × 37	Omitting extensions (see text)
Cen A.	38 × 31	Omitting extensions (see text)
3C 317.	60 × 34	. . . .
3C 338.	53 × 32	*
Cyg A.	48 × 32	. . . .
3C 465.	66 × 29	. . . .

* Minkowski (1961a) has photoelectrically measured a diameter of the major axis of 68 kpc to an isophote of 25 mag/sq. sec of arc.

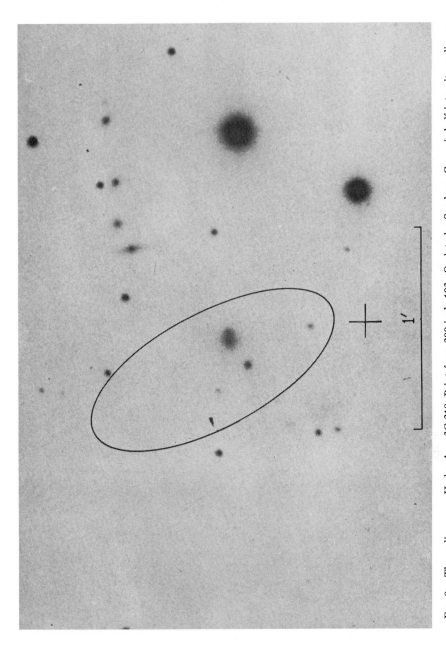

FIG. 9.—The radio source Hydra A = 3C 218. Print from 200-inch 103a-O plate by Sandage. Curve is half-intensity radio contour; the cross represents the mean error in the radio position.

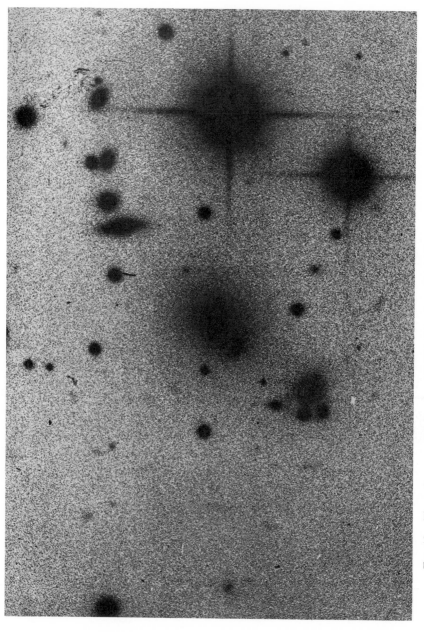

Fɪɢ. 10.—The radio source Hydra A = 3C 218. Print from 200-inch 103a-O plate + GG 1 filter by Baade

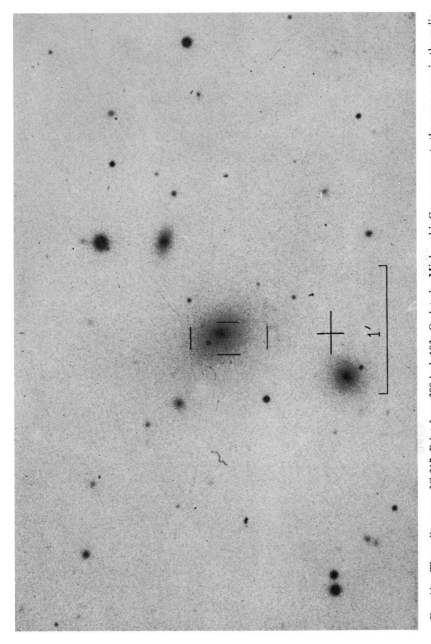

Fig. 11.—The radio source 3C 317. Print from 200-inch 103a-O plate by Minkowski. Cross represents the mean error in the radio position; short lines give positions of radio half-intensity.

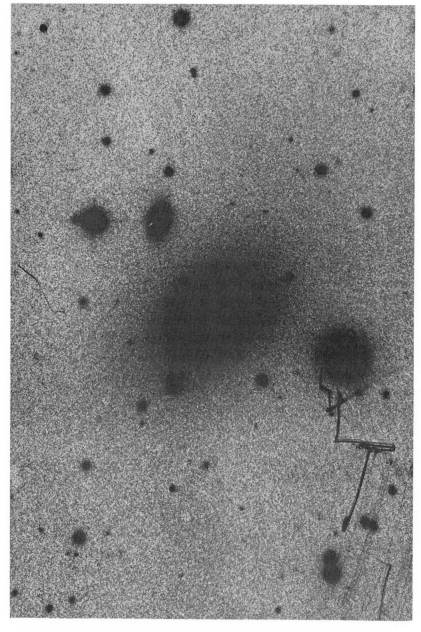

Fig. 12.—The radio source 3C 317. Print from 200-inch 103a-D plate + GG 11 filter by Minkowski

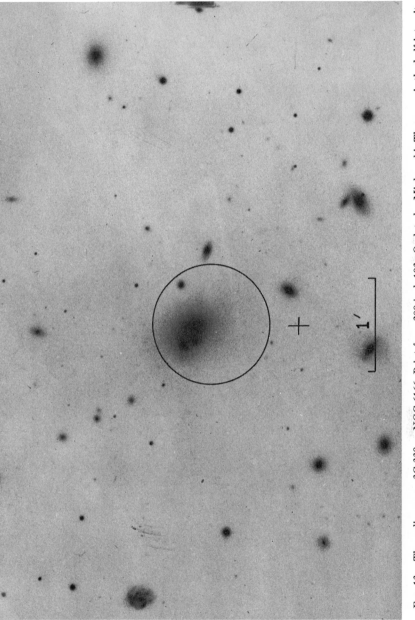

Fig. 13.—The radio source 3C 338 = NGC 6166. Print from 200-inch 103a-O plate by Minkowski. The curve is the half-intensity radio contour; the cross represents the mean error in the radio position.

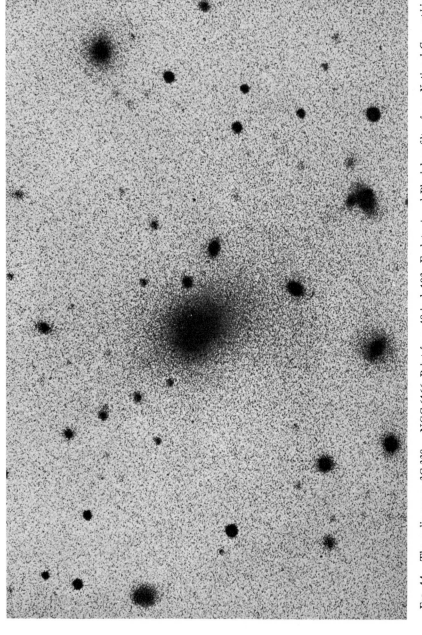

FIG. 14.—The radio source 3C 338 = NGC 6166. Print from 48-inch 103a-E plate + red Plexiglass filter from *National Geographic Society–Palomar Observatory Sky Survey.*

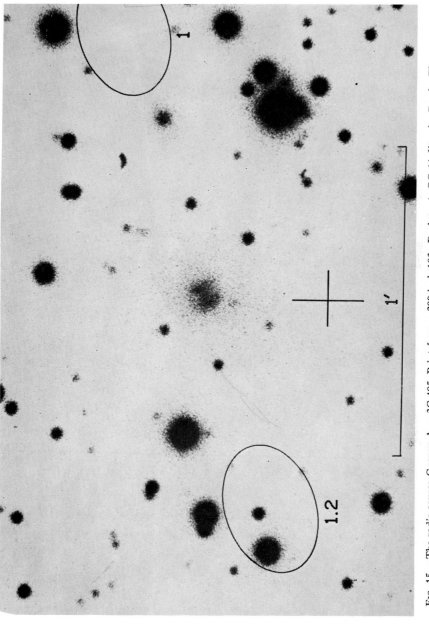

Fig. 15.—The radio source Cygnus A = 3C 405. Print from a 200-inch 103a-D plate + GG 11 filter by Baade. The cross represents the mean error in the radio position. The curves are half-intensity radio contours.

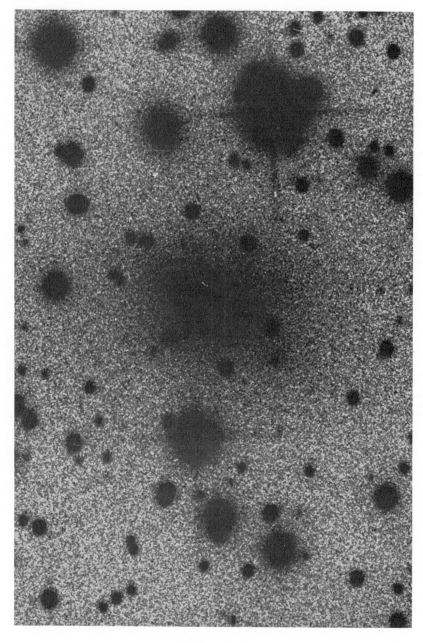

FIG. 16.—The radio source Cygnus A = 3C 405. High-contrast print from same plate as Fig. 15

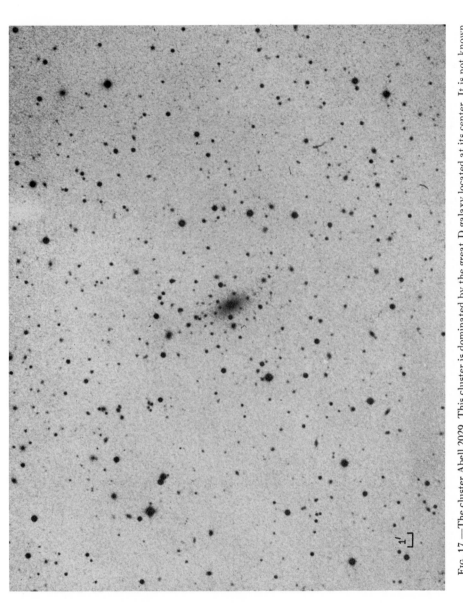

FIG. 17.—The cluster Abell 2029. This cluster is dominated by the great D galaxy located at its center. It is not known to be a radio source; however, its appearance is similar to that of some strong radio sources. 48-inch 103a-E plate + red Plexiglass filter from *National Geographic Society–Palomar Observatory Sky Survey.*

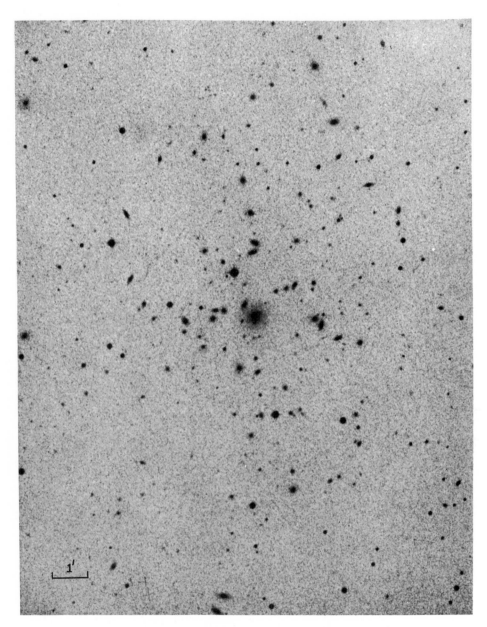

FIG. 18.—The cluster Abell 2670. See legend and data for Fig. 17

IX. RADIO SOURCES AND CLUSTERS OF GALAXIES

Figures 7–16 illustrate radio galaxies which are located in clusters. In each case, the radio galaxy dominates the cluster in which it is located, and is of the D form-class (elliptical-like nucleus, surrounded by an extensive envelope). Figures 17 and 18 show clusters Abell 2029 and 2670, both of which are dominated by centrally located D galaxies of supergiant dimensions. In these respects they resemble the radio sources illustrated in Figures 7–16; however, the supergiant D galaxies illustrated in Figures 17 and 18 are not known to be radio sources.

The galaxies which obviously occur in clusters are indicated in the notes to Table 1. Some of the clusters are not included in Abell's catalogue (Abell 1958) for one of several reasons: they fall outside the region of the sky he considers; they are of richness 0 (for

TABLE 5

OCCURRENCE OF RADIO SOURCES AS A
FUNCTION OF RICHNESS OF CLUSTER

Richness	No. of Radio Sources	Normalized Frequency of Cluster Richness (Abell)
No cluster........	10*	....
Poor cluster.......	9	....
Richness 0........	7	....
Richness 1........	7	22.4
Richness 2........	7	7
Richness 3........	0	1.2
Richness 4........	1	0.11
Richness 5........	0	0.02

* The quasi-stellar objects have been excluded from this table, but would be found in this category.

which his list is incomplete); or they are too faint to be included in his catalogue. For these clusters the richness group has been estimated in the manner used by Abell. The richness of the Virgo cluster was determined from the material of de Vaucouleurs (1961), and that of the Fornax I cluster was derived from material supplied by Zwicky (private communication). Table 5 gives the number of identifications as a function of richness of the cluster in which they are located. At least two of those in the "no cluster" category are known to be in small groups of about six galaxies. The quasi-stellar sources have been omitted, since for 3C 47 and 3C 147 no plate material exists on which any cluster of galaxies could be seen. 3C 48 and 3C 273 are not located in clusters of galaxies.

Table 5 shows that about 50 per cent of the parent galaxies are in clusters of richness greater than or equal to 0.[5] Further, one-third of the galaxies are in clusters having a richness ≥ 1. On the other hand about 20 per cent occur either as single objects or at least in very small groups of galaxies. In the last column of Table 5 the expected occurrence of the various richness groups is calculated, based on the clusters in Abell's catalogue. The expected frequency is normalized to agree at richness 2. The number of galaxies expected in the first three categories is very much higher than that in richness 2. The comparison between the second and third columns shows that the radio sources tend to occur in clusters of richness about 2. They probably occur with equal probability in clusters of richness greater than 2, but the number of identifications is not sufficient to make any statement.

[5] The association of radio sources and clusters of galaxies is not a new idea (see Minkowski, *Problems of Extragalactic Research*, ed. G. C. McVittie [New York: Macmillan Co., 1962], p. 201, and other references given there).

We are indebted to Dr. Allan Sandage for the determinations of the distances for several spiral galaxies; we are also indebted to Drs. Sandage, Minkowski, Zwicky, E. M. Burbidge, and W. Tifft for the use of plate material. We wish to thank also Dr. Arp for the reproduction of his remarkable multi-negative print of For A.

One of us (W. W. M.) wishes to acknowledge continued financial support from the Office of Naval Research for his project on the classification of the forms of galaxies. He also wishes to express his deepest thanks to Dr. I. S. Bowen, director of the Mount Wilson–Palomar Observatories, and to Dr. J. L. Greenstein, for the privileges extended to him as guest investigator. The work in radio astronomy at the California Institute of Technology is supported by the United States Office of Naval Research under contract Nonr 220(19).

REFERENCES

Abell, G. O. 1958, *Ap. J. Suppl.*, **3**, 211.
Allen, L. R., Anderson, B., Conway, R. G., Palmer, H. P., Reddish, V. C., and Rowson, B. 1962, *M.N.*, **124**, 477.
Arp, H. 1964, *Ap. J.*, **139**, 1378.
Baade, W., and Minkowski, R. 1954a, *Ap. J.*, **119**, 206.
———. 1954b, *ibid.*, p. 215.
Bolton, J. G., and Clark, B. G. 1960, *Pub. A.S.P.*, **72**, 29.
Burbidge, E. M., and Burbidge, G. R. 1959, *Ap. J.*, **129**, 271.
———. 1962, *Nature*, **194**, 367.
Burbidge, G. R., Burbidge, E. M., and Sandage, A. R. 1963, *Rev. Mod. Phys.*, **35**, 947.*
Conway, R. G., Kellermann, K. I., and Long, R. J. 1963, *M.N.*, **125**, 261.
Gardner, F. F., and Whiteoak, J. B. 1963, *Nature*, **197**, 1162.
Goldstein, S. 1962, *A.J.*, **67**, 171.
Greenstein, J. L. 1961, *Ap. J.*, **133**, 335.
———. 1962, *ibid.*, **135**, 679.
Greenstein, J. L., and Matthews, T. A. 1963, *Nature*, **197**, 1041.*
Hazard, C. 1963, *M.N.*, **126**, 489.
Hazard, C., Mackey, M. B., and Shimmins, A. J. 1963, *Nature*, **197**, 1037.*
Heeschen, D. S. 1961, *Ap. J.*, **133**, 322.
Heeschen, D. S., and Meredith, B. 1961, *Pub. N.R.A.O.*, **1**, 121.
Humason, M. L., Mayall, N. U., and Sandage, A. R. 1956, *A.J.*, **61**, 97.
Johnson, H. M. 1963, *Pub. N.R.A.O.*, **1**, 251.
Kellermann, K. I. 1963, Thesis, California Institute of Technology.
Kerr, F. J. 1962, *Sky and Telescope*, **24**, 254.
Lequeux, J. 1962, *Ann. d'ap.*, **25**, 221.
Maltby, P. 1961, *Nature*, **191**, 793.
———. 1962, *Ap. J. Suppl.*, **7**, 124.
Maltby, P., Matthews, T. A., and Moffet, A. T. 1963, *Ap. J.*, **137**, 153.*
Maltby, P., and Moffet, A. T. 1962, *Ap. J., Suppl.* **7**, 141.
Mathewson, D. S., and Rome, J. M. 1963, *Observatory*, **83**, 20.
Matthews, T. A., and Sandage, A. R. 1963, *Ap. J.*, **138**, 30.*
Mills, B. Y., Slee, O. B., and Hill, E. R. 1958, *Australian J. Phys.*, **11**, 360.
———. 1960, *ibid.*, **13**, 676.
Minkowski, R. 1958, *Pub. A.S.P.*, **70**, 143.
———. 1960, *Ap. J.*, **132**, 908.
———. 1961a, *A.J.*, **66**, 558.
———. 1961b, *Proceedings of the Fourth Berkeley Symposium on Mathematical Statistics and Probability*, ed. J. Neyman (Berkeley: University of California Press), **4**, 245.
Morgan, W. W. 1958, *Pub. A.S.P.*, **70**, 364.
Rowson, B. 1963, *M.N.*, **125**, 177.
Sandage, A. R. 1961a, *Ap. J.*, **133**, 355.
———. 1961b, *ibid.*, **134**, 916.
Schmidt, M. 1963, *Nature*, **197**, 1040.*
Schmidt, M., and Matthews, T. A. 1964, *Ap. J.*, **139**, 781.*
Seielstad, G. A., Morris, D., and Radhakrishnan, V. 1963, *Ap. J.*, **138**, 602.
Sersic, J. L. 1960, *Zs. f. Ap.*, **51**, 64.
Vaucouleurs, G. de. 1961, *Ap. J. Suppl.*, **6**, 213.
Wade, C. M. 1960, *Observatory*, **80**, 235.
———. 1961, *Pub. N.R.A.O.*, **1**, 99.
Zwicky, F. 1959, *Hdb. d. Phys.*, ed. S. Flügge (Berlin: Springer-Verlag), **53**, 390.
———. 1963a, *C.R.*, **257**, 2240.
———. 1963b, Reported in *Carnegie Inst. Washington Yearbook*, No. **62**, p. 32.

THE STRUCTURE OF THE EXTRA-GALACTIC RADIO SOURCES

chapter 11

C. Hazard

The extra-galactic radio sources have generally been considered to fall into two main classes, (*a*) "normal galaxies" with a total emission at meter wavelengths of the order or less than 10^{21} W $(c/s)^{-1}$ ster.$^{-1}$; (*b*) "radio galaxies" with a corresponding total emission of up to about 10^{27} W $(c/s)^{-1}$ ster^{-1}. There is no clear-cut definition of a normal galaxy, but a galaxy is generally considered to be "normal" if it exhibits no obvious optical pecularity and its total emission is not greatly in excess of that from the Galaxy or the Andromeda Nebula (M31). They have been studied by surveying the brightest of the nearby galaxies, usually using a pencil-beam technique. About fifty of these bright nebulae have now been detected as radio emitters and for the most part these are spirals of type Sb or Sc. The few irregular-type galaxies which have been detected appear to be weaker radio emitters relative to their light output than the spirals by about 3 mag., while none of the nearby elliptical galaxies has been detected, and they also appear to be weak radio emitters. It is convenient to express the ratio of radio to light emission by a radio index $R = m_R - m_{pg}$, and it is found that for spiral galaxies the value of R is $+1.3$ with an r.m.s. dispersion of ± 0.7; the values of R for irregulars and ellipticals are $+$ and >3, respectively.

The "radio galaxies" are associated with giant galaxies, usually elliptical, with absolute photographic magnitudes of the order of -20. Some, such as NGC 4486 (Virgo A) with its well-known jet, are obviously peculiar, but more usually there is no distinguishing optical feature. The values of R range from about -1 for NGC 1068 to -13 for Cygnus A. It is this very large range in the values of R relative to the small dispersion of ± 0.7 found for the nearby spirals that justifies the separation of the radio sources into "normal" and "radio" galaxies.

THE STRUCTURE OF NORMAL SPIRAL GALAXIES

M31 is the most intensively studied of the normal spirals. It was found that in this case about 90 per cent of the radio emission arises in an extensive corona which envelops the visible nebula and about 10 per cent in a small central concentration, and it appeared likely that the majority of the normal spirals had a similar structure. Recent work has

---

C. Hazard, the University of Sydney, Australia.

shown that the situation is more complex and that the normal spirals range from objects like M31 to objects like NGC 253 where the radiation arises in a source comparable in size to the nucleus of the galaxy. In view of the large differences in the distribution of radio brightness from galaxy to galaxy, the small dispersion in the measured values of the radio index implying a small dispersion in absolute radio magnitude appears rather puzzling.

As the possession of an extensive corona is apparently not common to all spiral nebulae, it is unlikely that supernovae, which occur in all spirals, are the source of the high-energy electrons responsible for the coronal emission by synchroton radiation. The observations of NGC 253 and similar objects where the emission is highly concentrated to the nucleus suggest rather that it is the nucleus itself which is the source of the relativistic electrons. The mechanism is probably catastrophic and may resemble that responsible for the emission from abnormal elliptical galaxies where the conditions are similar to those in the central region of a spiral. It may be that, whereas the lifetime of an excited elliptical galaxy is comparatively short, the lifetime of a spiral is prolonged by the trapping of electrons emitted from the excited nucleus in the magnetic fields associated with the spiral structure. This would account for the fact that so far none of the nearby elliptical galaxies but the majority of the bright spirals have been observed as radio sources. If this assumption is correct, then not all of the bright spirals should be detectable radio emitters, a conclusion supported by the results of an unpublished 237 Mc/s survey in which a number of bright spirals were not detected, although they would have been above the detection limit if the radio index were constant for all spirals.

THE STRUCTURE OF "RADIO GALAXIES"

It is generally considered that the isotropically distributed Class II sources, that is, the majority of the sources with a galactic latitude $|b|$ greater than about 10°, are associated with the "radio galaxies." The general structure of these sources may therefore be investigated by studying the diameters and brightness distributions of these high-latitude sources. For a few of the more intense and extended sources the brightness distributions have been studied in some detail using either narrow pencil-beam or interferometer techniques and where optical identifications are available the brightness distributions related to the structure of the optical galaxy. Where such a comparison has been possible, for example, Cygnus A and Centaurus A, it is found that in general the two distributions are radically different. The radio source is generally larger than the associated optical galaxy; it is often double, with the components situated on either side of the visible object; it may be single but apparently not coincident with its associated galaxy or even associated with two visible galaxies. For the majority of sources, however, the radio source is so small that only a general idea of its structure can be obtained and a detailed comparison with the optical object is not possible. Thus most of the information on the structure of the radio galaxies is of a statistical nature based on studies of the diameter distributions of the Class II sources. The two most extensive investigations are the long base-line interferometer observations made at the California Institute of Technology, both groups being concerned with a statistical investigation of the high-latitude Class II sources listed in the Cambridge 3C catalogue and the catalogue of Mills, Slee, and Hill.

Caltech Observations

These observations carried out by Maltby and Moffett covered a total of 195 sources of which 174 were probably extragalactic. Of these 75 were resolved, and all but 13 were found to be complex. Of the 55 complex sources, 15 had two components of equal intensity, 40 had two components of unequal intensity, and 7 were found to contain a bright core surrounded by an extensive halo. The 21 galactic sources were found in general to consist of a single emitting region.

Jodrell Bank Observations

A total of 384 sources was studied, 324 from the 3C list and 60 from the list of Mills, Slee, and Hill (hereinafter abbreviated as "MSH"). The observations were made at a frequency of 158.5 Mc/s using an interferometer at a number of base lines up to a maximum of 100 km. corresponding to a resolution of about 1 sec. The detailed analysis was restricted to 133 sources with a flux density of 12×10^{-26} W m^{-2} (c/s)$^{-1}$ and galactic latitude $|b| \geq 12°$. Of these 133 sources, 50 per cent were found to have angular sizes of $\geq 23''$ and 90 per cent to have an angular size of $\geq 3''$, on the assumption of a single circular Gaussian distribution. However, it was clear from a comparison of the fringe visibilities at the different base lines that a single Gaussian component was not an adequate model for the majority of the sources but that a large fraction must be complex; it was suggested that at least 30 per cent must be double.

A more detailed study of 55 of the sources common to the list of Maltby and Moffett indicated that at least 23 must be multiple, and, allowing for selection effects, it was suggested that at least two-thirds of the 55 sources were multiple. Assuming the sources to be double, the ratio of median separation to median component size is about 4.1. Thus, like the Caltech observations, the Jodrell Bank observations indicate that a large fraction of the extra-galactic sources are complex in structure.

However, the Jodrell Bank observations with their high resolution revealed one more interesting fact about the radio sources. Of the 133 sources analyzed, 12 have been identified with "radio galaxies" for which redshifts are available, and consequently the linear sizes of the radio sources can be calculated. It was found that the average linear size of these sources was about 25 kpc which is comparable to the average size of a galaxy. Yet 10 sources were found to have angular sizes less than the asymptotic limit (1.7") for objects of size 25 kpc in the steady-state model and 22 to have sizes less than the corresponding limit (5") in an Einstein–de Sitter model. This was the first indication of the existence of a third class of source, the starlike radio sources, which have been discussed in some detail in earlier papers. We will for convenience call these sources "stellar galaxies," although when the first few of these small diameter sources, namely, 3C 48, 3C 196, and 3C 286, were identified, it was thought that they were peculiar stars in the Galaxy. It was not until the identification of 3C 273 with a thirteenth-magnitude stellar object made possible by the accurate position obtained by the method of lunar occultations and the measurement of its redshift by M. Schmidt that it was recognized that, rather than being stars in the Galaxy, they were in fact a new type of astronomical object. As we now know, both 3C 273 and 3C 48 are extra-galactic objects some 3 mag. brighter than the brightest known field and cluster galaxies, yet with dimensions comparable to the size of a galactic nucleus rather than the Galaxy itself.

LUNAR OCCULTATION OBSERVATIONS

The Method of Lunar Occultations

The long base-line interferometer observations show that a study of the radio sources, in particular the "stellar galaxies," requires a resolution of a fraction of a second of arc. In addition, if the source is to be identified and the radio and optical data compared, then accurate positions (to the order of 1") must be measured not only for the whole source but also for the individual components. The only technique which seems to fulfil these requirements is "the method of lunar occultations." This method can be used either to carry out a survey of the radio sources or to measure the positions and investigate the structure of sources for which occultation predictions are available. Both methods require a large steerable telescope such as the 250-foot and the 210-foot instruments at Jodrell Bank and Parkes, respectively, although for the abovementioned sources much useful work can be carried out with smaller instruments. The survey technique has been described by the author, and an account of such a survey will be published shortly. A survey of this type is useful for detecting and measuring the positions of weak sources not already catalogued. However, the majority of radio sources with a flux density sufficiently high to enable the occultation curves, and hence the source structure, to be studied in detail are already catalogued and reasonably accurate occultation predictions available. In these cases the following observing procedure is adopted. At approximately 30 min. before the predicted time of occultation, the aerial beam is directed toward the source and the received power recorded throughout the period of the occultation. The passage of the source behind the Moon is revealed by a sharp fall in level as the source disappears behind the Moon's limb followed by a corresponding rise as it reappears. At high frequencies where the areal beam is small compared to the size of the Moon and the Moon's contribution to the received power is large compared to that from the source, the motion of the Moon through the aerial beam produces a severe gradient in the received power. This makes difficult the detection of the relatively small change in flux due to the occultation of the source and necessitates the use of a small receiver gain. To overcome this difficulty, instead of tracking the source the aerial beam is used to track the Moon's limb at the calculated points of immersion and emersion.

To a close approximation the limb of the Moon may be considered as a straight diffracting edge, and, for an ideal receiver with zero time constant and band width, the observed occultation-curve for a point source is a straight-edge diffraction pattern. For a source of finite size the observed pattern is the convolution of the straight-edge diffraction pattern with the one-dimensional (or strip) brightness distribution of the source in a direction perpendicular to the limb of the Moon at the point of occultation. The diffraction lobes are therefore smeared out in a manner depending on the size and structure of the source. As the observed pattern represents the progressive obscuration of an infinite plane wave, it is clear that it embodies all Fourier components of the strip distribution of brightness both in amplitude and phase and that it can be inverted by a suitable procedure to recover this distribution. A method of carrying out this inversion has been described by Scheuer. The structure can also be inferred from the amplitude of the diffraction lobes; indeed, as the size of a Fresnel zone at the limit of the Moon is only $10''$ at 410 Mc/s and $6''$ at 1420 Mc/s, it is possible to distinguish structure as small as $1''$ from a simple inspection of the observed occultation-curve. The fundamental limitations to the degree of resolution attainable are set by (1) the finite size of the Moon; (2) confusion by weak sources near the limit of the Moon at the time of occultation of the source under observation; (3) the irregularities in the Moon's limb; and (4) the finite size of the aerial system. The limitations set by both (1) and (2) are probably of the order of $0.01''$. That set by (3) is difficult to estimate as it depends on the form of the irregularities but is probably of the same order. Surprisingly, the limitations set by the aerial system is more serious. The aerial system may be considered as a probe which samples the radiation field of the diffraction pattern as it moves across the ground and therefore smooths out all details of the pattern comparable in size to the aerial aperture. Consequently, the resolution is limited to the angle subtended by the Earth at the Moon's distance, and for the Parkes telescope this is about $0.04''$. However, this is still smaller than the limitation imposed by the finite-receiver time constant and band width of an actual receiver, the time constant imposing a limit of about $0.3''$/sec and the band width a limitation which varies with frequency but is about $0.3''$ for a 1 per cent band width at 1420 Mc/s and $0.6''$ at 410 Mc/s.

For each complete occultation observed the times of immersion and emersion define two positions for the center of the Moon and hence two circles of radii equal to the respective semidiameters of the Moon. The points of intersection of these two circles then give two possible positions of the source, one on either side of the Moon's path and perpendicular to its direction of motion. The ambiguity in position can be resolved by

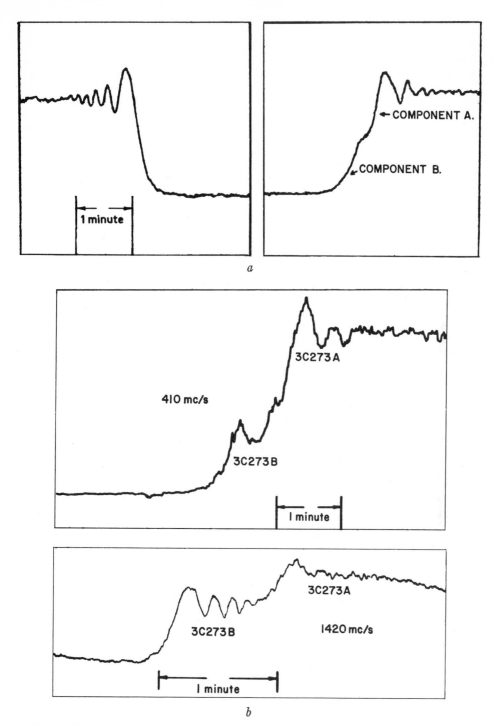

Fig. 1.—(a) 410 Mc/s occultation-curves of 3C 273 as observed on August 5, 1962. (b) 410 Mc/s and 1420 Mc/s immersion-curves of October 26, 1962.

observing a second occultation, although for the stronger sources the positions are already known with sufficient accuracy to make this unnecessary. The positional accuracy depends on the circumstances of the occultation and the angular size of the source, but for the small angular size sources it is possible to estimate the times of occultation, either from the lobe pattern or from the brightness distribution derived using the method of Scheuer, to an accuracy of about 0.1 sec. corresponding to a positional accuracy of the order of or less than 0.1″. In practice the accuracy is limited by uncertainties in the position of the limb of the Moon to about 1″.

The diameter measurements of the equivalent strip source always refer to a direction perpendicular to the Moon's center, and in general the observations at immersion and emersion refer to two different axes across the source. Observations of further occultations define additional axes and hence give a detailed picture of the source structure.

The Structure of 3C 273

The first source to be studied in detail using the occultation technique was 3C 273. The structure of this source was deduced from observation of two occultations on August 5 and October 6, 1962, at frequencies of 136 Mc/s, 410 Mc/s, and 1420 Mc/s. Figure 1, *a* shows the immersion-curves of August 5 as observed at 410 Mc/s. The double nature of the source is shown by the marked step at the 50 per cent point of the immersion-curve, while the absence of this step on the emersion-curve indicates that the source is oriented in such a way that the two components reappeared almost simultaneously. The prominent diffraction fringes show that the angular sizes of both components must be considerably less than 10″, which is the order of size of a Fresnel zone at the Moon's limb. The double nature of the source is more clearly shown in Figure 1, *b*, which shows the 410-Mc/s and 1420-Mc/s immersion-curves of October 26, 1962. At 1420 Mc/s, the smaller angular size of Component B relative to Component A is clearly shown by the more prominent diffraction fringes.

The structure of 3C 273 as deduced from the 410 Mc/s-observations is illustrated in Figure 2. At this frequency, the flux from Component A is approximately twice that from Component B. However, the spectrum of A is steeper than that of B, the spectral index (n) of A being -0.9 compared to a value of 0.0 for B; it is assumed that, in each case, the spectrum is of the form $S \propto f^n$. It follows that the relative fluxes of the two components vary with frequency being approximately equal at about 900 Mc/s, while at 1420 Mc/s Component B is the stronger of the two (see Fig. 1, *b*). The source widths indicated in Figure 2 are the widths of an equivalent strip source. However, an analysis of the fringe amplitudes recorded at both 410 Mc/s and 1420 Mc/s shows that in neither case can the patterns be fitted to a uniform strip or a Gaussian brightness distribution. The 1420 Mc/s observations of B can be explained by assuming that this source consists of a central bright core about 0.5″ wide contributing about 80 per cent of the total flux imbedded in a halo of equivalent width of about 7″. Source A appears to have a similar structure with a central core about 2″ in diameter at 410 Mc/s. There is an apparent variation of component width with frequency, the equivalent widths apparently increasing with decrease in frequency. This suggests that the spectrum becomes steeper in the outer regions of the sources, that is, in the regions of lower emissivity.

A more detailed analysis of the 1420-Mc/s observations has recently been carried out using the method of reduction suggested by Scheuer. The source distribution calculated for position angle 83° using an equivalent beam width of 1.2″ is given in Figure 3. This analysis in general confirms the conclusion given above. Component B is just resolved with the 1.2″ beam and indicates a half-width of 0.6″, while A has a half-width of 1.5″. However, one interesting new feature is revealed. Thus, rather than a halo surrounding Component B, there appears to be a concentration of four weak sources. These do not appear to be artifacts of the reduction procedure, although it is possible that they are produced by some weak external interference. However, this seems unlikely, especially as the rest of the distribution appears so smooth; indeed on a close inspection of the original record the two inner sources are clearly visible. It is well known that Component B is coincident with a starlike object of large redshift and it would appear that Component A is the result of an explosion which occurred in this object at least 10^5 years ago. It would appear that these weaker sources near B are the result of other weaker or more recent explosions.

More recently two further occultations of 3C 273 have been observed, one by Hazard and Mackey at Parkes on March 11, 1963, using frequencies of 1420 Mc/s and 3000 Mc/s and the other by Hughes and Maxwell at Fort Davis using an 85-foot telescope operating at a frequency of 960 Mc/s. The Parkes observations are particularly inter-

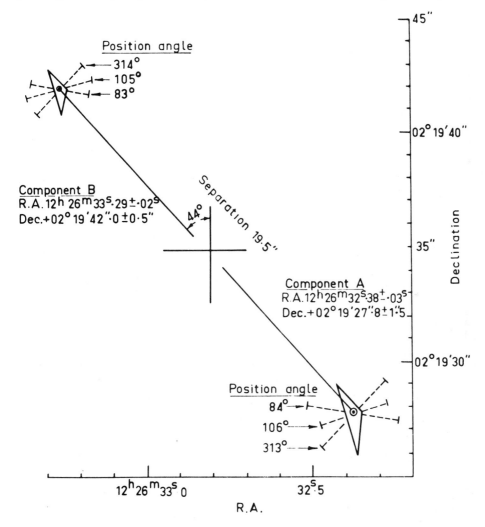

Fig. 2.—Structure of 3C 273. The sides of the full line triangles represent the position of the Moon at the times of occultation. The broken lines represent the widths of the equivalent strong source at 410 Mc/s for each of the indicated position angles.

esting in that they represent an extremely rare occurrence, a grazing occultation in which Component B passed through the first diffraction minimum but not behind the actual limb of the Moon and Component A was not occulted. Figure 4 shows a facsimile of the observed occultation-curves. The 3000-Mc/s record is disturbed by frequent changes in level due to difficulties in accurately tracking the edge of the Moon. At 1420 Mc/s, where the beam is larger, the tracking accuracy is not so important and the diffraction fringes are clearly visible. This record is difficult to analyze in detail as the position angle varies continuously throughout the occultation from 186° at 17^h10^m to 225° at 17^h40^m. However, there is a clear asymmetry between the immersion- and emersion-curves indicating an asymmetry in the source structure; it appears that the source is elongated along a line joining the two components. As the resolution was limited to about 0.3″ by the time constant of 1 sec, the asymmetry also confirms the finite size of source B and shows it to be greater than 0.3″.

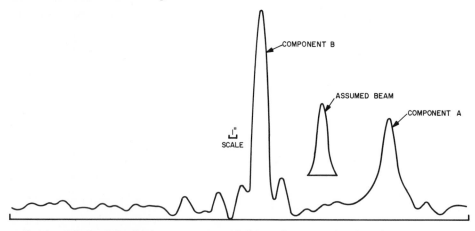

Fig. 3.—Calculated distribution across source 3C 273 at a frequency of 1420 Mc/s and position angle 83° as seen smoothed by a beam of half width 1.2″.

The observations of Hughes and Maxwell are chiefly of interest in that they refer to position angles of 186° and 240° at immersion and emersion, respectively. That is, the position angle at emersion corresponds to the direction of the axis joining the two main components of 3C 273, a direction not covered in the original Parkes observations. A comparison of the immersion- and emersion-curves confirms a suggestion based on these early observations that Component A is elongated along the direction of the jet which extends away from the starlike object.

FURTHER OCCULTATION OBSERVATIONS

Radio Data

Since the original observations of 3C 273 the Parkes telescope has been used to study a number of other sources also at frequencies of 136, 410, and 1420 Mc/s. In the earlier observations the telescope was used to track the position of the source, but more recently the observations have been carried out by tracking the edge of the Moon at the estimated position of occultation. The resolution limit as set out by the time constant and band width was in all cases about 0.5″.

Up to the present, fifteen occultations have been observed. These occultations, which were all predicted by H.M. Nautical Almanac Office, cover a total of eight sources, one being the well-known galactic source, the Crab Nebula. The observations of the Crab

Nebula show that the 1420- and 410-Mc/s distribution are similar and both agree with the optical distribution. We are here more concerned with the structure of the remaining seven sources which appear to be Class II sources and hence are probably extra-galactic. The estimated positions and relevant details of the structure of these sources are summarized in Tables 1 and 2 together with the data on 3C 212 which was observed using the 250-foot radio telescope at Jodrell Bank.

Except for 3C 212 all the sources observed have a complex structure and all have components of angular size less than about 10″. The data in Table 1 are intended only

TABLE 1

Source	Flux at 410 Mc/s in 10^{-26} W m^{-2}(c/s)$^{-1}$	Approximate Angular Size of Components	Approximate Component Separation	Approximate Temperature of Components at 410 Mc/s (° K)	Notes on Radio Source
3C 15...........	10	2″	10″	10^7	Three well-resolved components of approximately equal angular size and fourth component which is either extended or complex
3C 39A..........	2.5	$\left.\begin{array}{l}4″\\10″\end{array}\right\}$	30″	$\left\{\begin{array}{l}10^6\\10^5\end{array}\right\}$	Double
39B.........	2				
3C 212..........	12	7″×15″	....	10^6	Single elliptical source
3C 245..........	8	≤0″.5	3″	>10^8	Close double, components of approximately equal flux and angular size
3C 273A.........	45	$\left.\begin{array}{l}2″\\0″.5\end{array}\right\}$	19″.5	$\left\{\begin{array}{l}10^8\\10^9\end{array}\right.$	Double, spectral index of Component A=−0.9: spectral index of Component B=0.0
273B.........	22				
MSH 12+04A.....	4	15″	4′(A–B)	10^5	Triple, components spread about 5′, Component A appears double. Individual components of A≤5″. Spectral index of A steeper than that of B and C
12+04B.....	2	12″	....	10^5	
12+04C.....	2	20″	1′(B–C)	$5×10^4$	
MSH 14−121A....	7.5	$\left.\begin{array}{l}≤ 0″.5\\3″\end{array}\right\}$	37″	$\left\{\begin{array}{l}>10^8\\10^6\end{array}\right.$	Double, each component may be complex
14−121B....	1.5				
MSH 20−118A....	3	$\left.\begin{array}{l}12″\\>30″\end{array}\right\}$	1′	$\left\{\begin{array}{l}10^5\\10^4\end{array}\right.$	Apparently double but probably even more complex
20−118B....	1.5				

to indicate the general structure of the sources and there are indications that Component A of MSH 12 + 04 and both components of MSH 14 − 121 may themselves be complex. The quoted positional errors are maximum values and comprise both the errors in estimating the times of disappearance and reappearance at the Moon's limb and also the uncertainty in the position of the limb. The position given for MSH 12 + 04 refers to the strongest component, as from the single occultation analyzed it is not possible to pair with certainty the immersion and emersion times of the weaker components. No positions are yet available for 3C 39 and MSH 20 − 118, since for these sources the immersion and emersion, respectively, occurred below the horizon of the telescope and hence in each case only a single occultation-curve was observed.

The complex nature of the sources is clearly shown by the records reproduced in Figures 5–8.

Figure 5 shows the emersion of MSH 12 + 04 as observed on January 15, 1963, and shows clearly the three main components. The double nature of Component A is revealed by applying the Scheuer method of analysis. The measurements were made by

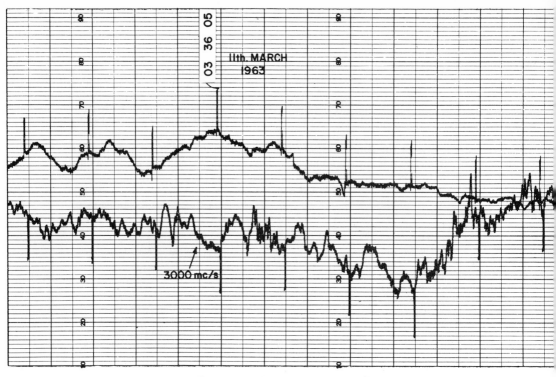

Fig. 4.—Grazing occultation of 3C 273

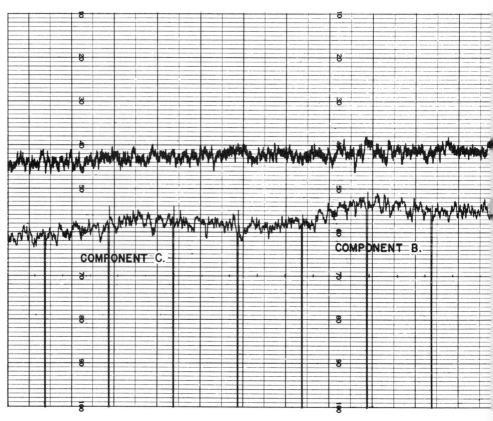

Fig. 5.—Emersion of MSH 12 + 04 on January 15, 1963, showing the three main components. The lower curve was taken at a frequency of 410 Mc/s. The upper curve is the 136 Mc/s record and is disturbed by interference at about the time of emersion of Component A.

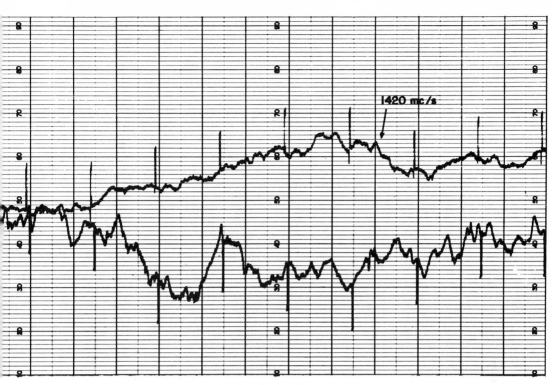

FIG. 4.—*Continued*

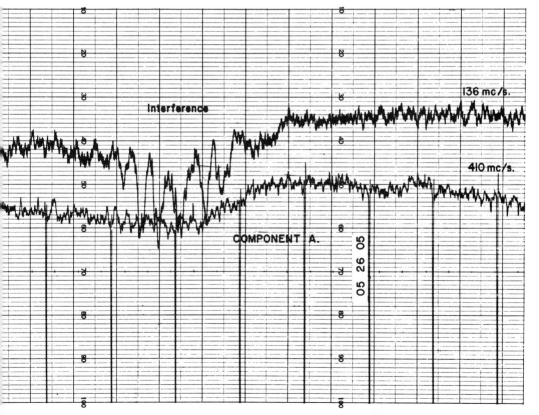

FIG. 5.—*Continued*

TABLE 2

SOURCE	Position of Radio Source (1950) R.A.	Error (±) (sec.)	Decl.	Error (±)	Position of Optical Object (1950) R.A.	Decl.	Notes on Optical Object
3C 15 A.....	00ʰ 34ᵐ 30.48ˢ	0.07	−01°25′ 34″	1″	....	....	Elliptical galaxy, $m_{pg} \approx +16$
15 B.....	00 34 30.90	.1	−01 25 42	1	00ʰ 34ᵐ 30.7ˢ	−01°25′ 40″	
15 C.....	00 34 30.93	.2	−01 25 52	2	....	....	
3C 212.....	08 55 55.8	.3	+14 21 23	2	08 55 55.7	+14 21 26	Possibly starlike object, $m_{pg} \approx +19.5$
3C 245.....	10 40 05.89	.06	+12 20 17.4	1	10 40 06.0	+12 20 17.9	Starlike object, $m_{pg} \approx +18$
3C 273 A.....	12 26 32.38	.03	+02 19 27.8	1.5	....	....	End of faint jet extending from stellar object
273 B.....	12 26 33.29	.02	+02 19 42.0	0.5	12 26 33.35	+02 19 42.0	Starlike object, $m_{pg} = +13$
MSH 12+04A.....	12 15 06.3	.2	+03 56 34	3	12 15 06.7	+03 56 26	Member of dense cluster of galaxies ($m_{pg} \approx +18$). Components B and C appear to be associated with other members of the cluster
MSH 14−121A.....	14 53 12.70	.03	−10 56 58.6	0.5	14 53 12.7	−10 56 42	Starlike object, $m_{pg} \approx +17$. Faint jet appears to project to south
14−121B.....	14 53 11.82	0.06	−10 56 24.1	1.0	14 53 12.0	−10 56 19	Faint jet nebulosity to north of stellar object, $m_{pg} \approx +19.5$

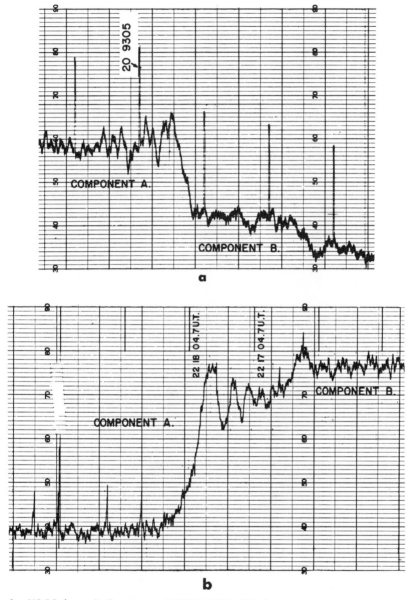

Fig. 6.—410 Mc/s occultation-curves of MSH 14-121. This is a composite record, the immersion (*b*) being that of December 22, 1962, and the emersion (*a*) that of May 8, 1962.

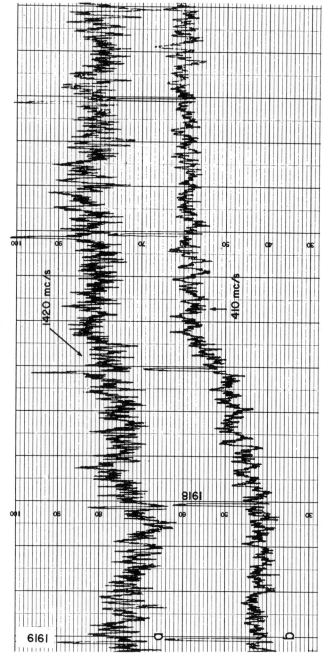

Fig. 7.—Emersion curve of 3C 39 as observed at (a) 1420 Mc/s, (b) 410 Mc/s.

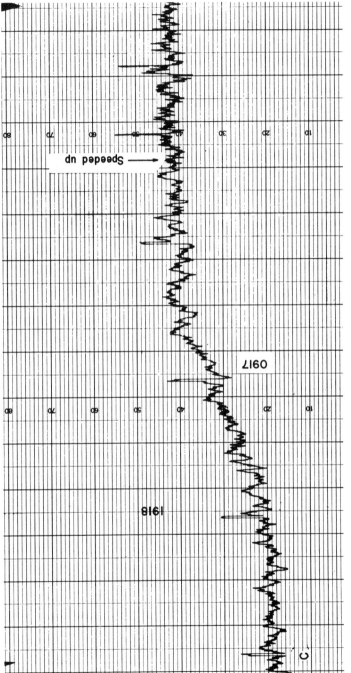

Fɪɢ. 7.—c, Emersion curve of 3C 39 at 136 Mc/s

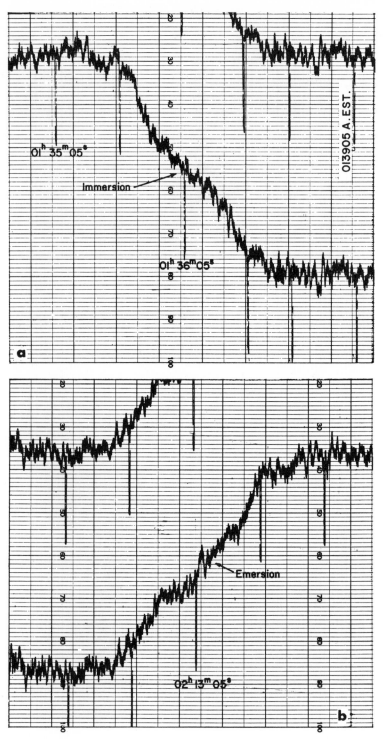

FIG. 8.—410 Mc/s occultation of 3C 15 on September 5, 1963: (a) immersion-curve, (b) emersion-curve.

tracking the position of the source, and the sloping base line is due to the passage of the Moon through the aerial beam.

Figure 6 shows a typical two-component source MSH 14 − 121 where the two components are well separated. The extremely small angular size of Component A is shown by its extensive diffraction pattern which may be compared with that of 3C 273 shown in Figure 1. The diffraction fringes extend out to the limit set by limitations of band width and time constant indicating that this component is not resolved and is certainly less than, possibly much less than, 0.5″ in diameter. Some evidence of beating is visible

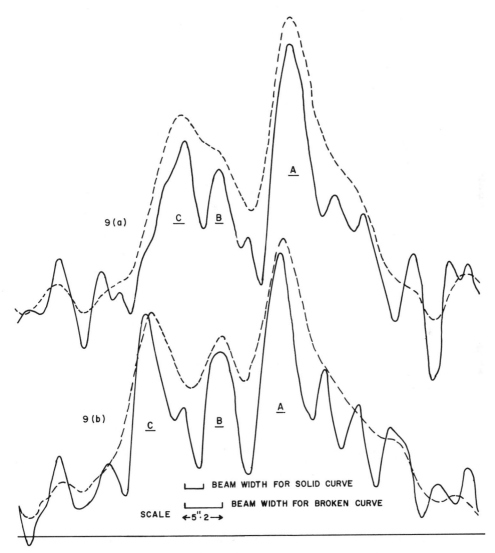

FIG. 9.—Distribution across 3C 15 as deduced from the curves given in Fig. 8. Solid curves represent the distribution as seen smoothed by a beam of width 2.6″ and broken lines the distribution as seen smoothed by a beam of 5.2″.

in the diffraction pattern indicating that Component A itself may be complex. There is some evidence that Component B is also complex.

3C 39, illustrated in Figure 7, shows another example of a double source where the individual components are of larger angular size and separation and no diffraction fringes are visible.

A rather different type of record is illustrated in Figure 8, which shows an occultation of 3C 15. The complex nature of the source is revealed by the sharp changes in slope of the occultation-curves. The curves are so complex, however, that the structure cannot be deduced by a simple inspection of the record as in the case of the well-resolved doubles. These curves have therefore been analyzed in detail again using the method of Scheuer. The results of this analysis are given in Figure 9. There are three well-defined components plus a broad component which may itself be complex.

Thus the occultation observations confirm the interferometer observations in showing the complex nature of the sources but indicate that the degree of complexity is often greater than that of a simple two-component model. Not only are the sources complex but, as pointed out above, all have structure less than 10″. Indeed that such a large percentage of sources show prominent diffraction fringes indicating structure of the order of less than 1″ was one of the most surprising features of this investigation.

There is some evidence that in 3C 273 the sizes of the individual components vary with frequency. What is certain is that the over-all appearance of a source can vary with frequency, for in the case of both 3C 273 and MSH 12 + 04 the spectra of the individual components are different; in the latter case the spectrum of Component A is markedly steeper than that of the other components; indeed it is the only component visible in the 136-Mc/s records. The variation of spectral index in the double source 3C 273 tends to rule out a torus model for this type of source and suggests that the double sources do in fact consist of two spatially separated components. A further feature of Table 1 is the very high temperature observed in all the sources, particularly the doubles 3C 245, 3C 273, and MSH 14 − 121, where the effective temperature at 410 Mc/s exceeds $10^{8°}$ K and may be as high as $10^{10°}$ K.

Optical Identifications

A search has been made of the Sky Survey plates in the region of the six radio positions available and has resulted in a possible identification in each case. The results of this investigation are summarized in Table 2; the quoted optical positions should be accurate to better than about 10″ in all cases. The close agreement between the optical and radio positions leaves little doubt that the identifications are correct. We have already heard a great deal about the structure of 3C 273, the most intensively studied of the "stellar galaxies," and we will therefore confine our attention to the remaining five sources in Table 2.

3C 15

The elliptical galaxy identified with 3C 15 is shown in Figure 10 and optically appears to be quite normal. Component B of the radio source appears to coincide with the Galaxy itself while the Components A and C straddle the optical image but are scarcely resolved from it.

3C 212

The optical counterpart of 3C 212 is the faintest object so far identified with an extragalactic radio source. Its relatively large radio size is perhaps more characteristic of the familiar elliptical radio galaxies than with a 3C 273- or 3C 48-type object and its identification as a "stellar-type" radio source must be considered tentative.

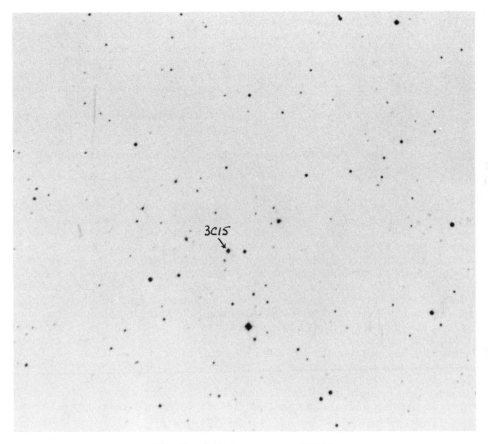

Fɪɢ. 10.—Optical counterpart of 3C 15

3C 245

Other than the suggested optical counterpart of 3C 245, which appears to be stellar on both the red and blue plates, there is no other object above the plate limits within about 1' of the radio position (see Fig. 11).

Preliminary spectral observations by M. Schmidt have confirmed that 3C 245 is indeed a "stellar" galaxy, but no redshift is yet available. The double nature of 3C 245 together with its small component size and separation had already suggested that it was a similar object to 3C 273 but possibly even more distant.

MSH 12+04

This is a particularly interesting source consisting of three well-separated components. Component A which is itself double has been identified with a faint member of a dense cluster of galaxies. The final positions of Components B and C have not yet been determined, but they lie close to other faint members of the cluster, and there seems little doubt that they are associated with these cluster members. Component A is the only component visible at 136 Mc/s, showing that it has a steeper spectrum than B and C.

This is the first time that three apparently unrelated members of a cluster have been identified as radio sources. It would be of great importance if one or more should turn out to be a stellar galaxy, as a comparison of the redshift with those of brighter cluster members would then disciminate between a gravitational and recessional origin for the redshift of objects like 3C 273.

MSH 14−121

As in the case of 3C 245, the double nature of the source and the small angular size of the individual components suggested on the basis of the radio data alone that this was another 3C 273-type object. However, unlike 3C 245 where only a single starlike object lay near the radio position, in this case there are three optical objects near the radio positions. These three objects lie in a line at position angle 340°, the same position angle is estimated for the two radio components. The central object marked (a) in Figure 12 appears to be stellar on the blue plate, while in the red there appears to be an addition a faint jet extending to the south. North-following these is a faint nebulosity which is not visible on the reproduction but whose position is indicated by (b). South-preceding there is another object probably a galaxy marked by (c). The coordinates of Component A do not agree with those estimated for any of the optical objects; the right ascension agrees with that of A, but the declination is closer to that of (c), which is −15°10'. In addition the separation of the radio components (37″) is not in agreement with the separation of the optical objects: 30″ between (a) and (c) and 25″ between (a) and (b). However, the position of Component B agrees closely with that of the optical component (b). Thus, the most probable interpretation is that Component B represents radio emission from the faint nebulosity (b), while Component A lies near the end of or beyond the faint jet projecting to the south of the starlike object (a). This would account for the agreement between the right ascensions of the radio and optical Components A and (a) and also the discrepancy between their estimated declinations. Whatever the details of the structure of the source, there is no doubt that it is associated with the central stellar object. As in the case of 3C 255 preliminary spectral observations have confirmed its unusual nature, but again no redshift is as yet available.

CONCLUDING REMARKS

Even if we neglect 3C 212 as a possible "stellar galaxy" out of eight sources observed, three appear to be definitely associated with stellar objects. Matthews and Sandage have noted that of the twenty-five brightest extra-galactic sources north of declination

F𝐼G. 11.—Identification of 3C 245

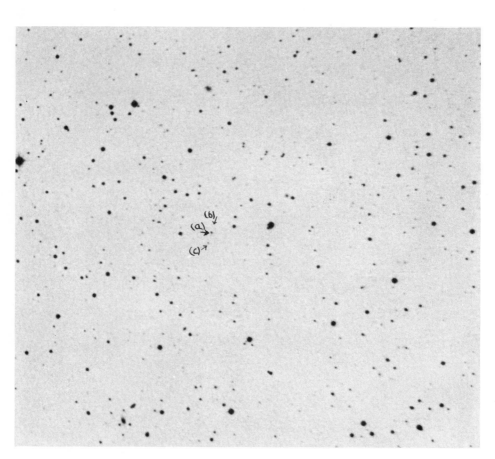

Fig. 12.—Identification of MSH 14-121

−47°, at least five, and possibly seven, are starlike. Combining the two sets of observations and remembering that 3C 273 is common to both source lists, we see that the "stellar galaxies" comprise 25–30 per cent of the total.

The three "stellar galaxies" studied here are all associated with double radio sources and, apart from a possible difference in the ratio of component separation to component size, appear to have a similar radio structure to the majority of the more common "radio galaxies." This is at least suggestive of a common type of origin, and the stellar objects could in fact represent the optical manifestation of a catastrophic phase in the formation of a radio galaxy. As in the "normal galaxies," the radio emission also appears to originate in a catastrophic event in the nucleus of the galaxy; it may be that they represent similar events of a less violent nature due to the smaller masses involved.

It is interesting to note that the six sources for which positions accurate to the order of 1″ have been obtained by the occultation technique have all been identified. Of these six only the complex source MSH 21 + 04 appears to be associated with a cluster of galaxies, the "stellar galaxies" all appearing to be isolated objects. This latter source illustrates one of the difficulties in obtaining identifications of the weak complex sources, for the mean position of the three components is several minutes of arc away from the three associated optical objects. In addition it may be noted that, as in the case of 3C 273, the spectrum of the individual components and hence the mean position of the source varies with frequency. Indeed if the observations of 3C 273 had been carried out only at a frequency of the order of 100 Mc/s, then the position measured would have been that of Component A, which differs by 20″ from the position of the associated thirteenth-magnitude stellar object. Thus, for the weaker sources in particular, apparent discrepancies between the optical and radio positions of associated objects are to be expected.

The occultation work described here was carried out with M. B. Mackey of the Radiophysics Laboratory, Sydney, while the author was a guest observer at Parkes from the Narrabri Observatory of the School of Physics of the University of Sydney. The accurate positions were derived by W. Nicholson of H.M. Nautical Almanac Office and the source distributions calculated by J. Sutton of the School of Physics, University of Sydney.

BRIGHTNESS DISTRIBUTION IN DISCRETE RADIO SOURCES IV. A DISCUSSION OF 24 IDENTIFIED SOURCES

chapter 12

P. MALTBY, THOMAS A. MATTHEWS, AND A. T. MOFFET

I. INTRODUCTION

At present there is no way of determining the distance of a radio source from radio observations alone. Thus it is fortunate that a number of radio sources can be identified with optical objects, because the optical red shift is known to be a reliable distance indicator. If the distance of a source is known, the observed radio intensities and brightness distributions can be used to obtain the total luminosity and the projected linear dimensions of the emitting regions. Estimates can then be made of the physical conditions within the source.

In previous papers, observations of radio-source brightness distributions at a wavelength of 31 cm have been described (Moffet 1962, Paper I; Maltby 1962, Paper II), and radio descriptions of a number of extragalactic sources have been given (Maltby and Moffet 1962, Paper III). Identifications are available for some of these objects, and in the present paper we consider a group of 24 identified sources for which the radio positions and brightness distribution data are complete, or nearly so. The identifications are used to provide distances and hence to obtain some of the intrinsic parameters of the radio sources. The radio positions, measured with the Caltech interferometer (Matthews and Read, in preparation), have been combined with the radio brightness distributions to show the relative location of radio and optical counterparts in the various types of sources.

The 24 sources considered here include some previously identified sources (see Bolton 1960), as well as some new identifications which have resulted from the Caltech programs of position and brightness distribution measurements. These and other identifications will be the subject of a forthcoming article by Matthews; hence a detailed discussion of the evidence for these particular identifications will not be given here.

II. OBSERVATIONAL DATA

Optical and radio data for the sources are given in Table 1. Column 1 contains the name or 3C catalogue number (Edge, Shakeshaft, McAdam, Baldwin, and Archer 1959) of each source, while column 2 gives NGC numbers, where they exist, for the associated optical objects. In column 3 are given the photographic magnitudes of the optical objects. These were estimated for us by E. R. Herzog from the blue plates of the National Geographic Society–Palomar Observatory Sky Survey. The estimates should be correct to

P. MALTBY, Institute for Theoretical Astrophysics, University of Oslo, Norway. THOMAS A. MATTHEWS and A. T. MOFFET, California Institute of Technology Radio Observatory.

Reprinted from the *Astrophysical Journal*, **137**, 153–163, 1963.

TABLE 1—OPTICAL AND RADIO PROPERTIES OF 24 IDENTIFIED SOURCES

Source (1)	NGC (2)	m_{pg} (3)	cz (4)	$r \cdot h$ (Mpc) (5)	$M_{pg}-5\log h$ (6)	Emission Lines (7)	Source Type (8)	Angular Diameter (') (9)	Angular Separation (') (10)	$h\cdot$Linear Diameter (kpc) (11)	$h\cdot$Linear Separation (kpc) (12)	Diam. (13)	Sep. (14)
								Projected Source Dimensions				**Radio Size/Opt. Size**	
3C 33		15.7	17800[a]	178	−20.9	em!	U		3.8		200		19
3C 40	541–545 547	13.4+13.2 +13.4	5320[b,c]	53	−20.7	—	U		5.7		88		6
3C 66		14.2	6450[c]	65	−20.8	—	U	<0.5	6.6	<1.6	125	<0.1	11
3C 71	1068	9.5	1130[d]	11	−20.9	em!	N						
3C 75		14.9+15.2	7220[e]	72	−19.8	—	E	1.2+1.2	2.8	25+25	59	7+7	17
3C 78	1218	14.8		(98)	−20.0	—	S	1.0				3	13
For A	1316	9.6	1730[d]	17	−21.8	em	U	18+18[k]	(29)	89+89	140	9	14
3C 98		15.3	9200[a]	92	−20.0	em!	U		3.4		91		
3C 198		17.8	25000[a]	250	−19.8	em!	H	<1+3.5		250		70	
Hyd A		15.1	15900[e]	160	−21.5	em!	H	1.0+5.0		46+230		10+50	
3C 219		19.4	52000[a]	520	−19.6	—	E	0.85+0.85	1.9	130+130	290	14+14	30
3C 270	4261	12.0	2090[d]	11*	−18.5	—	E	2.7+2.7	4.7	8.6+8.6	15	2+2	3.5
Vir A	4486	10.0	1220[d]	11*	−20.5	em	H	0.6+6.5		1.9+21		0.3+3.5	
3C 278	4782–3	13.2+13.6	4300[e]	43	−20.3	—	S	2.2		28		3.5	
Cen A	5128	7.5	470	4[j]	−21.3	em	E	3+3	7.1	3.5+3.5	8.3	0.25	0.6
							U	100+100[l]	200[l]	120+120	240	5	10
3C 295		20.9[f]	138000[f]	1380	−20.1	em!	N	0.08[m]		32			
3C 310		16.2+16.2		(200)			(E)		2.1	(140)	(120)	~3	
3C 315		17.8+18.3		(390)			(S)						21
3C 327		17.2		(280)		em	U	1.2	3.5		(290)	10	21
3C 338	6166	13.6[g]	9080[g]	91	−21.6	em!	S	1.2		32		8	21
Her A		19.3	46200[h]	460	−19.5	em!	E	0.75+0.75	1.95	100+100	260	10+10	25
3C 353		13.5[c]		(65)		em!	U	1.4+1.4	≥2.5	(26+26)	(≥50)	8+8	~15
Cyg A		15.1[i]	17100[i]	170	−21.1	em!	E	0.7+0.7	1.58	35+35	79	4+4	10
3C 442	7236–7	14.5+13.8	7860[h]	79	−21.1	em	S	3.0		69		10	

NOTES TO TABLE 1

* Assumed distance for the Virgo Cluster.

[a] M. Schmidt, private communication.

[b] Zwicky (1961).

[c] Minkowski (1961b), corrected velocities for 3C 40, 3C 66, and 3C 75 from private communication; M_{pg} for 3C 353 corrected for 4^m absorption.

[d] Humason, Mayall, and Sandage (1956).

[e] Greenstein (1961).

[f] Minkowski (1960b).

[g] Minkowski (1961a).

[h] Greenstein (1962).

[i] Baade and Minkowski (1954a), M_{pg} corrected for 2.1^m absorption.

[j] Sersic (1960).

[k] Wade (1961).

[l] Bolton and Clark (1960).

[m] Allen, Palmer, and Rowson (1960).

within 0.5 mag. for galaxies brighter than $m_{pg} = 17$, with a somewhat greater uncertainty for fainter objects.

Radial velocities for 19 of the selected objects are listed in column 4, together with references indicating their origin. Seven of these measurements have been made recently at the Palomar Observatory and have been communicated to us in advance of publication. We are deeply indebted to Drs. M. Schmidt, J. L. Greenstein, and R. Minkowski for permission to make use of these important results.

On assuming a value for the Hubble parameter of $H_0 = 100\,h$ km s^{-1} Mpc^{-1}, the radial velocities have been converted to the distances given in column 5. The distances and the apparent magnitudes have been used to derive absolute magnitudes, as given in column 6. The absorption within our own galaxy was assumed to be 0.25 csc b mag. In the cases where the radio source is identified with a multiple galactic system, the absolute magnitude of the brightest component has been given. No redshift correction has been applied to the absolute magnitudes, as it is not entirely clear that the usual redshift corrections are applicable without modification. The more distant objects, for which this correction would be greater than a few tenths of a magnitude (Humason, Mayall, and Sandage 1956), all have spectra characterized by strong emission lines. However, there seems to be no significant difference in absolute magnitude between objects with normal spectra and objects with spectra showing strong emission lines.

The mean of the absolute magnitudes in column 6 is $\bar{M}_{pg} - 5 \log h = -20.5$, with a standard deviation of 0.8 mag. Approximate distances have been derived for the remaining five galaxies on the assumption that they have absolute magnitudes equal to this mean. These distance values, inclosed in parentheses, are given in column 5. If the true M_{pg} of one of these objects should differ from the assumed mean value by an amount equal to the standard deviation in the mean, the derived distance would be in error by a factor of 1.5.

In column 7 the presence of strong emission lines in the optical spectrum is indicated by *em!*. If emission lines are present but not strong, an *em* is entered. A dash indicates that no emission lines are observed in the spectrum.

The letters in column 8 give the structural classification of the sources, as defined in Paper III. Sources with two equal intensity components are designated by an "E"; sources with unequal components by a "U"; core-and-halo objects by an "H"; simple, roughly circular sources by an "S"; and objects which were not resolved in our investigation by an "N." Columns 9 and 10 contain the angular dimensions of each source, while the corresponding linear dimensions in the plane perpendicular to the line of sight are given in columns 11 and 12. The radio diameters refer to half-intensity diameters of Gaussian models approximating the various components of the sources. Full details have been given in Paper III.

For each source the ratios of the radio dimensions to the optical diameter of the galaxy identified with the source are given in the last two columns. If more than one galaxy is involved, then the optical diameter refers to the largest galaxy of the group. The angular diameters of the galaxies were measured on the red plates of the Sky Survey. The true extent of a galaxy is several times larger than the size measured on the Sky Survey plates (Humason, Mayall, and Sandage 1956, Appendix A). The over-all extent of a radio source is also several times greater than the half-intensity diameter. Thus the ratios in column 13 should be reasonable comparisons of radio and optical diameters, while those in column 14 may exaggerate the separation of the radio source from the galaxy.

The distance of an object with red shift $z = \Delta\lambda/\lambda$ has been assumed to be equal to cz/H_0. In fact, the distances which should be used in determining linear dimensions and distance moduli contain additional terms which are non-linear in z (see, for example, Sandage 1961a). The coefficients of these additional terms depend on the cosmological model which correctly describes the universe, and a wide choice of models is compatible with current observational data (Sandage 1961b). Hence no attempt has been made to include these non-linear terms. The general effect would be to make the distant objects smaller and brighter than is indicated in Table 1. Some specific examples will be given in connection with the computation of the energies of the sources.

Figures 1, 2, and 3 give combined radio and optical pictures of several of the sources, indicating the position of the radio-emitting regions with respect to the associated galaxies. The circles indicate the approximate size of the various radio components. In the asymmetrical double sources there is more uncertainty about the component sizes, and they are indicated with dashed circles. The numbers give the relative intensities of the components. The photographs of the galaxies in Figures 1 and 2 have been copied from the red plates of the Sky Survey. The photograph of NGC 5128 in Figure 3 was copied from a red plate taken with the 48-inch Schmidt telescope by R. Minkowski.

III. REMARKS ON INDIVIDUAL SOURCES

The following remarks will serve to describe the objects in Figures 1–3 and to give references for those identifications which have previously been reported.

3C 33.—This identification was first suggested by Dewhirst (see Elsmore 1959). As can be seen in Figure 1, *a*, the galaxy lies very close to the centroid of the radio emission.

3C 40.—Minkowski (1958) originally suggested that this source might be associated with the close pair of elliptical galaxies NGC 545–547, although he pointed out that an accurate position by Mills was definitely earlier in right ascension. Our position and brightness distribution, shown in Figure 2, *a*, indicate that the source has two unequal components, with the radio centroid southwest of NGC 545–547 in the direction of a third elliptical galaxy, NGC 541. According to Zwicky (1961), there is a luminous bridge connecting NGC 545–547 to NGC 541, with a fainter extension toward the spiral seen in the lower right-hand corner of Figure 2, *a*. It seems possible that all three galaxies, which are the brightest members of a cluster, may be associated with the source.

3C 66.—The identification of this source with a single galaxy having a jetlike feature is due to Minkowski (quoted by Harris and Roberts 1960; see also Bolton 1960). The radio structure, shown in Figure 2, *b*, very much resembles that of 3C 40. In this case, however, the galaxy lies close to the radio centroid.

3C 71.—This source has been identified with the well-known Seyfert galaxy NGC 1068 (Seyfert 1943; Mills 1955; Burbidge, Burbidge, and Prendergast 1959; Woltjer 1959). The position and diameter measurements confirm the suggestion of Burbidge *et al.* and of Woltjer that the radio emission comes from the nucleus of the galaxy. The radio spectrum is remarkably flat.

3C 75.—Minkowski (1960a) suggested that this source could be identified with a close pair of galaxies. As can be seen in Figure 1, *b*, the radio source consists of two roughly equal components whose centroid falls about 1′ northeast of this pair. Closer to the radio centroid there is an inconspicuous galaxy of about $m_{pg} = 18$, but for the purposes of this paper we shall assume that the correct identification is the fifteenth-magnitude pair. Recent measurements by Read (private communication) indicate that the source components may not be so nearly symmetrical as was indicated in Paper III. The position of the radio centroid will not be changed appreciably, however. It is possible that another member of the cluster of galaxies, of which the double is a member, may also be associated with the radio source.

3C 78.—The identification with NGC 1218 has been noted by Mills (1960) and by Bolton (1960). Figure 1, *c*, shows that the radio structure is simple and fits nicely over the galaxy.

Fornax A.—The radio source is large, about 1° in over-all extent, and is thus heavily resolved by the Caltech interferometer at its closest spacing. Wade (1961) has shown that the source has two components of unequal intensities and diameters. The centroid of the radio emission lies within the optical boundaries of NGC 1316. The identification with

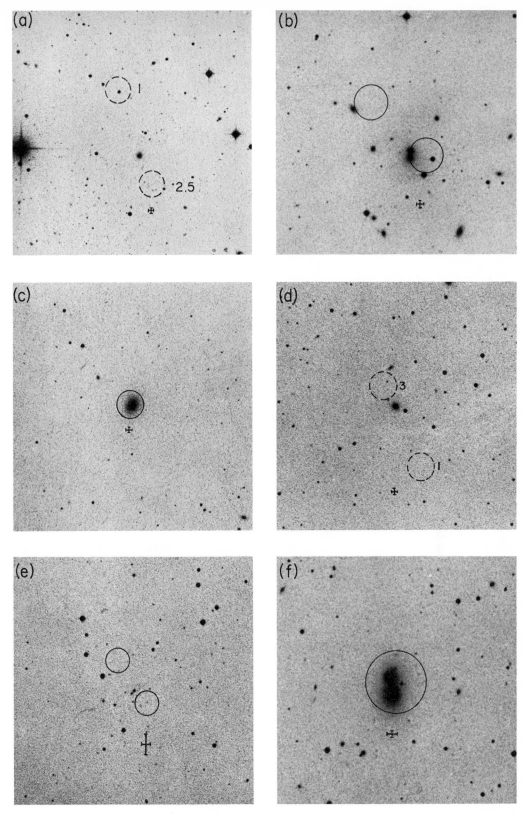

Fig. 1.—Radio and optical brightness distributions for (a) 3C 33, (b) 3C 75, (c) 3C 78, (d) 3C 98, (e) 3C 219, (f) 3C 278. The cross below each source indicates the probable error limits in the placement of the radio object with respect to its optical counterpart. North is at the top, and east is to the left. Each field is 10′ × 10′.

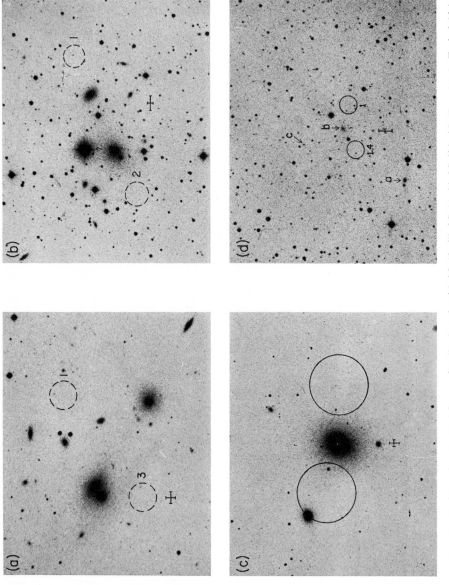

Fig. 2.—Radio and optical brightness distributions for (a) 3C 40, (b) 3C 66, (c) 3C 270, (d) Hercules A. Each field is 10' × 12'. See legend for Fig. 1 for other details.

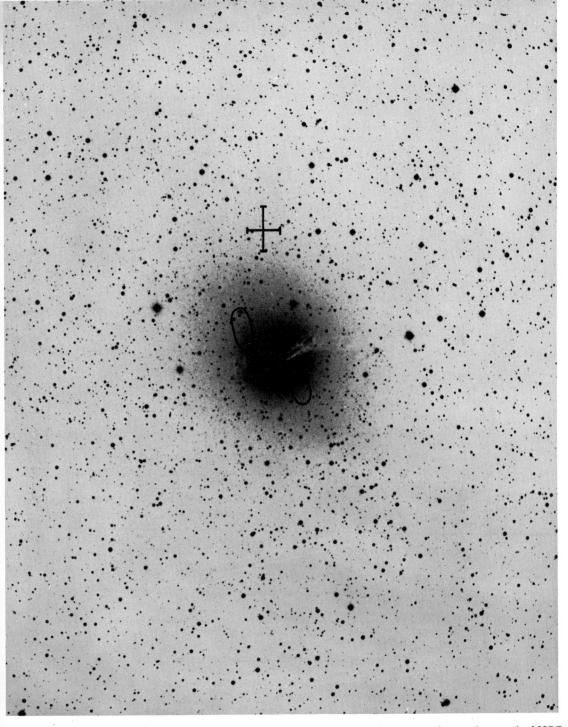

Fig. 3.—Radio brightness distribution for the central component of Centaurus A superposed on a photograph of NGC 5128. Field is 50′ × 40′. See legend for Fig. 1 for other details.

NGC 1316 was suggested independently by Shklovskii and by de Vaucouleurs (see the review by Minkowski 1957).

3C 98.—The CTA position measurements first suggested this identification (Harris and Roberts 1960; Bolton 1960), and it now seems quite certain. The centroid of the unequal double source lies very close to the galaxy, as is shown in Figure 1, *d.*

3C 198.—The radio source consists of a 3′.5 halo with a rather faint core of small diameter. It coincides in position with a loose cluster of galaxies. The brightest member of this cluster has a slightly asymmetrical image on the red Sky Survey plate, and Schmidt has found strong emission lines in its spectrum. The ratio of radio to optical size for this source is particularly large; the linear diameter of the radio source of 250 h^{-1} Mpc is among the largest known.

Hydra A.—The source consists of a large halo with a non-circular core. Measurements by Lequeux and Heidmann (1961) have shown that about 20 per cent of the flux from the core originates in a component of very small diameter. The optical identification, first noted by Minkowski, is a very close pair of elliptical galaxies having a common envelope (Dewhirst 1959).

3C 219.—The identification with a pair of nineteenth-magnitude galaxies was suggested by Dewhirst (1959). Figure 1, *e*, shows that the two components of the source straddle these galaxies, which are the two brightest members of a cluster. Sandage has obtained a red plate with the 200-inch telescope, and it shows that the fainter, southern member of the pair has jetlike extensions in position angles 120° and 240°. In addition, there is a faint bridge between the galaxies. A spectrum obtained by Schmidt shows that the northern object has strong emission lines. The linear size and the ratio of radio to optical size are both very large.

3C 270.—The identification with NGC 4261 is due to Mills, Slee, and Hill (1958). It seems to be well confirmed by the present data, as shown in Figure 2, *c.* The galaxy is a normal elliptical.

Virgo A.—This was one of the very earliest identifications (Bolton, Stanley, and Slee 1949). Extensive optical studies have been reported by Baade and Minkowski (1954*b*), Baade (1956), and Hiltner (1959). The radio measurements, which were reviewed in Paper III, show that a 7′ halo surrounds a small-diameter core that is presumably to be associated with the jet in NGC 4486. The measurements of Lequeux and Heidmann (1961) have shown that the core consists of two components with an east-west spacing of 0′.5. Baldwin and Smith (1956) have found evidence at meter wavelengths for a very extended halo component with a diameter of about 50′. In the absence of spectral information about this component, we shall ignore it in computing the total energy requirements for the radio source. The core will be assumed to consist of two cylindrical components, each 1.5 h^{-1} kpc long and 0.6 h^{-1} kpc in diameter.

3C 278.—The identification with the close pair of galaxies NGC 4782–4783 was first suggested by Mills, Slee, and Hill (1958). The galaxies have been discussed by Greenstein (1961). Figure 1, *f*, shows that they lie, at least in projection, within the single radio source.

Centaurus A.—The identification with NGC 5128 was made by Bolton, Stanley, and Slee (1949). Optical data on this galaxy have been given by Baade and Minkowski (1954*b*) and by Burbidge and Burbidge (1959). The radio emission comes from two extended regions on opposite sides of the galaxy and from two small regions situated within the galaxy (see review in Paper III; also Maltby 1961). The central source is shown superposed on the galaxy in Figure 3. The photograph was printed rather darkly, in order to show the outer regions of the galaxy. The major axis of the central radio source is seen to correspond roughly with the direction of elongation of these outer regions.

3C 295.—This object has been discussed by Minkowski (1960*b*). Allen, Palmer, and Rowson (1960) have found its east-west angular diameter at meter wavelengths to be 4″.5. Although the brightness distribution is not well known, this source has been included here because of its high luminosity and its relatively small ratio of radio to optical diameter. In order to calculate the energy requirements, we shall assume that the source is spherical, with an angular diameter equal to the measured east-west diameter.

3C 310, 3C 315.—These identifications were made by Dewhirst (1959) and are confirmed by subsequent position measurements. Data on the radio structure of these sources are not so complete as for most of the others in Table 1.

3C 327.—The identification was given by Bolton (1960). Our radio position and brightness distribution differ from those published by the Cambridge group (Elsmore, Ryle, and Leslie 1959; Leslie 1961), but the latter measurements were probably influenced by the source of comparable intensity situated about 1° to the southeast.

3C 338.—The identification with the NGC 6166 group of galaxies has been discussed in detail by Minkowski (1958, 1961). The radio source is of class S and agrees well in position with the group of galaxies.

Hercules A.—The correct identification seems to be that suggested by Williams, Dewhirst, and Leslie (1961, their "object b"). It is confirmed by our position and brightness distribution measurements and by a spectrum taken by Greenstein (1962). As seen in Figure 2, *d*, the galaxy, which has an unusual distribution of intensity, lies near the centroid of the two radio components. The sharp image 3″.3 northwest of the galaxy is probably a foreground star.

3C 353.—A seventeenth-magnitude elliptical galaxy noted by Mills (1960) agrees well with the position of this strong source. The amount of galactic absorption and hence the distance derived from the apparent magnitude are rather uncertain.

Cygnus A.—The optical features of this object have been described by Baade and Minkowski (1954*a*); the radio features are summarized in Paper III.

3C 442.—This source in many ways resembles 3C 278. A spectroscopic investigation of NGC 7236–7237 is described by Greenstein (1962).

IV. RADIO AND OPTICAL PROPERTIES

The sources shown in Figures 1–3 illustrate the variety of combinations of radio and optical structure that seem to occur. Not all the combinations are illustrated, since no example of the core-and-halo type of radio source is shown. Among the examples available so far, there seem to be no particular correlations of the optical appearance (e.g., close double galaxy, single galaxy, distortions, etc.) with any of the classifications of radio structure. The galaxies identified with radio sources exhibit a wide range of peculiarities on the direct photographs. Some galaxies have unusual absorption features, while others have barely visible jetlike features. A few of the identifications show no peculiarities. Some of the identifications are close binary or multiple systems of galaxies which are imbedded in a common envelope. A few of these pairs of galaxies have highly distorted envelopes and nuclei. More subtle peculiarities will undoubtedly be noticed when the galaxies are studied more intensively (see below).

As was shown in Paper III, an important result of the present investigation of source brightness distributions is that a majority of all the extragalactic sources consist of two widely separated components. The examples of this type of source which have been illustrated in the present paper show that in these cases the radio-emitting regions are usually well separated from the associated galaxy. The galaxy is typically found at, or very close to, the centroid of the radio emission. A few cases in which the optical object may be displaced from the radio source have already been noted and discussed in Section III.

Spectral information is available for 19 of the identifications listed in Table 1. Ten of these show unusually strong emission lines; the others show no spectral peculiarities. There seems to be a correlation between the intrinsic radio emission from the source and the occurrence of unusually strong emission lines in the spectrum. The probability of occurrence of the λ 3727 emission line in elliptical galaxies (Osterbrock 1960) is near 15 per cent, and the strength of the emission line is from weak to moderate. The seven sources in Table 2 having $L \gtrsim 5 \times 10^{41}$ ergs/sec and for which spectra exist, all have strong to very strong emission lines. Of the nine sources having $L \lesssim 5 \times 10^{41}$ ergs/sec and for which spectra exist, two (3C 71 and Vir A) have strong emission lines, three (Cen A, 3C 338, and 3C 442) have emission lines of the intensity found occasionally in normal ellipticals, and the other four show no emission lines in their spectra. The frequency of occurrence of emission lines is higher in the later-type systems, and so the significance of the above remarks must await a discussion of galaxy types and of the emission spectra.

Many of the radio sources are much larger than the size of the galaxy involved; some are only a few times the optical size. A few are smaller than the associated galaxy; for instance, 3C 71 is less than one-tenth the size of NGC 1068.

Two of the large radio sources—Hydra A and 3C 198—are identified with galaxies in clusters. They are both core-halo type objects, and the linear diameters of the halos are 230 and 250 kpc, respectively. These very large sizes might be due to the influence of other members of the cluster, but we have no indication that this is so. However, with these large sizes it is very probable that one or more other galaxies exist inside the radio-emitting region. There are at least two double radio sources having separations >170 kpc whose optical counterparts are members of clusters (3C 219 and 3C 327). Again the sizes are larger than the average separation between the galaxies in clusters.

Several of the galaxies identified with radio sources show an unusual distribution of light across the galaxy. Minkowski (1961a) has mentioned the lack of a central concentration in NGC 6166, and Greenstein (1961, 1962) has found similar unusually flat light-distributions in NGC 4782 and NGC 7237, each one a member of a pair of galaxies, and also in the galaxy identified with Hercules A (object b). Several other identifications also show the same effect to a varying degree—for instance, 3C 465 (NGC 7720), 3C 295, 3C 433, and probably 3C 33, 3C 88, and 3C 98. Not all identifications have this property; for instance, M87 seems normal in this respect.

V. LUMINOSITIES AND ENERGY REQUIREMENTS

When the distance of a source is known, as well as its flux density as a function of frequency, the radio luminosity may be calculated. We have done this for the sources described above, using the distances given in Table 1 and spectral information from a variety of observers. We have assumed a simple power-law dependence of the flux over the frequency range of 10^7–10^{10} c/s. The observed intensities have not been corrected for displacements in wavelength due to Doppler shifts because of our limited knowledge of the spectral behavior near the cutoff frequencies. For each source the power emitted (L) between the above frequency limits and the spectral index which gives a best fit to the observed intensities are given in Table 2.

It is seen that the luminosities have a range of nearly five decades, from weak emitters, such as 3C 71 and 3C 270, to the three strongest sources, Cygnus A, 3C 295, and Hercules A. As has already been mentioned, the luminosity distance, which should properly be used in deriving the total luminosity from the observed radiation flux, is a function of the cosmological model. The distance in Table 1 was assumed to be cz/H_0, which happens to be the correct luminosity distance for a closed, elliptical universe characterized by a deceleration parameter q_0 equal to $+1$ (Sandage 1961a; see also Sandage 1961b). Smaller values of q_0 would yield higher values for the luminosities of the distant sources, with the steady-state model $(q_0 = -1)$ giving a correction of $(1 + z)^2$. Thus, in a steady-state universe, 3C 295 would be more luminous than Cygnus A.

It is generally believed that non-thermal radio emission is produced by the synchrotron mechanism. As several authors have demonstrated, the theory of synchrotron emission permits an estimate of the energy requirements for a source, once the emitting volume and the radio luminosity and spectral index are known. Using rather limited data on the physical sizes of radio sources, Burbidge (1959) has already shown that the energy requirements for the more luminous sources are very great. We have thought it worthwhile to repeat these calculations for the sources described in this paper, inasmuch as the information presented here on source sizes and luminosities is considerably more detailed than that which has previously been available. We follow here the derivations of the Burbidges (G.R. 1956b; G.R. and E.M. 1957). Burbidge has given a short discussion of the assumptions underlying these calculations (1956a).

It is known that a non-thermal spectrum characterized by an intensity proportional to ν^x, where x is the usual spectral index, may be produced by a cloud of electrons circulating in a magnetic field H (in the following, H denotes the effective magnetic field) and having a number spectrum which varies with energy as E^{2x-1}. Each electron radiates most strongly near its critical frequency, given by $\nu_c \propto HE^2$; hence the cutoff frequencies assumed for the radio spectrum can be used to assign rough cutoff energies for

TABLE 2

REQUIRED MAGNETIC-FIELD STRENGTHS AND ENERGIES

Source	Spectral Index	Emitted Power (ergs/sec)	Volume (cm³)	H (oersted)	E_t (ergs)
3C 33..............	−0.70	4.0×10^{42}	4.3×10^{69}	3×10^{-5}	3×10^{59}
3C 40..............	−0.85	1.6×10^{41}	1.0×10^{68}	4×10^{-5}	1×10^{58}
3C 66..............	−0.65	3.7×10^{41}	2.1×10^{68}	3×10^{-5}	2×10^{58}
3C 71..............	−0.25	7.4×10^{39}	$<6.4\times10^{64}$	$>9\times10^{-5}$	$<4\times10^{55}$
3C 75..............	−0.65	2.8×10^{41}	4.8×10^{68}	2×10^{-5}	2×10^{58}
3C 78..............	−0.35	7.0×10^{41}	3.7×10^{68}	3×10^{-5}	3×10^{58}
For A..............	−0.75	2.5×10^{41}	2.2×10^{70}	8×10^{-6}	1×10^{59}
3C 98..............	−0.65	8.6×10^{41}	6.0×10^{68}	3×10^{-5}	5×10^{58}
3C 198..............	−0.95	1.6×10^{42}	2.4×10^{71}	8×10^{-6}	1×10^{60}
Hyd A $\{$core....	−0.65	1.0×10^{43}	1.5×10^{69}	5×10^{-5}	3×10^{59}
Hyd A $\{$halo....	−0.65	1.4×10^{42}	1.9×10^{71}	1×10^{-5}	3×10^{60}
3C 219..............	−0.70	2.2×10^{43}	6.7×10^{70}	2×10^{-5}	2×10^{60}
3C 270..............	−0.70	2.3×10^{40}	2.0×10^{67}	3×10^{-5}	2×10^{57}
Vir A $\{$core....	−0.30	1.6×10^{41}	2.5×10^{64}*	3×10^{-4}	2×10^{56}
Vir A $\{$halo....	−0.95	1.3×10^{41}	1.4×10^{68}	3×10^{-5}	1×10^{58}
3C 278..............	−0.85	1.4×10^{41}	3.4×10^{68}	2×10^{-5}	2×10^{58}
Cen A $\{$core....	−0.70	4.8×10^{40}	1.3×10^{66}	8×10^{-5}	7×10^{56}
Cen A $\{$halo....	−0.95	1.6×10^{41}	5.3×10^{70}	6×10^{-6}	2×10^{59}
3C 295..............	−0.50	4.4×10^{44}	5.0×10^{68}	2×10^{-4}	1×10^{60}
3C 310..............	−0.95	3.8×10^{42}	5.7×10^{69}	3×10^{-5}	4×10^{59}
3C 315..............	−0.80	6.3×10^{42}	4.2×10^{70}	2×10^{-5}	1×10^{60}
3C 327..............	−0.75	6.5×10^{42}	1.6×10^{70}	2×10^{-5}	7×10^{59}
3C 338..............	−1.10	5.0×10^{41}	5.0×10^{68}	4×10^{-5}	5×10^{58}
Her A..............	−0.90	1.1×10^{44}	3.1×10^{70}	5×10^{-5}	5×10^{60}
3C 353..............	−0.45	2.2×10^{42}	5.0×10^{68}	4×10^{-5}	7×10^{58}
Cyg A..............	−0.75	4.4×10^{44}	1.3×10^{69}	2×10^{-4}	3×10^{60}
3C 442..............	−1.10	2.6×10^{41}	5.0×10^{69}	2×10^{-5}	1×10^{59}

* Assumed to consist of two cylindrical components, each 1.5 kpc long and 0.6 kpc in diameter.

the electron spectrum. The electron spectrum can then be integrated between cutoffs to give the total electron energy,

$$E_e = C\,\frac{L}{H^2}\left(\frac{2+2x}{1+2x}\right)\frac{E_l^{2x+1}-E_h^{2x+1}}{E_l^{2x+2}-E_h^{2x+2}}.$$

Here E_l and E_h are the low and high cutoff energies, L is the radio luminosity, and C is a constant, approximately equal to 422.3 for c.g.s. units. If the cutoff frequencies are regarded as fixed, while the field strength H is left as a free parameter, the electron energy may be written as

$$E_e = C'LH^{-3/2},$$

where C' now includes a slow dependence on the cutoff frequencies and on the spectral index.

Let a be the ratio of heavy-particle energy, E_p, to the electron energy, E_e. The value of a is somewhat uncertain. Burbidge (1959) uses $a = 100$ on the assumption that the energy E_p is gradually transferred to secondary electrons produced by heavy-particle interactions. However, this process can be effective only in regions where the heavy-particle density is $\gtrsim 10^{-2}$ cm^{-3}.

The magnetic field energy E_m may be set equal to $H^2/8\pi$ times the volume occupied by the field. It has been customary in treatments such as this to assume that the magnetic field and the relativistic particles trapped in it are homogeneously distributed over the source volume. This may be the case, but it may also be that the source consists of tangled filaments and knots filling only a portion of the source volume. We let this portion be given by a filling factor ϕ. Then, if r is the radius of the emitting region, the magnetic field energy is

$$E_m = \phi \tfrac{4}{3}\pi r^3 \frac{H^2}{8\pi} = \phi \frac{H^2 r^3}{6}.$$

The total energy of the source (including the magnetic field and particles) is then given by

$$E_t = (1 + a) C'LH^{-3/2} + (\phi H^2 r^3)/6.$$

As can be seen from the dependence of the two terms on H, the total energy will have a minimum not far from the value of H for which the particle and field energies are equal. The functional dependences of the minimum energy and of the field required for minimum energy are as follows:

$$E_{min} \propto (1 + a)^{4/7} \phi^{3/7} L^{4/7} r^{9/7},$$

$$H(E_{min}) \propto (1 + a)^{2/7} \phi^{-2/7} L^{2/7} r^{-6/7}.$$

It is seen that these quantities are most strongly dependent on the radius of the emitting region, which emphasizes the need for accurate brightness distributions in order to determine the physical characteristics of radio sources. The field is seen to be quite insensitive to changes in a or ϕ, the total energy only moderately so.

On the assumption that $a = 100$, that $\phi = 1$, and that the field and particle energies are equal, the total energy requirements and the magnetic field have been calculated for each source, using the physical size obtained in Table 1, column 10. The results appear in the last two columns of Table 2. It is seen that the sources of small physical diameter, such as 3C 71 and the core of Virgo A, have magnetic fields near 10^{-4} oersted and comparatively low energy requirements of about 10^{56} ergs. The large, very luminous sources have energy requirements between 10^{60} and 10^{61} ergs.

As was mentioned earlier in this paper, the linear diameter of a source has been assumed to equal the product of the angular diameter and the distance. For the more distant sources, non-linear terms which depend on the choice of world model should be included in this calculation. As an example of the effect of this correction, the linear dimensions in Table 1 should be reduced by a factor of $(1 + z)^{-1}$ for a steady-state universe or by $(1 + z)^{-2}$ for a "$q_0 = +1$" universe. The correction for the source diameter will enter into the calculation of the energy, as will the correction for the source luminosity. The effects nearly cancel in the case of the steady-state universe, but for the case of $q_0 = +1$ the energy (E_t) of 3C 295 would be reduced by a factor of $(1 + z)^{-18/7} \approx 0.38$.

VI. DISCUSSION

In three of the sources examined, the radio core component is double (Centaurus A, Virgo A, and probably Hydra A). It is tempting to suppose that these double cores represent new sources which have recently been formed in the nuclei of their respective galaxies and which may in time add to the radio halos already surrounding these galaxies. 3C 71 is even smaller in proportion to the galaxy and may also be such a "new" source. The observations further suggest that a radio source is formed in or near the nucleus of a galaxy; initially its diameter is of the order of 10^3 pc or less. As the two components of a source grow older, they move away from the galaxy; at least some of the double sources finally reach distances of about 150 kpc from the galaxy and diameters of about 100 kpc. The energy input for the radio source probably lasts for only a relatively short interval of time when the components are near the galaxy, and subsequently the source lives on its stored energy. Since a given electron radiates away its energy in a time shorter than the minimum source lifetime found below, the radiating electrons cannot form the main energy reservoir.

Using this hypothesis, one may derive from the sizes of the sources some information about their ages. In Hercules A we detect emission from a distance of at least 180 h^{-1} kpc from the galaxy; in 3C 219 a projected distance of 210 h^{-1} kpc is observed. In Centaurus A there is quite definitely emission at a distance of $5°2$, or about 360 kpc (Bolton and Clark 1960). An expansion velocity equal to the speed of light would give a minimum age for these objects of the order of 10^6 years. An expansion velocity typical of the velocity, v_A, of hydromagnetic wave propagation in a galactic halo—$v_A \sim 2 \times 10^8$ cm/sec, assuming $n \sim 10^{-3}$ cm^{-3} and $H \sim 3 \times 10^{-5}$ oersted—would give very much greater ages of the order of 10^8–10^9 years.

A rough upper limit on the source lifetimes may be obtained from total energy considerations. The total mass-energy of a large galaxy is $\sim 10^{66}$ ergs. It is difficult to imagine an efficiency greater than $\sim 10^{-4}$ for any process which might convert the mass of stars into clouds of high-energy particles and magnetic fields. This suggests that our minimum total energies for the stronger sources of $\sim 10^{61}$ ergs (Table 2) are also close to the maximum energies which the sources have ever possessed. Dividing 5×10^{60} ergs by a radiation rate of 10^{44} ergs/sec, we obtain an estimated remaining lifetime of $\sim 10^9$ years.

A very high total energy is required to explain the observed radio emission of the more luminous sources. For seven sources in Table 2, E_t is more than 10^{60} ergs. These energies could be reduced if the ratio of E_p to E_e were much smaller or if the filling factor were much less than unity. On the other hand, if the magnetic and particle energies are not approximately equal, then the total energy must be larger. An amount of energy equal to 10^{60} ergs is perhaps best visualized as the total mass energy of 5×10^5 stars of solar mass; all this energy must be available in the form of relativistic particles and magnetic-field energy. The energy problem in radio sources has recently been considered by Shklovskii (1960), Hoyle (1961), and Burbidge (1961). The variety of the mechanisms proposed is probably the best indication of the theoretical difficulties which this problem presents.

We wish to thank Drs. J. L. Greenstein, R. Minkowski, A. R. Sandage, M. Schmidt, and F. Zwicky for their interest in the problem of identifying radio sources and for informing us of the results of their observations in advance of publication. We are most grateful to Dr. E. R. Herzog for his kindness in estimating for us the apparent magnitudes of the galaxies in Table 1. The continuing interest of G. J. Stanley, the director of the Owens Valley Observatory, is gratefully acknowledged. R. B. Read has given us valuable information on source declinations. One of us (P.M.) has been the recipient of a Fulbright Travel Grant and a grant from the Norwegian Research Council for Science and the Humanities. During the final preparation of this article, one of us (A.T.M.) has been a Fulbright Scholar visiting at the Observatory of the University of Bonn, Germany. He wishes to thank Professor F. Becker for the generous hospitality afforded him there. The program in radio astronomy at the California Institute of Technology is supported by the United States Office of Naval Research under contract Nonr 220(19).

REFERENCES

Allen, L. R., Palmer, H. P., and Rowson, B. 1960, *Nature*, **188**, 731.
Baade, W. 1956, *Ap. J.*, **123**, 550.
Baade, W., and Minkowski, R. 1954*a*, *Ap. J.*, **119**, 206.
———. 1954*b*, *ibid.*, p. 215.
Baldwin, J. E., and Smith, F. G. 1956, *Observatory*, **76**, 141.
Bolton, J. G. 1960, introductory talk at the session on discrete sources, U.R.S.I. General Assembly, London; also 1960, *Obs. California Inst. Technol.*, No. 5.
Bolton, J. G., and Clark, B. G. 1960, *Pub. A.S.P.*, **72**, 29. .
Bolton, J. G., Stanley, G. J., and Slee, O. B. 1949, *Nature*, **164**, 101.
Burbidge, E. M., and Burbidge, G. R. 1959, *Ap. J.*, **129**, 271.
Burbidge, E. M., Burbidge, G. R., and Prendergast, K. H. 1959, *Ap. J.*, **130**, 26.
Burbidge, G. R. 1956*a*, *Ap. J.*, **123**, 178.
———. 1956*b*, *ibid.*, **124**, 416.
———. 1959, *Paris Symposium on Radio Astronomy*, ed. R. N. Bracewell (Stanford, Calif.: Stanford University Press), p. 541.
———. 1961, *Nature*, **190**, 1053.
Burbidge, G. R., and Burbidge, E. M. 1957, *Ap. J.*, **125**, 1.
Dewhirst, D. W. 1959, *Paris Symposium on Radio Astronomy*, ed. R. N. Bracewell (Stanford, Calif.: Stanford University Press), p. 507.
Edge, D. O., Shakeshaft, J. R., McAdam, W. B., Baldwin, J. E., and Archer, S. 1959, *Mem. R.A.S.*, **68**, 37.
Elsmore, B. 1959, *Paris Symposium on Radio Astronomy*, ed. R. N. Bracewell (Stanford, Calif.: Stanford University Press), p. 337.
Elsmore, B., Ryle, M., and Leslie, P. R. R. 1959, *Mem. R.A.S.*, **68**, 61.
Greenstein, J. L. 1961, *Ap. J.*, **133**, 335.
———. 1962, *ibid.*, **135**, 679.
Harris, D. E., and Roberts, J. A. 1960, *Pub. A.S.P.*, **72**, 237.
Hiltner, W. A. 1959, *Ap. J.*, **130**, 340.
Hoyle, F. 1961, *Observatory*, **81**, 39.
Humason, M. L., Mayall, N. U., and Sandage, A. R. 1956, *A.J.*, **61**, 97.
Lequeux, J., and Heidmann, J. 1961, *C.R.*, **253**, 804.
Leslie, P. R. R. 1961, *M.N.*, **122**, 371.
Maltby, P. 1961, *Nature*, **191**, 793.
———. 1962, *Ap. J. Suppl.*, No. 67.
Maltby, P., and Moffet, A. T. 1962, *Ap. J. Suppl.*, No. 67.
Mills, B. Y. 1955, *Australian J. Phys.*, **8**, 368.
———. 1960, *Australian J. Phys.*, **13**, 550.
Mills, B. Y., Slee, O. B., and Hill, E. R. 1958, *Australian J. Phys.*, **11**, 360.
Minkowski, R. 1957, *I.A.U. Symposium*, No. 4: *Radio Astronomy*, ed. H. C. van de Hulst (Cambridge, England: Cambridge University Press), p. 107.
———. 1958, *Pub. A.S.P.*, **70**, 143.
———. 1960*a*, *Proc. Nat. Acad. Sci.*, **46**, 13.
———. 1960*b*, *Ap. J.*, **132**, 908.
———. 1961*a*, *A.J.*, **66**, 558.
———. 1961*b*, *Proceedings of the Fourth Berkeley Symposium on Mathematical Statistics and Probability*, ed. J. Neyman (Berkeley, Calif.: University of California Press), **4**, 245.
Moffet, A. T. 1962, *Ap. J. Suppl.*, No. 67.
Osterbrock, D. E. 1960, *Ap. J.*, **132**, 325.
Sandage, A. R. 1961*a*, *Ap. J.*, **133**, 355.
———. 1961*b*, *ibid.*, **134**, 916.
Sersic, J. L. 1960, *Zs. f. Ap.*, **51**, 64.
Seyfert, C. K. 1943, *Ap. J.*, **97**, 28.
Shklovskii, I. S. 1960, *Astr. J. U.S.S.R.*, **37**, 945; trans. in *Soviet Astr.—AJ*, **4**, 885.
Wade, C. M. 1961, *Pub. Nat. Radio Astr. Obs.*, **1**, 99.
Williams, P. J. S., Dewhirst, D. W., and Leslie, P. R. R. 1961, *Observatory*, **81**, 64.
Woltjer, L. 1959, *Ap. J.*, **130**, 38.
Zwicky, F. 1961, paper given at I.A.U. Symposium No. 15, "Problems of Extragalactic Research," *Proceedings*, in press.

PART IV

QUASI-STELLAR

RADIO SOURCES

THE QUASI-STELLAR RADIO
chapter 13 SOURCES 3C 48 AND 3C 273

Jesse L. Greenstein and Maarten Schmidt

I. INTRODUCTION

The present paper deals with optical objects of *stellar* appearance that have been associated with radio sources. The first radio source so identified was 3C 48, for which Matthews, Bolton, Greenstein, Münch, and Sandage (1960) announced the stellar appearance of the associated optical object. Subsequently, the radio sources 3C 196 and 3C 286 were identified with similar optical objects (Matthews and Sandage 1963), as was the source 3C 147 (Schmidt and Matthews 1964). The optical spectra of these four quasi-stellar objects appeared quite dissimilar, and no satisfactory identifications of the emission features could be obtained. The identification of the radio source 3C 273 with a bright object of stellar appearance provided a clue when it was found that its spectrum could be understood on the basis on an unexpectedly large redshift (Schmidt 1963). The spectrum of 3C 48, although of a rather different nature, could be explained by an even larger redshift (Greenstein and Matthews 1963).

The present discussion is limited to the *quasi-stellar radio sources* 3C 48 and 3C 273; the observational data are given in Sections II and III. The possibility of interpreting the redshift as the gravitational effect of either very dense or very massive objects is discussed in Section IV. The finally adopted interpretation of these quasi-stellar radio sources as distant, superluminous objects in galaxies, or intergalactic objects, is discussed in the remaining sections.

II. THE SOURCE 3C 273

A remarkably detailed study of the radio source 3C 273 has been made by Hazard, Mackey, and Shimmins (1963) using lunar occultations. They found that the source is double, with a separation of 19.5" between the components. Component A has a diameter of 4" at 400 Mc/s, and a spectral index of 0.9. Component B has a diameter of 3" at 400 Mc/s, with a spectral index near zero. This component has a core with a diameter of about 0.5" which contributes about half the flux at higher frequencies (Hazard, private communication). The position of each of the components was determined with an accuracy of around 1".

The two components coincide almost precisely with a thirteenth-magnitude star and the end of a faint jet. Figure 1 shows an enlarged portion of a 200-inch photograph taken by Sandage. The star is 1" east of Component B and the end of the jet 1" east of Com-

Jesse L. Greenstein and Maarten Schmidt, Mount Wilson and Palomar Observatories, Carnegie Institution of Washington and California Institute of Technology.

Reprinted from the *Astrophysical Journal*, **140**, 1–34, 1964.

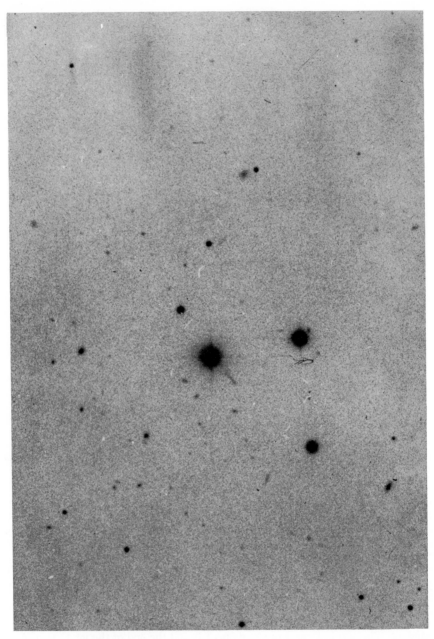

FIG. 1.—Enlarged portion of 200-inch photograph of 3C 273 (from a 103a-D plate taken by A. R. Sandage); north is up, east to left. The weak narrow jet visible in position angle 223° reaches to about 20″ from the quasi-stellar object.

ponent A. The jet is between 1″ and 2″ in width, begins 11″ and ends 20″ from the star. This is one of the few radio sources where one of the two components coincides with the optical object. Another case may be M87 where an asymmetric jet is also present.

Spectra of the star were taken in December, 1962, and January, 1963, with the prime-focus spectrograph at dispersions of 190 and 400 Å/mm. Figure 2 shows a spectrum with original dispersion of 400 Å/mm. The broad emission lines were found in a pattern resembling the Balmer series with an unexpectedly large redshift, $z = \Delta\lambda/\lambda_0 = 0.158$ (Schmidt 1963). The identification with the Balmer series was confirmed by Oke's (1963) observation of $H\alpha$ redshifted to λ 7590 ± 10 Å. The wavelength of 7590 Å is strongly affected by its chance superposition on the head of the atmospheric A-band of O_2. An infrared spectrum taken by Schmidt shows $H\alpha$ as an asymmetrical double wide line, the faint red component at 7617 Å corresponding with the first minimum in the absorption of the O_2-band. Thus, the wavelength of $H\alpha$ cannot be obtained with high accuracy.

TABLE 1

EMISSION LINES IN 3C 273

WAVELENGTH*		IDENTIFICATION	λ/λ_0
λ	λ_0		
3239..........	2798	Mg II	1.1576
4595..........	3970	$H\epsilon$	1.1574
4753..........	4101	$H\delta$	1.1590
5032..........	4340	$H\gamma$	1.1594
5200–5415......	(4490–4675)	....	
5632..........	4861	$H\beta$	1.1586
5792..........	5007	[O III]	1.1568
6005–6190......	(5186–5345)	....	
6400–6510......	(5527–5622)	....	
		Weighted mean....1.1581±0.0004	

* A sharp, weak line at 4318 Å is possibly λ 3727 [O II] emission.

Table 1 contains the observed wavelengths and identifications. Besides the Balmer lines, the identifications involve the Mg II doublet at about 2800 Å, and the strongest forbidden line of [O III]. The fit is quite satisfactory for the identifiable lines. The mean redshift is 0.1581 ± 0.0004; this internal mean error corresponds to about ±4 Å per line and is quite reasonable for the dispersion and line quality. The identified lines are about 50 Å wide. No detailed explanation of the broad lines can be given, although the $\lambda\lambda$ 4490–4675 group (possibly also present in 3C 48) could be the blend of He II, C III, C IV, and N III found in hot emission-line stars or in Type II supernovae. Interstellar Ca II absorption lines have been found by Preston (private communication), and subsequently also on a Palomar spectrum with a dispersion of 85 Å/mm. This plate also shows a weak, sharp emission line at 4318 Å, corresponding to λ 3727 of [O II]. It has the correct shift, but cannot come from the same physical volume or have been formed under the same excitation conditions as the other lines.

The continuum is blue with a nearly flat energy distribution, bluer than that of the quasi-stellar objects discussed by Matthews and Sandage (1963). The apparent brightness of the star is $m_V = +12.6$, or a flux of 3.5×10^{-25} erg cm^{-2} sec^{-1} (c/s)$^{-1}$ at λ 5600, according to Oke (1963). According to new measures by Oke, the Balmer gradient is not steep. His further measurements provide information on the excitation mechanism, and on the relative importance of Paschen, Balmer, and synchrotron continua.

Smith and Hoffleit (1963) have inspected the Harvard Patrol plates and found that

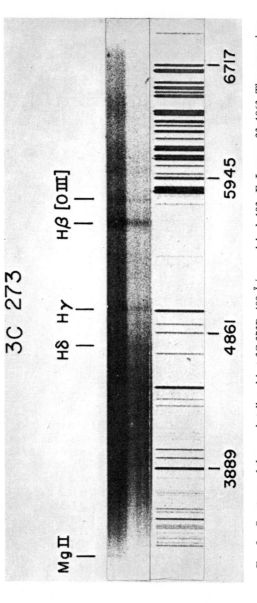

Fig. 2.—Spectrum of the quasi-stellar object 3C 273B, 400 Å/mm original, 103a-F, January 23, 1963. The comparison spectrum is H + He + Ne. Exposure over the upper half of slit was three times that over the lower half. Redshifted emission lines of H and [O III] are indicated; also the barely visible line of Mg II, confirmed on denser exposures.

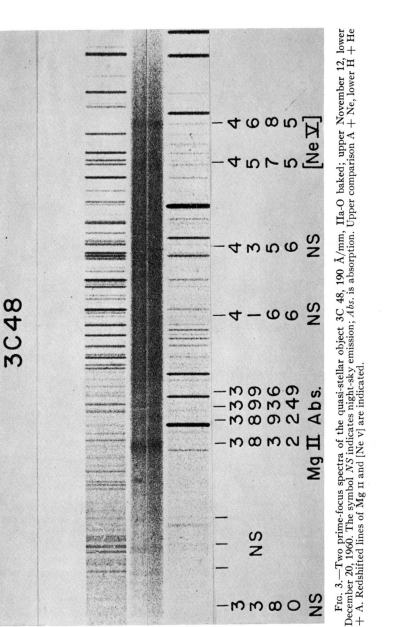

Fig. 3.—Two prime-focus spectra of the quasi-stellar object 3C 48, 190 Å/mm, IIa-O baked; upper November 12, lower December 20, 1960. The symbol *NS* indicates night-sky emission; *Abs.* is absorption. Upper comparison A + Ne, lower H + He + A. Redshifted lines of Mg II and [Ne V] are indicated.

the brightness of the star is nearly the same as it was 80 years ago. They report fluctuations up to 0.4 mag. with a rough period of about 10 years and scattered brightenings of a month's duration. Sharov and Efremov (1963) reported similar variations.

The proper motion is less than 0.01″/yr according to Luyten (1963), and less than 0.001″/yr according to Jefferys (reported at this conference and the December 1963 AAS meeting).

III. THE SOURCE 3C 48

The radio source is smaller than 1″ and apparently single. The photographic image of 3C 48 is stellar except for faint reddish wisps about 12″ N.-S. by 5″ E.-W. The star is 3″ north of the center of these weak features, whose distribution of intensity is irregular (Matthews and Sandage 1963).

TABLE 2

PROBABLE REAL LINES WITH IDENTIFICATIONS IN 3C 48*

Int.	λ	λ₀	Quality	Identification	λ/λ₀
10 E.....	3832.3	{2796 / 2803}	Broader than average	Mg II	1.3697:
1 A.....	3892	....	Sharp	?	....
1 A.....	3934.7	3933	Sharp	Ca II, interstellar?	....
1 A.....	3969	3968	Sharp	Ca II, interstellar?	....
2 E.....	4048.2	4047	Broad	Hg I, night sky	....
1 E.....	4065.7	2975:	Broad	[Ne v]	1.3667:
0 A.....	4139	....	Broad		....
0 A.....	4151	....	Broad		....
1 E.....	4166	....	Broad	Probably night sky	....
0 E.....	4205.3	....	Sharp		....
3 E.....	4356	4358	Sharp	Hg I, night sky	....
0 A.....	4553.7	....	Broad		....
3 E.....	4575	3346	Broad	[Ne v]	1.3673
5 E.....	4685.0	3426.	Broad	[Ne v]	1.3676
5 E.....	5097	{3726 / 3729}	Sharp	[O II]	1.3676
1 E.....	5136	....	Sharp		....
3 E.....	5288	3869	Sharp	[Ne III]	1.3668
10 E.....	5935	4340	Broad	Hγ	1.3675
2 E.....	6349:	4640–50	Broad		....
20 E.....	6646	4861	Very broad	Hβ	1.3672

Weighted mean (λ/λ₀) ...1.3675 ± 0.0002

* It is possible that [O III] is present and strong at the extreme red end of the plate sensitivity.

The first spectra of the stellar object, obtained in October, 1960, by Sandage, were sufficiently abnormal to show that this object was not an ordinary star or an extragalactic nebula of moderate redshift. An excellent spectrum at dispersion 190 Å/mm by Münch and several by Greenstein at dispersions of 190 and 400 Å/mm in 1961 established the existence of a nearly featureless continuum extending far into the ultraviolet and of weak, broad, emission lines not observed in normal or peculiar stars. Some details were reported by Greenstein and Münch (1961).

Figure 3 shows two spectra (6-hour exposures) of the blue region, original dispersion 190 Å/mm; the faint emission features are real, broad, and of low contrast. The colors ($B - V = +0^m41$, $U - B = -0^m59$) are not far from those of a cool white dwarf and indicate the extension of the spectrum into the ultraviolet. A trace of weak, sharp, Ca II absorption lines is seen, and also, on one plate, a line near λ 3888. The stationary H- and K-lines are interstellar and are somewhat strong for the high latitude and low dispersion used.

Table 2 contains a list of lines, measured at least twice, from which all obvious night-sky lines and dubious stellar lines have been omitted. Most of the features of Table 2 are probably real. Figure 4 is a sketch of the most significant features, in the blue, derived from the mean of direct-intensity tracings of two plates at 190 Å/mm, uncorrected for plate sensitivity. The exposures, 5–6 hours in length, have airglow features, the Herzberg bands of O_2, some city mercury lines, and slight traces of N_2 and N_2^+ (low-latitude aurorae). Broad minima are suspected in the blue, at observed λλ 4230, 4310. The λ 3832 feature has a half-width of 35 Å, as compared to the other weaker emissions, which average 23 Å.

The coincidence in wavelength of the strong emission feature in 3C 48 (at 4685 Å) with

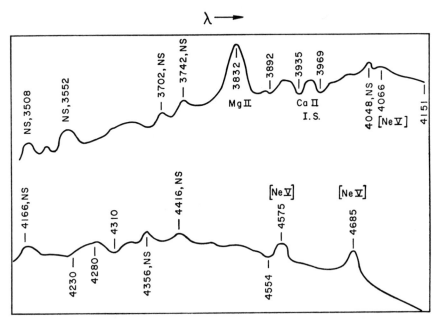

FIG. 4.—Mean of two microphotometer tracings of 3C 48 (not on an intensity scale). There is a possible slight contamination of λλ 3935, 3969 by moonlight. *NS* means night-sky emissions. Red-shifted lines of Mg II and [Ne v] are indicated.

the λ 4686 line of He II figured importantly in earlier attempts to explain the spectrum as that of a star of zero redshift. After the discovery by Schmidt of a large redshift in the Balmer spectrum of 3C 273 it was found that the strongest lines in 3C 48 can be identified (see Table 2) using a redshift $\Delta\lambda/\lambda_0 = 0.3675 \pm 0.0003$ (Greenstein and Matthews 1963). The wavelength of the blended Mg II resonance doublet is somewhat discrepant, possibly caused by self-absorption in an expanding envelope. A recently obtained low-dispersion spectrum at 760 Å/mm in the red shows the redshifted hydrogen lines Hγ and Hβ. A direct-intensity tracing is shown in Figure 5. The rapid drop in the 103a-F plate sensitivity at longer wavelengths and the presence of the atmospheric B-band make identifications from λ 6700 to λ 6850 difficult. But there is some evidence for a broad sensitivity maximum here, not measured, but corresponding to the redshifted wavelengths of the N1 and N2 [O III] lines. These have been confirmed by spectral scans by Oke. The hydrogen lines are 80 Å wide near the continuum level, suggesting a Doppler half-half-width of 1100 km/sec. There is a possible broad feature whose corrected wavelength is near λ 4643.

IV. THE POSSIBILITY OF GRAVITATIONAL REDSHIFTS

Redshifts as large as those found for 3C 48 and 3C 273 have thus far only been encountered in distant galaxies. Both sources have a dominant optical component with an angular diameter of less than 1″, simulating the appearance of a star. The observed redshifts cannot be explained as velocity shifts of ordinary stars; the low upper limit to the proper motion of 3C 273 in conjunction with a transverse velocity of the same order as the observed redshift would lead to a minimum distance of 10 Mpc, and an absolute magnitude higher than − 16. We shall discuss in the present section a possible interpretation in terms of gravitational redshifts. We divide the considerations into those relevant to collapsed "neutron" stars and to very massive objects.

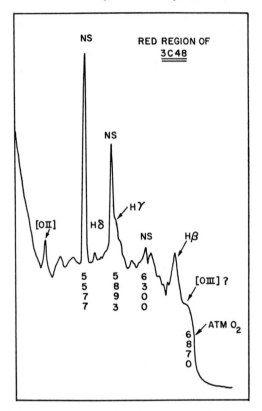

FIG. 5.—Microphotometer tracing of a low-dispersion spectrum of 3C 48 in the red, November 19, 1963. The source was near $V = 16^{m}5$ on all dates for which spectra of 3C 48 are reproduced.

Let us investigate the consequences of assuming that the redshift is of gravitational origin. The gravitational redshift is

$$\frac{\Delta\lambda}{\lambda_0} = \frac{GM}{Rc^2}$$

$$= 1.47 \times 10^5 \frac{M/M_\odot}{R},$$ (1)

where R is the mean radius in centimeters. The width w of the emission lines, though considerable, is but a small part of the redshift $\Delta\lambda$. If the line width is due solely to the variation of gravitational potential over the region containing ionized gases, they must be confined within a shell with thickness ΔR, such that

$$\Delta R/R = w/\Delta\lambda .$$ (2)

Table 3 shows some relevant data for the two sources.

Stars of very high density (approaching that of compressed nuclear matter) may result from the collapse of a massive star or of a supernova of Type II. A stable stellar nucleus could remain surrounded by a gaseous envelope. The gravitational potential energy of such dense objects approaches the rest-mass energy. The star will contain neutrons or, at higher densities, protons and hyperons. Work by Wheeler (1958), Cameron (1959), and Salpeter (1961) gives stable models in the range of central densities, ρ_c, 10^{15} to 10^{19} gm/cm^3. The gravitational redshift at their surface gives z in the range 0.1 up to about 0.6 (with considerable uncertainty at the upper bound). Unfortunately, the theory of collapsed stellar configurations is still in doubt and incomplete. Oppenheimer and Volkoff (1939) give a maximum redshift near $z = 0.11$ for a neutron gas with degenerate pressure. Cameron's models, with a specific nuclear repulsion law, apparently permit a larger mass and redshift. Cameron found for $\rho_c = 10^{13}$ gm/cm^2, $z = 0.002$; for $\rho_c = 10^{15}$, $z = 0.14$ (near 3C 273); and for $\rho_c = 2 \times 10^{15}$, $z = 0.35$ (close to 3C 48). Ambartsumian

TABLE 3

INTERPRETATION INVOLVING GRAVITATIONAL REDSHIFT

	3C 48	3C 273
$\Delta\lambda/\lambda_0$.........	0.367	0.158
w (Ångstroms)....	~30	~50
R (cm).........	$4.0 \times 10^5 \, M/M_\odot$	$9.3 \times 10^5 \, M/M_\odot$
$\Delta R/R$.........	0.016	0.07

and Saakyan (1961) have also studied the properties of the neutron-baryon stars and found an error in Cameron's application of his equation of state. Essentially, Ambartsumian and Saakyan (1961) first found that the maximum mass lay near 1.03 $M\odot$, at a density where hyperons were the most abundant constituent. Saakyan (1963) found that Cameron's masses, even with the latter's equation of state, were too large by a factor of approximately $\frac{3}{2}$. Ambartsumian and Saakyan find a maximum value of $M\odot/R_{km} = 0.28$ for an incompressible baryon gas, which gives a maximum $z = 0.42$. This is just above the observed value (0.37) for 3C 48. A general discussion by Bondi apparently will make possible evaluation of the maximum possible z. His present limit, $z < 1.5$, involves negative density gradients. A more useful limit, as low as $z < 0.6$, seems within the range of plausibility.

A much more positive argument arises from evaluation of the emission from ionized hydrogen. At an electron temperature T_e and electron density N_e the emissivity in Hβ is (Aller 1956)

$$E(H\beta) = 2.28 \times 10^{-19} \, N_e^2 T_e^{-3/2} b_4 \exp{(0.98 \times 10^4/T_e)} ,$$ (3a)

where b_4 measures the deviation from equilibrium population of the upper level of Hβ. We assume $T_e = 10^{4\,\circ}$ K, and a typical average nebular value of $b_4 = 0.16$. Then we compute

$$E(H\beta) = 1.0 \times 10^{-25} \, N_e^2 \text{ erg sec}^{-1} \text{ cm}^{-3} .$$ (3b)

The observed brightness of Hβ in 3C 273 is 3.4×10^{-12} erg cm^{-2} sec^{-1}. Equating this to the emission from a volume, V, of ionized hydrogen at a distance, r, yields the relation

$$10^{-25}\, V\, N_e{}^2 = 3.4 \times 10^{-12}\, 4\pi r^2 \,. \tag{4a}$$

Here $V = 4\pi R^2 \Delta R$, and $\Delta R = 0.07\, R$ is obtained in Table 3 from the width of the emission lines. Finally we have

$$N_e{}^2 R^3 r^{-2} = 4 \times 10^{14}\ \mathrm{cm}^{-5} \,. \tag{4b}$$

Let us first consider the possibility of a collapsed body of nearly normal stellar mass. The absence of observable proper motion makes a distance less than 100 pc very unlikely. Introducing this minimum distance into equation (4b) leads to the inequality

$$N_e{}^2 R^3 \geq 4 \times 10^{55}\ \mathrm{cm}^{-3} \,. \tag{4c}$$

If the mass of the object is 1 $M\odot$, then $R \approx 10^6$ cm, from Table 3, and we need $N_e \geq 6 \times 10^{18}$ cm^{-3}. This density is very much larger than the maximum electron density of about 10^8 cm^{-3} which is imposed by the appearance of a forbidden line in the spectrum. This enormous discrepancy cannot be removed by any other choice of T_e, or of b_4, in equation (3a), and we are forced to the conclusion that the spectrum of 3C 273 cannot be explained by gravitational redshift near a star of about 1 $M\odot$. Similar conclusions can be reached with regard to 3C 48, in which the forbidden lines are very strong, making the upper limit to N_e even lower.

The total luminosity in Hβ at $N_e = 6 \times 10^8$ cm^{-3} exceeds 10^{30} erg sec^{-1}. A black body of $R = 10^6$ cm and $T = 10^4$ ° K emits 7×10^{24} erg sec^{-1}; therefore the emission-line flux exceeds that from a black body, which is impossible. In fact, so high an electron density would result in a largely neutral gas opaque to its own radiation. The monochromatic flux at Earth from an object of radius R cm at a distance of r_{pc}, using the infrared approximation to the black body, is

$$F_\nu d\nu = 10^{-73} \left(\frac{R}{r_{\mathrm{pc}}}\right)^2 T\nu^2 d\nu\ \mathrm{erg\ sec}^{-1}\ \mathrm{cm}^{-2}(\mathrm{c/s})^{-1} \,. \tag{5}$$

With $R = 10^6$ cm, $r_{\mathrm{pc}} = 10^2$, $\nu = 6 \times 10^{14}$, we have $F_\nu \approx 4 \times 10^{-36}\, T$ erg sec^{-1} cm^{-2} (c/s)$^{-1}$ at 5000 Å. Since the observed $F_\nu \approx 4 \times 10^{-25}$ for 3C 273, we require that $T = 10^{11}$ ° K if the black-body radiation of a 10-km star is to produce the continuum.

The discovery of hyperdense stars would be of great interest in theoretical physics; our conclusions suggest that optical detection is hopelessly difficult. From the theoretical physics side, in addition, if only neutron degeneracy determines the pressure, the redshifts already observed are too large to be explained in this manner.

Another possible interpretation of a gravitational redshift, from equation (1), is that it arises in an object of very great mass and moderate radius, e.g., $10^8\, M\odot$ and $R = 10^{14}$ cm. We disregard for the moment questions regarding the stability of such a configuration. If such an object is located in or near our Galaxy, an additional limiting condition on its distance can be derived from its gravitational perturbations on the local dynamics of the Galaxy. The acceleration for stars near the Sun due to a single radio source certainly should be less than 10 per cent of that of the whole Galaxy, which gives

$$M/M\odot \leq 10^{-35}\, r^2 \,. \tag{6}$$

The emission in Hβ, from equation (3b), yields a flux at the Earth of

$$F(\mathrm{H}\beta) = 10^{-25}\, N_e{}^2 R^2\, \Delta R\, r^{-2} \,. \tag{7}$$

Combining equations (1), (6), and (7),

$$r^4 \geq N_e^{-2}(\Delta R/R)^{-1} \, (\Delta\lambda/\lambda_0)^3 \, 10^{114.5}F(H\beta) \,, \tag{8a}$$

$$M/M\odot \geq N_e^{-1} \, (\Delta R/R)^{-1/2}(\Delta\lambda/\lambda_0)^{3/2} \, 10^{22.2} \, [F(H\beta)]^{1/2} \,. \tag{8b}$$

The $H\beta$ fluxes are 3.4×10^{-12} and 4.4×10^{-14} erg cm^{-2} sec $^{-1}$ for 3C 273 and 3C 48, respectively; the redshifts and $\Delta R/R$ from Table 3 give approximately the same results for the two sources:

$$r_{\rm pc} > 8 \times 10^6 \, N_e^{-1/2} \,,$$
$$M/M\odot > 7 \times 10^{15} \, N_e^{-1} \,. \tag{9}$$

We will see that the spectra, containing forbidden lines, are not consistent with an N_e very different from 10^7 cm^{-3} for 3C 273, and a somewhat lower value, 10^5 cm^{-3} for 3C 48. The resulting values are for 3C 273, $r_{\rm pc} \geq 2500$, $M/M\odot \geq 7 \times 10^8$ and for 3C 48 $r_{\rm pc} \geq 25000$ and $M/M\odot \geq 7 \times 10^{10}$. These minimum values are derived for the unlikely case of a gravitational perturbation 10 per cent that of the attraction of the Galaxy. From the structure of the equations, when we lower this upper limit to the perturbation, we increase the mass and radius in equation (9). The high latitude of 3C 273 ($b = 60°$) and the fact that the above mass and distance are minimum values make it quite safe to conclude that the interpretation of the redshift as a gravitational effect also requires an extragalactic nature for these quasi-stellar objects. We are reminded here of the gravitationally collapsing masses investigated by Hoyle and Fowler (1963; see also Fowler and Hoyle 1964) with a view to gaining some understanding of the origin of the very large energies required in the strong extragalactic radio sources. At present, there is no assurance from the theory, and it may even be viewed as unlikely, that 10^{11} $M\odot$ within a radius of 0.01 pc are stable. If gravitational implosions should occur, it is difficult to see what train of theoretical arguments would lead to a gaseous shell of fixed radius and 10^{-4} pc thickness. Under large gravitational attraction, only a very narrow range of temperature (or explosion velocities) could produce such a scale height. It is difficult also to understand why the density distribution would be such as to make the emission lines quite symmetrical. On this hypothesis the red wing would originate in the inner part and the blue wing in the outer part of a thin shell.

   We believe that the postulation of stable, or nearly stable, objects of size less than 1 pc, with masses near those of galaxies, in nearby intergalactic space is not really justified at present. Consequently, we reject gravitational redshift as a basis for explanation of the large redshifts observed in 3C 48 and 3C 273. If stable, massive configurations exist, we must re-examine this possibility. The mass-radius relation would have to be such as to give larger gravitational redshifts for fainter objects. Although the range of shifts is small (a factor of 3 with recent discoveries), if we interpret the shifts as cosmological we deduce consistent optical and radio absolute fluxes for sources at various redshifts. The unprecedented combination of redshift, apparent luminosity, and appearance of 3C 48 and 3C 273 will require an unorthodox explanation.

V. EMISSION LINES IN A SUPERLUMINOUS GALAXY

   Let us assume as the surviving hypothesis that the redshifts for 3C 48 and 3C 273 are cosmological redshifts. With a Hubble constant of 100 km sec^{-1} Mpc^{-1} the distances are 1100 and 474 Mpc, respectively. The absolute visual magnitudes become about -25 and -26, respectively, making these objects the brightest yet known in the universe.

   The upper limits for the angular diameters of the optical starlike components, from visual inspection, are $1''$ for 3C 48, and $\frac{1}{2}''$ for 3C 273, corresponding to 5 kpc, and 1 kpc, respectively. The southern end of the optical wisps of 3C 48 is at a distance of about 50 kpc in projection. The end of the jet in 3C 273 is also at a projected distance of about 50 kpc from the quasi-stellar object. If these features have been ejected from the central objects, this event took place at least 2×10^5 years ago.

At these distances, corrections to luminosities depend on the specific world model. For an approximate determination of the fluxes in the emission lines we use the formulae given by Sandage (1961) based on Mattig (1958). For the energy contained within an emission line, in which we integrate over the entire profile, the correction to the inverse-square law is of the form $(1 + z/2)^2$ if the cosmological constant and deceleration parameter are zero. It is $(1 + z)^2$ for the steady-state model. We use the $(1 + z/2)^2$ correction in Table 4 to obtain the luminosity, L, in each line from the measured equivalent widths, W. Note that the emission-equivalent widths, in units of the neighboring continuum, are only poorly determined, because of the low contrast and width of the lines. In addition we used interpolated estimates of the flux in the continuum, as measured by Matthews and Sandage (1963) for 3C 38 and Oke (1963) for 3C 273.

The spectra observed are not too different from those of planetary or diffuse nebulae, except for the presence of Mg II, hitherto undetected because of terrestrial ozone absorption, but probably present in other nebulae. In the study of spectra of emission regions it is the distribution over various levels of ionization that introduces the greatest uncertainty in the determination of element abundances. This problem exists even more strongly for the spectra at hand, since the ultraviolet radiation field is unknown.[1] We have tried to circumvent the problem as well as possible by comparing the spectra with those of planetary nebulae and normalizing our computations to give intensities observed in planetaries of similar excitation. We assume that the chemical composition of the emitting regions is "normal," and that the electron temperature is $\theta_e = 0.3$ (slightly higher than normal). (See Appendix I for a detailed discussion of θ_e.)

We have revised and improved the expressions given by Aller (1954) for η_2, the deviation from thermodynamic equilibrium in the levels producing the nebular lines; we use, in particular for [O II], the work of Seaton and Osterbrock (1957) and compute the populations of the $^2D_{5/2}$ and $^2D_{3/2}$ levels separately before adding the intensities. The predicted emission per cubic parsec is given in Table 5 on a scale where O+ and O++ have the same abundance, taken as 10^{-4} that of hydrogen, and where Ne++ and Ne++++ are taken as 10^{-5} that of hydrogen; we assume $N(H^+) = N_e$. Where more than one nebular line is present, the sum of the intensities is given. Elements like Ne and O have a concentration near this value, and the distribution over the various ionization levels could re-

---

[1] *Note added in proof.*—The levels of ionization of common elements have been computed approximately by House (*Ap. J. Suppl.*, 8, 307, 1964) for coronal conditions, far from Boltzmann equilibrium in the absence of ultraviolet quanta. Collisional ionization is balanced by collisional and radiative recombinations. House's computations were made specifically for laboratory or solar plasma, i.e., very high electron density, 10^{15} cm^{-3}. At lower electron density, they are incorrect if radiative ionization rates are in any way appreciable. For us, the most critical question is whether the weakness of [O II] in 3C 273 could arise from such anomalous collisional ionization; we give below his values of the logarithm of the fractional concentration of an ion, in units of the total number of all ions of that element present, as a function of T_e in eV (1 eV = 11600° K).

EQUILIBRIUM	LOG N(ION)/N(ELEMENT)				
	$T=1$ eV	1.8 eV	3 eV	6 eV	10 eV
O+/O	−1.5	0.0	−0.2	−1.9	−4.9
O++/O		−4.5	−0.8	−0.3	−1.7
Ne++/Ne		−5.0	−1.4	−0.1	−1.5
Ne++++/Ne				−5.0	−0.8
Mg+/Mg	0.0	−0.7	−2.6	−3.8	−4.9

Inspection shows that there is no T_e which makes O+ weak and leaves O++ present without highly ionizing Mg+. Consequently, the weakness of [O II] in 3C 273 is confirmed as a density effect even if the ionization is collisional. The presence of [Ne III] and [Ne v] in 3C 48 requires $T_e > 2$ eV, i.e., higher than we used, and their weakness in 3C 273 suggests $T_e < 3$ eV. The probable values of electron temperature in the collisional case do not differ much from those obtained by our use of an analogy with planetary nebulae.

sult in Table 5 being approximately correct. The table also contains the predicted intensity of the hydrogen line, Hβ, per pc^3, derived from equation (3a). We use higher temperature $\theta_e = 0.3$, $b_4 = 0.16$, and normal composition instead of equation (3b) to give results tabulated in Table 5.

The Appendix contains a detailed study of the [Ne v] and Mg II lines. A very serious problem, comparable to that of Lyman-α, is raised by the high opacity in the Mg II lines. The strength of Mg II results from its high abundance, the low energy required, 4.42 eV, and the large collisional cross-section, $\Omega \approx 25$. The latter has been estimated by van Regemorter (1960a, b) for collisions of moderate energy. From his work, the Ca II resonance doublet has $\Omega \approx 6$, and since the normal abundance ratio Ca/Mg is near 0.06,

TABLE 4

EMISSION-LINE LUMINOSITIES

		3C 48	3C 273
r Mpc		1100	474
$(1+z/2)^2$		1.40	1.16
$4\pi r^2(1+z/2)^2$ cm^2		2.0×10^{56}	3.1×10^{55}
W(Ångstroms):	Hβ	28	86
	Mg II	10*	11*
	[Ne v]	6*	Absent
	[O II]	12*	Absent?
	[O III]	Present	24*
L (erg sec^{-1}):	Hβ	6.4×10^{42}	8.8×10^{43}
	Mg II	3.1×10^{42}*	4.0×10^{43}*
	[Ne v]	1.7×10^{42}*	. . . .
	[O II]	3.3×10^{42}*	?
	[O III]	Present	3.1×10^{43}*

* The sum of W of the two lines of each doublet is given, except for W of [O III], which is for λ 5007 only. L is the sum over each doublet.

TABLE 5

PREDICTED LUMINOSITIES IN FORBIDDEN LINES, Hβ AND MG II

($\theta_e = 0.3$; log $E(X)$ in erg sec^{-1} pc^{-3})

LOG N_e CM^{-3}	LOG ρ $M\odot$ PC^{-3}	LOG $E(X)$					
		[O II]*	[O III]*	[Ne III]†	[Ne v]†	Hβ	Mg II‡
2	0.4	35.1	35.7	34.8	34.7	34.0	33.4
3	1.4	37.0	37.7	36.8	36.7	36.0	35.4
4	2.4	38.7	39.7	38.8	38.7	38.0	37.4
5	3.4	40.0	41.7	40.8	40.7	40.0	39.4
6	4.4	41.0	43.5	42.7	42.7	42.0	41.4
7	5.4	42.0	44.8	44.6	44.6	44.0	43.4
8	6.4	43.0	45.8	46.1	46.2	46.0	45.4

* The ions of oxygen, O$^+$/O^{++}, vary greatly from one planetary nebula to another; the ratio is often less than 0.1. We adopt O/H $= 10^{-3}$, O$^+$/H $= 3 \times 10^{-5}$, and O^{++}/H $= 5 \times 10^{-4}$.

† The mean abundance used is Ne/O $= 0.2$ and the ions are spread evenly over Ne^{++} to Ne^{++++}, i.e., Ne^{++}/H $= 7 \times 10^{-5}$. Lower excitation planetaries have Ne^{++}/Ne^{++++} greater than unity.

‡ The abundance Mg/H is taken as 3×10^{-5}. The very rough ionization equilibrium in planetaries varies enormously at the low ionization-potential end, but $(1 - x_{Mg^+})$ is taken as 10^{-3}, with Mg^{++} assumed dominant.

the product of abundance times cross-section is near 0.015. The ionization of Ca^+ would also be greater than that of Mg^+, so that the great strength of Mg II is not completely unexpected; Daub (1963) had derived its intensity in discussing planetary nebulae. In the rocket solar spectra, the Mg II resonance doublet is outstandingly strong (Friedman 1963). The collisional de-excitation of the upper level of the Mg II line is negligible for $N_e < 10^{15}$ cm^{-3}. The emission of Mg II summed over the two lines is

$$E(\text{Mg \textsc{ii}}) = N_2 h\nu A_{21} = N_i(\text{Mg}^+) N_e \frac{\Omega_{12}}{g_1} C h\nu 10^{-4.42\theta_e}, \qquad (10)$$

where

$$C = 8.54 \times 10^{-6} T_e^{-1/2}.$$

Let $N_i(\text{Mg}^+)$ be $Z_x N_e$, where $Z_x N_e$ represents the Mg^+/H ratio. Then if Mg^+ were the dominant stage of ionization of Mg, $\log Z_x = -4.5$ using its normal solar abundance. Retaining x_{Mg^+}, its level of second ionization as a parameter, gives the effective number $\log N_i(\text{Mg}^+) = -4.5 + \log (1 - x_{\text{Mg}^+}) + \log N_e$. We neglect recombination as a source

TABLE 6

COMPARISON OF OBSERVED AND PREDICTED LINE INTENSITIES
(NORMALIZED TO Hβ)

	LOG $E(X)/(\text{H}\beta)$			
	[O II]	[O III]	[Ne III]	[Ne V]
3C 48....................	−0.3	Present	(−0.6):	−0.6
NGC 7027................	−0.8	+1.2	−0.1	−0.1
Table 5, $N_e = 10^5$...........	0.0	+1.7	+0.8	+0.7
Correction based on NGC 7027....	−0.8	−0.5	−0.9	−0.8
IC418....................	+0.3	+0.2	−1.5	Abs.
Table 5, $N_e = 10^3$............	+1.0	+1.7	+0.8	+0.7
Correction based on IC418........	−0.7	−1.5	−2.3	−2.3

of population of the upper level of the λ 2800 doublet. Finally, the emission per cubic parsec in the Mg II doublet is

$$E(\text{Mg \textsc{ii}}) = 2.6 \times 10^{32} N_e^2 (1 - x_{\text{Mg}^+}). \qquad (11)$$

It is very difficult to estimate the level of ionization of Mg^+ as compared to O^{++} or Ne^{++} or Ne^{+++}. The latter are usually the dominant states of ionization in high-excitation planetary nebulae. The results given by Aller and Menzel (1945) and Aller (1954) indicate a quite flat distribution of concentration over the various ions with O^+/O^{++} near 0.1. The data on NGC 7009 and 7027 obtained by Aller suggest, after considerable extrapolation, that Mg^+, with an ionization potential of 15 eV, is 10^{-3} of total Mg, the balance being Mg^{++}, with an 80-eV ionization potential. Consequently, in Table 5 we have assumed $1 - x_{\text{Mg}^+} = 10^{-3}$.

The energies are large enough so that only a few cubic parsecs are needed, if $N_e > 10^5$, to match the observed emission-line strengths. We cannot view the predicted relative intensities as final, because of the uncertainties of abundances and concentration of ions. In Table 6 we give observed line intensities (O'Dell 1963) in the high-excitation planetary nebula, NGC 7027 (which has $\log N_e = 3.7$, $\theta_e = 0.3$) and repeat the row, $\log N_e = 5$ from Table 5. Note that 3C 48 runs parallel to NGC 7027, except that it has stronger

[O II], weaker [Ne V], and possibly weaker [Ne III], for which only a rough estimate can be given. The corrections to Table 5 suggested by NGC 7027, on the average, are a factor of -0.8 in the logarithm, but the variations are smaller than a factor of 10. Just as in planetary nebulae, we have a considerable range of ionization level, with 3C 48 and 3C 273 differing very appreciably. The presence of strong [O III] in 3C 48 may be suggested by the results shown in Figure 5 where there seems to be a strong, excess emission longward of Hβ. Oke kindly informs us that photoelectric scans have, in fact, shown that [O III] is present. The rough intensities in 3C 48 give corrections which are not very different from those suggested by NGC 7027 and suggest a slightly lower level of ionization, since [O II] is stronger and [Ne V] weaker. We adopt a set of corrections shown in the fourth line of Table 6 and recompute part of Table 5, shown in Table 7A. No correction to the predicted Mg II intensities is made, since observations in planetary nebulae are not available. The correction to the O and Ne ionic concentrations may reflect peculiarities of ionization, a slightly lower than normal abundance, or most probably a wide variation in density and size of the emitting region for different ions.

TABLE 7A

CORRECTED PREDICTED EMISSIVITIES FOR 3C 48; RADIUS AND HYDROGEN MASS
DERIVED FROM OBSERVED Hβ LUMINOSITY

LOG N_e CM^{-3}	LOG $E(X)$, ERG SEC^{-1} PC^{-3}						LOG R_{pc}	LOG $M(H)/$ $M\odot$
	[O II]	[O III]	[Ne III]	[Ne V]	Mg II	Hβ		
2	34.3	35.2	33.9	33.9	33.4	34.0	+2.73	9.2
3	36.2	37.2	35.9	35.9	35.4	36.0	+2.06	8.2
4	37.9	39.2	37.9	37.9	37.4	38.0	+1.39	7.2
5	39.2	41.2	39.9	39.9	39.4	40.0	+0.73	6.2
6	40.2	43.0	41.8	41.9	41.4	42.0	+0.06	5.2
7	41.2	44.3	43.7	43.8	43.4	44.0	−0.61	4.2
log $L(X)$ observed	42.5	(Strong)	(Present)	42.2	42.5	42.8	....	....

The spectrum of 3C 273 is similar to that of a low-excitation planetary nebula in that it shows no [Ne V] or [Ne III]. However, no low-excitation planetaries are known in which the λ 3727 line of [O II] is weak or absent, as is the case in 3C 273. The most likely explanation is that the electron density is considerably higher than the values of 10^3 to 10^4 cm^{-3} usually encountered in planetary nebulae.

In Table 6 we attempt to obtain corrections for 3C 273 also, with less certain results. The [O III] line λ 5007 is present, but is not strong. No clear evidence for the presence of [O II] λ 3727 is found, although on one higher-dispersion plate (85 Å/mm) a trace of a sharp line is seen at the correct wavelength, allowing for redshift. We compare the spectrum of 3C 273 with that of the low-excitation planetary nebula IC418. The planetary shows weak [Ne III] (3C 273 shows none), and the [O III] line λ 5007 is about 1.5 times Hβ in strength. In 3C 273 this line is about $\frac{1}{3}$ Hβ in strength, suggesting either lower ionization of O or a very high density. Table 5 shows that the low ratio of [O II]/[O III] requires very high density. It seems best to use the corrections to Table 5 derived from IC418 in Table 6; Table 7B gives the predicted emissions. The [O II] line seems to be present, but very faint and with anomalous structure; the predicted [O II]/[O III] ratio changes by 60 from $N_e = 10^4$ to $N_e = 10^7$ cm^{-3}. While our observations do not require so large a ratio they are consistent with the high-density case.

Comparing relative line intensities in C3 48 with a planetary nebula suggests that it has a high ionization level. A high density, less than that at which forbidden lines weaken with respect to permitted lines, is suggested by data in Table 7A. An upper limit, $N_e \leq 3 \times 10^5$ cm^{-3}, is suggested, with $N_e < 10^5$ cm^{-3} a more probable value. For 3C 273, in Table 7B, with fewer lines observed, a lower limit, $N_e > 3 \times 10^5$ cm^{-3}, is suggested by the weakness of [O II], and $N_e \leq 3 \times 10^7$ cm^{-3} is suggested by the presence of [O III]. The upper limit of N_e in 3C 273 can also be estimated[2] from the observed wavelength of Hγ, which for high density would be affected by the λ 4363 line of [O III]. For $\theta_e = 0.3$ and $N_e = 3 \times 10^7$ we derive from formulae given by Aller (1956) that the λ 4363 line would have a strength about 60 per cent of that of Hγ, leading to a shift of $+10$ Å relative to Hγ in the observed, redshifted wavelength of the blend. As may be seen from Table 1, the value of z for Hγ is larger than the average redshift by an amount corresponding to about 6 Å in observed wavelength. Since the individual wavelengths are not better than about 4 Å, an electron density of 3×10^7 cm^{-3} is just possible for the assumed T_e of 16800° K.

TABLE 7B

CORRECTED PREDICTED EMISSIVITIES FOR 3C 273; RADIUS AND HYDROGEN MASS
DERIVED FROM OBSERVED Hβ LUMINOSITY

LOG N_e CM^{-3}	LOG $E(X)$, ERG SEC^{-1} PC^{-3}						LOG R_{pc}	LOG M(H)/ $M_{\odot}$
	[O II]	[O III]	[Ne III]	[Ne V]	Mg II	Hβ		
4	38.0	38.2	36.5	36.4	37.4	38.0	$+1.75$	8.3
5	39.3	40.2	38.5	38.4	39.4	40.0	$+1.08$	7.3
6	40.3	42.0	40.4	40.4	41.4	42.0	$+0.42$	6.3
7	41.3	43.3	42.3	42.3	43.4	44.0	-0.25	5.3
8	42.3	44.3	43.8	43.9	45.4	46.0	-0.91	4.3
log $L(X)$ observed	(Weak)	43.5	....	....	43.6:	43.9	....	....

We adopt an electron density $N_e = 3 \times 10^4$ cm^{-3} in 3C 48, and $N_e = 3 \times 10^6$ cm^{-3} in 3C 273. The uncertainty in each value of N_e is a factor of 10 on either side. The volume emissivity in Hβ is 10^{30} N_e^2 erg sec^{-1} pc^{-3}. We obtain the form of the relationships between R, N_e, and the observed $L(H\beta)$ as

$$\log R_{pc} = \tfrac{1}{3} \log L(H\beta) - \tfrac{2}{3} \log N_e - 10.21 ,$$

$$\log M(H)/M_{\odot} = \log L(H\beta) - \log N_e - 31.61 .$$

(12)

Radii and hydrogen masses computed from the observed Hβ luminosities of 3C 48 and 3C 273 are listed in the last columns of Tables 7A and 7B. For 3C 48, with $N_e = 3 \times 10^4$ cm^{-3} we find $R = 11$ pc, $M = 5 \times 10^6$ $M_{\odot}$, while for 3C 273, $N_e = 3 \times 10^6$ cm^{-3} leads to $R = 1.2$ pc, $M = 6 \times 10^5$ $M_{\odot}$. The effect of the uncertainty in N_e, which we estimate to be ± 1 in the logarithm, on the final R and M of the gas cloud is easily estimated from equation (12).

VI. AGES, LIGHT VARIATIONS, AND ENERGY SUPPLY

The southern end of the optical wisps of 3C 48 is at a distance of about 50 kpc, in projection, from the quasi-stellar object. The end of the jet of 3C 273 is also at a pro-

[2] We owe this remark to Dr. N. Woolf.

jected distance of about 50 kpc from the quasi-stellar object. If these features have been ejected from the central object, this must have taken place at least 2×10^5 years ago.

The upper limits to the angular diameters of the optical, starlike components from visual inspection are 1″ for 3C 48 and 0.5″ for 3C 273, corresponding to diameters of 5 kpc and 1 kpc. The widths of the emission lines correspond to 2000 and 3000 km/sec, respectively. These speeds are much larger than the escape velocities of about 100 km/sec, determined from the mass of hydrogen and the radius of the emission-line region. If material is indeed escaping from a very small inner region with the observed velocities, and if we may assume that these velocities represent the mean expansion velocity in the past, we obtain from the upper limit of size a maximum age of 2×10^6 years for 3C 48 and of 3×10^5 years for 3C 273. It would be more realistic to use here the diameters of the gaseous emission regions as determined in the preceding section. Together with the above velocities, these lead to ages of 10^4 and 10^3 years for 3C 48 and 3C 273, respectively.

These ages are considerably smaller than the minimum ages mentioned above. One possibility is that several events have occurred, one 2×10^5 years earlier than the other. Alternatively, the ages derived from the size of emission regions and the line widths would be meaningless if the emission regions are *not* expanding.[3] In that case there must be a mass of about $10^9 M\odot$ at the center of the gas cloud. The presence of a mass of this order is also attractive in view of the energy requirements to be discussed presently.

The discovery of light variations in 3C 48 by Matthews and Sandage (1963) and in 3C 273 by Smith and Hoffleit (1963) imposes quite stringent conditions on the light-travel time across these objects. The brighter object, 3C 273, has been studied for a long period. Smith and Hoffleit (1963) and Smith (1964) give results which may be summarized as follows: (1) there are small cyclic variations with a period of about 13 years; (2) flashes lasting of the order of a week or a month may occur, during which the object is up to 1 mag. brighter; and (3) in 1929 a sharp drop in brightness of $0^m.4$ occurred, after which normal brightness was restored by 1940. The cyclic variations with a period around 13 years present no problems as far as the light-travel time is concerned; the diameter of the optical model of the gas cloud for 3C 273 found in Section V is 7 light-years.

Were the 13-year period a rotation at 1500 km/sec, which is compatible with the line width, the object would be only 10^{16} cm in radius. If there is an "oscillation," it does not follow the $P\rho^{1/2}$ law for the mass and radius deduced. If there were an oscillation, it would require information transfer at nearly the velocity of light.

The flashes, which may last for a week or a month, do not necessarily put a restriction on the size of the object as a whole. Consider a region one light-month, i.e., 7×10^{16} cm, in radius. An event affecting this entire volume would be blurred by light-travel time over about one month. The matter is quite transparent when highly ionized. But when compressed, when recombination occurs, its hydrogen will be opaque in the ultraviolet. At $N_e = 10^7$ cm^{-3} the recombination time is about 3 days; there are 5×10^{23} atoms per cm^2, and if neutral, the hydrogen will have an ultraviolet opacity of 5×10^6. But an opaque sphere of this size radiates about 10^{46} erg sec^{-1} at $T = 10^4$ ° K, comparable to the visual luminosity of the flashes in 3C 273. (We have obviously neglected the problem of transfer and of the conversion of ultraviolet quanta into visual radiation,

---

[3] Electron scattering broadens emission lines when the density is high. The scattering optical depth, t, would be near 10 for 3C 273 and 1 for 3C 48. At a fixed hydrogen-line strength, t varies as $R^{-1/2}$; thus the effectiveness of scattering arises from the small size. Thermal electron velocities are $600(T_e/10^4)^{1/2}$ km/sec, so that an initially sharp emission line would be broadened to a width, at half-intensity, of 1000 km/sec at 10000° K. Multiple electron scattering slows the diffusion of quanta out of the H II region and, therefore, further slows the light variations. In both sources the emission lines have greater velocity widths, and in addition the line profiles seem to vary from line to line. For example, [O III] is sharper than Hβ in 3C 273, and [O II] is sharper than Hγ or [Ne V] in 3C 48. Only if T_e were greater than 10^5 ° K and the sizes less than a parsec would electron and Compton scattering dominate the line widths.

but the order of magnitude of the energy radiated is satisfactory.) A sudden cooling and density condensation thus results in a large and rapid increase of the thermal continuum. There would seem to be no severe problem in understanding the short duration of light flashes if there is such a filamentary or condensation structure, but there is an energy-content problem. Let the gas have m electron volts per proton-electron pair. A sphere one light-month in radius at $N_e = 10^7$ cm^{-3} contains $3 \times 10^{46} m$ ergs, so that the energy supply is sufficient for $3m$ seconds. Thermal energies give $m \approx 3$, ionization energies $m \approx 13$, and kinetic energies (at 1000 km/sec) $m \approx 6000$. Thus a maximum flash duration of only a few hours is possible for a region a light-month in radius. Larger total available energies and lifetimes occur only when velocities of 10^4 km/sec or larger are present.

Brief consideration of known means of supplying energy to produce light variations in the gas cloud yields largely negative results. Secondary nuclear-energy sources could be found in shock waves colliding at high velocities, heating to an equivalent temperature of 10^8 ° K at 1000 km/sec. The reaction rates (Milford 1959; Greenstein 1957) are such as to yield about $10^{34} M/M\odot$ erg sec^{-1}, where M is the mass of gas involved in the collision, from such nuclei as deuterium (lower temperatures) or C^{12} colliding with protons. Obviously only a small fraction of Mc^2 is so released. Supernova explosions usually produce about 10^{50} ergs of visible radiation in the 10^6 sec of their maxima; this is a barely detectable addition to the light of even 3C 48, for example. Supernovae may be sources of radioactive elements produced in the so-called r-process, sources too small, however, to maintain the enormous observed luminosities of the gas cloud for the total life span, 10^5 years. Short-lived decays yield about $2 \times 10^{40} M/M\odot$ erg sec^{-1}, for a mean lifetime near 30 days, but this is small compared to the energy required for the light flashes, unless multiple supernova detonations occur.

Colgate and Cameron (1963) have computed the efficiency and rate of conversion into visible light of the kinetic energy of a supernova shock wave colliding with an interstellar gas cloud of 10^{-16} gm cm^{-3} density. They assume that supernovae of 100 $M\odot$ are formed and release 3×10^{54} ergs in their explosion, i.e., about $2 M\odot c^2$, mostly in fast particles. This is very large compared to the observable radiative output of a supernova. They can obtain, by an ingenious mechanism, up to 5×10^{46} erg sec^{-1} total light, of which about one-tenth might be in the visible. It should be remembered that the large energy output of $2 M\odot c^2$ is not justified by any observed feature of a supernova light-curve or spectrum. The total input from the explosion of many such objects could explain the total light and its variability. Whether their model of multiple Type II supernova explosions really applies to these objects, for which nothing is known thus far about stellar content (if any), remains an open question. Their suggestion for rapid conversion of shock-wave energy into light may be an important one when the physical conditions within the gas cloud are better known. Similarly, shock waves around the outer fringe of the gas cloud may be the site of high-energy particle production for synchrotron emission.

While short-lived flashes can be thought of as localized phenomena, this does not apply to long-term decreases below the normal level of brightness. Such a steep drop occurred in 1929, with a decrease of 0.4 mag. for 3C 273 within a period of 7 months. This requires a light-travel time of 7 months across a volume containing at least 40 per cent of the source's radiation, implying a radius of not more than 0.3 pc. The gas cloud would have just this radius for the upper limit of the electron density, 3×10^7 cm^{-3}, derived in Section V.

For 3C 48 less detailed information is available over long periods (Smith and Hoffleit 1961). No secular variation and no fluctuations exceeding 0.3 mag. were found. However, photoelectric observations (Matthews and Sandage 1963; Sandage 1964) have shown it to be variable. The optical flux has changed by a factor of 1.4, apparently independent of wavelength, over a period of 600 days. This variation is too large to be caused by the emission lines only. The radius of the object emitting the continuum cannot be more than 1 pc. If the emission lines originate in this body, the electron density from Table 7A would have to be 10^6 cm^{-3}. This density is somewhat higher than the upper limit of 3×10^5 cm^{-3} derived from the emission-line spectrum in the previous section.

The above discussion suggests that the continuum radiation in 3C 48, and probably also in 3C 273, originates from a smaller volume than the emission-line spectrum. Perhaps the continuum is connected with the body of about 10^8 or 10^9 $M\odot$, which we suspect to be present in these sources (see below, and Sec. IX). The optical continuum in 3C 48 may be synchrotron radiation according to Matthews and Sandage (1963). This would shift the burden of explaining the light variations to models concerned with the non-thermal radiation. Obviously, continuing accurate spectrophotometry in absolute units of the emission lines and their intensity relative to the continuum in both objects would be of great value in further studies of the light variations. Increases in electron temperature or in synchrotron background decrease the apparent emission-line strength; the added synchrotron optical continuum could disappear in a few days. Increase in the thermal electron density causes a quadratic increase in brightness of hydrogen lines and continua but no relative change. The decay time is inversely proportional to the density, with a time constant of $a_H N_e$. According to Aller (1956), $a_H \approx 2 \times 10^{-8}$ days^{-1} cm^3. Thus if $N_e \geq 10^7$ cm^3, hydrogen light variations would occur in 5 days or less, after a sudden brightening caused by an increase of N_e. The time dependence of relative concentrations of ions of oxygen is shown by Aller (1956, Fig. IV:6). He finds recombination rates near one day for $N_e = 10^7$ cm^{-3}, permitting rapid variations in 3C 273. At the lower density of 3C 48, variations with a time scale of a year are plausible. The low intensity of [O II] in 3C 273 cannot be explained as a non-equilibrium ionization level, frozen in for the full 10^5-year time scale, without an unacceptably low N_e.

We have noted several times the fundamental question of the total energy supply. The total radiation from 3C 273 amounts to about 10^{54} ergs per year. If the sources are at least 2×10^5 years old, at constant luminosity, we are faced with the inescapable fact that the energies in the observable gas are insufficient. Thermal and ionization energies are trivial, only a few electron volts per proton. For a source of mass $M/M\odot$ and luminosity $L/L\odot$, the total energy released in t years needs to be $10^{-16} t(L/L\odot)/(M/M\odot)$ ergs per proton. Since, for 3C 273, the gas cloud has an L/M or more than 10^7 and $t > 10^5$, each proton must supply 10^{-3} ergs, of about 10^9 eV. From nuclear physics, only complete annihilation of matter is adequate. If the ordinary nuclear yield of a few MeV per nucleon is the energy source, there must be a nuclear-energy reservoir of several hundred times greater mass than the gas cloud we observe. If gravitational collapse were capable of yielding radiant energy near Mc^2, only 10^5 $M\odot$ is required; but if the more plausible value of the efficiency is only a few per cent (Fowler and Hoyle 1964) we require the energy from gravitational collapse of more than 10^7 $M\odot$. Energy production through nuclear processes is less efficient by another factor of 10. If all the energy has come from nuclear fusion, we require a mass of at least 10^8 $M\odot$. We saw above that a mass of about 10^9 $M\odot$ would stabilize the fast-moving gas; this object may well be the source of the total energy emitted by the quasi-stellar components of 3C 48 and 3C 273. Continued flow of energy from this massive component into the gaseous nebula is required, and thence into the large radio-emitting region.

VII. FREE-FREE EMISSION, ABSORPTION, AND FARADAY ROTATION

The enormous strength of the hydrogen emission lines in 3C 273 and 3C 48 suggests that free-free emission may be large in either optical or radio wavelengths. An expression for the absorption, per cm, including stimulated emission was derived by Elwert (1948); it does not differ substantially from those more recently derived, e.g., by Oster (1961).

$$k_\nu = \frac{8\pi\, e^6\, N_e^2}{3\,(6\pi)^{1/2}\, c\,(m k T_e)^{3/2}\nu^2}\left[\frac{3^{1/2}}{\pi}\ln\frac{(2kT_e)^{3/2}}{4.22\, m^{1/2}\, e^2\nu}\right]. \tag{13}$$

If we denote the bracketed term as $g_{\rm III}$, we get in cgs units

$$\tau_{ff} = 0.017\, g_{\rm III}\frac{N_e^2 R}{\nu^2 T_e^{3/2}}, \tag{14a}$$

$$g_{\rm III} = 10.6 + 1.9 \log T_e - 1.3 \log \nu . \tag{14b}$$

From radio to optical frequencies with $\theta_e = 0.3$, $g_{\rm III}$ drops from about 8, at 100 Mc/s, to unity in the optical range. There, a quantum-mechanical expression for the Gaunt factor replaces equation (14b) for $g_{\rm III}$.

Since the emissivity in a Balmer emission line (eq. [3a]) and τ_{ff} (eq. [14]) at radio frequencies both depend primarily on $N_e^2\, T_e^{-3/2}$, we can determine their ratio practically independently of N_e and T_e. For $\theta_e = 0.3$, $b_4 = 0.16$, $g_{\rm III} = 8$, the ratio is

$$\tau_{ff}/E({\rm H}\beta) = 1.3 \times 10^{18}\, \nu^{-2}\, R ,$$

$$\tau_{ff} = 1.3 \times 10^{18}\, \nu^{-2}\, R\, L({\rm H}\beta)/V , \tag{15}$$

$$\tau_{ff} = 3 \times 10^{-20}\, L({\rm H}\beta)(\nu\, R_{\rm pc})^{-2} .$$

We found in the preceding section that the radius of the emission region of 3C 273 may be about 1 pc. The luminosity in Hβ is 9×10^{43} erg/sec. The opacity will be large for frequencies less than 10^{12} c/s, i.e., over the whole radio spectrum down to wavelengths of 0.3 mm. If we were to give the radius the maximum value, 500 pc, permitted by the stellar appearance and radio diameter, the opacity would still be large for frequencies less than 3×10^9 c/s. This would require that the flux density below 3000 Mc/s be proportional to ν^2. However, the observations show Component B of 3C 273 to have a flux density almost independent of frequency (Hazard, Mackey, and Shimmins 1963).

The probable radius of 3C 48, if $N_e = 3 \times 10^4$, is about 10 pc. In that case the gaseous emission region would be optically thick in free-free for frequencies below 10^4 Mc/s. At the upper limit to its size, near 1500 pc, it would become optically thick and the spectrum would turn downward below 300 Mc/s, well within the usual radio-frequency range. This is also not observed. Thus, that part of the volume of these sources containing the gases emitting the optical line spectrum (as well as the continuous spectrum of 3C 273) cannot also produce the radio-frequency spectrum. Any radio-frequency emission produced in the dense gas cloud is therefore limited to the black-body radiation of an optically thick cloud, i.e., to a brightness temperature equal to the relatively low electron temperature.

No substantial optical emission can occur from the volume containing the radio-frequency synchrotron electrons. The radio-frequency optical depth $\tau_{ff} \geq 1$ if $N_e R_{\rm pc}^{1/2} \geq 2\nu$ Mc/s. Thus, if a volume of radius 500 pc produces non-thermal radio noise at $\nu = 10^2$ Mc/s, then $N_e < 10$ cm^{-3}. Thus our dense, massive, expanding or turbulent gaseous nebula must be surrounded by a relatively low density region containing high-energy electrons. A model with shock fronts expanding into a near vacuum and maintaining this very large density gradient could provide the necessary geometry for particle acceleration, with the massive gas clouds providing some of the driving force required.

There exists a large effect of the thermal electron cloud and the magnetic field required by synchrotron theory on the original polarization of the synchrotron radiation. The Faraday rotation is, in radians,

$$\Delta\theta = 81\lambda^2 \int N_e B_{||}\, dR_{\rm pc} , \tag{16}$$

where λ is in cm, $B_{||}$ is the parallel component of the field, and the integral is taken over dR in parsecs. Thus in our typical model for the gas, with $R_{\mathrm{pc}} \approx 1$ and $N_e \approx 3 \times 10^6$ in 3C 273, and $R_{\mathrm{pc}} \approx 10$, $N_e \approx 3 \times 10^4$ in 3C 48, the rotations are $\Delta\theta \approx 10^9 \lambda^2 B$ and $10^7 \lambda^2 B$, respectively, when $B_{||} = B$. So large a rotation could depolarize the radiation rapidly within the normally used decimeter band widths, if B is greater than 10^{-5} gauss.

Thus on two grounds, the absence of free-free absorption and the existence of intrinsic source polarization and only moderate Faraday rotation, as is observed in these sources (see Sec. VIII), we can exclude models in which the radio-frequency synchrotron radiation comes from the same volume of space as the emission lines. The optical synchrotron radiation could do so, but if it does, its good fit in 3C 48, after reasonable extrapolation onto the radio-frequency curve, would be accidental. Since according to Oke the optical continuum in 3C 273 is largely free-free, the radio and optical continua are quite unrelated in 3C 273. We will see that a satisfactory synchrotron model can be derived for the energy and magnetic field. For 3C 48, at least, the optical and radio continuum could be produced in the same volume, possibly just outside the dense gas cloud. With our upper limit of $N_e = 10$ cm^{-3} in this outer region, collisional losses by higher-energy particles need not be large.

The existence of spatial inhomogeneities of density and temperature under these circumstances is quite plausible. Threadlike, filamentary structures are common in supernova shells, radio sources, and solar prominences. The emission lines could arise in cool condensations in a much hotter and more massive envelope. At 10^8 ° K and the same $N_e^2 R$, the opacity from equation (14a) is reduced by a million. The hot gas is optically thin except for $\nu < 500$ Mc/s, and has a nearly flat spectrum. For 3C 273, with $N_e^2 R_{\mathrm{pc}}^3 = 2 \times 10^{13}$,

$$L_\nu(ff)\, d\nu = 2 \times 10^{32} e^{-h\nu/kT_e} T_e^{-1/2} d\nu \; ,$$

$$L(ff) = 3 \times 10^{42} T_e^{1/2} \text{ erg sec}^{-1} \; . \tag{17}$$

At $T_e = 10^4$ ° K most of the energy is in the visible, but at $T_e = 10^8$ ° K, it lies in the far ultraviolet. If the quantity $N_e^2 R^3$ were the same for the hot and cold gas, the hot gas would have one-tenth the visual luminosity, but one hundred times the total radiated energy. A lower T_e for the hot gas gives too low a brightness temperature and a wrong energy distribution for free-free emission to be the source of the observed radiation. The reason for so great a temperature differential, from 10^8 to 10^4 ° K, is hard to find, as is the energy source to balance the high value of $L_{ff} = 3 \times 10^{46}$ erg sec^{-1} from the hot gas. The large ultraviolet flux would be a source of excessive ionization, since 10^8 ° K is equivalent to 10 keV, rather than the observed ionization level, which is below 0.1 keV. Therefore, the hypothesis of large temperature fluctuation leads to no useful model. Density fluctuations are very plausible, and require that proper averages be taken over the quantities $N_e^2 R^3$ in emission, $N_e^2 R$ or $N_e R$ in absorption.

VIII. MODELS FOR FIELD AND PARTICLE ENERGIES FROM SYNCHROTRON EMISSION

Our goal is to determine the order of magnitude of the energies in magnetic field and particles required to explain the radio continuum, and perhaps the optical continuum, as synchrotron radiation. Matthews and Sandage (1963) have shown that the energy distribution of 3C 48 at radio wavelengths can be extrapolated smoothly to also account for the optical continuum. This allows interpretation of the whole continuum radiation as synchrotron radiation with critical frequency of about 6×10^{14} sec^{-1}. The optical continuum of 3C 273 cannot be smoothly joined with the radio continuum of Source B. The source has a flux density at radio wavelengths that is several hundred times larger than the flux density at optical wavelengths. Yet the latter shows a slight increase with increasing wavelength, according to Oke (1963). This does not rule out the possibility that part of the optical continuum is synchrotron. Conversely, the smooth fit of radio and optical continuum in 3C 48 does not guarantee the synchrotron origin for the latter. We will consider models of magnetic field and particle energies with and without optical synchrotron radiation.

An investigation of the bolometric correction for optical synchrotron emitters has been made by Greenstein (1964), who has also studied the far-ultraviolet synchrotron radiation as a possible source of ionization in radio galaxies. The results are that there is a minimal value to the bolometric correction, near 1.3 mag., when the cutoff frequency lies near the optical frequency, i.e., $\nu_c \approx 10^{15}$ sec^{-1}. If a high-energy tail is added to the distribution of energies of the relativistic electrons, sufficient ultraviolet synchrotron radiation can be emitted to account for ionization up to 100 eV without greatly increasing the bolometric correction. The absolute visual magnitude of 3C 48 is about -25; for 3C 273, M_v is of the order of -26, and since 3C 273 is quite blue it is bolometrically the brighter of the two by far. The minimum bolometric correction for synchrotron radiation raises M_b to -27.4. Consequently, we must consider the problem of producing over 10^{46} erg sec^{-1} of optical synchrotron radiation in a small volume. The energy distributions of 3C 48 and 3C 273B place quite different requirements on the cutoff frequency; $\nu_c \approx 6 \times 10^{14}$ sec^{-1} for 3C 48 and either a larger value for 3C 273B, if its blue continuum is synchrotron, or a much lower value if it is free-free. We will study different values of ν_c, from 6.3×10^{14} sec^{-1} to 6.3×10^{10} sec^{-1}, and obtain models for the luminosities corresponding to the cutoff energies. In addition, we cannot be certain that the optical and radio continua arise from the same volume. The light variability, probably largely in the continuum, suggests a much smaller volume if the optical radiation is synchrotron in origin.

Assume that the relativistic electrons giving radiated energy of power-law index $n = (m - 1)/2$ have a number density given by a power law:

$$N(E) \, dE = \frac{N_0 V \, dE}{E^m} . \tag{18}$$

The total particle energy content in electrons and protons is

$$U_p = p \int_{E_1}^{E_2} N(E) E \, dE = \frac{p N_0 V}{2 - m} E^{2-m} \Big|_{E_1}^{E_2}, \tag{19}$$

where we have assumed that heavy particles carry $(p - 1)$ times the energy of the electrons. The total synchrotron radiation over all frequencies is approximately

$$L = 2.4 \times 10^{-3} B^2 \frac{N_0 V}{3 - m} E^{3-m} \Big|_{E_1}^{E_2}. \tag{20}$$

The cutoff frequency ν_c is defined by a dimensionless parameter β,

$$\beta \equiv \frac{\nu_c}{6.3 \times 10^{18}} = B E_2^2 . \tag{21}$$

The lifetime, in days, of an electron of energy E, in ergs, is

$$t_{1/2}(E) = (206 B^2 E)^{-1} . \tag{22}$$

The energy content in the magnetic field is

$$U_M = \frac{B^2 V}{8\pi} , \tag{23}$$

and for convenience let the total particle energy $U_p = a U_M$.

For values of m well below 2, only E_2 is needed in equations (19) and (20), since $E_2 \gg E_1$. It is of interest to investigate briefly the case $m = 1$, corresponding to a flat spectral energy distribution ($n = 0$), such as that exhibited by the bluer quasi-stellar objects. The luminosity is then

$$L = 0.03 \, U_M U_p \frac{E_2}{V \, p} , \tag{24}$$

and we obtain

$$L = \frac{0.03 \, a \, U^2_M \beta^{1/2}}{p \, V B^{1/2}} . \tag{25}$$

For a quick reconnaisance, equation (25) is useful. We will assume that the optical and radio emission arises in the same region, of radius R_{pc} (in parsecs). The magnetic field B (in gauss) is given as a function of L (in erg sec^{-1}) and the parameters a, β, and p as

$$\log B = \tfrac{2}{7} \log \frac{pL}{a} - \tfrac{6}{7} \log R_{pc} - \tfrac{1}{7} \log \beta - 14.79 . \tag{26}$$

We have an upper limit to R_{pc} from the angular diameter, and L is known. The total energy, $(1 + a)U_M$, is obtainable from

$$\log U = \log (1 + a) + \tfrac{4}{7} \log \frac{pL}{a} + \tfrac{9}{7} \log R_{pc} - \tfrac{2}{7} \log \beta + 25.11 . \tag{27}$$

For $p = 1$ (no protons) and $a = 1$, the usual equipartition assumption, we obtain values of B which may at first seem reasonable. Using $L = 2.5 \times 10^{46}$ erg/sec for 3C 273, $\beta = 10^{-4}$ (i.e., $\nu_c = 6.3 \times 10^{14}$ sec^{-1}) and adopting $R_{pc} = 500$ (see below), we find the value of $B = 5.4 \times 10^{-4}$ gauss. The most energetic "optical" electrons present have $E_2 = 0.4$ erg or 250 BeV and a lifetime, $t_{1/2}$, of 100 years. But the derived U (the sum of U_p and U_M) is too small—only 3×10^{56} erg, an energy supply sufficient to maintain the present total optical energy output for only 400 years. (This maximum time scale is evaluated from $t_0 = U/L$, i.e., assuming constant luminosity and complete conversion of both U_p and U_M into radiation.) If the total particle energy is 100 times that of the electrons, i.e., $p = 100$, then for $a = 1$ the field is $B = 2 \times 10^{-3}$ gauss, and the total energy content 4×10^{57} ergs, sufficient for at most 5000 years at the present rate of radiation if the entire proton energy can eventually be converted into relativistic electrons. The total energy can be increased if we admit non-equipartition of energies of field and particles, but the gain is by a factor of less than 10 for values of a between 0.01 and 100. In non-equipartition cases, there is possibly some preference for values of a less than unity, if we think that the magnetic fields cause particle acceleration, i.e., B greater than in the equipartition case.

In further considerations of the properties of 3C 273, and in finding the energies involved in a model for 3C 48, we will account for the properties of each source specifically. We have adopted $p = 100$, i.e., the relativistic proton (or heavy particle) total energy store 99 times that of the electrons. Burbidge (1956) evaluated the direct production of electrons or positrons from meson decay in energetic stationary proton–cosmic-ray collisions, giving $p \approx 30$. At the very best, neutrino- and gamma-ray losses insure that $p > 10$. Only a direct electron injection could give small p. We give the parameters of interest in Table 8. For given values of n, ν_c, L, and E_1 the field strength B determines E_2, N_0V, and U_p through equations (19)–(21). For 3C 48 we use $n = 0.67$ and $\nu = 6.3 \times 10^{14}$ sec^{-1} ($\beta = 10^{-4}$) from a discussion by Matthews and Sandage (1963) to derive data given in Table 8 for Case A. Case B in the table is based on $\nu_c = 6.3 \times 10^{10}$ sec^{-1} ($\beta = 10^{-8}$), i.e., the optical continuum has a non-synchrotron origin or arises in a smaller volume with larger B. Because n is larger than 0.5, the total particle energy depends strongly on the lower-energy cutoff of the relativistic electron spectrum, E_1. We will take this as 100 MeV for electrons, assuming that at lower energy they are lost by inelastic collisions so that $E_1 \approx 1.6 \times 10^{-4}$ erg. Since the volume occupied by the radio emission is not directly measured, in order to make the problem concrete, for the energy-supply time scale, t_0, we have assumed an undetectably small synchrotron process volume of 10^9 pc^3 for Cases A and B, the same as the observed radio volume of the core of 3C 273B (see below). Lovell (private communication) informs us that 3C 48 is still unresolved at 180000 λ.

From our analysis of the emission lines, and from the light variations, we believe that the optical radiation of 3C 48 comes largely from a small volume that is less than about 10 pc in radius. In Case C we assume that the optical continuum is of synchrotron origin,

TABLE 8

PARTICLE AND MAGNETIC ENERGIES IN ERGS FOR
SYNCHROTRON MODELS OF 3C 48

($n = 0.67$, $m = 2.34$)

CASE A

LUMINOSITY ALL SYNCHROTRON; $\nu_c = 6.3 \times 10^{14}$ SEC^{-1}, $L = 2 \times 10^{46}$ ERG SEC^{-1};
RADIO AND OPTICAL CONTINUUM FROM 10^9 PC^3 VOLUME

LOG B	LOG E_2 (erg)	LOG N_0V	LOG U_p	LOG U_M	TIME SCALES	
					log $t_{1/2}(E_2)$ (days)	log t_0 (yrs)
0........	−2.0	50.1	53.8	63.1	−0.3	9.3
−1........	−1.5	51.7	55.5	61.1	+1.2	7.3
−2........	−1.0	53.4	57.2	59.1	+2.7	5.3
−3........	−0.5	55.1	58.8	57.1	+4.2	5.0
−4........	0.0	56.7	60.5	55.1	+5.7	6.7
−5........	+0.5	58.4	62.2	53.1	+7.2	8.4

CASE B

LUMINOSITY OF SYNCHROTRON ORIGIN ONLY AT RADIO FREQUENCIES; $\nu_c = 6.3 \times 10^{10}$,
VOLUME $V = 10^9$ PC^3; $L = 10^{45}$ ERG SEC^{-1}

LOG B	LOG E_2 (erg)	LOG N_0V	LOG U_p	LOG U_M	TIME SCALES	
0........	−4.0	48.7	52.5	63.1	1.7	10.6
−1........	−3.5	50.4	54.2	61.1	3.2	8.6
−2........	−3.0	52.1	55.8	59.1	4.7	6.6
−3........	−2.5	53.8	57.5	57.1	6.2	5.1
−4........	−2.0	55.4	59.2	55.1	7.7	6.7
−5........	−1.5	57.1	60.8	53.1	9.2	8.3

CASE C

LUMINOSITY OF SYNCHROTRON ORIGIN AT OPTICAL FREQUENCIES; $\nu_c = 6.3 \times 10^{14}$
FROM 4×10^3 PC^3 INNER CORE; $L = 2 \times 10^{46}$ ERG SEC^{-1}

LOG B	LOG E_2 (erg)	LOG N_0V	LOG U_p	LOG U_M	TIME SCALES	
+1........	−2.5	48.4	52.2	59.7	−1.8	5.9
0........	−2.0	50.1	53.8	57.7	−0.3	3.9
−1........	−1.5	51.7	55.5	55.7	+1.2	2.1
−2........	−1.0	53.4	57.2	53.7	+2.7	3.4

has $n = 0.67$ and $\nu_c = 6.3 \times 10^{14}$ sec^{-1}, but arises from a volume $V = 4 \times 10^3$ pc^3. The radio-frequency spectrum has low total luminosity in 3C 48, compared to that in optical frequencies, so we can still use $L = 2 \times 10^{46}$ erg sec^{-1}.

The source 3C 273 has a more complicated structure at radio wavelengths. We shall not here consider Source A that is associated with the optical jet. Source B, associated with the quasi-stellar object, has an extended part with a diameter of about 4″ with a central component with a diameter of about 0.5″ (see Hazard's paper herein), or about 1.1 kpc. We shall only be concerned with this core of 3C 273B. Accordingly, we have adopted for the source of continuum radiation in Cases A and B a volume of 10^9 pc^3, corresponding to a radius of about 500 pc. Observations at Michigan (see Dent and Haddock's paper herein) suggest that 3C 273B may have a flat radio-frequency spectrum at very high frequencies. We have assumed for 3C 273B (core) a flux density of about 10^{-25} W m^{-2} (c/s)$^{-1}$, independent of frequency (i.e., $n = 0$, $m = 1$). At the distance of 3C 273 this corresponds to a flux of about 3×10^{33} erg sec^{-1} (c/s)$^{-1}$. We have actually used the total luminosities given in Table 9, Case A for $\nu_c = 6.3 \times 10^{13}$ sec^{-1}, and Case B with $\nu_c = 6.3 \times 10^{13}$ sec^{-1}. In Case A the cutoff was arbitrarily placed in the infrared, in such a way that synchrotron radiation is negligible in the visual range. Since m is rather smaller than 1, the values of U_p and L depend mostly on E_2, very little on E_1. We have again used $p = 100$, in deriving data given in Table 9.

Inspection of Tables 8 and 9, Cases A and B, shows that in all cases equipartition between field and total particle energies (with the assumed $p = 100$) is reached at a magnetic-field strength of between 10^{-3} and 3×10^{-3} gauss. The corresponding upper limits to the lifetime $t_0 = (U_M + U_p)/L$ at present luminosity for optical synchrotron radiation are almost 10^5 years and 10^4 years for 3C 48 and 3C 273, respectively. The maximum lifetime t_0 for radio radiation in 3C 48 is barely larger than that for the optical synchrotron radiation, i.e., about 10^5 years. The maximum lifetime t_0 for radio radiation in 3C 273 is 10^6 years. The decay times for the "optical" electrons in 3C 48 are 10 years, for $B = 3 \times 10^{-3}$ gauss, and about 100 times longer for the highest-energy electrons producing radio frequencies. Thus variability of the continua is plausible on optical but not on radio frequencies.

There is no particular reason why in these sources there should be equipartition between field and particle energies. The range of magnetic field which is plausible for these non-equipartition cases is limited by the following considerations. If there is a magnetic field in the gaseous emission-line region, we might interpret the line broadening as an Alfvén velocity. Since $v_A \approx 2.2 \times 10^{11} BN_e^{-1/2}$, from the observed $v = 10^8$ cm sec^{-1}, we obtain $B = 0.1$ gauss for the inner region of 3C 48. It is improbable that B in the radio-emitting region is larger than in the gas clouds, so we should use $B < 10^{-1}$ gauss. We have already shown from Faraday rotation and from the lack of free-free self-absorption at radio frequencies that N_e is small in the outer region; an Alfvén velocity q times that of light requires that $B = 0.14 \; qN_e^{1/2}$, again setting the upper limit to the field at $B < 0.5 \; q$ gauss.

The observed Faraday rotation also carried information about B (cf. eq. [16]). Gardner and Whiteoak (1963) give for 3C 273 a Faraday rotation of -8.2 radians per m^2. The polarizations observed, ranging from $2\frac{1}{2}$ per cent at 21-cm wavelength to 4 per cent at 10-cm wavelength, must be due to Component B, which has a much flatter spectrum than Component A. Seielstad (1963) derived a rotation of $+11 \pm 6$ radians per m^2 for 3C 273, and $+48 \pm 9$ radians per m^2 for 3C 48. We find from these small rotations and equation (16) that $N_e B$ is about 10^{-8} to 10^{-7} for both sources, if $R \approx 500$ pc. The requirement that no free-free absorption in the radio-emitting region occurs sets an upper limit to N_e of about 10 cm^{-3} (cf. Sec. VII). The corresponding lower limit of 10^{-8} in B is quite low. Since the field must be larger, the small rotation observed requires very low N_e.

Arguments leading to the value of the field strength B in these sources will involve the age of the objects and the possibility of a steady renewal of the high-energy electrons from some unknown central source, as in the Crab Nebula. This very interesting question of evolution of radio sources and the interchange between energy modes, U_p and U_M, is outside the scope of the present paper. If there is a steady renewal from an unknown energy source of the high-energy electrons, the values of t_0 listed in Tables 8 and 9 are lower limits. It should be noted that, if there is no such steady injection of high-energy particles and magnetic energy from the unknown source, t_0 must be a quite generous upper limit to the past lifetime, because it assumes complete conversion of the total energy content of the source into synchrotron radiation from electrons, neglecting col-

TABLE 9

PARTICLE AND MAGNETIC ENERGIES, IN ERGS, FOR
SYNCHROTRON MODELS OF 3C 273B

$(n = 0, \; m = 1)$

CASE A

LUMINOSITY ALL SYNCHROTRON;* $\nu_c = 6.3 \times 10^{13}$ SEC^{-1}, $L = 2 \times 10^{47}$ ERG SEC^{-1};
RADIO AND OPTICAL CONTINUUM FROM 10^9 PC^3 VOLUME

LOG B	LOG E_2 (erg)	LOG N_0V	LOG U_p	LOG U_M	TIME SCALES	
					log $t_{1/2}(E_2)$ (days)	log t_0 (yrs)
0.	−2.5	55.2	54.7	63.1	0.2	8.3
−1.	−2.0	56.2	56.2	61.1	1.7	6.3
−2.	−1.5	57.2	57.7	59.1	3.2	4.3
−3.	−1.0	58.2	59.2	57.1	4.7	4.4
−4.	−0.5	59.2	60.7	55.1	6.2	5.9
−5.	0.0	60.2	62.2	53.1	7.7	7.4

CASE B

LUMINOSITY OF SYNCHROTRON ORIGIN ONLY AT RADIO FREQUENCIES; $\nu_c = 6.3 \times 10^{10}$ SEC^{-1},
$L = 2 \times 10^{44}$ ERG SEC^{-1}; VOLUME $= 10^9$ PC^3

0.	−4.0	55.2	53.2	63.1	1.7	11.3
−1.	−3.5	56.2	54.7	61.1	3.2	9.3
−2.	−3.0	57.2	56.2	59.1	4.7	7.3
−3.	−2.5	58.2	57.7	57.1	6.2	6.0
−4.	−2.0	59.2	59.2	55.1	7.7	7.4
−5.	−1.5	60.2	60.7	53.1	9.2	8.9

CASE C

LUMINOSITY OF OPTICAL CORE IS OF SYNCHROTRON ORIGIN FROM SMALL VOLUME $= 1$ PC^3,
$\nu_c = 6.3 \times 10^{15}$ SEC^{-1}; $L = 5 \times 10^{46}$ ERG SEC^{-1}

+1.	−2.0	51.6	51.6	56.1	−2.3	+1.8
0.	−1.5	52.6	53.1	54.1	−0.8	−0.2
−1.	−1.0	53.6	54.6	52.1	+0.7	+0.3
−2.	−0.5	54.6	56.1	50.1	+2.2	+1.8
−3.	+0.5	55.6	57.6	48.1	+3.2	+3.3

* The very high luminosity in Case A arises as follows: There is considerable difficulty in assuming the optical radiation to be of synchrotron origin, according to Oke. In this model we extrapolate the flat radio spectrum to the infrared and set a cutoff energy such that it does not contribute to the visual and blue continuum. If ν_c is reduced, L is reduced in proportion.

lisional losses in U_p and the dissipation of the field, U_M, by loss of flux lines, when, in fact, the efficiency is probably quite low.

One most interesting case for which we may evaluate the energy density is given in Tables 8 and 9 and labeled Case C. Here the optical continuum is interpreted as synchrotron radiation from the same inner volume containing a gas nebula which produces the emission lines. In 3C 48 the radius was 10 pc or more; in 3C 273, less than 1 pc. The differences in the derived properties arise largely from the difference in volumes. The equipartition values of B are near 0.1 gauss, and the total energies are 10^{56} and 10^{53} erg, respectively. The lifetime of the high-energy electrons is a few days, but t_0 is 100 years and 1 year for 3C 48 and 3C 273. These total lifetimes, based on exhaustion of the energy supply, are near the radius, measured in light years, i.e., relativistic particles, even traveling in straight lines, would barely traverse the volume before their energy must be exhausted.

Even more startling is the energy density of relativistic particles. At equipartition in 3C 273B (Case C, $a = 1$, $p = 100$), we find $B \approx 0.5$ gauss, $U_p = 3 \times 10^{53}$, i.e., 0.01 erg cm^{-3}, 6×10^9 eV cm^{-3}. If we evaluate an equivalent temperature from U_p, we find $T = 1000°$ K. The gas has $N_e k T \approx 10^{-5}$ erg cm^{-3}, but if we include translational energy $\frac{1}{2}\rho v^2$, it has 0.05 erg cm^{-3}. Thus, the cosmic rays have nearly the same energy as the observable gas. The energy density of radiation near the surface is ≈ 0.05 $L/R^2 c \simeq 0.02$ erg cm^{-3} also. The loss rate to the high-energy protons can be evaluated from the nuclear collisions with stationary protons, which have a cross-section of 4×10^{-26} cm^2. The lifetime of the protons against collision is 10 years. The synchrotron lifetime for high-energy electrons is near 10^5 sec. The inverse Compton effect is large and should be evaluated. The energy loss is measured by $c\sigma_0\gamma^2 u$, where σ_0 is the Compton cross-section, 6.6×10^{-25} cm^2, $\gamma = E/m_0 c^2$ is the electron energy and u is the photon energy density. With values used of L and R in Case C, an electron loses energy at the rate of 4×10^{-8} erg sec^{-1}, or has a lifetime of 2×10^5 sec. If we slightly increase u or γ the inverse Compton effect can be very important compared to synchrotron losses. It is suggestive that the balance is so close; if inverse Compton effect dominates, the photons are "heated" by the cosmic rays, and therefore the thermal gas will also be heated. The proton nuclear collisions produce an energy loss of U_p/τ where τ is their nuclear-collision lifetime; this is about 10^{45} erg sec^{-1}, less than the luminosity by 1–2 orders of magnitude. Thus, the small radius model for optical synchrotron radiation is nearing the boundaries of the plausible. At much higher energy concentrations (i.e., higher luminosities from so small a volume), other physical effects may provide a limit.

IX. THE JET, 3C 273A

The stronger radio source in 3C 273 is associated with a visible jet about 1.5″ × 10″. We have no conclusive spectroscopic or colorimetric data as to the nature of its continuum, nor even an accurate apparent magnitude. The radio-frequency observations suggest an index $n = 0.77$ and a flux of 4.2×10^{-25} W m^{-2} (c/s)$^{-1}$ at 400 Mc/s. Let us assume that the entire radiation is synchrotron and has $\nu_c = 6.3 \times 10^{14}$ sec^{-1}, as does 3C 48. We then predict the optical apparent magnitude of the jet and find it to be 16^{m}6, brighter than seems plausible for an object not much brighter than the sky background. A spectral index of $n = 0.9$ and the same ν_c predicts an apparent magnitude near 19^m, which is probably more nearly correct. The total luminosity of the jet is not very sensitive to the frequency range adopted, varying as $\nu_c^{0.1}$, and is found to be 2×10^{44} erg sec^{-1}. The volume producing optical radiation is observed to be about 3×10^{11} pc^3. If we use our equations for the case $a = 1$, we find $B \approx 6 \times 10^{-4}$ gauss, $E_2 \approx 200$ BeV, the total energy $U = 2 \times 10^{60}$ erg. For other values of B, with $p = 100$, the results are given in Table 10. Note that especially if $U_M > U_p$ the lifetime of the highest-energy electrons becomes short, suggesting that the electron acceleration processes must continue, even in this source of very low energy density, 10^{-7} erg cm^{-3}. The total lifetime, t_0, however, is very long, more than 10^8 years, so that a single event storing 10^{60} erg and occurring 10^5 years ago could easily provide the required energy. At constant luminosity, the total radiation in 10^5 years is 10^{57} erg, a small fraction of the minimum U of 10^{60} erg. We cannot yet make a full study of 3C 273A. The details of radio structure of the jet are not as simple as the simple cylindrical model we adopt. There is a brightening at the far end, and there consequently may be density and field fluctuations.

If the optical luminosity is not of synchrotron origin, our analysis would be modified only slightly. Cutting ν_c to 6×10^{10} sec^{-1}, and using the radio power-law index of 0.77 gives $L = 10^{44}$ erg sec^{-1}. If we examine analogous solutions for 3C 48 and 3C 273B in Tables 8 and 9 (Case B) and change the volume to 3×10^{11} pc^3, the minimum energy is then 4×10^{58} erg, $B = 3 \times 10^{-4}$ gauss and t_0 is 10^7 years.

It is of course possible that the jet has hydrogen emission rather than synchrotron continuum. From equation (3b) the Hβ luminosity from 3×10^{11} pc^3 is $10^{42} N_e^2$ erg sec^{-1}, the total hydrogen emission is about $3 \times 10^{43} N_e^2$ erg sec^{-1}. From $L = 10^{44}$ erg sec^{-1} we obtain $N_e = 1.7$ cm^{-3}, or a mass of 10^{10} $M\odot$, a rather high value; such an N_e is not excluded by considerations of radio-frequency opacity (eq. [15]), but could give large Faraday rotation (eq. [16]). So far, one spectrum of the far end of the jet has been obtained. It shows only a weak, bluish continuum.

TABLE 10

SYNCHROTRON RADIATION FROM THE JET, 3C 273A

($L = 2 \times 10^{44}$ erg sec^{-1}; $\nu_c = 6.3 \times 10^{14}$ sec^{-1};
$n = 0.9$; volume $= 3 \times 10^{11}$ pc^3)

LOG B	LOG E_2 (erg)	LOG $N_0 V$	LOG U_p	LOG U_M	TIME SCALES	
					log $t_{1/2}(E_2)$ (days)	log t_0 (yrs)
−2..........	−1.0	52.4	57.4	62.2	2.7	10.4
−3..........	−0.5	54.3	59.3	60.2	4.2	8.5
−4..........	0.0	56.2	61.2	58.2	5.7	9.4

X. DISCUSSION

We have considered the explanation of the observed redshifts in terms of (1) Doppler effect from a high-velocity star, (2) gravitational redshift, and (3) cosmological redshift.

The first two alternatives have been shown to lead to an extra-galactic nature of the object. In case 1 the small proper motion results in a distance measured in megaparsecs and a luminosity closer to that of galaxies than of stars. The four quasi-stellar objects with known velocity are all receding from us (Schmidt and Matthews 1964). These facts, when combined with the problem of how to accelerate an apparently very large star (or stellar system) to velocities that are an appreciable fraction of that of light, make case 1 an exceedingly unlikely interpretation.

We have shown that alternative 2 also leads to an extra-galactic nature of these objects. In fact, the mass would have to be of the order of that of a galaxy or more. It seems rather likely on the basis of current theoretical work that objects of such a mass, condensed to a diameter of less than 1 pc, cannot be stable and thus cannot exist for any length of time. The thinness of the surrounding emission-line shell would also be a problem. Altogether, we believe that it is quite unlikely (but not definitely disproven) that gravitational redshifts explain the spectrum of the quasi-stellar objects.

Accordingly, we have adopted the interpretation of the redshifts as cosmological redshifts. The ensuing lengthy astrophysical discussion of the emission spectra gave radii for the gaseous nebulae of about 1 pc for 3C 273, and 10 pc or more for 3C 48. The light variations seem to require even smaller sizes for the source of optical continuum radiation, especially for 3C 48. The non-thermal character of the radio spectrum shows that it must originate outside the gas cloud which emits the emission lines. We find it attractive to think of a model in which a small inner core produces most of the optical continuum, surrounded by a gas cloud producing the emission lines and thermal continuum. This would itself be surrounded by the radio-emitting regions.

The models for optical continuum synchrotron radiation from an inner volume small enough to admit of the light variations encounter serious difficulties. The high energy-density in a region containing a gaseous nebula produces rapid loss of cosmic-ray protons; the electrons are lost rapidly by either inverse Compton-effect or synchrotron radiation, so that it is nearly impossible to maintain the high-energy particle supply.

An important parameter in further considerations regarding the quasi-stellar objects is their age, i.e., their lifetime as objects producing large optical luminosity from an intrinsically small volume. Let us consider the consequences of two quite different estimates of their age, namely, 10^3 years and 10^6 years.

Age 10^3 years.—This is the age, to an order of magnitude, that follows from the size of the gaseous nebula and the interpretation of the widths of the emission lines as caused by expansion. It also seems a lower limit to the possible age of 3C 273, because the secular decrease in optical light amounts to less than 0.1 mag. per century (Smith 1964). The total energy output would amount to 10^{57} ergs, or the rest-mass energy of about 500 suns. This amount can be supplied by nuclear fusion of 10^5 $M_\odot$ of hydrogen to helium. Such a mass is less than that of the gases producing the emission lines; the expansion of the fast-moving gas would be unimpeded. Any of the synchrotron emission models in Tables 8 and 9 (Cases A and B) would have sufficient energy content to maintain present radiation over 10^3 years. *Not* explained by so short an age would be the radio halo of 3C 273B, the radio source 3C 273A and the jet, or the optical wisps near 3C 48. We assume here that all these features originated in what is now the quasi-stellar object. Their existence requires either a number of separate events, or a much larger age.

Age 10^6 years.—The above objections are met if we assume an age of about 10^6 years. Total energy output would amount to 10^{60} ergs, requiring gravitational collapse of a large mass or the nuclear energy for 10^8 $M_\odot$ of hydrogen. This would probably involve a total mass of some 10^9 $M_\odot$. Such a mass could stabilize the large internal motions of the observed H II region at the radius of a few parsecs, derived from the electron density and the intensity of the emission lines. Synchrotron emission models (Tables 8 and 9) with $B \approx 10^{-3}$ gauss (close to equipartition of energies) do not have sufficient energy content to last for 10^6 years at present luminosity. Either there is a steady injection of high-energy particles or a non-equipartition of energy. In the latter case we would consider field of 0.01–0.1 gauss most likely.

We discussed above a model of the quasi-stellar objects consisting of an optical-continuum source (radius < 1 pc) surrounded by an emission region (radius $\approx$ 1 pc [3C 273], $\approx$ 10 pc [3C 48]) and by a radio-emitting region. If there is indeed an object with a mass of about 10^9 $M_\odot$ present in these objects, then, presumably, this would be inside the small optical-continuum source. The radius of the 10^9 $M_\odot$ object could have any value below 1 pc. Its gravitational redshift, if any exists, cannot easily be observed because the observed redshift of emission lines refers to a distance from this mass of about 1 pc, where the gravitational effect is negligible. The radius of a Schwarzschild sphere is $2GM/c^2$, about 10^{-4} pc for such a mass. It would be important to know whether continued energy and mass input from such a "collapsed" region are possible.

It is not yet possible to establish the role of these quasi-stellar radio sources in the evolution of galaxies or radio galaxies. No trace of a galaxy around these objects has been found as yet. It is not certain at present that this really excludes the possibility of a galaxy being present; seeing and scattering in the photographic emulsion make detection of a low surface-brightness galaxy, containing a stellar object 100 times brighter, very difficult.

The quasi-stellar sources might have been thought to be a precursor stage of the radio galaxies. Their radio luminosities are about equal to that of the most intense radio galaxies. However, the linear sizes of the radio-emitting regions in the quasi-stellar sources show a range quite similar to that seen in the radio galaxies (Schmidt and Matthews 1964). This does not support the idea that radio galaxies start their radio life as a quasi-stellar source. Either the quasi-stellar stage can occur at any time in the life of a radio galaxy, or the two phenomena may be completely unrelated, with the quasi-stellar objects primary intergalactic condensations.

TABLE 11

RÉSUMÉ OF DATA ON QUASI-STELLAR SOURCES

	3C 48	3C 273
z	0.367	0.158
r (Mpc)	1100	474
Luminosities (erg sec^{-1}):		
Hβ	6×10^{42}	9×10^{43}
Visual	10^{45}	4×10^{45}
Radii (R_{pc}):		
Optical	<2500	<500
Radio	<2500	500
H II region	≥ 10	1
H II region:		
N_e cm^{-3}	$\leq 3 \times 10^4$	3×10^6
$M/M_\odot$	$\geq 5 \times 10^6$	6×10^5
v (km/sec)	1000	1500
Equipartition synchrotron models		
L (erg sec^{-1}):		
Case A	2×10^{46}	2×10^{47}
Case B	10^{45}	2×10^{44}
Case C	2×10^{46}	5×10^{46}
U (erg):		
Case A	10^{58}	2×10^{58}
Case B	2×10^{57}	3×10^{57}
Case C	4×10^{55}	4×10^{53}

In Table 11 we give a final résumé of the properties of possible models. The "distance" r is obtained simply from czH^{-1}, with $H = 100$ km sec^{-1} Mpc^{-1}. The Hβ luminosity is observed; the N_e refers to the H II regions producing permitted and forbidden lines, the internal velocity, v, is deduced from the line widths. The N_e in 3C 273 is determined from the weakness of [O II]; in 3C 48 a wide range is possible, and we give nearly the largest acceptable. The angular diameter gives the sizes, but R(H II) is derived from L(Hβ) and N_e, so the masses depend on $N_e R^3$. The total luminosity is well determined for the visual region, but bolometric corrections may be large. If the radiation is of synchrotron origin, for various ν_c, the L becomes fixed, and the total L and U are given in the last columns.

We are much indebted to J. B. Oke for as yet unpublished information on the photoelectric scans of the continuum of 3C 273 and of the red region of the spectrum of 3C 48; we are grateful to many colleagues for very stimulating discussions and for much observational data before publication.

APPENDIX I

ELECTRON TEMPERATURES

Although the present material is not sufficient for a quantitative analysis, the appearance on three plates of what seems to be the auroral line, λ 2973 of [Ne v], gives the possibility of estimating the electron temperature in 3C 48 by a new method. The situation is the same as for λ 4363 of [O III] except that λ 2973 will be important at higher electron temperatures. It may be observable in planetary nebulae from rockets or satellites. Consequently, an approximate derivation of the ratio of the auroral to the nebular lines of [Ne v] was made. The various terms in the general expression for b_3/b_2, the populations of states 3 and 2, were evaluated approximately to determine which could be neglected. The collisional cross-sections are only poorly known. The results are

$$\frac{b_3}{b_2} = \frac{C(\Omega_{12}+\Omega_{23}) + A_{21}g_2}{C(\Omega_{13}+\Omega_{23}) + A_{32}g_3}, \tag{AI.1}$$

$$\frac{E_{32}}{E_{21}} = 1.13 \times 10^{-4.17\theta_e}\left(\frac{1+4.5\times10^{-6}N_e/T_e^{1/2}}{1+2.2\times10^{-6}N_e/T_e^{1/2}}\right). \tag{AI.2}$$

Equation (AI.2) gives the ratio of the intensity of the auroral line E_{32} to E_{21}, the sum of the intensities of the two nebular lines. Note that if the term involving $N_e/T_e^{1/2}$ is less than unity, i.e., low N_e, one asymptotic limit to the intensity ratio for one of the nebular lines, λ 3426, is

$$\frac{E(\lambda 2973)}{E(\lambda 3426)} = 1.55 \times 10^{-4.17\theta_e}, \tag{AI.3}$$

and if N_e is very high, the other limit is

$$\frac{E(\lambda 2973)}{E(\lambda 3426)} = 3.2 \times 10^{-4.17\theta_e}. \tag{AI.4}$$

As a function of N_e the coefficient of $10^{-21000/T_e}$ changes only by a factor of 2. The crossover to equation (AI.4) occurs for $T_e = 20000°$ at $N_e > 6 \times 10^7$ cm^{-3}, a very high electron density, so that equation (AI.3) is the expression for most nebulae and for 3C 48. Consequently, the uncertainty of the cross-sections proves not to be a serious factor. If λ 2973 appears at all (i.e., with an intensity ratio to λ 3426 of even 0.1), we know that T_e is above 15000° K. It can become quite strong if $T_e > 20000°$ K; since λ 2973 is weak in 3C 48, it is improbable that $T_e > 40000°$ K.

From observation of planetary nebulae, we find associated with the small changes of T_e large changes in the relative intensity of forbidden lines of different ions; the direct effects of change of T_e are relatively small in the excitation of the nebular lines. In the absence of knowledge of the source of ionization (radiation from stars or synchrotron electrons or by collision), it seems impossible to do more than set a lower limit to T_e from the relative intensity of the forbidden lines. Inspection of spectra of planetary nebulae shows large variations in the [O II]/[O III] and [O II]/[Ne v] ratios, although no low-excitation objects resemble 3C 273 in the small [O II]/[O III] ratio, which is here a density effect. But if the auroral line of [Ne v], and other nebular and permitted lines of 3–4.4 eV excitation are to be present, very low T_e is excluded.

The hydrogen-line spectrum of 3C 273 excludes very high T_e, because of the reduced visibility of a hydrogen line superposed on the Paschen and free-free continua. The addition of synchrotron continuum will reduce the intensities predicted here. We can derive a rough theoretical expression for the ratio of Hβ to the continua on which it is superposed, and for the discontinuity in emission at the Balmer limit. The bound-free plus free-free, neglecting the quantum-mechanical g-factors, is

$$E_{ff+bf}d\nu \propto \frac{N_e^2 h\, d\nu}{T_e^{3/2}}\, e^{-h\nu/kT_e}\left(\frac{kT}{2Rh} + \sum \frac{10^{13.54\theta_e/n'^2}}{n'^3}\right), \tag{AI.5}$$

with R the Rydberg. The summation is to be taken over those series whose n'th limits are longward of the observed frequency, ν. The bound-bound is

$$E_{bb} \propto \frac{N_e^2 b_n 2 hR}{T_e^{3/2} n'^3 n^3} 10^{13.54\theta_e/n^2}, \tag{AI.6}$$

where n' is the lower level and n the upper level. Let us write $E_{bb} = E_{ff+bf}\Delta\nu$, so that $\Delta\nu$ is the equivalent width, in frequency units, of a line, $n \rightarrow n'$, in terms of the neighboring hydrogen continua (neglecting two-photon emission). Then we obtain for Hβ, with $n = 4$, $n' = 2$, and $b_4 = 0.16$ (assumed constant) an expression for $\Delta\nu$ independent of N_e,

$$\Delta\nu = 2.2 \times 10^{12} \times 10^{3.39\theta_e} \frac{62.4\theta_e}{1 + 62.4\theta_e \Sigma (1/n'^3) 10^{13.54\theta_e/n'^2}}. \tag{AI.7}$$

The exponential dominates for large θ_e, and the equivalent width of Hβ is large; if $\theta_e < 0.1$ the free-free emission (represented by unity in the denominator) becomes large and the lines are weak. The values of $\Delta\nu$ are 4×10^{14} sec^{-1} at $\theta_e = 0.5$, 10^{14} sec^{-1} at $\theta_e = 0.3$, and 2×10^{13} sec^{-1} at $\theta_e = 0.1$. The summation permits evaluation of the Balmer emission discontinuity, which is a factor of over 20 at $\theta_e = 0.5$; no such jump is observed. The predicted and observed equivalent widths do not agree until $\theta_e = 0.05$, where $\Delta\nu = 8 \times 10^{12}$ sec^{-1}, as compared to 86 Å in 3C 273, which gives the same $\Delta\nu$. This value of θ_e is a minimum value because any nonthermal or additional thermal component in the continuum over that predicted from equation (AI.5) would reduce the observed strength of Hβ in units of the total continuum. The use of $b_4 = 0.16$ is also questionable; this is an average "observed" value in typical planetaries. Perhaps the range $0.1 \leq \theta_e \leq 0.3$ is a reasonably correct first approximation. Oke is discussing his photoelectric scans of the 3C 273 continuum and hydrogen lines in detail, including the two-photon emission, which is very blue.

The effect of increasing the electron temperature above the value of $17000°$ ($\theta_e = 0.3$) adopted in this paper is to reduce the predicted Hβ fluxes by $T_e^{-3/2}$. The behavior of the forbidden lines is quite complicated. If we could continue to use the standard expressions for b_2/b_1 (the deviations from Boltzmann populations), then the important terms are of the form

$$\frac{b_2}{b_1} \approx \frac{1}{1 + \text{const.} \, T_e^{1/2}/N_e}. \tag{AI.8}$$

Note that the "high-density" limit ($b_2/b_1 \rightarrow 1$) is approached when $N_e/T_e^{1/2}$ becomes large. Therefore, an increase from T_e to T_e' causes the high-density limit to be reached at a new value, $N_e'^2 = N_e^2(T_e/17000)$. The weakness of [O II], λ 3727, was critical in our discussion of 3C 273. Raising T_e to $50000°$ results in an increase of N_e' by $3^{1/2}$; the Hβ emission-line luminosity is given by $N_e'^2/T_e'^{3/2}$, which is now $3^{-1/2}$ of the originally adopted values. Not all forbidden lines would change in the same way, since more complicated formulae than equation (AI.8) are required as the higher states become well populated. The very high electron temperatures might more grossly change the various ionization equilibrium. Another effect is strengthening of the auroral line of [O III] at 4363 Å. We derived in Section V an upper limit to the electron density of 3×10^7 cm^{-3} from the observed wavelength of the blend of Hγ and the λ 4363 line. If T_e were high, this upper limit to the electron density would be reduced to a value between 10^7 and 3×10^6 cm^{-3}.

A very high electron temperature, say $\theta_e < 0.1$, has still another consequence if the helium/hydrogen ratio is normal. Lines of a hydrogenic element like He II arise from levels of binding energy Z^2R/n^2. The line of He II corresponding to Hβ has $n' = 4$, $n = 8$, $Z = 2$, and an emission proportional to

$$\frac{N(\text{He II}) \, N_e Z^6 b_8}{T_e^{3/2} n'^3 n^3} 10^{13.54 \, Z^2 \theta_e/n^2}. \tag{AI.9}$$

If $b_8(\text{He II}) = b_4(\text{H})$, the Pickering series line equals $H\beta$ only if $N(\text{He II}) = N_e$; however, for $\lambda\,4686$, $n' = 3$, $n = 4$, the binding energy is larger, and $\lambda\,4686 = H\beta$ at $N(\text{He II}) = 0.03\,N_e$, if $\theta_e = 0.1$. Since neither He I or He II is observed so far, the electron temperature may not be very high.

APPENDIX II

SELF-ABSORPTION

A few additional considerations of the possible self-absorption of the emission lines, forbidden and permitted, are necessary. The large broadening suggests that the problem is less serious than in planetary nebulae; the velocity width of $\pm 10^8$ cm/sec in 3C 48 and 3C 273 spreads the absorption coefficient over a frequency width $\Delta\nu_D = 4 \times 10^{12}$ sec^{-1}. If there are $N_i(X)$ ions of element X per cm^3, the mean optical depth across a sphere of radius R, in a forbidden line arising from the ground state, is

$$\langle \tau \rangle_\nu = \frac{\pi\,e^2}{m\,c}\,\frac{2R N_i(X)}{\Delta\nu_D}\,\frac{g_2 A_{21}}{g_1}\,\frac{m\,c^3}{8\pi^2 e^2 \nu^2}. \tag{AII.1}$$

Converting to R_{pc}, $g_2/g_1 = 1$, $N_i(X) \approx 10^{-4}\,N_e$ for strong forbidden lines, and evaluating $\langle \tau \rangle_\nu$ at the undisplaced frequency $\nu = 7 \times 10^{14}$ sec^{-1}, we find

$$\langle \tau \rangle_\nu \approx 10^{-8} A_{21} R_{\text{pc}} N_e. \tag{AII.2}$$

The values of A_{21} range from about 10^{-1} to 10^{-4} sec^{-1}, so that $\langle \tau \rangle_\nu$ approaches unity for such strong lines as [Ne V] and [O III] only if $R_{\text{pc}}N_e > 10^9$ and for [O II] if $R_{\text{pc}}N_e > 10^{12}$. Thus, in general, the forbidden lines have low mean optical depth of 10^{-2} to 10^{-5}.

Are the emitting volumes also transparent in the Balmer lines? This may depend on the method of excitation, radiative or collisional. Consider first recombination in a nebula optically thick in Lyman-α. Then the population of the level $n = 2$ is given by

$$N_2 = \frac{g_2 b_2}{2}\,N_e^2 \left(\frac{h^2}{2\pi m k}\right)^{3/2} 10^{3.39\theta_e} T_e^{-3/2}. \tag{AII.3}$$

Since Lyman-α is optically thick, $b_2 \approx 1$. We obtain the mean absorption in $H\beta$ proportional to N_2 from equations (AII.1) and (AII.3) as

$$\langle \tau \rangle_\nu(H\beta) \approx 7.8 \times 10^{-12} b_2 10^{3.39\theta_e} T_e^{-3/2} R_{\text{pc}} N_e^2. \tag{AII.4}$$

Note that if $b_2 \approx 1$, $\theta_e \approx 0.3$, $\langle \tau \rangle_\nu(H\beta) \approx 4 \times 10^{-17} R_{\text{pc}}N_e^2$. From Table 7B, or equation (12), note that $N_e^2 R_{\text{pc}} \approx 2 \times 10^4 N_e^{4/3}$, which is about 5×10^{13} for $N_e = 10^7$ cm^{-3}. Therefore, $\langle \tau \rangle_\nu$ $(H\beta)$ is at most 0.002, at the high-density limit of N_e suggested by the weakness of [O II]. Since lower values of density are probable for 3C 48, it appears that $H\beta$, and also $H\gamma$ and the Balmer continuum are optically thin.

A separate consideration is needed for the case where the radiation field is neglected and the ionization as well as the excitation is by collision. For collision, $b_2 \approx 1$. Chamberlain (1953) computes the collisional ionization and excitation of hydrogen over suitable ranges of θ_e. His values of b_n are compared with those in the recombination case in his Tables 2 and 3. For low n, collision and recombination differ by about a factor of only 2 if the nebula is optically thick in the Lyman lines. The Balmer decrements also do not differ greatly, especially at high T_e. No modification in the conclusions drawn from equation (AII.4) are necessary.

APPENDIX III

THE INTENSITY OF Mg II EMISSION IN
AN OPTICALLY THICK NEBULA

We find from equation (AII.2) that the optical thickness of the Mg II resonance line is large, since $A_{21} \approx 10^8$ sec^{-1}. The concentration of Mg II is $Z(\mathrm{Mg})(1 - x_{\mathrm{Mg^+}})N_e$, which we will denote by aN_e; the number of atoms per cm^3 in the ground level is then $N_1 = aN_e$. Let us first consider the standard collisional treatment, which we will find leads to a significant contradiction. We resolve this by study of the effect of the nebular radiation itself on the population of the upper level. Consider a two-level atom with collisional excitation and de-excitation rates F_{12} and F_{21}, respectively, and a spontaneous decay probability of A_{21}. The population of the upper level N_2 is obtained from a collisional value, $b_2(\mathrm{coll.})$, given by the steady-state condition

$$N_2 A_{21} + F_{21} = F_{12} \tag{AIII.1}$$

and the collisional rates

$$F_{12} = \frac{8.54 \times 10^{-6}}{T_e^{1/2}} \frac{N_1 N_e \Omega 10^{-\theta x}}{g_1}, \qquad F_{21} = \frac{8.54 \times 10^{-6}}{T_e^{1/2}} \frac{N_2 N_e \Omega}{g_2}. \tag{AIII.2}$$

The value of $b_2(\mathrm{coll.})$ so obtained is small, and therefore collisional de-excitation can be neglected, so that $b_2(\mathrm{coll.})$ simplifies to

$$b_2(\mathrm{coll.}) = \frac{8.54 \times 10^{-6}}{T_e^{1/2}} \frac{N_e \Omega}{g_2 A_{21}} \approx 10^{-15} N_e. \tag{AIII.3}$$

The rate of emission for the optically thin case is obtained from either the total number of collisions within the volume V, or from the number of atoms in the upper state times A_{21}. The lumnosity in Mg$^+$ is then, as used before in equation (10),

$$E(\mathrm{Mg^+}) = \frac{8.54 \times 10^{-6} a N_e^2 \Omega h\nu 10^{-4.42\theta_e}}{T_e^{1/2} g_1} \frac{4\pi R^3}{3} \quad (\tau_\nu < 1). \tag{AIII.4}$$

But the optical depth is, in fact, very large; through an object of radius R, with a total Doppler width of $\Delta\nu_D$, the mean line absorption averaged over the line is $N_1 B_{12} h\nu \, 2R/\Delta\nu_D \approx 10^{-2} N_e R_{\mathrm{pc}}$. We can show that unless the synchrotron radiation is much larger than the black-body radiation, we can neglect both the normal black-body-stimulated emission and that stimulated by the synchrotron radiation.

The atomistic equation of transfer valid over the frequency range $\Delta\nu_D$ within the line can be taken as

$$dI_\nu = - N_1 B_{12} h\nu I_\nu d s + \frac{N_2 A_{21} h\nu d s}{4\pi}, \tag{AIII.5}$$

which leads to

$$-\frac{dI_\nu}{h\nu N_1 B_{12} d s} = I_\nu - \frac{g_2 b_2(\mathrm{coll.}) A_{21}}{g_1 4\pi B_{12}} e^{-h\nu/k T_e}. \tag{AIII.6}$$

With the optical depth defined as $dt_\nu = -h\nu N_1 B_{12} ds$ the transfer equation becomes

$$\frac{dI_\nu}{dt_\nu} - I_\nu = -\frac{b_2(\mathrm{coll.})}{4\pi} \frac{2 h\nu^3}{c^2} e^{-h\nu/k T_e}. \tag{AIII.7}$$

If we take the simple geometry of a plane-parallel slab, the emergent intensity is $I_\nu(0)$, constant over $\Delta\nu_D$,

$$I_\nu(0) = \frac{2 h\nu^3}{c^2} e^{-h\nu/k T_e} \frac{b_2(\mathrm{coll.})}{4\pi} [1 - e^{-t_\nu(2R)}], \tag{AIII.8}$$

where $t_\nu(2R)$ is the total optical thickness. The energy emitted, as evaluated from equation (AIII.8), must be multiplied by the band width $\Delta\nu_D$ and proves to be the thermal emission times b_2, if $t_\nu(2R)$ is very large. For a plane the flux is $\pi I_\nu(0)$. The total luminosity is then, for $t_\nu = \infty$,

$$E(\text{Mg}^+) = \frac{2\,h\nu^3}{c^2}\,10^{-4.42\theta_e}\pi R^2 b_2(\text{coll.})\Delta\nu_D\,. \qquad \text{(AIII.9)}$$

We have here integrated over the entire line width $\Delta\nu_D$, and evaluated a surface emission, in contrast to the volume emission given by equation (AIII.4). It can be shown that if $t_\nu(2R)$ is small in equation (AIII.8), the total luminosity approaches that given by equation (AIII.4) within a trivial factor of $2\pi/(4\pi/3)$. If a spherical geometry had been used this factor would be unity.

Returning to the optically thick case of equation (AIII.9), we compute the surface emissivity, which is now linearly dependent on N_e but independent of the abundance of Mg, as essentially that of a black body reduced by the factor $b_2(\text{coll.})$, i.e.,

$$E(\text{Mg}^+) = \frac{8.54 \times 10^{-6}N_e\Omega}{T_e^{1/2}g_2A_{21}}\frac{2\,h\nu^3}{c^2}\,10^{-4.42\theta_e}\pi R^2\Delta\nu_D$$

$$\qquad \text{(AIII.10)}$$

$$\approx 8 \times 10^{19}\Delta\nu_D N_e R_{\text{pc}}^2 \approx 3 \times 10^{32}N_e R_{\text{pc}}^2 \text{ erg cm}^{-3}\text{ sec}^{-1}\,.$$

If we apply this result to 3C 273, with $E = 4 \times 10^{43}$ and $N_e = 10^7$, we find the large radius of 140 pc, where all other lines gave $R \approx 1$ pc. We believe that the radius is 1 pc and that a new approach to the excitation mechanism is required by the intense radiation field of the line itself. The actual flux at the surface in the Mg II line reaches the enormous value of 10^6 erg cm^{-2} sec^{-1}, approximately equal to daylight.

The absorbed radiation within the Mg$^+$ resonance line is multiply scattered, as long as ionizations or absorptions from its upper level can be neglected. The problem of the emergent intensity of the diffused light is equivalent to the largely unsolved problem of Lyman-a in a planetary nebula with internal motions. The diffusion of the λ 2800 radiation differs from that of Ly-a in that its upper level is populated easily by collision (only 4.4 eV excitation) as against recombination for Ly-a (10.2 eV). The upper level of the resonance lines of Mg$^+$, 3^2S–3^2P^0 ($\lambda\lambda$ 2795.5, 2802.7) communicates by the absorptions of 3^2P^0–3^2D ($\lambda\lambda$ 2798.0, 2790.8) to levels which can reradiate these strong, nearly coincident ultraviolet lines or, by forbidden transitions 3^2D–4^2S or 3^2D–3^2S, return to the ground state. The population of 3^2P^0, however, seems to be too small at reasonable N_e to complicate the situation in any significant way beyond the two-level pure scattering problem. At $N_e = 10^7$ cm^{-3} and $b_2 \approx 10^{-9}$ if the optical depth is of the order of 10^5, only one scattering in 10^4 leads to an "absorption" process, i.e., the scattering albedo is very near unity.

We cannot neglect, therefore, the effect of radiative excitation on the population of the upper level, and proceed to re-evaluate b_2, including both radiative and collisional effects. Equation (AIII.1) should be rewritten as

$$N_2(A_{21}+B_{21}4\pi J_\nu)+F_{21} = N_1B_{12}4\pi J_\nu+F_{12}\,, \qquad \text{(AIII.11)}$$

where J_ν is the mean intensity in the line over all directions. The terms involving the stimulated emission ($N_2 B_{21} 4\pi J_\nu$) and collisional de-excitation F_{21} are, in fact, small. We follow an analysis by Münch (1962) to whom we are indebted for several interesting discussions. We obtain the result that $b_2(\text{rad.} + \text{coll.}) \approx b_2(\text{rad.})$ is

$$b_2(\text{rad.}+\text{coll.}) = \frac{[\,(8.5 \times 10^{-6}N_e\Omega)/(T_e^{1/2}g_1A_{21})\,]+\mathfrak{J}\,e^{h\nu/kT_e}}{[\,(8.5 \times 10^{-6}N_e\Omega)/(T_e^{1/2}g_1A_{21})\,]+\mathfrak{J}+1}\,. \qquad \text{(AIII.12)}$$

Here the effective mean intensity is

$$\mathfrak{J} = \frac{c^2 4\pi}{2 h\nu^3} \frac{J_\nu}{\Delta\nu_D} \tag{AIII.13}$$

and must be derived from the radiation field in the line itself. In equation (AIII.12) in the numerator, only the second term proves to be appreciable and in the denominator only unity. Therefore, the best estimate of b_2(rad. + coll.) is

$$b_2(\text{rad.} + \text{coll.}) \approx \frac{c^2}{2 h\nu^3} 4\pi J_\nu e^{h\nu/k T_e}. \tag{AIII.14}$$

As before, the line width is $\Delta\nu_D$, so that the luminosity for an optically thick nebula from equation (AIII.8) becomes

$$I_\nu(\text{Mg}^+) = J_\nu. \tag{AIII.15}$$

Equation (AIII.15) represents merely the conservation of energy, i.e., that every resonance quantum absorbed within the volume ultimately is emitted at the surface, except for the small neglected factors in equation (AIII.12). The b_2 derived in equation (AIII.14) is linear in J_ν; if we take the observed flux from 3C 273 at the surface and compute J_ν from $J_\nu \approx \frac{1}{2}F_\nu$, we find b_2(rad. + coll.) $\approx 2 \times 10^{-5}$, or b_2(rad.) $\approx 2 \times 10^{10}$ b_2(coll.)$/N_e$. Thus we have an increase in the predicted radiation by about 2000, or a required radius of $R \approx 1$ pc, as computed earlier from the total volume emissivity. A more detailed study of this problem would involve us in a very difficult problem. A major simplification in this case is that the Mg^+ analog of Balmer-α is here coincident with the Ly-α transition of Mg^+, because of the wide spacing of the 3^2S, 3^2P^0, and 3^2D levels. We have neglected recombination in the population of 3^2P^0 throughout this paper. No computations have been made of the value of b_2 for recombination; the energy levels are widely split and the degeneracy which makes hydrogen relatively simple is absent. If we treat the Mg^+ ion as if it were hydrogenic, the approximate value of the recombination emission is $10^{32} b_2 N_e^2 R_{\text{pc}}^3$ or about b_2 10^{45} erg sec^{-1} for 3C 273. Thus unless b_2(recombination) exceeds 10^{-2} there is little likelihood of pure recombination being important. If recombination computations can be carried through for this complex case and b_2 is large, it is possible that an additional emission varying as $N_e^2R^3$ would then be found. In that case the $N_e^2R^3$ required would be less than that predicted in this paper.

REFERENCES

Aller, L. H. 1954, *Ap. J.*, **120**, 401.
———. 1956, *Gaseous Nebulae* (New York: John Wiley & Sons), p. 162.
Aller, L. H., and Menzel, D. H. 1945, *Ap. J.*, **102**, 239.
Ambartsumian, V. A., and Saakyan, G. S. 1961, *Astr. Zh.*, **38**, 785.
Burbidge, G. R. 1956, *Ap. J.*, **124**, 416.
Cameron, A. G. W. 1959, *Ap. J.*, **130**, 884.
Chamberlain, J. W. 1953, *Ap. J.*, **117**, 387.
Colgate, S. A., and Cameron, A. G. W. 1963, *Nature*, **200**, 870.
Daub, C. T. 1963, *Ap. J.*, **137**, 184.
Dent, W. A., and Haddock, F. T. 1964, *Quasi-stellar Sources and Gravitational Collapse*, ed. I. Robinson, A. E. Schild, and E. L. Schucking (Chicago: University of Chicago Press) (in press).
Elwert, G. 1948, *Zs. f. Naturf.*, **3a**, 477.
Fowler, W. A., and Hoyle, F. 1964, *Quasi-stellar Sources and Gravitational Collapse*, ed. I. Robinson, A. E. Schild, and E. L. Schucking (Chicago: University of Chicago Press) (in press).
Friedman, H. 1963, *Space Science*, ed. D. P. Le Galley (New York: John Wiley & Sons), p. 579.
Gardner, E. F., and Whiteoak, J. B. 1963, *Nature*, **197**, 1162.
Greenstein, J. L. 1957, *Radio Astronomy*, ed. H. C. van de Hulst (Cambridge: Cambridge University Press), chap. 32.
———. 1964, *Ap. J.* (in press).
Greenstein, J. L., and Matthews, T. A. 1963, *Nature*, **197**, 1041.*
Greenstein, J. L., and Minkowski, R. 1953, *Ap. J.*, **118**, 1.
Greenstein, J. L., and Münch, G. 1961, *Ann. Rept. Dir. Mt. Wilson and Palomar Obs.* (Carnegie Inst. of Washington Yearbook), p. 80.

Hazard, C. 1964, *Quasi-stellar Sources and Gravitational Collapse*, ed. I. Robinson, A. E. Schild, and E.
    L. Schucking (Chicago: University of Chicago Press) (in press).
Hazard, C., Mackey, M. B., and Shimmins, A. J. 1963, *Nature*, **197**, 1037. *
Hoyle, F., and Fowler, W. A. 1963, *M.N.*, **125**, 169.
Luyten, W. J. 1963, *Pub. Astr. Obs. Minnesota*, Vol. **3**, No. 13.
Matthews, T. A., Bolton, J. G., Greenstein, J. L., Münch, G., and Sandage, A. R. 1960, Am. Astr.
    Soc. meeting, New York; *Sky and Telescope*, 1961, **21**, 148.
Matthews, T. A., and Sandage, A. R. 1963, *Ap. J.*, **138**, 30.*
Mattig, W. 1958, *A.N.*, **284**, 109.
Milford, S. N. 1959, *Ap. J.*, **130**, 465.
Münch, G. 1962, *Ap. J.*, **136**, 823.
O'Dell, C. R. 1963, *Ap. J.*, **138**, 1018.
Oke, J. B. 1963, *Nature*, **197**, 1040.*
Oppenheimer, J. R., and Volkoff, G. M. 1939, *Phys. Rev.*, **55**, 374.
Oster, L. 1961, *Rev. Mod. Phys.*, **33**, 525.
Regemorter, H. van. 1960a, *Ann. d'ap.*, **23**, 817.
———. 1960b, *M.N.*, **121**, 213.
Saakyan, G. S. 1963, *Astr. Zh.*, **40**, 82.
Salpeter, E. 1961, *Ap. J.*, **134**, 669.
Sandage, A. R. 1961, *Ap. J.*, **133**, 355.
———. 1964, *Ap. J.*, **139**, 416.
Schmidt, M. 1963, *Nature*, **197**, 1040.*
Schmidt, M., and Matthews, T. A. 1964, *Ap. J.*, **139**, 781.*
Seaton, M. J., and Osterbrock, D. E. 1957, *Ap. J.*, **125**, 66.
Seielstad, G. A. 1963, thesis, California Institute of Technology.
Sharov. A. S., and Efremov, Y. N. 1963, *Inform. Bull. on Var. Stars*, No. 23.
Smith, H. J. 1964, *Quasi-stellar Sources and Gravitational Collapse*, ed. I. Robinson, A. E. Schild, and
    E. L. Schucking (Chicago: University of Chicago Press) (in press).
Smith, H. J., and Hoffleit, D. 1961, *Pub. A.S.P.*, **73**, 292.
Wheeler, J. A., with Harrison, B. K., and Wakano, M. 1958, *La Structure et l'évolution de l'univers*,
    Solvay Conf. (Brussels: R. Stoops), p. 124.

GALACTIC INTERSTELLAR ABSORPTION LINES IN THE
chapter 14 # SPECTRUM OF 3C 273

DAVID R. W. WILLIAMS

A number of observers have tried to estimate the distance of 3C 273. Schmidt (1963) suggested that the radio source 3C 273 may be associated either with a nearby starlike object of unusual characteristics, or with an extremely bright extragalactic nebula of large cosmological redshift ($Z = 0.158$). I describe observations which may enable us to decide if 3C 273 is a galactic or an extragalactic object.

Dr. G. Preston, of Lick Observatory, obtained a number of optical spectra of the object at 48 Å/mm in which the interstellar H- and K-lines of Ca II are visible; a typical spectrum is shown in Figure 1. Dr. R. Minkowski suggested subsequently that a search should be made for the 21-cm hydrogen-absorption line in the radio spectrum. In the case of the bright radio sources near the galactic plane, it is possible to position the source among the spiral arms of the Galaxy. This is done by observing the deep absorption lines in the profiles and then identifying the radial velocity of the absorbing cloud with that of the spiral arms in the direction of the source. In the case of 3C 273 at a galactic latitude of $+64°$ no spiral structure is visible in the emission profile and an alternative method had to be sought.

In the radio work a hydrogen-line receiver of a scanning type was used in conjunction with the 85-ft. aperture radio telescope of the University of California Radio Astronomy Observatory at Hat Creek. The receiver employed a parametric amplifier and used a double-frequency comparison method; a digital output permitted the use of a computer reduction program.

At the time the measurements were made, a survey of the absorption spectra in the radio sources in the galactic plane was in progress, and this was then extended to cover the more intense of the high latitude sources.

We obtained comparison spectra at points on a hexagonal grid centered on the source and one full beam width away (45′), together with the spectrum in the position of the source. We always took the spectra in sets of three (comparison point, source, comparison point) to secure homogeneity in the results. In this way small linear drifts are averaged out, and the reality of the differential profile is insured.

Twenty-seven individual spectra are used in the analysis, and the average of the six

DAVID R. W. WILLIAMS, University of California, Berkeley.

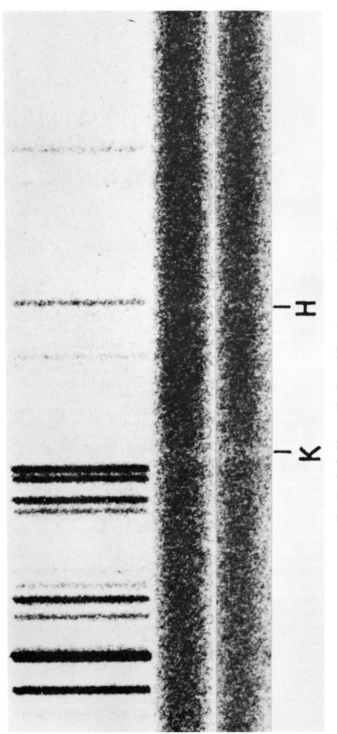

Fig. 1.—Optical interstellar lines of Ca II in spectrum of 3C 273

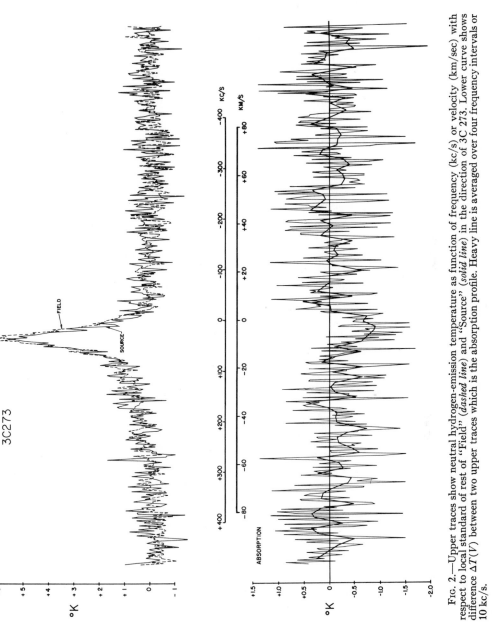

Fig. 2.—Upper traces show neutral hydrogen-emission temperature as function of frequency (kc/s) or velocity (km/sec) with respect to local standard of rest of "Field" (*dashed line*) and "Source" (*solid line*) in the direction of 3C 273. Lower curve shows difference $\Delta T(V)$ between two upper traces which is the absorption profile. Heavy line is averaged over four frequency intervals or 10 kc/s.

normalized comparison points is plotted as the "Field" dashed line in the temperature versus frequency plot of Figure 2. The frequencies and velocities are reduced to local standard of rest. The average of the spectra in the direction of 3C 273 is shown in the solid upper trace and marked "Source." The difference in temperature $\Delta T(V)$ between the "Field" and "Source" spectra becomes the absorption profile plotted in the lower part of Figure 2.

The receiver band width used in the observations is 16.5 kc/s, the interval plotted on the frequency scale is 2.5 kc/s, which corresponds to the 9-sec interval over which the receiver output is integrated and then digitized. The lower heavy curve shows averages over four frequency intervals or 10 kc/s and has correspondingly less noise present. In the frequency-switched receiver the source does not produce a displacement of the baseline so that the antenna temperature T_a of the source is obtained from a separate record of the receiver total power output. Also, in the double-comparison method, the difference in T_a at the line frequency and points ± 2 Mc/s away is measured simultaneously so that the change in T_a due to the spectral index of the source is averaged out across the region of interest.

TABLE 1

Source	ΔT (° K)	T_a (° K)	τ_{pk}*	(N_{tot}/T_s) atoms/cm²/° K	T_s (° K)
3C 273............	0.7	4.6	0.15	$(2.03 \pm 0.20) \times 10^{18}$	33
3C 274 = M87.......	4.0	24	0.17	$(1.61 \pm 0.20) \times 10^{18}$	43

* τ_{pk} is the opacity at the peak of the absorption line.

The opacity $\tau(V)$ may then be computed as a function of velocity from the relation

$$T_a - \Delta T(V) = T_a \cdot e^{-\tau(V)} .$$

Hence we can evaluate the quantity $(N_{tot}/T_s)_{3C\ 273}$, where N_{tot} is the total number of atoms in line of sight to the source having spin temperature T_s, from

$$\left(\frac{N_{tot}}{T_s}\right)_{3C\ 273} = 1.835 \times 10^{13} \int \tau(V) \cdot dV .$$

At this point we can proceed no further in the discussion of the number of atoms in line of sight unless we specifically know the spin temperature.

There is another possibility, however, that we make a comparison between this source and another in the same region of the sky. If this source is extragalactic, we can compute the spin temperature for the region, or alternatively, normalize N_{tot} to T_s and make the assumption that T_s is constant over the region involving the two sources. The source-absorption spectrum was therefore obtained for the nearby radio source 3C 274 which has been identified with M87 and is known to be extragalactic. Hence the value $(N_{tot}/T_s)_{3C\ 274}$ is calculated and applies to all the atoms in line of sight. We now make the reasonable assumption that T_s has the same value for 3C 273 and 3C 274 at galactic latitudes $b_1{}^{II} = 64°$ and $b_2{}^{II} = 74°$, respectively; then we can compare $(N_{tot}/T_s)_{3C\ 273}$ with $(N_{tot}/T_s)_{3C\ 274}$ directly. If the galactic neutral hydrogen is distributed in the form of layers parallel to the galactic plane, then when 3C 273 and 3C 274 are both extragalactic

$$\frac{(N_{tot})_{3C\ 273}}{(N_{tot})_{3C\ 274}} = \frac{\text{cosec } 64°}{\text{cosec } 74°} = 1.07 .$$

The observed values for the two sources are given in Table 1.

From the tabulated values

$$\frac{(N_{\text{tot}})_{3C\ 273}}{(N_{\text{tot}})_{3C\ 274}} = 1.26 \pm 0.28$$

in agreement with the expected value of 1.07 within experimental error and consistent with the assumption that 3C 273 is extragalactic. The values for T_s in the final column are calculated on this assumption, knowing the emission temperature in the "field" regions. These values are to be compared with 110° K found in the galactic plane, and are to be expected for high latitude H I.

A comparison between the velocity of the radio and optical lines reduced to the local standard of rest is given in Table 2. It may be inferred that within the limits of error the

TABLE 2

Optical velocity..................... -1 ± 8 km/sec
Radio velocity....................... -4 ± 1 km/sec

same feature is being observed in the optical and radio domains. Interstellar lines are usually observed in stars which are at considerable distances from the galactic plane and Münch and Zirin (1961) list no high latitude star with a Z distance less than 230 pc.

A recent discussion by Robinson, van Damme, and Koehler (1963) attempts to decide whether 3C 273 is galactic or extragalactic by comparing the opacities τ and τ' in front of the two sources 3C 270 and 3C 273 at one frequency, at the peak of the emission line. The fractional opacities they measured varied greatly on two occasions so that the quantity $\tau - \tau'$ may not have too much significance. However, the conclusion from their results is in agreement with our own, that 3C 273 is beyond all the local hydrogen and therefore extragalactic.

REFERENCES

Münch, G., and Zirin, G. 1961, *Ap. J.*, **133**, 11.
Robinson, B. J., Damme, K. J. van, and Koehler, J. A. 1963, *Nature*, **199**, 990.
Schmidt, M. 1963, *Nature*, **197**, 1040. *

chapter 15 THE PROPER MOTION OF 3C 273

WILLIAM H. JEFFERYS

At the suggestion of Dr. Harlan Smith, an investigation of the absolute proper motion of 3C 273 was undertaken at Yale University. This parameter is of importance, for if it is large, then 3C 273 is certainly nearby: on the other hand, if the proper motion is zero within the measuring error, the probability that the object is within a certain distance, determined by the mean error of the observed proper motion, is very small.

The measures from fourteen plates covering the period 1887–1963 were used in the investigation, including seven from the Harvard Observatory, four from the Van Vleck Observatory, and three from the *Astrographic Catalogue*. Up to forty-eight reference objects were measured on a plate for the accurate determination of the proper motion of the reference system through systematic proper motions. They were also used for the determination and elimination of certain systematic errors due to the differences between the types of observational material (the problem of inhomogeneous material). This can be done by comparing the probability distribution function of the proper motions of the reference stars as predicted by statistical astronomy with that actually observed, and adjusting various parameters (plate constants) in order to bring the two distributions into the best agreement. In practice, an equivalent adjustment is made by the method of least squares, as extended by Brown (1955).

The systematic errors are those associated with magnitude, color, and position; magnitudes and colors were determined from a blue and a visual plate lent by the Warner and Swazey Observatory and measured at the Van Vleck Observatory. The required systematic proper motions were predicted from material compiled by Vyssotsky and Williams (1948).

The positions are expanded in a polynomial of low degree in the relevant parameters:

$$\Sigma a_{ijkl} x^i y^j c^k m^l - \xi - \mu \Delta t = 0 , \tag{1}$$

where ξ is the so-called standard coordinate of the star at a given, constant epoch; μ is the proper motion; Δt is the difference between the epoch of the plate and the given epoch; a_{ijkl} are plate constants (each plate has its own set of plate constants); x and y are the measured coordinates of the star; c its color index; and m its magnitude. When we adjoin to such equations of condition equations describing predicted systematic proper motions,

$$\mu = \mu^{(\text{systematic})} , \tag{2}$$

WILLIAM H. JEFFERYS, Yale University Observatory.

219

and equations for any reference positions obtained from standard catalogues,

$$\xi + \mu\Delta t = \xi^{(\text{catalogue})} \, , \tag{3}$$

we can form the resulting set of equations into a set of normal equations. We solve them for the plate constants, a_{ijkl}, and star constants, ξ and μ, by methods described elsewhere (Eichhorn 1960; Jefferys 1963).

In the present problem the resulting set of normal equations was a system of approximately four hundred equations in as many unknowns. But certain simplifications in their structure make the solution much less laborious than it would appear at first sight.

Among the star constants resulting from this solution is the proper motion of 3C 273, determined within the system of the FK3, since all the reference material was computed within the FK3 system. After correction for the rotation of the system of the FK3 with respect to an inertial system, the absolute proper motion of 3C 273 is found to be

$$\mu_a = +0.0009'' \pm 0.0025''/\text{yr}$$

and

$$\mu_\delta = -0.0012'' \pm 0.0025''/\text{yr} \, .$$

This result may be interpreted as follows: in the first place, the object is located with respect to the Sun at approximately right angles to the solar peculiar velocity vector. We use now the formula

$$V_t = 4.74\mu d \, , \tag{4}$$

where V_t is the transverse velocity of an object relative to the Sun, in km/sec; μ is the proper motion of the object, in seconds of arc per year; and d is the distance to the object, in parsecs (1 pc = 3.26 light-years = 3.08×10^{18} cm). Since the solar motion is about 20 km/sec, equation (4) predicts under such conditions that motion of the object would almost certainly be detected if it were much closer than 2000 pc (excluding the unlikely possibility that the object travels parallel to the Sun at the same speed).

In a similar manner, the object is in a high galactic latitude; and at such a distance it is unlikely to be traveling around the Galaxy with the same direction and speed of the Sun. Since the latter is about 200 km/sec, equation (4) predicts that it is unlikely that the object is much closer than 20000 pc, which puts it effectively out of the Galaxy.

The results reported here are confirmed by similar research by Luyten (1963) on the proper motions of 3C 273 and similar objects. In no case was he able to detect a significant proper motion.

The author would like to express his thanks to Drs. H. J. Smith, H. K. Eichhorn, and W. J. Luyten for their comments and suggestions; to Mr. James Gibson for taking the four plates from Van Vleck Observatory; and to the directors of the various observatories for their loan of plates and equipment. This research was supported from a grant by the National Science Foundation, and part of it was accomplished while the author was studying under a National Science Foundation Graduate Fellowship.

REFERENCES

Brown, D. C. 1955, *Ball. Res. Lab. Rept.* No. 937.
Eichhorn, H. K. 1960, *Astr. Nachr.*, **285**, 233.
Jefferys, W. H. 1963, *A.J.*, **68**, 111.
Luyten, W. J. 1963, *Pub. Astr. Obs. Minnesota III*, No. 13.
Vyssotsky, A. N., and Williams, E. T. R. 1948, *Pub. McCormick Obs.*, Vol. **10**.

chapter 16 LIGHT VARIATIONS OF 3C 273

HARLAN J. SMITH

INTRODUCTION

When the first quasi-stellar radio sources were discovered it seemed reasonable (e.g., Sandage 1961) to suspect them to be very peculiar, unstable, starlike objects in the Galaxy. This hypothesis implied that their brightness might be variable, either explosively in the past or perhaps continuing at present. To test this hypothesis on the first quasi-stellar source, 3C 48, an exhaustive search (Smith and Hoffleit 1961) of the Harvard Observatory historical photographic collection yielded seventy-five plates with images of the source adequate for rough estimates of visual magnitude. Within a total scatter of 0.4 mag. there was no conclusive evidence for variation or for secular change of brightness greater than 0.1 mag. over the interval 1899 to 1949. On the other hand, recent photoelectric work (Sandage 1964) has shown that irregular variations of several tenths of a magnitude are present in 3C 48 as well as other quasi-stellar sources. But practically all of these objects—ranging from $m = 16$ to $m = 19$—are difficult to study even with large telescopes, and are at best poorly represented in historical plate collections. The discovery that 3C 273 is associated with a quasi-stellar object brighter than $m = 13$ was thus important in providing the first and probably the only such source bright enough to be reached with relatively modest telescopes and to be recorded on thousands of older stellar photographs. Preliminary discussion of most of these plates and of some recent photoelectric observations form the principal subject of this paper.

HISTORICAL PLATE MATERIAL AND ANALYSIS

The Harvard Observatory photographic plate collection includes material up to a century old taken by several dozen cameras and telescopes ranging from 60-inch reflectors and 24-inch refractors down to patrol cameras of $1\frac{1}{2}$-inch aperture. While nearly all of the refractors contributed at least a few plates to the present analysis, the principal weight of the historical light-curve of 3C 273 rests on material from the 16-inch MC, the 12-inch MA, the 8-inch B, the 3-inch RH and RB, and the $1\frac{1}{2}$-inch AC. Although the aberrations of the cameras are not identical with respect to star color, completion of astrophotometer measures and reductions using a number of comparison stars of different colors will make it possible to reduce the different plate series more closely to a common system; preliminary checks have shown such differences to be small compared with the variations observed.

HARLAN J. SMITH, University of Texas.

221

Practically all of the historical Harvard plates are untreated blue emulsions, giving magnitudes essentially on the old "pg" system; the few yellow- or red-sensitive plates encountered were rejected from the present analysis.

Through a co-operative Yale Observatory project with Dorrit Hoffleit, assisted by Eugene and Helen Milone, Güner Omay, P. Raju, Hamid Rizavi, T. Slebarski, Zeki Tüfekcioglu, and particularly Charles Martin, some five thousand blue plates on the region of 3C 273 were located in the Harvard plate stacks and examined; nearly half showed the quasi-stellar image clearly enough to warrant eye estimation of its brightness interpolated in a sequence of adjacent comparison stars (Fig. 1 and Table 1).

Comparison star magnitudes for the photographic light-curve first published (Smith and Hoffleit 1963a) were derived by visual comparison with adjacent Selected Area 104 and the Harvard Standard Region at 12^h, $4°30'$. A slightly improved set, derived from iris photometry of a pair of Warner and Swasey Schmidt plates, was used for the latter half of the Harvard visual work as well as (with minor revisions) for Sonneberg and

TABLE 1

MAGNITUDES OF COMPARISON STARS FOR 3C 273

	PROVISIONAL YALE PHOTO-GRAPHIC	IRIS PHOTOMETER		McDONALD PHOTOELECTRIC		
		Sharov and Efremov	Warner and Swasey Plates	B	B−V	U−B
K........	11.6	....	11.60	11.79	1.46	+1.80
A........	12.0	....	12.07	12.38	0.66	+0.13
B........	12.4	12.29	12.26	12.57	0.44	−0.05
C........	12.6	12.56	12.70	12.75	0.99	+0.59
D........	12.8	12.81	12.82	13.04	0.53	−0.02
E........	13.1	13.04	13.10	13.24	0.66	+0.10
F........	13.8	....	13.66	13.85	1.09	+0.80
G........	13.9	....	13.64	13.99	0.61	+0.11

Heidelberg magnitudes. Sharov and Efremov (1963a), in their independent discovery of the variation of 3C 273, published a closely similar set of iris photometer magnitudes. All of these sets of comparison star magnitudes are similar enough so that magnitudes of 3C 273 derived from them have so far been used uncritically in the provisional visual light-curve; some changes in form and amplitude will appear when corrections to the final comparison star photographic magnitude system are made. Photoelectric measures for the comparison stars were obtained during 1963–1964 on a number of nights at the McDonald Observatory; means of these also appear in Table 1. In particular, the B magnitudes were used in reducing iris photometer measures of some of the plates as described below. The photoelectric magnitudes indicate a zero-point error of about 0.20 mag. in the older photographic sequences—3C 273 thus being a little fainter than given in data and curves previously published.

Individual eye estimates of 3C 273 magnitudes from the Harvard plates were made either by D. Hoffleit or the author. The principal difficulty in making the estimates arose from lens aberrations which generated images of slightly different quality as a function of the color and brightness of the star. But since the variations of 3C 273 described in this paper appear in long runs of plates taken with a single lens, as well as consistently between plates taken with different lenses, the results from all Harvard cameras have been averaged together. The principal Harvard plate series with good scale for this work terminate around 1953. Fortunately, from 1952 through 1957 the Harvard New Mexico Super-Schmidt meteor cameras often photographed the region; despite the only

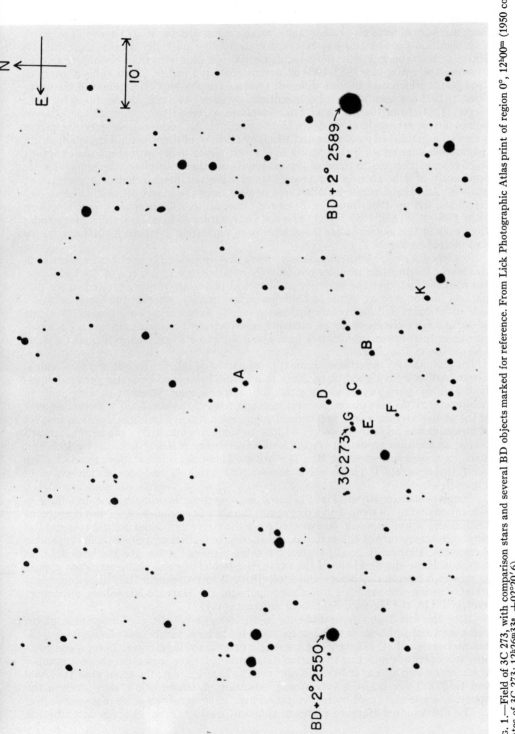

Fig. 1.—Field of 3C 273, with comparison stars and several BD objects marked for reference. From Lick Photographic Atlas print of region 0°, 12ʰ00ᵐ (1950 co-ordinates of 3C 273: 12ʰ26ᵐ33ˢ, +02°20ʹ6).

0.2 mag. precision available from each of these small-scale films, averages of results from large numbers of films give rather stable mean magnitudes for 3C 273 over this interval.

A significant amount of non-Harvard material has gradually became available. H. Huth, of Sonneberg, kindly provided some 190 eye estimates from Sonneberg patrols covering the entire gap 1953–1963 as well as scattered earlier results (plus a group of 1964 points which may be on a different photometric system). The weight of the curve prior to 1915 has been increased substantially by ninety-two magnitudes taken by E. L. Geyer (1964) from the old Wolf asteroid plates at Heidelberg (thirteen more Geyer points fall at various later times up to the present). An additional seventy-five points were earlier published by Sharov and Efremov (1963b); of these, seventeen non-doubtful magnitudes determined by iris photometer mostly from 40-cm astrograph plates appear to have weights equal to those of typical points of other collections; the remainder are apparently of substantially lower weight and have not been included in the present analysis. Additional points include three in 1963 from the Maria Mitchell Observatory (Hoffleit), five in 1962 from the Bamberg Observatory (Kippenhahn), and fifteen in 1929, 1930, 1958, and 1959 from the Lowell Observatory (Giclas, H. Smith). Magnitudes from each of the sources so far listed have been separately averaged by 100-day means and plotted in Figure 2.

Readers unfamiliar with variable-star work may question the use of eye estimates in this work. Justification includes not only the relative ease and speed of the technique, but also the fact that the majority of historical plates are rather unsuited to iris diaphragm photometry by virtue of their low image quality, whereas the eye is normally able to integrate and interpolate with some facility even among poor images. Precision of such an eye estimate, when an extremely good adjacent comparison sequence is available as in the present case, ranges from about 0.05 to 0.2 mag. depending on the scale and quality of the plate.

Iris photometry, nevertheless, can approximately double the weight of an individual determination from a good plate. Since in addition it largely eliminates personal equations and also permits partial correction for color equations, an effort is being made to photometer all possible plates. So far it has been possible to obtain only a limited amount of iris photometer data on a well-defined comparison star system. Specifically, a first set of measures was made by E. and H. Milone on some five hundred of the better Harvard plates; an additional nineteen Goethe Link Observatory plates at Indiana, for 1953 and 1962, have been measured by Mrs. D. Owings. These measures, reduced for each plate using the complete B photoelectric sequence of Table 1, lead to the light-curve of Figure 3.

The eye-estimate curve (Fig. 2), based on over two thousand plates, has the significant advantage of more detailed coverage than the photometer-curve, but it also contains more "noise" as would be expected from the larger individual point errors and the heterogeneous nature of the material, estimators, reduction techniques, and sequences. Agreement is generally good between the three principal series: the Harvard data, as dots, constitute the backbone of the curve, the Heidelberg and Sonneberg data appear as crosses, respectively, before and after 1930. Where approximately time-coincident 100-day means are available for intercomparison, the Harvard-Heidelberg differences average 0.118, the Harvard-Sonneberg differences 0.112.

After the mid-1920's improvements in the sensitivity of the photographic plates being used and additions of new camera series led to large numbers of plates giving well-exposed images of 3C 273, hence to a strongly determined light-curve. There is considerably more latitude in fitting the earlier data, although close inspection shows a number of features which appear to be significant even in Figure 2 (e.g., the crests near JD 12000 and 15500). There is also a very strong indication, discussed below, that much of the apparent scatter is caused by real variation over intervals of the order of a year or less.

The five hundred Harvard plates of sufficient quality to be readily reduced by iris photometry give the curve of Figure 3. Individual-plate internal probable errors for the 3C 273 magnitudes average only 0.05 mag., as determined by the scatter in the comparison star astrophotometer readings from a least-squares fit for each plate. Accordingly, although with serious gaps in coverage where satisfactory Harvard plates were not available, Figure 3 provides the more definitive light-curve for all intervals having a sufficient density of points. It also has the advantage of being on a nearly perfect Pogson scale of magnitudes, whereas most of the older visual values were reduced using the provisional comparison star magnitudes now known to be relatively incorrect by more than a tenth of a magnitude, leading to the spuriously smaller amplitude and distorted form of variation seen in Figure 2.

Close inspection or superposition of the curves shows remarkably detailed agreement. The principal apparent discrepancy is the long, shallow minimum centered around 1900 on the photometer-curve. But even here agreement can be reached without serious forcing if we note that the apparently contradictory 1902 maximum in the visual data arises largely from a strong 1901–1903 series of Harvard points so far unavailable for confirmation in the photometer data. Another apparent anomaly, the high point at JD 35000 in Figure 3, is probably the only seriously unreliable point in the photometer-curve, since it is the only one depending entirely on extreme small-scale plates and may well be affected by blending.

In the following interpretations, it will be assumed that the excellent agreement which is found where checking is possible shows that Figure 2 can be used to establish the character of variations between the relatively well-observed sections of Figure 3.

RESULTS

Several conclusions are immediately evident from Figures 2 and 3.

a) Secular Stability

As proved to be the case with 3C 48, the immense luminosity ($M \sim -26$) of 3C 273 is not a recent or transient phenomenon, at least in the ordinary nova or supernova sense, since the apparent magnitude has shown little if any secular change in 78 years. The slow but rather striking apparent decline of 0.2 mag/century in the visual-estimate light-curve remarked on earlier (Smith and Hoffleit 1963a) should now be given low weight compared with the almost perfect secular constancy indicated by the more uniform and impersonal isophotometer measures. Iris photometry of more of the difficult early plates is urgently needed to settle this point.

b) Variability with a Time Scale of Years

After 1929, an apparently quasi-periodic variation dominates the light-curve, prior to 1929 the variation is of smaller amplitude and more confused character. The relatively sharply defined minima fall around 1932, 1947, and 1958; their corresponding but much broader maxima appear around 1939, 1952, and 1963(?). These intervals suggest an average period of about 13 years, but would also be consistent with a period decreasing from 15 to 11 years since 1929, coupled with a decreasing amplitude. With considerably less credibility, earlier and shallower minima can be placed or extrapolated around 1884(?), 1895, 1905, 1914(?), 1919(?), and 1925; maxima around 1892, 1901, 1909, 1917, 1923(?), and 1928. These intervals average about 8 years, but also suggest a decreasing period accompanying a decreasing amplitude. Indeed, a linear period-amplitude relation would be roughly consistent with these data.

c) Variability with a Time Scale of Months

Plots of individual-plate magnitudes with sufficient time resolution frequently indicate non-random runs of rising or falling brightness. While almost any arbitrarily chosen period of several years shows this effect, it is particularly striking and interesting over several intervals which are quite rich in data. Figure 4 contains the individual-plate iris photometer values for the period immediately before, during, and after the "1929 crash"; Figure 5 shows similar details of variation around the 1939 maximum. To draw only the weakest conclusion, 3C 273 is able to show increases or decreases of brightness amounting to some 0.5 mag. in extreme cases (more commonly about 0.2 mag.) over periods of many months. Such fluctuations, superimposed on the slower quasi-periodic

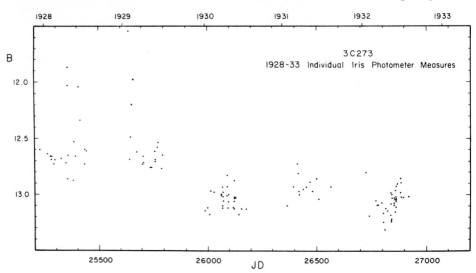

Fig. 4.—Individual iris photometer magnitudes of 3C 273 for the period 1928–1932, showing details of the break in 1929 and of other significant variations taking place over intervals short with respect to a year.

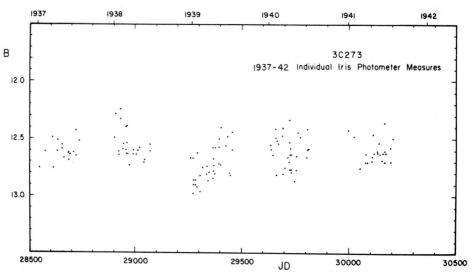

Fig. 5.—Individual iris photometer magnitudes of 3C 273 for the period 1937–1941, showing details around the maximum of the first long cycle after 1929.

variation, help to confuse whatever pattern it may have. A harmonic analysis now under way should be able to suggest whether or not the components of variation with different time scales are simply part of a random spectrum.

d) Flashes—Variability with a Time Scale of Days

About 1 per cent of the Harvard plates indicated on visual inspection that 3C 273 was abnormally bright by 0.5 mag. or more, an amount ranging from about 3–5 standard deviations above the particular 100-day mean. However, practically all of the bright points were called at least questionable by either Hoffleit or Smith, and accordingly fail to appear in Figure 2 which includes only non-questionable points. Several of these plates were more or less successfully measured by the iris photometer, giving an apparently different set of flash points in Figure 3. The reality of these points is difficult to assess. It is well known that photographic irregularities, particularly near the plate limit as is true for much of this material, can produce abnormally bright images; also in one case a 10th-mag. image at the position of 3C 273 actually turned out to be that of an

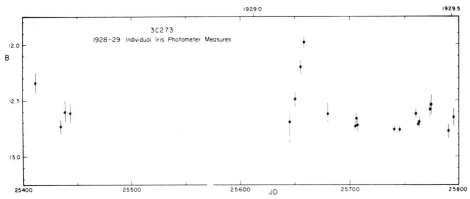

FIG. 6.—Individual iris photometer magnitudes of 3C 273 for 1929–1930, shown on an expanded time scale to increase the credibility of some of the minor fluctuations, also to permit direct comparison with Fig. 7. Error bars are probable errors, computed from least-squares fit to comparison-star astrophotometer readings for each plate.

asteroid! The only instance of several successive good astrophotometer points appearing to take part in the same flash occurred in 1929 (Fig. 6), where a flarelike rise with amplitude of about 0.7 mag. and rise time of about 10 days is suggested. Other apparent though questionable flash points occur on nights within several hours of a plate with a normal image. As provisional conclusions, it is probable that 3C 273 in an interval as short as 1–2 weeks, and possibly in an interval as short as a day, can become up to 0.5 mag. brighter than normal. But photoelectric confirmation is required before these conclusions can be regarded as established beyond reasonable doubt.

PHOTOELECTRIC OBSERVATIONS

Sandage (1964) has made available photoelectric magnitudes and colors of 3C 273 obtained at the Mount Wilson and Palomar Observatories during February–May and December of 1963. At the McDonald Observatory at least one observation using the 36-inch reflector has been made by G. Malik or W. Kunkel on most of the practicable nights from December, 1963, through February, 1964. Figure 7 shows the photoelectric points (V mag.) in detail; the same measures appear as 100-day means of B in Figure 3. Exact coincidence between the Mount Wilson and McDonald systems cannot be expected, particularly for an object of such anomalous spectral energy distribution as

3C 273; the anomalous spectrum also makes these observations more sensitive to atmospheric extinction corrections. The photoelectric data suggest that 3C 273 is moving steeply off the 1963 maximum, but that the variation is of a much smoother character than is indicated by the scatter in the photographic material (Figs. 4–6). Support for the more vigorous variations indicated by much of the older photographic data comes less from photoelectric photometry of 3C 273 than from the 3-year run of photoelectric observations of 3C 48 (Sandage 1964). It is of course highly desirable to keep 3C 273 under as continuous surveillance as possible, photoelectrically, photographically, and even visually, in order to detect and follow the details of variations and to look for associated spectral changes at critical times.

DISCUSSION

The variations found over the last 77 years in 3C 273 admit several possible explanations, depending in part on which features are accepted as real.

Perhaps the simplest interpretation asserts that the variation is irregular, in the sense

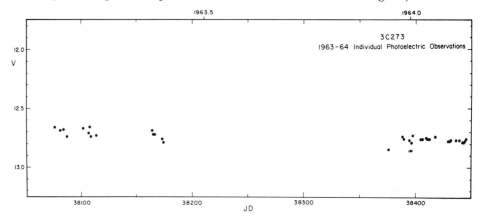

Fig. 7.—Individual photoelectric magnitudes of 3C 273 from Mount Wilson (JD 38078–38375) and McDonald (JD 38388–38431).

in which irregular variable stars show activity which is not periodic (although there can be substantial concentrations in certain frequency regions of the power spectrum). This may turn out to be correct, and to be explicable in terms of some such mechanism as changing opacity in a substantial hydrogen cloud, as has been proposed in somewhat different contexts by J. Greenstein and by A. Young.

But it is also interesting to see what properties might follow in terms of a more speculative reading of the light-curve. Specifically, I have suggested that the optical observations of variability may be interpreted as arising in large part from damped oscillations having coupled period and amplitude. On this view, in 1929 the 3C 273 system experienced an impulse followed by an oscillation which has now damped to about 0.7 the original amplitude and period. A similar impulse would have occurred around 1870, prior to the beginning of photographic recording; for this case, only the decay phase is observed.

Interpreting the light-curve as an oscillation permits some order-of-magnitude arguments as to the possible nature of the oscillating object. On the assumption that gravitational forces dominate the oscillation, the period versus mean density relation takes the conventional form $P(\bar{\rho})^{1/2} \sim G^{1/2} = 4 \times 10^{3}$ cgs, where G is the gravitational constant. Ignoring the apparent amplitude-dependence of the period (with its indication that non-linear terms are important in the oscillation), a mean period of 10 years (3×10^8 sec) roughly fits the observations, whence

$$\bar{\rho} \sim 2 \times 10^{-10} \text{ gm cm}^{-3} \, .$$

The magnitude data make possible three very weak, but consistent and independent, estimates of the order of size of the principal luminous source. First, if a coherent flash can change the brightness of the object by 0.5 magnitude in as short a time as a week or less, considerations of light travel time from the various portions of the surface require a radius for the principal emitting object which may be as small as several light days and is not greater than several light weeks, viz., somewhere in the range $1–4 \times 10^{16}$ cm. (It is, of course, possible that each flash comes from a separate small portion of a larger object—hypernovae with $M \sim -27$—but this additional hypothesis is not required for the present argument.)

Quite independently, the basic hypothesis of gravitational pulsation requires the region partaking of the 10-year pulsation to be of a size S commensurate with the velocity of sound C and the period of oscillation, that is $S \sim CP$. Although the value is not critical, the high energy output per gram of matter suggests that a mean effective temperature of at least $10^{7 \, \circ}$ K may be appropriate to most of the object. If the composition is primarily hydrogen, C is then around 10^8 cm sec^{-1}, from which the characteristic size again appears to lie between 10^{16} and 10^{17} cm.

The photoelectric color indices ($B - V = +0.2$; $U - B = -0.9$), while not those of proper stars, are in the B–A spectral class range. The spectrum shows strong hydrogen lines, plus apparent infrared and ultraviolet anomalies. But should a substantial near-black-body continuum be present, the color indices are consistent with an effective temperature around $1.5 \times 10^{4 \, \circ}$ K, corresponding to surface emission of about 3×10^{12} erg cm^{-2} sec^{-1}. From the absolute magnitude, the total optical emission of 3C 273 is about 1.5×10^{46} erg sec^{-1}. The total emitting area required to produce this luminosity, 5×10^{33} cm^2, yields once again

$$R \sim 2 \times 10^{16} \text{ cm} \, .$$

Since this value is entirely consistent with the two previous estimates, it will be used in the remaining arguments.

The mean density and radius give at once the mass of the object,

$$\mathfrak{M} \sim 6 \times 10^{39} \text{ gm} \doteq 3 \times 10^6 \, \mathfrak{M}\odot \, .$$

with an uncertainty of one or two powers of ten.

While no other direct observational estimate of the mass follows from the photometric data, a further indirect indication derives from the emission requirements. Specifically—for a given luminosity—the smaller the mass, the greater the energy radiated per unit mass. For $10^6 \, \mathfrak{M}\odot$, this is already well over 10^7 erg gm^{-1} sec^{-1}. Such a burning rate would exhaust the available thermonuclear sources in about 10^4 years, while the potential energy liberated by this mass falling to the present radius would produce only a comparable amount of energy (unless, of course, the object has high central mass concentration). Such a time limit seems small in view of the requirement that the system must be older than 10^5 years as judged by the separation of the jet from the core. To be sure, the luminosity may have been less in the past; also the pulsation does not depend on the mass exterior to the present radiating surface—a large amount of matter may have been thrown out in earlier stages of the system, as in fact the jet indicates. But if the present picture is even generally correct, it seems more reasonable to accept the higher range of masses in the core of 3C 273.

Rotation also presents interesting problems. If the core of 3C 273 has collapsed from more normal galactic dimensions, original motions must have led to insupportably large rotations before the present small core size was approached, requiring the passing of angular momentum to outer elements of gas. However, one would expect the present rotation to be close to the allowable limit, namely $v < (G\mathfrak{M}/R)^{1/2}$, from which the surface velocity of rotation follows (for the above numerical values) as $v \sim 1000$ km sec^{-1}; such a velocity would produce rotational broadening of spectral lines equal to some 50 Å. While this is the amount of broadening observed in the emission lines of 3C 273, the coincidence may not be significant since most of the lines would probably be formed in parts of an extended atmosphere at very much larger radii.

An alternate explanation of the quasi-periodic decade cycle of Figures 2 and 3 is suggested by the striking similarity of the light-curve to those of W UMa variables, in terms of the relatively sharp minima and 0.7 mag. amplitude of variation—effects produced by a highly distorted, contact eclipsing-binary pair of stars. Two objects of 10^6 $\mathfrak{M}\odot$, with centers separated by the characteristic size found above (2×10^{16} cm), would have an orbital period of about 25 years, giving successive eclipses at half that interval, as observed (this argument being essentially the same as the one in the previous paragraph). The principal drawback to this explanation is the difficulty in forcing the observations to fit a regular period even with very liberal allowance for irregular photometric disturbances, or in accepting the mass and/or radius changes which would be required if irregular orbital motion is to be permitted.

The above arguments are the basis for the numerical values given last year (Smith and Hoffleit 1963b) for the properties of 3C 273.

In summary, the proposed picture for this quasi-stellar source is of a core of radius $\sim 2 \times 10^{16}$ cm and mass probably $> 10^7$ $\mathfrak{M}\odot$, producing most of the energy of the system, the core being either a close binary or more probably a single object undergoing damped oscillations as a result of unspecified impulses (perhaps connected with instabilities in gravitational collapse). The core is surrounded by a hydrogen envelope one or two orders of magnitude larger, as required to produce the emission lines, and with an outer radio-emitting shell source three orders of magnitude larger yet (the required relativistic electrons also originating in activity in the massive core). This picture is in no proper sense a model; indeed, it may be that no object able to satisfy these parameters can exist. But it is interesting that rather conventional interpretations of the photometric data lead to even so much of a self-consistent picture. Continuous current observations, exhaustive photometry of the old plates, detailed harmonic analysis of the final results, and more information on the relative intensities of emission lines and adjacent continuum during variations are among the observational approaches which can test these notions.

In addition to individuals acknowledged above, I thank F. Lopez, C. Michelis, and G. Fendley for help with the data; F. Whipple, A. Skumanich, and J. Warwick for stimulating discussions of some of these matters; and the Harvard Observatory for the opportunity to work with its uniquely valuable historical plate collection.

REFERENCES

Geyer, E. L. 1964, *I.A.U. Comm. 27, Information Bull.*
Sandage, A. 1961, *Sky and Telescope*, **21**, 148.
———. 1964, *Ap. J.*, **139**, 148.
Sharov, A. S., and Efremov, Y. N. 1963a, *I.A.U. Comm. 27, Information Bull.* No. 23, April 18.
———. 1963b, *Astr. Zhur.*, **40**, 950.
Smith, H., and Hoffleit, D. 1961, *Pub. A.S.P.*, **73**, 292.
———. 1963a, *Nature*, **198**, 650. *
———. 1963b, *A.J.*, **68**, 292 (also *I.A.U. Comm. 27, Information Bull.* No. 27, May 18).

OPTICAL IDENTIFICATION OF
3C 48, 3C 196, AND 3C 286 WITH
chapter 17 STELLAR OBJECTS

Thomas A. Matthews and Allan R. Sandage

I. INTRODUCTION

One of the major programs of the Owens Valley Radio Observatory of the California Institute of Technology is the determination of precise positions of discrete radio sources. The radio observations are made with the two 90-foot antennas working as an interferometer at several spacings ranging from 200 to 1600 feet. The east-west direction is used to determine right ascension and the north-south direction to find declination. The observational technique for declination measurements has been described by Read (1963), and the entire problem and results will be discussed elsewhere by Matthews and Read. Errors in determination of position in both right ascension and declination can now be made smaller than 5 seconds of arc under favorable conditions. With this high positional accuracy, the search for optical identification is now much more efficient than similar searches made several years ago, and a number of new identifications have already been made (Bolton 1960; Maltby, Matthews, and Moffet 1963; Matthews and Schmidt, unpublished).

Identifications to date by all workers have shown that radio sources are associated with galactic nebulae, supernovae remnants, and external galaxies both "normal" and peculiar. The distribution of discrete sources above $b = \pm 20°$ is isotropic and has usually been attributed to galaxies alone. No star, except the sun, has previously been identified with a radio source. The purpose of this paper is to present evidence for the identification of three radio sources with objects which are starlike in their appearance on direct photographs and in their photometric and spectroscopic properties.[1]

Thomas A. Matthews, Owens Valley Radio Observatory, California Institute of Technology.
Allan R. Sandage, Mount Wilson and Palomar Observatories, Carnegie Institution of Washington and California Institute of Technology.

Reprinted from the *Astrophysical Journal*, 138, 30–56, 1963.

[1] Since this paper was written, two more similar objects have been identified—3C 273 (Schmidt 1963) and 3C 147—for which M. Schmidt has obtained the necessary confirmatory spectra. Thus at least 20 per cent of the apparently strongest radio sources are this type of object.

II. RADIO AND OPTICAL PROPERTIES OF THE THREE SOURCES

Our attention was drawn to 3C 48, 3C 196, and 3C 286 as peculiar radio objects because of their high radio surface brightness. Measurements of the brightness distribution (Maltby and Moffet 1962) along both a north-south and an east-west base line at the Owens Valley Radio Observatory with a maximum base line of 1600 wavelengths showed that these three sources are single, with radio diameters of less than 30 seconds of arc. The Jodrell Bank observations of brightness distribution with four base lines from λ 2200 to λ 61000 (Allen, Anderson, Conway, Palmer, Reddish, and Rowson 1962) have shown that, even at the longest base line of λ 61000, 3C 48 is unresolved in the east-west direction, which means that the radio diameter is less than 1 second of arc east-west. Rowson (1962) has shown also that the diameter is less than 1 second of arc in the north-south direction. However, the Jodrell Bank observations do show some structure in 3C 196 and 3C 286 in the east-west direction. The simplest two-component model fitting the east-west intensity distribution for 3C 196 is that 75 per cent of the flux comes from a halo of about 12″ diameter, while the remaining 25 per cent of the flux is in an unresolved core of less than 1″ diameter.[2] For 3C 286, 40 per cent of the flux comes from a halo of diameter ⌣20″, and the remaining 60 per cent is again in an unresolved core of diameter less than 1″. We are indebted to H. P. Palmer for the data prior to publication, upon which these diameters are based.

These small radio diameters, together with the large observed radio flux, initially suggested that the three sources might be additional examples of distant galaxies of large redshift such as 3C 295, which shows a similar radio surface brightness. Consequently, when precise radio positions were available, direct photographs were made of each field with the 200-inch telescope in the near red spectral region (103a-E plates plus Schott RG1 filter).

The first object studied was 3C 48 (Matthews, Bolton, Greenstein, Münch, and Sandage 1961). A direct plate was taken on September 26, 1960, with every expectation of finding a distant cluster of galaxies, but measurement of the plate gave the unexpected result that the only object lying within the error rectangle of the radio position was one which appeared to be stellar. The stellar object was associated with an exceedingly faint wisp of nebulosity running north-south (surface brightness ∼23 mag/arcsec^2 in V) and measuring 12″ by 5″ (N-S × E-W). The stellar object lies about 3″ north of the center of the nebulosity. The peculiarity of the nebulosity, together with the excellent agreement between the radio position and the optical object, made it almost certain that an identification had been achieved. But the nature of the optical source remained in doubt because in late 1960 the existence of radio stars was not generally considered a serious possibility.

Two spectrograms were taken with the prime-focus spectrograph at the 200-inch on October 22, 1960. One covered the blue-green region from λ 3100 to λ 5000 with a dispersion of 400 A/mm. The other covered the region from λ 3100 to about λ 7000 on an Eastman 103a-F plate with a dispersion of 800 A/mm. The blue-violet spectrum is extremely peculiar, the only prominent features being several strong, very broad emission lines. The three strongest occur at λ 4686 (intensity 4), λ 4580 (2), and λ 3832 (6). The broad emission line at λ 3832 is the most striking feature and as yet has not been identified. The most obvious identification of the λ 4686 line is with He II. If this is correct, then the measured wavelength of λ 4686.2 ± 1 shows that the radial velocity of the object must be less than 100 km/sec. The lines could not be identified with any plausible combination of red-shifted emission lines. The total width of the two strongest lines at half-intensity points is about 22 A for λ 4686 and about 30 A for λ 3832. The half half-widths, expressed in km/sec, would indicate a velocity field (either random or systematic) within which the emission lines are formed of about 1200 km/sec for the

---

[2] Recent measurements of flux (Conway, Kellermann, and Long 1963) suggest that 3C 196 may be all core. A spuriously high close-spacing flux was the only evidence of a halo.

λ 3832 line and 700 km/sec for the λ 4686 line. No strong emission lines are present in the red, although several faint ones do exist. In particular, Hα is definitely absent. Spectrograms of higher dispersion were subsequently obtained by Greenstein and Münch, and a complete discussion of the spectroscopic features will be given by them.

Photometric observations of the 3C 48 optical object confirm its peculiar nature. On October 23, 1960, the photometry gave $V = 16.06$, $B - V = 0.38$, $U - B = -0.61$, colors which are similar to, but not identical with, old novae (Walker 1957) and to some white dwarfs (Greenstein 1958), but are quite different from ordinary stars and galaxies. This point will be discussed later in this section.

An effort was made in the case of 3C 48 to resolve the optical image. On a night of good seeing a series of exposures ranging from 10 minutes to 15 seconds was made at the 200-inch prime focus (scale = 11.06 arcsec/mm) on Eastman 103a-O plates. On the shortest-exposure plate (15^s) the image diameter of 3C 48 was measured to be 0.09 mm, which corresponds to $1''$ of arc. This is the same diameter as images of stars of the same apparent brightness on the plate. The image of 3C 48 on all plates is sharp and appears to be stellar.

A second-epoch Sky Survey plate was taken by W. C. Miller on January 18/19, 1961,

TABLE 1

Photometric Data for the Three Radio Stars

Object	Date	V	$B - V$	$U - B$	Remarks
3C 48.....	Oct. 23/24, 1960	16.06	0.38	−0.61	
	Nov. 19/20, 1960	16.02	.48	− .61	60-inch
	Jan. 12/13, 1961	16.11	.42	− .61	
	Jan. 13/14, 1961	16.13	.39	− .61	
	Jan. 14/15, 1961	16.02	.49	− .60	
	Jan. 16/17, 1961	16.13	.40	− .59	
	Aug. 17/18, 1961	16.31	.40	− .52	
	Oct. 11/12, 1961	16.333	.340	− .579 ⎫	Taken 15 minutes apart
	Oct. 11/12, 1961	16.289	.393	− .555 ⎭	
	Dec. 4/5, 1961	16.44	.35	− .57	Obs. by Baum
	Dec. 5/6, 1961	16.40	.42	− .64	Obs. by Baum
3C 196.....	Mar. 31/1, 1962	17.79	.57	− .43	
3C 286.....	June 2/3, 1962	17.25	0.26	−0.91	

with the 48-inch Schmidt to check for a detectable proper motion. This plate was centered identically with the base plate O 30 of the original Sky Survey taken on December 21/22, 1949, giving an 11-year interval. Inspection of the two plates in a blink comparator showed no detectable proper motion relative to neighboring comparison stars. The proper motion is less than $0''.05$/yr (a value which could have been detected by this method).

Optical photometry of 3C 48 continued sporadically during 1961, with the results given in Table 1. The most striking feature of these data is that the optical radiation varies! Unfortunately, our time resolution is very poor. The only evidence for short-term fluctuations is the data obtained on October 11/12, 1961, where the observations listed were made in a time interval of 15 minutes. We believe that the observed difference in intensity between these times is probably real because the local standard star D (see Fig. 2) was observed after each of the 3C 48 observations. The differences between the measurements of D were only $\Delta V = 0^m.007$, $\Delta(B - V) = 0^m.007$, and $\Delta(U - B) = 0^m.010$, whereas the 3C 48 differences are $\Delta V = 0^m.044$, $\Delta(B - V) = 0^m.053$, and $\Delta(U - B) = 0^m.024$.

The probable errors for most of the data of Table 1 are less than $\pm 0^m.02$ except for the 60-inch telescope data of November 19/20, 1960, where the error is $\pm 0^m04$. We therefore conclude that the night-to-night variations and those over the 13-month interval are undoubtedly real. It remains for future observations to determine whether short-term fluctuations with a time scale of minutes exist in the optical radiation similar to those found and studied in old novae by Walker (1954, 1957). The work of Smith and Hoffleit (1961) shows that there have been no large systematic variations in the magnitude of 3C 48 over the last 60 years.

Special observations for the constancy of the radio flux at 1420 Mc/s were made at the Owens Valley Radio Observatory by K. Kellermann for more than a week in February, 1962, to see whether similar fluctuations are present in the radio-flux data. No variation greater than 3 per cent was detected, the probable error of a single observation being about 1.2 per cent. Comparison with flux levels determined 4 months earlier showed no variation within the probable error of about 5 per cent. Although the data are not con-clusive, our present data suggest that the radio flux of 3C 48 is constant, while the optical flux varies by at least a factor of 1.4 in an interval of 13 months.

Following the identification of 3C 48, the other two sources were found in the same way. For both 3C 196 and 3C 286, the only objects on the direct photographs within the error rectangles have a stellar appearance. Furthermore, the stellar object in the position of 3C 196 is also associated with an exceedingly faint wisp of nebulosity that appears as a tail in position angle 120° on the stellar image. The wisp is slightly curved and has dimensions of only $3'' \times 1''$, so it is smaller than the nebulosity associated with 3C 48. The nebulosity near 3C 196 is extremely difficult to see on a 103a-D plate behind a GG11 filter exposed for 50 minutes but is easily seen on a plate taken for us by W. A. Baum on 103a-E emulsion behind red plexiglas for 60 minutes. We have no plates of 3C 48 taken on 103a-D emulsion for comparison, but on a 103a-F plate behind Schott RG2 (126-minute exposure) and on a 103a-E + Schott RG2 (90-minute exposure), as well as on several 103a-O plates, the 3C 48 nebulosity is visible and stronger than that associated with 3C 196. We have not detected nebulosity around 3C 286, but again the only available plate is a 103a-D + GG11, which, in view of the extreme difficulty of detecting the wisp in 3C 196 with this emulsion and filter combination, does not allow us to conclude that 3C 286 has no nebulosity.

The colors and magnitudes of the stellar objects at the radio positions of 3C 196 and 3C 286 were measured photoelectrically with the 200-inch and were found to be quite unusual, as was 3C 48. The available data, determined on only one night for each, are listed in the last two rows of Table 1. The colors of all three sources are plotted in Figure 1, which also shows three solid lines: (C) the normal main-sequence relation for luminos-ity class V stars, (B) black-body radiators, and (A) objects whose energy distribution per unit frequency interval is of the form $F(\nu) \propto \nu^{-n}$. Lines are marked on curve A for various n-values ranging from $n = 0.0$ to $n = 2.0$ in steps of 0.2. This form of the energy spectrum is that predicted for synchrotron radiation under certain conditions, as ex-plained in Section III. The lines B and C were computed by the methods of Appendix A. The black-body line differs slightly from that computed by Arp (1961) for reasons ex-plained in Appendix A. Note that the three radio sources fall close to line A. The only other known stellar sources in this general region of the diagram are old novae (Walker 1957, Table 1) and a very few white dwarfs. Most white dwarfs fall on or below the black-body line. Those old novae that do not have composite spectra are plotted as crosses in Figure 1 to illustrate the point. We are indebted to R. Kraft for unpublished spectral data on the old novae.

M. Schmidt has obtained spectra of both 3C 196 and 3C 286, and their spectral peculiarities again confirm that we are dealing with unusual stellar objects. Schmidt reports that, at a dispersion of 400 A/mm, 3C 196 has a continuous spectrum with no prominent features either in emission or in absorption (contrary to 3C 48). He also re-ports (1962) from several spectrograms that 3C 286 has a spectrum showing one emission line at λ 5170 and possibly one absorption feature at λ 4390. The observed features are not the same as those observed in 3C 48.

Finally, a second-epoch Sky Survey plate of 3C 286 was obtained with the 48-inch Schmidt on April 6/7, 1962, by J. Berger. Comparison in the blink comparator with the base Survey plate O 131 taken on June 5/6, 1950, showed that 3C 286 has no detectable proper motion over the 11-year interval. This puts an upper limit to the motion of 0″05/yr.

Table 2 summarizes the radio and optical position measurements now available for these three sources. The quoted radio positions are those that were determined before the optical identifications were made. The radio right ascension measurements are due to T. A. Matthews, the radio declination measurements are due to R. B. Read (1962). After the preliminary measurements of the 200″ plates for optical position were made by Matthews to identify the stars, the final measurements of the plates were done by R. F. Griffin, and the precise optical positions of Table 1 are due to him. The agreement be-

TABLE 2

RADIO AND OPTICAL POSITIONS FOR THREE RADIO STARS

Source	α(1950.0)	ϵ_α	δ(1950.0)	ϵ_δ	Remarks
3C 48.......	01ʰ 34ᵐ 50ˢ3	0ˢ6	+32° 54′ 20″	2″	Radio
	01 34 49.82	.04	+32 54 20.2	0.5	Optical
3C 196.......	08 09 59.6	.4	+48 22 06	2.6	Radio
	08 09 59.41	.05	+48 22 07.9	0.5	Optical
3C 286.......	13 28 50.8	.4	+30 45 55	6.5	Radio
	13 28 50.74	0.04	+30 45 59.5	0.5	Optical

tween the radio and optical positions is excellent and strongly substantiates the reality of the identifications. The quoted errors of Table 2 are r.m.s. values.

Figures 2, 3, and 4 are finding charts for the optical objects. In Figure 1 for 3C 48 the two photometric comparison stars B and D are shown. They have been used as local standards in the photometry done after August 17/18, 1961, and have adopted values for star B of $V = 13.53$, $B - V = 0.50$, $U - B = 0.00$; and for star D of $V = 14.54$, $B - V = 0.66$, $U - B = 0.05$. Local standards will be determined around 3C 196 and 3C 286 in the future when these objects are followed more closely.

III. POWER-SPECTRUM DATA

a) The Radio Data

We have compiled and tabulated the available radio-flux data for the three sources in Tables 3, 4, and 5. The measurements are from many sources, either in the literature or from unpublished data from the Owens Valley Radio Observatory generously made available by Kellermann and Bartlett. The references are listed at the bottom of Table 5. The flux values are in units of 10^{-26} watts (meter)$^{-2}$ (c/s)$^{-1}$ and have been taken directly from the various authors with no attempt to put the various absolute calibrations on a strictly homogeneous system. The power spectra in the radio range from 160 to 3200 Mc are shown in Figures 5, 6, and 7. Probable errors are given in the tables where known. As a guide, the size of a 10 per cent probable error is shown in Figures 5, 6, and 7.

The data are most complete for 3C 48, and it is evident from Figure 5 that no single straight line can be drawn through all the points. The best compromise single spectral index that satisfies all the points except the three in the 3000 Mc region is −0.59. Since

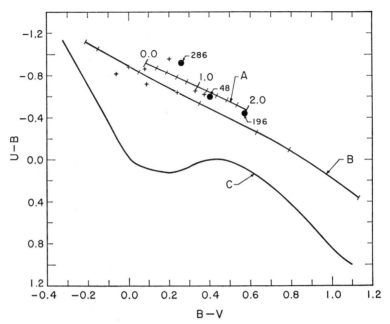

FIG. 1.—The two-color diagram for various types of objects. Line C is for unreddened main-sequence stars, line B is for black-body radiation, and line A is for sources whose energy distribution is of the form $F(\nu) = \nu^{-n}$. Values of n from 0.0 to 2.0 are marked along curve C. Colors for the three radio stars are plotted as filled circles. Colors for a few old novae are shown as crosses. The tics on curve B indicate values tabulated in Table A3.

TABLE 3

RADIO-FLUX MEASUREMENTS FOR 3C 48

Observer	ν (Mc/s)	$F(\nu)*$	ϵ_p (Per Cent)	References†
RSE 01.01..........	81	80	....	1
2C 133.............	81	102	....	2
BSS 92.............	100	60	20	3
3C.................	159	50	22	4
HBH...............	159	60	....	5
ERL...............	178	43	10	6
CIT(K).............	475	33	6	7
CIT(K).............	710	26.0	2	7
Heeschen..........	750	21.6	10	8
CIT(MM)..........	958	20.4	5	9, 10
CIT(K).............	1420	16.1	2	7
Goldstein..........	1423	17	5	11
CIT(B).............	2841	9.2	5	12
Heeschen..........	3000	7.4	9	8
CIT(K).............	3200	8.1	11	7

* The flux unit is 10^{-26} W m^{-2}(c/s)$^{-1}$.

† The references are given at the bottom of Table 5.

TABLE 4

RADIO-FLUX MEASUREMENTS FOR 3C 196

Observer	ν (Mc/s)	$F(\nu)$*	ϵ_F (Per Cent)	References[†]
Whitfield.....	38	125	56	13[‡]
RSE 08.01....	81	100	....	1
2C 724.......	81	124	....	2
BSS 84.......	100	70	20	3
3C..........	159	66	30	4
HBH........	159	40	50	14
ERL........	178	66	10	6
CIT(K).......	710	25.2	1.2	7
Heeschen.....	750	25.7	10	8
CIT(MM)....	958	19.4	4	9, 10
CIT(K).......	1420	14.9	.3	7
Goldstein.....	1423	17ˉ	8	11
CIT(B).......	2841	7.5	5	12
Heeschen.....	3000	6.7	10	8
CIT(K).......	3200	7.1	20	7

* The flux unit is 10^{-26} W m^{-2}(c/s)$^{-1}$.

† The references are given at the bottom of Table 5.

‡ Confused record.

TABLE 5

RADIO-FLUX MEASUREMENTS FOR 3C 286

Observer	ν (Mc/s)	$F(\nu)$*	ϵ_F (Per Cent)	References[†]
2C 1120.......	81	50	....	2
3C...........	159	30	23	4
ERL.........	178	22	10	6
CIT(K).......	710	19.1	5	7
CIT(MM)....	958	18.8	7	9, 10
CIT(K).......	1420	16	2 5	7
Goldstein......	1423	17	6	11
CIT(B).......	2841	12	6	12

* The flux unit is 10^{-26} W m^{-2}(c/s)$^{-1}$.

† References for Tables 3, 4, and 5 are as follows:

1. Ryle, M., Smith, F. G., and Elsmore, B. 1950, *M.N.*, **110**, 508.
2. Shakeshaft, J. R., Ryle, M., Baldwin, J. E., Elsmore, B., and Thomson, J. H. 1955, *Mem. R.A.S.*, **67**, 106.
3. Bolton, J. G., Stanley, G. J., and Slee, O. B. 1954, *Australian J. Phys.*, **7**, 110.
4. Edge, D. O., Shakeshaft, J. R., McAdam, W. B., Baldwin, J. E., and Archer, S. 1960, *Mem. R.A.S.*, **68**, 37.
5. Brown, R. H., and Hazard, C. 1959, *M.N.*, **119**, 297.
6. Elsmore, B., Ryle, M., and Leslie, P. R. R. 1960, *Mem. R.A.S.*, **68**, 61.
7. Kellermann, K. I., 1962, private communication.
8. Heeschen, D. S., and Meredith, B. L. 1961, *Pub. Nat. Radio Astr. Obs.*, **1**, 121.
9. Moffet, A. T. 1962, *Ap. J. Suppl.*, **67**, 93.
10. Maltby, P. 1962, *Ap. J. Suppl.*, **67**, 124.
11. Goldstein, S. J. 1962, *A.J.*, **67**, 171.
12. Bartlett, J. F. 1962, private communication.
13. Whitfield, G. R. 1960, *M.N.*, **120**, 581.
14. Brown, R. H., and Hazard, C. 1953, *M.N.*, **113**, 123.

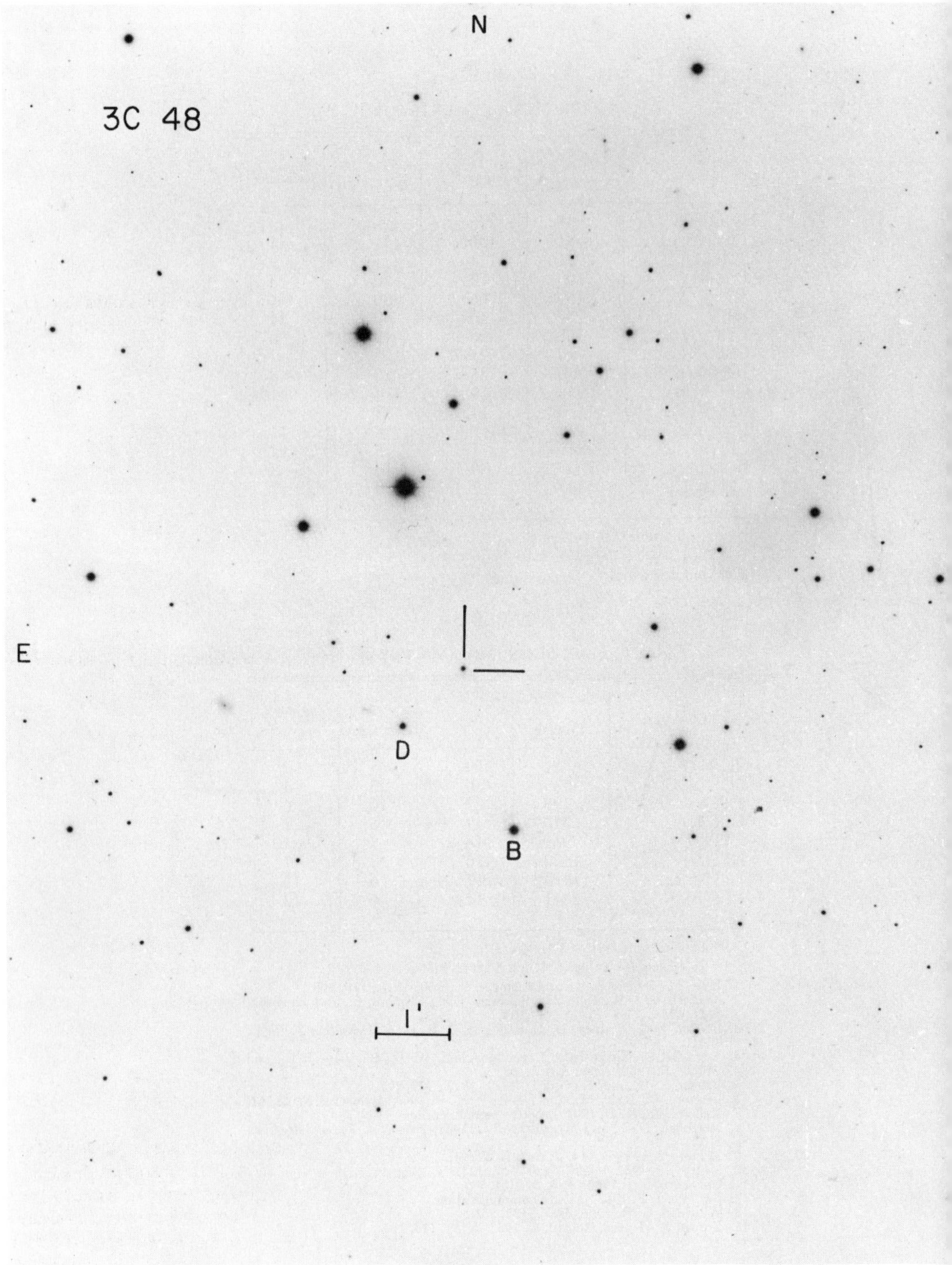

Fig. 2.—Finding chart for 3C 48 taken from a 10-minute exposure with the 200-inch. Local photometric standard stars B and D are marked. The data are $V = 13.53$, $B - V = 0.50$, $U - B = 0.00$ for star B; $V = 14.54$, $B - V =$ 0.66, and $U - B = 0.05$ for star D. The plate used was a 103a-O + GG 13.

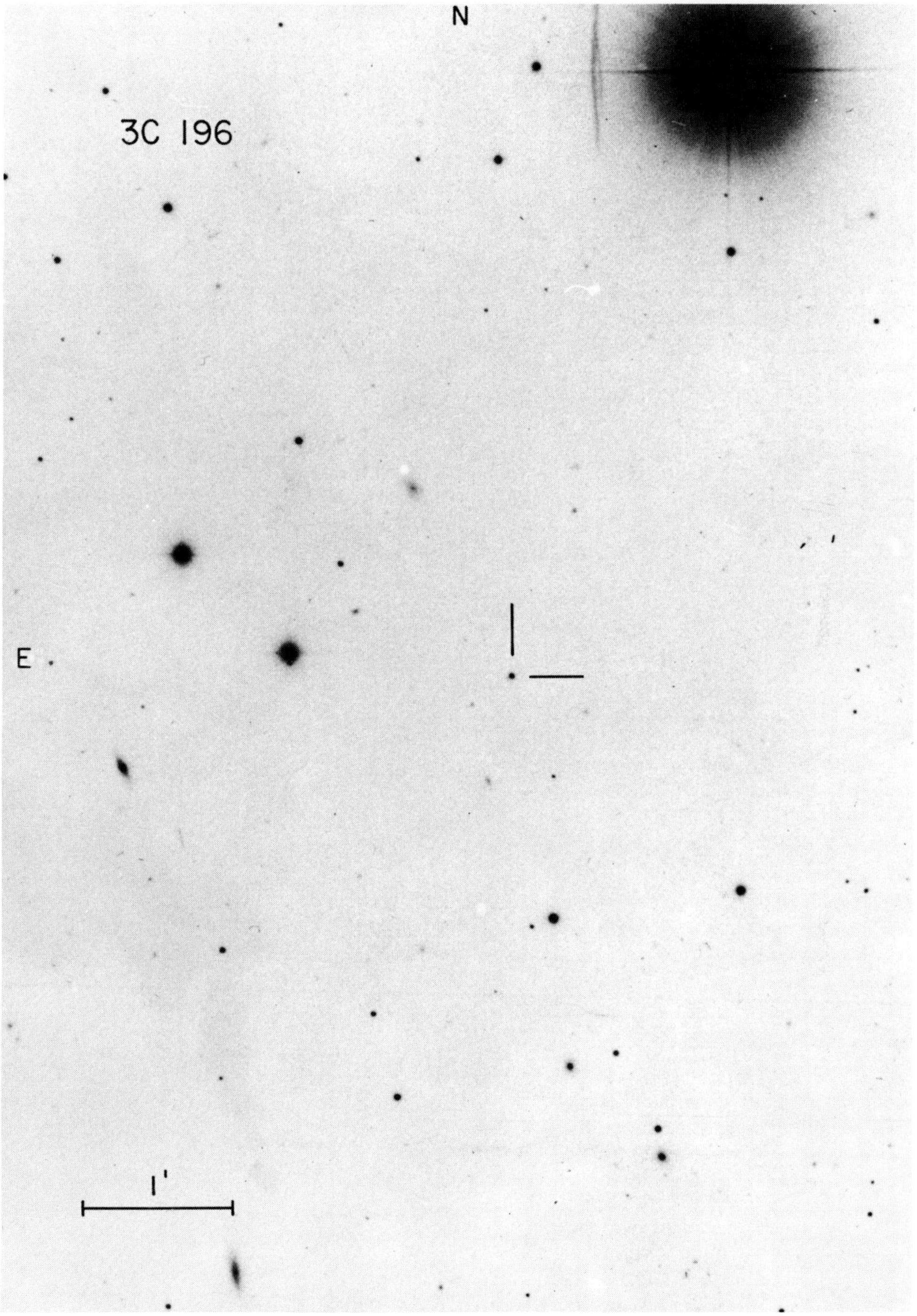

FIG. 3.—Finding chart for 3C 196. The plate used was a 103a-E + Red filter

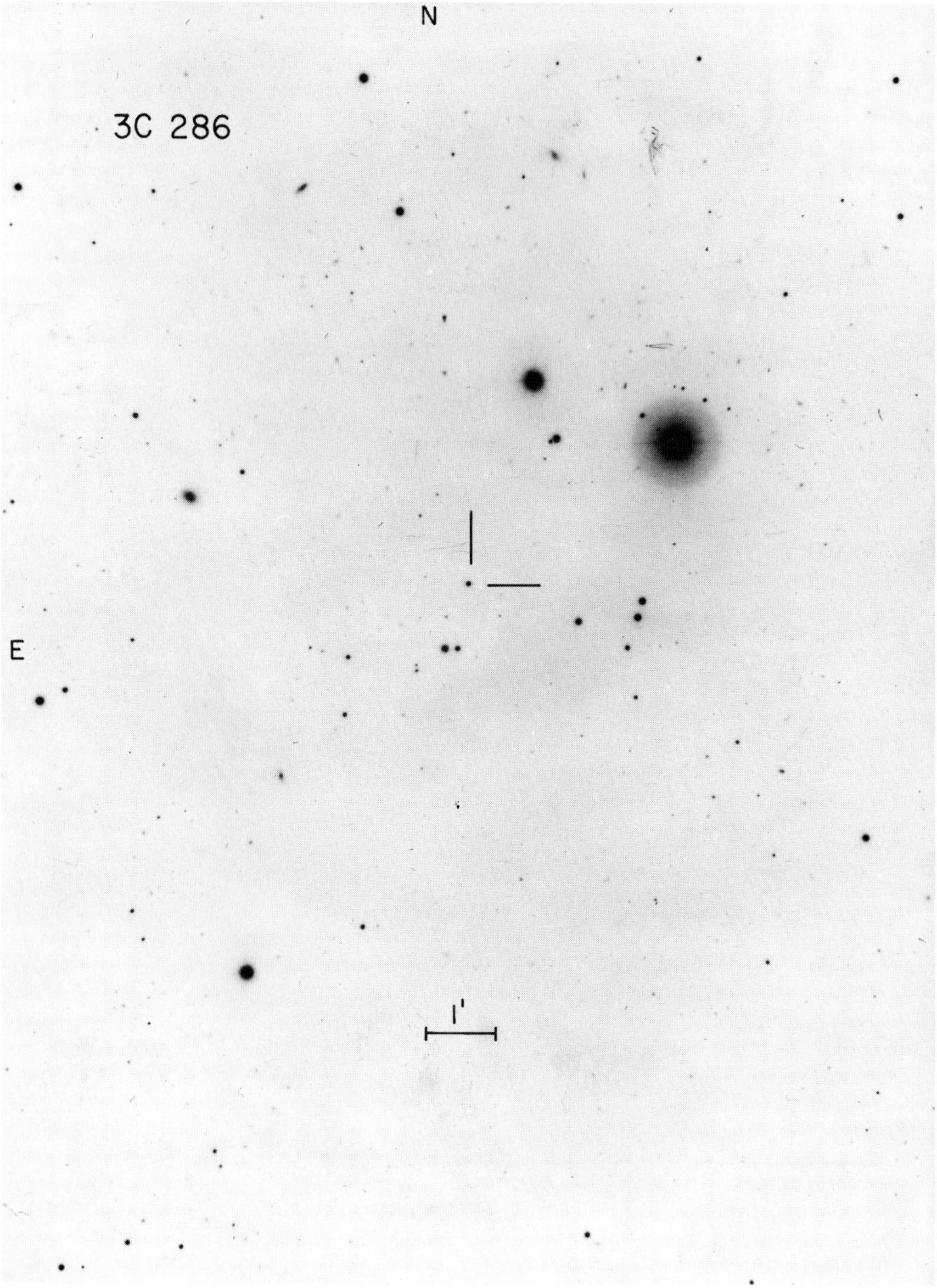

Fig. 4.—Finding chart for 3C 286. The plate used was a 103a-D + GG 11

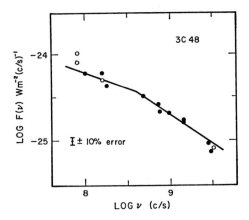

Fig. 5.—The radio power spectrum of 3C 48 taken from Table 3. The two straight lines have slopes of −0.67 and −0.47. The slope of −0.67 is that required in Fig. 8 to fit the optical data. The open circles denote observations of lower weight.

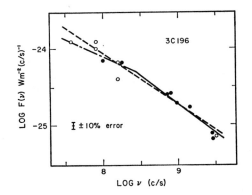

Fig. 6.—The radio power spectrum for 3C 196 taken from Table 4. The dotted line has a slope of −0.67 and gives the best representation of the radio data over the entire range. The solid line for $\nu >$ 4×10^8 c/s has a slope of −0.74, as required in Fig. 10 to fit the optical data.

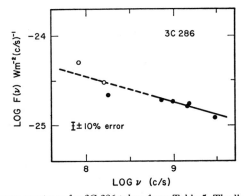

Fig. 7.—The radio power spectrum for 3C 286 taken from Table 5. The line has a slope of −0.28

these three high-frequency observations carry so much combined weight, we conclude that a single spectral index is not acceptable. We have arbitrarily fitted segments of two power laws to the data with indexes $n_1 = -0.47$ for frequencies lower than $\nu = 7 \times 10^8$ c/s and $n_2 = -0.67$ for $\nu > 7 \times 10^8$ c/s. Kellermann, Long, Allen, and Moran (1962), using unpublished low-frequency flux measurements, believe that the low-frequency spectral index is even flatter than $n = -0.47$. They have suggested that a high-energy cutoff is responsible for the curvature seen in the radio spectrum. However, in view of the optical data to be discussed later, we wish to suggest that it might be interpreted as the low-energy cutoff of the electrons producing the synchrotron radiation. The possibility of a low-frequency cutoff is not discussed further here because of the limited observational data.

The index -0.67 fits the 3C 48 radio data for $\nu > 7 \times 10^8$ c/s quite well, and we shall see later in this section that an extension of $F(\nu)$ into the optical region, using the synchrotron radiation theory with $n = -0.67$, predicts the observed optical flux with remarkable accuracy.

Figure 6 shows that the data for 3C 196 also cannot be well represented by a single spectral index, although most of the points (except the three near $\nu = 3000$ Mc/s) do fall near the dashed line of index -0.67. We shall show later that the optical data, if all the observed optical flux is assumed to be due to synchrotron radiation, require $n = -0.74$, and this is shown as a solid line in Figure 6 for $\nu > 4 \times 10^8$ c/s. The behavior of the flux at low frequencies is not well determined; one suggestion is shown by the dash-dot line.

The few data available for 3C 286 suggest that the radio spectral index has the very low value of $n = -0.28$, but more observations at low and high frequencies are needed to confirm the result. Recent flux data below 400 Mc/s measured at Cambridge suggest that the spectrum of 3C 286 also flattens at the low-frequency end (Conway, Kellermann, and Long 1963).

b) The Optical Data

The U, B, V values of Table 1 have been converted to absolute flux units by the methods of Appendix B and have then been compared with the radio data. For 3C 48 we have adopted mean values $V = 16.20$, $B - V = 0.40$, $U - B = -0.59$ for this comparison, rather than treating each of the observations separately. We were fortunate in asking W. A. Baum to measure U, B, V magnitudes of 3C 48 during his Palomar run in December, 1961, because, in addition to these three colors, he measured the star in his eight-color system, which extends from 3700 to 9800 A, and he has made these data available to us for discussion.

Table 6 summarizes the available optical data. The effective frequencies for the U, B, V observations are directly computed from the effective wavelengths worked out in Appendix B and given in columns 4, 5, and 6 of Table B1 for different values of the effective index n. The value of n was estimated for each of the three sources from their observed $B - V$ values by comparing them with column 3 of Table B1. Baum's data were converted to absolute units by force-fitting them, over the frequency interval in common, to the absolute calibration of the U, B, V points given in the first three rows of Table 6. The flux unit in Table 6 is 10^{-29} W m^{-2} (c/s)$^{-1}$.

The radio and optical data are plotted together in Figure 8. The straight line with its family of termination-curves A, B, and C is, under certain conditions (see below), the theoretical power spectrum for an assemblage of relativistic electrons whose number in energy range E to $E + dE$ is

$$N(E)\,dE = KE^{-\beta}dE \qquad (1)$$

for $E_1 < E < E_2$, where E_1 and E_2 are the low- and high-energy cutoffs. The well-known theory of synchrotron radiation, summarized by Oort and Walraven (1956), by Woltjer

(1958), by Burbidge (1956), and by others, predicts the power at frequency ν radiated by the electron assemblage to be of the form

$$F(\nu) = 1.171 \times 10^{-22} K H_{\perp}^{(\beta+1)/2} L^{(\beta-1)/2} \nu^{-(\beta-1)/2} \int_{a_2}^{a_1} a^{(\beta-3)/2} F(a) \, da \qquad (2)$$

in units of ergs sec^{-1} cm^{-2} (c/s)$^{-1}$. Here $H_{\perp}$ is the component of the magnetic-field strength perpendicular to the velocity vector of the electron; $L = 1.608 \times 10^{13}$ if the electron energy E is expressed in Bev, $L = 6.269 \times 10^{18}$ if E is in ergs, and a relates the frequency of observation ν with the low and high critical frequencies ν_1 and ν_2 by

$$a_1 = \frac{\nu}{\nu_1}; \qquad a_2 = \frac{\nu}{\nu_2}, \qquad (3)$$

TABLE 6

OPTICAL FLUX FOR THE THREE RADIO STARS

Object	$\nu \times 10^{-14}$ (c/s)	$B(\nu)$*	ϵ_F (Per Cent)	Remarks
3C 48......	8.32	0.669	1	$U = 16.01$
	6.77	0.958	1	$B = 16.60$
	5.42	1.29	1	$V = 16.20$
	8.07	0.718	1	
	7.09	0.900	1	
	5.94	1.19	1	
	5.46	1.35	1	
	5.31	1.46	1	Baum eight-color data
	4.50	1.94	3	reduced to $V = 16.20$
	3.99	1.78	4	
	3.53	2.24	12	
	3.04	2.26	14	
3C 196.....	8.32	0.124	2	$U = 17.93$
	6.77	0.195	2	$B = 18.36$
	5.41	0.302	2	$V = 17.79$
3C 286.....	8.35	0.421	2	$U = 16.60$
	6.81	0.416	2	$B = 17.51$
	5.44	0.403	2	$V = 17.25$

* The units for $F(\nu)$ are 10^{-29} W m^{-2}(c/s)$^{-1}$.

where the critical frequencies are given by

$$\nu_1 = LH_{\perp}E_1^2; \qquad \nu_2 = LH_{\perp}E_2^2. \qquad (4)$$

The function $F(a)$ has been tabulated by Vladimirsky (1948), by Oort and Walraven (1956), and by Westfold (1958). In the following calculations we shall assume that the low-frequency cutoff, ν_1, is below 10^7 c/s. To compute the theoretical flux for frequencies greater than 10^8 c/s, we can put $a_1 = \infty$ with good accuracy. In what follows we also put $H_{\perp}$ equal to a constant and thereby ignore the possibility of magnetic-field gradients. (Such gradients will give a different F distribution from the constant H model, as will a model such as has been postulated for the Crab [Oort and Walraven 1956], where different regions of the source contain electrons of different energies.) Under these assumptions, equation (2) becomes

$$F(\nu) = D\nu^{-(\beta-1)/2} \int_{a_2}^{\infty} a^{(\beta-3)/2} F(a) da$$

$$= D\nu^{-(\beta-1)/2} I(a_2),$$

(5)

where D is a constant and where

$$I(a_2) = \int_{a_2}^{\infty} a^{(\beta-3)/2} F(a) da.$$

(6)

If the frequency of observation ν is far enough removed from the high-frequency cutoff (i.e., $a_2 \leq 0.01$ or $\nu_2 \geq 100 \nu$), then the theoretical energy spectrum will be a power law of index $(\beta - 1)/2$, in good general agreement with Figures 5, 6, and 7.

If we now require that all the optical flux of 3C 48 be synchrotron emission alone, then Figure 8 shows that the high-frequency cutoff, ν_2, is near 10^{15} c/s, since the optical points are fainter than the extrapolated $\nu^{-0.67}$ relation. $I(a_2)$ has been found by numerical integration of equation (6), with $\beta = 2.43$ corresponding to a spectral index -0.67.

Once the value of β is fixed, the only free parameter in equation (5) is the lower limit of the integral a_2. Curves A, B, and C of Figure 8 are predicted spectra for critical frequencies ν_2 of 3×10^{14} c/s, 6×10^{14} c/s, and 10^{15} c/s, respectively. Figure 9 shows more detailed calculations in the optical range compared with the data of Table 6. The six curves are for cutoff frequencies ranging from 4×10^{14} to 10^{15} c/s. A frequency of $\nu_2 = 7 \times 10^{14}$ c/s provides a remarkably good fit to all of the data.

The detailed calculations show that deviations from the simple power law $F(\nu) \propto \nu^{-n}$ occur if the frequency of observation is closer to the critical frequency ν_2 than $a_2 = 0.01$. For $a_2 > 0.01$, the [log, log] plot is no longer a straight line but, over small intervals in frequency, $F(\nu)$ can still be adequately represented by an "effective index n" which will be larger than $(\beta - 1)/2$. Over the optical range of the U, B, V, filters ($8.4 \times 10^{14} > \nu > 5.5 \times 10^{14}$) the effective index for 3C 48 is about 1.5 (rather than 0.67, which holds for $a_2 < 0.01$), and this explains why the plotted point for 3C 48 in Figure 1 lies close to and below curve A near the value for $n = 1.3$. It is important to note that, although curve A of Figure 1 was computed using the theoretical synchrotron power law of equation (5) with $a_2 = 0$, objects which lie close to curve A are not necessarily synchrotron radiators. The close fit of observations to curve A only means that, over the very small frequency range between the U and the V filters, the energy distribution can be approximated by $F(\nu) \propto \nu^{-n}$ with the n appropriate to the particular position on curve A.

Finally, with regard to Figures 8 and 9, it should be mentioned that the value of the spectral index, $(\beta - 1)/2$, is quite critical for a good fit of the optical data. The first calculations for 3C 48 were made with an index of 0.59, as suggested by the best over-all fit to the radio data of Figure 5. The fit of those calculations to the optical data was much poorer than in Figure 9, with deviations over the U–V interval ranging to 0^m3. Consequently, in making the fit of Figure 9, there are in effect the two adjustable parameters β and ν_2. However, β can be adjusted only within the limits imposed by the detailed radio data of Figure 5 and Table 3.

Similar calculations were made for 3C 196 and 3C 286 and are shown in Figures 10 and 11. In the case of 3C 196, Figure 10 shows that equation (5) gives a satisfactory tie-in between the radio and optical data if the high-frequency cutoff is about 4×10^{14} c/s. But again it should be emphasized that this does not in itself prove that the optical radiation is due to synchrotron emission. However, Figures 8 and 10 are so similar that it would be surprising if the optical emission were not somehow related to the radio flux. On the other hand, Figure 11 shows that the situation must be more complicated for 3C 286. We can derive a curve such as B which will pass through one of the optical

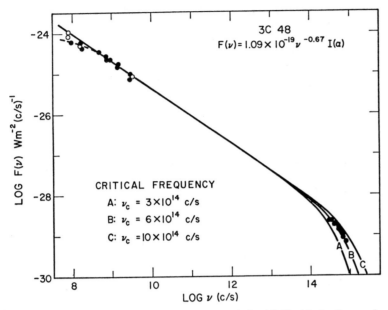

FIG. 8.—Comparison of the radio and optical power levels for 3C 48 with the theory of eq. (5). The optical data are from Table 6.

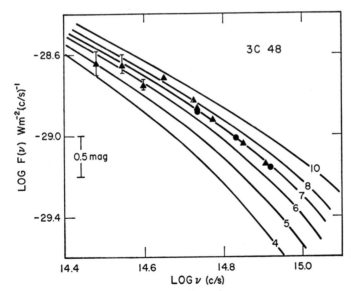

FIG. 9.—Detailed plot of the optical data for 3C 48 (Table 6) compared with theoretical curves from eq. (5) for various cutoff frequencies. The critical frequencies at the high-energy cutoff are given on the curves in units of 10^{14} c/s.

points (which, of course, is always possible as long as the optical flux is less than, or equal to, the $\nu^{-(\beta-1)/2}$ relation extrapolated from the radio region), but no change of parameters can predict the observed color of 3C 286, as we have done for 3C 48 and 3C 196. Consequently, we conclude that the optical radiation of 3C 286 cannot be due to synchrotron emission with the assumptions we have made. The high-frequency cutoff must occur at frequencies between 10^{11} and 10^{13} c/s, and most, if not all, of the observed radiation from the 3C 286 star is probably thermal. A more complex electron energy distribution or magnetic-field variations could, of course, be used to explain the optical radiation as due to synchrotron radiation.

In addition to the agreement of theory and observation in Figures 8, 9, and 10, an indirect argument might be used to suggest that the optical flux is synchrotron radiation.

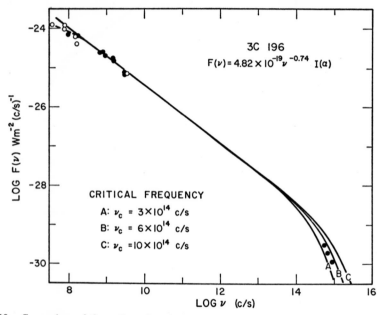

Fig. 10.—Comparison of the radio and optical power levels for 3C 196 with the theory of eq. (5). The optical data are from Table 6.

The argument concerns the explanation of the fluctuations of the optical intensity of 3C 48. The time for an electron to lose half its original energy E (in Bev) is given (Oort and Walraven 1956) by

$$t_{1/2} = \frac{3.05}{H_\perp^2 E} \text{ days}. \tag{7}$$

The energy of the electrons which emit the large majority of the optical radiation is related to the magnetic field through equation (4), because individual electrons radiate mainly near their own critical frequency. Putting $\nu = 7 \times 10^{14}$ in equation (4) gives $E = 6.6 \, H_\perp^{-1/2}$ Bev, and, substituting in equation (7), we have

$$t_{1/2} = \frac{0.462}{H_\perp^{3/2}} \text{ days (for } \nu = 7 \times 10^{14} \text{ c/s)} \tag{8}$$

for the decay time of electrons responsible for optical radiation. In the radio frequencies, the decay time is very much longer. If $\nu = 1000$ Mc/s, then equation (4) requires $E = 7.9 \times 10^{-2} H_\perp^{-1/2}$ Bev, which, from equation (7), gives

$$t_{1/2} = \frac{387}{H_\perp^{3/2}} \text{ days (for } \nu = 10^9 \text{ c/s)}. \tag{9}$$

If the synchrotron radiation is steady, new electrons must be injected at or accelerated to energy E at just the rate necessary to replace electrons degraded in energy from E because of their own radiation. If this steady state is not exactly maintained, then the distribution function of equation (1) is not exactly maintained, and the radiated power will fluctuate with the time scales of equation (7). A comparison of equations (8) and (9) shows that the time scale of variations for the radio frequencies is 840 times longer than the optical time scale, which might then explain why the radio flux is observed to remain constant over the same time intervals as those in which the optical radiation fluctuates.

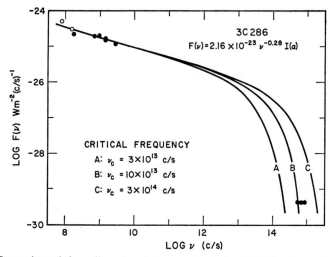

FIG. 11.—Comparison of the radio and optical power levels for 3C 286 with the theory of eq. (5). The optical data are from Table 6.

The *amplitude* of the fluctuations will be determined by the fluctuation in the number of electrons radiating or by any change in the mean magnetic field seen by these electrons. The number of electrons being observed by a radio receiver is 900 times the number observed by the V filter. This takes into account the electron spectrum (eq. [1]), the band widths used at the two frequencies (radio, $\Delta\nu = 2 \times 10^7$ c/s; optical, $\Delta\nu = 8.6 \times 10^{13}$ c/s), and the band width into which an electron radiates at the two frequencies. About 10 per cent of the radio electrons come from electrons which previously radiated in the optical region; thus the presence of radio intensity fluctuations depends primarily on the constancy of the injection mechanisms at energies at from 0.1 to 1 Bev. Equation (8) shows that the optical-flux variation on a time scale of a day would require $H_\perp$ to be about 1 gauss, and therefore the optical electrons would have an energy about 6 Bev according to equation (4).

With the synchrotron mechanism in mind, we requested W. A. Hiltner to measure the optical polarization of 3C 48, which he did at the McDonald Observatory in late 1960, and he reports that any polarization is less than 2 per cent. This negative result may mean either that the optical radiation is thermal or that the magnetic fields are sufficiently tangled that the net polarization observed, when averaged over the region of emission, is immeasurably small.

IV. SOME PHYSICAL PARAMETERS EVALUATED FROM THE SYNCHROTRON THEORY

Further insight into the physical conditions that may exist in these stars can be gained by using the synchrotron mechanism to calculate the magnetic field and minimum total energy required to produce the observed radiation. In doing this, we follow the computational methods of Burbidge (1956; see also Burbidge and Burbidge 1957). Parallel calculations have been carried out by assuming, first, that the synchrotron spectrum extends into the optical region as in Figures 8, 9, and 10 and, second, that the optical radiation is thermal and the high-frequency cutoff occurs at $\nu_2 = 10^{10}$ c/s. The total flux emitted by the source is given by

$$L = 4\pi r^2 \int_{\nu_1}^{\nu_2} F(\nu)\, d\nu, \tag{10}$$

where r is the distance (L is not to be confused with the constant in eqs. [2] and [4]). In making the integration, the flux spectral distribution has been assumed to be of the form $F(\nu) \propto \nu^{-n}$ between the lower cutoff frequency ν_1 and the upper cutoff frequency ν_2. Using the distribution of electron energies given by equation (1) and noting that the rate of radiation of a single electron is $dE/dt = -2.368 \times 10^{-3}\, H_\perp^2 E^2$ ergs sec^{-1}, then

$$L = 2.368 \times 10^{-3} H_\perp^2 K \int_{E_1}^{E_2} E^2 N(E)\, dE, \tag{11}$$

where E is in ergs, L in ergs (sec)$^{-1}$, and $H_\perp$ in gauss. The total energy of relativistic electrons is E_e and is given by

$$E_e = K \int_{E_1}^{E_2} E N(E)\, dE. \tag{12}$$

We also make the assumption (see Burbidge 1959) that the heavy-particle energy, E_p, is 100 times the electron energy, E_e.

The energy in the magnetic field is

$$E_m = \frac{H^2}{8\pi} V, \tag{13}$$

where V is the volume of the emitting region. If we now assume that the total energy $(E_m + E_e + E_p)$ is a minimum, then it can be shown that

$$E_m = \tfrac{3}{4}(E_p + E_e). \tag{14}$$

From equations (10), (11), (12), (13), and (14) we can solve for the minimum total energy, $E_T = E_m + E_p + E_e$:

$$E_T(\text{min.}) = 4.586 \times 10^{17}\, [CL(1)]^{4/7} S^{9/7} r^{17/7}, \tag{15}$$

where S is the angular diameter in arcseconds and $L(1)$ is the emitted flux if the source is at a distance of 1 parsec. The value of C is a slow function of spectral index n and of the upper and lower energy cutoffs and is given by

$$C = 4.805 \times 10^8 \left(\frac{\beta - 3}{\beta - 2}\right)\left[\frac{1 - (\nu_2/\nu_1)^{-(\beta-2)/2}}{1 - (\nu_2/\nu_1)^{-(\beta-3)/2}}\right].$$

The magnetic field H, which produces the minimum value of E_T, is

$$H(E_T \text{ min.}) = 3.819 \times 10^{-4}[CL(1)]^{2/7} S^{-6/7} r^{-2/7} \text{ gauss} . \tag{16}$$

An interesting result of equation (16) is that the magnetic field depends almost entirely

TABLE 7

PHYSICAL PARAMETERS AT AN ASSUMED DISTANCE OF 1 PARSEC

SOURCE	$M_V(1)$	$V(1)$ (cm³)	$\nu_2 \approx 10^{10}$ c/s				ν_2*			
			$L(1)$ (erg/sec)	$H(1)$ (gauss)	$E_T(1)$ (ergs)	$\tau(1)$ (years)	$L(1)$ (erg/sec)	$H(1)$ (gauss)	$E_T(1)$ (ergs)	$\tau(1)$ (years)
3C 48	21									
Core $S=1''$			1.8×10^{39}	1.39×10^{26}	0.20	1.2×10^{37}	12	6.18×10^{27}	0.22	1.5×10^{37}	0.33
$S=0''.1$			1.8×10^{36}	1.39×10^{26}	1.4	6.4×10^{35}	0.62	6.18×10^{27}	1.6	7.8×10^{35}	0.017
3C 196	23									
Halo			3.0×10^{42}	9.89×10^{25}	0.022	2.7×10^{38}	370	2.04×10^{27}	0.041	9.2×10^{38}	61
Core $S=1''$			1.8×10^{39}	3.30×10^{25}	0.14	5.9×10^{36}	24	6.82×10^{26}	0.25	2.0×10^{37}	4.8
$S=0''.1$			1.8×10^{36}	3.30×10^{25}	0.99	3.1×10^{35}	1.2	6.82×10^{26}	1.8	1.0×10^{36}	0.25
3C 286	22									
Halo			1.4×10^{43}	6.28×10^{25}	0.010	2.6×10^{38}	550	9.70×10^{27}	0.017	7.2×10^{38}	9.9
Core $S=1''$			1.8×10^{39}	9.42×10^{25}	0.15	6.9×10^{36}	9.9	1.46×10^{28}	0.25	1.9×10^{37}	9.18
$S=0''.1$			1.8×10^{36}	9.42×10^{25}	1.1	3.6×10^{35}	0.51	1.46×10^{28}	1.8	1.0×10^{36}	0.0092

* The upper cutoff frequencies used are: 3C 48 $\nu_2 = 7 \times 10^{14}$ c/s; 3C 196 $\nu_2 = 4 \times 10^{14}$ c/s; 3C 286 $\nu_2 = 10 \times 10^{12}$ c/s

TABLE 8

SCALING FACTORS FOR OTHER DISTANCES

r (pc)	$M_V - M_V(1)$	$V(r)/V(1)$	$L(r)/L(1)$	$H(r)/H(1)$	$E_T(r)/E_T(1)$	$\tau(r)/\tau(1)$
1	0	1	1	1	1	1
10	-5	10^3	10^2	0.52	2.7×10^2	2.7
10^2	-10	10^6	10^4	0.27	7.2×10^4	7.2
10^3	-15	10^9	10^6	0.14	2.0×10^7	20
10^4	-20	10^{12}	10^8	0.072	5.2×10^9	52
10^5	-25	10^{15}	10^{10}	0.037	1.4×10^{12}	140

on the angular size and only slightly on the distance.

The ratio $\tau = E_e/L$ is a measure of the time scale of replenishment of the relativistic electrons or of the lifetime of the source itself if no replenishment occurs. Under the assumptions that have been made, the total energy E_T is 236 times E_e.

Since we do not have any good estimate of the distance to these sources, the values of $L(1)$, $V(1)$, $H(1)$, $E_T(1)$, and $\tau(1)$ are given in Table 7 for a distance of 1 parsec. The value of the absolute visual magnitude M_V is also given. Table 8 gives the various scaling factors to calculate the parameters for other distances. The angular size of 3C 48 has only an upper limit, as do the cores of 3C 196 and 3C 286. In order to indicate the effects of size, the tables have been computed for two assumed sizes of 1.0 and 0.1 arcsecond.

The most interesting feature of Table 7 is the large value of magnetic field necessary in each of the radio core components. The value is almost independent of the assumed cutoff frequency but does depend on the assumed size. The value of $H = 0.20\ S^{-6/7}$ $r^{-2/7}$ gauss for 3C 48 is not far from the estimate of 1 gauss found necessary in Section IIIc to explain the observed optical intensity fluctuations; this perhaps adds further weight to the suggestions of optical synchrotron radiation.

For a mean distance of 100 pc, as is suggested in Section VI, for 3C 48 values of total energy $E_T = 1.1 \times 10^{41}\ S^{9/7}$ erg and of the magnetic field $H = 0.054\ S^{-6/7}$ gauss are almost completely independent of cutoff frequency. The cores of the three objects all have similar values for these quantities. The time scale τ depends on cutoff frequency and is $\tau(\nu^2 \doteq 10^{10}\text{ c/s}) = 86\ S^{9/7}$ years or $\tau(\nu_2 = 7 \times 10^{14}\text{ c/s}) = 2.4\ S^{9/7}$ years. Since S is less than $1''$, both these time scales are very short and indicate either that the star must be continuously supplying relativistic electrons or that the production of secondary electrons and the acceleration of particles are efficient processes. In either case a continuing supply of relativistic electrons must be made available on a short time scale by some process if the magnetic field we have assumed is correct. But it should be pointed out that the requirement for replenishment need not hold if we discard the requirement of minimum total energy. If the magnetic field is arbitrarily made very much smaller than computed above, τ can be made arbitrarily long because $\tau \propto H^{-3/2}$. Thus, if later investigations prove it difficult to find a continuing supply of electrons, τ can be made as long as the lifetime of the source by lowering H. Further investigation of the optical variations may show whether or not the optical radiation is indeed due to the synchrotron mechanism and thus determine the value of H.

V. FREQUENCY OF OCCURRENCE OF STARLIKE RADIO SOURCES

In a compilation of radio sources in order of apparent flux which are north of $\delta = -47°$, there are 24 sources whose flux is greater than 19×10^{-26} W m^{-2} (c/s)$^{-1}$ at 958 Mc/s. This listing omits all probable galactic nebulosities (i.e., H II regions, supernovae remnants, etc.) by considerations of identification, size, radio structure, galactic location, and radio spectrum. Twelve of the 24 have been identified with galaxies, and one other probably so. Three are starlike objects. Of the remaining 8, only 4 might be starlike objects, since they have extremely small diameter components.[3] Thus at least $\frac{3}{24}$ (or 12 per cent), and at most $\frac{7}{24}$ (or 29 per cent), of the strongest apparent radio sources could be starlike objects.

The radio stars seem to be characterized by having a considerable fraction of their flux coming from a very small diameter ($\leq 1''$). There are 18 sources in the Jodrell Bank diameter measures (Allen *et al.* 1962) which are of this type and which have not already been identified with galaxies. These 18 sources include 4 of the 5 known starlike objects. Their list comprises 91 per cent of all 3C sources having $S \geq 12 \times 10^{-26}$ W m^{-2} (c/s)$^{-1}$ at 178 Mc/s. Thus 5.6 per cent of their 324 sources could be starlike objects. This is a lower limit, since the fifth starlike radio source (3C 273) has, in addition to a very small component, a double radio structure resembling other extragalactic radio sources. The 18 sources above do not include such objects.

VI. APPROXIMATE DISTANCE IF GALACTIC

If the starlike objects belong to the Milky Way system, then we may make a rough estimate of the distance of the closest such object to us.

The number of stellar sources that a 3C type of survey would find in both hemispheres would be approximately $0.056 \times 461 \times 2$, or about 50. If this is the total number of such objects in the Galaxy (volume $= 10^{11}$ pc^3), then the nearest object to the sun would be about 650 pc away. On the other hand, let us consider the 18 objects mentioned in Section V which have an isotropic distribution over the sky. If these objects are in the

---

[3] Two of these, 3C 147 and 3C 273, have subsequently been shown to be similar to 3C 48.

galactic plane, that is, if they are uniformly distributed throughout a sphere of radius 300 pc, then the nearest neighbor would be 90 pc away.

The absence of any observable proper motions suggests that the minimum distance of the objects is about 60 pc. These estimates are very rough, but they indicate that the objects are approximately 100 pc away, if they belong to the Galaxy. The mean absolute magnitude of the three objects would then be $M_v = +12$.

VII. 3C 48 AS A GALAXY

After this paper had been submitted, new evidence strongly suggests that 3C 273, another similar object, has an appreciable redshift ($z = 0.158$; Schmidt 1963). The spectrum of 3C 48 can also be understood if it also has a redshift (Greenstein and Matthews 1963). This section has been included to discuss the observational data for 3C 48 under the assumption that it is a galaxy.

a) The redshift of $z = 0.3675$ for 3C 48 (Greenstein and Matthews 1963) can be interpreted as a distance of 1100 Mpc using a Hubble constant of $H = 100$ km/sec (Mpc)$^{-1}$. Using this distance to calculate the absolute magnitude of the optical object gives the value in Table 9 which has been corrected for the effects of the redshift[4] but not for interstellar absorption. The absolute magnitudes for 3C 48 and 3C 273 are compared

TABLE 9

ABSOLUTE MAGNITUDES BASED ON
$H = 100$ KM/SEC 10^6 PC

Object	cz (Km/Sec)	m_V*	M_V†
3C 48.............	110000	16.2	−24.3
Neb 3C 48........	110000	18.7	−22.8
3C 273...........	47500	12.6	−25.6
Cyg A...........	16830	14.1	−22.1
3C 295...........	138000	20.9	−21.3
Field and cluster‡...	....	....	−22.3

* Not including K correction. For Cyg A includes 1ᵐ35 absorption and 0ᵐ75 incompleteness.
† Includes K correction.
‡ On the system of the first brightest.

to other more normal radio galaxies 3C 295 and Cygnus A and to the brightest field and cluster galaxies known (Humason *et al.* 1956). 3C 48 is about 2 mag. brighter optically than the brightest field and cluster galaxies and 2.6 mag. brighter than the average of 3C 295 and Cygnus A. Table 9 shows that 3C 273 is even brighter.

The observed radio and optical size of 3C 48 of ≤ 1 second of arc means that the radio and optical flux is coming from a diameter of ≤ 5500 pc. In the case of 3C 273 (Hazard, Mackey, and Shimmins 1963, Schmidt 1963), the diameter of the core of com-

[4] The bolometric magnitude must be corrected for the K effect due to the shift of the spectrum under the measuring bands. This is composed of two terms, one due to the change of band width of the filters relative to the spectrum being measured and the other due to the wavelength-dependent effect of reducing heterochromatic magnitudes to bolometric (see eq. $B7$ of Humason, Mayall, and Sandage 1956). For an effective index of $n = 2$, the second term is zero. The first term is always 2.5 log $(1 + z)$. Hence, since $n \approx 1.5$ for 3C 48, we neglect the selective term and adopt a total correction 2.5 log $(1 + z)$ which is 0ᵐ34 for 3C 48. For 3C 295 and Cygnus A, the K correction of Humason *et al.*, Table BIII, was applied. These corrections are only approximate for two reasons: (1) only the first term (cz/H) in the distance equation (Sandage 1961, eq. [50]) has been used; and (2) the selective K term is not known exactly. However, they suffice for our present purpose. Except for Cygnus A, no correction for absorption in our own Galaxy has been applied.

ponent B is ≤ 1000 pc. The faint nebulosity visible around 3C 48 is 56 kpc long if at 1100 Mpc. The nebulosity is probably not a faint underlying galaxy for several reasons. (1) It is much larger than one would expect for a galaxy at that distance. (2) The appearance of the nebulosity does not resemble a galaxy in outline or in the distribution of brightness. (3) The bright object having a stellar appearance on direct plates is not centrally located (see Sec. II). It is 16 kpc from the center of the visible nebulosity. (4) The integrated apparent magnitude of the nebulosity omitting the "star" is $m_v \approx 18.7$. Its absolute magnitude, given in Table 9, is brighter than the brightest of known cluster galaxies and is 1 mag. brighter than the average of 3C 295 and Cygnus A, which are normal radio galaxies. In the case of more normal and radio galaxies, the nucleus of the galaxy is usually the brightest part and contributes heavily to the absolute magnitude. The integrated absolute magnitude for the nebulosity around 3C 48 does not include the effect of any such nucleus.

TABLE 10

PHYSICAL PARAMETERS FOR 3C 48 AT DISTANCE 1.1×10^9 PC

SIZE	V (cm³)	$\nu_2 = 10^{10}$ c/s				$\nu_2 = 5 \times 10^{14}$ c/s			
		L (ergs/sec)	H (gauss)	E_T (ergs)	τ (years)	L (ergs/sec)	H (gauss)	E_T (ergs)	τ (years)
$S=1''$...	2.4×10^{66}	3.82×10^{44}	9.1×10^{-4}	1.8×10^{59}	6.4×10^4	2.01×10^{46}	1.0×10^{-3}	2.4×10^{59}	1.6×10^3
$S=0''.1$..	2.4×10^{63}	3.82×10^{44}	6.6×10^{-3}	9.4×10^{57}	3.3×10^3	2.01×10^{46}	7.6×10^{-3}	1.2×10^{58}	83
		3.82×10^{44}	2.9×10^{-4}	1.0×10^{60}	1.8×10^5	2.01×10^{46}	2.9×10^{-5}	5.3×10^{61}	1.8×10^5

If the nebulosity was produced by some phenomenon (say an explosion) at some time in the past, then from its visible extent we can infer that the event occurred $\geq 1.8 \times 10^5$ years ago. The minimum corresponds to assuming that the expansion has occurred at the velocity of light and that there are no projection effects.

b) Physical parameters.—The physical parameters for 3C 48 at a distance of 1.1×10^9 pc have been computed in exactly the same manner as in Section IV. The results are given in Table 10. Note that the value of the magnetic field for minimum total energy is near 10^{-3} gauss, much lower than suggested in Section IV, and not far from other radio galaxies (Maltby *et al.* 1963). The total energies required are also similar to, but lower than, some of the other radio galaxies. However, note that the time scales are all very short compared with the 1.8×10^5 years suggested above. We can resolve this difficulty in one of two ways: (1) The nuclear region of the galaxy has been continuously producing high-energy particles throughout its lifetime. The total energy required since birth, then, is 5×10^{59} ergs ($\nu_2 = 10^{10}$) or 3×10^{61} ergs ($\nu_2 = 5 \times 10^{14}$). (2) The magnetic field is lower by at least the amount required to make the lifetime equal to 1.8×10^5 years. The physical parameters required, under this latter hypothesis, are given in the last row of Table 10. There is no dependence on the size of the object. The total energy required in both these cases is becoming uncomfortably large and will be even larger if H is made any smaller.

c) Optical fluctuations.—The observation of the optical-flux variations (Sec. III) becomes more important if these objects are galaxies, since we normally do not think of the light from galaxies as varying. A time scale of 6 months for the variations implies a size of the emitting region of ≤ 0.15 pc on the basis of light-travel time across the object. If we are seeing statistical variations of a number of similar events, about 10 such events would be happening simultaneously, and the emission region would be at least 10 times larger. The variations *could* still be due to decay of optical synchrotron electrons in a magnetic field of $\sim$1 gauss (see Sec. III). This is not inconsistent when we note that the total energy depends very little on which hypothesis we use in the previous subsection. Thus, without changing the total energy requirements very much, we can choose the magnetic field and adjust the emitting volume to fit. The discussion of the lack of radio fluctuations would be the same as in Section III.

We wish to express our appreciation to the many people who have let us use their unpublished material. In particular, we should like to thank Baum and Hiltner for their photoelectric photometry, Greenstein and Schmidt for information of the spectra, Griffin for his accurate optical positions, Read for his precise radio declinations, Kellermann and Bartlett for their radio-flux data, and Palmer for letting us use the Jodrell Bank data at large spacings before publication. We have also had useful discussions with Greenstein and Schmidt, and we wish to express our appreciation to them.

The Radio Astronomy program at the California Institute of Technology is supported by the United States Office of Naval Research under contract Nonr 220(19).

APPENDIX A

THEORETICAL $U-B$, $B-V$ COLORS FOR SPECTRAL DISTRIBUTIONS OF ARBITRARY FORM

In many applications it is desirable to compute the colors on the U, B, V system of radiant sources with given energy distributions. This can be done, once the transmission functions $S(\lambda)$ of the U, B, V system are known. Melbourne showed (1960) that the $S(\lambda)$ functions tabulated by H. L. Johnson (1955) as representing the system will not predict exactly the observed $U - B$, $B - V$ colors for real stars of known energy distributions unless a systematic zero-point correction of $0^{\mathrm{m}}17$ is added to the computed natural $u - b$ magnitude and a correction of $-0^{\mathrm{m}}13$ is applied to the computed natural $b - v$ magnitude before applying Johnson's empirically determined transformation equation (5) of *Ap. J.*, **117**, 313, 1953. These corrections assume that there is no color equation between the theoretical colors based on $S(\lambda)$ and the $U - B$ and $B - V$ values adopted for standard stars in the sky. In this appendix we confirm Melbourne's zero-point procedure for $B - V$ colors by showing that his adopted $S(\lambda)$ functions predict the natural colors $(b - v)_0$ outside the atmosphere for seven real stars such that the regression line of $(b - v)_0$ on the known $B - V$ colors has a slope of 1.00. However, this is not the case in $U - B$, where the adopted $S(\lambda)$ functions predict $(u - b)_0$ colors with a longer base line than the observed $U - B$; i.e., a color equation exists. The equations derived in this appendix can be used to convert theoretical calculations based on the adopted $S(\lambda)$ to the empirical U, B, V system. Predicted $U - B$, $B - V$ colors for *any* arbitrary flux distribution function $F(\lambda)$ can be obtained therefrom.

Table A1, taken from Melbourne's thesis, lists the transmission functions for the theoretical photometric system designated by u, b, v. As anticipated in the last paragraph, this system, aside from zero-point corrections, is close to, but not identical with, U, B, V. The $S(\lambda)$ functions were constructed by A. D. Code from Johnson's tabulated values for zero air mass by applying the monochromatic extinction of the atmosphere for 1 and 2 air masses as determined from spectrum scanner observations (Code, as tabulated by Melbourne 1960, Table 2). We have tabulated these functions because they are needed in what follows and they appear nowhere in the literature. The $S(\lambda)$ for 1 air mass was tabulated by Arp (1961) in his discussion of $U - B$, $B - V$ colors for black bodies, but $S(\lambda)_0$ and $S(\lambda)_2$ are needed for a full treatment of the problem.

The $S(\lambda)_1$ and $S(\lambda)_2$ functions of Table A1 were used to operate on the relative energy distributions $F(\lambda)$ for seven real stars. The $F(\lambda)$ data were obtained from Minnaert (1953, Table 1), Code (1960), and Melbourne (1960). Code and Melbourne tabulate $2.5 \log F(\nu)$, where $F(\nu)$ is the energy flux per unit frequency interval. The $F(\nu)$ values were converted to relative energy flux per wavelength interval $F(\lambda)$ by multiplying $F(\nu)$ by λ^{-2}. The seven stars chosen were either relatively free from Fraunhofer lines or, as in the case of the sun (Minnaert 1953, Table

1), the continuum level was already adjusted to compensate for the effect of the lines.

Theoretical colors on the natural system of $S(\lambda)$ for 1 and 2 air masses were computed from

$$(u-b)_i = 2.5 \log \frac{\int_0^\infty S_b(\lambda)_i F(\lambda)\, d\lambda}{\int_0^\infty S_u'(\lambda)_i F(\lambda)\, d\lambda}, \qquad i = 1 \text{ or } 2, \text{ (A1)}$$

TABLE A1
ADOPTED TRANSMISSION FUNCTIONS AFTER MELBOURNE AND CODE*

$\lambda \times 10^{-2}$ (A)	$S(\lambda)_0$		$S(\lambda)_1$, 1 Air Mass			$S(\lambda)_2$, 2 Air Masses		
	b_0	v_0	u_1	b_1	v_1	u_2	b_2	v_2
30....			0.025			0.025		
31....			0.250			0.060		
32....			0.680			0.170		
33....			1.137			0.375		
34....			1.650			0.675		
35....	0.000		2.006	0.000		1.000		
36....	0.015		2.250	0.006		1.250	0.000	
37....	0.100		2.337	0.080		1.390	0.040	
38....	0.500		1.925	0.337		1.125	0.250	
39....	1.800		0.650	1.425		0.600	0.870	
40....	3.620		0.197	2.253		0.140	1.745	
41....	3.910		0.070	2.806		0.030	2.025	
42....	4.000		0.000	2.950		0.000	2.200	
43....	3.980			3.000			2.290	
44....	3.780			2.937			2.290	
45....	3.500			2.780			2.200	
46....	3.150			2.520			2.050	
47....	2.700	0.000		2.230			1.840	0.000
48....	2.320	0.020		1.881	0.020		1.580	0.020
49....	1.890	0.280		1.550	0.175		1.325	0.175
50....	1.530	1.180		1.275	0.900		1.079	0.830
51....	1.140	2.170		0.975	1.880		0.840	1.570
52....	0.750	2.970		0.695	2.512		0.580	2.150
53....	0.500	3.300		0.430	2.850		0.360	2.420
54....	0.250	3.250		0.210	2.820		0.180	2.425
55....	0.070	3.000		0.055	2.625		0.050	2.270
56....	0.000	2.700		0.000	2.370		0.000	2.035
57....		2.320			2.050			1.780
58....		2.000			1.720			1.530
59....		1.670			1.413			1.255
60....		1.280			1.068			0.985
61....		0.920			0.795			0.745
62....		0.650			0.567			0.505
63....		0.430			0.387			0.340
64....		0.260			0.250			0.220
65....		0.175			0.160			0.140
66....		0.125			0.110			0.100
67....		0.100			0.081			0.080
68....		0.070			0.061			0.055
69....		0.050			0.045			0.030
70....		0.030			0.028			0.025
71....		0.020			0.017			0.010
72....		0.010			0.007			0.000

* Tabulated are the transmissions of two aluminum reflections, filters, 1P21 photomultiplier, and atmosphere for zero, 1, and 2 air masses.

with a similar equation for $(b - v)_1$ and $(b - v)_2$. In an obvious notation the subscripts refer to 1 or 2 air masses. Results for the seven stars are listed in Table A2, where the *observed* $U - B$, $B - V$ colors are shown in columns 2 and 3; the *computed* natural colors $(b - v)_1$, $(b - v)_2$ in columns 4 and 5; $(u - b)_1$, $(u - b)_2$ in columns 6 and 7; and the differences $k_{12} \equiv (b - v)_2 - (b - v)_1$ and $k_{56} \equiv (u - b)_2 - (u - b)_1$ in columns 8 and 9. Note that k_{12} and k_{56} represent the color extinction between sec $Z = 2$ and sec $Z = 1$ and therefore are related to the usual extinction coefficients, defined by

$$k_{12} \equiv k_1 - k_2(b - v)_0,$$ \hfill (A2)

$$k_{56} \equiv k_5 - k_6(u - b)_0.$$ \hfill (A3)

As was expected, the extinction coefficients k_{12} and k_{56} are color-dependent according to our calculations (i.e., k_2 and k_6 are not zero). From Table A2 it is easily shown that

$$k_{12} = 0.102 - 0.024(b - v)_0,$$ \hfill (A4)

TABLE A2

COMPUTED AND OBSERVED COLORS FOR THE SEVEN CALIBRATING STARS

Star (1)	$(B-V)_{obs}$ (2)	$(U-B)_{obs}$ (3)	$(b-v)_1$ (4)	$(b-v)_2$ (5)	$(u-b)_1$ (6)	$(u-b)_2$ (7)	k_{12} (8)	k_{56} (9)	$(B-V)_c$ (10)	$(U-B)_c$ (11)
10 Lac..........	−0.20	−1.04	−0.994	−0.864	0.284	0.743	0.130	0.459	−0.21	−1.05
η UMa	− .21	−0.68	− .984	− .857	0.683	1.121	.127	.438	− .20	−0.68
HD 19445......	+ .46	−0.24	− .338	− .223	1.182	1.596	.115	.414	+ .46	−0.22
HD 140283.....	+ .48	−0.20	− .288	− .174	1.161	1.567	.114	.406	+ .51	−0.24
σ Boo........	+ .37	−0.09	− .436	− .320	1.332	1.725	.116	.393	+ .36	−0.08
α Lyr........	+ .00	−0.01	− .839	− .714	1.410	1.762	.125	.352	− .05	−0.01
Sun...........	+0.62	+0.10	−0.196	−0.090	1.512	1.933	0.106	0.421	+0.61	+0.08

which is in excellent agreement with observational determinations of extinction on good nights over the last 10 years on Mount Wilson. The extinction coefficient k_{56} cannot be represented by such a simple equation over the range of $(u - b)_0$ covered by our seven calibrating stars. The value of k_6 depends on $(u - b)_0$ itself, which shows that equation (A3) does not represent the broad-band ultraviolet-blue extinction. The variation of k_6 with $(u - b)_0$ has been found observationally (Johnson, unpublished communication). It should be emphasized that, in setting up the $U - B$ system in 1953, Johnson *intentionally put* $k_6 = 0$ to avoid the great complication involved in the reduction procedure of $k_6 = f[(u - b)_0]$. Therefore, if we are to compare theoretically computed $u - b$ indices with $U - B$ values assigned to real stars, we must ignore the color variation of k_{56}, even though $k_6 \neq 0$ in nature. The adopted $U - B$ values for stars in the sky therefore contain slight inconsistencies with a purely theoretical system. Consequently, in the following we shall relate the computed $(u - b)_1$ values directly to $U - B$ rather than use the theoretical k_{56} value from Table A2 to obtain $(u - b)_0$ from $(u - b)_1$ in the usual way [i.e., $(u - b)_0 = (u - b)_1 - k_{56}$] and then to find $(u - b)_0 = f(U - B)$. We tried this latter procedure, which is theoretically correct because it takes the non-zero k_6 term into account, but the correlation of $(u - b)_0$ and $U - B$ was non-linear, deviating by $\pm 0\overset{m}{.}05$ from a straight line. The foregoing explanation is believed to be correct (i.e., small, residual inconsistencies in the actual $U - B$ values) because the non-linearity was eliminated in a plot of $(u - b)_1$ versus $U - B$. Conversations with Harold Johnson after these calculations were completed confirm that this is undoubtedly the case.

With the foregoing precepts and with the data of Table A2, the following extinction and color equations can be derived. From equation (A4) and from the definition of extinction coefficients, which is

$$(b-v)_0 = (b-v)_{\sec\,Z} - [k_1 - k_2(b-v)_0]\sec Z , \qquad \text{(A5)}$$

it follows that

$$(b-v)_0 = 1.024(b-v)_1 - 0.104 . \qquad \text{(A6)}$$

With $(b-v)_0$ now known by using equation (A6) and the $(b-v)_1$ values of Table A2, we corre-

TABLE A3

BLACK-BODY LINE IN THE $U-B, B-V$ DIAGRAM

T_e	PRESENT		ARP	
	$U-B$	$B-V$	$(U-B)_A$	$(B-V)_A$
∞	-1.28	-0.44	-1.33	-0.46
25000.....	-1.13	-0.21	-1.17	-0.23
20000.....	-1.06	-0.15	-1.09	-0.17
12000.....	-0.83	$+0.05$	-0.84	$+0.04$
8000.....	-0.53	$+0.35$	-0.52	$+0.34$
6000.....	-0.26	$+0.63$	-0.22	$+0.61$
5000.....	-0.10	$+0.79$	-0.05	$+0.78$
4000.....	$+0.36$	$+1.13$	$+0.37$	$+1.12$
3300.....	$+0.78$	$+1.44$	$+0.83$	$+1.44$
3000.....	$+1.07$	$+1.67$	$+1.14$	$+1.66$

TABLE A4

$U-B, B-V$ COLORS FOR SOURCES WITH $F(\nu) = C\nu^{-n}$

n	$(u-b)_1$	$(b-v)_1$	$U-B$	$B-V$
0.0........	0.440	-0.697	-0.90	0.10
0.2........	.487	$-$ .648	$-$ .86	.15
0.4........	.534	$-$ .600	$-$ .82	.20
0.6........	.582	$-$ .551	$-$ .77	.25
0.8........	.629	$-$ .503	$-$ .73	.30
1.0........	.677	$-$ .454	$-$ .68	.34
1.2........	.724	$-$ .406	$-$ .64	.39
1.4........	.772	$-$ .358	$-$ .60	.44
1.6........	.820	$-$ .310	$-$ .55	.49
1.8........	.868	$-$ .263	$-$ .51	.54
2.0........	0.916	-0.215	-0.46	0.58

late $(b-v)_0$ with the observed $B-V$ for the seven calibrating stars. The result is

$$B-V = 1.00(b-v)_0 + 0.91 \qquad \text{(A7)}$$

or

$$B-V = 1.024(b-v)_1 + 0.81 , \qquad \text{(A8)}$$

which shows that there is no color equation between Table A1 and the $B-V$ system if the extinction is treated in this way.

The $U-B$ situation is different. No extinction values were applied to $(u-b)_1$ to obtain $(u-b)_0$, for the reasons previously discussed. Direct comparison of $(u-b)_1$ and $U-B$ from Table A2 gives the well-determined relation

$$U - B = 0.921\,(u - b\,)_1 - 1.308\,, \tag{A9}$$

which is the color equation between the *observed* $U - B$ system and the *theoretical* $(u - b)^1$ system.

An objection might be raised to our procedure in that, in actual fact, we may not know the true $F(\lambda)$ for the seven calibrating stars of Table A2 because of the effects of line blanketing, with the result that our predicted $(u - b)_1$ colors may be in error. While this objection may be true for σ Boo and, to a lesser extent, for α Lyr with its strong hydrogen lines, it is not true for the other stars. 10 Lac and η UMa are so hot as to have few lines; HD 19445 and HD 140283 are cool subdwarfs with extremely weak Fraunhofer lines, and the blanketing effect is almost nil, while the effect in the sun has been corrected for by Minnaert before giving his $F(\lambda)$ of his Table 1 (1953). Therefore, we interpret the slope coefficient in equation (A9) to differ significantly from 1.00 and suggest that a color equation exists. We are not completely confident of the result because of the blanketing problem, but we accept it for the present.

Equations (A8) and (A9) solve the problem. To compute $U - B$ and $B - V$ for any arbitrary energy distribution $F(\lambda)$, proceed as follows: (1) Use the $S(\lambda)_1$ functions of Table A1 and use equation (A1) to compute natural colors $(u - b)_1$ and $(b - v)_1$. (2) Use equations (A8) and (A9) to find $U - B$ and $B - V$. A check on the internal consistency of this procedure is made by applying the equations to the seven calibrating stars. Comparison of the computed colors in columns 10 and 11 of Table A2 with the observed colors of columns 2 and 3 shows good agreement.

The above procedure differs from that used by Arp (1961), in that we have used a color equation (A9) to the $U - B$ system, whereas Arp had none. Our zero points also differ slightly. Table A3 shows the difference between Arp's calculations of the black-body line and our own. The difference is very small.

In the theory of synchrotron radiation, energy distributions of the form $F(\nu) \propto \nu^{-n}$ (flux per unit frequency interval) are found. Calculation of $U - B$ and $B - V$ values have been made for these distributions for various values of n ranging from 0.0 to 2.0 in steps of 0.2. The sources were assumed to radiate as $F(\lambda) \propto \lambda^{n-2}$ (per unit wavelength interval). The results are given in Table A4 and have been discussed in the body of the paper.

APPENDIX B

CONVERSION OF U, B, V OPTICAL DATA TO ABSOLUTE FLUX UNITS

The most recent calibration of the energy flux in absolute units arriving from a star of apparent visual magnitude $V = 0$ is due to Willstrop (1960). We adopt Willstrop's Table 1 for the energy flux per A at λ 5390 for stars of $V = 0.00$ and take the known relative energy distribution-curves for stars of different $B - V$ values to compute the absolute flux calibrations at the effective wavelengths of the U, B, and V points for stars of $U = B = V = 0$.

a) Effective Wavelengths for the U, B, V Filters

The effective wavelength of any filter system depends on the energy distribution $F(\lambda)$ of the source which is measured with the system. We define the effective wavelength in the usual way by

$$\lambda = \frac{\displaystyle\int_0^{\infty} \lambda S(\lambda) F(\lambda)\, d\lambda}{\displaystyle\int_0^{\infty} S(\lambda) F(\lambda)\, d\lambda} \tag{B1}$$

and compute $\bar{\lambda}$ for sources characterized by $F(\lambda) \propto \lambda^{n-2}$.

The effective wavelengths calculated from equation (B1) using the $S(\lambda)$ function from Table A1 are for the u, b, v natural system, which is related to the U, B, V system via equations (A7),

(A8), and (A9) of Appendix A. From these equations and from $\bar{\lambda}_u, \bar{\lambda}_b, \bar{\lambda}_v$ for 1 air mass, we can obtain $\bar{\lambda}_U, \bar{\lambda}_B, \bar{\lambda}_V$ for the actual U, B, V system as follows.

The relation between two color systems, characterized by effective wavelengths λ_1, λ_2, and λ_3, λ_4, when the measurements are made on black bodies is

$$\frac{(CI)_{1,\,2}}{(CI)_{3,\,4}} = \frac{(1/\lambda_1) - (1/\lambda_2)}{(1/\lambda_3) - (1/\lambda_4)}. \tag{B2}$$

TABLE B1

ADOPTED EFFECTIVE WAVELENGTHS AND CONVERSIONS TO ABSOLUTE
FLUX UNITS FOR THE U, B, V SYSTEM FOR SOURCES WHICH
RADIATE AS $F(\nu) = C\nu^{-n}$

n (1)	$U-B*$ (2)	$B-V*$ (3)	$\bar{\lambda}_U$ (4)	$\bar{\lambda}_B$ (5)	$\bar{\lambda}_V$ (6)	$F(\nu)_U$† (7)	$F(\nu)_B$† (8)	$F(\nu)_V$† (9)
0.0.....	−0.91	0.10	3585	4383	5502	1.79	4.13	3.81
0.2.....	− .86	.15	3586	4387	5505	1.80	4.15	3.82
0.6.....	− .77	.25	3593	4408	5515	1.81	4.18	3.84
1.0.....	− .68	.34	3598	4412	5525	1.82	4.21	3.87
1.4.....	− .60	.44	3604	4431	5534	1.83	4.26	3.90
2.0.....	−0.46	0.58	3610	4440	5545	1.84	4.31	3.94

* $U - B$ and $B - V$ taken from Table A4 of Appendix A.
† The unit on the flux is 10^{-23} W m^{-2}(c/s)$^{-1}$ for a star of $U = B = V = 0$ apparent magnitude.

For sources we are considering, where $F(\lambda) \propto \lambda^{n-2}$, the correct relation will be

$$\frac{(CI)_{1,\,2}}{(CI)_{1,\,2}} = \frac{\log(1/\lambda_1) - \log(1/\lambda_2)}{\log(1/\lambda_3) - \log(1/\lambda_4)}, \tag{B3}$$

but, for color systems where the effective wavelengths are very close to one another, equations (B2) and (B3) give nearly identical answers. We use equation (B2) in the following.

The effective wavelength of V was obtained by assuming $\bar{\lambda}_V \equiv \bar{\lambda}_v$ for $S_v(\lambda)_0$ in equation (B1). This gives $\bar{\lambda}_V$ listed in column 6 of Table B1 for various n-values. The $\bar{\lambda}_B$ follows from equation (B2) and equation (A8) as

$$\frac{1}{\bar{\lambda}_B} = \frac{1}{\bar{\lambda}_V} + 1.024\left(\frac{1}{\bar{\lambda}_{b1}} - \frac{1}{\bar{\lambda}_{v1}}\right), \tag{B4}$$

where $\bar{\lambda}_{b1}$ is the effective wavelength of the natural b system for 1 air mass and likewise for v in $\bar{\lambda}_{v1}$. A check on the above procedure is available from equation (A7), which requires that $\bar{\lambda}_B = \bar{\lambda}_{b0}$. The check was made and was found to be excellent. Column 5 of Table B1 gives $\bar{\lambda}_B$.

For the ultraviolet, equation (A9) requires

$$\frac{1}{\bar{\lambda}_U} = \frac{1}{\bar{\lambda}_B} + 0.921\left(\frac{1}{\bar{\lambda}_{u1}} - \frac{1}{\bar{\lambda}_{b1}}\right), \tag{B5}$$

where all quantities on the right side are now known or were computed from equation (B1). Column 4 of Table B1 gives $\bar{\lambda}_U$ for the various n-values.

b) Calibration of Magnitudes in Absolute Flux Units

Willstrop, in his Table 1 (1960), gives absolute monochromatic fluxes at $\lambda = 5390$ A, a wavelength which differs from $\bar{\lambda}_V$. We need the ratio $F(\bar{\lambda}_V)/F(5390)$ to correct Willstrop's values to monochromatic fluxes at $\bar{\lambda}_V$. For the sources we are considering, where $F(\lambda) = C\lambda^{n-2}$, it follows that

$$\log \frac{F(\lambda_V)}{F(5390)} = (n-2)\log \left(\frac{\lambda_V}{5390}\right). \tag{B6}$$

From equation (B6), from Willstrop's Table 1, and from the conversion of flux units in ergs cm^{-2} sec^{-1}A^{-1} to W m^{-2}(c/s)$^{-1}$ by multiplying the former by $10^5 \lambda^2/c$ to get the latter, we obtain the flux at $\bar{\lambda}_V$ for a source of visual magnitude $V = 0$ tabulated in column 9 of Table B1, which is one of the three answers we require. The flux at the effective wavelengths of the B and U bands are now found as follows. For a given index n (for example, $n = 2$), the flux in the source at the wavelengths $\bar{\lambda}_V$ and $\bar{\lambda}_B$ are in the ratio $(\nu_V/\nu_B)^{-2} = 1.5596$ (for $n = 2$) per unit frequency interval. Thus, if the visual magnitude of the source were 0.00, the absolute flux density in W m^{-2} (c/s)$^{-1}$ at $\bar{\lambda}_B = 4440$ A would be 0.6412 times the flux at $\bar{\lambda}_V$, which we have previously calculated and listed in Table B1. But Table A4 or Table B1 shows that $B - V = +0.58$ for $n = 2$, or $B = +0.58$ by the requirement that $V = 0.00$. Hence the flux at $\bar{\lambda}_B = 4440$ for a source of index $n = 2$ corresponding to a *blue magnitude 0.00* will be 4.31×10^{-23} W m^{-2} (c/s)$^{-1}$. Similar calculations were made for all cases and are tabulated in Table B1, and these numbers solve the problem.

REFERENCES

Allen, L. R., Anderson, B., Conway, R. G., Palmer, H. P., Reddish, V. C., and Rowson, B. 1962, *M.N.*, **124**, 477.
Arp, H. C. 1961, *Ap. J.*, **133**, 874.
Bolton, J. G. September, 1960, U.R.S.I. General Assembly, London, *Obs. California Inst. Technology*, No. 5.
Burbidge, G. R. 1956, *Ap. J.*, **124**, 416.
————. 1959, *Paris Symposium on Radio Astronomy*, ed. R. N. Bracewell (Stanford, Calif.: Stanford University Press), p. 541.
Burbidge, G. R., and Burbidge, E. M. 1957, *Ap. J.*, **125**, 1.
Code, A. D. 1960, *Stellar Atmospheres*, ed. J. L. Greenstein (Chicago: University of Chicago Press), chap. 2.
Conway, R. G., Kellermann, K. I., and Long, R. J. 1963, *M.N.*, **125**, 261.
Edge, D. O., Shakeshaft, J. R., McAdam, W. B., Baldwin, J. E., and Archer, S. 1959, *Mem. R.A.S.*, **68**, 37.
Greenstein, J. L. 1958, *Hdb. d. Phys.*, ed. S. Flügge (Berlin: Springer Verlag), **50**, 161.
Greenstein, J. L., and Matthews, T. A. 1963, *Nature*, **197**, 1041.*
Hazard, C., Mackey, M. B., and Shimmins, A. J. 1963, *Nature*, **197**, 1037.*
Humason, M. L., Mayall, N. U., and Sandage, A. R. 1956, *A.J.*, **61**, 97.
Johnson, H. L. 1955, *Ann. d'ap.*, **18**, 292.
Kellermann, K. I., Long, R. J., Allen, L. R., and Moran, M. 1962, *Nature*, **195**, 692.
Maltby, P., Matthews, T. A., and Moffet, A. T. 1963, *Ap. J.*, **137**, 153.*
Maltby, P., and Moffet, A. T. 1962, *Ap. J. Suppl.*, No. 67, p. 141.
Matthews, T. A., Bolton, J. G., Greenstein, J. L., Münch, G., and Sandage, A. R. 1961, *Sky and Telescope*, **21**, 148.
Melbourne, W. G. 1960, *Ap. J.*, **132**, 101.
Minnaert, M. 1953, *The Sun*, ed. G. P. Kuiper (Chicago: University of Chicago Press), chap. 3.
Oort, J. H., and Walraven, T. 1956, *B.A.N.*, **12**, 285.
Read, R. B. 1963, *Ap. J.*, **138**, 1.
Rowson, B. 1962, submitted to *M.N.*
Sandage, A. R. 1961, *Ap. J.*, **133**, 355.
Schmidt, M. 1962, *Ap. J.*, **136**, 684.
————. 1963, *Nature*, **197**, 1040.*
Schwinger, J. 1949, *Phys. Rev.*, **75**, 1912.
Smith, H. J., and Hoffleit, D. 1961, *Pub. A.S.P.*, **73**, 292.
Vladimirsky, V. V. 1948, *Zhur. Eksp. Theoret. Fiz.*, **18**, 392.
Walker, M. F. 1954, *Pub. A.S.P.*, **66**, 230.
————. 1957, *Non-stable Stars*, ed. G. H. Herbig (Cambridge: Cambridge University Press), p. 46.
Westfold, K. C. 1958, *Ap. J.*, **130**, 241.
Willstrop, R. V. 1960, *M.N.*, **121**, 17.
Woltjer, L. 1958, *B.A.N.*, **14**, 39.

THE OPTICAL IDENTIFICATION
OF THREE NEW RADIO OBJECTS
chapter 18 # OF THE 3C 48 CLASS

M. Ryle and Allan R. Sandage

The identification of the radio sources 3C 48, 3C 196, and 3C 286 with an entirely new class of optical object (Matthews and Sandage 1963), and the subsequent discovery that objects of the class possess large redshifts (Schmidt 1963), have opened up powerful new possibilities for study of the cosmological problem. Because so few of these objects are known, many of their physical and spatial properties are, for the moment, obscure. For this reason a systematic search for additional objects of this type has been started at the Mount Wilson and Palomar Observatories and at the Mullard Radio Astronomy Observatory.

At this writing, accurate new radio positions have been obtained at Cambridge by Mrs. Margaret Clarke for eighty-eight objects in the revised 3C Catalogue. The errors of these new positions are generally of the order of ± 1 second of time in right ascension and ± 1 minute of arc in declination—errors which are small enough to give significant identification with optical objects brighter than $B = 19$ by using the Palomar Sky Survey prints. M. S. Longair has found galaxies on the Sky Survey prints in the majority of the eighty-eight source positions. In four of the cases no galaxy was found but rather a starlike image was present very close to the radio position—a circumstance which suggested the possibility of an identification with a 3C 48-type object. Two of these four objects are 3C 9 and 3C 245, whose revised radio positions are given in Table 1.

It has been possible to make positive identifications at Mount Wilson and Palomar from these suggestions. The method is based on the unusual ultraviolet excess shown in optical wavelengths by objects of this type as found by Sandage when the identification of the first members of the class was made (Matthews and Sandage 1963, Fig. 1). The excess is so great that ordinary photographic techniques are sufficient to show the anomaly as illustrated in Figure 1a. Here the field of 3C 245 is shown in a double exposure taken on blue-sensitive Eastman 103a-O emulsion with the 100-inch telescope.

M. Ryle, Mullard Radio Astronomy Observatory, Cavendish Laboratory, University of Cambridge. Allan Sandage, Mount Wilson and Palomar Observatories, Carnegie Institution of Washington, California Institute of Technology.

Reprinted from the *Astrophysical Journal*, **139**, 419–421, 1964.

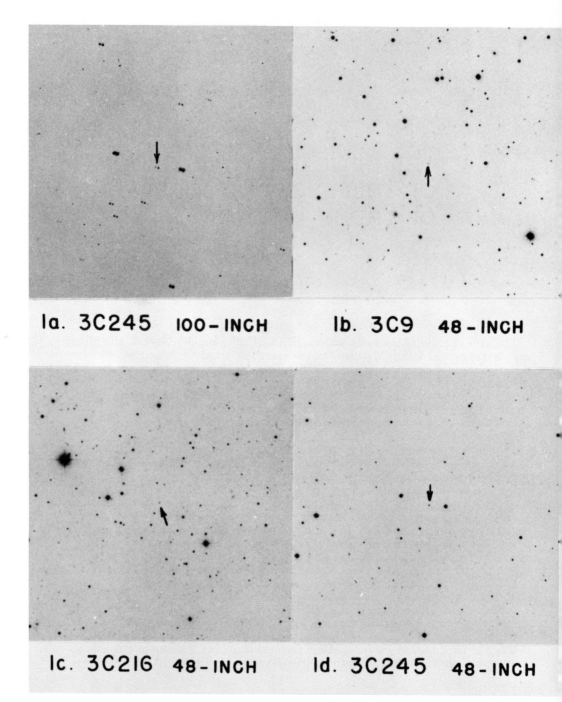

Ia. 3C245 100-INCH   Ib. 3C9 48-INCH

Ic. 3C216 48-INCH   Id. 3C245 48-INCH

Fig. 1.—Identification charts for 3C 9, 3C 216, and 3C 245. Figure 1a shows the discovery technique using the ultraviolet excess criteria. The left image was taken behind a Schott GG 13 filter which, together with an Eastman 103a-O plate, defines a band pass from $\lambda \simeq 3900$ Å to $\lambda \simeq 5000$ Å. The right image was taken behind a Schott UG 2 filter which transmits from $\lambda \simeq 3200$ Å to $\lambda \simeq 3900$ Å. Figures 1b, 1c, and 1d are from the Palomar Sky Survey prints.

The left image was taken behind a Schott GG 13 filter which, together with the *a*-O plate, defines a band pass from $\lambda = 3900$ Å to $\lambda = 5000$ Å. The right image was taken on the same plate behind a Schott UG 2 filter which transmits from $\lambda = 3200$ Å to $\lambda = 3900$ Å. The ultraviolet excess of the radio object is clearly seen.

A color plate of this type was also taken of the 3C 9 field with positive results. Figures 1*b* and 1*d* show the identification of the 3C 9 and 3C 245 objects on reproductions made from the Palomar Sky Survey prints.

A general search program using the color technique has now been started in order to find all objects of this type in the revised 3C Catalogue and in selected regions of the forthcoming 4C Catalogue. Besides 3C 9 and 3C 245, whose identifications were first suggested from their radio positions alone, a third object, 3C 216, was discovered by the color technique in the first two nights of the general survey at the 100-inch reflector. The optical object is shown in Figure 1*c* as reproduced from the Palomar Sky Survey prints.

TABLE 1

REVISED RADIO POSITIONS OF TWO SOURCES

Name	$a(1950.0)$	$\delta(1950.0)$
3C 9.........	$00^h17^m49^s9 \pm 0^s5$	$+15°24'3 \pm 0'5$
3C 245.......	$10\ 40\ 05.9 \pm 0.5$	$+12\ 19.6 \pm 0.5$

TABLE 2

PHOTOELECTRIC DATA

Object	V	$B-V$	$U-B$
3C 9..............	18.21	0.23	-0.74
3C 216............	18.48	.49	$-.60$
3C 245............	17.29	0.46	-0.82

Three-color photoelectric observations made with the 200-inch Hale reflector on December 11/12, 1963, confirmed that the three objects marked in Figure 1 are indeed the radio sources. The data are given in Table 2. The $B - V$ and $U - B$ colors are singularly peculiar compared with normal stars but are similar with the photoelectric values of all five previously known objects of this class (3C 48, 3C 147, 3C 196, 3C 273, and 3C 286), which removes all doubt of the optical identifications.

The initial success of this survey suggests that many more objects of this type remain to be found. When a representative sample of these objects is available for study, such questions as the occurrence or non-occurrence of the objects in clusters of galaxies, the spatial distribution and the distribution over the plane of the sky, the presence or absence of light variations, the connection of the optical to the radio spectrum, the absolute luminosities and the dispersion about a mean, and the form of the redshift–apparent magnitude relation can be studied.

REFERENCES

Matthews, T. A., and Sandage, A. R. 1963, *Ap. J.*, **138**, 30. *
Schmidt, M. 1963, *Nature*, **197**, 1040.*

INTENSITY VARIATIONS OF 3C 48, 3C 196, AND 3C 273 IN

chapter 19   # OPTICAL WAVELENGTHS

ALLAN R. SANDAGE

The optical objects which have so far been identified with radio sources of the 3C 48 type are unlike anything heretofore known. Maarten Schmidt's remarkable discovery (1963) that members of the class possess large redshifts showed that objects of this type are not only located at large distances from the Galaxy but also that they are the most luminous objects known in the universe. For example, 3C 48 radiates the enormous power of 1.3×10^{46} erg/sec over the optical region extending from $\lambda_0 = 2340$ Å to $\lambda_0 = 4390$ Å as computed from (1) the observed flux of 1.0×10^{-29} W/m^2 cs at $\lambda = 5000$ Å (see Matthews and Sandage 1963, Table 6); (2) a redshift of $\Delta\lambda/\lambda_0 = 0.3675$ (Greenstein and Matthews 1963); (3) the band pass of the optical spectral region from $\lambda = 3200$ Å to $\lambda = 6000$ Å in the laboratory system; and (4) an assumed distance of 1.0×10^9 pc obtained from the redshift and a Hubble constant of 100 km/sec 10^6 pc.

In view of these high-power levels, it is exceedingly surprising that variations in the optical flux have been observed in 3C 48, 3C 196, and 3C 273. Three-color photoelectric observations of 3C 48 on the UBV system were made in October, 1960, as part of the discovery procedure (Matthews and Sandage 1963). Photoelectric observations have been continued to the present with the results shown in Figure 1 and Table 1. These data show that the optical flux has changed by a factor of 1.4 at all three wavelengths over a period of approximately 600 days. This corresponds to a *change* of power output by about 4×10^{44} erg/sec—a value so large that the reality of the variation might well be questioned. The probable error of a single measurement in each color is about $\pm 0^m.02$, a value which is twenty times smaller than the observed variation. Because of this fact and because (1) two comparison stars which were observed before or after each observation of 3C 48 were constant to within $\pm 0^m.03$ and (2) the light-curves in all three colors are in phase, there can be no doubt that the long time-scale variation shown in Figure 1 is real. On the other hand, the short-term fluctuations near JD 2437600 and 2438300 with a characteristic period of 50 days are not well established, even though the ampli-

ALLAN R. SANDAGE, Mount Wilson and Palomar Observatories, Carnegie Institution of Washington and California Institute of Technology.

Reprinted from the *Astrophysical Journal*, **139**, 416–419, 1964.

tude of the variations is somewhat larger than the probable error. Special observations were made on three nights (October 22/23, 1962, October 23/24, 1962, and October 14/15, 1963) to monitor very short-term fluctuations of the order of minutes or hours. No variation greater than the probable error of $\pm 0^m02$ was observed over a time span of three hours on each of the three nights. Therefore, short-term fluctuations larger than 2 per cent appear to be absent.

The photoelectric data are less complete for 3C 273. Nevertheless, the results given in Table 2 show beyond doubt that the flux also varies for this object. This result is consistent with the more extensive photographic data of Smith and Hoffleit (1963) and of Sharov and Efremov (1963), which suggest large optical variations. That the variation shown in Table 2 is significant can be proved by noting that the observed magnitude of a nearby comparison star in the field of the radio object is constant to within about $\pm 0^m02$ over the entire interval of 10 months, whereas the magnitude of 3C 273 has

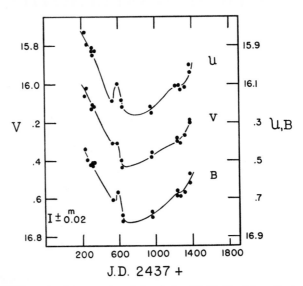

Fig. 1.—The light-curve in three wavelength bands for 3C 48. The left ordinate is the scale for V magnitudes. The right ordinate is the scale for U and B magnitudes. The data are from Table 1.

decreased by about 0^m20.

The data for 3C 196 consist of observations on only three nights over an interval of 20.5 months but these show beyond doubt that a variation has also taken place in this object. The data are given in the second part of Table 2 where it is seen that a change of 0^m24 in V occurred between May 15/16, 1963, and December 11/12, 1963, a value which is considerably larger than the probable error.

Because the first three objects studied have shown variability, it now becomes important to monitor all objects of the class (nine are known at this writing). The cause of the light variations is unknown at present, but whatever the mechanism, it apparently does not change the wavelength dependence of the optical radiation by a large factor because Tables 1 and 2 show that both $B - V$ and $U - B$ have remained nearly constant. It is of course important to extend the wavelength coverage, especially into the radio region, to decide between various mechanisms. Among many possible causes of the optical variations might be (1) a change in the high-frequency cut-off of relativistic electrons by new injections and subsequent energy decay, if indeed the optical flux is

TABLE 1
Photoelectric Data for 3C 48

Date	JD 2437+	V	B	U	B−V	U−B	Remarks
Oct. 24, 1960...	231.8	16.06	16.44	15.83	0.38	−0.61	....
Nov. 20, 1960...	258.8	16.02	16.50	15.89	.48	− .61	....
Jan. 13, 1961...	312.8	16.11	16.53	15.92	.42	− .61	....
Jan. 14, 1961...	313.8	16.13	16.52	15.91	.39	− .61	....
Jan. 15, 1961...	314.8	....	16.51	15.91	....	− .60	....
Jan. 17, 1961...	316.8	16.13	16.53	15.94	.40	− .59	....
Aug. 18, 1961...	529.8	16.31	16.71	16.19	.40	− .52	....
Oct. 12, 1961...	584.8	16.31	16.67	16.10	.36	− .57	Mean of 2
Dec. 5, 1961...	638.8	16.44	16.79	16.22	.35	− .57	Data by Baum
Dec. 6, 1961...	639.8	16.40	16.82	16.18	.42	− .64	Data by Baum
Oct. 23, 1962...	960.8	16.38	16.80	16.25	.42	− .55	Mean of 5
Oct. 24, 1962...	961.8	16.36	16.77	16.22	.41	− .55	Mean of 5
July 23, 1963...	1233.8	16.30	16.69	16.11	.39	− .58	....
July 24, 1963...	1234.8	16.29	16.66	16.11	.37	− .55	....
Aug. 26, 1963...	1267.8	16.31	16.69	16.13	.38	− .56	Data by Eggen
Oct. 15, 1963...	1317.8	16.27	16.67	16.12	.40	− .55	Mean of 4
Dec. 11, 1963...	1374.8	16.20	16.57	16.00	.37	− .58	Mean of 2
Dec. 12, 1963...	1375.8	16.20	16.62	16.04	0.42	−0.58	....

TABLE 2
Photoelectric Data for 3C 273 and 3C 196

Date	JD 2438+	V	B	U	B−V	U−B	Remarks
				3C 273			
Feb. 17, 1963...	077.8	12.66	12.80	11.91	0.14	−0.89	Mean of 5
Feb. 21, 1963...	081.8	12.69	12.82	11.93	.13	− .89	Data by Eggen
Feb. 24, 1963...	084.8	12.68	12.79	11.90	.11	− .89	Data by Eggen
Feb. 27, 1963...	087.8	12.74	12.87	11.96	.13	− .91	Data by Eggen
Mar. 14, 1963...	102.8	12.67	12.82	11.93	.15	− .89	Data by Kowal
Mar. 19, 1963...	107.8	12.71	12.87	11.96	.16	− .91	Data by Kowal
Mar. 20, 1963...	108.8	12.66	12.83	11.89	.17	− .94	Data by Kowal
Mar. 21, 1963...	109.8	12.74	12.89	11.99	.15	− .90	Data by Kowal
Mar. 26, 1963...	114.8	12.73	12.75	11.97	.02	− .78	Mean of 3
May 15, 1963...	164.8	12.69	12.87	12.04	.18	− .83	Mean of 2
May 16, 1963...	165.8	12.72	12.88	12.03	.16	− .85	....
May 17, 1963...	166.8	12.72	12.88	12.04	.16	− .84	....
May 24, 1963...	173.8	12.76	12.89	12.01	.13	− .88	....
May 25, 1963...	174.8	12.79	12.96	12.07	.17	− .89	....
Dec. 12, 1963...	375.8	12.85	13.05	12.18	0.20	−0.87	Mean of 3
	JD 2437+			3C 196			
Apr. 1, 1962...	755.8	17.79	18.35	17.91	0.56	−0.44	....
May 16, 1963...	1165.8	17.69	18.31	17.99	.62	− .32	....
Dec. 12, 1963...	1375.8	17.45	18.05	17.56	0.60	−0.49	....

caused by synchrotron radiation (but here the color index of the optical light should change); (2) a variation of the electron density of a high-temperature gas ($T_e = 50000°$ K) radiating by free-free and free-bound emission; and (3) storage and release of energy by an Eddington valve process similar to that in pulsating variables.

Systematic observation of all members of this class of objects is now under way, and it may eventually be possible to establish if the variations occur in all objects of this type and if the variations are periodic or of a random nature.

REFERENCES

Greenstein, J. L., and Matthews, T. A. 1963, *Nature*, **197**, 1041.*
Matthews, T. A., and Sandage, A. R. 1963, *Ap. J.*, **138**, 30.*
Schmidt, M. 1963, *Nature*, **197**, 1040.*
Sharov, A. S., and Efremov, Y. N. 1963, *Russ. A.J.*, **40**, 950.
Smith, Harlan J., and Hoffleit, D. 1963, *A.J.*, **68**, 292.

REDSHIFTS OF THE QUASI-STELLAR RADIO SOURCES 3C 47 AND 3C 147

chapter 20

MAARTEN SCHMIDT AND THOMAS A. MATTHEWS

The purpose of this letter is to communicate the identifications of the radio sources 3C 47 and 3C 147 as quasi-stellar objects with large redshifts. The positions of the radio sources given in Table 1 were determined in the course of an extensive program of

TABLE 1

OBSERVED DATA FOR 3C 47 AND 3C 147

Source	$\alpha(1950)$	$\delta(1950)$	$S(400 \text{ Mc/s})$ $10^{-26} \text{ Wm}^{-2} (\text{c/s})^{-1}$	n
3C 47:				
Radio.......	$01^h 33^m 40^s.6 \pm 1^s.0$	$+20°41'56'' \pm 8''$	12.9 ± 0.5	-0.89 ± 0.04
Opt.........	$01\ 33\ 39.8 \pm 0.2$	$+20\ 42\ 11\ \pm 3$	....	....
3C 147:				
Radio.......	$05\ 38\ 44.1 \pm 0.5$	$+49\ 49\ 39\ \pm 3$	46.3 ± 2.3	-0.56 ± 0.06
Opt........	$05\ 38\ 43.5 \pm 0.1$	$+49\ 49\ 43\ \pm 1$	....	....

position determinations carried out with the California Institute of Technology twin interferometer in the Owens Valley. The declinations have been published by Read (1963), the position of the optical object in 3C 147 by Griffin (1963). The table also gives the flux density at 400 Mc/s and the spectral index (Kellermann 1963). Existing interferometric data on 3C 47 (Maltby 1962; Allen, Anderson, Conway, Palmer, Reddish, and Rosen 1962) show that it may have a halo of 2' in diameter containing 75 per cent of the flux and a core of 4" diameter. Alternatively, the source may be a double with a component separation of about 70". The source 3C 147 is probably a double with separation 2".4, each component being smaller than 1", but a possible alternative is an elliptical distribution with axes of 1".9 by less than 1" (Rowson 1963).

MAARTEN SCHMIDT, Mount Wilson and Palomar Observatories, Carnegie Institution of Washington and California Institute of Technology. THOMAS A. MATTHEWS, Owens Valley Radio Observatory, California Institute of Technology.

Reprinted from the *Astrophysical Journal*, **139**, 781–785, 1964.

The position of the radio source 3C 47 practically coincides with that of a starlike object of visual magnitude 18; this object is notably blue on the plates of the National Geographic Society–Palomar Observatory Sky Survey. Spectra taken with the prime-focus spectrograph of the 200-inch telescope with a dispersion of 400 Å/mm in November, 1963, showed emission lines at $\lambda\lambda$ 3986, 4885, and 5510. These wavelengths could be represented to within a few Ångstroms (Table 2) on the assumption that they are lines of Mg II, [Ne V], and [Ne III], with a redshift $z = (\lambda - \lambda_0)/\lambda_0$ of 0.425. On this basis the N_1 line of [O III] would be expected at 7135 Å. Two spectra taken on 103a-U plates in December, 1963, did show the line at 7136 Å, as well as the fainter N_2 line of [O III]. The fact that Hβ was not detected must be due to the low speed of both F and U plates at the wavelength of interest. A broad band of emission observed around 6200 Å is a blend of Hγ and the λ 4363 line of [O III]. The widths of the other lines are about 20 Å. The λ 3727 line of [O II] is quite weak. The λ 3346 line of [Ne V], which should be about three times fainter than the one at λ 3426, is suspected on one of the plates. The λ 3968 line of [Ne III] is seen quite weakly, as expected; its wavelength has not been measured.

TABLE 2

WAVELENGTHS AND IDENTIFICATIONS OF
EMISSION LINES IN 3C 47

λ	Identif.	λ_0	1.425 λ_0
3986	Mg II	2798	3987
4885	[Ne V]	3426	4882
5310	[O II]	3727	5312
5510	[Ne III]	3869	5513
6200	Hγ, [O III]	4340, 4363	6185, 6217
7072	[O III]	4959	7066
7136	[O III]	5007	7135

With a Hubble constant H of 100 km/sec per Mpc the nominal distance czH^{-1} of 3C 47 becomes 1275 Mpc, and its absolute visual magnitude about -23. This object clearly belongs to the class of *quasi-stellar radio sources*, such as 3C 273 (Schmidt 1963) and 3C 48 (Greenstein and Matthews 1963). These objects of stellar appearance have optical luminosities considerably larger than those of the brightest galaxies.

The position of the radio source 3C 147 is close to that of a compact group of three faint stars, of visual magnitudes about 18, 19, and 20. At first the twentieth-magnitude object was suspected to be a galaxy related with the radio source. A spectrum in the blue with the slit across it and the eighteenth-magnitude object taken in October, 1962, showed no emission lines in the fainter object. The spectrum of the brighter object appeared to have unusually high brightness in the ultraviolet relative to that in the blue. Spectra taken subsequently in the visual region showed several emission features near 5800 Å. The first spectra seemed to indicate that the emission features were variable in wavelength and intensity; as a consequence, a considerable number of spectra, mostly with a dispersion of 400 Å/mm, was taken of this object. The weak, low-contrast emission features are determined by a small number of grains in the unwidened spectra. Some of the weak emission lines originally suspected have not been found on subsequent plates and most probably do not exist. Variability in the lines that do exist has not been confirmed.

Two emission lines exist without any doubt. Their observed wavelengths are 5760 and 5976 Å. The width of the lines is about 30 Å. All individual measures of wavelengths are given in Table 3. There are two values of the redshift z for which these two lines can be identified with emission lines often seen in planetary nebulae, radio galaxies, and quasi-stellar objects. If $z = 0.229$ the lines would be identified with the $\lambda\,4686$ line of He II and Hβ, respectively. The intensity ratio of the lines does not favor this explanation: the line at 5760 Å is two to three times stronger than the one at 5976 Å; however, the He II line is usually much fainter, and never brighter, than Hβ in planetary nebulae. All available spectra were searched for other lines at the wavelengths predicted on the basis of the above redshift. None were found, notably not those of [O III] and [Ne V] that are always seen in high-excitation planetaries and radio galaxies that show the He II line. The combined evidence makes the above value for the redshift quite unattractive.

The alternate value of the redshift is 0.545, on which basis the two lines are identified with the $\lambda\,3727$ line of [O II] and the $\lambda\,3869$ line of [Ne III], respectively. A search for

TABLE 3

INDIVIDUALLY MEASURED WAVELENGTHS AND IDENTIFICATIONS
OF EMISSION LINES IN 3C 147

Plate No.	Wavelength (Å)				
N 1818(1)..........	....	....	5291:	5760	5976	....
(2)..........	....	....	....	5762:	5981:	....
1852..........	....	....	....	5754:	5980:	....
1854(1)..........	4843:	....	5758	5972:	....
(2)..........	4836	5287	5755	5975	6127
(3)..........	....	....	5762	....	....
1856..........	....	....	5759	5976	....
1858..........	....	....	5762	5975	6126:
1860..........	....	5288:	5763	5970	....
1879..........	....	....	5757	....	....
1882..........	....	5296:	5762	5976	6136
2132..........	....	....	5761	5978	6137
Mean λ..........	4839:	5290:	5760	5976	6132
Identif..........	O III	[Ne V]	[O II]	[Ne III]	[Ne III]
λ₀..........	3133	3426	3727	3869	3968
1.545 λ₀..........	4840	5293	5759	5977	6130

other lines to be expected on the basis of this redshift was moderately successful. The $\lambda\,3968$ line of [Ne III] could be found near 6130 Å on four exposures. Individually uncertain measurements were made of an emission feature near 5290 Å on four plates, and of a feature near 4840 Å on two plates (cf. Table 3). The wavelengths of these emissions correspond closely to that of the $\lambda\,3426$ line of [Ne V] and that of the $\lambda\,3133$ line of O III, respectively. Although the reality of these emissions on each individual plate is uncertain, the small range in measured wavelengths and the fact that the five features detected are those that are strongest in the relevant range of wavelengths in the planetary nebula NGC 7027 (Aller, Bowen, and Wilson 1963) leave little doubt that the redshift $z = 0.545$ is indeed correct. This redshift is the largest one determined so far, exceeding that of 3C 295 (0.461, Minkowski 1960) by about 20 per cent. The corresponding nominal distance czH^{-1} of 1635 Mpc yields an absolute visual magnitude of about -25, where we have corrected for about 1 magnitude absorption in the Galaxy (Sandage 1964).

Redshifts are now available for four quasi-stellar radio sources. The main results are collected in Table 4. The "size" given is the separation of the two components of the radio source on the assumption that it is indeed double. The radio luminosities have been computed by integration of the power law for the flux density to an assumed emitted frequency of 10^{11} c/s. The lower emitted cutoff frequency was assumed to be 10^7 c/s unless stated otherwise in Table 4. The major uncertainty in the calculated radio luminosities comes from the uncertainty in the upper cutoff frequencies. Both luminosities and linear sizes have been computed on the basis of an evolving world model with zero cosmological constant and deceleration parameter $q_0 = 0$ (Sandage 1961).

All four sources are seen to have very large radio luminosities, of the same order as that of the most powerful radio galaxies Cyg A, Her A, and 3C 295. The quasi-stellar source 3C 147 has the largest radio luminosity, 2×10^{45} erg/sec, equal to that of the intrinsically brightest radio galaxy, 3C 295. The radio spectrum of 3C 147 shows marked curvature at the low-frequency end (Conway, Kellermann, and Long 1963). The total optical luminosities of the objects depend to a large extent on the bolometric correction. They probably range roughly from 10^{45} to 10^{46} erg/sec, and are for each source larger than the radio luminosity. Sandage has measured the colors of all these objects and will discuss them shortly.

The source 3C 47 is the weakest member of the group, both in radio output and in optical luminosity; it also has the largest radio size and might be the oldest member of

TABLE 4

DATA FOR FOUR QUASI-STELLAR RADIO
SOURCES WITH KNOWN REDSHIFTS

Source	z	M_v	L (Radio)* (erg/sec)	"Size" (Radio) (kpc)
3C 47.........	0.425	−23	1.5×10^{44}	250
3C 48.........	.367	−25	4.7×10^{44}	< 3
3C 147........	.545	−25	2.0×10^{45}	10
3C 273........	0.158	−26	3.1×10^{44}	40

* Computed by integration between emitted frequencies of 10^7 c/s and 10^{11} c/s, except for the following lower limits of observed frequency: 10^8 c/s for 3C 48, 5×10^7 c/s for 3C 147, 10^9 c/s for component B of 3C 273.

the group. In addition it has a straight spectrum at low frequencies, unlike the other quasi-stellar sources. The optical flux for 3C 47 falls on or above a straight-line extrapolation of the unusually steep radio spectrum. This is quite different from the other quasi-stellar objects for which the optical flux is well below the straight-line extrapolation (Matthews and Sandage 1963).

The optical spectra of these four quasi-stellar objects vary more among themselves than those of radio galaxies (Schmidt 1964). The λ 3727 line of [O II] is prominent in 3C 48 and 3C 147, weak in 3C 47, probably absent in 3C 273. The λ 2798 doublet of Mg II first found in 3C 273 is also prominent in 3C 48, clearly present in 3C 47, but weak or absent in 3C 147. These differences are presumably due to variations in ionization, excitation, electron temperature and density (Greenstein and Schmidt 1964). A practical consequence is that the redshift of a quasi-stellar object cannot be determined with reasonable certainty from a single emission line only. For that reason an attempt by Shklovsky (1963) to determine the redshift of the quasi-stellar radio source 3C 286 from a single emission line (Schmidt 1962) must be considered premature until at least one other emission feature has been detected and identified.

One of us (M. S.) wishes to thank Dr. I. S. Bowen for a valuable discussion. The other (T. A. M.) has conducted this investigation under the program of research in radio astronomy at the California Institute of Technology which is supported by the United States Office of Naval Research under contract Nonr 220(19).

REFERENCES

Allen, L. R., Anderson, B., Conway, R. G., Palmer, H. P., Reddish, V. C., and Rosen, B. 1962, *M.N.*, **124**, 477.
Aller, L. H., Bowen, I. S., and Wilson, O. C. 1963, *Ap. J.*, **138**, 1013.
Conway, R. G., Kellermann, K. I., and Long, R. J. 1963, *M.N.*, **125**, 261.
Greenstein, J. L., and Matthews, T. A. 1963, *Nature*, **197**, 1041.*
Greenstein, J. L., and Schmidt, M. 1964, *Ap. J.*, **140**, 1.*
Griffin, R. G. 1963, *A.J.*, **68**, 421.
Kellermann, K. I. 1963, thesis, California Institute of Technology.
Maltby, P. 1962, *Ap. J. Suppl.*, **7**, 124.
Matthews, T. A., and Sandage, A. R. 1963, *Ap. J.*, **138**, 30.*
Minkowski, R. 1960, *Ap. J.*, **132**, 908.
Read, R. B. 1963, *Ap. J.*, **138**, 1.
Rowson, B. 1963, *M.N.*, **125**, 177.
Sandage, A. R. 1961, *Ap. J.*, **133**, 355.
———. 1964, private communication.
Schmidt, M. 1962, *Ap. J.*, **136**, 684.
———. 1963, *Nature*, **197**, 1040.*
———. 1964, in preparation.
Shklovsky, I. S. 1963, *Astr. Circ. U.S.S.R.*, No. 250.

THE BRIGHTNESS OF 3C 273

chapter 21   AT 2.2 μ

Harold L. Johnson

The recent optical identification of the radio object 3C 273 with a thirteenth-magnitude starlike object (Schmidt 1963) has provided the incentive for an attempt to measure the brightness of this object at 2.2 μ (magnitude K). It has a visual magnitude of 12.7 (Sandage 1964) and, if its radiation is indeed due to the synchrotron process, might be bright enough at 2.2 μ to be measurable with our infrared photometer. The attempt to measure 3C 273 at 2.2 μ was successful and the following K magnitude was obtained:

$$K = 9.5 \pm 0.2 \text{ (p.e.) mag} .$$

The total time of observation was about 4 hours, including guiding time; of this time, one-half was spent measuring the object-plus-sky and the rest, the sky alone. The data

TABLE 1

THE PHOTOMETRY OF 3C 273

Object	V	$U-V$	$B-V$	$V-R$	$V-I$	$V-K$
3C 273.........	12.72	−0.74	+0.14	+0.33	+0.83	+3.2

were taken as five independent observations and the probable error, above, was computed from the comparison of these five observations. The photometer was mounted on the 28-inch telescope of the Lunar and Planetary Laboratory.

Our data for 3C 273, combined with those of Sandage (1964), are listed in Table 1. For the *UBV* photometry, the averages of Sandage's measures are given. Sandage has shown that the brightness of the object is variable but, even so, the data of Table 1 may be of considerable significance.

Harold L. Johnson, Lunar and Planetary Laboratory, University of Arizona, Tucson, Arizona.

Reprinted from the *Astrophysical Journal*, **139**, 1022–1023, 1964.

If we compute, by the process outlined elsewhere (Johnson 1964), the absolute energy fluxes from the object, the data of Table 2 are obtained. We agree with Oke (1963) that the spectral energy distribution for 3C 273 is quite unlike that of any known star. The energy distribution is relatively flat from the ultraviolet to the red; it begins to rise at the *I* filter (0.87 μ) and continues to rise out to the *K* filter (2.2 μ). These data appear to

TABLE 2

THE ABSOLUTE FLUX FROM 3C 273

OBJECT	FILTER BAND					
	U	*B*	*V*	*R*	*I*	*K* (watts/m²/c/s)
3C 273..........	3.0	3.2	3.2	3.0	3.6	9.2×10^{-28}

agree with the idea that the source of radiation in 3C 273 might be the synchrotron process.

It may be of interest to note here that the amount of power from 3C 273 which came from the 28-inch telescope and entered the photometer was approximately 8×10^{-15} watts. The actual power incident upon the lead-sulphide cell was reduced to about 3×10^{-15} watts by losses in the filter, field lens, etc., in the photometer.

REFERENCES

Johnson, H. L. 1964, *Bull. of the Tonantzintla and Tacubaya Obs.*, in press.
Oke, J. B. 1963, *Nature*, **197**, 1040.*
Sandage, A. 1964, *Ap. J.*, **139**, 416.
Schmidt, M. 1963, *Nature*, **197**, 1040. *

ON THE MECHANISM OF
RADIATION OF THE GALAXY

chapter 22 3C 273B

V. L. Ginzburg, L. M. Ozernoy, and S. I. Syrovatzkii

The extra-galactic radio source 3C 273B, identified (Schmidt 1963) with a starlike object of the twelfth magnitude, is an example of a recently discovered new type of extra-galactic object. This galaxy[1] is exceptionally bright ($M_v = -26.5$) and has a very small size ($D \sim 4 \times 10^{16}$ cm; this estimate follows from the observations of the irregular changes of the brightness per week; see Smith and Hoffleit [1963] and Sharov and Efremov [1963]). Together with the peculiarities of the spectrum (Oke 1963) this points to a highly unusual nature for that object.

Because of this, it is interesting to investigate the possibility that the continuous optical radiation of the galaxy 3C 273B is connected with magnetobrems (synchrotron) mechanism. Making such an assumption, already expressed in the literature, we will survey the corresponding energy requirements and some observational consequences.

According to Oke (1963) the optical spectrum $I_\nu \sim \nu^{-\alpha}$ of the object 3C 273B has in the interval between $\nu_1 = 3.6 \times 10^{14}$ Hertz and $\nu_2 = 9.1 \times 10^{14}$ Hertz negative spectral index $\alpha = -0.28$. Thus, the exponent of the energy spectrum of the electrons $N(E) \sim E^{-\gamma}$ should be equal $\gamma = 2\alpha + 1 = 0.44$. Under stationary conditions, such a character of the spectrum points to a continuous output of the electrons from the radiating region with a strong field. Actually, for the concentration of the electrons $N(E)dE$ in the stationary case the continuity equation in the energy space is valid:

$$-\frac{\partial}{\partial E} [C(E) N(E)] = q(E). \tag{1}$$

Here $C(E) = -dE/dt$ and $q(E)dE$ is the number of electrons with the energy in the interval $\{E, E + dE\}$, supplied by the sources. For the magnetic as well as the Compton

V. L. Ginzburg, L. M. Ozernoy, and S. I. Syrovatzkii, P. N. Lebedev Physical Institute, Academy of Sciences, U.S.S.R.

[1] Object 3C 273B is most probably not a star cluster, but a "superstar" (Hoyle and Fowler 1963). Thus, we use the term "galaxy" for this object only in a conditional sense in the absence of established terminology.

damping, the loss $C(E) = $ const. E^2 and so, with $N(E) = $ const. $E^{-\gamma}$, the power of the source is

$$\int Eq\,(E)\,dE = (\gamma - 2)\int C\,(E)\,N\,(E)\,dE .$$

Obviously, for $\gamma < 2$ the output of the "sources" is negative and for $\gamma < 1$ its absolute value is greater than the loss. The use of the stationarity condition is based on the following arguments. The galaxy 3C 273B has been photographed for 76 years (Smith and Hoffleit 1963; Sharov and Efremov 1963), and the diminishing of the brightness amounts to or rather does not exceed 0.2^m per century (Smith and Hoffleit 1963). If this diminishing is real, then according to the exponential law, the luminosity goes down e times in 550 years. Obviously, this value gives the lower limit of its age. Meanwhile, as one will see from what follows, the characteristic time of the loss of the radiated electrons is much smaller.

The electrons should leave the radiating region. This restricts its effective dimensions, l; namely, l cannot noticeably exceed the displacement of a relativistic electron during the characteristic time of energy loss T.

We make the convention that $l = cT/3$, i.e., the electrons leave with mean velocity $v \simeq c/3$ (very likely, l is even smaller). Then taking into account the loss due to magnetic and Compton damping, we have

$$l = \frac{cT}{3} = \frac{c}{3}\left(\frac{4}{9}\,\frac{e^4 H^2}{m^3 c^5}\,\frac{E}{m\,c^2} + \frac{4}{3}\,c\,\sigma_0 W_\varphi\,\frac{E}{m^2 c^4}\right)^{-1} , \tag{2}$$

where H is the intensity of the magnetic field; E is the energy of the electron;

$$\sigma_0 = \frac{8\pi}{3}\left(\frac{e^2}{m\,c^2}\right)^2 = 6.65 \times 10^{-25}\ \text{cm}^2$$

is the Thomson cross-section, and W_φ is the energy density of radiation.

Assume that the full energy of the relativistic electrons

$$W_e = \frac{H^2}{8\pi}\,V ,$$

where V is the volume of the radiating region. Under these conditions, the energy of the electrons and the field is near to the minimal. Thus (see Ginzburg and Syrovatzkii [1963], p. 115)

$$W_e = 0.19\left[A\,(\gamma, \nu)\,\frac{L_\nu}{4\pi}\right]^{4/7} (6D^2 l)^{3/7} , \tag{3}$$

where $L_\nu = 4\pi F_\nu R^2$ is the spectral luminosity for the frequency ν, D is the linear size of the optical source, l is the thickness of the radiating layer ($l \ll D$, $V = \pi D^2 l$), and R is the distance to the source. The intensity of the electrons is here chosen $I_e(E) = c/4\pi N(E) = KE^{-\gamma}$. One should remember, however, that using for $\gamma < 2$ the coefficient $A(\gamma, \nu)$ in equation (3) corresponds to the assumption about the power character of the spectrum of the electrons in a very large energy interval. In order to get the minimal value W_e, we assume that all the radiation of an electron with the energy $E = E_m(\nu)$ is at the frequency ν and the power spectrum of the electrons ranges only from the energy $E_m(\nu_1)$ to $E_m(\nu_2)$ where

$$E_m(\nu) = m\,c^2\sqrt{(4\pi m\,c/3\,e\,H_\perp)(\nu/0.29)} = 5.1 \times 10^2\sqrt{\nu/H}\ \text{eV} \tag{4}$$

is the energy of the electrons whose spectral maximum of radiation occurs at the frequency ν.

In $A(\gamma, \nu)$ one has to put $y_2(\gamma) = y_1(\gamma) = 0.24$ and $a(\gamma) = 0.31 \times (0.24)^{\gamma-1/2}$.

According to data of Hazard et al. (1963), Smith and Hoffleit (1963), and Oke (1963), we put[2]

$$R = 1.6 \times 10^{27} \text{ cm}, \quad L_\nu(\lambda = 5600 \text{ Å}) = 3.5 \times 10^{-25} \, 4\pi R^2 = 1.1 \times 10^{31} \text{ erg/sec Hertz}$$

(the same result one gets if one assumes the optical luminosity $L = 1.3 \times 10^{46}$ erg/sec and $\Delta\nu \sim 10^{15}$). $D \simeq 4 \times 10^{16} \, \zeta$ cm. With these values

$$W_e \simeq 4.4 \times 10^{42} l^{3/7} \, \zeta^{6/7} \text{ erg}, \qquad H \simeq 1.5 \times 10^5 \, l^{-2/7} \, \zeta^{-4/7} \text{ oersted}. \tag{5}$$

TABLE 1

Source	φ	D (cm)	a	$F_{960\text{MHz}}$ (erg/cm² sec Hertz)	L_p (erg/sec)	W_e (erg)	H (oersted)
A:							
Nucleus......	2″	1.6×10^{22}⎫	0.9	1.25×10^{-22}⎫	2.5×10^{43}	1.2×10^{57}	1.2×10^{-4}
Halo........	6″	4.8×10^{22}⎭		1.25×10^{-22}⎭		4.9×10^{57}	4.6×10^{-5}
B:							
Nucleus......	0″.5	4×10^{21}⎫	0	$2.0\ \times10^{-22}$⎫	2.3×10^{43}	1.0×10^{56}	2.7×10^{-4}
Halo........	7″	5.6×10^{22}⎭		$0.5\ \times10^{-22}$⎭		1.3×10^{57}	1.9×10^{-5}

For the magnetobrems radiation in the discussed frequency interval are responsible electrons with the energy

$$E_m \simeq 1.3 \times \nu^{1/2} \, l^{1/7} \, \zeta^{2/7} \text{ eV}. \tag{6}$$

At the surface of the object, the energy density of the photon radiation gives $W_\varphi = 5.4 \times 10^{13} \, \zeta^{-2}$ eV/cm³. Using equations (5) and (6) and solving equation (2) with respect to l with $E_m = E_m(\nu_2)$, we find

$$l = 2.6 \times 10^{11} \, \zeta^{3/2} \text{ cm}, \quad V = 1.3 \times 10^{45} \, \zeta^{7/2} \text{ cm}^3, \quad W_e = 3.5 \times 10^{47} \, \zeta^{3/2} \text{ erg},$$
$$H = 82 \, \zeta^{-1} \text{ oersted}, \quad E_m(\nu_1) = 1.1 \times 10^9 \, \zeta^{-1} \text{ eV}, \quad E_m(\nu_2) = 1.7 \times 10^9 \, \zeta^{-1} \text{ eV}. \tag{7}$$

At the same time, for example, the losses due to the Compton scattering are 3 times less than to the magnetobrems radiation (for every ζ).

For the comparison, we will consider the energy requirements for the relativistic electrons of the components A and B of the radio source 3C 273, whose magnetobrems nature of the radiation is without doubt. In Table 1 are given spectral indices and sizes of both components from Hazard et al. (1963) and also computed spectral densities of the radiation flow of the separate components from the data about the total flow (Harris

[2] In the Einstein–de Sitter model, the photometric distance from 3C 273 is 5 per cent smaller and the optical luminosity 40 per cent smaller than the cited values. We will neglect these differences as the accuracy of the observational data is not too great. We notice, in particular, that the cited value D at $\zeta = 1$ gives, most likely, the lower limit. Thus, a number of the following quantitative estimates necessarily have a tentative character.

and Roberts 1960) and spectral data (Hazard *et al.* 1963). In the last three columns are given radio luminosities

$$L_p = 4\pi R^2 \int_{\nu_1}^{\nu_2} F_\nu d\nu$$

(in all the cases, it was assumed that $\nu_1 = 10^8$ Hertz and $\nu_2 = 3 \times 10^9$ Hertz), energy of the relativistic electrons, and the mean value for the intensity of the magnetic field. We emphasize that these estimates for the total energy are minimal (in particular, here as well as in eq. [5], the energy of the proton-nucleus component of the cosmic rays was not taken into account). The characteristic duration of the emission of radiation for the nucleus of the radio source B is $T_p \simeq W_e$, nucleus$/L_p \simeq 10^{13}$ sec, and for the halo of both sources $T_p \simeq 3 \times 10^{14}$ sec.

For the optical source the time of the emission of radiation $T_0 \simeq W_e/L \simeq 30 \, \zeta^{3/2}$ sec, even if one takes into account only losses for the optical radiation $L = 1.3 \times 10^{46}$ erg/sec. Thus, in the case of the magnetobrems nature of the optical radiation of the galaxy 3C 273B, one should have practically continuous generation of the relativistic electrons with the characteristic energy (Hazard *et al.* 1963). Taking into account the Compton losses of the electrons, their leaving the region emitting optical frequencies and also their optical radiation inside the interval $\nu_1 \leq \nu \leq \nu_2$, the power of injection of the relativistic electrons amounts to, probably, not less than 10^{47} erg/sec. For $T = 10^3$ years, this corresponds to the injection energy $W > 3 \times 10^{57}$ erg. Such an energy is by no means unusual for galaxies. At the same time, the necessity of assuring the given power of injection imposes important requirements on the models of the "superstars."

The optical radiation of the galaxy 3C 273B is not polarized (Moroz and Yesipov 1963). Thus, it could have also quite non-magnetobrems nature.[3] If the radiation of the object is a bremsstrahlung origin (free-free and free-bound transitions) then according to the peculiarities of the spectrum, it cannot be considered to be black-body radiation (Oke 1963). Here one has, however, some other possibilities. We mention only that a sphere with the radius $R = 2 \times 10^{16} \, \zeta$ cm will radiate $L = 10^{46}$ erg/sec if its effective temperature $T_{eff} \simeq 13700° \, \zeta^{-1/2}$. As it was said one cannot consider the radiation to be black, but the cited value T_{eff} from our point of view does not exclude the possibility of a bremsstrahlung mechanism of the radiation of the object. At the same time, the character of the spectrum of other starlike extra-galactic sources makes the hypothesis about the bremsstrahlung nature of the radiation much less probable (this remark is due to I. S. Shklovskii).

The fundamental question of the mechanism of the optical radiation of the galaxy 3C 273B can be, in principle, solved in a different way as follows:

If the mechanism of the optical radiation of the galaxy 3C 273B is magnetobrems, then this galaxy should be also the source of an exceptionally powerful γ-radiation. In the collision of a relativistic electron with the energy $E \ll (mc^2)^2/\langle\epsilon\rangle$ with photons with the average energy $\langle\epsilon\rangle$, there are created γ-rays with the average energy

$$E_\gamma = \tfrac{4}{3}\langle\epsilon\rangle\left(\frac{E}{mc^2}\right)^2. \tag{8}$$

If the average energy of photons $\langle\epsilon\rangle \simeq 2$ eV, then with $E \sim (1 \div 3) \times 10^9 \, \zeta^{1/2}$ eV one gets γ-rays with the energy $E_\gamma \sim (10^7 \div 10^8) \, \zeta$ eV (see also Ginzburg and Syrovatzkii [1964] and Felton and Morrison [1963]). The total flux of the γ-rays is equal to the Compton losses, i.e., in our case equals, e.g., 5×10^{45} erg/sec. Thus, on the Earth, the

---

[3] The opposite statement is, of course, not true, as the magnetobrems radiation can, as the result of several reasons (Ginzburg and Syrovatzkii 1963) be completely depolarized.

flux of γ-rays $F_\gamma \simeq 5 \times 10^{45}/4 \pi R^2 \simeq 1.6 \times 10^{-10}$ erg/cm^2 sec. For the γ-rays with the average energy $E_\gamma \sim 10^7 \zeta$ eV this corresponds to the flux of

$$F_\gamma^* = \frac{F_v}{E_\gamma} \sim 10^{-5} \zeta^{-1} \text{ photon cm}^2 \text{ sec .} \tag{9}$$

According to Ginzburg and Syrovatzkii (1964) the intensity of the Compton γ-rays for $I_e(E) = K_e E^{-0.44}$ equals

$$I_\gamma(E_\gamma) = \tfrac{2}{3} \sigma_0 W_\varphi K_e (m c^2)^{0.56} (\tfrac{4}{3}\epsilon)^{-1.28} E_\gamma^{-0.72} . \tag{10}$$

So, calculating the radiation toward us over a half-sphere,

$$F_\gamma(E_{\gamma 1} \leq E \leq E_{\gamma 2}) = \frac{\pi D^2 l}{2R^2} \int_{E_{1\gamma}}^{E_{2\gamma}} I_\gamma(E_\gamma) \, dE_\gamma \simeq 5 \times 10^{-6} \zeta^{-1} \text{ photon cm}^2 \text{ sec} , \tag{11}$$

where we took the values

$$E_{\gamma_1} = 2.7 \times 10^6 \zeta \text{ eV and } E_{\gamma_2} = 10^8 \zeta \text{ eV .}$$

Limits E_{γ_1} and E_{γ_2} correspond to the limits $E_1 = 5 \times 10^8 \zeta^{1/2}$ eV and $E_2 = 3 \times 10^9 \zeta^{1/2}$ eV (see eq. [8]). Such a widening of the energy interval of the electrons as compared with that used in equation (7) is used to calculate approximately the contribution from the electrons radiating light outside the interval of the visible frequencies. Equation (11) agrees with the estimate (9). One has to note that the flux (11) is very great. It suffices to say that the expected intensity of the galactic γ-rays gives $I_\gamma \leq 10^{-4}$ photon/cm^2 sec sterad (see Ginzburg and Syrovatzkii [1964]); for a γ-telescope with an opening angle 10° this corresponds to a flux $F_\gamma^* < 3.10^{-6}$ photon/cm^2 sec. The necessity of measuring the flux of γ-rays from galaxy 3C 273B is obvious.

REFERENCES

Felton, J. E., and Morrison, P. 1963, *Phys. Rev. Letters*, **10**, 453.
Ginzburg, V. L., and Syrovatzkii, S. I. 1963, *The Origin of the Cosmic Rays* (Moscow).
———. 1964, *J.E.T.F.*, **46**, 1865.
Harris, D. E., and Roberts, J. A. 1960, *Pub. A.S.P.*, **72**, 237.
Hazard, C., Mackey, M. B., and Shimmins, A. J. 1963, *Nature*, **197**, 1037. *
Hoyle, F., and Fowler, W. A. 1963, *Nature*, **197**, 533.*
Moroz, V. I., and Yesipov, V. R. 1963, *Information Bulletin on Variable Stars*, No. 31, Commission 27 of I.A.U.
Oke, J. B. 1963, *Nature*, **197**, 1040.*
Schmidt, M. 1963, *Nature*, **197**, 1040.*
Sharov, A. S., and Efremov, J. N. 1963, *Information Bulletin on Variable Stars*, No. 23, Commission 27 of I.A.U. (*Soviet Astr.—A.J.*, **40**, 950).
Smith, H. J., and Hoffleit, D. 1963, *Nature*, **198**, 650.*

chapter 23

ON THE MAGNETIC FIELDS OF COLLAPSING MASSES AND ON THE NATURE OF SUPERSTARS

V. L. GINZBURG

The discovery of superstars (starlike extra-galactic objects 3C 48, 3C 273B and others; see Greenstein, Matthews, Oke, and Schmidt [1963]); and the attempts to find the mechanism of the formation of radio galaxies called attention to the problem of the gravitational collapse of the large masses of gas (Hoyle, Fowler, Burbidge, and Burbidge 1963; Zeldovitch 1963). It is still not clear in what manner and under what conditions a cloud of gas or a protostar with a mass reaching $10^8 \, M \odot$ can form and collapse as a single entity. Also, it has not been shown that, if one takes into account that the problem is not completely spherical, the gravitational collapse can really lead, at least in some cases, to the appearance of the observable superstars and powerful explosions which are responsible for the formation of radio galaxies. Nevertheless, it is fully justified to try now to analyze different possibilities and astrophysical data, proceeding from the assumption of the collapse of large masses (in the following they will be called protostars). In Hoyle *et al.* (1963) such an analysis proceeds in two directions, the first of which is connected with going outside the limits of the real physical notion (the introduction of a C-field with negative-energy density, the assumption about the "creation" of matter). Such attempts seem to us, at least, premature, and we will base the following discussion on the general theory of relativity without any modifications. The second possibility discussed in Hoyle *et al.* (1963) is connected with taking into account the fact that a collapsing protostar has a gravitational field (at a distance $r \gg R_g = 2GM/c^2$ the gravitational potential has the Newtonian value $\varphi = -[GM/r]$). Therefore, the collapsing protostar contributes to the dynamics of the system—a cluster of galaxies, a single galaxy, or a double star, one of whose components collapses. In the co-moving system of coordinates, the time of the collapse τ is of the same order as the time of fall of a freely falling particle in a field with a potential $\varphi = -(GM/r)$. From this, as well as more rigorously from Hoyle *et al.* (1963) and Oppenheimer and Snyder (1939), we get the value $\tau \sim (G\rho_0)^{-1/2}$, where $\rho_0 = (3M/4\pi R_0^3)$ is the initial density of the protostar (initial radius $R_0 \gg R_g$). As for an outside observation (in the region with quasi-Galilean metric) the surface of the collapsing protostar reaches gravitational radius only after an infinite time, this surface could be, in principle, observed for fairly long. However,

V. L. GINZBURG, P. N. Lebedev Institute of Physics, Academy of Sciences, U.S.S.R.

283

the diminishing of the surface and the deflection of the light rays (Oppenheimer and Snyder 1939) causes a decrease in luminosity, and thus it is hardly possible to observe the surface of a collapsing star at any later stage of its collapse. The detection of such an object by the deflection of the light rays coming from other sources and passing near it also requires extremely favorable conditions.

In connection with the above remarks, we consider it worthwhile to determine the possible role of the magnetic field of a collapsing protostar.

During an isotropic compression of a sufficiently well conducting protostar with an initial field H_0, this field, due to the conservation of flux $\int H d\rho \sim HR^2$, will increase according to the law

$$H(R) = H_0 \left(\frac{\rho}{\rho_0}\right)^{2/3} = H_0 \left(\frac{R_0}{R}\right)^2. \tag{1}$$

Understanding by $H(R)$ the field at the surface and assuming the field inside the protostar to be a dipole field, we can consider that the effective magnetic moment of the protostar changes according to the law

$$\mu(R) \sim H(R)R^3 \sim H_0 R_0^2 R \sim \mu(R_0)\frac{R}{R_0}, \qquad H(r) \sim \frac{H_0 R_0^2 R}{r^3},$$

TABLE 1

Example	$M/M_\odot$	R_0 (cm)	ρ_0 (g/cm³)	$\tau \sim (G\rho_0)^{-1/2}$ (sec)	R_g (cm)	H_0 (oersted)	$H(R \sim R_g)$ (oersted)
1.............	10^8	10^{19}	10^{-16}	3.10^{11}	10^{13}	10^{-3}	10^9
2.............	10^3	10^{12}	1	3.10^3	10^8	1	10^8
3.............	1	10^{11}	1	3.10^3	10^5	1	10^{12}

where $H(r)$— field at a distance $r > R$ from a protostar with the radius R. For a non-relativistic computation we cannot consider the region $R \lesssim R_g$. If, however, one puts $R = \xi R_g$, then the estimations of the orders of magnitude are good with $\xi \simeq 2 \div 3$. This means that for the rough estimations below one can put $R \sim R_g$. In Table 1 we give three completely arbitrary examples. It is obvious that the strong fields can be attained only if during the time of the collapse τ the field will not fade out as a result of a finite conductivity σ. From this follows the condition (see Pikelner [1961]; we put $R \sim R_g$):

$$\tau \ll t_0 \sim \frac{4\pi\sigma(R_g)R_g^2}{c^2}. \tag{2}$$

For the stars of the same type as the Sun $\sigma_0 \sim 10^{16}$, and if the average temperature during the compression were constant then $\sigma(R_g) \sim \sigma_0$ and $t_0 \sim 10^6$; for examples 1 and 2 for the average temperature of the Sun we get $t_0 \sim 10^{22}$ and $t_0 \sim 10^{12}$ sec. In all the cases, condition (2) is satisfied.[1]

Therefore, for the collapsing protostars, one can expect the conservation of field, although the finite conclusion cannot be drawn before the more consistent determination of the conductivity of the object for $R \sim R_g$.

[1] Condition (2) is too strong so long as we compare the time during which R changes from R_0 to $R \sim R_g$ (time of falling) with the time of damping in the already compressed state. The time of fall from the distance $\sim R_g$ is of the order $\tau_0 \sim R_g/c$. Thus, the necessary condition of the conservation of field probably has the form $\tau_0 \ll t_0$, i.e., $\sigma(R_g) \gg c/4\pi Rg = c^3/8\pi GM$.

The magnetic energy of the protostar

$$W_M(R) \sim \frac{H^2}{8\pi}\frac{4\pi}{3}R^3 \sim H_0^2 R_0^3 \frac{R_0}{R} \sim W_M(R_0)\frac{R_0}{R}$$

(see equation [1]). The energy $W_M(R_0)$ is negligible in comparison with the gravitational energy $|\Omega(R_0)| \sim GM^2/R_0$ and obviously

$$\frac{W_M(R)}{|\Omega(R)|} \sim \frac{W_M(R_0)}{|\Omega(R_0)|}.$$

For the examples given above, this ratio is of the order 10^{-6} (for $M \sim 10^8\ M\odot$) and $\sim 10^{-16}$ (for $M \sim M\odot$). At the same time in the first of these cases, the absolute value $W_M(R_g) \sim 10^{56}$ is quite large ($|\Omega(R_g)| \sim M_c^2 \sim 10^{62}$ for $M \sim 10^8\ M\odot$).

More important, of course, is the problem of the change of the magnetic field during the relativistic stage of the collapse. We hope to discuss this problem in Ginzburg and Ozernoy (1964), and now in connection with it, however, we can make some remarks. One can show that in the Schwarzschild metric (see, e.g., Landau and Lifschitz [1953]) the field of a constant magnetic dipole has the form (the dipole is directed along the axis $\theta = 0$):

$$H_r = \frac{2\cos\theta}{r^3}f(r)\mu, \qquad H_\theta = \frac{\sin\theta}{r^3}\psi(r)\mu,$$

$$f(r) = \frac{3r^3}{R_g^3}\left[\ln\left(1 - \frac{R_g}{r}\right) + \frac{R_g}{r} + \frac{1}{2}\left(\frac{R_g}{r}\right)^2\right], \qquad (3)$$

$$\psi(r) = \frac{3r^2}{R_g^2}\left[\frac{1}{1 - R_g/r} + 2\frac{r}{R_g}\ln\left(\frac{R_g}{r}\right) + 1\right]\sqrt{1 - R_g/r}.$$

Of course, $f(r) \to 1$ and $\psi(r) \to 1$ for $r \gg R_g$. From expression (3) it follows that the dipole field approaching gravitational radius increases unboundedly ($f[r] \simeq -3\ln[1 - R_g/r]$ and $\psi[r] \simeq 3[1 - R_g/r]^{-1/2}$ for $r \to R_g$). In such a field, the component of the energy momentum tensor $T_0^0 = -(H^2/8\pi)$ increases as $(1 - [R_g/r])^{-1}$ and the total energy of the field outside the protostar

$$W_{M,\ \text{rel}}(R) = -2\pi\int_0^\pi\int_R^\infty T_0^0\left(1 - \frac{R_g}{r}\right)^{-1/2}r^2\sin\theta\,d\theta\,dr \to \frac{6\mu^2}{R_g^3}\left(1 - \frac{R_g}{R}\right)^{-1/2}$$

for $R = R_g + \epsilon$, $\epsilon \ll R_g$. In other words, in comparison with the non-relativistic value $W_M(R_g) \sim \mu^2/R_g^3 \sim H_0^2 R_0^4/R_g$ here appears a factor $(1 - R_g/R)^{-1/2}$. Therefore, if the magnetic moment μ does not tend to zero[2] when the surface of the collapsing star approaches the singular sphere, the role of the magnetic energy becomes important and one has to take into account its influence on the collapse.

The mass of the star

$$M = -\frac{4\pi}{c^2}\int T_0^0 r^2\,dr$$

[2] As is shown in Ginzburg and Ozernoy (1964) in simple case μ tends to zero for $R \to R_g$.

and thus the corresponding contribution of the external magnetic field is characterized by the expression

$$\Delta M = \frac{1}{2\,c^2} \int_0^\pi \int_R^\infty H^2 r^2 \sin\theta\, d\theta\, dr \simeq \frac{6\,\mu^2}{R_g{}^3 C^2} \ln \frac{R_g}{R - R_g}$$

for $R \to R_g$. For $\Delta M \sim M$ an explosion could take place (then the expulsion of the matter would proceed, probably, mainly in the direction of the magnetic poles). Obviously, even for $\mu \sim H_0 R_0^2 R_g$, $\Delta M \ll M$ as long as

$$\ln \frac{R_g}{R - R_g} \ll \frac{M\,c^2}{W_M(R_g)} \sim \frac{GM^2}{H_0^2 R_0^4},$$

i.e., for a long time after the collapse has begun.

In view of all this the possibility of the existence of a gigantic magnetosphere surrounding large collapsing protostars seems to us possible. The presence of a magnetosphere, of course, completely changes the appearance of the collapsing protostar from the point of view of an outside observer. Thus, for example 1 even at the distance $R \sim 10^{15} \sim 10^2\,R_g$ the field $H \sim 10^3$, which will cause large Zeeman splitting of the spectral lines. The rotation of the plane of polarization of the radio waves will be observable at even larger distances.[3] Such effects are, however, of secondary importance in comparison with the possible role of the radiation belts around a collapsing magnetic protostar. Relativistic and non-relativistic particles forming those belts are the source of the electromagnetic waves belonging to radio, optical, and X-ray frequencies. It suffices to say that the cyclotron frequency of an electron $\omega_H = eH/mc = 1.76 \times 10^7\,H$ in example 1 ($M \sim 10^8\,M_\odot$) reaches the value 10^{16}. In this case, for instance, an electron with the energy $\sim 10^7$ eV will radiate mainly at the frequency $\omega_m \sim \omega_H (E/mc^2)^2 \sim 10^{19}$ ($\lambda_m \sim 1$ Å). The energy of the particles in the belts can be comparable with the magnetic energy, i.e., for example 1, it can reach 10^{56} erg. We do not see any reasons why this value should not be greater by several orders of magnitude (see above). Note that, assuming the magnetobrems mechanism of the radiation of the superstar 3C 273B, we got (Ginzburg, Ozernoy, and Syrovatzkii 1963) for an object with the radius $R \sim 10^{16}$ cm value $H \simeq 10^2$ and the energy supply $W \sim 3.10^{57}$ erg, necessary for supporting the radiation for a period of 10^3 years. In example 1, the field $H \sim 10^2$ at the distance $r \sim 2.10^{15}$ cm. Therefore, we think it is possible to hypothesize that "superstars" are not gigantic non-equilibrium stars but are radiation belts around large collapsing magnetic protostars. The development of this hypothesis is connected with the necessity of analyzing large numbers of problems, e.g., the role of manetobrems losses and the mechanism of the acceleration of particles in belts (the magnetic field of a collapsing protostar is variable, and therefore in its magnetosphere one has to take into account effect of the induced electric field. Note that to explain the mechanism of the flow of energy from the collapsing prototar into interstellar space Hoyle et al. (1963) assume the existence of the C-field. If a protostar has a magnetosphere, such a flow is possible as a result of known mechanisms. From this point of view, to explain the "gain" of energy in the Crab Nebula (see, e.g., Hoyle et al. [1963]), one could consider that the collapsing supernova of 1054 A.D. is surrounded by a powerful enough magnetosphere (even for $M \sim M_\odot$ the field energy in the magnetosphere W_M may be even much smaller than

---

[3] E.g., for the polarized radio waves coming from discrete sources (Ginzburg 1960; Ginzburg and Pisareva 1963) and passing through the neighborhood of the collapsing magnetic protostar, one can observe a noticeable rotation of the plane of polarization at a distance which is many orders of magnitude larger than R_g. At the same time, the deflection of the light rays in the gravitational field of the star is equal $a = 2R_g/R$ (the minimum distance between the ray and the protostar $R \gg R_g$) and can hardly be noticed for $R \gtrsim 10^2\,R_g$.

$Mc^2 \sim 10^{54}$ to explain the observations). As has been already mentioned, such a magnetosphere can be, in principle, also a source of X-ray radiation. Such a possibility is interesting in connection with the discovery of a discrete source of the X-rays (Giacconi, Gursky, Paolini, and Rossi 1962, 1963; see also Ginzburg and Syrovatzkii [in press]).

The author is grateful to J. B. Zeldovitch, I. D. Nevikov, and L. M. Ozernoy for valuable remarks.

REFERENCES

Giacconi, R., Gursky, H., Paolini, F., and Rossi, B. 1962, *Phys. Rev. Letters*, **9**, 439.
———. 1963, *ibid.*, **11**, 530.
Ginzburg, V. L. 1960, *Radiophysics (Izvestya VIIZ)*, **3**, 341.
Ginzburg, V. L., and Ozernoy, L. M. 1964, *J.E.T.P.*, Vol. 47.
Ginzburg, V. L., Ozernoy, L. M., Syrovatzkii, S. I. 1964, Astronomical Preprint No. 267 (1963), *Doklady Akad. Nauk.* (in Russian).
Ginzburg, V. L., and Pisareva, V. V. 1963, *Radiophysics (Isvestya VIIZ)*, **6**, 877.
Ginzburg, V. L., and Syrovatzkii, S. I. (in press), *Doklady Acad. Sci. U.S.S.R.*
Greenstein, J. L., Matthews, T. A., Oke, J. B., and Schmidt, M. 1963, *Nature*, **197**, 1040.
Hoyle, F., Fowler, W. A., Burbidge, G. R., and Burbidge, E. M. 1963, *Nature*, **197**, 533.
Landau, L., and Lifschitz, E. 1963, *The Classical Theory of Fields* (Cambridge, Mass.: Addison-Wesley Publishing Co.).
Oppenheimer, J. R., and Snyder, H. 1939, *Phys. Rev.*, **56**, 455.
Pikelner, S. B. 1961, *Foundations of the Cosmical Electrodynamics*, *Physmatgiz*, Sec. 10.
Zeldovitch, J. B. 1963, *Astr. Zhur.*, No. 250.

PART V

ORIGIN OF RADIO

SOURCES

THEORIES OF THE ORIGIN
chapter 24 OF RADIO SOURCES

E. Margaret Burbidge and G. R. Burbidge

I. INTRODUCTION

The problem of the enormous energy required to explain the radio sources is not a new one; it has been with us since the time that (1) Baade and Minkowski (1954) identified one of the strongest radio sources in the sky (Cygnus A) with a rather distant external galaxy; and (2) Dombrovsky (1954) and Oort and Walraven (1956) found the polarization predicted by Shklovsky (1953) in the optical radiation from the Crab Nebula radio source, thus, verifying the theory that the emission was synchrotron radiation. According to this theory, one can calculate the energy required in high-speed electrons and positrons and in magnetic field, for synchrotron radiation to be emitted at a rate given by the measured power output and frequency dependence of the radiation from sources at known distances. The calculations are well known (cf. Burbidge 1956a, b; 1959), and have recently been carried out with the newest observational data by Maltby, Matthews, and Moffet (1963).

The usual calculations assume that the energy is equally divided between that contained in the high-energy particles and the energy of the magnetic field, since this division gives the minimum energy requirements. Two sets of values are usually tabulated for the identified radio sources: one in which the minimum energy in field and in electrons and positrons (which are the radiating particles) is calculated, and one in which allowance is made for the presence of high-energy protons. The latter calculation is made because most suggested energy sources require, as the final stage in producing high-energy electrons, some kind of Fermi-type acceleration process, and this would necessarily produce accelerated protons as well. Burbidge (1956a) and Ginzburg (1957) suggested that the electrons were secondary particles produced by interaction between the ambient gas and the accelerated protons; multiple production theory then gave the value of 100 as a reasonable estimate for the factor by which the proton energies exceed the electron energies needed to explain the emission.

This factor of 100 is customarily used in the more recent calculations. It has not been re-examined, and since the energy requirements are so enormous, even without this factor, we would like to draw the attention of theoretical workers to the need for a critical reappraisal of the amount of energy which may be present in the proton flux.

The largest energy requirements discussed by Hoyle and Fowler (see pp. 17–27)

E. M. Burbidge and G. R. Burbidge, University of California, San Diego.

are greater than the minimum energies for another reason. The radio sources in many cases lie well outside the galaxies in which they originate, and the regions where the radio emission is observed are the volumes which must contain the relevant magnetic fields. Magnetic fields of 10^{-4} or 10^{-5} gauss, which come from the calculations assuming equipartition, are much larger than can reasonably be expected to exist in intergalactic space. Thus the magnetic fields are almost certainly smaller than the equipartition values and the *total* energies consequently higher. We then arrive at the figure of approximately 10^{62} ergs for the content of the most energetic radio sources. The possible consequences of the dominance of particle energies over magnetic-field energies are interesting: the strong radio galaxies may contribute appreciably to the general cosmic-ray flux (Burbidge 1962a; Burbidge and Hoyle 1964; Burbidge 1964).

A good part of the following sections will be found in detail in a paper by Sandage and ourselves (Burbidge, Burbidge, and Sandage 1963).

TABLE 1

	Luminosity of Nucleus (erg/sec)	Energy Emitted in Emission Lines (erg/sec)
NGC 1068*........	20×10^{42}	2.7×10^{42}
1275.........	19×10^{42}	....
3516.........	25×10^{42}	1.2×10^{42}
4051.........	1×10^{42}	....
4151.........	16×10^{42}	$\begin{cases} 1.2 \times 10^{42} \text{ (hydrogen wings)} \\ 2.2 \times 10^{42} \text{ (remainder)} \end{cases}$
7469.........	52×10^{42}	....
M82.............	....	2×10^{40} (Hα only)
Cygnus A........	400×10^{42} (luminosity of whole optical system)	$\simeq 200 \times 10^{42}$

* New measure by A. R. Sandage.

II. VIOLENT EVENTS IN GALAXIES: RELATION BETWEEN STRONG RADIO SOURCES, QUASI-STELLAR RADIO SOURCES, AND SEYFERT GALAXIES

The galaxies that are strong radio emitters and the quasi-stellar radio sources can be related with another manifestation of short-lived energy release, taking place in the nuclei of Seyfert galaxies (Seyfert 1943). The latter have the following characteristics:

1. They have small, intensely bright nuclei (less than 25 pc in diameter in NGC 4151, for example, for which Sandage made a critical measurement, and which is shown in Fig. 1).

2. The spectra of their nuclei show strong emission lines, sometimes of high excitation.

3. These emission lines are very broad, indicating, if this is Doppler broadening, velocities of 1000–3000 km/sec. The hydrogen lines are usually broader than lines of other elements.

The direct link with radio galaxies comes about because two galaxies are common to both categories: NGC 1068 (Fig. 1) and NGC 1275 (Fig. 2). The former is a relatively weak radio source, with only some 10^2 times the output from normal galaxies, but the latter is a strong source. Table 1 shows the total optical radiation emitted by some of these objects, and that emitted in the emission lines (mostly from the work of Seyfert), together with, for comparison, that emitted in optical radiation by M82 (from the work of Lynds and Sandage 1963) and by the very strong radio source Cygnus A. It is likely that the Seyfert galaxies represent a milder manifestation of the same kind of violent event that must be postulated to explain the radio sources; possibly one may be wit-

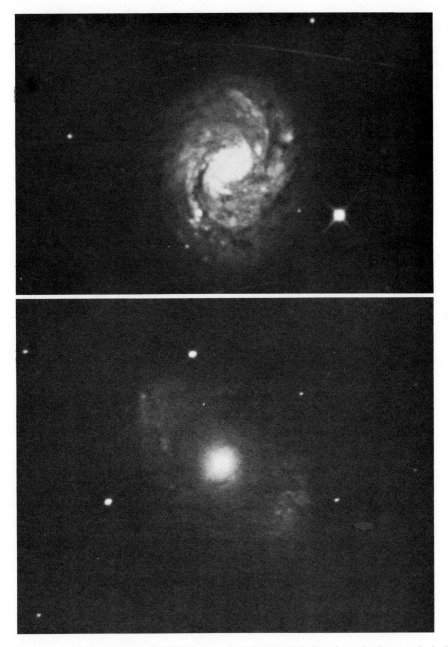

Fig. 1.—Two Seyfert galaxies, NGC 1068 (*upper*) and NGC 4151 (*lower*). Both photographed with McDonald 82-inch telescope on Eastman Kodak 103a-0 emulsion, no filter. North at top, west at left in both; scale: 1 mm = 2.7″ in both.

Fig. 2.—Radio galaxy NGC 1275 (Lick 120-inch telescope; Eastman Kodak 103a-0 emulsion, no filter). Main plate is 45^m exposure, showing outer filaments and dust structure; inset is 5^m exposure, showing structure in center. North at top, west at left; scale (same in both): 1 mm = 1.4″.

nessing an earlier stage in the event, or the event may be occurring in a different kind of galaxy.

The very large velocities indicated by the broad emission lines link the Seyfert galaxies to the quasi-stellar radio sources rather than to the ordinary radio galaxies. Schmidt (1963) noted that the widths of the identified spectral features in 3C 273 were 50 Å; if this is Doppler broadening, it indicates a velocity range of ± 1500 km/sec, which lies right in the range observed in Seyfert nuclei. In contrast to this, spectra of radio galaxies, other than those which are also Seyfert galaxies, do not have very broad lines. Indeed, some have no emission lines at all, and the excitation is usually low. The excitation in the quasi-stellar radio sources also tends to be lower than in the Seyfert nuclei.

From high-energy resolution studies of NGC 1068, Walker (1963) has found that the nuclear region consists of separate cloud complexes moving about in a disordered fashion with relative velocities $\sim 10^3$ km/sec. This was earlier found to be the case in NGC 4151 by O. C. Wilson (unpublished). The large velocities in the Seyfert nuclei imply Mach numbers of 10–100; these will lead to a high rate of energy dissipation and heating. Further, these velocities exceed the escape velocity from the nuclear region and gas must be leaking out from it.

Estimates of the kinetic energy present in the nucleus can be made if the gas density can be calculated, as has been done by Woltjer (1959) (using Seyfert's photometry) in NGC 4151 and NGC 1068. Bearing in mind the uncertainties, we estimate the resulting kinetic energy to be $10^{55\pm2}$ ergs. It is interesting that this is of the same order as that estimated from the *radio emission* of NGC 1068 to be present in magnetic-field and high-energy particles (4×10^{55} erg if protons dominate; 3×10^{53} if only electrons are present). It is also of the same order of magnitude as the kinetic energy in the moving Hα filaments of M82—2×10^{55} erg (Lynds and Sandage 1963).

Ten per cent of this kinetic energy of 10^{55} erg, if dissipated in the disk of a galaxy such as NGC 1068, containing, say, $10^8 M\odot$ of gas, would be sufficient to impart motions of 50 km/sec. It is interesting that Walker (1963) has observed considerable anomalous velocities in the gas in the spiral arms of NGC 1068, whose velocities were analyzed by Burbidge, Burbidge, and Prendergast (1959) in terms of rotation of the galaxy.

There is one further connection between the Seyfert galaxies and the quasi-stellar radio sources that we would like to point out. It has been suggested that, at the distance of 3C 273, if there were a normal galaxy surrounding the bright starlike object, it should be visible on the existing photographs (the faint jet is plainly visible). If there is no such underlying galaxy, then the object must be different in kind from a radio galaxy such as NGC 5128. Now in many of the Seyfert galaxies, almost all the light is concentrated in the bright nucleus and the surrounding galaxy is much fainter than a normal galaxy (NGC 4151, NGC 7469, NGC 5458, and NGC 3516, shown in Figs. 1, 3, and 4, are examples of this). This is not the case in all Seyfert galaxies; NGC 1068 (Fig. 1) and NGC 3227 (Fig. 4), for example, have outer parts of normal luminosity. We feel, however, that it may be a significant feature. It brings to mind many questions: are the Seyfert galaxies with faint outer parts and the quasi-stellar radio sources objects of low mass? Of low angular momentum and initial turbulent velocity? Are they objects at an early evolutionary stage, about which a normal galaxy will later form? These are highly speculative questions which we cannot answer.

The lifetime for the energetic phenomena occurring in nuclei of Seyfert galaxies is about 2×10^4 years, from the time taken for gas moving with the observed velocities to escape from the observed nuclear dimensions. The time for the observed optical emission from the nuclei to exhaust the calculated store of kinetic energy is 2 orders of magnitude longer than this, i.e., $\sim 10^6$ years. The estimated frequency of Seyfert galaxies among normal galaxies then indicates that the Seyfert phenomenon is likely to be recurrent 100 times or more during the total lifetime of the galaxy. The estimated lifetimes for radio galaxies, as discussed earlier, are thought to be $\sim 10^6$–10^7 years, while a time scale of $\sim 10^5$ years is indicated for 3C 273.

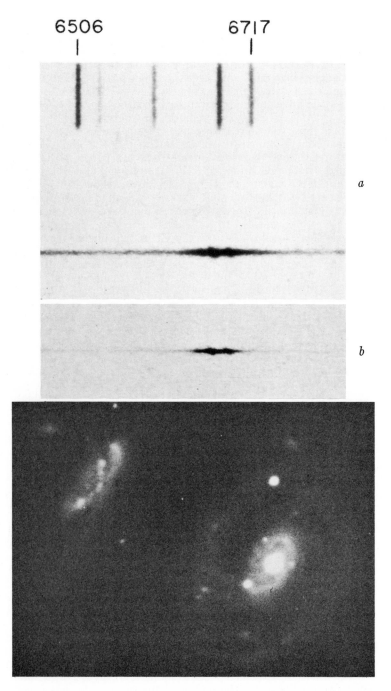

FIG. 3.—*Upper:* Spectrum of nucleus of Seyfert galaxy NGC 7469 (Lick 120-inch prime focus: 20^{m} exposure at a, 5^{m} exposure at b), showing very broad Hα and [N II] λ 6583 emission, with narrow inclined cores. *Lower:* NGC 7469 and its companion *(left)* IC 5283 (Lick 120-inch telescope, Eastman Kodak 103a-0 emulsion, no filter). North at left, east at top; scale: 1 mm = 1.5″.

Fig. 4.—Three Seyfert galaxies (all with McDonald 82-inch telescope, on baked Eastman Kodak IIa-0 emulsion, no filter). *Upper:* NGC 3227 (with its elliptical companion NGC 3226); scale: 1 mm = 2.9″. *Lower left:* NGC 3516, *lower right:* NGC 5548; scale for both: 1 mm = 2.6″. North at left, east at top in all.

The evidence for linking the violent events in Seyfert galaxies, quasi-stellar radio sources, and the strong radio-emitting galaxies is reviewed in more detail in the paper already mentioned (Burbidge *et al.* 1963).

III. POSSIBLE SOURCES OF ENERGY FOR RADIO GALAXIES

A variety of proposals have been made in the last decade to explain the energy for outbursts in galaxies of the magnitude required to explain the radio emission. Which energy source is responsible has considerable bearing on the types of particles ejected and also on the form of the particle energy spectrum. The possible energy sources can be considered in three groups. They are (*a*) energy which are released by the interaction of a galaxy with material that was previously unconnected with it; (*b*) internal energy in a galaxy in the form of rotational energy, turbulent energy, or magnetic field energy which is released by some catastrophic process; (*c*) energy which is released in the evolution of stars. Included here is the gravitational energy released when stars are formed, the nuclear energy released in thermonuclear explosions, and rest-mass energy which is released if the star goes to a highly collapsed phase.

In category (*a*) the first proposal was that the energy was released in collisions between galaxies (Baade and Minkowski 1954). It is clear now that this argument cannot be sustained either on theoretical grounds or on the basis of the identifications of radio sources (cf. Burbidge 1961). In addition to the arguments given in that latter reference, the observational evidence now available shows that a large number of the sources of violent activity are centered on single galaxies, and the violence appears to start at their centers. NGC 1275 (see Fig. 2) still presents an ambiguous situation in that it may be two systems in collision, but, as Minkowski has pointed out, the gas which has a velocity of 3000 km/sec relative to the main galaxy, if it is part of a colliding galaxy, should have a nucleus associated with it, and there is no sign of such a nucleus. The large velocity difference might well be due to just such an outburst as that postulated in M82, only of a more violent nature. We shall return to a consideration of the velocity field in NGC 1275 later.

A second proposal which falls into category (*a*) is that the energy is produced by the interaction of material in the galaxy with antiparticles or antimatter and the subsequent annihilation. This was proposed by Burbidge (1956*b*) and Burbidge and Hoyle (1956). The general difficulty with this hypothesis is that one needs a mechanism for separating matter and antimatter, whatever cosmology one is working with, and with antigravity ruled out by the arguments of Schiff (1959), this does not appear to be possible. The attraction of the hypothesis, at the time it was proposed, was that it provided electrons and positrons directly, without the need for the large flux of high-energy protons, and hence the energy requirements were reduced; although an acceleration process was needed, which would necessarily accelerate protons as well as electrons and positrons, at least the latter would be injected into this process at energies above the low energies where electron acceleration is relatively inefficient.

The most recent proposal in category (*a*) is that made by Shklovsky (1962) in which it is supposed that a galaxy interacts with material that has come from outside. He specifically considered the case of M87, and argued that the material accreted by such a massive system falls into the center. Energy is released and material in the central region is accelerated outward in the form of plasma jets. While the rate at which material falls in is estimated by Shklovsky to be about 10 $M\odot$/year, and this is compatible with the normal accretion rate for a galaxy of mass of the order of 10^{12} $M\odot$ in a medium of density $\sim 10^{-29}$ gm/cm^3, the details of this process are not at all clear. In particular, it is not obvious how the acceleration occurs, or why infall of material should always give rise to a violent event which appears to emanate from the center. Thus we see that all of the proposals which fall into category (*a*) have difficulties associated with them.

We next turn to the processes involved in category (b). In its process of formation a proto-galaxy must dissipate energy both by radiation and by the generation of large-scale motions in the fragmentation which is required if stars are to form (cf. Hoyle 1953). It might be asked whether the violent release of energy in some systems is associated with this stage of evolution. The obvious objection to this is that the vast majority of systems in which violent events are taking place are well organized and often highly evolved galaxies, i.e., the elliptical galaxies. M82 may be in a fairly early stage of evolution as deduced from the integrated spectral type of A5 and the large amount of uncondensed material, but it does not appear to be at the very early stage at which the dissipation of energy in this way is important. Of the peculiar systems catalogued by Vorontsov-Velyaminov (1959) and studied by us and others, some are thought to be systems at an early stage of evolution; none of these have been identified with radio sources. A possible exception to this is NGC 4038–39, which is one of the weaker of the identified radio sources.

The question therefore arises as to whether any of the internal energy in a well-developed galaxy could be released suddenly to give rise to a violent event. The only proposal of this type which has been made is that by Hoyle (1961) who argued that, in galaxies with considerable amounts of gas containing magnetic flux and large angular momenta, galactic flares could arise through discharges following the winding up of the magnetic fields in the centers. This mechanism is similar to that proposed by Gold and Hoyle (1960) for the generation of solar flares. While the model proposed by Hoyle is not unattractive, it suffers from the disadvantage that the discharge conditions cannot be reached unless there is a large amount of gas already present in the galaxy, and also a large amount of angular momentum per unit mass. This means that massive systems with high rotations containing large amounts of uncondensed material are the obvious candidates to produce violent events. However, most of the galaxies in which violent events are seen do not fulfil all of these conditions. The elliptical galaxies which are massive often contain little gas and probably have little angular momentum. The Seyfert galaxies, while they do contain considerable amounts of gas and are fast-rotating, do not appear to have sufficiently large masses or mass concentrations.

Finally, therefore, we come to the processes which are contained in category (c). Ginzburg (1961) has attempted to show that high-energy particles can be produced in the early stages of formation of a galaxy when gravitational energy is released. However, as we have described earlier it appears that none of the galaxies from which radio sources have emanated are systems which are recently formed.

As will be seen in what follows, energy release following star formation and evolution appears to give the best hope of explaining the phenomena. The observations of the Crab Nebula and other supernova remnants in our Galaxy show that in, or following, stellar explosions the necessary conditions for a synchrotron source to appear are produced. Also, only in stellar explosions (novae and supernovae) are velocities generated of the magnitude seen in the Seyfert nuclei. Thus it is natural to suppose that the violent outbursts in galaxies are the result of multiple supernova outbursts or their equivalent in energy output.

Shklovsky (1960) argued simply that the supernova rate must have been very considerably enhanced so that some 10^6 or more supernovae have gone off at a rate of about 1 per year in an object like M87. However, he had no argument as to why this should occur. Since supernovae only occur at the end of a star's evolution, it is not reasonable to take this view unless it is supposed that the outbursts (i) are causally connected, or, (ii) unless stars of very great mass are continuously being formed and evolve very rapidly. Cameron (1962) considered the rapid formation and evolution of massive stars in the nuclear region of elliptical galaxies. His calculations, however, neglected turbulent motions in the gas at the centers of such galaxies (Burbidge 1962b).

Burbidge (1961) proposed that a chain reaction of supernovae could be caused in the nucleus of a galaxy if one supernova went off naturally and the stellar density was sufficiently high so that other stars could be exploded. It was estimated that the star density required if such a mechanism were to work must be of the order of $10^6 \simeq 10^7$ stars/pc^3 and it was pointed out that there was no observational argument against this, particularly for the elliptical galaxies. Even higher star densities may be acceptable. The difficulty lies in understanding how a detonation wave can propagate even if sufficient light nuclei are present. This problem has not been solved, partly because the geometry involved is exceedingly difficult to handle. Also modern ideas concerning supernova outbursts suggest that an integral part of the normal supernova process is a catastrophic collapse. The chain reaction mechanism would not lead to this. Finally, if the magnitude of the energy released suggests that gravitational (rest-mass) energy is involved, this cannot be expected to occur by such a mechanism.

Since the theory of the release of gravitational energy by the formation, rapid evolution, and collapse of objects with masses as great as $10^8 \, M\odot$ has been fully discussed here by Hoyle and Fowler (see also Hoyle, Fowler, Burbidge, and Burbidge 1964), we shall not discuss this further here. We would like to mention one further possibility: that of a rapidly accelerating process of star collision leading to what might be called a "phase change" of matter in the nuclei of galaxies. Two independent investigations along these lines are under way at present: one by Gold at Cornell, and one by Ulam at Los Alamos. Since Gold is reporting about his work in this volume, we would just like briefly to discuss Ulam's ideas.

Of the radio galaxies which are close enough to be observed optically in detail, the strongest sources tend to be highly luminous, massive, mainly stellar systems, often with a characteristic extended luminosity distribution (cf. Matthews, Morgan, and Schmidt in this volume). Figures 5 and 6 illustrate this. Figure 5 is an ultraviolet photograph of NGC 6166 (3C 338), in the cluster Abell 2199, taken with the Lick 120-inch telescope. Resolution in the radio observations is not sufficient to place the emission in any one component of this multiple elliptical, but the probability is that the optically unusual component—the brightest, very extended galaxy with the small ultraviolet nucleus— is responsible. Apart from the ultraviolet nucleus (which is mainly [O II] λ 3727 emission), the lack of central concentration of the light and the great outer extent, in comparison with other galaxies in the cluster, is to be noted. Minkowski has found a very large velocity dispersion of the stars in the nuclear region.

Figure 6 shows NGC 4782–3 (3C 278), photographed with the Lick 120-inch telescope. The difference in nuclear concentration in the two components of this double (already noted by Greenstein [1961] from the light distribution in his spectra), and the asymmetrical outer isophotes, are to be noted. There is no evidence for any appreciable amount of gas in this object; the outer isophotes must be due to asymmetrical stellar orbits.

Ulam is considering the motions in a small group of stars as a pilot problem in considering a bigger assembly. The question he asks first is: If a collision between two stars occurs, is a third star likely to collide in a shorter time than the time taken for the first two? Very probably this is the case. We do not know what the energy release in a stellar collision would be, but if a rapidly accelerating process of this type could lead to the agglomeration of the whole nuclear region, we should have a way of producing the 10^6– $10^8 \, M\odot$ objects whose subsequent history might follow the course described by Hoyle and Fowler. Further, during such an agglomeration, which would occur by energy exchange among stars, many stars would be thrown into orbits carrying them far from the nucleus, thus providing the greatly extended light distributions observed.

IV. CONCLUSION: THEORETICAL REQUIREMENTS

Let us collect together the observational facts that a successful theory of radio sources has to account for:

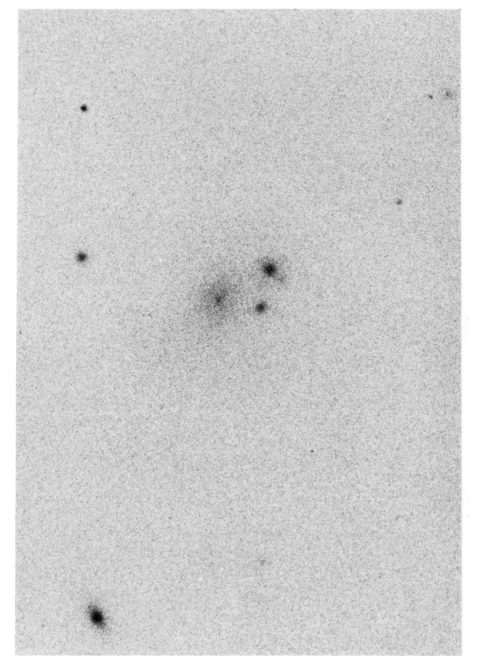

Fig. 5.—Negative print of multiple elliptical radio source NGC 6166 (north at top, west at left). Photographed with 120-inch Lick telescope on baked Eastman Kodak IIa-0 plate through Schott UGl filter and Ross corrector (isolating small wavelength region around redshifted λ 3727). Scale: 1 mm = 0.76″. Note lack of central concentration and great outer extent of brightest component; also small *UV* nucleus (appearance of small cross about center is spurious, due to flaw in two-stage reproduction).

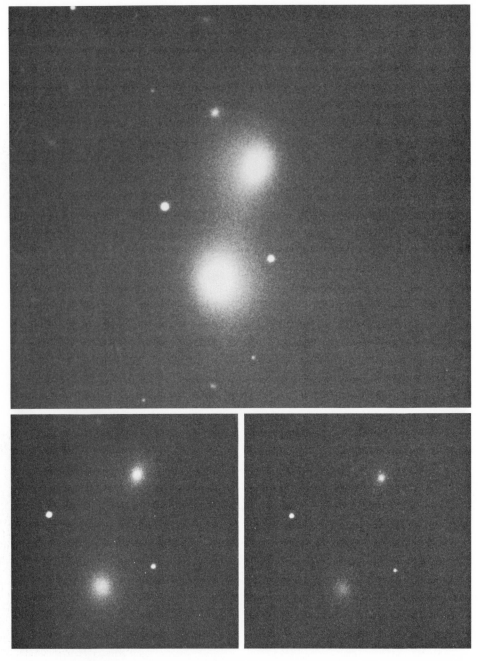

FIG. 6.—Double elliptical radio source NGC 4782–3. Three exposures (45^m, 15^m, 5^m) with 120-inch Lick telescope on Eastman Kodak 103a-D emulsion through Schott GG 11 filter. Note asymmetrical light distribution in longest exposure, and different light distribution in centers of two components. For all, north is at top, west at left; scale is 1 mm = 1.3″.

1. The most important is a means of obtaining the very large energies, already referred to many times here.

2. The energy must be supplied in the right mode, i.e., in the form of high-energy particles and magnetic fields. In stressing the energy requirements, there is sometimes a tendency not to pay enough attention to this point. Although the magnetic energy may be already present in the form of galactic or intergalactic fields, there must be an efficient way of producing and accelerating high-energy electrons. For those radio sources which emit synchrotron radiation in optical frequencies, the lifetimes of the radiating electrons are no more than 10^2–10^3 years so, in general there must be a way of continuously supplying or reaccelerating these particles.

3. The lifetimes ($\sim10^6$ years) of radio sources (and the shorter lifetimes of the explosive phenomena in Seyfert nuclei), together with the spatial frequency of these objects, show that the violent outbursts can be recurrent. Indeed, it is well known that in the Centaurus A source (NGC 5128), the radio brightness distribution shows that the results of more than one outburst can be seen now. A satisfactory theory of radio sources must explain how recurrent outbursts can take place in any one galaxy. For example, if the formation, rapid evolution, and implosion of gas masses of $\sim10^8$ $M_\odot$ are responsible, then we have to be able to do this more than once in a galaxy's lifetime. Similarly, if a "phase change" of matter in the center of a galaxy takes place, through rapidly accelerated stellar collisions and agglomeration, then this process has to be able to recur.

4. The theory has to account for the type of galaxy that is most likely to become a radio source, namely, spherical (low angular momentum), massive, mainly stellar systems with a somewhat unusual distribution of light and hence of stellar orbits. What is the relation of this to the *lack* of a galaxy of normal brightness around at least one of the quasi-stellar radio sources, and around the nuclei of some Seyfert galaxies?

5. The characteristic double radio sources have to be explained. What relation does this radio distribution bear to any axis of symmetry in the galaxy of origin—for example, the axis of rotation? Apparently, in one case there is a considerable component of velocity in the line of sight which could be interpreted as being due to rotation about an axis along the line joining the two sources (Matthews, Morgan, and Schmidt, this volume). In NGC 5128, rotation of the gaseous system coexisting with the well-known broad dust lane occurs about an axis perpendicular to the dust line, i.e., about an axis which is inclined by 20°–30° to the long axis of the main outer radio distribution (Burbidge and Burbidge 1959; Bolton and Clark 1960).

Turning from the radio distribution, that is, the distribution of high-energy particles, in typical radio galaxies, let us consider the distribution of more quiescent gaseous material ejected from a radio galaxy. We have two examples, M82 and NGC 1275. Lynds and Sandage have deduced an outward velocity ~1000 km/sec along the minor axis for the extensive filaments emitting Hα light in M82. We have some spectra taken with the 82-inch telescope at the McDonald Observatory in several position angles, from which we hope to deduce the velocity field of the exploding gas in more detail. Dr. Vera Rubin is working on these plates at the moment, and she has the results of measurements of one plate in position angle 83°, i.e., at $\sim20°$ to the major axis. It is interesting that the velocity gradient is greater than either Mayall's rotational velocity gradient along the major axis (Mayall 1960) or the explosive velocity gradient along the minor axis (Lynds and Sandage 1963); it is about 9 km/sec per second of arc.

In NGC 1275, we have obtained spectra in many position angles with the 120-inch telescope at Lick Observatory. We are working on these at present, in the hope of plotting out the velocity field in relation to the outer gaseous filaments which have a big velocity with respect to the central galaxy (+3000 km/sec in the line of sight [Minkowski 1957]). We find that there is ionized gas around the main galaxy, and the emission lines produced by this gas are inclined, giving the biggest velocity gradient in position angle 10°–20°. It may be seen from Figure 2 that the extended outer filaments (where

Minkowski found the big velocity displacement) are located north and west of the galaxy, mainly in position angle 110°–120°, i.e., roughly perpendicular to the direction of our biggest velocity gradient. Our velocity gradients amount to a few hundred km/sec; we have found no run of velocities filling in the range from 5200–8200 km/sec nor any velocities showing a big negative displacement. If our measures indicate rotation of the galaxy, then the axis of rotation lies roughly in the direction of the big displaced velocity. This would support the concept of ejection along the axis of rotation, as in M82.

6. Finally, we have to understand the role played by dust in radio sources. The presence of dust in an otherwise normal-looking galaxy has come to be accepted as a good indication that a tentative identification with a radio source was in fact correct (M84 [Wade 1960] is an example). The broad dust lane in NGC 5128 has already been referred to. The dust pattern in the radio source NGC 1316 (Fornax A) is another good case. It can be seen in Figure 7 that the dust has an unusual structure—rather like that in NGC 1275—and extends close into the center but not through it (the dust lane seen in the shortest exposure in Fig. 7 is slight eccentric). A faint dark structure, possibly dust, was found in the brightest component of NGC 6166 (E. M. Burbidge 1962). Among the Seyfert galaxies, a curious dust bar near the center can be seen in NGC 3227 (Fig. 4). The very chaotic and remarkable dust structure in M82 is one of its most striking features.

In conclusion, we have to emphasize that theory is still in an unsatisfactory state as regards accounting for the data described above. While we think there is a connection between Seyfert galaxies, on the one hand, and the radio galaxies and quasi-stellar radio sources on the other, we do not know to what extent the differences are differences in kind, in degree, or in time (i.e., stage of development of the aftermath of an explosion). The effect of recurrent outbursts may be to supply a considerable extragalactic component of cosmic radiation throughout space (Burbidge 1962a, 1964; Burbidge and Hoyle 1964). If gravitational collapse of massive objects occurs, there may be a considerable amount of "hidden mass" in existence in the universe. If outbursts have occurred in the past in present-day quiescent galaxies like our own, the effect of the degraded energy supply fed into kinetic energy and thermal motions on the generation of non-circular velocities and even on the renewal of spiral structure in galaxies are possibilities to be considered.

This research has been supported in part by grants from the National Science Foundation and NASA (NsG-357).

REFERENCES

Baade, W., and Minkowski, R. 1954, *Ap. J.*, **119**, 215.
Bolton, J., and Clark, B. G. 1960, *Pub. A.S.P.*, **72**, 29.
Burbidge, E. M. 1962, *Ap. J.*, **136**, 1134.
Burbidge, E. M., and Burbidge, G. R. 1959, *Ap. J.*, **129**, 271; see also *Nature*, **194**, 367, 1962.
Burbidge, E. M., Burbidge, G. R., and Prendergast, K. H. 1959, *Ap. J.*, **130**, 26.
Burbidge, G. R. 1956a, *Phys. Rev.*, **103**, 264.
———. 1956b, *Ap. J.*, **124**, 416.
———. 1959, *Paris Symposium on Radio Astronomy*, ed. R. N. Bracewell (Stanford, Calif.: Stanford University Press), p. 541.
———. 1961, *Nature*, **190**, 1053.
———. 1962a, *Progr. Theor. Phys. Japan*, **27**, 999.
———. 1962b, *Nature*, **194**, 964.
———. 1964, *Proc. Int. Conf. on Cosmic Rays, Jaipur, India* (in press).
Burbidge, G. R., Burbidge, E. M., and Sandage, A. R. 1963, *Rev. Mod. Phys.*, **35**, 947.
Burbidge, G. R., and Hoyle, F. 1956, *Nuovo Cimento*, **4**, 558.
———. 1964, in preparation.
Cameron, A. G. W. 1962, *Nature*, **194**, 963.
Dombrovsky, V. A. 1954, *Dokl. Akad. Nauk SSSR*, **94**, 1021.
Ginzburg, V. L. 1957, *Usp. Fiz. Nauk*, **51**, 343.

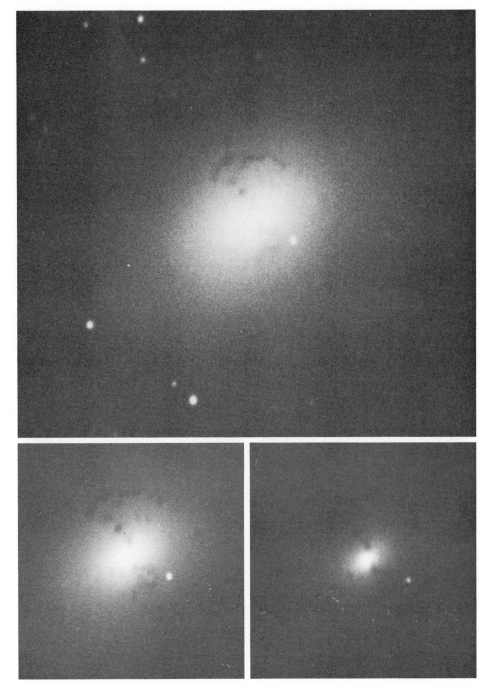

FIG. 7.—NGC 1316 (Fornax A radio source), showing dust structure. Exposures of 30ᵐ (*upper*), 8ᵐ (*lower left*), and 2ᵐ (*lower right*), all at prime focus of 82-inch McDonald telescope on baked Eastman Kodak IIa-0 emulsion, no filter. North at top, west at left; scale in all is 1 mm = 2.8″.

————. 1961, *Astr. Zhur.*, **38**, 380 (trans.: *Soviet Astr.*, **5**, 282).
Gold, T., and Hoyle, F. 1960, *M.N.*, **120**, 89.
Greenstein, J. L. 1961, *Ap. J.*, **133**, 335.
Hoyle, F. 1953, *Ap. J.*, **118**, 513.
————. 1961, *Observatory*, **81**, 39.
Hoyle, F., Fowler, W. A., Burbidge, G. R., and Burbidge, E. M. 1964, *Ap. J.*, **139**, 909.
Lynds, C. R., and Sandage, A. R. 1963, *Ap. J.*, **137**, 1005.*
Maltby, P., Matthews, T. A., and Moffet, A. T. 1963, *Ap. J.*, **137**, 153. *
Mayall, N. U., 1960, *Ann. d'ap.*, **23**, 344.
Minkowski, R. 1957, *I.A.U. Symposium on Radio Astronomy*, No. 4 (Cambridge: Cambridge University Press), p. 107.
Oort, J. H. and Walraven, T. 1956, *B.A.N.*, **12**, 285.
Schiff, L. 1959, *Proc. Nat. Acad. Sci.*, **45**, 69.
Schmidt, M. 1963, *Nature*, **197**, 1040.*
Seyfert, C. K. 1943, *Ap. J.*, **97**, 28.
Shklovsky, I. S. 1953, *Dokl. Akad. Nauk SSSR*, **90**, 983.
————. 1960, *Astr. Zh.*, **37**, 945 (trans.: *Soviet Astr.*, **4**, 885).
————. 1962, *ibid.*, **39**, 591.
Vorontsov-Velyaminov, B. A. 1959, *Atlas and Catalogue of Interacting Galaxies* (Moscow).
Wade, C. M. 1960, *Observatory*, **80**, 235.
Walker, M. F. 1963, Ann. Rept. Lick Obs., *A.J.*, **68**, 643.
Woltjer, L. 1959, *Ap. J.*, **130**, 38.

STUDY OF THE DISTRIBUTION OF IONIZED HYDROGEN IN

chapter 25 # SOME RADIO GALAXIES

G. Courtès, M. Viton, and P. Véron

It has been suggested that the synchrotron spectrum of certain radio sources could be extended in the direction of high frequencies, higher than the Lyman frequency. This ultraviolet energy would then be responsible for the excitation of the observed hydrogen clouds. This would be the case for the filaments of the Crab Nebula (Woltjer 1958) and for the hydrogen emission nebula observed in M82 by Lynds and Sandage (1963).

If the radio emission of galaxies is due to synchrotron radiation, the fine structure of these radio sources will be the same as the structure of the magnetic field; unfortunately, the resolving power of the big radio telescopes now in use is not sufficient to study this structure. However, if the ionization process described above is sufficiently effective, one can expect to find clouds of ionized hydrogen in the regions of radio-synchrotron emission and therefore obtain the magnetic-field structure. This is the reason why we have systematically studied the distribution of ionized hydrogen in neighboring radio galaxies.

The observational method is the one described by Courtès and Cruvellier (1961). The Newton focus of the 193-cm telecsope of Haute Provence Observatory is equipped with a focal length reducer which increases the over-all aperture from $f/5$ to $f/1$. An interference filter with a peak of transmission approximately centered on the Hα wavelength, redshifted by the velocity of the galaxy, is placed at the Newton focus.

These are the preliminary results:

The galaxies we have considered are NGC 1275, NGC 3034 (M82), NGC 4258, NGC 5194–5 (M51), and NGC 6946. Table 1 gives the characteristics of the interference filters, the emulsions, and the time exposure used.

NGC 1275

NGC 1275 (Fig. 1, *a*) is one of the galaxies with emitting nucleus studied by Seyfert (1943); the emission is not restricted to the nucleus. Minkowski (1957) has spectrographically studied the distribution of ionized material which consists of two clouds of respective radial velocities: 5200 km/s and 8200 km/s.

G. Courtès and M. Viton, Marseille Observatory. P. Véron, Meudon Observatory.

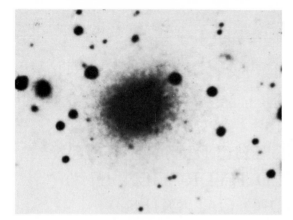

FIG. 1a.—NGC 1275, comparison plate

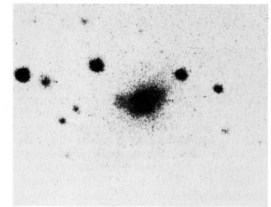

FIG. 1b.—NGC 1275, filter 50 Å
[N ɪɪ] + 5000 km/sec.

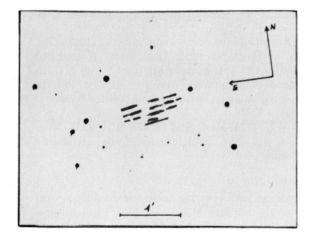

FIG. 1c.—NGC 1275, reconstitution of the emission nebula with 5160 km/sec using the spectara of Minkowski.

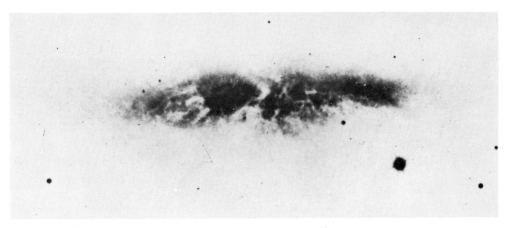

FIG. 1d.—M82, comparison plate

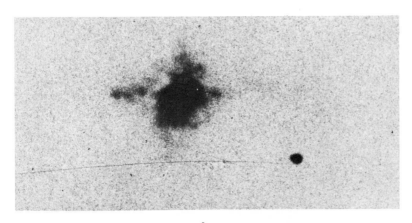

FIG. 1e.—Filter 6 Å, Hα + 225 km/sec

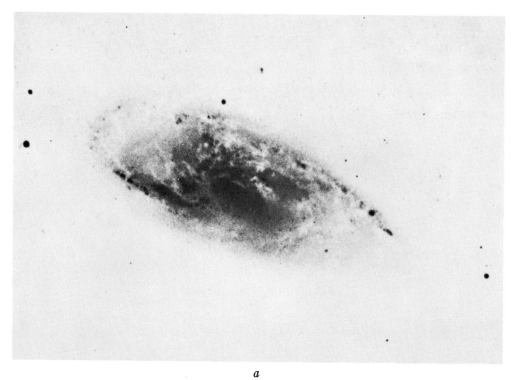

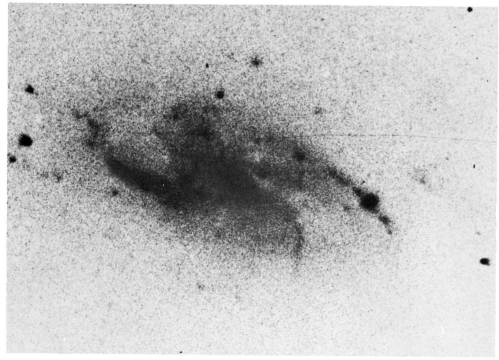

FIG. 2.—*a*, NGC 4258; *b*, filter 50 Å, Hα + 0 km/sec

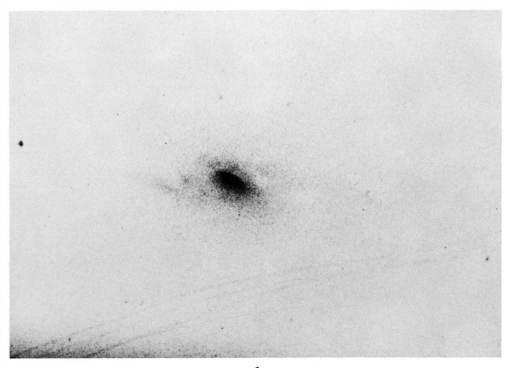

c

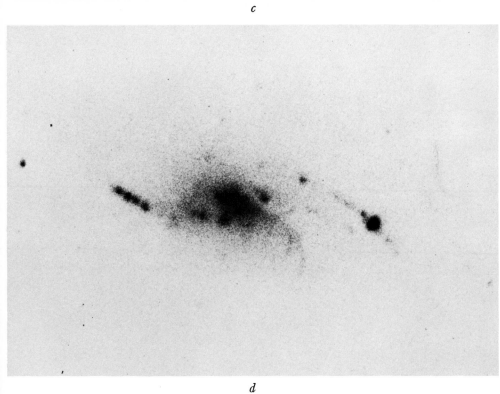

d

FIG. 2.—*c*, NGC 4258, comparison plate; *d*, NGC 4258, filter 6 Å, Hα + 310 km/sec

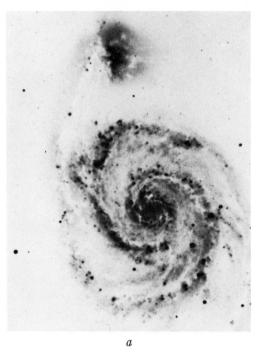

a

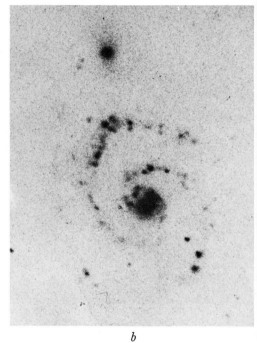

b

c

Fig. 3.—*a*, NGC 5194–5;
b, NGC 5194–5, filter 6 Å, Hα + 310 km/sec;
c, NGC 5194–5, comparison plate.

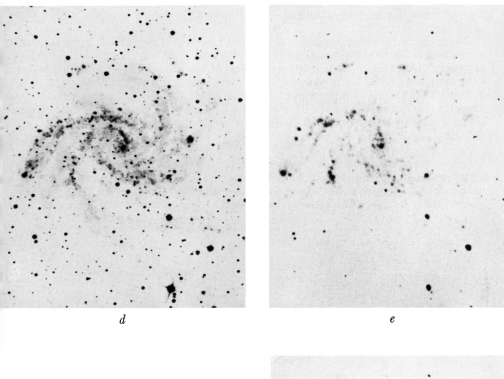

d

e

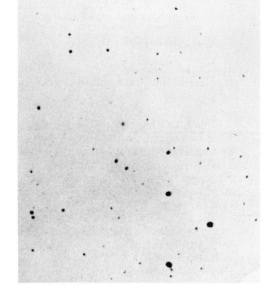

f

Fig. 3.—d, NGC 6946;
  e, NGC 6946, filter 4 Å, Hα + 0 km/sec;
  f, NGC 6946, comparison plate.

Figure 1, *c*, gives a reconstitution of the emitting cloud with radial velocity 5200 km/sec, following the spectra published by Minkowski in the region of the 3727-Å line of [O II].

The maximum of the transmission of the filter used here is at the 6584-Å line of [N II] with a redshift of 5000 km/sec. Figure (1, *b*) shows the distribution of the ionized cloud of velocity 5200 km/sec for the external regions of the galaxy; this distribution is the same as the one found by Minkowski. The dimensions of the cloud are approximately 2′ E.W., 1′ N.S. NGC 1275 is a powerful radio source (3C 84) with a nucleus 10″ in diameter (Lequeux 1962*a*) and with a halo of 4′5 ± 1′0 (Maltby and Moffet 1962). Its global spectral index is 0.65 ± .05 (Boischot *et al.* 1963).

NGC 3034 (M82) (FIG. 1, *d*)

In the central region, west of the absorption band which crosses the main body of the galaxy, one can see a big mass of ionized hydrogen, the brightest part of which has approximately the dimensions of the radio source (3C 231), that is, 45″ in diameter (Lequeux 1962*b*). Its right ascension coincides with the one of the radio source measured by

TABLE 1*

NGC	Radial Velocity (km/sec) (1)	Radial Velocity at Peak Transmission (2)	Band Width (Å) (3)	Emulsion (4)	Exposure Time (5)
1275.......	5160	[N II]+5000 km/sec	50	103a-F	4ʰ
3034.......	263	Hα + 225 km/sec	6	103a-F	2
4258.......	420	Hα + 310 km/sec	6	103a-E	5 45ᵐ
5194–5.....	438+542	Hα + 310 km/sec	6	103a-E	2
6946.......	38	Hα + 0 km/sec	4	103a-E	3

* Col. (1) gives the radial velocity of the nebula following Humason, Mayall, and Sandage (1956); col. (2) gives the corresponding radial velocity for Hα or [N II] (6584 Å) at the point of best transmission of the filter; col. (3) gives the band width of the filter in Å. The comparison plates have been taken with emulsion 103a-D with a red filter VR1 (Parra-Mantois).

Heidmann (1963) (Fig. 1, *e*). This emitting hydrogen cloud has emitting filaments pointing to the North and to the South (Lynds and Sandage 1963).

NGC 4258 (FIG. 2, *a*)

This galaxy has already been studied by Courtès and Cruvellier in 1961. In addition to some H II regions excited by hot stars, visible on plates exposed in blue light, they show the existence of a huge arm crossing the nucleus (Fig. 2, *b*). The more selective filter used here (9 Å instead of 50 Å) increases the contrast between the Hα-emission and the continuum of the stars in the region of the arm south of the nucleus and shows a remarkable structure of filaments (Fig. 2, *c* and *d*). But the radial velocity of the galaxy and its rotation are such (Burbidge, Burbidge, and Prendergast 1963) that the filter transmission for the part of the arm north of the nucleus is insufficient, and this part of the arm becomes invisible. On the other hand, the filter of 9 Å does not let through [N II] (6584 Å). Only the hydrogen is thus detected. NGC 4258 is a weak radio source (7,9.10⁻²⁶ W m⁻²hz⁻¹ at 159 Mhz) detected first by Hanbury Brown and Hazard (1953) and studied later by Heeschen (1961).

NGC 5194–5 (M51) (FIG. 3, *d, e, f*)

A weak radio emission is detected at the position of NGC 5194 (2,5.10⁻²⁶ W m⁻² hz⁻¹ at 1430 Mhz), and one cannot tell if this comes from NGC 5194 or from NGC 5195 (Heidmann 1963). The plate in Hα light shows many H II regions with classical aspect. All of them are probably excited by hot stars, but no emitting cloud has been associated with the radio source (Fig. 3, e).

NGC 6946 (FIG. 3, a, b, c)

NGC 6946 is a weak radio source ($6,6.10^{-26}$ W m^{-2} hz^{-1} at 159 Mhz) studied by Heeschen (1961). Many H II regions appear showing the spiral arms of the galaxy (Fig. 3, b); no one of them can be associated with a radio emission.

NGC 598 (M33)

This galaxy has been studied by Courtès and Cruvellier (1961) with the interference filter used for NGC 6946. In addition to many classical H II regions, one observes in emission a jet which seems to be coming out of the nucleus. M33 is a weak radio source, the dimensions of which are larger than the optical dimensions (Heidmann 1963).

CONCLUSION

These first results show that it is possible to find big regions of ionized hydrogen in the nuclear regions of galaxies by using very selective interference filters and taking the pictures at the Hα-line. The excitation of these regions cannot be attributed to hot stars and is related perhaps to the presence of radio-synchrotron emission in these galaxies. The plates further show numerous new classical H II regions.

It is interesting to note that jets or filaments in emission in close relation to the nucleus of the galaxies are not only located in exceptionally strong radio galaxies. More observations are needed with high monochromatic selectivity to show if this kind of emission feature is a general property of early-type spirals. It is possible that they would have been missed because of the poor selectivity of the color filters conventionally used in the photography of galaxies.

REFERENCES

Boischot, A., et al. 1963, Ann. d'ap., 26, 85.
Burbidge, E. M., Burbidge, G. R., and Prendergast, K. H. 1963, Ap. J., 138, 375.
Courtès, G., and Cruvellier. 1961, C.R., 253, 218.
Hanbury Brown, R., and Hazard, C. 1953, M.N., 113, 123.
Heeschen, D. S. 1961, Pub. N.R.A.O., Vol. 1, No. 9.
Heidmann, J. 1963, Ann. d'ap., 26, 343.
Humason, M. L., Mayall, N. U., and Sandage, A. 1956, A.J., 61, 97.
Lequeux, J. 1962a, Ann. d'ap., 25, 221.
———. 1962b, C.R., 255, 1865.
Lynds, C. R., and Sandage, A. 1963, Ap. J., 137, 1005.
Maltby, P., and Moffet, A. 1962, Ap. J. Suppl., 7, 141.
Minkowski, R. L. 1957, I.A.U. Symposium No. 4, p. 107.
Seyfert, C. K. 1943, Ap. J., 97, 28.
Woltjer, L. 1958, B.A.N., 14, 39.

EVIDENCE FOR AN EXPLOSION IN THE CENTER OF THE GALAXY M82

chapter 26

C. R. LYNDS AND ALLAN R. SANDAGE

I. INTRODUCTION

Although generally classified as an irregular galaxy, M82 is far from being typical of that class of objects. The highly oblong shape of the galaxy suggests a flattened system seen nearly edge-on. However, aside from this, there is little evidence of any regularity of form. On photographs in blue or visual light, the galaxy presents a chaotic mixture of luminous patches and dark lanes (Fig. 1). The integrated spectral type of A5 (Humason, Mayall, and Sandage 1956) contrasts strongly with the color index, $B - V = +0.91$ (de Vaucouleurs 1961). Evidence has been found by Morgan and Mayall (1959) that this discrepancy between spectral type and color index is due to the reddening produced by a large amount of dust in M82. This dust evidently is also responsible for the dark lanes which overlie the face of the galaxy.

One of the most remarkable features of M82 is the system of luminous filaments which extend to about 2 minutes of arc north and south of the galaxy in the direction of the minor axis (see Fig. 1). The National Geographic Society–Palomar Observatory Sky Survey plates show the filaments, as well as the galaxy, to be considerably fainter in the violet than in the red. Previously it might have been supposed that the filaments were subject to the same reddening from dust as the main body of the galaxy, but now it appears most likely, from data reported herein, that a large fraction of the radiation from the filaments is contributed by Hα.

Radio observations of M82 (Lynds 1961) have shown that the galaxy is a radio source with a spectral index of approximately 0.2, nearly the same as that found for the Crab Nebula radio source. By analogy with the Crab Nebula, it was suggested that the radio emission from M82 was due to the synchrotron mechanism and that the synchrotron

C. R. LYNDS, Kitt Peak National Observatory, operated by the Association of the Universities for Research in Astronomy, Inc., under contract with the National Science Foundation. This paper is No. 28 of *Contributions from the Kitt Peak National Observatory*. A. R. SANDAGE, Mount Wilson and Palomar Observatories, Carnegie Institution of Washington and California Institute of Technology.

Reprinted from the *Astrophysical Journal*, **137**, 1005–1021, 1963.

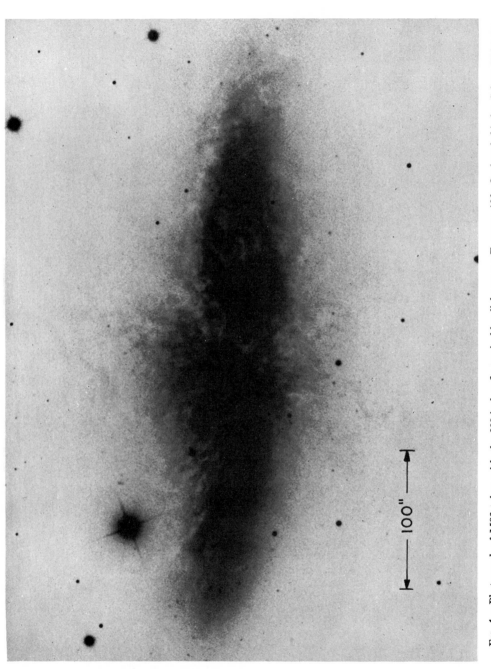

FIG. 1.—Photograph of M82 taken with the 200-inch reflector in blue light on an Eastman 103a-O plate behind a Schott WG2 filter (λλ 3600–5000 A). The cardinal directions are skewed on this reproduction, with north pointing down and to the right at about 30° to a vertical line and east pointing up and to the right at about 30° to a horizontal line.

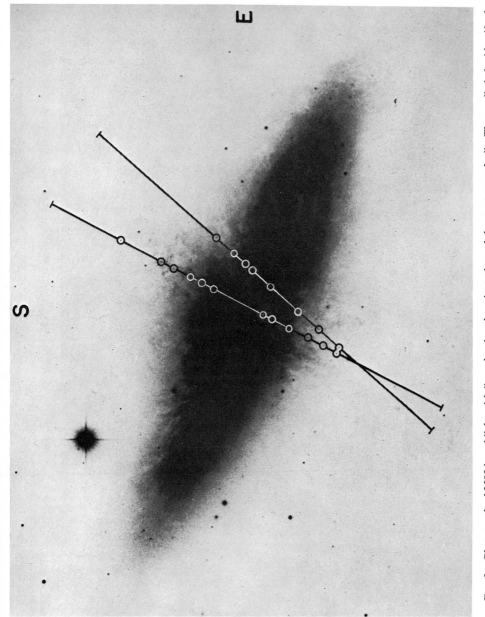

FIG. 2.—Photograph of M82 in red light with lines showing the orientations of the spectrograph slit. The small circles identify the positions at which radial-velocity measurements were made. The reproduction of M82 shown here was made from the same plate as was Fig. 7.

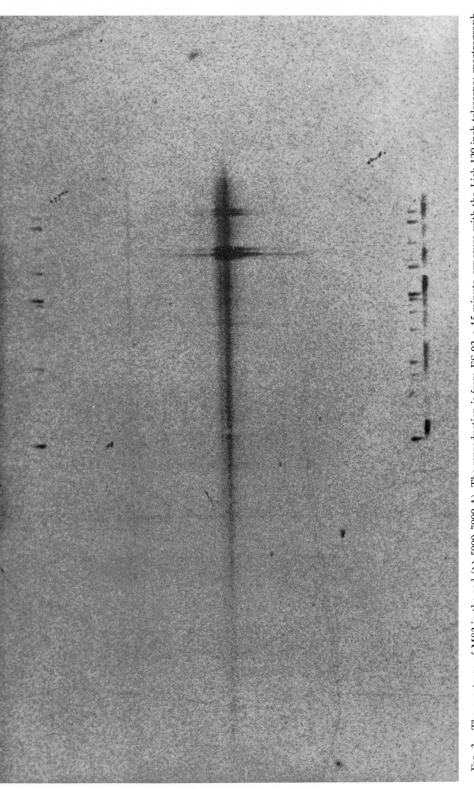

Fig. 3.—The spectrum of M82 in the red (λλ 5000–7000 A). The reproduction is from ES-92, a 15-minute exposure with the Lick 120-inch telescope; spectrograph slit oriented at 335° position angle. The comparison spectrum is due to neon.

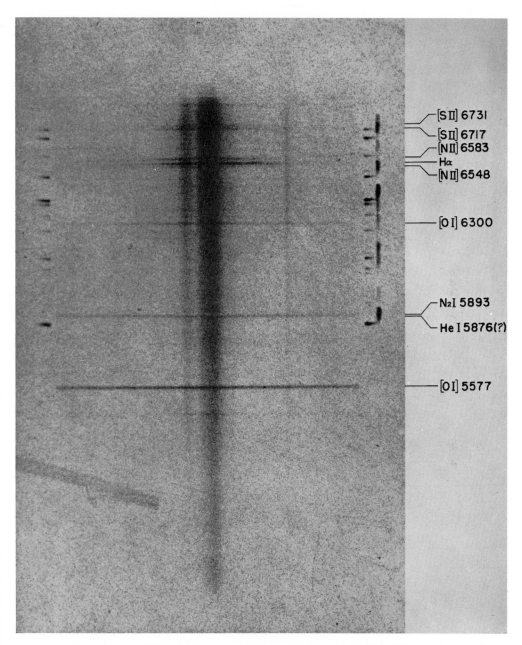

FIG. 4.—The spectrum of M82 and its system of filaments taken with the Lick 120-inch telescope. The reproduction is from ES-93, a 2-hour exposure for which the slit of the spectrograph was oriented at 335° position angle.

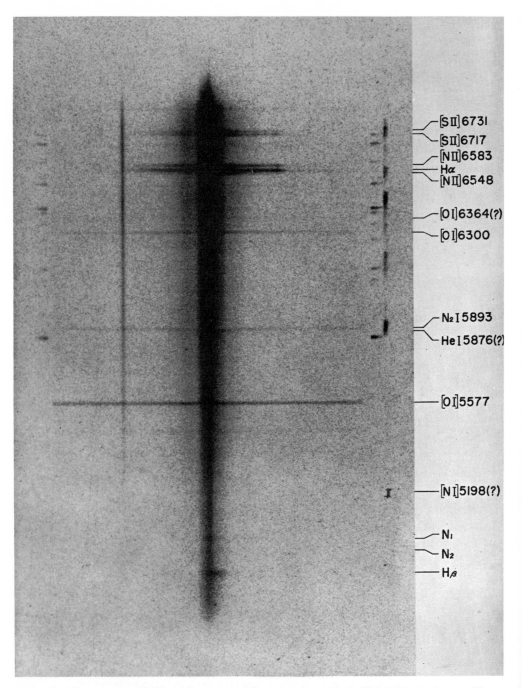

[SⅡ]6731
[SⅡ]6717
[NⅡ]6583
Hα
[NⅡ]6548

[OⅠ]6364(?)

[OⅠ]6300

N₂Ⅰ5893
HeⅠ5876(?)

[OⅠ]5577

[NⅠ]5198(?)

N₁
N₂
Hβ

Fɪɢ. 5.—The spectrum of M82 and its system of filaments taken with the Lick 120-inch telescope. The reproduction is from ES-94, a 2-hour exposure for which the slit of the spectrograph was oriented at 322° position angle.

continuum extended into the optical region and was responsible for the optical radiation from the filaments of M82.

After unsuccessful photographic attempts by both Lynds and Sandage to detect optical polarization, Elvius and Hall (1962a, b) have found polarization by using photo-electric methods. They have measured 10–15 per cent polarization in the filaments and only 2–3 per cent polarization in the main body of the galaxy. The polarization measurements in the filaments show electric vector orientations roughly parallel to the major axis of the galaxy or perpendicular to the radial pattern of the filaments, a point important for our subsequent discussion.

II. NEW OBSERVATIONS

a) Spectra

During March, 1962, three spectra of M82 in the Hα region were obtained with the prime-focus nebular spectrograph of the Lick Observatory 120-inch reflector. These plates are listed in Table 1, together with the corresponding exposure times and slit

TABLE 1

SPECTRA OF M82

Plate	Exposure Time	Slit P.A.
ES-92............	15 min.	335°
ES-93............	2 hr.	335°
ES-94............	2 hr.	322°

orientations. The emulsion used was Eastman 103a-F, and the dispersion is approximately 360 A/mm. All three spectra were obtained with a slit width of 2.7 seconds of arc and a slit length of 5 minutes of arc. The slit of the spectrograph was centered on the galaxy, with orientations roughly perpendicular to the major axis of the galaxy. For all three spectra the slit passed over the prominent star approximately 1.2 minutes of arc north preceding the nucleus of M82 and had position angles as given in the third column of Table 1. The spectrograph was rotated through approximately 180° between exposures ES-93 and ES-94. The slit positions on M82 are shown on Figure 2.

The three spectra of M82 are reproduced in Figures 3, 4, and 5. In addition to the usual night-sky lines, [O I] 5577, 6300 (and possibly 6364), and Na I 5893, the spectra show Hα, [N II] 6548, 6583, and [S II] 6717, 6731 in emission, and Na I 5893 in absorption. There is some evidence for the presence of [O I] 6300 and He I 5876. Weak [O I] 6364 is present, but it is impossible to determine whether it arises from the galaxy or from the night sky. On the original of ES-92 it is possible to see evidence of strong Hα absorption underlying the emission, thus tending to confirm an early integrated spectral type for the stellar content of M82. On ES-93, in the out-of-focus 5000 A region, Hβ and N1, N2 of [O III] appear in emission. On this plate there is also a faint indication of [N I] 5198 in emission. For ES-93 the slit of the spectrograph crosses the most intense emitting region of M82, located just west of the main dark band crossing the galaxy. Judging from the relative intensities of Hβ and N1, the excitation class (Aller 1956) of this part of M82 is between 2 and 3. It will be noticed that the region of strongest Hβ is not coextensive with the region showing the strongest continuous spectrum.

Referring to Figures 4 and 5, it is seen that, in general, little or no continuum was recorded outside the fairly well-defined main body of the galaxy. On the other hand, the emission lines of [N II] and [S II] and Hα are seen to extend well beyond the main boundary of M82. In fact, Hα and λ 6583 can be traced to nearly 2 minutes of arc from the center of the galaxy. This is almost the maximum extent of the system of filaments shown on the Sky Survey "E" plate. It now appears that the relatively great strength of the filaments as shown on red-sensitive plates is due largely to the Hα and λ 6583 emission lines.

The relative intensities of the emission lines are somewhat abnormal when compared with the spectra of typical planetary nebulae (Wyse 1942). Compared with Hα, the emission lines of [S II] and [N II] are stronger than average. In addition, there is an interesting variation in the intensity ratio Hα:[N II]6583. This ratio varies from about 3:1 in some regions just north of the galaxy to approximately 1:1 in the faint filaments south of the galaxy—a variation which is shown in Figure 6, taken from a microphotometer tracing of plate ES-94 made along Hα and λ 6583. The curves represent opacity (reciprocal transmission) as the microphotometer slit was scanned along the emission lines. The abscissa is angular distance from the foreground star located about 80 seconds

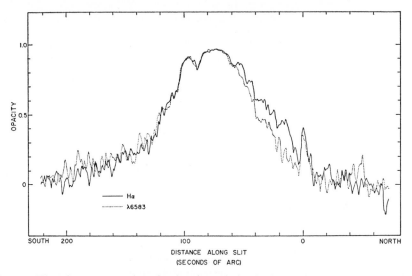

Fig. 6.—Microphotometer tracings showing the variation in the relative intensity of Hα and λ 6583 on the spectrogram ES-94. The scanning slit of the microphotometer was made very short and was scanned along the lines individually in a direction perpendicular to the dispersion.

of arc north of the center of M82. Figure 6 shows that Hα is substantially stronger than λ 6583 from 20 seconds to 80 seconds north of the galaxy center, but to the south the lines are of nearly equal intensity. Furthermore, the original plates show that the ratio Hα:λ 6583 is noticeably greater for the intense emission region crossed by the slit of ES-92 and ES-93 than it is for the relatively low surface-brightness region of the galaxy crossed by the slit of ES-94. Similar variations in the relative intensity of Hα and λ 6583 have been found by Burbidge and Burbidge (1962) in certain types of spiral galaxies.

It will be noticed that there are numerous condensations in the Hα line and the lines of [N II] and [S II]. These features may be identified with corresponding areas of emission in Figure 2. However, most of the detail of the direct plates remains unresolved on the spectra because of the small scale in the focal plane of the spectrograph camera (approximately 1.3 minutes of arc per mm). There appears to be some irregularity of the position in wavelength of the various knots in the emission lines, indicating differential velocities of the order of 50 km/sec. A possible dispersion in the radial velocity of the fine structure included within the knots is difficult to detect at the dispersion of the present spectra.

One characteristic feature of the filament spectra that can be seen upon careful in-

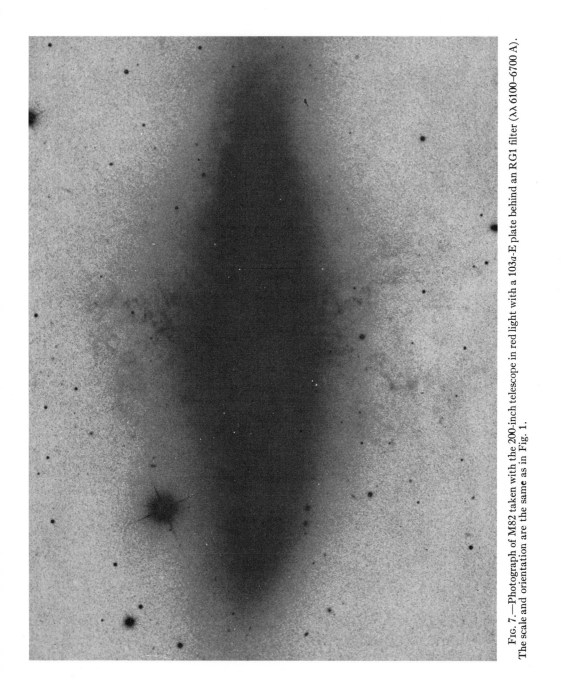

Fig. 7.—Photograph of M82 taken with the 200-inch telescope in red light with a 103a-E plate behind an RG1 filter (λλ 6100–6700 A). The scale and orientation are the same as in Fig. 1.

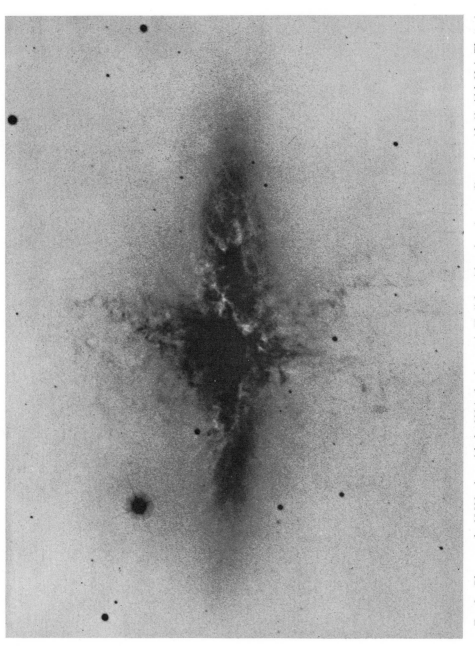

FIG. 8.—Photograph of M82 taken with the 200-inch telescope in Hα light with an interference filter of total half-width 80 A. The scale and orientation are the same as in Fig. 1. The print has been automatically dodged to increase the latitude of the photographic paper, as explained in the text. We conclude from the asymmetry of the dust pattern that the northwest (lower) edge of M82 is the near side.

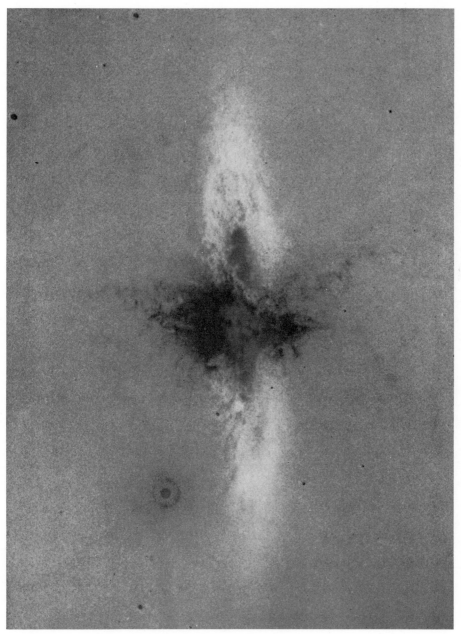

Fig. 9.—A composite photograph of M82 obtained by "subtracting" a photovisual plate (Fig. 10) from the Hα plate of Fig. 8

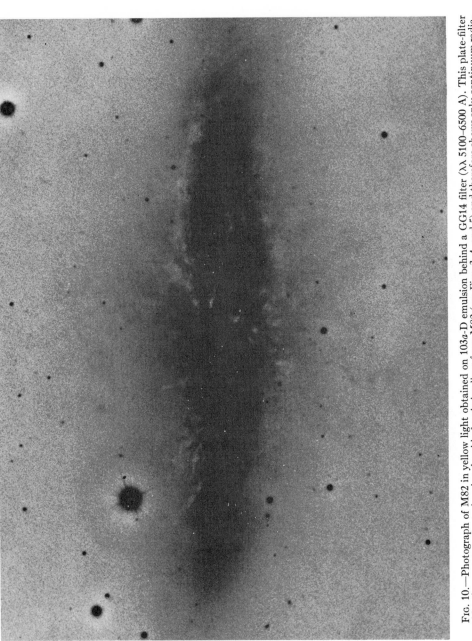

FIG. 10.—Photograph of M82 in yellow light obtained on 103a-D emulsion behind a GG14 filter (λλ 5100–6500 A). This plate-filter combination covers a spectral region devoid of emission lines from M82 (see Figs. 3, 4, and 5) and therefore shows only continuum radiation. It is seen that some of the filaments radiate in the continuum as well as in Hα. The illustration has been printed very dark, in order to show this effect.

spection of Figures 4 and 5 is the pronounced inclination of the emission lines relative to the comparison lines.[1] The inclination of the lines is in the sense that the material in the filaments north of the galaxy is receding and the material south of the galaxy is approaching. Velocity measurements relating to this effect will be treated in Section III.

b) Direct Photographs

Figure 7 is a reproduction from a plate taken in December, 1955, with the Palomar 200-inch reflector on 103a-E emulsion behind a Schott RG1 filter—a plate and filter combination which passes radiation between λ 6100 and λ 6700 A. The delicate filamentary structure perpendicular to the major axis is clearly seen extending to at least 2 minutes of arc on either side of the M82 major axis, which, when compared with the spectra, leaves no doubt that the filaments are due to a localized emission of radiation rather than to an irregular absorption of a continuous background of radiation.

To increase the contrast between the filaments and the background of sky, additional plates were taken with the 200-inch in March, 1962, using an Hα interference filter of 80 A total half-width (transmits the [N II] lines in addition to Hα). Figure 8 is a reproduction from a 3-hour interference-filter exposure made with a 103a-E emulsion. The filamentary structure is massive and lies perpendicular to the major axis of the galaxy. Figure 8 has been automatically dodged to increase the latitude of the paper print, but otherwise shows faithfully the structure. The dodging technique, developed by W. C. Miller, consists of making a low-density printing negative from a printing positive made from the original plate, then superimposing exactly this negative with the glass positive in the photographic enlarger and printing through the combination. Without this procedure, the denser regions of the original plate are lost. We are much indebted to Mr. Miller for using his characteristic skill in making this and other reproductions of the direct plates shown herein.

The filaments in Figure 8 show some regularity. The more extended part of the structure on the south-following part of the minor axis displays segments of two closed loops, one of which is bright and the other faint and somewhat fragmentary. These loops lie slightly to the east of the minor axis on the south side and reach at least 120 seconds of arc into the halo. On the original plate they can be seen to attach onto the main body of the galaxy through two intense Hα emission spikes. At least four other loops of smaller extension can be traced on the south side, and these terminate in the halo at a point 40 seconds of arc from the major axis on the boundary which separates a high-intensity region from the two low-intensity filaments. The filamentary structure on the north side of the major axis is not nearly so regular, but faint extensions can be traced to 190 seconds of arc from the major axis on this side. The general appearance of Figure 8 as regards the loops is that of a solar prominence photographed in Hα.

Figure 9 gives another representation of the filamentary system and was made by photographically "subtracting" the image of the galaxy in yellow light (103a-D plus GG14) from the Hα plate of Figure 8. A positive film was made from the original Hα plate, which was then superimposed with the original 103a-D negative, and the two were printed together. The resulting photograph clearly shows that the Hα filaments are predominantly perpendicular to the major axis of the galaxy.

The linear extent of the filamentary system is enormous. Here and in the following sections, we adopt a distance modulus $m - M = 27.5$, or a distance of 9.76×10^{24} cm, based on the membership of M82 in the M81 group (Sandage 1962). At this distance, a projected length of 190 seconds of arc on the sky corresponds to approximately 3000 pc. Hence we are dealing with a heretofore unknown but major element in the description of M82.

---

[1] In view of the rather remote possibility of a systematic instrumental effect, it is reassuring to note that the spectrograph orientation was reversed between ES-93 and ES-94.

Figure 10 is a reproduction of a long-exposure plate taken on an Eastman 103a-D plate behind 2 mm of GG14 filter—a combination which accepts radiation from λ 5050 to just shortward of Hα. Although there are no strong emission lines in this wavelength interval (see Figs. 3, 4, and 5), some of the filaments are visible on the reproduction, in particular the faint streamer on the northwest side of the minor axis and parts of the brightest extended loop on the south minor axis. We do not believe this is to be due to Hα radiation leaked to the plate because a special series of red-leak tests showed that the 103a-D emulsion is 220 times less sensitive at λ 6563 A than the 103a-E emulsion. This factor is so large relative to the intensity ratio of the filaments shown between Figure 8 and Figure 10 that we conclude that some of the filaments *radiate weakly in the continuum as well as in Hα*. If the filaments outline lines of magnetic flux as in solar prominences, then we conclude that continuum radiation of these filaments is connected with

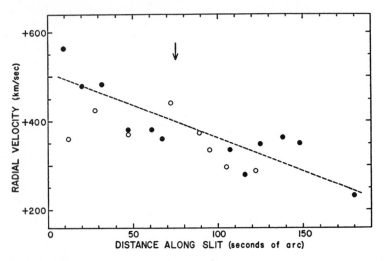

Fig. 11.—Measurements of the radial velocity of the filaments at various positions along the slit of the spectrograph. The filled circles and open circles represent velocities obtained from ES-93 and ES-94, respectively. The dashed curve is a least-squares straight line fitted to the observations from ES-93. The arrow in the upper part of the figure indicates the approximate center of the galaxy.

the magnetic field, and this is the basis for our later calculation of the synchrotron emission. In addition to these filaments, the original plate of Figure 10 shows a faint, semi-uniform surface emission over the entire volume of the halo, which we also later attribute to synchrotron emission from electrons moving in a magnetic field threading this entire volume. Figure 10 has been deliberately overprinted in an attempt to show this feature.

III. MOTIONS OF THE FILAMENTS

The three spectra, ES-92, 93, and 94, have been measured for radial velocity. Corrections have been made for the effects of slit curvature, the earth's motion, and the motion of the sun with respect to the local group. The solar-motion correction was made following the procedure of Humason *et al.* (1956).

The measurements of the main body of the galaxy yielded radial velocities of 300 km/sec for ES-92, 350 km/sec for ES-93, and 400 km/sec for ES-94. The difference in velocity given by ES-93 and ES-94 may possibly be due to real differential motion between the parts of the galaxy covered by the two slit positions. However, the difference between the velocities shown by ES-92 is believed to be an exposure-time effect arising from differential motions along the slit. The measurements have an estimated internal precision of about 25 km/sec; however, the absolute accuracy of the measurements is not known, since the spectrograph has been in operation only a short time and its velocity system has not as yet been well established. It is felt that little significance can be attached to any differences between the present velocity measurements of M82 and those published by Humason *et al.* (1956), which gave +400 km/sec from the Mount Wilson data and +410 km/sec from the Lick material.

The positions at which velocity measurements were made along Hα and λ 6583 are indicated by the circles in Figure 2. The corrected velocities for these positions have been plotted in Figure 11. The abscissa is the same as that in Figure 6 and is the distance in seconds of arc south from the reference star located approximately 75 seconds north of M82. The arrow in the upper part of the figure indicates the approximate center of the galaxy. The filled circles represent the velocities obtained from ES-93, for which the slit was oriented perpendicular to the major axis of the main outline of the galaxy. It is seen that the tilt of the emission lines, mentioned in Section II, is well represented by the measurements. A linear velocity relation, established by a least-squares fitting to the observed velocities, is shown as a dashed line in Figure 11. The measured velocities are not of sufficient weight to warrant the determination of a velocity relation of higher than the first order in the angular distance from the center of the galaxy. The linear velocity relation has a slope of 1.5 km/sec per second of arc and crosses the plane of the galaxy at about 400 km/sec. However, the quoted velocity at the crossover point may be of little significance for the reasons mentioned above.

The open circles in Figure 11 represent the radial velocities obtained from ES-94, for which the slit made an angle of approximately 13° with respect to that for ES-93. The abscissa is the same as before, that is, angular distance along the slit; however, depending on the interpretation given to the observed velocities, account should be taken of the projection angle between the two slit orientations. Aside from the discrepancy at about 65 seconds north of the galaxy, there is general agreement between the velocity relationships shown by the two spectra. Although measurements were not actually made as far south on ES-94 as on ES-93, visual inspection of the spectra confirms a general decrease in radial velocity to the south for both spectra.

Mayall's observations (1960) show that the spectrum of M82 has inclined lines when a spectrographic slit is placed along the major axis. These data suggest that the galaxy is rotating about its minor axis as in normal systems, with an average gradient of 1.4 km/sec per second of arc, which gives a minimum total mass of 2.7×10^{10} solar masses, using an adopted distance of 9.76×10^{24} cm. The interpretation of Mayall's data as rotation seems highly likely, even though we have observed radial velocities of the filaments with the slit placed 90° to Mayall's direction. It is, of course, possible that the total angular momentum vector is not along one of the principal axes of inertia, in which case there would be components of the rotational velocity along *both* the major and minor axes of the projected image and inclined lines would then be produced, as observed, when the slit is placed along *either* of these axes. But this seems so unlikely that we, for the moment, reject such a possibility and suggest that Mayall's data give the rotational curve for the galaxy and, therefore, that our data show that the filaments are in systematic motion perpendicular to the fundamental plane.

Our data can be reproduced if the fundamental plane is tilted slightly to the line of sight so that a component of the filament motion along the minor axis appears as a radial velocity. Such a geometry seems plausible because the observed axial ratio of the best-fitting ellipse to Figure 10 is $\beta/a = 0.175$. Most of the flattened galaxies of the S0–Sc type have true axial ratios of $b/a \simeq 0.10$ (see Pl. 8 of NGC 4762 and Pl. 25 of six nearly edge-on galaxies in the *Hubble Atlas* ["Carnegie Institution of Washington Publications," No. 618]).

The inclination angle of the fundamental plane of M82 to the line of sight can be computed from Hubble's formula (1926)

$$\cos^2 i = \frac{1 - (\beta/a)^2}{1 - (b/a)^2},$$

(1)

which gives $i = 8°23'$ if $b/a = 0.10$, or $i = 9°56'$ if $b/a = 0$ (the flat-disk assumption). In all subsequent calculations, we adopt $i = 8°23'$.

Having established the possibility of systematic motions of the filaments, we now inquire as to the direction of the velocity field—a problem which is solved only if identification of the near side of the galaxy can be made. Following Hubble (1943), we have adopted the asymmetry of absorption lanes across the galaxy face as the primary tilt criterion, a point well taken by the established small dispersion in the height of the distribution of dust in the principal planes of other galaxies. Figure 8 then requires that the northwest side of M82 be nearest to the observer. The radial-velocity curve of Figure 11 shows that the filaments on this side of the projected image are receding, which then requires that the matter on both sides of the major axis be *moving away from the fundamental plane. The filaments appear to be expanding from the center of the galaxy!*

This expansion is approximately linear (see Fig. 11) and of the form $\rho(\theta) = \mu\theta$, where $\rho(\theta)$ is the radial velocity of a particular angular segment of a filament at an angular distance θ from the center of M82 and $\mu = 1.5$ km/sec per second of arc, a value found earlier in this section. If $v(r)$ is taken to be the true velocity of expansion at a true distance r from the center of M82 along the minor axis, then $\mu = 0.664$ km sec^{-1} pc^{-1} or 2.15×10^{-14} cm sec^{-1} cm^{-1}, where the inclination angle has been taken into account.

In the absence of deceleration, a linear velocity-distance relation has the unique property that the time for every element to travel along its path from a common point of origin to its presently observed position is a constant for all segments of the filaments. This time is μ^{-1}, which in our case is 1.47×10^6 years. It is the interval from the present epoch to that time in the past when all matter in the filaments was near the center of the galaxy. Deceleration has undoubtedly occurred but will be neglected in our following exploratory calculations because of lack of precise data. When more extensive radial-velocity measurements are available and when the mass distribution of M82 is known, a more complete description can be made, taking deceleration into account.

IV. THE PROPOSED MODEL

Data from the last section require that an expulsion of material has occurred from the nuclear regions of the galaxy in what appears to have been an explosion. It looks as if the filamentary material in the halo is partially confined to loops which are assumed to outline magnetic field lines [as, for example, in the case of the Crab Nebula (Baade 1956)] carried from the disk by the matter in its outward motion. Although the initial explosion may have been isotropic, the debris cannot move freely in the fundamental plane because of the magnetic pressure built up by compression or, perhaps more importantly, because of the high probability of inelastic collisions with gas which may be associated with the abundant dust which covers the plane. Most of the expanding matter will move poleward in the directions of least constraint. If this material is to carry the magnetic field, then the kinetic energy of the filaments must be greater than the total magnetic energy carried with it. Estimates in Section VI of the magnetic-field strength (computed from the synchrotron theory) and of the mass of the filaments (computed from the observed Hα flux) indeed suggest that this may be the case.

By some mechanism, not understood, a large fraction of the explosion energy may be put into relativistic electrons which spiral in the magnetic field, producing the observed radio emission and the continuous optical emission in the halo. The polarization observed by Elvius and Hall (1962a, b) midway in the halo can be explained in this way because the polarization plane is perpendicular to the predominant orientation of the filaments, as required by theory.

The remaining problem is to find the source of excitation of the emission lines in the optical spectrum. The observed recombination spectrum resembles that of planetary and gaseous nebulae of low excitation. Forbidden emission lines of N II, S II, and possibly O III are present in addition to the emission lines of hydrogen. The relativistic electrons cannot be the excitation source because they pass through the cold gas with no appreciable interaction. The character of the line spectrum requires that the recombining electrons have average energies of only a few electron volts ($T \simeq 10000°$ K). Consequently, two energy systems coexist in the filaments of M82: a high-energy electron component, giving rise to the synchrotron emission, and the low-energy electrons, which produce the recombination emissions and excitation for the forbidden lines. Following Woltjer's (1958) discussion of a similar situation in the Crab Nebula, we postulate in Section VII that the ionization of the hydrogen is produced by the optical synchrotron radiation below the Lyman limit—a radiation source which substitutes for the more usual hot-star radiation in emission nebulae in our own Galaxy.

The plan of the remainder of this paper is to carry through calculations based on this model so as to estimate the magnitude of the relevant parameters.

V. THE FILAMENTS: ELECTRON DENSITY, MASS, AND KINETIC ENERGY

The electron density in the filaments can be determined by standard methods, once the volume emissivity E is known in absolute units (ergs cm^{-3} sec^{-1}) for any of the Balmer lines. We can determine E from M82, provided that (1) the apparent Hα flux received at the earth (ergs cm^{-2} sec^{-1}) is known, (2) the distance of the galaxy is known, and (3) the volume occupied by the filaments can be estimated. Unfortunately, we have no direct measurement of the apparent Hα flux but have resorted to an estimate of the intensity of the filaments on the Hα interference filter plate relative to the sky brightness at λ 6563, whose absolute surface brightness can be determined approximately. Photoelectric measurement of the sky brightness at λ 6260 A was made by Lynds with the 20-inch reflector at Palomar on a night when the aurora was active, with the result that $S(\lambda$ 6260 A$)_{sky} = 5.3 \times 10^{-31}$ w m^{-2} cps^{-1} per square second of arc. The absolute calibration of the photometer was made by observing several stars of known apparent magnitude and then using the sun as a standard in the normal way. This flux density can be compared with Allen's tabulation (1955), which gives $S(\lambda$ 6500 A$)_{sky} = 2.0 \times 10^{-31}$ w m^{-2} cps^{-1} per square second of arc. As a compromise, we adopt the specific sky brightness to be $S(H\alpha)_{sky} = 2.5 \times 10^{-31}$ w m^{-2} cps^{-1} per square second of arc.

It is estimated by visual inspection of the Hα plate that the radiation flux in Hα from the entire filament system is equivalent to the flux from the sky over an area of 1.2×10^4 square seconds of arc. The total band width of the Hα interference filter is 80 A to half-power points (or $\Delta\nu = 5.57 \times 10^{12}$ cps), which, after calculation, gives the observed Hα flux density as 1.7×10^{-11} erg cm^{-2} sec^{-1} (or 5.6 Hα photons cm^{-2} sec^{-1}) at the earth's surface. This is admittedly a crude estimate; but, as the electron density varies as the square root of this number, we can obtain the electron density N_e to within a factor of 10 (provided that we know the volume-filling factor) even if the value of $S(H\alpha)$ is in error by a factor of 100. Such accuracy for N_e is adequate for our purpose. The observed Hα flux requires that the total power radiated by the filaments of M82 in Hα be $4\pi D^2 S(H\alpha) = 2.0 \times 10^{40}$ ergs sec^{-1} if $D = 9.76 \times 10^{24}$ cm is the distance to M82.

We now require the volume emissivity of the filaments of M82. This quantity can be found, once the geometry of the system has been specified. (In this discussion it should be recognized that, to some extent, the geometry of the system of filaments was implicitly involved in the foregoing estimate of the Hα flux density.) For this it is assumed that the filaments are contained in the volume common to a sphere of radius $R = 1550$ pc (100 seconds of arc) centered on the nucleus of M82 and a cone (extending symmetrically to either side of the nucleus) of apex half-angle 60° whose axis of symmetry coincides with the minor axis of the galaxy. This geometry gives the total volume containing the filaments as $V = 2\pi R^3/3 = 2.29 \times 10^{65}$ cm^3. The Hα emission is not uniformly distributed throughout the volume but is concentrated in the filaments. Inspection of the Hα plate suggests a volume-filling factor of approximately $7^3 = 343$, which is a guess based on our simple geometry and the observed dimensions of the filaments. The volume contained within the filaments is $V_f = V/343 = 6.68 \times 10^{62}$ cm^3. Therefore, the average volume emissivity of the filaments is 3×10^{-23} erg cm^{-3} sec^{-1}.

The well-known theory of the hydrogen recombination spectrum, due principally to Menzel and his co-workers,[2] gives the volume emissivity in Hα as

$$E_{H\alpha} = \frac{6.54 \times 10^{-19} b_3 \, g_{32} N_i N_e}{T_e^{3/2}} \exp\left(\frac{1.75 \times 10^4}{T_e}\right) \tag{2}$$

in erg cm^{-3} sec^{-1}, where N_i and N_e are the proton and electron densities in particles per cm^3, T_e is the electron temperature, b_3 measures the departure of the population of the third quantum level from what it would be in thermodynamic equilibrium, and g_{32} is the Gaunt factor which Baker and Menzel (1938) tabulate as 0.757. The quantity b_3 depends on the physical conditions of the radiation field and has a value near 0.1 for a situation where the filaments are optically thick in the Lyman continuum (Baker and Menzel, case B). Adopting $b_3 = 0.1$, $T_e = 10^4 \,^\circ$K, and $N_i = N_e$ requires that

$$E_{H\alpha} = 2.85 \times 10^{-25} N_e^2 \tag{3}$$

in erg cm^{-3} sec^{-1}. Our observed emissivity of 3×10^{-23} erg cm^{-3} sec^{-1} then requires $\langle N_e \rangle = 10.3$ particles per cm^3 for the average density in the filaments.

The total amount of material responsible for the recombination radiation is evidently $\langle N_e \rangle V_f = 7 \times 10^{63}$ protons $= 1.2 \times 10^{40}$ gm or 5.8×10^6 solar masses, which is very high, representing as it does 2×10^{-4} of the total mass of the galaxy.[3]

In computing the kinetic energy of the hydrogen in the filaments, we shall adopt the geometry of the system outlined above. For the distribution of the material in the filaments, we shall consider two cases: (a) the electron density in the filaments is a constant for all distances r from the center of M82, $N_e(r) = \langle N_e \rangle$, and (b) the electron density is given by

$$N_e(r) = \frac{\langle N_e \rangle}{26}\left(53 - 40\frac{r}{R}\right). \tag{4}$$

For both cases the velocity relation adopted is that determined in Section III, namely,

$$v(r) = \mu r, \tag{5}$$

where $\mu = 2.15 \times 10^{-14}$ cm sec^{-1} cm^{-1}. In addition, the fraction of space occupied by the filaments, $\Lambda(r)$, is assumed to be of the form

$$\Lambda(r) = \frac{\Lambda}{2}\left(5 - 4\frac{r}{R}\right), \tag{6}$$

where Λ is the reciprocal of the volume-filling factor adopted earlier in this section. Equation (6) has the properties that $\Lambda(R) = \Lambda/2$ and that the average value of $\Lambda(r)$ taken over the whole volume of space is equal to Λ, i.e.,

$$\langle \Lambda(r) \rangle = \frac{3}{R^3} \int_0^R \Lambda(r) \, r^2 dr = \Lambda. \tag{7}$$

[2] Contained in a series of articles in the *Astrophysical Journal* beginning with Vol. 85.

[3] It should be pointed out that this may be an upper limit to the mass of the visible matter because the volume-filling factor may be larger than we have estimated. If the angular diameters of the filaments are smaller than they appear on our plates ($\sim 2''$ of arc) due to seeing difficulties, then V_f is decreased, N_e is increased, but the product $V_f N_e$ is decreased by $V_f^{1/2}$, which gives a smaller total mass than computed above. Of course there may be a large additional mass of invisible neutral hydrogen.

Equation (4) has the property that $N_e(R) = \langle N_e \rangle / 2$ and that the total mass of the system is conserved, that is,

$$2\pi m_{\mathrm{H}} \int_0^R \Lambda(r) N_e(r) r^2 dr = \tfrac{2}{3}\pi R^3 \Lambda \langle N_e \rangle m_{\mathrm{H}} . \tag{8}$$

It is obvious that case a will exactly reproduce the value of the Hα flux from which the average electron density was originally determined. This is not true for case b; a computation of the Hα flux gives a value about 10 per cent too large, indicating that the adopted value of $\langle N_e \rangle$ should be reduced by about 5 per cent to be appropriate for this particular electron-density distribution.

The total kinetic energy of the system of filaments is

$$\epsilon_k = \pi m_{\mathrm{H}} \int_0^R \Lambda(r) N_e(r) [v(r)]^2 r^2 dr , \tag{9}$$

which, when integrated, gives $\epsilon_k \simeq 2.4 \times 10^{55}$ ergs to within about 20 per cent for both cases a and b, showing that the kinetic energy is relatively insensitive to the exact distribution of matter within the system. This estimate is an upper limit to ϵ_k because, as

TABLE 2

RADIO OBSERVATIONS OF M82

Frequency (kMc)	$S(\nu) \times 10^{26}$ (w m^{-2} cps^{-1})	Reference
0.158	12	Brown and Hazard (1953); Edge, Shakeshaft, McAdam, Baldwin, and Archer (1959)
0.71	10.7	California Institute of Technology Radio Observatory, unpublished
0.75	8	Lynds (1961)
1.423	8.6	Goldstein (1962)
3.0	6.15	Lynds (1961)
3.2	6.5	California Institute of Technology Radio Observatory, unpublished

previously mentioned, we may have overestimated the total mass of the filaments.

If the magnetic field is assumed to be constant throughout the volume, the total magnetic energy will be

$$\epsilon_M = \tfrac{1}{12} R^3 H^2 = 9.1 \times 10^{63} H^2 \text{ ergs} , \tag{10}$$

where H is the field strength in gauss. For a field strength of 2×10^{-6} gauss, obtained in Section VI, equation (13) gives a magnetic energy of 3.6×10^{52} ergs, which is about three orders of magnitude smaller than the kinetic energy of the moving filaments. This insures that the material ejected from the central region of M82 was sufficiently energetic to carry a substantial magnetic field from the galaxy.

VI. THE SYNCHROTRON RADIATION

The available radio-frequency observations of the M82 radio source are given in Table 2. The first column gives the frequency in kilomegacycles; the second column, the flux density in units of 10^{-26} w m^{-2} cps^{-1}; and the third column is the reference. On the basis of the presence of optical polarization of the filaments found by Elvius and Hall (1962a, b), we suggest that some or all of the radiation from the filaments, as well as from the background halo recorded on the photovisual plate, arises from the optical synchrotron continuum. We have attempted to estimate this synchrotron flux using the 103a-D +

GG14 photograph (Fig. 10) in the same way that we previously used for the Hα flux. However, there is a question of the degree to which the discrete emission lines contribute to the photographic image of the filaments on this plate. The emission lines of interest are Hα and N1. The test already described in Section II shows that the 103a-D emulsion is down by a factor of 220 relative to the 103a-E emulsion at the wavelength of Hα and, therefore, that the effect of Hα radiation on the photovisual plate is negligible. Further-more, the GG14 filter transmits only 20 per cent of the radiation at the N1 line (deter-mined by measurement of the actual filter used), which suggests, by comparison of the intensities of the emission lines in the spectra of the filaments of M82, that the effect of N1 on the photovisual plate can also be neglected.

The photographic density of the filaments and of the semiuniform halo which fills the conical volume was compared with the density due to the night sky, for which we have adopted a surface brightness of 7×10^{-32} w m^{-2} cps^{-1} per square second of arc. In this

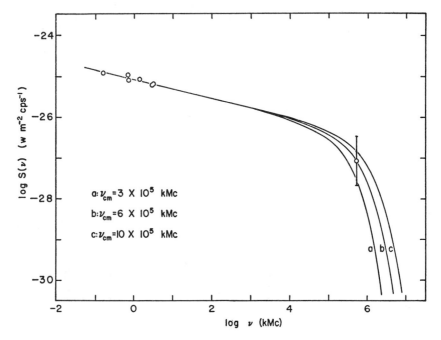

FIG. 12.—The syncrotron spectrum of the M82 filaments. The circles represent the observed spectrum, and the curves give theoretical spectra for different values for the cutoff frequency (the frequency corre-sponding to the high-energy cutoff of the electron energy distribution).

manner the flux density of the visual synchrotron emission of the entire source is esti-mated to be 8.5×10^{-28} w m^{-2} cps^{-1} at the effective wavelength of 5550 A ($\nu = 5.4 \times 10^{14}$ cps).

If we now make the assumption that the flux at radio frequencies is generated in the same volume of M82 as is the optical synchrotron radiation, we can determine the power spectrum of the source over the range $\nu = 1.6 \times 10^8$ cps to 5.4×10^{14} cps. The radio-frequency flux densities given in Table 2 and the above estimate of the optical flux density (with an estimated error of ± 1.5 mag.) are plotted in Figure 12. The indicated spectral index is about 0.23, and the cutoff frequency would seem to be between 10^{14} and 10^{15} cps. The three curves represent the theoretical synchrotron spectra having cutoff frequencies of 3×10^{14}, 6×10^{14}, and 10^{15} cps, as determined later in this section.

A general development of the theory of synchrotron radiation has been given in a well-known article by Schwinger (1949). The theory has been put in a form useful for astronomical problems by Oort and Walraven (1956), by Woltjer (1958), and by Burbidge in a series of articles (cf. 1956). The results of interest for us are that an assemblage of electrons with an energy distribution

$$N(E)dE = kE^{-\beta}dE \tag{11}$$

moving in a magnetic field H will radiate at frequency ν with a flux density

$$P(\nu) = 1.171 \times 10^{-22} kL^{(\beta-1)/2}(H \sin \theta)^{(\beta+1)/2} \nu^{-(\beta-1)/2}$$

$$\times \int_{a_m}^{\infty} a^{(\beta-3)/2} F(a) \, da \text{ erg sec}^{-1} \text{ cps}^{-1}, \tag{12}$$

where $L = 1.608 \times 10^{13}$, θ is the pitch angle of the electron orbits, a_m is the ratio of ν to the frequency radiated by electrons at the high-energy cutoff E_m, and $F(a)$ is a function tabulated by Oort and Walraven (1956) and by others. The high-frequency cutoff is given by

$$\nu_{cm} = LH \sin \theta E_m^2, \tag{13}$$

where E_m denotes the maximum energy reached by the electron distribution (E_m in 10^9 ev if ν is in cps). In our calculations we have adopted $\langle \sin \theta \rangle = \pi/4$ and $\langle \sin \theta^{(\beta+1)/2} \rangle = \frac{3}{4}$, corresponding to an isotropic velocity distribution and a uniform magnetic field.

From the observed radio-frequency spectral index of 0.23, we deduce from equation (12) that $\beta = 1.46$. Also, from the radio data the flux density at 3 kMc is $S(3 \text{ kMc}) = 6.4 \times 10^{-26}$ w m^{-2} cps^{-1} = 6.4×10^{-23} erg sec^{-1} cm^{-2} cps^{-1}, which gives, for the total power emitted at $\nu = 3$ kMc in a bandwidth of 1 cps,

$$P(3 \text{ kMc}) = 4\pi D^2 S(3 \text{ kMc}) = 7.66 \times 10^{28} \text{ ergs sec}^{-1} \text{ cps}^{-1}, \tag{14}$$

where we have again adopted a distance modulus for M82 of 27.5. Upon substitution of equation (14) in equation (12), we find that

$$k = 4.0 \times 10^{49} H^{-(\beta+1)/2}, \tag{15}$$

where the integral has been evaluated numerically, using the $F(a)$ tables and the asymptotic form $F(a) = 2.15 a^{1/3}$ for $a = \leq 0.001$.

By combining the relation for k (eq. [15]) with equation (12), we have the theoretical synchrotron spectrum,

$$S(\nu) = 3.2 \times 10^{-24} \nu^{-0.23} G(\nu) \tag{16}$$

in w m^{-2} cps^{-1}, where

$$G(\nu) = \int_{a_m = \nu/\nu_{cm}}^{\infty} a^{(\beta-3)/2} F(a) \, da, \tag{17}$$

which is the function only of ν, once ν_{cm} is specified.

Equations (16) and (17) have been used to compute theoretical spectra for three different assumed values of the high-frequency cutoff ν_{cm}. Equation (17) was integrated numerically over the range of $F(a)$ covered by the tables of Oort and Walraven (1956) and was extended to the limits analytically, using the well-known asymptotic forms of $F(a)$. For small a_m, the analytical extension is trivial. For $a_m > 10$, the asymptotic form of $F(a)$ requires that

$$G(\nu) = 1.26 \int_{a_m = \nu/\nu_{cm}}^{\infty} a^{-0.27} e^{-a} da \qquad (18)$$

(with $\beta = 1.46$), which can be integrated by parts to give an asymptotic series where only the first term need be kept, giving

$$G(\nu) = 1.26 \left(\frac{\nu}{\nu_{cm}}\right)^{-0.27} e^{-\nu/\nu_{cm}}, \qquad \text{for } \frac{\nu}{\nu_{cm}} > 10. \quad (19)$$

Three theoretical spectra computed from equation (16) in this manner are shown in Figure 12, where the values of ν_{cm} are 3×10^{14}, 6×10^{14}, and 10^{15} cps. For $\nu < 10^{13}$ cps, a_m is nearly zero, and $G(\nu)$ is a definite integral with effective limits between 0 and ∞ and is therefore a constant. Hence, in this frequency range, the three spectra are nearly identical and follow a power law, as is observed at radio frequencies. However, the differences between the spectra in the optical region are substantial, and the importance of an accurate value of the observed optical flux density is apparent if ν_{cm} is to be well determined. Figure 12 shows that ν_{cm} could be as low as 2×10^{14} cps or as high as 2×10^{15} cps and still fit the one optical observation. We adopt $\nu_{cm} = 6 \times 10^{14}$ cps in subsequent calculations.

Making use of equation (11) and our determination of k (eq. [15]), we find that the total energy in relativistic electrons is

$$\epsilon_R = k \int_0^{E_m} E N(E) dE$$

$$= \frac{4 \times 10^{49}}{2 - \beta} \left(\frac{4\nu_{cm}}{\pi L}\right)^{(2-\beta)/2} H^{-3/2} \qquad (20)$$

$$= 2.1 \times 10^{50} H^{-3/2} \text{ Bev},$$

$$\epsilon_R = 3.36 \times 10^{47} H^{-3/2} \text{ ergs}, \qquad (21)$$

where any error introduced by assuming the lower limit of the integral to be zero will be negligible. Although the quantity ν_{cm} is not well determined, the total energy is seen to be relatively insensitive to its precise value. Even if ν_{cm} is in error by a factor of 10, the error in ϵ_R will be less than a factor of 2.

In previous considerations of the energy balance in radio sources (see, e.g., Burbidge 1956), it has been customary to introduce here an assumption of equality between the energy stored in the relativistic electrons (eq. [21]) and the energy ϵ_M stored in the magnetic field [eq. [10]]. Doing this would give $H = 2 \times 10^{-5}$ gauss for M82, but this leads to some problems in the time scale and the total energy by the following argument. Equation (21) shows that this value of H requires $\epsilon_R = 3.7 \times 10^{54}$ ergs for the energy now stored in the electrons, which should be compared with the total energy radiated by the synchroton process in the past 1.5×10^6 years. Integration of the power spectrum of equation (16) over the entire frequency range from 10^8 cps to 6×10^{14} cps gives 1.64×10^{-9} erg cm^{-2} sec^{-1} for the apparent synchrotron flux. Multiplication by $4\pi D^2$ and by the time of 1.5×10^6 years gives 9×10^{55} ergs radiated in the lifetime of the M82 source, a number which is large compared with the 3.7×10^{54} ergs now stored in the electron reservoir. Therefore, electrons would have to be continuously injected into the system from an unseen energy reservoir to maintain the present rate of radiation for 1.5×10^6 years. And it would appear that a Fermi-type acceleration mechanism which transfers part of the energy contained in the magnetic field to the particles cannot be the replenishment source because, on the foregoing assumptions, the total energy in the field is only 3.7×10^{54} ergs, which is small compared with the 9×10^{55} ergs required. Therefore, the field cannot be pumped for 9×10^{55} ergs unless the field itself is periodically regenerated.

The need for continuous injection of high-energy electrons can be seen in another way by considering the time for the optical electrons to lose one-half of their initial energy, which is

$$T_{1/2} = \frac{8.35 \times 10^{-3}}{(H \sin \theta)^2 E_0} \text{ years} . \qquad (22)$$

This gives $T_{1/2}$(optical) $= 2.5 \times 10^4$ years (using $E_0 = 1.5 \times 10^3$ Bev obtained from eq. [13] with $\nu_{\rm em} = 6 \times 10^{14}$ cps and $H = 2 \times 10^{-5}$ gauss). This time is much smaller than the lifetime of radio M82.

Following Burbidge (1956), we had originally supposed that the unseen energy reservoir might be high-energy protons which collided with the quiescent cool protons in the filaments, producing mesons which would subsequently decay into the required electrons. Burbidge (1956) estimates that 10 per cent of the collision energy of the bombarding protons finally appears in the relativistic electron gas. This means that, if each bombarding proton were to make one collision in the lifetime of the system, at least 9×10^{56} ergs must reside in the high-energy protons. But the probability of a single bombarding proton colliding with the quiescent hydrogen in the halo and the filaments in time t is not 1.0 but $c\sigma Nt$, where σ is the collision cross-section ($\simeq 4 \times 10^{-26}$ cm^2/proton), c is the velocity of light, and N is the number of target protons per cm^3. Spitzer has pointed out to us that the high energy protons, if they exist, cannot be confined in the filaments because their energy density is much higher than the magnetic-field energy density; hence N must be much smaller than 10, which applied only in the filaments. Even if we take the average density over the halo to be as high as 0.1, the number of collisions per bombarding proton in 1.5×10^6 years will be 6×10^{-3}, and the energy store in these protons must then be $9 \times 10^{56}/6 \times 10^{-3} = 1.5 \times 10^{59}$ ergs, which is very high. Consequently, unless the total energy of the system is as high as 10^{59} ergs, the assumption of equipartition between ϵ_R and ϵ_M may not apply to M82.

Spitzer has suggested that a way to reduce the total energy of the problem is to require that ϵ_R be equal to, or greater than, the energy radiated over the lifetime of the M82 radio source. This assumption is equivalent to saying that the energy put initially into the electron gas was high enough to maintain the observed radiation for at least 1.5×10^6 years. Equation (21) then requires that $3.36 \times 10^{47} H^{-3/2} > 9 \times 10^{55}$ ergs, which gives $H < 2.5 \times 10^{-6}$ gauss. We have adopted this point of view, which eliminates the necessity of a continuous injection or reacceleration of electrons to maintain the observed synchrotron flux. We then require that the initial "explosion" put at least $\sim 10^{56}$ ergs into the high energy electrons. But we wish to emphasize that we have discussed only two of the many possibilities of the energetics of the system. Until we have an independent way of estimating H, the problem has no unique solution, although it may be fair to say that the total energy must be at least as high as 10^{56} ergs and is probably less than 10^{60} ergs.

As in other radio source problems, these energy levels are extremely high. An energy of 10^{56} ergs is equivalent to the total emission of about 10^6 supernovae. This result seems inescapable. We observe radio emission from an expanding filament system whose expansion time is 1.5×10^6 years, and this requires that at least 10^{56} ergs have been emitted if the synchrotron emission extends into the optical region. Arguments in the next section, which are in addition to those already given, suggest that the electron radiation probably does extend below the Lyman limit and, therefore, that these minimum power levels obtain.

The nature of the initial explosion in the central regions of M82 is an enigma. But M82 may be the first recognized case of a high energy explosion originating in the central regions of a galaxy, and as such may provide features required for a general explanation of many extragalactic radio sources. In passing, it is interesting to note that Hoyle and Fowler (1963) have recently postulated an explosion mechanism involving the gravitational collapse of a massive ensemble of gas which can generate as much as 10^{62} ergs. Also, Ambartsumian (1961) for many years has considered similar problems concerned with energies in the nuclei of galaxies.

VII. EXCITATION OF THE EMISSION LINES

The problem of the radiation source for the low excitation emission lines observed in the filaments was outlined in Section IV. Some source other than stellar must be found because of the lack of any evidence for stars in the halo of M82. Furthermore, the high energy particles can play no direct role in the problem. Following Woltjer's discussion (1958) of the Crab Nebula, we have calculated the number N_L of photons below the Lyman limit for two of the theoretical synchrotron spectra of Figure 12. If the optical synchrotron radiation below the Lyman limit is the ionization source for the hydrogen recombination spectrum, then N_L must be about 3.3 times larger than the number of Hα photons emitted (see, e.g., Zanstra 1961), provided that the filaments are optically thick to Lyman continuum radiation.

One can determine N_L by dividing equation (16) by $h\nu$ and integrating over all $\nu >$ 3.29×10^{15} cps ($\lambda = 912$ A). For values of $\nu_{\rm cm}$ in the optical region, the main contribution from $F(\alpha)$ (in eq. [17]) occurs within the range of the $F(\alpha)$ tables, and numerical techniques yield a good determination of N_L. The resultant photon flux at the earth is 0.09 photon cm^{-2} sec^{-1} for $\nu_{\rm cm} = 6 \times 10^{14}$ cps and 1.2 photons cm^{-2} sec^{-1} for $\nu_{\rm cm} = 10^{15}$ cps. These values correspond to the upper two spectra represented in Figure 12. N_L is evidently extremely sensitive to $\nu_{\rm cm}$. We estimated in Section V that the observed Hα photon flux from M82 was 5.6 photons cm^{-2} sec^{-1}, with a possible error of a factor of 10–100. Adopting this estimate as correct requires N_L to be approximately 18 for the excitation mechanism to work, a condition not met even for $\nu_{\rm cm} = 10^{15}$ cps. There are two ways out of the difficulty: (1) the estimated Hα flux must be reduced by a factor of about 16, in which case our calculated electron density of the filaments would be decreased by a factor of 4, decreasing in like fashion the mass and the kinetic energy in the filaments; or (2), the value of $\nu_{\rm cm}$ must be put to about 2×10^{15} cps ($N_L = 12$ photons cm^{-2} sec^{-1}), which is quite possible if our estimate of the synchrotron flux at λ 5550 A is only a little too low. Obviously, the problem cannot be solved without accurate photometric measurements of the Hα and optical continuum flux from the filaments, but we can conclude that, to within the accuracy of our present data, the far ultraviolet synchrotron emission could be the excitation mechanism producing the low-energy recombination spectrum observed in the filaments.

VIII. CONCLUSIONS

In conclusion, it may be well to summarize our tentative knowledge of M82 and point out certain striking similarities between phenomena observed in the filaments of M82 and those observed in the Crab Nebula. First of all, the radio-frequency spectra of M82 and the Crab Nebula are very similar and are among the "flattest" known. Both objects show a strong optical emission-line spectrum, requiring a source of excitation other than that which is normally provided by ultraviolet stellar radiation. In both the Crab Nebula and M82 we find a filamentary structure emitting polarized continuum radiation with electric vector orientations roughly perpendicular to the filament orientations. Expansion velocities of about 1000 km/sec are indicated in both systems.

We have proposed that approximately 1.5 million years ago there took place an extremely energetic expulsion of material from the central regions of M82. The expulsion was confined to regions near the minor axis of the galaxy, because of pressure in the disk, and was sufficiently energetic to dominate the magnetic field existing in the disk of the galaxy. By some unknown mechanism, relativistic electrons reaching energies of about 5×10^{12} ev were created in the "explosion," and these have radiated radio and optical noise by the synchrotron process for the lifetime of the system. If the magnetic field is lower than 2×10^{-6} gauss, the decay time for the most energetic electrons is longer than the lifetime, and no replenishment is necessary. Calculations indicate that it may be possible to account for the excitation of the observed optical emission lines by means of the synchrotron radiation shortward of the Lyman limit.

C. R. Lynds is grateful to A. E. Whitford, director of the Lick Observatory, for observing privileges extended, and to G. Herbig and T. Kinman for valuable assistance and advice. Also, this author wishes to acknowledge many stimulating discussions with N. U. Mayall. A. R. Sandage wishes to acknowledge very helpful conversations with J. L. Greenstein, D. Lynden-Bell, G. Münch, and especially L. Spitzer for his comments on the energy problem. Both of us acknowledge the fine photographic work of W. C. Miller.

REFERENCES

Allen, C. W. 1955, *Astrophysical Quantities* (London: Athlone Press), p. 125.

Aller, L. H. 1956, *Gaseous Nebulae* (London: Chapman & Hall), p. 66.

Ambartsumian, V. A. 1961, "Problems of Extragalactic Research," *Trans. I.A.U.* (London: Academic Press), Vol. **XI B**, 145.

Baade, W. 1956, *B.A.N.*, **12**, 312.

Baker, J. G., and Menzel, D. H. 1938, *Ap. J.*, **88**, 52.

Brown, R. Hanbury, and Hazard, C. 1953, *Nature*, **172**, 853.

Burbidge, E. M., and Burbidge, G. R. 1962, *Ap. J.*, **135**, 694.

Burbidge, G. R. 1956, *Ap. J.*, **124**, 416.

Edge, D. O., Shakeshaft, J. R., McAdam, W. B., Baldwin, J. E., and Archer, S. 1959, *Mem. R.A.S.*, **68**, 37.

Elvius, A., and Hall, J. S. 1962a, *A.J.*, **67**, 271.

———. 1962b, *Sky and Telescope*, **23**, 255.

Goldstein, S. J. 1962, *A.J.*, **67**, 171.

Hoyle, Fred, and Fowler, William A. 1963, *Monthly Notices of Royal Astronomical Society*, in press.

Hubble, Edwin. 1926, *Ap. J.*, **64**, 321.

———. 1943, *ibid.*, **97**, 112.

Humason, M. L., Mayall, N. U., and Sandage, A. R. 1956, *A.J.*, **61**, 97.

Lynds, C. R. 1961, *Ap. J.*, **134**, 659.

Mayall, N. U. 1960, *Ann. d'ap.*, **23**, 344.

Morgan, W. W., and Mayall, N. U. 1959, *Science*, **130**, 1421.

Oort, J. H., and Walraven, Th. 1956, *B.A.N.*, **12**, 285.

Sandage, A. R. 1962, "The Distance Scale," *Proc. I.A.U. Symposium*, No. 15 (New York: Macmillan Co.), p. 359.

Schwinger, J. 1949, *Phys. Rev.*, **75**, 1912.

Vaucouleurs, G. de. 1961, *Ap. J. Suppl.*, **5**, 233.

Woltjer, L. 1958, *B.A.N.*, **14**, 39.

Wyse, A. B. 1942, *Ap. J.*, **95**, 356.

Zanstra, H. 1961, *Quart. J. R.A.S.*, **2**, 137.

EVIDENCE FOR THE OCCUR-
RENCE OF VIOLENT EVENTS IN
chapter 27 # THE NUCLEI OF GALAXIES

G. R. Burbidge, E. Margaret Burbidge, and
Allan R. Sandage

I. Introduction

It is generally believed that the vast majority of galaxies are massive condensations of matter which reached equilibrium configurations billions of years ago and have essentially remained unchanged ever since. Since they are in equilibrium under gravitational forces (magnetic forces are undoubtedly negligible in the bulk of the matter, which is condensed into stars), no significant departures from this equilibrium can be expected as the galaxy evolves in time, unless gravitational forces comparable in magnitude to the forces exerted in the gravitational potential of the galaxy are encountered. The only situation in which such effects will occur is when galaxies collide, and the most probable place of occurrence of collisions is in clusters.

It is therefore self-evident that unless outside influences come into play, once the equilibrium configuration is reached the distributions of mass and angular momentum do not change in a galaxy in its life history. On the other hand, the form and the distribution of gas and dust in a galaxy may change drastically through the processes of stellar evolution, and through the differential galactic rotation. Since in spiral and irregular galaxies the gas and dust are a very conspicuous feature and play an important role in the classification scheme, it is possible that the outward appearance of galaxies may change drastically as a function of time. Spiral structure is a most important example of this. While the problem of the persistence of spiral structure remains unsolved, the characteristic time scale that must be associated with changes in this structure is the period of rotation at different distances from the center. A reasonable average value for this time is 10^8 yr.

Until recently this time scale has been the shortest which has been thought to be associated with galaxies taken as a whole, as far as structural changes or changes in rate of evolution of energy output are concerned. It is our purpose in this paper to describe

G. R. Burbidge and E. Margaret Burbidge, University of California, San Diego. Allan R. Sandage, Mount Wilson and Palomar Observatories, Carnegie Institution of Washington and California Institute of Technology.

Reprinted from *Reviews of Modern Physics*, **35**, 947–972, 1963.

a number of phenomena, all associated with the nuclei of galaxies, which may suggest that in these nuclei there may take place violent events manifested by a very large energy output and a time scale as short as 10^6 yr.

Some account of the phenomena described has been given previously in the literature, but we have considered it worthwhile to review all the evidence together.

II. Optical Data

(1) Nuclei of Seyfert Galaxies

There are nine known galaxies which have nuclei satisfying the following criteria [eight of the twelve originally listed by Seyfert (1943), and a further system described by Burbidge and Burbidge (1962a)]:

(i) They have small, very bright nuclei.

(ii) The spectra of the nuclei may contain emission features not normally seen in the spectra of galaxies, indicating higher excitation than that required to produce [O III] and [Ne III].

(iii) The emission features, or at least the hydrogen emission lines, must be of great width, which if interpreted as Doppler motions, correspond to velocities in the range ± 500 to ± 4250 km/sec, according to Seyfert (1943).

It is this last criterion which puts these galaxies in a class by themselves.

Since Seyfert's investigation of NGC 1068, 1275, 3516, 4051, 4151, and 7469, further studies using nebular spectrographs and direct photography have been made of NGC 1068, 7469, 1275, 4051, and 4151 (Burbidge, Burbidge, and Prendergast 1959, 1963; Minkowski 1957; Baade and Minkowski, see Woltjer 1959). NGC 1068 is shown in Fig. 1. Investigations of NGC 1275 and NGC 3227 are being made by the authors. If we consider now a composite of all of these investigations the following preliminary model emerges.

The Nucleus

A Seyfert galaxy has a very small bright nucleus in which high-excitation features are seen. Attempts to measure the diameter of the nucleus in, e.g., NGC 4151 show that its size on the photographic plate is set by the seeing. Figure 2 shows a short exposure of NGC 4151 showing the telescope diffraction pattern produced by the nucleus. The true diameter is $< \frac{1}{2}''$ corresponding at a distance of 10 Mpc to < 25 pc. The widths of the emission features, particularly the Balmer series, correspond to Doppler motions in the range given by Seyfert, which we will take to be of the order of 1000–3000 km/sec. These widths are difficult to determine with precision but there is no doubt that the range quoted by Seyfert is approximately correct. However, in all cases the width of the hydrogen lines is significantly greater than the width of the other features, particularly in NGC 3516. In two cases, NGC 4151 and 1068, the nuclei have been observed at larger scale and higher dispersion than that used in normal nebular investigations. This work has been carried out on NGC 4151 by Wilson (1956), on NGC 1068 by Walker (1962), and on both galaxies by Sargent (1963). These results show that there is a very considerable amount of structure in the broad emission bands, showing that the emitting region consists of separate cloud complexes moving about in a disordered fashion with velocities of the order of 1000 km/sec or more with respect to each other. A possible explanation of the broader features which are seen in the hydrogen emission lines is that an outer shell of gas at lower density is expanding outward at somewhat higher velocities than the velocities in the disordered motions of the separate cloud complexes. In any case, the structure in the broadened lines, and the greater widths of the hydrogen lines compared with the outer emission lines, all strongly support the idea that the broadening seen is Doppler broadening.

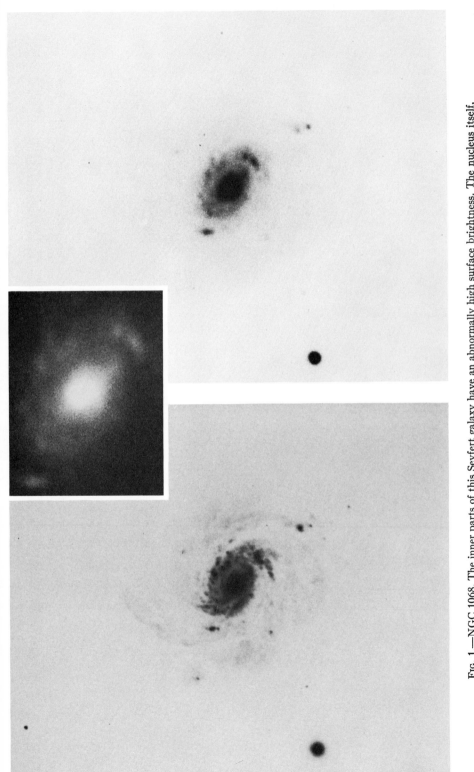

FIG. 1.—NGC 1068. The inner parts of this Seyfert galaxy have an abnormally high surface brightness. The nucleus itself, burned out in these photographs, is exceedingly small and bright. The left photograph, taken with the 200-in. telescope, is a 1-min exposure on a 103a-O plate behind a GG 13 filter. The right photograph is a 30-min exposure on a 103a-E plate behind an Hα interference filter of 80 Å total half-width. The insert is an enlarged portion of the Hα plate. There is some suggestion of an Hα filament coming from the central region.

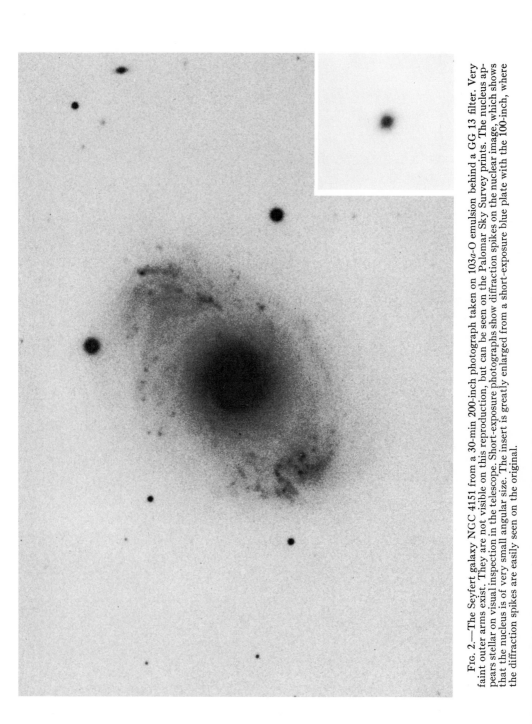

FIG. 2.—The Seyfert galaxy NGC 4151 from a 30-min 200-inch photograph taken on 103a-O emulsion behind a GG 13 filter. Very faint outer arms exist. They are not visible on this reproduction, but can be seen on the Palomar Sky Survey prints. The nucleus appears stellar on visual inspection in the telescope. Short-exposure photographs show diffraction spikes on the nuclear image, which shows that the nucleus is of very small angular size. The insert is greatly enlarged from a short-exposure blue plate with the 100-inch, where the diffraction spikes are easily seen on the original.

Conditions outside the Nuclei

In the cases of NGC 1068, 7469, 3227, and 1275, spectra taken in good seeing show that, immediately outside the regions where the broad emissions are seen, only the emission lines characteristic of more quiescent ionized gas are seen, i.e., Hα, [N II] λ 6583, and [O II] λ 3727. These features are narrow and tilted. While there are some deviations from symmetry in these cases, and these may well be due to the gas moving in noncircular motions in the nuclei, for NGC 1068 and 7469, the systems studied in the most detail so far, it appears that the inclinations of these narrow emission components are predominantly due to the rotations of the galaxies. They appear to be consistent with the normal rotation curves for spiral galaxies in as far as they have been observed (measurements have been made out as far as 3.5 kpc from the nucleus in the case of NGC 7469). It is possible, however, that this simple explanation does not hold for NGC 1275. The masses that are derived for these inner parts based on the rudimentary rotation curves are of the order of several times 10^{10} $M\odot$. It seems clear therefore that the disordered motions seen in the nuclear regions are far in excess of the escape velocities in the centers. A photograph of NGC 1068 taken through an Hα filter shows a curious double flare coming from one side of the nucleus (Fig. 1), which may represent the escape of gas from the nuclear region.

NGC 1068 and 7469 both have outer rings of low luminosity with diameters of the order of 30 kpc. NGC 4151 also has faint outer spiral arms, with a pitch different from that of the inner arms, and NGC 3227 has two broad rather smooth outer structures; these may be seen in Fig. 3.

NGC 1275 is still being studied, and discussion of it is more tentative. Figures 4 and 5 show various features of this galaxy, including many small patches of luminosity surrounding it which appear to be connected with it, and radially directed streaks which show strongest on the photograph taken in mainly Hα light. However, the nucleus of this galaxy shows the Seyfert characteristics, and immediately outside this region narrow tilted lines are seen. This galaxy was first investigated by Minkowski (1959). He showed that an outer mass of gas is present whose spectrum has a separate and discrete set of emission lines, indicating a velocity of 3000 km/sec with respect to the nucleus. This result has been confirmed by spectra obtained more recently. Since NGC 1275 is in the center of the Perseus cluster of galaxies, Minkowski's argument that this should be interpreted as a collision between two galaxies is still, on the basis of the spectroscopic evidence, an entirely reasonable one, and cannot be directly discounted. However, the background to the interpretation at the time it was made was that strong radio sources were produced by collisions between galaxies, and of course, NGC 1275 is such a strong source. It appears now that the concept of collisions being responsible for radio sources must be abandoned (for a summary of the reasons for this see, for example, Burbidge 1961). Consequently, if we continue to argue that NGC 1275 is a collision on the basis of the spectroscopic evidence, then we have to suppose that in this galaxy an event has taken place which has led it to become a strong radio source, while at the same time it is by chance in collision with another system. The alternative explanation is that the material which is seen to have a velocity of 3000 km/sec with respect to the nucleus of NGC 1275 has been driven out of the central part of this galaxy. This material is present in a broad structure extending over a distance of the order of 10–20 kpc from the center.

(2) M82

This system is the well-known irregular galaxy in the M81 group. A description has been given by Sandage (1961) and its rotation has been measured by Mayall (1960). The galaxy, which is elongated, shows a considerable amount of filamentary structure outside the main body, particularly in the region of the minor axis. A major development has been the investigation by Lynds and Sandage (1963) in which Hα filter photography

Fig. 3.—NGC 3226–3227. Taken on a 103a-O plate with the 82-inch McDonald telescope. The spiral NGC 3227 has a bright nucleus and broad emission lines characteristic of the Seyfert galaxies. Very faint outer structure, like an incompleted ring, are easily seen on the original plate. Similar structures are known to exist in the other Seyfert galaxies NGC 1068, 4151, and 7489.

Fig. 4.—NGC 1275 and surrounding galaxies in the Perseus cluster, from a 103a-O plate taken by Humason with the 200-inch telescope, showing the extensive system of filaments.

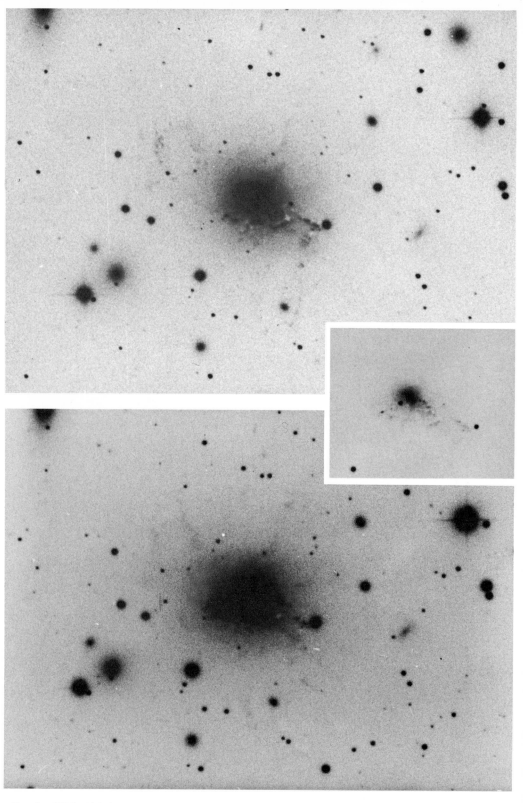

Fig. 5.—NGC 1275 photographed in three different wavelengths. The upper is from Humason's 30-min 103a-O plate (λ 3500–4800 Å); the bottom is from a 180-min exposure taken on a 103a-F plate behind an RG 1 filter (λ 6000–6800 A); the insert is a short exposure of the nucleus taken in the ultraviolet from a 100-inch plate by Baade (λ 3300–3900 Å). The filamentary structure visible on both the blue and Hα plates extends to about 80 sec of arc on either side of the nucleus, which corresponds to about 30 kpc linear dimension (based on $H = 75$ km/sec 10^6 pc).

shows a tremendous flux of emission in the central region with limited extensions in the direction of the major axis and long filaments of emission in the direction of the minor axis above and below the main body of the galaxy. Figures 6, 7, and 8 show that these filaments are emitting mainly in the Hα line. These filaments extend to distances of the order of 3–4 kpc above and below the main body of the galaxy. Spectra taken with the slit aligned along the minor axis show tilted Hα, and this indicates that material is either being ejected or is falling in along the minor axis. Sandage and Lynds have concluded from their study of the orientation of the galaxy that the observations are best interpreted by supposing that material is streaming out from the center in the direction of the minor axis. Making very approximate estimates to correct for projection they have concluded that the velocity at which the material is moving outward is about 1000 km/sec.

(3) NGC 5128

This galaxy consists of a large elliptical component with a broad band containing gas and dust lying across its equatorial region. Spectroscopic observations along this band (Burbidge and Burbidge 1959) show that it is rotating, and the rotation curve is roughly linear, with a total velocity difference from one edge to the other of about 600 km/sec. Only the emission features characteristic of normal ionized hydrogen regions are seen. Observations of the stellar content of the system above and below the dark lane (Burbidge and Burbidge 1962b) show that this also is rotating, but more slowly than the belt of gas and dust. The observations appear to be best interpreted by supposing that the dust and gas lie in a ring which is rotating outside the main body of the galaxy.

(4) M87

The characteristics of this giant elliptical galaxy are well known. The jet, which is due to synchrotron emission, appears to emanate from the nucleus. Fig. 9 shows the jet as it appears in a rather short exposure. The energetics of this will be discussed later. That ionized gas is also present in the nucleus is clear from the presence of a strong [O II] λ 3727 line (Osterbrock 1960). In contrast to many ellipticals in which this line indicates that a small amount of ionized gas is present, the line here is strong and the profile is asymmetrical and may be called double with a difference in velocity (apart from the broadening indicating random motions which are comparable with those of the stars) of about 900 km/sec. Osterbrock has considered that this may be associated with the radio source and optical jet centered on M87. One component gives a recession velocity corresponding to the value for the stars of the galaxy, while the other is shifted to the violet by 900 km/sec. This may indicate that gas is moving outward from the nucleus with this high velocity. However, the velocity of escape from this massive galaxy is comparable with this value. Consequently gas which is moving outward in this way may not be able to escape.

A remarkable feature of M87 is the very large number of globular clusters associated with it, greatly exceeding the number associated with any other galaxy in the Virgo cluster. We may wonder whether these are in any way connected with the fact that this is a radio galaxy; judging by the radio brightness distribution, discussed in Sec. III (4) it may indeed be a recurrent radio source. We return to this point later.

All of the systems we have described so far are galaxies with redshift velocities at maximum of about 5000 km/sec (for NGC 1275 and NGC 7469). Consequently they are sufficiently big and bright so that studies of their optical characteristics in different parts can be made without too much difficulty. Apart from the Seyfert galaxies these systems have become of especial interest because they were identified as galaxies which are associated with strong radio sources. Consequently these are not necessarily all of the bright galaxies in which such circumstantial evidence for nuclear activity exists, although it

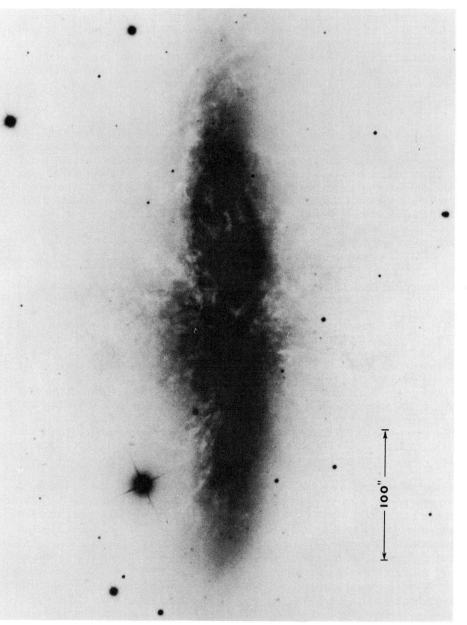

Fig. 6.—M82 from a 30-min 103a-O plate behind a GG 13 filter with the 200-inch telescope (from Lynds and Sandage 1963).

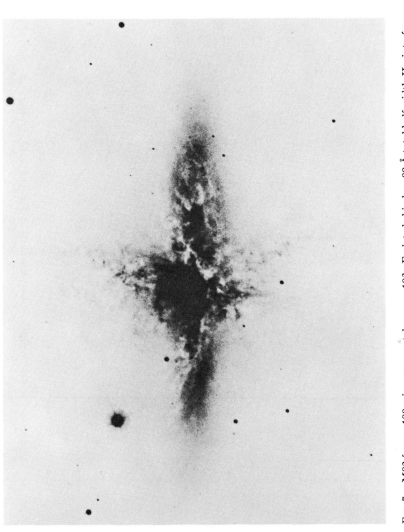

FIG. 7.—M82 from a 180-min exposure taken on a 103a-E plate behind an 80 Å total half-width Hα interference filter, showing the massive Hα filamentary structure on both sides of the fundamental plane (from Lynds and Sandage 1963).

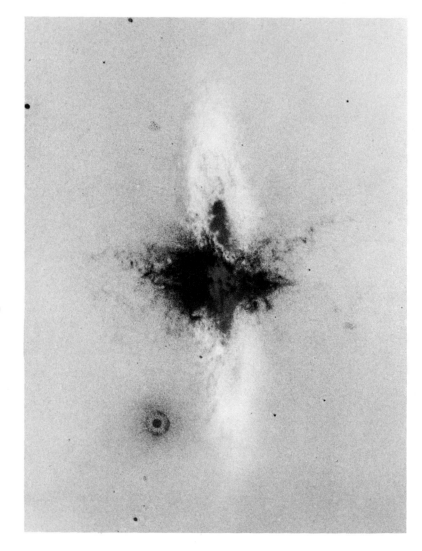

FIG. 8.—Photographic "subtraction" of a yellow plate (103a-D + GG 11) of M82 from the Hα plate of Fig. 7, showing that the Hα emission region is confined predominantly to the minor axis of the galaxy.

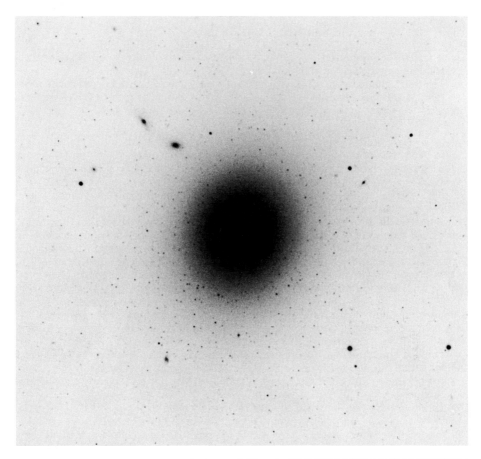

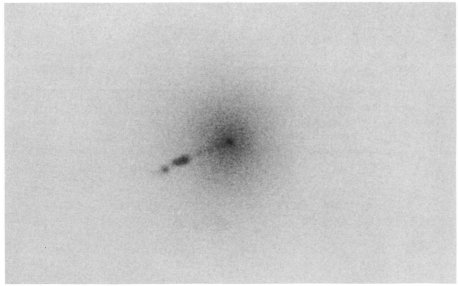

FIG. 9.—*Top:* M87 from a 30-min 103*a*-O plate taken with the 200-inch showing the large number of globular clusters in the halo of the galaxy. *Bottom:* A highly enlarged short-exposure blue plate of M87 taken with the 100-inch showing the well-known jet starting from a very intense nucleus. The jet is 18 sec of arc in length, measured from the nucleus to the outer condensation. This corresponds to about 1100 pc linear dimension if $m - M = 30.6$, neglecting projection effects.

is probable that the survey of Seyfert galaxies is fairly complete out to distances corresponding to redshifts of 5000 km/sec.

The radio sources associated with some of these galaxies are discussed in the following section. In this discussion of the optical data we wish now to turn to the optical characteristics of distant galaxies identified with strong radio sources.

(5) CYGNUS A, 3C 295, AND OTHER FAINT RADIO SOURCE GALAXIES

In 1953, Baade and Minkowski (1954) identified an extragalactic object associated with the very strong radio source Cygnus A. This system has a recession velocity of +16830 km/sec, and an apparent magnitude (uncorrected) m_{pg} of +17.90 ($m_{pv} = 16.22$, C.I. = +1.68). There is undoubtedly a considerable amount of galactic absorption and reddening. Baade and Minkowski assumed $2^m.1$ of photographic absorption. With allowance for the diaphragm used not admitting all the light from the galaxy, their estimated corrected value was $m_{pg} = 15.05$. The spectrum shows strong emission lines due to Hα, [O I], [O II], [O III], [N II], [Ne III], and [Ne V]. As Baade and Minkowski pointed out, this spectrum, as far as these features are concerned, resembles the spectra of Seyfert nuclei. In this respect it satisfies criterion (ii) given in the discussion of these objects. About 50% of the total luminosity of the galaxy is emitted in the emission lines. In two other respects this system differs from the Seyfert galaxies. First, the emission lines do not have great broadening, and second, the emission comes from a much more extended region than is the case in the Seyfert nuclei. With a value for the Hubble constant of 75 km/sec/Mpc (Sandage 1958) the extent of the strong emitting region is about 6 kpc. Although the continuous spectrum may be due to stars, no absorption features have so far been identified in this spectrum [more recently, further spectra of Cygnus A have been obtained by Herbig and Schmidt (private communication)]. Consequently the character of the underlying stars in the system is unknown.

The determination of more precise radio source positions has led recently to the identification of a number of very faint galaxies associated with these sources. Minkowski (1960) identified the source 3C 295 with a system with a redshift $z = 0.46$ on the basis of a single emission line at λ 5448 which appears to be [O II] λ 3727. Recently Schmidt (1962a) has obtained spectra of a number of galaxies which have been identified as sources of radio emission. A number of these show very strong emission lines similar to those observed in the spectrum of Cygnus A and the Seyfert galaxies. Since these galaxies are very faint and small in angular size, very little is known about them other than these indications from the spectra that there is a large mass of highly excited gas present. In the case of Cygnus A, the energy output in the emission lines is of the order of 10^{44} erg/sec.

We have described so far galaxies which show either evidence for peculiar conditions in the nuclei from optical investigations alone, or peculiarities both from the optical and spectroscopic standpoints and which also are radio emitters. However, there is one final group of galaxies which have been identified as being associated with strong sources of radio emission, but which have no spectral peculiarities, and whose systemic optical peculiarities, if present, are concerned with the density distribution of the stars or with the presence of dust. We mention a few of these in the next subheading.

(6) OTHER SINGLE, DOUBLE, AND MULTIPLE E OR S0 SYSTEMS

NGC 4782–83 (3C 278) is a pair of elliptical galaxies with a recession velocity of +4300 km/sec. Spectra were obtained by Page (1952) and Greenstein (1961). These show only the absorption features seen in normal elliptical galaxies and no emission lines. The degree of central concentration of the stars is greater in one component than in the other and the outer isophotes of both are not symmetrical about the line joining their centers.

NGC 7236–37 (3C 442) is another pair of elliptical of S0 galaxies for which spectra have been obtained by Greenstein (1962). Apart from a weak [O II] λ 3727 line seen in NGC 7237, only the absorption features of normal elliptical galaxies are seen. The recession velocity is +8100 km/sec. Again, the degree of concentration of luminosity is different in the nuclei of the two components.

NGC 545–547 is another double elliptical system and a radio source has been identified with it. No abnormal features are seen in the spectra.

NGC 6166 (3C 338) is a multiple elliptical system lying in a cluster of galaxies. No abnormal emission features are seen in the spectra of the three components. However, [O II] λ 3727 is seen in the center of the brightest component (Minkowski 1961) which also has a very small, bright ultraviolet nucleus (E. M. Burbidge 1962). The distance of this system is about 121 Mpc. The brightest member of the NGC 6166 group shows some structure which is probably due to obscuring clouds (Burbidge 1962) and the degree of central condensation in this galaxy is very different from that in the other members of the multiple and also from that in the other cluster members, in that this galaxy is of much greater diffuseness and diameter.

NGC 1316 (Fornax A) has been classified S0 and its spectrum shows no emission features in the blue. A spectrum obtained at the McDonald Observatory shows one emission line in the red; from the known redshift of this galaxy, the line is [N II] λ 5583. In this system a considerable amount of dust is clearly seen at some distance from the center. The dust arms extend inwards to the central region of the galaxy. Figure 10 shows these arms, which, after coming out radially, turn sharply and continue as spiral arms, somewhat in the way the luminous spiral arms join on to the ends of the bars in barred spirals. This dust structure somewhat resembles that visible alongside the luminous outer structure in NGC 1275 (Fig. 5). Interstellar absorption due to dust may explain why [N II] λ 6583 is seen while [O II] λ 3727 is absent.

NGC 4261 (3C 270) is an apparently normal single elliptical or S0 galaxy.

III. Radio Data

Apart from the Seyfert galaxies, all of the systems described in Sec. II are strong sources of radio emission, and in general it was this discovery which led to their being investigated by optical methods. It is widely accepted now that the radio radiation is emitted by relativistic electrons (and positrons) moving in weak magnetic fields, and for assumed values of the magnetic field the total energy in particles and field can be calculated if the size of the source is known. The total energy calculated when it is supposed that the magnetic energy is equal to the particle energy is the minimum energy required on the basis of this theory to explain the energy radiated. All of the sources, with the exception of NGC 1068, are much larger than the volumes occupied by the galaxies as far as the stars, gas, and dust are concerned. However, whatever the ultimate origin of the energy for these sources may be, it is most likely to have been released initially in the nuclei, since the greatest concentration of matter is there. This is borne out by the source in NGC 1068, and by other evidence, suggesting that material and high-energy particles have been shot out from the center. Consequently the energy presently contained in the radio sources gives some indication of the energy released in these nuclei. Moreover, the distribution of radio emission in the sources gives information about the ejection mechanism from the nucleus.

With these points in mind we summarize the information available on the radio emission from the galaxies described above.

(1) SEYFERT GALAXIES

Among this class of galaxy only NGC 1068 and NGC 1275 are known to be radio sources, and they show quite different characteristics. NGC 1068 contains a highly concentrated source with a diameter of 600 pc or less at the center of the galaxy.

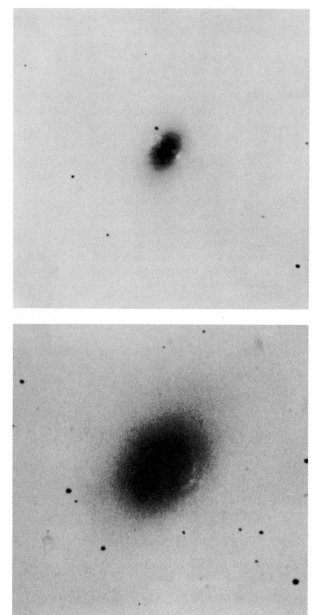

Fig. 10.—Two exposures of the radio source NGC 1316 taken on 103*a*-O emulsion with the 82-inch telescope. A very extensive outer envelope exists, which can be seen on plates taken with the 48-inch Schmidt, but is not visible on these reproductions.

This radio source is between 1 and 2 orders of magnitude stronger than normal galaxies such as our Galaxy and M31, and it is therefore considered to be a weak radio source on a scale which goes all the way from about 10^{38} erg/sec for our Galaxy to an emission rate of about 10^{45} erg/sec for Cygnus A and Hercules A. However, in view of the general idea which we are developing here that the nuclei are the ultimate sources of energy, NGC 1068 is of great importance. It would be important to study the other Seyfert galaxies besides NGC 1275, and measure the radio output from them. It is reasonable to suppose that they also contain small sources radiating at power levels comparable with that in NGC 1068, to within a factor of 10.

The radio source centered on NGC 1275 has been studied in considerable detail. The work of Leslie and Elsmore (1961) and Maltby and Moffet (1962) shows that this source has a complex structure, a central source with a diameter of about 1' (= 20 kpc) coinciding approximately with the galaxy, and a more extended halo distribution with a size of about 90 kpc, most of which is probably associated with NGC 1275. The energetics of these sources are discussed in Sec. IV.

(2) M82

This is a comparatively weak radio galaxy with a very flat radio spectrum (spectral index = 0.2). A discussion of the radio characteristics of the system has been given by Lynds (1962) and Lequeux (1962) has shown that it is a very small source at the center of the optical galaxy (cf. Sec. VI). A very interesting feature of this galaxy is that it appears that optical synchrotron radiation is present in the filamentary structure described earlier. This has been established by the work of Elvius and Hall (1962), who found that the continuous optical emission in the halo regions shows linear polarization amounting to about 10%. The properties of this radiation and the model described by Lynds and Sandage (1962) are described in Sec. V.

(3) NGC 5128

This galaxy lies at the center of the largest radio source so far discovered, though it is not the most powerful radio emitter. The source has a complex structure with a central core and a very extended distribution with dimensions of about 0.7 Mpc by 0.25 Mpc (Bolton and Clark 1960). The extended source has two components. The central source also has two components (Twiss, Carter, and Little 1960; Maltby 1961) with dimensions of about 5.5 × 2.4 kpc separated by a distance of about 8.5 kpc. The elongation of this radio source structure is approximately in the direction of the minor axis of the galaxy as determined by the rotation curve in the dust and gas (Burbidge and Burbidge 1959). Recently, Gardner and Whiteoak (1962) have shown that this radio source has a high degree of linear polarization (38%) at a frequency of 1500 Mc. The energetics of this source are also discussed in Sec. IV.

(4) M87

The synchrotron emission from this galaxy consists of three components. These are:

(i) The jet. This is due to synchrotron emission in the optical frequency range. The measurement of a high degree of polarization of this by Baade (1956) by photographic methods and by Hiltner (1959) by photoelectric techniques confirmed the original prediction of Shklovsky (1955) that this jet consisted of synchrotron radiation. The energetics of the jet were worked out by Shklovsky (1955) and Burbidge (1956). The jet clearly comes from the center of the galaxy and provides one of the most direct pieces of evidence that violent events originate in the nuclear regions. The radio emission consists of two components, a core and halo (Biraud, Lequeux, and LeRoux 1960; Maltby and Moffet 1962).

(ii) The core source is elongated with a diameter of about 0.6' = 3 kpc. The position angle of the major axis of this elongated source is 300°, while the position angle of the jet is 290°. This strongly suggests that the core source and the jet are genetically connected, as was earlier suggested by Baade and Minkowski (1954). The core source consists of two components according to Lequeux and Heidmann (1961) with an east-west separation of about $0.5' = 2.5$ kpc.

(iii) There is a halo distribution which has a diameter of about $6.5' \approx 30$ kpc (Maltby and Moffet 1962).

(5) CYGNUS A

This is one of the most powerful of the radio sources so far studied. It consists of two components almost equal in intensity (Jennison and Das Gupta 1953). The observed separation of the components is a slowly varying function of wavelength. The separation is of the order of $1.5'$, which corresponds to about 100 kpc, while the size of each component is about 40 kpc, and there is some evidence that each component is elongated in the direction of the line joining the two centers. The optical object Cygnus A is situated approximately centrally between these two components.

(6) HERCULES A

This system falls into the group containing Cygnus A, 3C 295, and others because the optical object identified with the radio source (Williams, Dewhirst, and Leslie 1961; Maltby, Matthews, and Moffet 1962) shows a strong [O II] λ 3727 line (Greenstein 1962) which contributes much of the light emitted by the system. This radio source is also one of the most powerful sources so far identified. The recession velocity is $+46000$ km/sec and the radio source is double with a separation of about 300 kpc between the two components each of which has a diameter of about 100 kpc.

In our discussion of the optical data we included in the category of Cygnus A, Hercules A, and 3C 295, a number of other radio sources which have been identified with optical objects and which have spectra similar to Cygnus A (Schmidt 1962). Since redshifts are now available for these sources their sizes can be obtained, and the radio power levels are found to be quite similar to many of the systems which have been discussed above.

(7) OTHER SINGLE, DOUBLE, AND MULTIPLE E OR S0 SYSTEMS

NGC 4782–83 is identified with a radio source that has size of about $2' = 34$ kpc and is approximately circular (Maltby and Moffet 1962). For NGC 7236–37, with a recession velocity of $+8100$ km/sec, the size of the radio source is about $3'$ or 97 kpc. The diameter of the radio source identified with NGC 6166 is about $1' = 36$ kpc.

IV. EVIDENCE CONCERNING THE ENERGY RELEASED IN VIOLENT EVENTS

Estimates of the energy which has been released in the various systems we have described can be determined in a variety of ways. We have first the direct measurement of the optical or radio luminosities.

(1) OPTICAL LUMINOSITIES

Most of the data are from the work of Seyfert (1943) on the galaxies discussed earlier. He estimated the magnitudes of the nuclei of NGC 1068, 1275, 3516, 4051, 4151, and 7469, and by spectrophotometric methods determined the fraction of the energy currently being emitted in the emission lines in the cases of three of these systems, NGC 1068, 3516, and 4151. We show in Table I estimates of the energy being emitted by these nuclei, which we have obtained from Seyfert's work by assuming a value of H of 75 km/sec/Mpc. In this table we give the total luminosities of the nuclei and the fractions of the energies emitted in the emission lines where they are available. We also include in

Table I the estimate of the energy being emitted in the filaments in M82 in Hα light (Lynds and Sandage 1963). Also we give the luminosity of Cygnus A together with the fraction of the light emitted in the emission lines in this galaxy.

(2) RADIO LUMINOSITIES

A table of radio luminosities was given by Burbidge (1959) based on the data then available. Since that time many new identifications with optical systems have been made, and a second table has been compiled by Maltby, Matthews, and Moffet (1962). However, since the range of radio luminosities remains the same, we shall not give a tabulation here, but simply state that for the strong sources the radio output lies in the range 10^{40}–10^{45} erg/sec.

Optical synchrotron radiation is seen in M82 and M87. The energy radiated in optical synchrotron radiation in M87 was estimated by Burbidge (1959) to be about 2×10^{42} erg/sec. In M82 the continuous energy radiated in the filaments and the faint

TABLE I

	Luminosity of Nucleus (erg/sec)	Energy Emitted in Emission Lines (erg/sec)
NGC 1068[a]	20×10^{42}	2.7×10^{42}
1275	19×10^{42}	
3516	25×10^{42}	1.2×10^{42}
4051	1×10^{42}	
4151	16×10^{42}	1.2×10^{42} (hydrogen wings)
		2.2×10^{42} (remainder)
7469	52×10^{42}	
M 82		2×10^{40} (Hα only)
Cygnus A	400×10^{42} (luminosity of whole optical system)	$\simeq200\times10^{42}$

[a] New measure by one of us (A. R. S.)

luminous halo surrounding the system can be estimated from the work of Lynds and Sandage to be about 10^{41} erg/sec, where we have assumed that the radiation is emitted over a bandwidth of 1000 Å between 5000 and 6000 Å.

Direct estimates of the energy content in these systems can be made in two ways. First we can consider the evidence of mass motions derived from spectroscopic data, and second, we can obtain evidence for the energy content in high-energy particles and magnetic fields from the observed radio luminosities and the synchrotron theory. We now consider these in turn.

(3) KINETIC ENERGY IN MASS MOTIONS

The Seyfert galaxies show broad emission features which indicate velocities of the order of several thousand km/sec. The structure in these emission features can be interpreted in a number of ways. At one extreme we have the possibility that we are seeing large gas masses moving with random velocities of this order. Another possible interpretation is that we are seeing a fairly uniform gas in which shock fronts are moving with these extremely high velocities, and the gas which is radiating is that behind the shock fronts. In any case, since the motions which are seen are hypersonic with Mach numbers of the order of 10–100 it must be expected that the energy dissipation in such regions is very high. It is possible that these nuclei contain magnetic fields of considerable strength, perhaps $\sim10^{-4}$ G, so that hydromagnetic shocks are being propagated. In this case the Alfvén velocity $(H^2/4\pi\rho)^{1/2}$ and not the sound velocity is the significant quantity. However, only for very low densities and high magnetic field intensities is the Alfvén velocity significantly greater than the sound velocity.

To calculate the kinetic energy present in the rapidly moving ionized gas we must estimate the density. This can be done by using the absolute intensity of hydrogen emission lines, if an estimate of the electron temperature is made. Woltjer did this for NGC 1068 and NGC 4151 by using Hβ, and we have made some calculations using Hα. The total mass of ionized gas in the nuclei of NGC 1068 and NGC 4151 calculated by this method is of the order of 10^7 $M\odot$. This is a maximum value, as was pointed out by Woltjer, since if the radiating gas is concentrated into filamentary structure or any kind of denser clouds, which may very well be the case, the radiating efficiency is increased. Woltjer has attempted to estimate a minimum mass, but the method used is very uncertain. Thus we propose to use the maximum value only. The random motions in these nuclei lie in the range 1000–5000 km/sec. Hence a reasonable estimate for the kinetic energy present in the ionized gas is $\leq 10^{56}$–10^{57} ergs. Taking into account the uncertainties and real differences between the Seyfert nuclei, in the strength of the excitation, the degree of condensation of emitting gas, and the velocity dispersion, we reach the conclusion that the kinetic energy is $10^{55\pm2}$ ergs.

In M82, Lynds and Sandage have estimated that the total kinetic energy at present in the filaments which emit Hα is about 2×10^{55} ergs. They consider that this is an upper limit because they may have overestimated the mass in the filaments. However, it gives a possible lower limit to the total kinetic energy in the matter exploded from the center, since much of this may now be undetectable.

(4) ENERGY IN MAGNETIC FIELDS AND HIGH-ENERGY PARTICLES

It is well known that from the observed power output in synchrotron radiation the total energy now present in the sources in the form of magnetic field energy and high-energy particles can be calculated as a function of the magnetic field and of the energy of the particles. There are two uncertainties involved in determining these energies. First, we have no independent estimates of the magnetic field strengths in the sources, and second, it is reasonable to suppose that associated with the electrons (and positrons) there is a flux of high-energy protons which may contain the bulk of the particle energy. The arguments for this second conclusion have been described previously (cf. Burbidge 1959). The minimum total energy required to account for the observed emission is obtained when there is equipartition between the magnetic energy and the particle energy. Calculations were made on this basis for the identified radio sources by Burbidge (1956, 1959); similar calculations for the majority of the identified sources have been made more recently by Maltby, Matthews, and Moffet (1962).

If it is supposed that the energy in the proton flux is 100 times that in the electrons and positrons, then the total energy in particles and magnetic field for all of the sources described by Maltby *et al.* with the exception of NGC 1068, lies in the range 10^{57}–10^{61} ergs. The equipartition values of the magnetic field in these cases lie in the range 6×10^{-6}–3×10^{-4} G with the majority lying between 5×10^{-6} and 5×10^{-5} G.

If, on the other hand, the proton energy is only equal to the electron–positron energy, then the total energies lie in the range 10^{56}–10^{60} ergs and the equipartition magnetic field strengths are reduced by a factor of $(100)^{2/7} = 3.7$.

In the case of NGC 1068, the source is very small and the total energy is 4×10^{55} ergs if protons dominate and about 3×10^{53} ergs if protons are insignificant. The magnetic field strengths in two cases are 2×10^{-4} and 6×10^{-5} G, respectively.

In M87 and M82, where optical synchrotron radiation is seen, the conditions in these regions are thought to be rather different from those in the radio sources in general, essentially because the presence of this radiation means that electrons of very much higher energy are present, since $\nu_c \propto E^2$, so that, e.g., if the particles are radiating in the same magnetic field, electrons which radiate in the optical region (5×10^{14} cps) must have energies of the order of 10^3 greater than those which radiate in the radio region (taken as about 5×10^8 cps).

For the jet in M87 the corresponding values for the total energy in particles and magnetic field are 2.4×10^{55} ergs with $H = 7 \times 10^{-4}$ G if protons are dominant, and 1.7×10^{54} ergs with $H = 2 \times 10^{-4}$ G if electrons contribute much of the particle energy.

For M82 the equipartition condition considering the relativistic electrons alone gives a total energy of 7×10^{54} ergs with $H = 2 \times 10^{-5}$ G, while if the protons are dominant the total energy appears to be about 10^{56} ergs in a magnetic field of 8×10^{-5} G.

This concludes the summary of the data presently available on the current rate of energy dissipation in the sources and the energy reservoirs which are seen to be present. We turn next to a consideration of the time scales associated with these events.

V. Time Scales Associated with Violent Events

The different classes of object will be discussed in turn.

(1) SEYFERT NUCLEI

In these objects the time scales which can be derived are (a) those given by L/v, where L is the size of a nucleus and v is the velocity associated with the gas which is seen, and (b) the time scale for the energy at present in the form of kinetic energy of turbulent gas to be radiated in the emission lines. As far as (a) is concerned, for the nuclei we have $L \approx 100$ pc and $v \approx 2000$ km/sec so that $t = 2 \times 10^4$ yr. For (b), if we use the values given previously of about 10^{42} erg/sec as a rate of emission by the spectral lines and a total energy in the gas of $10^{55 \pm 2}$ ergs, then the time scale if all of the energy were dissipated in this way is $3 \times 10^{6 \pm 2}$ yr.

Since the velocities seen in the nuclei appear to be far in excess of the escape velocities, the gas will tend to escape very rapidly, except for that part which is brought to rest by inelastic collisions between gas clouds in the central region, or which is slowed down as it moves outward from the center by interaction with the gas in the disk. Thus, unless motions of the sort seen at present are being continuously generated, the time scale associated with these nuclei as they appear now must be very short, $\ll 10^6$ yr.

Another possible way of estimating a time scale is given by the optical data on NGC 1275. We have already discussed the data which show that gas is moving with respect to the nucleus of NGC 1275 with a velocity of about 3000 km/sec. As stated earlier, one interpretation is that of Minkowski, who supposes that we are seeing a collision between two previously separate galaxies. Alternatively, we may suppose that the gas which is seen at an average distance of about 20 kpc from the nucleus has been ejected from it. Then the maximum time, neglecting deceleration, which has elapsed since this event took place is L/v, where L is ≈ 20 kpc, and $v \approx 3000$ km/sec. This time is 7×10^6 yr. The fact that not a complete shell, but only a segment of a shell, is seen must then be explained as being due to different rates of cooling and recombination in different parts, so that Hα is only seen in a limited region.

(2) M82

In this galaxy the most direct method of estimating the time scale associated with the event is to determine the time taken for the filaments to have moved to their present positions above and below the main body of the system. Lynds and Sandage have made estimates of this time based on the velocities measured from their spectra along the minor axis. These spectra show in first order a linear velocity–distance relation. There are two uncertainties involved in making this estimate. One is that it has not been found possible to take account of the deceleration which must have occurred due to the interaction of the gas ejected in the violent event with the remainder of the gas present in the disk of the galaxy. Thus the time which has been derived by neglecting the deceleration is a maximum. Also there is some uncertainty in determining the tilt of the plane of rotation of the galaxy to the line of sight so that the correction which is applied to obtain true velocities of expansion is rather uncertain. Lynds and Sandage derived a time of 1.5×10^6 yr since the filaments started to move outward from the center. However, bearing in mind the uncertainties just mentioned, perhaps the time may be estimated to lie between the limits $5\text{--}20 \times 10^5$ yr.

A second time scale which can be derived is obtained from the half-lives of the electrons which are responsible for optical synchrotron radiation in M82. These half-lives depend critically on the assumed strength of the magnetic field in which the electrons radiate. If the half-life at a given frequency in a magnetic field of strength H_0 is t_0, then in a magnetic field of strength H_1 the half-life is $t_1 = t_0(H_0/H_1)^2$. For a value of $H = 2 \times 10^{-5}$ G, $t = 2.5 \times 10^4$ yr, and for a value of H of 7×10^{-5} G, $t = 2 \times 10^3$ yr.

Lynds and Sandage finally chose a value of the magnetic field of 2×10^{-6} G which gives $t = 2.5 \times 10^6$ yr. As they pointed out, this means that one generation of electrons with energies near 5×10^{12} eV will have continued to radiate for the lifetime of the source which they estimated from the rate of expansion of the filaments be to near 10^6 yr. If the magnetic field in the filaments is considerably stronger than this, perhaps having field strengths as large as the values given in the last paragraph, then many generations of electrons (of lower energies $\sim 10^{12}$ eV for $H = 7 \times 10^{-5}$ G) must have been generated in the lifetime of 10^6 yr.

Lynds and Sandage also pointed out that the structure of the filaments, the presence of optical synchrotron radiation, and the very flat radio spectrum in M82 are all reminiscent of the situation in the Crab Nebula. In that single supernova remnant with an age of about 10^3 yr, the best estimates of the magnetic field strength lie in the range $10^{-3}\text{--}10^{-4}$ G so that many generations of electrons must have been produced. Clearly the similarity between the stellar remnant and the situation in M82 cannot be taken very far because the scales and energetics of the systems are of entirely different orders of magnitude.

(3) M87

In this galaxy, as in M82, optical synchrotron radiation is seen, so that a time scale could be associated with this as was done for M82 in the discussion above. The minimum total energy required to explain this jet was given in the previous section and it suggests that the field lies between 2×10^{-4} and 7×10^{-4} G. Thus the electrons have energies in the range $2\text{--}4 \times 10^{11}$ eV, and their optical half-lives are of the order of 10^3 yr. As shown above, this time scale cannot be increased unless it is supposed that the magnetic field is much weaker, and in this case there is an imbalance between the energy of the particles and the field so that the particles cannot be contained. While we consider that this situation is probable for the extended radio sources, it does not appear likely here. Since the over-all time scale for the radio source in M87 is probably several orders of magnitude greater than 10^3 yr, then if the jet has been continuously present over the lifetime of the radio source, many generations of electrons must have been produced. These could either have come from the much larger flux of protons which may be trapped in the vicinity of the jet, or from continuous activity in the nucleus, as was recently proposed by Shklovsky (1962). There is certainly good reason to believe that many generations of optical electrons have been produced, since the core radio source is closely associated with the optical jet and it appears reasonable to suppose that it is the optical jet which has gradually increased the strength of the radio source by feeding electrons into it.

As was described in the first section, [O II] λ 3727 shows a displaced component indicating a velocity of 900 km/sec in the line of sight with respect to the center of mass of the galaxy. This appears to us to be comparable in magnitude with the random motions of the stars, so that the gas will not escape. However, Shklovsky (1962) has considered that this does indicate that gas is moving outward and is escaping from the nucleus. If this is the case, then the time scale associated with its escape from the nucleus is again given by L/v, where L is the dimension of the nucleus, and this time turns out to be about 3×10^4 yr.

(4) RADIO SOURCES IN GENERAL

The majority of the radio sources show no optical features from which time scales can be obtained. Thus the conditions all derive from the properties obtained by using the synchrotron theory. As described in the earlier sections, the magnetic fields associated with the minimum total energy required to explain the radio sources all appear to lie in the range 5×10^{-6}–10^{-4} G. The half-lives for radio electrons which emit near 100 Mc and thus have energies in the range 10^8–10^9 eV are then 3×10^8–7×10^5 yr.

Now, if a large proton flux is also present it might be thought that perhaps electrons could be produced by secondary interactions, so that the time scales given above would be less than the age of the source. However, this is probably not the case for the following reasons:

(a) The proton flux may not always be as powerful as has been suggested by the earlier arguments. This depends on the mechanism of generation of the particles.

(b) Even if the proton flux dominates as far as its energy content is concerned, the density of intergalactic gas in the large volumes occupied by the sources must be so low that nuclear collisions giving rise to secondary electrons are negligible unless the particles can be contained for times of order 10^9 yr or longer. Only in a source with a fairly high density of gas ($\sim 10^{-26}$ g/cm^3 or greater) can this secondary production process be significant. Such a high density in the large volumes of many sources implies the presence of unreasonably large concentrations of mass. Moreover, the containment of the particles also appears to be very difficult. Thus while the first generation of electrons may have arisen in a radio source in this way, many generations cannot be produced in the large halo regions unless reacceleration is an important mechanism operating there. However, in the case of M82, if such reacceleration takes place through a process in which energy is transferred from the moving filaments to the particles, the total energy in the filaments will be greater than the estimate given earlier.

Other arguments which bear on the time scales for the radio sources, and which are of more significance, are as follows. It has been pointed out elsewhere (Burbidge 1962) that these equipartition values for the magnetic field given above are very high for the large extended regions in which many of the radio sources exist. If it is considered that they are unreasonably large, as the authors believe, and if it is supposed that the average field strengths are much lower, perhaps $\sim 10^{-6}$ G, we are automatically led to the conclusion that $E_p \gg E_M$ in the sources at present. Consequently the particles must be expanding away very rapidly from their places of origin in the galaxies, and the times scales associated with the sources are then of the order of L/v, where L is the dimension of the source at present, and v is the appropriate velocity of expansion. If very large fluxes of particles are being ejected at relativistic velocities into a weak field with a much smaller energy content, then the time scale is presumably given by L/c and from the dimensions of the sources this gives times $\sim 10^6$ yr or less. If we are dealing with clouds of plasma which are expanding outward with hydromagnetic velocities, then the time scales are probably $\leq 10^8$ yr.

Radio spectra also give valuable information concerning the time scales to be associated with the radio sources. It is the electrons of highest energy which give the high-frequency part of the radio spectrum, as these have the shortest half-lives. Thus a measurement of the high-frequency cutoff can, in theory, give a measure of the time which has elapsed since the last generation of high-energy electrons was injected. The observational situation concerning high-frequency cutoffs is not clear as yet. However, we may take as an example Cygnus A. The minimum total energy required to explain the source gives a magnetic field strength near 10^{-4} G. Apparently no high-frequency cutoff is seen, even at 10000 Mc, and the half-lives for electrons which radiate at this frequency in a field of 10^{-4} G are about 3×10^5 yr. Thus we must conclude that either electrons have been continuously injected within the last 3×10^5 yr, or else the magnetic field is weaker than 10^{-4} G. Although we are inclined to believe this latter explanation, as discussed earlier, this leads to further complications, since if the fields are weaker, the particles of highest energy will tend to escape first, thus again producing a high-frequency cutoff; this is not seen. Probably the true situation in this source is a very complex one in which particles are produced over a fairly short time scale, while some escape from the sources rapidly.

Kardashev, Kuz'min, and Syrovatsky (1962) have attempted to derive an age for Cygnus A by using the fact that the radio spectrum shows a change in slope at about 1500 Mc. On the basis that the source giving rise to the particles is short-lived (i.e., is not stationary) they have found that the age is related to the frequency at which the spectrum changes slope by the relation

$$t = 17H^{-3/2}\nu^{-1/2} \text{ (Mc) yr.}$$

Thus if
$$H = 10^{-4} \text{ G}, \qquad \nu = 1500 \text{ Mc}, \qquad t = 5 \times 10^5 \text{ yr} .$$

And if
$$H = 10^{-5} \text{ G}, \qquad \nu = 1500 \text{ Mc}, \qquad t = 15 \times 10^6 \text{ yr} .$$

They pointed out that to fill the radio source in a time of the order of 10^6 yr demands velocities of the order of $\frac{1}{3}c$. However, many observers would not agree that there is a sharp change in slope at 1500 Mc.

Shklovsky (1960) attempted to determine the ages of Cygnus A and Centaurus A by supposing that the same type of event occurred in both, and that this arose by the expansion of vast plasma clouds outward at hydromagnetic velocities. The different sizes of the two sources then gave rise to ages of 10^6–10^7 yr (Cygnus A) and $\sim 10^8$ yr (Centaurus A).

We may summarize the discussion of the time scales associated with these violent events as follows: The small-scale optical phenomena indicate very short time scales of the order of 10^3–10^4 yr. Arguments based on the radio data suggest times mostly of the order of 10^5–10^6 yr and there is some indication that a number of events with characteristic time scales of 10^3–10^4 yr are required over a time of the order of 10^6 yr.

It has been pointed out (Burbidge 1962) that if time scales as short as 10^6 yr are general for these outbursts then to account for the fraction of galaxies which are now radio sources among all of the galaxies it must be concluded that the sources are recurrent in galaxies. The frequency with which such outbursts occur will depend on whether all types of galaxy are involved or whether only certain types of galaxy have the suitable conditions which lead to an outburst.

As was pointed out by Woltjer (1959) the Seyfert galaxies are a sizable fraction of all of the Sa and Sb galaxies down to the same magnitude limit—they make up about 3% of these and if we consider them among all galaxies to the same limiting brightness they are about 1%. Thus if the time scale associated with galaxies is $\sim 10^{10}$ yr and all galaxies go through this phase then it might be expected to last on the average about 10^8 yr. However, our other arguments have suggested much shorter time scales in the Seyfert nuclei, so that it might be argued that perhaps 100 events each with a time scale of the order of 10^6 yr takes place in a galaxy over a time of order 10^{10} yr. If only certain types of galaxy are involved then an even higher frequency has to be involved in them.

For the strong radio sources Burbidge (1962) estimated that 1 in 10^3–10^4 galaxies is currently a strong source. By the same argument as that given above, if the duration of the event is about 10^6 yr each galaxy will become a source 1 to 10 times in about 10^{10} yr. If only a certain fraction of the galaxies is physically able to generate such violent events —if say only the brightest 5% of the galaxies are involved—then in them the process must have occurred some 20–200 times.

Having described these properties based on the observational evidence associated with galaxies, we turn to a brief discussion of the starlike objects. After this we consider the general circumstances of the outbursts.

VI. Starlike Objects Associated with Radio Sources

A very recent development which bears on our understanding of violent events is concerned with the properties of the so-called radio stars. The identification of the radio sources 3C 48, 196, and 286 with what appeared to be stars in our own Galaxy has been described by Matthews and Sandage (1964). They measured the colors and magnitudes of these objects and obtained spectra of 3C 48. The spectral features are broad and weak in most cases and consequently there has been great difficulty in making any identifications with well-known lines (cf. Schmidt 1962b). However, the recent spectroscopic investigation of the starlike object associated with 3C 273 by Schmidt (1963) shows that this has a number of broad emission features which can be identified as Hβ, Hγ, Hδ, Hϵ, Mg II λ 2798, and [O III] λ 5007 which show a redshift $\Delta\lambda/\lambda_0 = 0.158$. Following this work, Greenstein and Matthews (1963) have now identified features in 3C 48 as Mg II λ 2798, [Ne V] λ 4685, [O II] λ 3727, [Ne V] λ 3346, [Ne III] λ 3868, and [Ne V] λ 2975 which show a redshift $\Delta\lambda/\lambda_0 = 0.368$. The observations of the energy distribution of 3C 273 over a wide wavelength region by Oke (1963) show a feature which is due to Hα with a redshift in agreement with Schmidt; they also show that the object is exceedingly blue and cannot be represented by a blackbody, so that part at least of the optical continuum radiation may be synchrotron radiation.

The spectrum lines are broadened by amounts which correspond to random motions of the order of 1000 km/sec, i.e., they are comparable with but less than the random velocities seen in the Seyfert nuclei.

If the redshifts are due to recession of the objects then it is clear that we are seeing the early stages of outbursts in the nuclei of very distant galaxies. For a value of the Hubble constant of 75 km/sec/Mpc the absolute magnitudes of 3C 48 and 3C 273 are $M_v = -24.9$ and -26.2, respectively [here the $(1 + z)^2$ corrections for number and energy effects having been taken into account using the equations discussed by Sandage (1961b).]

The radio source associated with 3C 48 is then comparable in strength to the strongest sources known, but the radio and optical dimensions are $\lesssim 5.5$ kpc. In the case of 3C 273, a small optical wisp or jet is associated with the object and one component of the radio source extends to a distance ~ 50 kpc from the starlike object which has a dimension $\lesssim 1$ kpc.

It may be argued, therefore, that such objects represent the first stages of evolution in a violent event in the nucleus of a galaxy, and at later stages the optical luminosity decreases and the radio source expands. The ages of such objects must be significantly less than the ages of the majority of extended radio sources and we may suppose from the scales involved that they lie in the range 10^3–10^5 yr.

However, 3C 48 has been shown by Matthews and Sandage (1963) to show variations in light of about 0.4 mag. over a period of about a year. This means that a small region within the volume of the optical source with a dimension $\lesssim 0.1$ pc has varied in light enough to have made the whole object change in brightness. Thus we must suppose that violent activity is still occurring in the source.

It is clear that if these objects are indeed distant galaxies no very short period light variations can be present. An observational program to see if this condition is fulfilled is therefore of great importance.

The alternative explanation of these redshifts is that they are gravitational in origin. It has already been proposed that small redshifts $\Delta\lambda/\lambda_0 = 0.005 - 0.05$, if they were found might indicate that the radio stars were highly evolved objects with neutron cores and masses of about 3 $M\odot$ (Burbidge 1963). However, in the cases of 3C 273 and 3C 48 the magnitudes of the redshifts and their constancy from line to line indicate a very small gravitational potential gradient and hence an unreasonably small volume in which forbidden lines are produced has led to this possibility being discounted. On the other hand, an intermediate situation in which it is argued that the gravitational redshifts arise at the surfaces of massive objects ($\sim10^5$ $M\odot$) with radii $\sim10^{11}$ cm and distances ~1 Mpc (similar in mass and distribution in space to intergalactic globular clusters) may be considered. There appears to be an upper limit for gravitational redshifts near $\Delta\lambda/\lambda_0 = 0.1$ for objects in which the gravitational field is static. If it can be shown that gravitational redshifts greater than this can never be observed then we shall have a firm theoretical basis for supposing that these objects are distant galaxies with nuclei which have exploded comparatively recently.

VII. Outbursts in Galaxies

The material that has been summarized in the previous section shows, in general, that:

(1) Violent events can originate in elliptical, spiral, or irregular galaxies. The data on irregulars come from M82 alone.

(2) The outbursts vary considerably in the amounts of energy released. All the energetic considerations show that the range is from 10^{55}–10^{61} ergs.

(3) These events produce effects which manifest themselves in a number of ways and these are seen to persist for periods of up to 10^6 yr after the first event occurred. However, activity over as short a time scale as 10^3 yr is indicated in some cases.

(4) Mass motions of many thousands of km/sec are generated.

(5) Very large fluxes of relativistic particles may be generated in the outbursts.

The mechanism which may lead to these events is discussed in the following section. However, it is necessary here to come to closer grips with the types of event which are possible. The most important point to stress first is that very large mass motions are involved. As far as we are aware, such velocities can be generated only in two ways— either in an explosion, which by necessity must involve the condensed material already present, or by an electromagnetic acceleration process, such as that seen in a discharge or in the acceleration of a plasma. Quite high random motions are present in the stars in the nuclei of galaxies, but they are an order of magnitude less than the velocities seen in the violent events described here. The mechanism of acceleration of gas clouds by the so-called rocket effect described by Oort and Spitzer (1955) and Biermann and Schlüter (1955) cannot be invoked since no mechanism of this type can generate velocities significantly higher than the velocity of sound. In our own Galaxy velocities $\geq 10^3$ km/sec have been observed only in supernova remnants, where they are attributed to the supernova outbursts, or in the sun, where they are associated with some forms of solar activity due to electromagnetic processes. It is thus natural that all of the proposed explanations for the occurrence of violent events in galaxies have suggested that the large velocities and the high-energy particles have been generated either by explosive processes or by electromagnetic acceleration processes.

The generation of very large mass motions in different types of galaxy will have different effects depending on the amounts of gas which are already present in the system. In a spiral galaxy there is a considerable concentration of gas in the disk, and the degree of concentration towards the center depends on the type of galaxy. In the irregular galaxy M82 there is obviously a tremendous amount of uncondensed gas and dust. In most elliptical systems there is apparently only a very small amount of ionized gas present, and the concentration of neutral gas is not shown. There are many systems showing the symmetry associated with ellipticals in which all that can be seen are stars and dust. These systems are not classified as ellipticals because of the presence of dust, but are usually put into the category of S0. The presence of such systems indicates that much uncondensed interstellar matter may be present in systems which differ markedly in their form and, to a lesser degree, in stellar content, from the spiral and irregular galaxies. In explosions that occur in nuclear regions of spiral and irregular galaxies, the role of the gas already present will be of importance. In some elliptical systems enough gas may be present to influence the development of the explosion, but in many cases there may be only a negligible amount of gas available.

The generation of very large fluxes of high-energy particles will also have different effects depending on the density of interstellar matter and the magnetic fields into which the particles are injected. The high-energy particles will give rise to a number of effects. If the flux consists of protons and electrons with relativistic energies we can consider the following situations.

(a) The gas and magnetic field have an appreciable density and energy content. In this case,

    (i) Relativistic electrons will radiate in the magnetic field thus providing a synchrotron source in the central region of the galaxy. As has been pointed out by Lequeux (1962), the very small radio sources which lie well within the confines of the optical galaxy and hence in the gas near the centers all tend to have rather flat spectra. These must arise because of the moderating effect of the comparatively dense gas.

    (ii) As the electrons lose energy by synchrotron emission they will radiate successively at lower frequencies, but, depending on the density of the gas and the strength of the magnetic field, an energy level will be reached at which the energy losses are predominantly due to atomic processes. When this level is reached the synchrotron emission will grow significantly weaker and the heating effect in the gas will be increased. In practice, since an electron spectrum of the form $N(E) = kE^{-n}$ is expected to be generated in the outburst, the synchrotron source and the heating will be coexistent in time and space.

    (iii) The relativistic protons will lose energy only by nuclear collisions in which electrons, positrons, gamma rays, and neutrinos will be the stable end products. The electrons and positrons will thus provide a source of synchrotron radiation, and ultimately of heating. Any low-energy nucleons will also provide a source of heating.

(b) In the case in which the particles are injected into a medium of very low or negligible density and very weak magnetic field the effects will be very different. In this case if $E_p \gg E_m$ the particles will be shot out of the galaxy and will rapidly escape. Synchrotron emission in the radio-frequency range will be seen only if the electrons pass through a region of suitable magnetic field strength. Moreover, when very little gas was present originally, secondary production of electrons and positrons by nuclear collisions cannot be an important effect.

This, then, summarizes some of the effects which the particles will have when they are injected at the center of a galaxy. However, in addition to this, in the first case, in which the ejected particles immediately become coupled to the magnetic field in the ambient gas already present, they will do work in expanding this gas. A much more important effect which gives rise to the outward motion in the gas in the central region if it is present, will be due, however, to the mass motions which are generated in the outburst.

As shown in a previous section, the data on the Seyfert galaxies suggest that the energy available in the form of ionized gas with velocities of several thousand km/sec lies in the range $10^{55\pm2}$ ergs. Although more energy may have originally been made available in these forms in some of the strong radio sources, we take only what is indicated in the Seyfert galaxies here, since in those systems we are presumably seeing an event in its early stages. The energy corresponds to about 10^6–10^7 $M\odot$ moving with velocities of 1000–3000 km/sec.

The escape velocity from the center of a normal spiral galaxy is only of the order of 500 km/sec, while for a massive elliptical system it may be as large as about 1500 km/sec. Therefore when a large amount of momentum is suddenly generated in the nuclear region of a galaxy it will push out material ahead of it and whether or not it will escape depends on the amount of gas present and its distribution. The directions in which it will escape will therefore depend critically on the original distribution of gas. In spiral galaxies this distribution is obviously strongly concentrated to the plane of rotation. In elliptical galaxies too, the uncondensed gas which is concentrated to the center will show an equilibrium distribution which is flattened if the system has an appreciable angular momentum. In this connection it must be remembered that even a spherical elliptical system may have a considerable net angular momentum. All that is required is that the stars form in the proto-galaxy before the gas reaches an equilibrium configuration characteristic of its angular momentum. In the subsequent evolution gas ejected from stars will collect in such an equilibrium configuration.

It is clear, therefore, what the sequence of events following the explosion will be. That part of the exploding gas with high linear momentum which is moving towards the comparatively thin sheet of gas in the plane will compress and push the original gas outward. Thus it will generate outward radial motions in the plane. Simple arguments based on the momentum balance show that, for example, if half of the momentum of 10^6 $M\odot$ traveling at 1000 km/sec is transmitted to the disk, where we assume that we have a characteristic thickness of 500 pc and a mean density of gas and dust of 10^{-24} g/cm³, then at a distance of about 1 kpc from the center the outward velocities will be about 50 km/sec. If the initial explosion generates 10^7 $M\odot$ at 3000 km/sec, then at a distance of about 4 kpc the outflow velocity will be about 50 km/sec.

In the direction of the minor axis the situation will be quite different. The total mass of gas in a sphere of radius 250 pc surrounding the center will be only about 10^6 $M\odot$ so that the sudden impulse involves a mass of comparable order to that which it encounters. Consequently the deceleration will be very limited, and the whole of the cloud will be blasted out in two cones whose axes are the axis of rotation of the galaxy.

It is thus clear that by this process the axis of symmetry of the results of the explosion will be always perpendicular to the equatorial plane. This will also apply to the high-energy particles, which, as described earlier, will cause only a local synchrotron source and heating in the plane, in the direction in which the gas is concentrated, but will be blasted out in the direction of the axis of rotation.

This then gives an obvious qualitative explanation of the well-known feature of many strong radio sources in which two strong components are seen lying along an axis in the system. In the case of NGC 5128, for example, there is both a large source lying approximately perpendicular to the plane of gas and dust, and a small double source which may be the result of a more recent event also lying along a line perpendicular to the plane of gas and dust. Spherical symmetry is also seen in some cases, and clearly these different distributions show that the form of the source depends on the total amount of gas which was originally present, and whether or not there was a preferred plane of symmetry due to the angular momentum originally present. If practically no quiescent gas was present then we might see the exploding gas in a spherical shell expanding with velocities of thousands of kilometers a second far from the center. This would be the gas generated in the explosion itself. It is this effect we may be seeing in NGC 1275. Since many double radio sources are centered on elliptical galaxies this necessarily implies that in these galaxies before the outburst took place enough gas was originally present to prevent the explosion being spherically symmetrical.

It is also required, to explain the extended radio sources, that the particles are shot out freely in these preferred directions, in order to avoid the well-known difficulties associated with the adiabatic expansion. This suggests that the magnetic field is weak and that the field configuration already has a radial form in the direction of the axis of rotation when the particles are shot into it. If there are successive outbursts, then it can be supposed that this configuration of the field has been produced by the first outburst involving the large-scale mass motions. In the first outburst the particles will move ahead of the shell so that this flux will encounter the original configuration. Provided that the energy density in the magnetic field and in the ambient gas is small enough the particles may be expected to be blasted straight through this material.

VIII. Mechanism of Outbursts

A very considerable number of proposals have been made to try to explain the source of the energy and the mechanisms by which outbursts of this type occur in galaxies. This problem at present is one of the most important of the unsolved problems of modern astronomy. The reasons for this, in the opinion of the authors, are as follows:

(1) The apparently short-lived character of the outbursts and the observed frequencies of the outbursts as seen in the Seyfert galaxies and in the radio sources, among the total population of galaxies, shows that the outburst may recur in galaxies. Since 10^{55}–10^{62} ergs are released in an outburst this energy dissipation may play an important role in the rate of evolution of the galaxy.

(2) The dissipation of this energy, much of which goes into the intergalactic medium, may continuously increase the energy density in the medium, particularly the cosmic-ray energy density. This energy increase is made at the expense of the condensed material in the galaxies.

It can be seen that these arguments are not without their cosmological implications, since they both bear on the evolution of galaxies and provide a reason for supposing that there is constant and energetic interaction between the condensed and uncondensed material in the universe. In fact, different assumptions about the structure of the universe in which we live, i.e., the cosmological model employed, will lead to different conclusions about the role that the outbursts play. For example, in the majority of the discussion concerning the outbursts which give rise to nonthermal radio sources, beginning with supernova remnants, it has been argued that in the explosions, plasma containing magnetic field is ejected, and high-energy particles are generated as well. If we take the conventional view, then it has been shown (Burbidge 1962) that, provided that the strong radio sources are short-lived, they build up a "local" intergalactic cosmic-ray density of the order of $10^{-13\pm1}$ erg/cm^3, in a time of the order of H^{-1}, i.e., in the lifetime of the universe in an evolutionary cosmology. On the other hand, the proponents of the hot universe version of the steady-state model (Gold and Hoyle 1959) have argued that the cosmic-ray density throughout space is of the order of 10^{-12} erg/cm^3. Consequently, in that picture, a strong radio source will arise if the magnetic field is increased sufficiently by the outburst and no particles need necessarily be produced by the outburst itself. [See a more recent discussion of this by Hoyle and Burbidge (1963).] However, this is not adequate to provide an optical source of synchrotron emission as appears to be present in M87 and M82, since for reasonable values of the magnetic field the particle energies must be far in excess of those created in the hot universe. Thus if this picture is accepted, it is still necessary to suppose that some acceleration of electrons has taken place in the source. It is necessary to add here that if electrons and positrons are produced by any other process, as for example in the annihilation of nucleons and antinucleons (cf. Burbidge and Hoyle 1956) local increases in the magnetic field will also give rise to a radio source.

The possible energy sources can be considered in three groups. They are:

(a) Energy which is released by the interaction of a galaxy with material that was previously unconnected with it.

(b) Internal energy in a galaxy in the form of rotational energy, turbulent energy, or magnetic field energy which is released by some castatrophic process.

(c) Energy which is released in the evolution of stars. Included here is the gravitational energy released when stars are formed, the nuclear energy released in thermonuclear explosions, and gravitational energy which is released if the star goes to a highly collapsed phase.

We now give a critical discussion of all of the proposals which have been made, each of which appears in one or other of the above categories.

In category (a) the first proposal which was made was that the energy was released in collisions between galaxies (Baade and Minkowski 1954). It is clear now that this argument cannot be sustained either on theoretical grounds or on the basis of the identifications of radio sources (cf. Burbidge 1961). In addition to the arguments given in the latter reference, the observational evidence now available shows that a very large number of the sources of violent activity are centered on single galaxies, and as discussed earlier, the violence appears to start at their centers. NGC 1275 still presents an ambiguous situation in that it may be two systems in collision but an alternative explanation has been discussed earlier in this paper.

A second proposal which falls into category (a) is that the energy is produced by the interaction of material in the galaxy with anti-particles or anti-matter and the subsequent annihilation. This was proposed by Burbidge (1956) and Burbidge and Hoyle (1956). The general difficulty with any hypothesis of this type is that the presence of anti-matter in the universe appears, from the point of view of fundamental physics, highly improbable, although all possibilities have not been explored.

The most recent proposal in this category is that made by Shklovsky (1962), in which it is supposed that a galaxy interacts with material which has come from outside. He specifically considered the case of M87, and argued that the material which is accreted by such a massive system falls into the center. Energy is released and material in the central region is accelerated outward in the form of plasma jets. While the rate at which material falls in is estimated by Shklovsky to be about 10 $M\odot$/yr, and this is compatible with the normal accretion rate for a galaxy of mass of the order of 10^{12} $M\odot$ in a medium of density $\sim 10^{-29}$ g/cm^3, the details of this process are not at all clear. In particular, it is not obvious how the acceleration occurs. However, if such a mechanism is supposed to be operative for violent events which occur in the nuclei of galaxies of all types, as is required from the observational arguments summarized above, then it is difficult to see how a process of infall of material could always give rise to a violent event which appears to emanate from the center. The infalling gas would first interact with gaseous material far from the center wherever it is present. Thus we see that all of the proposals which have been made which fall naturally into category (a) have very severe difficulties associated with them.

We next turn to the processes involved in category (b). In its process of formation a proto-galaxy must dissipate energy both by radiation and by the generation of large-scale motions in the fragmentation which is required if stars are to form (cf. Hoyle 1953). This fragmentation will eventually give rise to star clusters and associations. It might well be asked whether the violent release of energy in some systems is associated with this stage of evolution. The obvious objection to this is that the vast majority of systems in which violent events are taking place are well organized and often highly evolved galaxies, i.e., the elliptical galaxies. M82 may be in a fairly early stage of evolution as deduced from the integrated spectral type of A5 and the large amount of uncondensed material, but it does not appear to be at the very early stage of which the dissipation of energy in this way is important. None of the many peculiar systems catalogued by Vorontsov-Velyaminov (1960) and studied by us, and others, and which are thought in some cases to be systems of a very early stage of evolution, are associated with radio sources or other violent events. The only possible exception to this is NGC 4038–39, which is one of the weaker of the identified radio sources.

The question therefore arises as to whether any of the internal energy in a well-developed galaxy could be released suddenly to give rise to a violent event. The only proposal of this type which has been made is that by Hoyle (1961), who argued that in galaxies with considerable amounts of gas containing magnetic flux and large angular momenta galactic flares could arise through discharges following the winding up of the magnetic fields in the centers. This mechanism is similar to that proposed by Gold and Hoyle (1960) for the generation of solar flares. While the model proposed by Hoyle is not unattractive, it suffers from the disadvantage that the discharge conditions cannot be reached unless there is a very large amount of gas already present in the galaxy, and also a very large amount of angular momentum per unit mass. This means that very massive systems with high rotations and containing large amounts of uncondensed material are the obvious candidates to produce violent events. However, most of the galaxies in which violent events are seen do not fulfill all of these conditions. The elliptical galaxies which are massive, often contain little gas, and probably have little angular momentum. The Seyfert galaxies which do contain considerable amounts of gas and are fast rotating do not appear to have sufficiently large masses nor large mass concentrations.

Finally, therefore, we come to the processes which are contained in category (c). Ginsburg (1961) has attempted to show that high-energy particles can be produced in the early stages of formation of a galaxy when gravitational energy is released. However, as we have described earlier, it appears that none of the galaxies from which radio sources have emanated are systems which are recently formed.

As will be seen in what follows, energy release following star formation and evolution appears to give the best hope of explaining the phenomena. As described earlier, the observations of the Crab nebula and other supernova remnants in our Galaxy show that in, or following, such a stellar explosion the necessary conditions for a synchrotron source to appear are produced. Also, only in stellar explosions (novae and supernovae) are velocities generated of the magnitude seen in the Seyfert nuclei. Thus it is natural to suppose that the violent outbursts in galaxies are the result of multiple supernova outbursts or their equivalent in energy output. It is normally estimated that some 10^{50} ergs are emitted in a supernova outburst (this number is uncertain and in large part it is based on the observational side from studies of the Crab nebula and the supernova in IC 4182). However, the total amount of nuclear energy available in the conversion of one solar mass of hydrogen to helium is about 10^{52} ergs. It must be stressed, however, that this amount of energy cannot be released catastrophically. On the other hand, the upper limit to the gravitational energy which can be released if a configuration collapses to the Schwarzschild limit is about 10^{53} ergs. If we take the more conservative estimate of 10^{50} ergs then it is clear that the energy required to explain the various types of violent events described above demand explosions involving 10^5–10^{11} $M\odot$. This upper limit (corresponding to the energies in the most powerful radio sources) is so large that it alone may already indicate that the release of gravitational energy must be important. This possibility was first mentioned by Burbidge (1962b). However, we describe next the various proposals which have been made involving the stars.

Shklovsky (1960) has argued simply that the supernova rate must have been very considerably enhanced so that some 10^6 or more supernovae have gone off at a rate of about 1 per year in an object like M87. However, he gave no argument as to why this should occur. Since supernovae only occur at the end of a star's evolution it is not reasonable to take this view unless it is supposed that the outbursts (a) are causally connected, or, (b) unless stars of very great mass are continuously being formed and evolve very rapidly. It was proposed by Burbidge (1961) that a chain reaction of supernovae could be caused in the nucleus of a galaxy if one supernova went off naturally and the stellar density was sufficiently high so that other stars could be exploded.

It was estimated that the star density required if such a mechanism were to work must be of the order of 10^6–10^7 stars/pc^3 and it was pointed out that there was no observational argument against this, particularly for the elliptical galaxies. Even higher star densities may be acceptable. The difficulty lies in understanding how a detonation wave can propagate even if sufficient light nuclei are present. This problem has not been solved, partly because the geometry involved is exceedingly difficult to handle. Also, modern ideas concerning supernova outbursts suggest that an integral part of the normal supernova process is a catastrophic collapse due to a phase change in the material or neutrino emission at very high temperatures in an evolved core. The chain reaction mechanism would not lead to this. Finally, if the magnitude of the energy which is released suggests that gravitational energy release is involved, this cannot be expected by such a mechanism. These difficulties and unsolved questions have led some authors to consider a somewhat different approach. There is obviously only one other possibility left. This is to suppose that stars are formed and rapidly evolve in the nucleus of a galaxy to give rise to such events. This is essentially what was implied by Shklovsky in his 1960 attempt at understanding what is taking place in M87.

The first and quite fundamental question is to consider the formation of new stars in the nuclear region of a galaxy. This was considered briefly by Cameron (1962), who wrote down the condition for gravitational instability in a gas cloud containing a magnetic field with conditions which he considered were reasonable for a gas cloud in the central parts of an elliptical galaxy. Unfortunately, in deriving the critical condition, he omitted the contribution to the internal energy from the random motions in the gas. All indications from observations of the quiescent centers of galaxies suggest that either the gas has turbulent motions of comparable order to the motions of the stars (several hundred km/sec) or else ordered rotational motion of the same magnitude. In this case this contribution to the internal energy dominates (Burbidge 1962) and the critical mass becomes unreasonably large. Although the conditions can be improved by supposing that the initial density of the gas in the center is very much higher than assumed by Cameron (perhaps 10^{-22} g/cm^3 instead of 10^{-26} g/cm^3) there obviously is considerable difficulty in understanding how stars can be formed under such conditions. Two factors which do not have to be considered in star formation in spiral arms, but which must be taken into account here, and which have not been properly evaluated so far are:

(i) Star formation is taking place in a deep potential well at the center;

(ii) the star density is rather high,—at least $\sim$1000 stars/pc^3 and the proto-stars have got to condense in this medium.

The first of these conditions may help star formation. However, the effect of the second is more difficult to understand. It seems possible that these stars will have a general disrupting effect on a condensation because they will continuously stir the material and also tidally disrupt condensations.

However, it is possible that the observations of the state of the gas in the centers of galaxies may be misleading for this problem. The observations come from the ionized gas, and it is not impossible that the presence of such ionized gas indicates an abnormal state of activity. Our discussion of the relative strength of the Hα and [N II] λ 6583 emission lines in a wide range of spiral and elliptical galaxies (Burbidge and Burbidge 1962c, 1963) indicates that the electron energies determined from the strength of the lines and their relative intensities, are incompatible with excitation of the gas from the comparatively low luminosity stars which are present. This might suggest that what we are seeing in the majority of cases in which ionized gas appears strongly in the central region, is a remnant of the violent activity arising from an earlier outburst which has not yet died out completely. Obviously we have no observational information on the presence of neutral gas in the nuclear regions of galaxies apart from that in our own, but the ideal situation for star formation will be reached if gas, perhaps originally ejected from stars in an ionized state, slowly cools and condenses in the center.

If the time scale of the outburst is 10^6 yr or less, then if star formation and evolution are occurring, stars with masses $\sim$100 $M\odot$ or greater must be formed. The upper limit to the total mass involved is about 10^8 $M\odot$ if we suppose that it is gravitational energy and not nuclear energy which is mainly responsible. In many cases, however, the total energy in the outburst indicates that a lesser mass is involved. Thus we may need to consider a wide range of masses of star formation and evolution is responsible. If stars can be formed in the nucleus of a galaxy the masses depend on the degree of fragmentation which can occur. From the theoretical standpoint we have little indication at present of what is possible, though it is an obvious requirement that much larger masses must appear than is normally the case when stars are formed in spiral arms. Moreover the suggestion that continuous activity may occur with time scales of the order of 10^3–10^4 yr over a total period of about 10^6 yr may indicate that not just one sudden event corresponding to the evolution of single massive object occurs, but that a number of smaller masses may sometimes be involved. Thus the evolution of stars in the range 10^2–10^8 $M\odot$ must be investigated. The fragmentation is presumably controlled by the magnetic field conditions in the original medium, but no real understanding of this point is available as yet.

The first discussions of the evolution of stars with masses in the range 10^5–10^8 $M\odot$ have been made by Hoyle and Fowler (1963a, b). However, they have not discussed the formation process, but have begun by considering the main-sequence configurations of such objects. Their investigations suggest that the subsequent evolution will rapidly lead, following neutrino emission, to a collapse to a radius near to the Schwarzschild limit at which point relativity effects become of importance.

At this early stage in the investigation of these fascinating phenomena it must be stressed that the idea that gravitational energy release may explain these events is very attractive. However at the present time it must be emphasized that we have little idea of how such objects can first be formed in the nuclei of galaxies.

Conclusion

In this paper we have attempted to describe the many arguments which now suggest strongly that violent events occur in the nuclei of galaxies, that they are fairly frequent, and may have many effects on the structure and evolution of galaxies. Ambartsumian (1958 and other references given there) for many years has stressed the importance of events which occur in the nuclei of galaxies. Although he has described these in terms of the "splitting of the nuclei" of galaxies and has related this to his ideas concerning intrastellar matter, it is clear that our general conclusions follow rather closely his original thinking on these topics. It now seems difficult to underestimate the importance of these new concepts. We have described in some detail the observational evidence which leads to the conclusion that such events are of importance. However, there are many other effects which must be considered, few of which have been investigated as yet. Some of these are as follows:

(1) It seems probable that the type of weak galactic radio halo which is seen in M31 and other comparable nearby galaxies is produced by events such as those described. If this is so, an important feature of such a halo is that it will be a transient phenomenon with a lifetime in the range 5×10^7–10^9 yr. Other properties of such a halo have been described by Burbidge and Hoyle (1963).

(2) Some theories concerning the origin of cosmic rays must be revised if these ideas are correct. If particles are produced in the outbursts they may make a significant contribution to the intergalactic cosmic ray flux (Burbidge 1962a). In any case, if the halo in our own Galaxy is a transient phenomenon it can no longer be supposed that galactic cosmic rays alone are present in the Galaxy. If we take the view that the cosmic ray density everywhere is $\sim 10^{-12}$ erg/cm^3 (Gold and Hoyle 1959) then the radio sources appear because of the magnetic field and acceleration effects which take place in the outbursts.

(3) Noncircular motions in the disk of a galaxy will be produced by these outbursts. Thus the outward moving gas seen in our own Galaxy and departures from rotational motions seen in other spirals are easily explained by such effects.

(4) It is entirely possible that the outward radial motions generated in such explosive events in the disks of a spiral galaxy may be an important factor in explaining the appearance and maintenance of spiral structure. This question demands close study.

(5) It has frequently been argued (cf. proceedings of the Princeton Conference on Interstellar Matter in Galaxies 1963) that it is very difficult to account for the energy input into the interstellar gas in the disk of our Galaxy by means of processes involving normal O and B stars alone. It is clear that repeated outbursts in the nuclear regions of a galaxy of the type we have described here may contribute significantly to the energy input.

(6) It is well known that in the nuclei of some spiral galaxies a number of large ionized regions (hot spots) can be observed (cf. Morgan 1958). It is obvious that such features are probably associated with the occurrence of nuclear outbursts. Whether they indicate regions in which outbursts have taken place in the past, or whether they have something to do with the conditions which are building up prior to new outbursts demands investigation.

(7) If massive objects evolve rapidly or if the supernova frequency is vastly increased in the nuclear region of a galaxy element synthesis may be expected to go on at an enhanced rate there. Which of the many processes will be especially involved will not be clear until we have a definitive model of the mechanism of the outbursts. However, it has already been proposed (cf. Hoyle and Fowler 1963) that much of r-process material might be produced in this way.

(8) If violent events recur frequently in some types of galaxy, and a large amount of material is ejected from the nuclear regions it is possible that some of this material may not escape from the galaxy but condense into stars in the halo regions. It is perhaps suggestive that M87 which shows all of the signs of violent activity in its nucleus has more globular clusters than any other elliptical galaxy known. A survey of the elliptical galaxies in the Virgo cluster shows that M87 has more than ten times more globular clusters than any other elliptical there.

This research has been supported in part by a grant from the National Science Foundation.

It is a pleasure to thank W. C. Miller for his characteristically fine work in preparing the reproductions.

REFERENCES

Ambartsumian, V. A. 1958, Solvay Conference Reports.
Baade, W. 1956, *Astrophys. J.*, **123**, 550.
Baade, W., and Minkowski, R. 1954, *Astrophys. J.*, **119**, 215.
Biermann, L., and Schlüter, A. 1955, *Gas Dynamics of Cosmic Clouds* (North-Holland Publishing Company, Amsterdam), Chap. 27.
Biraud, F., Lequeux, J., and Le Roux, E. 1960, *Observatory*, **80**, 116.
Bolton, J. G., and Clark, B. G. 1960, *Publ. Astron. Soc. Pacific*, **72**, 29.
Burbidge, E. M. 1962, *Astrophys. J.*, **136**, 1134.
Burbidge, G. R. 1956, *Astrophys. J.*, **124**, 416.
———. 1959, *Paris Symposium on Radio Astronomy*, edited by R. N. Bracewell (Stanford University Press, Stanford, California), p. 541.
———. 1961, *Nature*, **190**, 1053.
———. 1962a, *Progr. Theoret. Phys. Japan*, **27**, 999.
———. 1962b, *Ann. Rev. Nucl. Sci.*, **12**, 507.
———. 1963, *Astrophys. J.*, **137**, 995.
Burbidge, G. R., and Hoyle, F. 1956, *Nuovo Cimento*, **4**, 558.
———. 1963, *Astrophys. J.*, **138**, 57.
Burbidge, E. M., and Burbidge, G. R. 1959, *Astrophys. J.*, **129**, 271.
———. 1962a (unpublished).
———. 1962b, *Nature*, **194**, 367.
———. 1962c, *Astrophys. J.*, **135**, 694.
———. 1963 (unpublished).

Burbidge, E. M., Burbidge, G. R., and Prendergast, K. H. 1959, *Astrophys. J.*, **130**, 26.
———. 1963, *Astrophys. J.*, **137**, 1022.
Cameron, A. G. W. 1962, *Nature*, **194**, 963.
Elvius, A., and Hall, J. 1962, *Astron. J.*, **67**, 271.
Gardner, F. F., and Whiteoak, J. B. 1962, *Phys. Rev. Letters*, **9**, 197.
Ginsburg, V. L. 1961, *Astron. J. USSR*, **38**, 380; *Soviet Astronomy*, **5**, 282.
Gold, T., and Hoyle, F. 1959, *Paris Symposium on Radio Astronomy*, edited by R. N. Bracewell (Stanford University Press, Stanford, California), p. 583.
———. 1960, *Monthly Notices Roy. Astron. Soc.*, **120**, 89.
Greenstein, J. L. 1961, *Astrophys. J.*, **133**, 335.
———. 1962, *Astrophys. J.*, **135**, 679.
Greenstein, J. L., and Matthews, T. A. 1963, *Nature*, **197**, 1041. *
Herbig, G. H. 1962 (private communication).
Hiltner, W. A. 1960, *Astrophys. J.*, **130**, 340.
Hoyle, F. 1953, *Astrophys. J.*, **118**, 513.
———. 1961 (private communication).
Hoyle, F., and Fowler, W. A. 1963a, *Monthly Notices Roy. Astron. Soc.*, **125**, 169.
———. 1963b, *Nature* (to be published).
Hoyle, F., and Burbidge, G. R. 1963 (to be published).
Jennison, R. C., and Das Gupta, M. K. 1953, *Nature*, **172**, 996.
Kardashev, V., Kuz'min, and Syrovatsky, S. I. 1962, *Astron. Zh.*, **39**, 216 [Trans.: *Soviet Phys.—A.J.*, **6**, 167].
Leslie, P., and Elsmore, B. 1961, *Observatory*, **81**, 14.
Lequeux, J. 1962, *Compt. Rend.*, **255**, 1865.
Lequeux, J., and Heidmann, J. 1961, *Compt. Rend.*, **253**, 804.
Lynds, C. R. 1961, *Astrophys. J.*, **134**, 659.
Lynds, C. R., and Sandage, A. R. 1963, *Astrophys. J.*, **137**, 1005. *
Maltby, P. 1961, *Nature*, **191**, 793.
Maltby, P., and Moffet, A. T. 1962, *Astrophys. J. Suppl.*, **7**, 141.
Maltby, P., Matthews, T., and Moffet, A. T. 1962, *Publ. Astron. Soc. Pacific*, **74**, 277.
———. 1962 (preprint).
Matthews, T. A., and Sandage, A. R. 1963, *Astrophys. J.*, **138**, 30.
Mayall, N. U. 1960, *Ann. Astrophys.*, **23**, 344.
Minkowski, R. 1957, *IAU Symposium on Radio Astronomy* (Cambridge University Press, Cambridge, England), p. 107.
———. 1960, *Astrophys. J.*, **132**, 908.
———. 1961, *Astron. J.*, **66**, 558.
Morgan, W. W. 1958, *Publ. Astron. Soc. Pacific*, **70**, 364.
Oke, J. B. 1963, *Nature*, **197**, 1040.*
Oort, J. H., and Spitzer, L. 1955, *Astrophys. J.*, **121**, 6.
Osterbrock, D. E. 1960, *Astrophys. J.*, **132**, 325.
Page, T. L. 1952, *Astrophys. J.*, **116**, 63.
Sandage, A. R. 1958, *Astrophys. J.*, **127**, 513.
———. 1961a, *Hubble Atlas of Galaxies* (Carnegie Institution of Washington, Washington, D.C.).
———. 1961b, *Astrophys. J.*, **133**, 355.
Sargent, W. L. W. 1963 (private communication).
Schmidt, M. 1962a (private communication).
Schmidt, M. 1962b, *Astrophys. J.*, **136**, 684.
———. 1963, *Nature*, **197**, 1040.
Seyfert, C. K. 1943, *Astrophys. J.*, **97**, 28.
Shklovsky, I. S. 1955, *Astron. Zh. USSR*, **32**, 215.
———. 1960, *Astron. Zh. USSR*, **37**, 945 [trans.: *Soviet Phys.—A.J.*, **4**, 885].
———. 1962, *Astron. Zh. USSR*, **39**, 591.
Twiss, R. Q., Carter, A., and Little, A. G. 1960, *Observatory*, **80**, 153.
Vorontsov-Velyaminov, B. A. 1960, *Atlas of Interacting Galaxies*, Moscow.
Walker, M. F. 1962 (private communication).
Williams, P. J., Dewhirst, D. W., and Leslie, P. 1961, *Observatory*, **81**, 64.
Wilson, O. C. 1956 (private communication).

RADIO STRUCTURE OF 3C 273 AND SPECTRA OF RADIO SOURCES

chapter 28

P. A. G. SCHEUER

This paper discusses first brightness distribution across 3C 273.

When the moon occults a small radio source, then, to a good approximation, a screen with a straight edge removes the flux density of successive narrow strips of the source. The observed course of the occultation is complicated by the fact that a Fresnel diffraction pattern is formed for each such strip. Fortunately, the diffraction effects only change the relative phases of the Fourier components of the true profile, without changing their relative weights, and therefore one can recover the occultation observations which would have been obtained if geometrical optics were valid, and hence the profile of the source. This is not the place to discuss technique (see Scheuer 1963); I shall merely state that the observations are swallowed by a computer, which is then ordered to produce (on an automatic curve-plotter) a profile of the source as it would be seen with a fan beam of some prescribed width. If one asks for better and better resolution, one is looking at narrower strips of the source (and looking at them for a shorter time), so that the signal-to-noise ratio on the profile becomes less favorable. Eventually one also reaches a limit of resolution set by the finiteness of the frequency band accepted by the receiver.

Dr. Hazard very kindly sent me photostat copies of his records of the occultations of 3C 273 observed at Parkes on 1962 August 5 and October 26, 1962 (Hazard, Mackey, and Shimmins 1963). Figure 1 is the profile derived from the emersion of August 5; on this occasion the limb of the moon was parallel to the line joining components A and B, and only one peak appears on the profile. In Figure 2 the components are well separated, and source A appears to have an extension between itself and source B. In Figures 1 and 2 the resolution is limited to 2″ by the receiver band width, and all that one can say about the dimensions of the sources of 410 Mc/s emission is that they are smaller than 2″.

Figure 3a shows the sources of 1410 Mc/s emission as observed with a Gaussian beam 1″ wide between half-power points. Source A now shows a halo about 3″ wide, but the larger extension noted in Figure 2 is too faint to be convincing. Nor am I convinced of the reality of the series of bumps around source B; it may yet be possible to obtain inde-

P. A. G. SCHEUER, Cavendish Laboratory, Cambridge, England.

pendent evidence about them from 410 Mc/s observations of the same immersion, but unfortunately these observations were spoiled (apparently by slipping of the recorder chart), and taken at their face value they lead to nonsensical profiles. As the main sources are not resolved by a 1″ beam, I tried a 0.3″ beam, using the same observations, and obtained the profile shown in Figure 3b. Both sources are now resolved; the core of source A is slightly less than 1″ in diameter, and source B is only 0.5″ in diameter, corresponding to linear dimensions of 2 kpc for source A and 1 kpc for source B.

The other topic that I want to discuss is the effect of the compactness of a radio source on its radio-frequency spectrum.

Most radio sources have spectra of the form $S \propto \nu^{-\alpha}$, where S = flux density, ν = frequency, and α is called the spectral index; generally α is between 0.5 and 1. On the customary log S–log ν-graphs, these spectra appear as straight lines of slope $-\alpha$. But a few sources have spectra that curl over at the low-frequency end, and these turn out to be among the most compact radio sources known, that is, those with the smallest angular diameters and the highest surface brightness (Kellerman, Long, Allen, and Moran 1962; Williams 1963; Bolton, Gardner, and Mackey 1963).

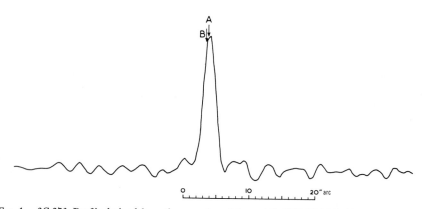

FIG. 1.—3C 273. Profile derived from the emersion of August 5, 1962 (410 Mc/s)

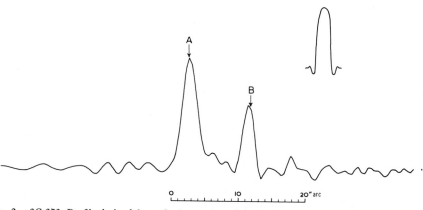

FIG. 2.—3C 273. Profile derived from the immersion of August 5, 1962 (410 Mc/s). The small diagram at upper right shows the apparent profile of a point source, in Figs. 1 and 2, due to the effect of receiver band width.

Figure 4 shows the spectra studied by Williams (1963). A number of reasons could be suggested for the behavior of these sources:

(i) A cut-off at the low-energy end of the energy distribution of the electrons responsible for synchrotron radiation.

(ii) Absorption by free-free transitions in ionized gas in or around the source. The relevant formulae are well known; if the gas is ionized hydrogen at 10000° K, absorption becomes important at frequencies below

$$\nu_{FF} \approx 20N \sqrt{\bar{L}} \text{ Mc/s},$$

where N is the number of electrons (and protons) per cm³ and L is the diameter of absorbing region in kpc.

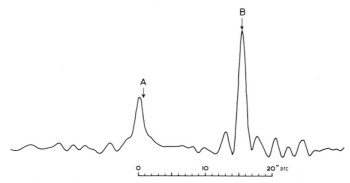

Fɪɢ. 3a.—3C 273. Profile derived from immersion of October 26, 1962 (1410 Mc/s; 1″ beam)

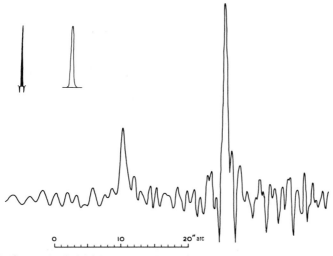

Fɪɢ. 3b.—3C 273. Profile derived from immersion of October 26, 1962 (1410 Mc/s; 0.3″ beam). The small diagram at upper left shows (*left*) the apparent profile due to receiver band width alone and (*right*) the 0.3″ Gaussian profile demanded by the computer program in compiling Fig. 3b.

(iii) Synchrotron self-absorption.

Le Roux (1961) has worked out the theory of the process in some detail, but a very simple calculation is quite adequate for interpreting the present astrophysical data. A single electron of energy $E = \gamma m_0 c^2$ radiates synchrotron radiation with the spectrum sketched in Figure 5; the intensity increases like $\nu^{1/3}$ up to the "critical frequency"

$$\nu_c = \nu_g \gamma^2 \ (\nu_g = \text{gyrofrequency} = eH/m_0 c)$$

and vanishes exponentially at higher frequencies.

Most of the radiation emitted from a radio source at frequency ν comes from electrons whose critical frequency ν_c is close to ν, for those with $\nu_c \ll \nu$ cannot emit such radiation and those with $\nu_c \gg \nu$ are comparatively rare (Fig. 6).

The energy of these "relevant" electrons is given by the formula for ν_c:

$$E_{\text{relevant}} = \gamma m_0 c^2 = m_0 c^2 \sqrt{\frac{\nu_c}{\nu_g}} = m_0 c^2 \sqrt{\frac{\nu}{\nu_g}}$$

and the kinetic temperature corresponding to this energy is given by $\bar{E} = 3\,kT$, the relativistic version of the more usual formula $\bar{E} = \frac{3}{2}\,kT$. If extrapolation of the high-

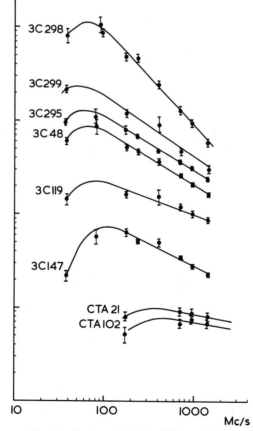

FIG. 4.—Spectra studied by Williams (1963)

frequency radio spectrum indicates a surface brightness, at frequency ν, greater than that of a black body at the kinetic temperature corresponding to the energies of the "relevant" electrons, then the source must be optically thick, and self-absorption is important. Thus the cut-off frequency ν_s for self-absorption is determined by the condition

$$\text{Extrapolated brightness temperature} = T_b = \frac{m_0 c^2}{3k} \sqrt{\frac{\nu_s}{\nu_0}}.$$

If the source in question has flux density S_0 at frequency ν_0 and a spectral index a, then

$$S_0 \left(\frac{\nu_0}{\nu_s}\right)^a = S_{\nu_s} = \frac{2k}{\lambda_s^2} \int T_b d\Omega = \frac{2k}{c^2} \nu_s^2 \Theta^2 T_b,$$

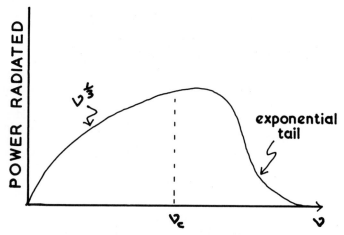

Fig. 5.—Spectrum of synchrotron radiation from one electron

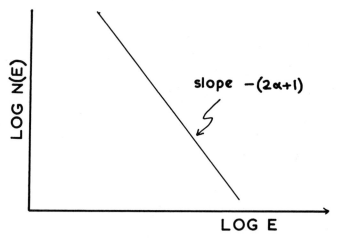

Fig. 6.—Energy distribution of electrons in a radio source

where Θ is the angular diameter of the source. Substituting in the condition for T_b gives

$$\nu_s{}^{2.5+a} \approx \frac{3}{2} \sqrt{\frac{eH}{m_0{}^3 c}} \frac{S_0 \nu_0{}^a}{\Theta^2}.$$

Note that ν_s depends mainly on the surface brightness S_0/Θ^2, and rather weakly ($\propto H^{0.15}$) on the magnetic field assumed to exist in the source. Williams (1963) finds that synchrotron self-absorption can account for the spectra he observed if the source diameters are a few tenths of a second of arc; the sources CTA 21 and CTA 102, with much higher cut-off frequencies, would need to have diameters of $\sim 0.01''$.

(iv) The Razin effect.

A fast electron gyrating in a magnetic field radiates a series of sharp spikes (synchrotron radiation) because, in that part of its orbit in which it approaches the observer, it is very nearly catching up with its own radiation. The ratio[1]

$$\frac{\nu_c}{\nu_{\text{orbit}}} = \frac{\text{Interval between spikes}}{\text{Width of a spike}} = \gamma^3 = \left(1 - \frac{v^2}{c^2}\right)^{-3/2},$$

so that the synchrotron radiation depends very critically on just how relativistic the electron is—just how close v, the electron's velocity, is to c, the speed of propagation of electromagnetic waves. If v is reduced very slightly, say from .9999c to .999c, ν_c falls by a large factor. So far as I know, Razin (1957) was the first to consider seriously the effect of increasing the "speed of light" by introducing a medium containing free electrons, so that the refractive index is less than 1. I have not yet been able to consult Razin's work, or two earlier papers by Tsytovich and by Ginzburg. Eidman (1958) has given a very general treatment, including gyrotropic media and the continuous transition to Čerenkov radiation ($\mu > 1$). Eidman's results are necessarily complicated, but once again a very rough and naïve calculation is sufficient for the immediate purposes of radio astronomy.

The refractive index μ of a plasma is given by $\mu^2 = 1 - (\nu_p{}^2/\nu^2)$ where ν_p is the plasma frequency; it is fairly safe to assume that we shall only be concerned with $\nu \gg \nu_p, \nu_g$, and the simple formula above is then a very good approximation to the full expression of magnetoionic theory. Thus we have to replace

$$\nu_c = \frac{eH}{mc} \gamma^3 = \frac{eH}{mc} \left(1 - \frac{v^2}{c^2}\right)^{-3/2},$$

which is valid in a vacuum, by

$$\nu_c = \frac{eH}{mc} \left(1 - \frac{v^2}{(c/\mu)^2}\right)^{-3/2} = \frac{eH}{\gamma m_0 c} \left[1 - \frac{v^2}{c^2}\left(1 - \frac{\nu_p{}^2}{\nu^2}\right)\right]^{-3/2}$$

$$= \frac{\nu_g}{\gamma} \left(\frac{1}{\gamma^2} + \frac{\nu_p{}^2}{\nu^2}\right)^{-3/2} \left(\text{neglecting } \frac{1}{\gamma^2} \frac{\nu_p{}^2}{\nu^2}\right).$$

Appreciable radiation occurs only when $\nu < \nu_c$. But ν_c is now itself dependent on ν, and the result is that the range for which $\nu < \nu_c$ now has a lower limit as well as an upper limit. The spectrum radiated by an electron resembles Figure 7b rather than

---

[1] The ν_{orbit} is not the same as ν_g, for ν_g, the ordinary gyrofrequency, refers to non-relativistic electrons: their relation is $\nu_g = \gamma \nu_{\text{orbit}}$.

Figure 5. For sufficiently low energies, the two limits meet, and synchrotron radiation from such electrons is extinguished altogether.

From the formula for ν_c, it is clear that radiation at frequency ν will be reduced appreciably below the vacuum value if ν_p/ν is comparable with $1/\gamma$ for the "relevant" electrons, i.e., those with $\gamma = \sqrt{(\nu/\nu_g)}$. Thus there is a low frequency cut-off where

$$\sqrt{\frac{\nu_g}{\nu}} \approx \frac{\nu_p}{\nu}, \qquad \text{i.e.,} \qquad \nu \approx \frac{\nu_p^2}{\nu_g}.$$

In fact, a little algebra shows that $(\nu/\nu_c) > 1$ for *all* values of γ (i.e., regardless of electron energy) if

$$\nu < \frac{3\sqrt{3}}{2}\frac{\nu_p^2}{\nu_g}.$$

Thus quite a sharp cut-off must appear in the spectrum in the neighborhood of

$$\nu_R = 3\frac{\nu_p^2}{\nu_g} \approx 15\frac{N}{H}\,\mathrm{Mc/s},$$

where N is once more the electron density in cm^{-3}, and H is the magnetic field in units of 10^{-6} gauss.

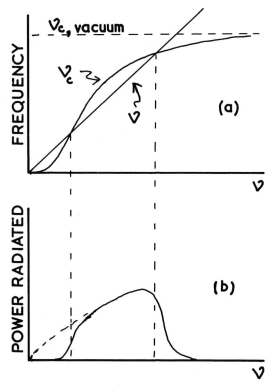

FIG. 7.—Spectrum of Razin radiation from one electron

I particularly wanted to mention Razin's work because it does not appear to have been noticed outside the Russian literature.

Concluding I would like to say that as far as possibility (i) is concerned, I think it is not likely to be important. The synchrotron radiation from one electron (in vacuo) never increases with frequency more rapidly than $\nu^{1/3}$, and a fortiori the same must be true of any distribution of electron energies. The flux density of 3C 147 increases much more rapidly than $\nu^{1/3}$ between 38 Mc/s and 178 Mc/s, so that for this source, at least, some other explanation must be found; the present data suggest to me that the same will be found in most other cases when we have more detailed spectra extending to lower frequencies.

However, possibilities (ii), (iii), and (iv) may all play a part, and each of these effects can be expected to occur only in compact sources: (ii) and (iv) require high electron densities and (iii) requires very high surface brightness. In the case of 3C 295, Williams (1963) considers that synchrotron self-absorption is the most plausible mechanism, for the radio-emitting regions are outside the associated galaxy, and therefore, presumably, in regions of low electron density. On the other hand, synchrotron self-absorption cannot account for the very sharp cut-off in the spectrum of the astonishing source discovered by Bolton *et al.* (1963); the flux of this source varies as rapidly as ν^3 at frequencies below the maximum, and synchrotron self-absorption would not give a variation more rapid than $\nu^{2.5}$.

One conclusion does not admit of much doubt; the radio-emitting regions must be very much larger and have far lower electron densities than the regions which Greenstein and his colleagues have found to be responsible for the emission of light from 3C 48 and 3C 273. The lunar occultation gave an estimate of 1 kpc for the diameter of 3C 273B; it is still possible that some finer structure exists within this source, but it is unlikely to be on a scale much smaller than 100 pc.

The computations were performed on EDSAC II at the Mathematical Laboratory of the University of Cambridge.

REFERENCES

Bolton, J. G., Gardner, F. F., and Mackey, M. B. 1963, *Nature*, **199**, 682.
Eidman, V. Ia. 1958, *J.E.T.P.*, **34**, 131 (also in *Soviet Phys. J.E.T.P.*, **34**, 91).
Hazard, C., Mackey, M. B., and Shimmins, A. J. 1963, *Nature*, **197**, 1037. *
Kellerman, K. I., Long, R. J., Allen, L. R., and Moran, M. 1962, *Nature*, **195**, 692.
Le Roux, E., 1961, *Ann. d'ap.*, **24**, 1.
Razin, 1957, dissertation, Gorki.
Scheuer, P. A. G. 1963, *Australian J. Phys.*, **15**, 333.
Williams, P. J. S. 1963, *Nature*, **200**, 56.

RADIO SPECTRA OF A VARIETY OF NON-THERMAL RADIO

chapter 29 SOURCES

W. A. Dent and F. T. Haddock

The flux densities of thirty-three non-thermal radio sources, including five quasi-stellar sources, have been measured at 8000 Mc/s (3.75 cm) with the 85-foot reflector at the University of Michigan. There are no previously reported flux-density values for most of these sources above 3200 Mc/s. The observed antenna temperatures have been corrected for the partial resolution of some of the sources by the 6′ antenna beam, for the measured linear polarization of the source, for the variation of aperture efficiency of the antenna when pointing at different parts of the sky, and for atmospheric extinction. The flux-density calibration has been made relative to the survey of the spectra of radio sources made by Conway, Kellerman, and Long (1963) for the frequency range 38–3200 Mc/s, by assuming that the spectra of the strongest sources Cassiopeia A, Taurus A, and Virgo A follow the law $S = S_0 \nu^a$ up to 8000 Mc/s, where a is a constant. It is estimated that the uncertainty in the absolute calibration may introduce a systematic error of 10 per cent into the measurements.

The results of the flux-density measurements are summarized in Figures 1 and 2. The plots corresponding to an individual spectrum have arbitrarily displaced ordinates to permit a compact presentation. The extension of the spectrum of each source by these measurements is indicated by the solid line. Nearly all of the observations shown for frequencies less than 8000 Mc/s were made by Conway *et al.* (1963).

All but four, or possibly five, of the sources are extragalactic. The four galactic supernova remnants—Cas A, Tau A, Tycho's Supernova, and Kepler's Supernova—have "straight" spectra and are shown in Figure 1, *a*. Sources whose spectra seem to indicate a "slight curvature" are displayed in Figure 1, *b*. The number which identifies the source in most cases is its number in the Cambridge University "3C" catalogue. The spectra of 3C 196 and 3C 433, both quasi-stellar sources, appear to show a curvature in the spectrum at high frequencies; while the source Cygnus A which has been suspected previously of having a curved spectrum appears to curve gradually over a wide range in frequency. The sources 3C 33, 3C 219, and 3C 353, in addition to having a spectrum similar to Cygnus A, consist of two emitting regions as does Cygnus A.

In Figure 2, *a*, are shown sources whose spectral index is definitely a function of fre-

W. A. Dent and F. T. Haddock, Radio Astronomy Observatory, University of Michigan.

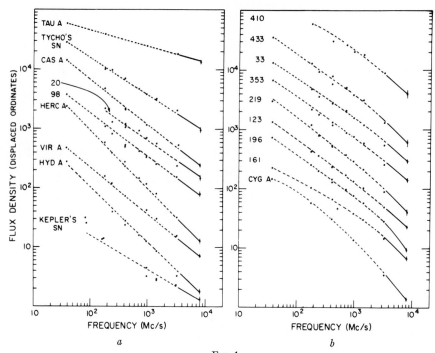

Fig. 1

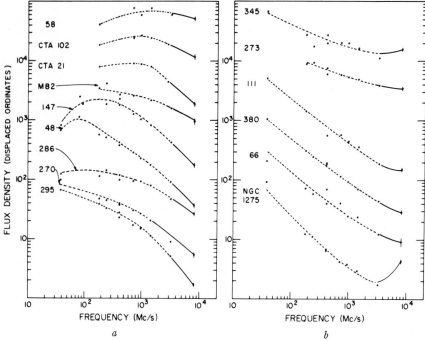

Fig. 2

quency. Three of the sources, 3C 48, 3C 147, and 3C 286, have been identified with quasi-stellar objects. The California Institute of Technology sources CTA 21 and CTA 102 have not been identified optically. These five sources have small radio diameters and very high brightness temperatures suggesting that pronounced curvature in the spectrum, especially at low frequencies, may be explained by the self-absorption of synchrotron radiation (Slish 1963; Williams 1963). The extragalactic sources 3C 270 and 3C 295 are both double radio sources with similar spectra. The linear size of the components of 3C 270 and the separation between the two components is similar to the size and separation of the components of 3C 295. However the brightness temperature of 3C 295 is 10^4 times that 3C 270. The curvature of these spectra and those in Figure 1, *b*, is due to a deviation from a simple power law for the electron energy spectrum. This deviation is very likely a result of the greater radiation losses of the more energetic electrons which are responsible for the high-frequency radiation.

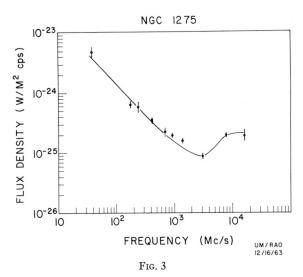

NGC 1275

FIG. 3

The spectra of those sources for which the flux density at 8000 Mc/s was greater than that predicted by a straight-line extrapolation are shown in Figure 2, *b*. Note that the quasi-stellar source 3C 273 is of this type. However, because of the large scatter in observational data for some of these sources, the indicated curvature in the spectra is not necessarily significant. No optical identifications have been made for the sources 3C 20, 3C 123, 3C 161, 3C 345, 3C 380, and 3C 410. Their small radio diameters suggest that some of them may be quasi-stellar.

One source with an obviously complex spectrum is the radio source NGC 1275 (Perseus A). To confirm the upward turn in the spectrum of NGC 1275 observations were made at 16300 Mc/s (1.84 cm). Figure 3 shows the results of this measurement plotted with the observations for the source shown in Figure 2, *b*. The spectrum of NGC 1275 appears to be nearly flat from 8000 to 16300 Mc/s, although the errors of the measured 16300 Mc/s flux density are large. The point depicted at this frequency is the average of two sets of observations each having an r.m.s. error of about 17 per cent. A further error in the absolute calibration of the antenna may be about 20 per cent at this frequency. The observations suggest that the source might be of a thermal origin having a unity optical depth near 8000 Mc/s. If this is the case, estimates of the electron temperature and density and the total mass of ionized gas, assuming complete ionization, can be made based on the apparent size and estimate of the distance to the source. The measured optical distance is 54 Mpc (1.6×10^{26} cm). No information is available concerning the apparent diameter of the source at 8000 Mc/s. An upper limit of 1' can be obtained from the present measurements. At 960 Mc/s the source is a 0.5' core imbedded in a weak 4.5' diameter halo (Moffet and Maltby 1962), whereas at 1420 Mc/s the halo is not observed and the core is about 10'' in diameter (Lequeux 1962). Assuming that the diameter is 10'' at 8000 Mc/s the electron kinetic temperature is found to be about 5000° K, the average electron density 170 cm^{-3}, and the total mass of the ionized hydrogen gas 4×10^9 $M\odot$ contained in a sphere 2600 pc in diameter. Thus the emitting region is much smaller than the galaxy (about 30000 pc in diameter). The emitting region may correspond to the very bright galactic nucleus which is a characteristic feature of a Seyfert galaxy such as NGC 1275.

Another source of interest is 3C 273. Its measured flux density at 8000 Mc/s is 27.7 ×

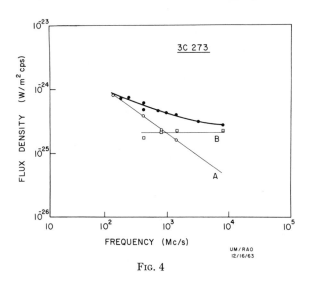

FIG. 4

10^{-26} W/m^2 c/s with a relative probable error of 6 per cent. This flux density is 26 per cent higher than that obtained from a straight-line extrapolation of observations made at lower frequencies. A weighted least-squares fit of first, second, and third order were applied to the observed spectrum of the source. Gauss's criterion indicated that the second-order curve gave the best fit, from which spectral indices of −0.36 at 300 Mc/s and −0.22 at 3000 Mc/s were computed. The spectral index is therefore a function of frequency. A source consisting of two emitting components of different spectral indices would produce a composite spectrum of this type.

An occultation of 3C 273 at 800 Mc/s was observed at the University of Michigan on December 9, 1963, by J. L. Talen (1963). The observation confirms the results of Hazard that the source is double. The components are found by Talen to have approximately equal flux densities at 800 Mc/s. If this ratio of the contributions from each component is combined with the ratios of Hazard, Mackey, and Shimmins (1963), at 410 Mc/s and 1420 Mc/s and with the observed composite spectrum of the source, the spectra of each component can be deduced. This is shown in Figure 4.

The spectrum of component A, associated with the optically observed jet, has a spectral index of −0.7. If its spectrum is extrapolated to give a flux density at 8000 Mc/s, the flux density of component B, associated with the quasi-stellar object, can be deduced at this frequency. The spectrum of component B must be flat out to 8000 Mc/s to account for the flattening of the observed composite spectrum. Since the spectra are shown on a logarithmic plot, any reasonable deviation of the extrapolated spectrum of component A from that of a straight line produces a small effect upon the flux density value of 22×10^{-26} W/m² c/s deduced for component B at 8000 Mc/s. The flat spectrum of component B is characteristic of a thermal source. However, the observed brightness temperature of 10^{9} ° K and the excessively large mass (about 10^{12} $M\odot$) required to explain this object would appear to exclude a thermal origin.

REFERENCES

Conway, R. G., Kellerman, K. I., and Long, R. T. 1963, *M.N.*, **125**, 313.
Hazard, C., Mackey, M. B., Shimmins, A. J. 1963, *Nature*, **197**, 1037.
Lequeux, J. 1962, *Ann. d'ap.*, **25**, 221.
Moffet, A. T., and Maltby, P. 1962, *Ap. J. Suppl.*, **7**, 141.
Slish, V. I. 1963, *Nature*, **199**, 682.
Talen, J. L. 1963, private communication.
Williams, P. T. S. 1963, *Nature*, **200**, 56.

ABOUT GRADIENTS
chapter 30   # OF GALAXIES

E. Vandekerkhove

The energy-curve of the nucleus of a galaxy may be characterized, in a particular region such as that of 5000 Å, by the gradient of its continuous spectrum. It is in this region that the Greenwich observers have well determined the value of this gradient (ϕ_{5000}) for some bright stars, which may then be chosen as comparison stars. This region is also particularly important because it is in its vicinity that photographic magnitudes and redshifts of the galaxies have been measured. The interpretation of those parameters as indicators of distance and of radial velocity have been used for the discussion of the redshift.

At the beginning of December, 1963, with the combined Schmidt telescope of the Uccle Observatory, I have obtained objective-prism spectra of o Ursae Majoris, Messier

TABLE 1

Galaxy	Type	Radial Velocity (km/sec)*	ϕ_{5000}
M81.............	Sc	71–77	3.28
M82.............	Irr.	400–410	2.00

Astronomical Journal, **61** (1956), 105–121, 122.

81, and Messier 82, where something like an explosion of the nucleus had been observed last year. For calibration purposes those spectra have been obtained on the same photographic plates (Eastman 103a-F), with the same exposure time, the same zenith distance, and the same developing conditions. The spectra have been transformed with a Zeiss microphotometer into registered curves (wavelength, transparency) which gave the results shown in Table 1.

The spectrum of M82 shows well a peak of emission in the region of Hα, but the continuum, in the region of 5000 Å, has an anomalous gradient; usually for the nucleus of a galaxy ϕ_{5000} increases with the radial velocity, and M82, whose radial velocity is larger than that of M81, has a lower value of ϕ_{5000}.

The continuous spectrum of M82 and its bluing are well represented in the region of 5000 Å by the low ϕ_{5000} value.

E. Vandekerkhove, Uccle Observatory, Belgium.

DIPOLE MAGNETIC FIELDS OF

chapter 31 ## GALACTIC DIMENSIONS

Howard D. Greyber

Since the spring of 1963, when the double-humped character of the geometry of many of the large extra-galactic radio sources became evident, I have been increasingly convinced that a dipole magnetic field centered at the optical object with its axis parallel to the line of centers of the inner pair of sources is important in explaining the asymmetric character of the radio radiation.

In 1960 such a large-scale organized dipole magnetic field of galactic dimensions was proposed by Greyber (1962) in order to explain the spiral pattern in normal spiral galaxies. Great skepticism met this idea because of the then widespread *conviction* that galactic-halo magnetic fields were small scale and randomly turbulent. However the beautiful photographs taken in the last two years by Halton Arp and Margaret Burbidge of peculiar and "interacting" galaxies (the Vorontsov-Velyaminov types) tend more and more to emphasize the large-scale order in objects of galactic dimensions.

In addition the remarkable work of A. Elvius (1962) has demonstrated the existence of a dipole magnetic field of galactic dimensions in M82, oriented exactly as predicted, with the dipole axis along the minor axis (and rotation axis) of the galaxy and, as close as can be measured, centered on the galactic nucleus. The recent (within the last 2 or 3 million years) central contraction and explosion in M82 has provided the energetic electrons, gas, dust, and magnetic field to permit observation of the dipole magnetic field. In our theory all spirals, normal and barred, possess such a magnetic field, although a much weaker field than in M82 is probably the usual case. A specific prediction of the model is that sufficiently close to the galactic nucleus the magnetic field should be in one direction along the spiral arm *above* the plane of the spiral galaxy and in the opposite direction *below* the plane.[1]

The "core-halo" radio sources would be interpreted in our model for radio galaxies as the case when we happen to observe the dipole magnetic field end-on. A double radio source represents in our theory the result of a giant gravitational contraction and consequent explosion with the generation of an enormous dipole magnetic field many times the size of the optical galaxy or "quasar" from the gravitational energy released. The two clouds of hot gas and relativistic electrons are expelled mainly along the minor axis (i.e., dipole magnetic-field axis). However if the event is an old one, the "clouds" may

---

Howard D. Greyber, Northeastern University.

[1] Very recently this has been verified for our local spiral arm by Morris and Berge (1964).

have been curved in their path by the magnetic field and lie now at an angle to the dipole axis (or minor axis, or rotation axis).

It is important to note that the line of centers of the inner radio sources in Centaurus A lies along the rotation axis of the optical object while the outer two concentrations lie at some 17° from this axis, in accord with the model. It is also significant to point out that, up to now, only in three optical objects, which are also strong radio sources, has the rotation axis been carefully measured: Centaurus A, M82, and 3C 33; and in all cases the rotation axis is also the line of centers of the radio sources! In M82, the rotation axis is shown to be also the axis of the galactic dipole magnetic field.

A reasonable mechanism for generating such a dipole magnetic field in astrophysical objects has been devised by Greyber (1964) and is being analyzed. The identical mechanism was proposed much earlier by Donald H. Menzel for the generation of a loop current during the formation of stars.

It should be noted that, on the basis of our theory, the common identification of some galaxies that are strong radio sources as giant ellipticals seems doubtful. The creation of spiral structure in galaxies and the evolutionary dynamics of strong radio galaxies and "quasars" are, in our model, very similar phenomena on different scales.

REFERENCES

Elvius, A. 1962, *Bull. Lowell Observatory*, No. 119.
Greyber, H. D. 1962, "On the Steady-State Dynamics of Spiral Galaxies," A.F.O.S.R. Rept. 2958.
———. 1964, 116th meeting, A.A.S., Flagstaff, Arizona, June, 1964, Abstr. 51a.
Morris, D., and Berge, G. L. 1964, *Ap. J.*, **139,** 1388.

PART VI

SUPERDENSE STARS

SUPERDENSE EQUILIBRIUM STARS

chapter 32

E. E. SALPETER

I. INTRODUCTION

I will restrict myself entirely to discussing spherically symmetric stars in hydrostatic equilibrium and mainly to stars with very high density and relatively low temperature, the so-called neutron stars. We now know that the "quasi-stellar objects," which seem to be the main topic of this volume, are *not* neutron stars. Nevertheless, neutron stars are theoretically likely to exist as remnants of some types of supernova explosions, but they will be hard to observe unless they are very close or very recent.

The theoretical study of *equilibrium* models for zero-temperature stars is also of some academic interest when considering gravitational collapse. For instance, one might find an upper limit M_{max} for the mass of an equilibrium zero-temperature star of any density. In that case, for a star which manages to lose all its angular momentum while still retaining a mass in excess of M_{max}, one will have to consider gravitational collapse into relativistic regimes. Or, if one finds an upper limit to the redshift from an equilibrium star and then observes a larger gravitational redshift from some object, one knows that the object must be under gravitational collapse. Studying the effects of general relativity on equilibrium models will give some insight into relativistic effects under the more complicated non-static situations, and so on.

The following is merely a short review with special emphasis on the points just mentioned. I review the equation of hydrostatic equilibrium first, discuss possible and impossible equations of state next, and then return to the results from actual stellar-model calculations. Finally, I will briefly mention some unpublished work of H. Bondi's.

II. THE EQUATIONS OF HYDROSTATIC EQUILIBRIUM

We first introduce units which are convenient for considering neutron stars. For the equation of state the natural units for mass are the neutron mass H and for length the Compton wavelength $(\hbar/Hc)$ of the neutron. The unit of particle number density is then of the same order of magnitude as n_0, the density at which the Fermi momentum of a

E. E. SALPETER, Laboratory of Nuclear Studies and Center for Radiophysics and Space Research, Cornell University.

This work was supported in part by the Office of Naval Research.

free neutron gas equals Hc. At other densities n the Fermi momentum p_F is given by

$$\frac{p_F}{Hc} = \left(\frac{n}{n_0}\right)^{1/3}, \qquad n_0 = 3.4 \times 10^{39} H/\text{cm}^3 = 5.7 \times 10^{15} \text{ gm/cm}^3. \tag{1}$$

With Hc^2 as the unit of energy, the unit of pressure P is then also defined.

To eliminate the gravitational constant from the stellar-structure equations we shall express masses and radii of neutron stars in terms of

$$R_0 = 2\sqrt{2\pi}(\hbar c/GH^2)^{1/2}(\hbar/Hc) = 13.6 \text{ km}$$

and

$$M_0 = 2\sqrt{2\pi}(\hbar c/GH^2)^{3/2}H = 9.2 \, M_\odot, \qquad M_0 \propto H^{-2}. \tag{2}$$

The dimensionless quantity $(GH^2/\hbar c)$ which occurs in these definitions is the gravitational equivalent (for neutrons) of the Sommerfeld fine-structure constant $e^2/\hbar c$, but has the much smaller numerical value 5.7×10^{-39}.

We now assume a star in complete hydrostatic equilibrium, the absence of any angular momentum, and assume the pressure P is purely isotropic everywhere. With these simplifying assumptions the theory of general relativity then leads to a single differential equation for pressure as a function of radial distance r. Using a particularly convenient one of the various choices of coordinate systems in general relativity (see Appendix), this equation can be written (Landau 1932; Oppenheimer and Volkoff 1939) in the form

$$\frac{dP}{dr} = -\frac{\rho}{r^2}\, m\, \left[\left(\frac{1+\xi}{1-2\phi}\right)\left(1+\frac{P}{\rho}\right)\right]$$

and

$$m(r) = \int_0^r 4\pi y^2 \rho(y)\, dy \equiv (4\pi r^3/3)\langle\rho(r)\rangle. \tag{3}$$

In this equation ξ and ϕ are two dimensionless functions defined by

$$\xi(r) = 4\pi r^3 P(r)/m(r) = 3P(r)/\langle\rho(r)\rangle$$

and

$$\phi(r) = m(r)/r, \tag{4}$$

and r, m have been expressed in units of R_0 and M_0 in equation (2); $\rho(r)$ is the total energy-density, which in our units equals the particle-number density (or rest-mass density) n *plus* contributions from kinetic energy and the potential energy from nuclear and all other forces *except* gravitational. The symbols ρ and P are expressed in terms of "proper coordinates" everywhere (in terms of which the velocity of light and neutron Compton wavelength are always unity) and therefore do not depend on the particular choice of coordinate system used in equation (3).

To solve equation (3) one still needs an "equation of state," which gives P as a function of ρ (or both P and ρ as functions of n). If the equation of state is known (see Sec. III) one simply assumes a central value ρ_c of density (and hence P_c) and integrates equation (3) outward until P falls to zero at some radial distance $r = R$, the "radius of the star." In this way one obtains the "gravitational mass" M_{gr},

$$M_{gr} \equiv m(R), \tag{5}$$

as a unique function of central density ρ_c. This quantity is the "observable" mass in the sense that, a large distance s *outside* of the star, the gravitational potential due to the star is M_{gr}/s. As will be discussed in Section V, the quantity $\phi(R) \equiv M_{gr}/R$ is related to the redshift with which light from the surface of the star is received far away.

If the relation between "total-energy density" ρ and the "particle number density" (or "rest-mass–energy–density") n of the baryons is known, one can also calculate another mass, the "proper rest mass" M_{pr}, by means of

$$M_{\mathrm{pr}} = \int_0^R 4\pi r^2 n(r)[1 - 2\phi(r)]^{-1/2} dr . \qquad (6)$$

M_{pr} (in our units) is simply the total number of baryons (neutrons, protons, and hyperons) present in the star. If the star had originally condensed from relatively cold and dilute matter, and the number of baryons has been conserved during its evolution, then M_{pr} also equals the total rest-mass energy of the original matter and $(M_{pr} - M_{gr})$ is the total amount of energy lost by the star to the outside world during its evolution.

Equation (3) is based on the full glory of the theory of general relativity. If classical gravitational theory had been used, the expression in braces in equation (3) would simply be replaced by unity. We shall see in Section V that $(1 - 2\phi)$ is at least of the order of magnitude of unity under all circumstances and in Section III that, at least for physically realistic equations of state, P/ρ and ξ are of order unity or less. The expression in braces is then at least roughly of order unity even in highly relativistic models, and the neglect of general relativity would not alter the qualitative nature of the results.

It is useful to estimate the rough order of magnitude of M_{gr} as a function of central density ρ_c and pressure P_c. Replacing the expression in braces by unity and applying dimensional analysis to equation (3) we conjecture that $\langle P \rangle$ is of the same order of magnitude as $\langle \rho \rangle M_{gr}/R$ where the angular brackets denote some kind of average over the star. Putting $R \sim [(M_{gr}/\langle n \rangle)]^{1/3}$ we find the order of magnitude relation

$$M_{\mathrm{gr}} \sim (\langle P \rangle / \langle \rho \rangle \langle n \rangle^{1/3})^{3/2} . \qquad (7)$$

In the next section we will therefore discuss $P/\rho n^{1/3}$ as a function of ρ (or n) for various equations of state. We are tempted to replace $\langle P \rangle$ by P_c and $\langle \rho \rangle$ by ρ_c in equation (7) to give an estimate for M_{gr} in terms of central conditions. We shall see in Section IV that this replacement leads to serious errors only under some special circumstances.

III. EQUATIONS OF STATE

Let us consider first a Fermi-Dirac gas of free, non-interacting neutrons at absolute zero temperature. The pressure P and energy-density ρ are then known exactly as a function of number-density n. We have simple order of magnitude relations for two extreme cases: (i) if $n \ll 1$ the neutrons are non-relativistic and the Fermi-energy E_F is proportional to p_F^2 (p_F is Fermi momentum), (ii) if $n \gg 1$ the neutrons are highly relativistic and $E_F \propto p_F$,

and
$$
\begin{aligned}
P/n &\sim E_F/Hc^2 \sim n^{2/3} , \quad & P/\rho n^{1/3} &\sim n^{1/3} \quad & \text{(if } n \ll 1\text{)} \\
P/n &\sim E_F/Hc^2 \sim n^{1/3} , \quad & P \approx \tfrac{1}{3}\rho , \quad P/\rho n^{1/3} &\sim n^{-1/3} . \quad & \text{(if } n \gg 1\text{)}
\end{aligned}
\qquad (8)
$$

Thus $P/\rho n^{1/3}$, the quantity which occurs in equation (7), has a maximum value at a finite density $n \sim \rho \sim 1$ where the neutrons are on the borderline of being relativistic. The quantity $P/n^{4/3}$ is very close to $P/\rho n^{1/3}$ for $n \ll 1$ but approaches a constant limiting value (instead of decreasing) as $n \to \infty$.

Consider next a fully ionized hydrogen gas at zero temperature but of high enough density so that the electrons can be considered as a non-interacting Fermi-Dirac gas. Because of the large proton-electron mass radio $H/m \approx 1836$, the electrons become relativistically degenerate at a density $n_1 \sim n_0(m/H)^3 \sim 10^6$ gm/cm³, much smaller than the equivalent density n_0 for protons or neutrons. For $n \ll n_0$ the pressure is mainly due to the electrons, but the energy-density ρ is mainly due to the protons and is close to n. The quantity $P/\rho n^{1/3}$ for ionized hydrogen as a function of n is shown in Figure 1 by the curve labeled "H." Note that it leads to a constant for $n \gg n_1$, as does the quantity $P/n^{4/3}$ (shown dotted in Fig. 1) for $n \gg n_0$.

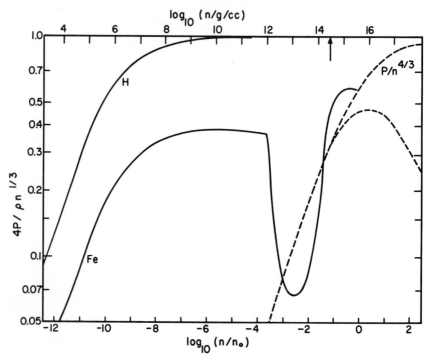

Fɪɢ. 1.—A combination of pressure and density plotted against density for various equations of state

The electron pressure for an ionized gas with given density n is proportional to $(n/\mu_e)^{4/3}$, where μ_e is the mean atomic weight per electron, $\mu_e = A/Z$. At low or moderate densities the most stable nuclei are those near Fe^{56} with $\mu_e = 2.15$ and the curve for $P/\rho n^{1/3}$ in Figure 1 labeled "Fe" represents electron pressure with constant μ_e for $n \lesssim 10^9$ gm/cm³. However, for $n \gtrsim 10^9$ gm/cm³ the Fermi energy of the electrons exceeds a few MeV, inverse beta-decays are now energetically favorable, and the equilibrium shifts to larger values of μ_e. Finally, when an electron Fermi energy of about 20 MeV is reached at $n \sim 10^{12}$ gm/cm³, neutrons become stable and the partial pressure due to the electrons remains constant as n is increased further.

For $n > 10^{13}$ gm/cm³ we are dealing mainly with a neutron gas, and $P/\rho n^{1/3}$ for a Fermi gas of non-interacting neutrons is shown by the broken curve in Figure 1. In reality we have to consider the effect on the neutrons of nuclear forces, which are attractive at separations $\geq 10^{-13}$ cm and repulsive at shorter range. Because of this change of sign of the nuclear potential, one finds that the actual pressure is less than that of non-interacting neutrons below about $n \sim 3 \times 10^{14}$ gm/cm³ (roughly the internal density of ordinary "nuclear matter") and is larger at greater densities. The solid curve in Figure 1 gives $P/\rho n^{1/3}$ for the most stable form of matter (at absolute zero temperature) at densities up to $n \sim 10^{15}$ gm/cm³.

The above discussion and Figure 1 give only a schematic view of the actual equation of state. Detailed discussions of more realistic equations of state have been given by a number of authors for purposes of application to neutron stars, and some results for stellar models are discussed in Section IV. An important range for these calculations are densities near and just below "nuclear" (say, $n \sim [1 \text{ to } 5] \times 10^{14}$ gm/cm³). In this range the equations of state (Wheeler *et al.* 1958; Cameron 1959; Salpeter 1960; Ambartsumyan and Saakyan 1962; Saakyan and Vartamian 1963) used so far in stellar models took account of nuclear forces essentially by semi-empirical extrapolation from "ordinary nuclear matter."

The last five years or so have seen some progress in explicit theoretical calculations for the nuclear many-body problem, starting with accurate experimental data on neutron-proton and proton-proton scattering. At high relative kinetic energies one is not justified in assuming a static two-nucleon potential, and the scattering data do not give the potential uniquely. These ambiguities are not very important for moderate densities; the properties of "ordinary nuclear matter" can be predicted quite well and explicit calculations for energy and pressure of a neutron gas up to similar densities, $n \sim 3 \times 10^{14}$ gm/cm³, should be quite reliable. It turns out that, at these and lower densities, the semi-empirical extrapolations overestimate the attractive and underestimate the repulsive part of the nuclear force, and the more accurate explicit calculations (Levinger and Simmons 1961) give higher pressures.

As the density n increases, the Fermi momentum p_F and energy E_F (and hence the relative kinetic energies of the neutrons) increase and the ambiguities due to the non-static nature of the nuclear potential become more serious very rapidly. At $n \sim 5 \times 10^{14}$ gm/cm³, where we have $p_F \sim 2 \times 10^{13}$ cm⁻¹ and $E_F \sim 55$ MeV, these ambiguities are beginning to be noticeable (Levinger and Simmons 1961) and should be quite serious by $n \sim 10^{15}$ gm/cm³. At still higher densities part of the neutron gas is converted into hyperons and some authors (Wheeler *et al.* 1958; Cameron 1959; Salpeter 1960; Ambartsumyan and Saakyan 1962; Saakyan and Vartamian 1963) have attempted to calculate the lowering of the pressure produced by this conversion, making simplifying assumptions about nucleon-hyperon forces. However, even the experimental data relevant to these forces are very meager and the theoretical ambiguities mentioned above are severe. At the moment any calculations of pressure for n appreciably greater than 1×10^{15} gm/cm³ must be considered as merely rough estimates.

Note that our ignorance of the equation of state sets in already at densities slightly less than $n_0 \sim 6 \times 10^{15}$ gm/cm³, where the neutrons become relativistic. In view of our ignorance it is useful to see what upper limits on pressure P or the ratio P/ρ are dictated, or at least suggested, by the theory of special relativity:

a) It had sometimes been conjectured that

$$P/\rho \lesseqgtr \tfrac{1}{3}, \tag{9}$$

where ρ is the energy density in the units discussed in Section II. This conjecture was based on two plausibility arguments. (i) For matter with isotropic pressure the quantity $(\rho - 3P)$ is an invariant combination under Lorentz transformations. For low-density matter this combination is positive, and the theory would be aesthetically more pleasing if it were also positive at high densities. (ii) For the special case of any mixture of electromagnetic radiation and Fermi-Dirac particles interacting only electromagnetically, ρ and P can be evaluated explicitly, and they satisfy the inequality in equation (9).

b) More recently there has been a trend toward a less stringent conjecture for two reasons: (i) Zel'dovich (1962) has constructed an explicit model for baryons interacting in a more complicated way than merely electromagnetically. For this model equation (9) is violated under some circumstances, although $P < \rho$ is always satisfied. This model was not meant to be realistic, but merely to provide a counterexample; nevertheless, it has enough resemblance to nuclear forces that one might expect equation (9) to be violated at high densities for real matter. (ii) Let Γ be the square of the sound velocity (in units of c) in a medium. With special relativity (as without) one has

$$(\partial P/\partial\rho)_{\text{adiab}} = \Gamma, \tag{10}$$

and Γ cannot exceed unity without violating special relativity. Strictly speaking the derivative in equation (10) refers only to dynamic processes, but it is at least a plausible conjecture to assume that equation (10) with $\Gamma < 1$ also holds for our static equation of state. Since $P \ll \rho$ at low densities, equation (10) with $\Gamma \leq 1$ then implies

$$P/\rho < 1. \tag{11}$$

Incidentally, a restriction on Γ in equation (10) also implies a restriction on how rapidly ρ and P can increase with n: For adiabates, ρ and n are related by means of

$$d\rho/dn = (\rho + P)/n. \tag{12}$$

If, in some density range from n_1, ρ_1, to n_2, ρ_2, the derivative Γ in equation (10) is constant, then one can integrate equation (12) to give

$$(\rho_2 + P_2)/(\rho_1 + P_1) = (n_2/n_1)^{1+\Gamma}. \tag{13}$$

Hence, if $\Gamma < 1$ then both ρ and P increase less rapidly than n^2; if $\Gamma \leq \frac{1}{3}$ then ρ and P increase at most as rapidly as $n^{4/3}$.

Figure 2 gives (somewhat schematically) the derivative $dP/d\rho$ for various equations of state: The curve labeled "free" is for a Fermi gas of non-interacting neutrons; the curve labeled "Cam" is for a simple analytic equation of state (Cameron 1959) based on semi-empirical extrapolation. This equation would violate the inequality in equation (10) for $\rho > 2 \times 10^{15}$ gm/cm³, but it is a non-relativistic formula and not applicable at these high densities. The broken curve is merely an estimate of an improved equation of state up to $\rho \sim 1 \times 10^{15}$ gm/cm³.

IV. STELLAR MODELS

With a given equation of state, the "observable" mass M_{gr} as a function of central density n_c is obtained by calculating a "stellar model" for each value of n_c, i.e., by integrating equation (3) numerically from the center out. If general relativistic effects are neglected, we have seen that the order of magnitude of M_{gr} should be given by equation (7), and for that reason we had plotted the combination $P/\rho n^{1/3}$ for various equations of state in Figure 1.

In Figure 3 we give the results of actual stellar model calculations for $M_{\text{gr}}(\rho_c)$ for various equations of state: The curve labeled "Opp." is for a non-interacting neutron gas (Oppenheimer and Volkoff 1939); the curve labeled "Cam." is for a semi-empirical equation of state (Cameron 1959) for neutrons alone with contributions from electron pressure neglected. The dashed curve is merely an estimate (partly based on some explicit

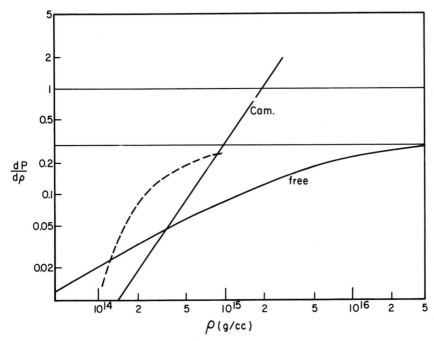

FIG. 2.—The derivative of pressure plotted against density

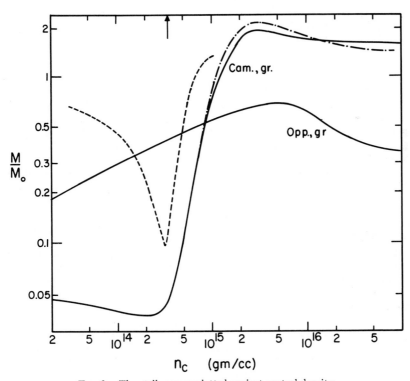

FIG. 3.—The stellar mass plotted against central density

calculations [Hamada and Salpeter 1961] at the lower dentities) of what the results will be like for a more complete equation of state.

Note the qualitative resemblance between the curves in Figures 1 and 3. For instance, both curves for a free neutron gas show a maximum at a finite value of the density, close to n_0. This feature of a maximum mass at finite density is related to the upper limit the ratio P/ρ is allowed to reach, but does *not* depend on any features of the theory of *general relativity* (which were all omitted in the derivation of eq. [7]). Some explicit model calculations (Saakyan 1963), which include special but omit general relativity, confirm that the *qualitative* features of the results can be understood without the general theory.

Equation (7) (and the curves in Fig. 1) would give values of mass M which decrease toward zero as the *average* density $\langle n \rangle$ increases from about n_0 to infinity. The explicit model calculations for M_{gr} as a function of *central* density n_c give a maximum value $M_{gr, max}$ for a finite value $n_{c, max}$, but M_{gr} decreases only slightly to a finite limiting value $M_{gr, lim}$ as $n_c \to \infty$. Consider a model with a very large value of $n_c \gg n_{c, max}$: The combination $P/\rho n^{1/3}$ is then indeed very small near the center, and the density decreases rapidly a short distance outside the center where the mass function $m(r)$ is still quite small. However, as the density $n(r)$ decreases with increasing r the combination $P/\rho n^{1/3}$ increases and reaches a maximum when $n(r) \sim n_{c, max}$. In this region the fall-off of density is much slower and most of the contribution to total mass M_{gr} and radius R comes from this region. Hence, as $n_c \to \infty$, the *average* density $\langle n \rangle$ as well as M_{gr} and R tend to a finite limit.

A similar effect takes place (Hamada and Salpeter 1961) when one follows the models from n_c about 10^{12} to about 3×10^{13} gm/cm³: In this density range the combination $P/\rho n^{1/3}$ in Figure 1 decreases appreciably with increasing density (in fact, P is mainly electron pressure and almost constant in this range). For $n_c \sim 10^{12}$ gm/cm³ the model calculations give $M_{gr} \sim 0.5 M\odot$, the same order of magnitude as does equation (7) with $\langle n \rangle$ replaced by n_c. However, for $n_c \sim 3 \times 10^{13}$ gm/cm³ (and any other value in between) the density and pressure decrease rapidly with increasing r near the center where $P/\rho n^{1/3}$ is small, but most of the contribution to mass and radius comes from the outer regions where $n(r) \sim 10^{12}$ gm/cm³ and $P/\rho n^{1/3}$ is larger. Over this rather large range of central densities n_c, the values for $\langle n \rangle$ and M change rather little.

In addition to the "observable" mass M_{gr}, the "proper rest-mass" M_{pr}, defined in equation (6), has also been evaluated for some models (Ambartsumyan and Saakyan 1963; C. Misner, unpublished). In Figure 3 the broken curve (dash-dot) near the curve for M_{gr} labeled "Cam., gr." is an estimate for M_{pr} for the same models (the numerical values for M_{pr} for these models given by Cameron [1959] are in error). Note that M_{pr} has a maximum value at the same central density $n_{c, max}$ as M_{gr}, so that the "binding energy" $(M_{pr} - M_{gr})$ is independent of n_c there and the star is in neutral equilibrium. For larger values of n_c the binding energy (as well as M_{gr} and M_{pr} separately) decreases with increasing n_c and in fact becomes negative for very large values of n_c. These qualitative features of the binding energy are present in all the models (similar features are even found for the physically quite different situation of very massive and hot stars [Iben 1963] which Fowler reported on).

The effects of general relativity are contained in the braces in equation (3). We shall see in Section V that the quantity $(1 - 2\phi)$ never decreases below a finite limit of order unity for any equilibrium model. As discussed in Section III, the inequalities $P/\rho < 1$ and $\xi < 3$ hold for any *realistic* equation of state and the expression in braces in equation (3) cannot exceed a finite value a few times larger than unity. However, if unrealistic equations of state (with arbitrary P/ρ) were allowed, the effects of general relativity could be dominant: Consider a series of models all with the same central density ρ_c but with different equations of state so that P/ρ (and ξ) is less than unity for some models but very large for others. The classical equation, equation (3) with the brace replaced by unity, is linear in pressure P and would lead to values of the mass M which increase indefinitely as $P/\rho \rightarrow \infty$. The fully relativistic equation (3), on the other hand, has the quadratic term ξP on the right-hand side. Consequently M_{gr} considered as a function of P/ρ (with ρ_c fixed) increases at first but comes to a maximum value for some finite value of $P/\rho \sim 1$ and then actually decreases with a further increase of P/ρ! Even with realistic equations of state, typical effects of general relativity can of course be seen in the *qualitative* results of model calculations.

One of the most important results of the model calculations is the numerical value of the maximum mass $M_{\mathrm{pr,\,max}}$ for any spherical zero-temperature equilibrium configuration. It is only for stars whose mass exceeds this value that we have to face the problem of eventual gravitational collapse. As Figure 3 shows the value of $M_{\mathrm{pr,\,max}}$ is about 0.6 $M_{\odot}$ for non-interacting neutrons and is most probably somewhere between 1.5 $M_{\odot}$ and 2.5 $M_{\odot}$ for more accurate equations of state.

It is very unlikely that $M_{\mathrm{pr,\,max}}$ exceeds 3 $M_{\odot}$, but this statement cannot be proved from relativity theory alone and is based in part on our knowledge of nuclear forces. Merely as an academic illustration, let us consider two equations of state which are quite incompatible with nuclear physics but would not violate relativity.

1. Imagine a strong repulsive force between neutrons whose range is larger than the neutron Compton wavelength by some factor $\eta \gg 1$. Relativity does not allow P/ρ to exceed unity, but with such a force P/ρ would be close to unity already at a relatively low density $n \sim n_0 \eta^{-3}$. Equation (7) then shows that the maximum value of the mass will occur when $n_c \sim n_0 \eta^{-3}$ and will be of the order of $M_0 \eta^{3/2}$, i.e., it would increase indefinitely with increasing η. In fact we know that the actual strong nuclear repulsive force has a range only slightly larger than the neutron Compton wavelength. Incidentally, this feature of the nuclear force is responsible for the fact that $M_{\mathrm{pr,\,max}}$ (and $M_{\mathrm{gr,\,max}}$) is larger by a factor of about 2 or 3 than it would be in the absence of nuclear forces and occurs at somewhat lower densities. We do not understand the forces or the equation of state in any detail for very much shorter ranges (higher densities) but, as outlined above, a very high pressure at high density would not increase M_{gr} and M_{pr} (and might in fact decrease it).

2. Consider an even more fictitious kind of *attractive* molecular force of enormous strength which can bind three neutrons into a stable "tri-neutron" with the energy release of most of the original rest-mass energy $3\,Hc^2$. This tri-neutron would then have a rest mass ζH, say, with $\zeta \ll 1$. Assume further that these tri-neutrons, which are Fermi-Dirac particles, do not interact with each other. The same stellar models would then apply as for non-interacting neutrons, except for scaling factors as shown in equation (2) with $M_0 \propto (\zeta H)^{-2}$. The maximum observable mass $M_{\mathrm{gr,\,max}}$ would then be about $0.6\,M_{\odot}\zeta^{-2} \gg M_{\odot}$ and $M_{\mathrm{pr,\,max}}$, which is essentially the number of neutrons, would even be of order $M_{\odot}\zeta^{-3}$.

There is good evidence from molecular and nuclear physics against the existence of such stable "tri-neutrons" or similar devices, but their existence would not violate relativity. Our present knowledge of nuclear physics cannot yet rule out strong attractive forces which come into play at very high densities. Stellar models have not yet been constructed for such equations of state, and it is conceivable that they might lead to larger values of M_{pr}. To summarize: Nothing can be proved rigorously, but I would bet reasonably long odds against $M_{\mathrm{pr,\,max}}$ exceeding 3 $M_{\odot}$.

V. BONDI'S LIMIT ON THE GRAVITATIONAL REDSHIFT

We have seen that no rigorous limits can be put on the gravitational mass M_{gr} of a zero-temperature equilibrium star (nor on its radius) unless some assumptions are made about the equation of state. On the other hand, Bondi (1964) has been able to derive a rigorous upper limit for the ratio $\phi(R) = M_{\mathrm{gr}}/R$ even if absolutely *no* restrictions are placed on the equation of state. This quantity is of particular physical interest because the redshift at a distant receiver for light emitted from the surface of the star is given by

$$\frac{\lambda + \Delta\lambda}{\lambda} = \frac{1}{\sqrt{1 - 2\phi(R)}}. \tag{14}$$

Bondi's work will be published shortly in the *Monthly Notices*, so I will only give a (distorted) "bird's-eye view" of it.

In equation (4) we had already defined two dimensionless functions of radial distance, $\xi(r)$ and $\phi(r)$. We had written the conditions for hydrostatic equilibrium in the form of equation (3), an equation for P with r as the independent variable. Bondi rewrites this

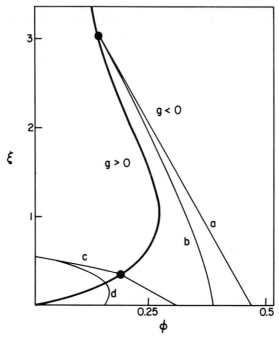

FIG. 4.—Tracks for stellar models in Bondi's $\xi = \phi$ plane

equation in a different form, essentially an equation for r and the quantity ϕ with the quantity ξ as the independent variable. This equation is of the form

$$\frac{dr}{r} = \frac{d\xi}{\phi} \frac{a(\varphi, \xi) + b(\varphi, \xi) d\varphi/d\xi}{g(\varphi, \xi)}, \tag{15}$$

where the functions a, b, and g are known polynomials.

In equation (3) one boundary condition was that $m = \phi = 0$ at $r = 0$ whereas P/ρ and ξ had finite values at the origin. The outer radius R (and hence $\phi[R]$) was determined as the value of r at which P (and hence ξ) is zero. In a plane representing ξ and ϕ (Fig. 4) the track of a stellar model from the center to the outer radius is then represented by a curve starting at $\phi = 0$ with a finite value of ξ and ending up at $\xi = 0$ with ϕ having a finite value $\phi(R)$, the quantity we are interested in. The thin curves c and d in Figure 4 might be two such tracks. For equation (15) one needs the equation of state (as one does for eq. [3]) and the initial value of ξ (instead of ρ_c) to determine a unique solution. Since it contains two derivatives instead of one, equation (15) is less suitable than equation (3) for numerical integrations but is more convenient for Bondi's analytic purposes.

The thick curve in the ξ-φ plane in Figure 4 represents the curve $g = 0$ which separates the two regions in which the denominator in equation (15) is positive and negative, respectively. The largest value of ϕ on this curve is 0.25 at $\xi = 1$. The ends of the tracks in Figure 4 correspond to $r = 0$ and $r = R$, respectively, and r must increase monotonically along this track (as ξ goes from its central value to zero)—if r were not monotonic there would be two different sets of (ξ, ϕ), i.e., two different sets of physical conditions, corresponding to the same value of $r!$ In the region with negative g the monotonic behavior of r then requires the numerator in equation (15) to be negative or zero. This gives a maximum value for the slope $d\phi/d\xi$ in terms of a and b, and this enables Bondi to derive an upper limit for $\phi(R)$ as follows:

Start with some point on the $g = 0$ curve in Figure 4 and follow the track to the point $\xi = 0$. The track for an actual model depends on the equation of state, but the *maximum* value of $d\phi/d\xi$ and hence of $\phi(R)$ is simply obtained by putting the numerator in equation (15) equal to zero ($dr/d\xi = 0$) everywhere. Curve a in Figure 4 represents such a case schematically, curve b one with a finite value of $dr/d\xi$. One can then start with a different point on the curve $g = 0$, repeat the porcedure and find which starting point gives the largest value for the maximum value which $\phi(R)$ can have. Bondi manages to do all this analytically, finds that $\xi = \infty$ is the optimum starting point and that

$$\phi(R) < 6\sqrt{(2)} - 8 = 0.485 . \tag{16}$$

Incidentally, this value is also an upper limit to $\phi(r)$ for any other value of r.

Equation (16) is a rigorous upper limit independent of any assumptions about the equation of state; in fact one would need highly unrealistic equations of state to come anywhere close to this limit (high value of P/ρ at low density, then an infinitely thin mass shell at a finite radius R, etc.). By placing various mild restrictions on the equation of state, Bondi has also obtained various (lower) values for the upper limit on $\phi(R)$. For instance, if he requires equations (9) and (10) with $\Gamma = 1$ to hold as well as adiabatic stability, he finds

$$\phi(R) < 0.31 , \qquad \Delta\lambda/\lambda < 0.615 . \tag{17}$$

A model track which corresponds to this upper limit is shown schematically by curve c in Figure 4.

To come close to the limit in equation (17) one needs a model for which P/ρ is close to $\frac{1}{3}$ at the center and $d\phi/dr$ is positive for all r, which requires $(3\rho\langle\rho\rangle)$ to be positive everywhere. This implies that the pressure must fall to zero at a finite density ρ which is not much smaller than the central value ρ_c. With realistic equations of state, an enormously larger decrease in ρ is required before the pressure vanishes. For such an equation of state the track will look something like curve d in Figure 4. For the correct equation of state, I would guess a value of $\phi(R) \approx 0.15$ for high-density models. If this guess is correct the maximum gravitational redshift from a stable object is then only $\Delta\lambda/\lambda \sim 0.3$. This is less than the redshift observed from at least one of the "quasistellar" objects, but Greenstein has in any case given us more convincing proofs that these objects are not "neutron stars" and that the redshifts are cosmological rather than gravitational (see also Appendix 2).

APPENDICES

1. THE COORDINATE SYSTEM FOR EQUATION (3)

Equation (3) holds for a coordinate system for which the line element ds is given by

$$ds^2 = e^v dt^2 - e^\lambda dr^2 - r^2(d\theta^2 + \sin^2\theta \, d\phi^2) . \tag{A1}$$

For our spherically symmetric equilibrium models, the quantities λ and ν are functions of r only. They are related to some of the variables used in Section II as follows:

$$e^{-\lambda(r)} = 1 - 2\phi(r), \qquad \frac{d\nu(r)}{dr} = -\frac{2}{P+\rho} \qquad \text{with} \qquad \nu(R) = -\lambda(R). \qquad \text{(A2)}$$

The gravitational redshift for light coming from radial distance r is given by

$$(\lambda + \Delta\lambda)/\lambda = \exp\left[-\tfrac{1}{2}\nu(r)\right]. \qquad \text{(A3)}$$

For light coming from the surface, $r = R$, this expression reduces to equation (14).

2. OBSERVABILITY OF NEUTRON STARS

Although we have only discussed zero-temperature stars in the text, the structure would not be altered greatly for finite central temperatures T_c up to, say, 10^9 ° K. It may be of interest to compare the radiation emitted by a hot neutron star with a typical white dwarf or hot main-sequence star. We have seen that typical masses of these three classes of stars are not very different. The main difference for a neutron star is that its radius R is smaller (and surface gravity g larger) by a factor of about 10^5 compared with a main-sequence star, about 10^3 compared with a white dwarf.

The atmospheric scale height is proportional to T_e/g and is very small for a typical neutron star (order of meters). The photospheric pressure is therefore higher than in the Sun, but of course quite low enough so that no neutrons could survive in or anywhere near the photosphere. In spite of the great difference in radius between a neutron star and a white dwarf their total bolometric luminosity L_{bol}, for the same central temperature, will be roughly similar.

Consider, for instance, a neutron star with $L_{bol} \sim 0.5$ $L\odot$ (brighter than typical white dwarfs). Its surface temperature T_e will then be about 1×10^6 ° K and its direct visual luminosity only about $10^{-7} L\odot$. If such a star were immersed in a region of gas, probably the best chance of detecting it would be via the "Strömgren sphere" it produces. For a gas density of $10\, H/\text{cm}^3$ the radius of this ionized region would be about 0.1 pc. Typical photons emitted directly from the star are in the very soft X-ray region of a few hundred electron volts. Their mean free path is roughly comparable with the radius of the Strömgren sphere (the helium in the gas contributes slightly more to the absorption than the hydrogen), and the edge of this sphere is quite diffuse, unlike the sharp boundaries typical for hot main-sequence stars.

Chiu (1964) has estimated that a newly formed hot neutron star (formed as a supernova remnant, say) cools sufficiently slowly so that a thousand years later its surface temperature T_e is about 10^7 ° K. For such a high surface temperature the concept of a Strömgren sphere is hardly applicable: typical photons emitted by such a star are in the X-ray region of several keV and have a very long absorption mean free path. One then gets very little conversion into visible light, but the X-rays could be detected directly.

REFERENCES

Ambartsumyan, V. A., and Saakyan, G. S. 1962, Soviet Astr.—A.J., 5, 601, 779.
Bondi, H., M.N. (to be published).
Cameron, A. G. W. 1959, Ap. J., 130, 884.
Chiu, H.-Y. 1964, Ann. Phys., 26, 364.
Hamada, T., and Salpeter, E. E. 1961, Ap. J., 134, 663.
Iben, I. 1963, Ap. J., 138, 1090.
Landau, L. 1932, Phys. Zeits. Sowjetunion, 1, 285.
Levinger, J. S., and Simmons, L. M. 1961, Phys. Rev., 124, 916.
Oppenheimer, J. R., and Volkoff, G. M. 1939, Phys. Rev., 55, 374.
Saakyan, G. S. 1963, Soviet Astr.—A.J., 6, 788.
Saakyan, G. S., and Vartamian, Y. L. 1963, Nuovo Cim., 30, 82.
Salpeter, E. E. 1960, Ann. Phys., 11, 309.
Wheeler, J. A., et al. 1958, Solvay Conference Report, p. 124.
Zel'dovich, Y. B. 1962, Soviet Phys. JETP, 14, 1143.

THE FORMATION OF NEUTRON STARS AND THEIR SURFACE

chapter 33 PROPERTIES

HONG-YEE CHIU

I. INTRODUCTION

About 30 years ago Chandrasekhar[1] proved that at zero temperature there is no equilibrium configuration for a star with a mass greater than $5.66/\mu_e^2 M\odot$ (μ_e is the ratio of mass number to atomic number; $M\odot$ = solar mass = 2×10^{33} gm). For a star made of elements other than hydrogen, the mass limit is around $1.4\ M\odot$. Oppenheimer and Volkoff (1939) extended Chandrasekhar's theory to the relativistic region. They found that, for a perfect Fermi gas, the relativistic mass limit is only $0.76\ M\odot$.

Massive stars exist. In order to avoid the difficulty of the mass-limit dilemma in stellar evolution discussions, it has been generally assumed that a massive star can always get rid of its mass before it comes to the end of stellar evolution. It is easy to see just from energetic grounds how erroneous this idea is (Sec. IIIa).

In this paper we discuss how a star reaches a dynamically unstable stage, the energetics during stellar collapse, and the observations of remnants of collapsed stars (neutron stars) if they can be observed at all. It is suggested that neutron stars may be visible in the 3–10-Å X-ray band for around a few thousand years.[2]

II. EVOLUTION OF PRE-SUPERNOVA STARS

a) Equations of Evolution

One possible mechanism (iron-helium phase change) for supernova collapse has been discussed extensively by Fowler and Hoyle (1960). In this paper we consider an alternative approach which does not depend upon certain simple assumptions (such as eq. [21] of this paper) which Hoyle and Fowler made in their paper.

When a star is contracting rapidly, one must include the acceleration in the equation of hydrostatic equilibrium. As long as the gravitational energy is small compared with

---

HONG-YEE CHIU, Goddard Institute for Space Studies and Columbia University.

[1] For a complete bibliography, see Chandrasekhar (1951).

[2] Chiu (1964) gives a somewhat detailed discussion of material not covered or only briefly mentioned here.

the rest energy of the star, we can use the non-relativistic approximation. Assuming spherical symmetry, the equation for hydrostatic equilibrium is

$$\frac{dP}{dr} = - \rho \frac{Gm}{r^2} - \rho \dot{v} , \tag{1}$$

where P is the total pressure, ρ the density, G the gravitational constant, m the mass contained in a sphere of symmetry of radius r; v is the radial velocity at r; and $\dot{v}$ is given by

$$\dot{v} = \frac{\partial v}{\partial t} + v \frac{\partial v}{\partial r} . \tag{2}$$

It is more convenient to use m as one of the two independent variables, since m is independent of t. Then equation (1) becomes

$$\frac{dP}{dm} = \frac{-Gm}{4\pi r^4} - \frac{\dot{v}}{4\pi r^2} . \tag{3}$$

From the definition of m we have

$$\frac{dr}{dm} = \frac{1}{4\pi r^2 \rho} . \tag{4}$$

Also, we have the equation of continuity

$$\dot{\rho} + \rho \ \text{div} \ v = \dot{\rho} + \rho \frac{\partial v}{\partial r} = 0 . \tag{5}$$

Before a star reaches the iron-helium stage, a contraction is induced by a neutrino process which dissipates stellar energy. Let the rate of energy dissipation per unit mass be $\epsilon_d(\rho, T)$ (in our notation ϵ_d has a positive sign). The energy balance equation is

$$-T \frac{dS}{dt} = \epsilon_d(\rho, T) , \tag{6}$$

where S is the entropy per unit mass. We have neglected ordinary radiative transfer processes. For the annihilation process (Chiu 1961) we have

$$\epsilon_d(\rho, T) = \frac{4 \times 10^{15}}{\rho} \left(\frac{T}{10^9} \right) \ \text{erg/gm sec} . \tag{7}$$

b) Approximate Solutions[3]

Let W be the gravitational energy of the star and E its total thermodynamic energy; then the total energy of the star E_T is given by

$$E_T = W + E . \tag{8}$$

The virial theorem gives

$$-W = (1 + \eta)E , \tag{9}$$

[3] Although we also use the simple relation $\rho \propto T^3$ here, our result only serves as an example and indicates directions of a more detailed calculation program whose preliminary result is also discussed here.

where η is a slowly varying constant depending on the gross thermodynamic properties of a star. For all cases, $1 > \eta > 0$. At $T \sim 6 \times 10^9 \,^\circ$ K, $\eta \approx 0.1$.

One can write approximately

$$W = -G \int \frac{m\,dm}{r} \approx -\frac{GM^2}{R}, \qquad (10)$$

where R is the radius of the star, and also

$$E = \int \epsilon dm \approx M \cdot R_g T, \qquad (11)$$

where ϵ, the thermodynamic energy per unit mass, is approximated by the expression for a perfect gas,

$$\epsilon = \tfrac{3}{2} R_g T, \qquad (12)$$

and R_g is the gas constant ($R_g = 8.2 \times 10^7$ in cgs units). From equations (10) and (11), the following relations are obtained:

$$T = \frac{GM}{R_g(1+\eta)} \frac{1}{R} \qquad (13)$$

and

$$W = -\eta E_T = -\eta M R_g T = -\frac{\eta G}{1+\eta} \frac{M^2}{R}. \qquad (14)$$

Since gravitational contraction is the only energy source available at $T \gtrsim 10^9 \,^\circ$ K,[4] above this temperature the energy-balance equation becomes

$$-\frac{dW}{dt} = \int \epsilon_d dm \approx M \epsilon_d(\rho, T). \qquad (15)$$

From equation (13) we can also obtain a dynamical relation between T and ρ. Since $M = \rho \tfrac{4}{3}\pi R^3$, the relation is

$$\rho = \frac{R_g^3}{4G^3 M^2} T^3 \equiv A T^3. \qquad (16)$$

From equations (14)–(16), we obtain the following relations:

$$-\frac{dR}{dt} = \frac{1+\eta}{\eta GM} \epsilon_d \frac{1}{A} \left[\frac{GM}{R_g(1+\eta)} \right]^6 \frac{1}{R^4} = \frac{C}{R^4} \qquad (17)$$

and

$$-\frac{d^2R}{dt^2} = -\frac{4C}{R^5} \frac{dR}{dt} = +\frac{4C^2}{R^9}. \qquad (18)$$

Since d^2R/dt^2 cannot exceed the gravitational acceleration at the surface of the star, from equation (18) we obtain a lower limit for R below which no hydrostatic equilibrium is possible

$$R > \left(\frac{4C^2}{MG} \right)^{1/7} = R_l. \qquad (19)$$

[4] Since the amount of nuclear energy left at $T \gtrsim 10^9 \,^\circ$ K is small, nuclear fuel will be consumed before the temperature of the star is so high that nuclear energy becomes an important term in eq. (6).

Let $M = 20\ M\odot$, $\eta = 0.1$, we find the limiting radius R_l to be

$$R_l \approx 10^9$$

$$C = 1.08 \times 10^{31}\ \text{(in cgs units)}.$$

The corresponding temperature as estimated from equation (16) is roughly $3 \times 10^{9}\ °\ \text{K}$. This temperature is below the iron-helium disintegration temperature ($\sim 6 \times 10^{9}\ °\ \text{K}$). However, we remark that the above estimate is very crude. The only conclusion we can draw is that qualitatively both *the annihilation neutrino process* and the *iron-helium disintegration process* are capable of causing a massive star to collapse, and a detailed analysis is necessary to tell which process acts first.

c) Simple Implications of Equation (6) (the Energy-Balance Equation)

From the sign of equation (6) we see that the entropy S is a decreasing function of t. For a gas that is not too degenerate, one finds

$$S \propto \ln\,(T^K/\rho)\,, \tag{20}$$

where $K = 1.5$ in a non-relativistic gas and $K = 3$ in the relativistic limit.

We can obtain a rough relation between average values of ρ and T for a star from the virial theorem. We have the simple relation

$$\rho \propto T^3\,. \tag{21}$$

Equation (21) holds for a normal star whose composition is homogeneous and whose self-gravitational energy is much less than its rest energy. Substituting equation (21) into equation (20), we find that as long as the gas is non-relativistic, S is a decreasing function of T, and equations (6), (20), and (21) are compatible. If the gas becomes relativistic, equations (20) and (21) give a constant S, independent of the temperature and density of the star. This is incompatible with equation (6), which states that S must decrease with time. Equation (6) describes the energy-balance relation and must be true. Hence equation (21) cannot hold in stars with strong neutrino emission. Since equation (21) is obtained with the assumption that the star is homogeneous, the breakdown of it also means that a star homogeneous in composition cannot remain homogeneous in structure in the presence of strong neutrino emission. In some parts of the star the density must rise much faster than the third power of T. This is demonstrated in the numerical example described below.

d) A Simple Numerical Example of the Development of a Degenerate Core in a Massive Star

Since $dR/dt \propto R^{-9}$, the acceleration term in equation (1) may be neglected until the very end of stellar collapse. We now present a model calculation. The pressure term includes the electron and positron pressure, radiation pressure, and ion pressure. All other quantities (pressure, energy, neutrino rate, etc.) are obtained from exact equations describing them.

The masses are taken to be $10\ M\odot$ and $20\ M\odot$, respectively, and the initial condition is arbitrarily set by the temperature-density relation

$$\rho \propto T^{1.5}\,. \tag{22}$$

The proportionality constant is determined by the mass. The initial temperature at the center is taken to be $10^{9}\ °\ \text{K}$.

It is found that the central density ρ_c has a very steep dependence on the central temperature T_c. We have

$$\rho_c \propto T_c^9 \; (M = 10 \, M\odot) \tag{23}$$

and

$$\rho_c \propto T_c^5 \; (M = 20 \, M\odot) . \tag{24}$$

The density and temperature profiles are shown in Figures 1–4. The amazing result is the following: initially we have a reasonable amount of temperature gradient, but it gradually disappears as the star evolves. There is a very heavy concentration of matter toward the center. In fact, in the 10 $M\odot$ model, when T_c (central temperature) is around 4×10^9 ° K, the center becomes quite degenerate.

From these two models, we can say that, in general, a degenerate core will develop in the core of a star with strong neutrino dissipation. In certain stars, the degenerate core may induce instability. The mass contained in the degenerate core must not exceed the Chandrasekhar mass limit. Once the mass limit is exceeded, there does not exist any equilibrium, and collapse may take place, independent of iron-helium conversion process.

The fact that the neutrino processes can induce a collapse is illustrated in Figure 5. In Figure 5, the central density is plotted as a function of time. It diverges at some finite time, meaning a collapse.

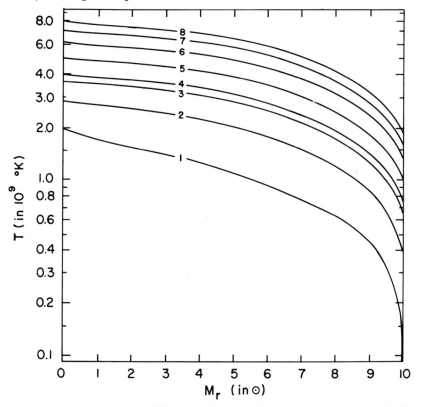

FIG. 1.—The temperature T of a $10 M\odot$ star is plotted as a function of the shell mass M_r (M_r is the mass contained inside a sphere of symmetry of radius r) for several time sequences (marked 1–8 in order of increasing time). The flattening of the temperature gradient is apparent.

These two models are highly simplified, but they indicate that conclusions based on simple qualitative arguments used previously to obtain pre-supernova models are not reliable. A full program to investigate pre-supernova models is under way.

III. ENERGETICS OF A COLLAPSING STAR—NEUTRINOS

a) *Impossibility of Ejecting Enough Matter To Become a White Dwarf*

In order that a massive core may eject enough mass to become a white dwarf, some physical mechanism must be present to eject almost all of its mass into space.

It is difficult to imagine a practical mechanism to achieve this. However, we shall now demonstrate on energetic grounds that a star cannot eject enough matter into space for the remaining star to become a white dwarf. The gravitational energy of a star is GM^2/R. Since no cold star of mass $>1.4\ M_\odot$ may exist (see Sec. I), an energy of the amount

$$\frac{G(M^2 - 2M_\odot{}^2)}{R}$$

is needed to dissociate the star from its gravitational binding. This energy must be

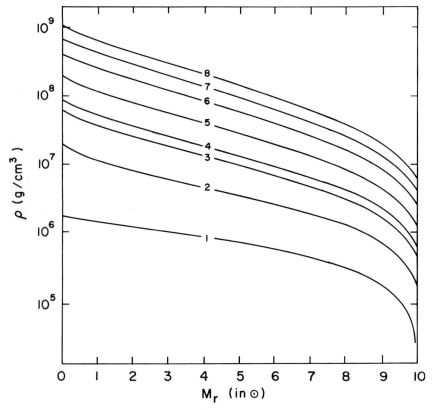

Fig. 2.—The density ρ as a function of M_r for the same star as in Fig. 1 and for the same time sequences. The development of a dense degenerate core is obvious.

supplied gravitationally by the remaining core of the star of mass around $M\odot$, radius r. Hence, to the first approximation

$$\frac{G(M^2 - 2M_\odot{}^2)}{R} \approx \frac{GM_\odot{}^2}{r}. \qquad (25)$$

Consider $M \approx 20\ M\odot$, and a radius of 10^9 cm (which corresponds to a temperature of around 1 MeV when instability occurs), we find $r \sim R/400$. The density of the remaining core will be $(400)^3 = 6.4 \times 10^7$ higher than that of the star before collapse takes place. From equation (16), the density at the instant of collapse is estimated to be roughly 10^7 gm/cm^3. Hence the remaining core will have a density of at least 10^{13} gm/cm^3, which is the density of a neutron star. If we apply results of our numerical model calculation, because there is a higher concentration of mass in the center, even less massive stars may have trouble getting rid of their mass.

This example is cited just to demonstrate that, when a massive star collapses, there is no possibility that the remaining core will be a white dwarf. Colgate further demonstrates

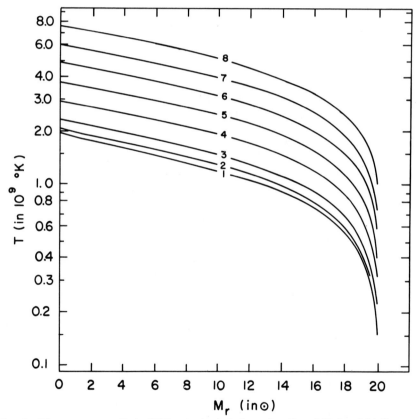

Fig. 3.—The temperature T of a $20M\odot$ star is plotted as a function of M_r for eight time sequences (marked 1–8). Note there is very little flattening of the temperature gradient as compared with that for a $10M\odot$ star.

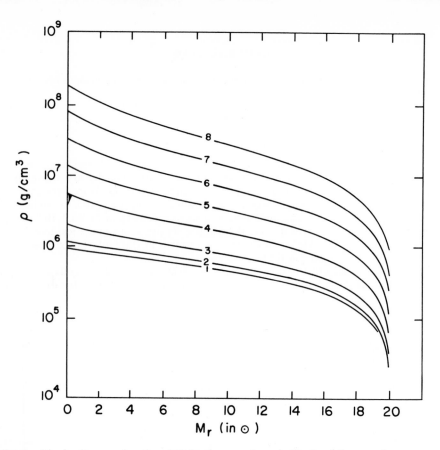

Fig. 4.—The density ρ as a function of M_r for the same star as in Fig. 3 and the same time sequences. The development of a dense core is obvious.

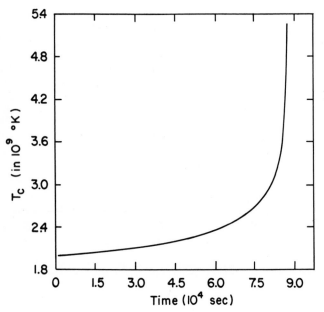

Fig. 5.—The central temperature T_c of the $10M_\odot$ star (described in Figs. 1 and 2) is plotted as a function of time. T_c diverges at some finite time.

that shock waves generated during the collapse phase will enable the star to achieve neutron star density at even lower stellar masses. Moreover, the energy released during gravitational collapse will be mostly in the form of neutrinos and cannot be of more than limited use.

b) Neutrino Losses during Stellar Collapse

The density ρ is related to the Fermi momentum p_F as follows:

$$\rho = \frac{1}{3\pi^2\hbar^3} p_F^3 = \frac{(m_y c)^3}{3\pi^2\hbar^3} x^3 \tag{26}$$

and

$$x = p_F/m_y c , \tag{27}$$

where m_y is the mass for the particle y. As we have seen, during the evolution of a star, at best $\rho \propto T^3$. For relativistic energy (for electrons) $E_F \approx p_F c$. Hence, at best, the degeneracy parameter E_F/kT will be a constant. Otherwise E_F/kT will always increase (gas becomes degenerate).

In the following, we shall assume that the ratio E_F/kT will be roughly 1. With this assumption, if we find the relaxation time for neutrino loss to be short compared with the dynamical time scale, then we can regard the gas as collapsing under zero temperature conditions.

At $T = 6 \times 10^9\,°\,K$ ($kT \sim 0.5$ MeV) the most dominant neutrino process is the annihilation process. This is because all other processes involve a threshold energy of the order of the energy difference between neutrons and protons. At higher temperature, the threshold becomes unimportant and all neutrino processes must be considered. Moreover, at low density ($\rho < 10^7$ gm/cm³, say) the mean free path of neutrinos is longer than the physical dimension of the star. At high density, the mean free path of neutrinos can no longer be considered long compared with the physical dimension of the star. The rate of dissipation of neutrinal energy is then less than the production rate.

At $kT \sim m_\mu c^2$, the creation of π-meson pairs and μ-meson pairs is not negligible. Because the neutrinos associated with the μ-meson do not interact with electrons to the lowest order, the dissipation of stellar energy through μ-neutrino production is more important. Table 1 lists the electron, π, μ-meson equilibrium densities as a function of temperature.

c) Neutrino Cross-Sections

When the energy difference between neutron and proton can be neglected, the cross-section for first-order neutrino processes is given by

$$\sigma \frac{v}{c} = CG^2 p_\nu^2 , \tag{28}$$

where G is the weak interaction constant, v is the relative velocity of the initial system of particles ($\sim c$) and p_ν is the final neutrino momentum; C is a numerical constant close to unity. Equation (28) is valid if $p_\nu \sim 1$ BeV/c.

d) Neutrino Losses during Collapse

As the density of the star increases, the mean free path of neutrinos becomes smaller. Once the mean free path of the neutrinos becomes smaller than the dimension of the star, the neutrino energy loss rate is no longer the same as the production rate. Let the radius of the star be R, the mean free path for neutrinos be λ, the total stellar neutrino energy content be U_ν, then the neutrino luminosity L_ν for a star is

$$L_\nu = \frac{U_\nu}{R/c \, (R/\lambda)} \, . \tag{29}$$

In equilibrium, U_ν (the neutrino energy density) is approximately the same as the radiation energy density).

A recent experiment demonstrated that there are two kinds of neutrinos, ν_e and ν_μ. In the lowest order, ν_e does not interact with μ-meson and ν_μ does not interact with electrons. Thus ν_μ can be scattered by an electron.

TABLE 1

ELECTRON, π-MESON, AND μ-MESON NUMBER DENSITIES
AS A FUNCTION OF TEMPERATURE

(T Measured in ° K, n in particles/cm³)

$\log_{10} T$	$\log_{10} n_e$	$\log_{10} n_\mu$	$\log_{10} n_\pi$
10.0.........	31.31	....	....
10.2.........	31.91	....	....
10.4.........	32.51	....	....
10.6.........	33.11	21.7	19.27
10.8.........	33.71	27.1	26.37
11.0.........	34.31	30.5	28.47
11.2.........	34.91	32.8	31.69
11.4.........	35.51	34.4	33.69
11.6.........	36.11	35.6	35.09
11.8.........	36.71	36.5	36.18
12.0.........	37.31	37.2	37.0
12.2.........	37.91	37.89	....
12.4.........	38.51	38.5	....
12.6.........	39.11	39.1	....

Since the average energy of ν_μ coming from π-decay and μ-decay is of the order of $m_\mu c^2$ (or less), inverse μ capture reaction cannot occur favorably. Until $kT \approx m_\mu c^2$ ($T \sim 10^{12}$ ° K), the number density for μ-mesons is small. At the temperature ($T = 1.6 \times 10^{11}$ ° K) when the loss of energy due to π-decay becomes very important, the mean free path for $\nu_\mu - \mu$ scattering is 10^8 cm, which is around the radius of the star ($\sim 7 \times 10^7$ cm). Hence μ-neutrinos can dissipate stellar energy rapidly while e-neutrinos cannot. Table 2 summarizes our result. The relaxation time for dissipating stellar energy is shortest at roughly $T = 6.3 \times 10^{10}$ ° K, and again at $T \sim 4 \times 10^{11}$ ° K. The corresponding relaxation times are roughly 3×10^{-3} and 10^{-4} sec, respectively. This is roughly the time scale for the star to relax to the zero temperature configuration discussed previously.

Since this time scale is of the same order of magnitude as that required for light to travel across the star, we conclude the core collapses under zero temperature conditions ($E_F/kT \gg 1$).

We have not included in our calculations the redshift of neutrinos due to the gravitational field of the star. The redshift caused by the gravitational field of the star will at most decrease the net loss energy rate by a factor of 2.

IV. STATIC STRUCTURE OF STARS AT ZERO TEMPERATURE

This problem is discussed in full detail by Salpeter in a separate paper in this volume.[5] We shall emphasize certain points.

[5] E. E. Salpeter, in this volume. A review and bibliography may be found in Chiu (1964).

As the density of matter approaches 10^{12} gm/cm³, inverse beta processes alter the composition of matter toward neutron-rich elements. At $\rho > 10^{12}$ gm/cm³, only free neutrons and a small amount of electrons and protons exist. At $\rho \sim 10^{15}$, hyperons begin to come into existence. The structure of a zero temperature star (made of a Fermi gas) as a function of the central density ρ_c is shown in Figure 6. We see the mass M first increases as the central density until $\rho_c \sim 10^9$ gm/cm³, then M decreases as ρ_c rises further. When ρ_c approaches 10^{13} gm/cm³, then M increases again. Very soon we come to a second maximum, and M decreases when $\rho_c > 10^{16}$ gm/cm³. It may be emphasized that the second maximum exists even for a perfect Fermi gas.

TABLE 2

NEUTRINO LOSS RATES IN A NEUTRON STAR

Density (gm/cm³)	Energy Density (erg/cm³)	Neutrino Production Rate (erg/sec cm³)		Mean Free Path (cm)		Radius of Star (cm)	Relaxation Time (sec)	
		ν_e	ν_μ	ν_e	ν_μ		ν_e	ν_μ
				$T = 10^{10}$ °K				
10^7	1.6×10^{26}	10^{26}	....	10^{10}	....	10^9	1	....
4×10^7	10^{27}	3×10^{27}	....	1.6×10^9	....	6.3×10^8	3×10^{-1}	....
1.6×10^8	6.3×10^{27}	2×10^{29}	4×10^{12}	2.5×10^8	>Star	4×10^8	3×10^{-2}	....
6.3×10^8	4×10^{28}	1.3×10^{31}	7×10^{21}	4×10^7	>Star	2.5×10^8	3×10^{-3}	....
2.5×10^9	2.5×10^{29}	10^{33}	9×10^{28}	6.3×10^6	>Star	1.6×10^8	0.1	3
				$T = 10^{11}$ °K				
10^{10}	1.6×10^{30}	EQ.	10^{31}	10^6	>Star	10^8	0.3	0.1
4×10^{10}	10^{31}	EQ.	2×10^{34}	1.6×10^5	>Star	6.3×10^7	0.5	5×10^{-4}
1.6×10^{11}	6.3×10^{31}	EQ.	2×10^{36}	2.5×10^4	>Star	4×10^7	1	3×10^{-5}
6.3×10^{11}	4×10^{32}	EQ.	5×10^{37}	4×10^3	>Star	2.5×10^7	....	10^{-5}
2.5×10^{12}	2.5×10^{33}	EQ.	EQ.	6×10^2	~Star	1.6×10^7	....	10^{-4}
				$T = 10^{12}$ °K				
10^{13}	1.6×10^{34}	EQ.	EQ.	....	~Star	10^7	....	10^{-3}

Since the interparticle spacing in typical neutron stars is of the order of 10^{-13} cm or less (roughly the size of elementary particles) it is not possible to exclude the structure of elementary particles from our discussion. However, some general results can still be obtained without particle physics. First, we examine the limitations on the equation of state.

a) The Unimportance of Quantum-gravitational Effects

A well-known theorem in Riemannian geometry[6] states that, in a given space with a non-Euclidean metric, it is always possible to find a coordinate transformation such that

[6] This is easily proven. The line element ds may be written as

$$d s^2 = {}_i\Sigma_j g_{ij} d x^i d x^i , \qquad \text{(i)}$$

where $\{g_{ij}\}$ is the metric tensor and $\{x^i\}$ is a general set of coordinates. Since $\{g_{ij}\}$ is a symmetric tensor, locally at any given point, the metric $g_{\mu\nu}$ may be reduced to that for a Minkowskian space, that is,

$$g'_{\mu\nu} = \begin{pmatrix} -1 & 0 & 0 & 0 \\ 0 & -1 & 0 & 0 \\ 0 & 0 & -1 & 0 \\ 0 & 0 & 0 & +1 \end{pmatrix}.$$

(30)

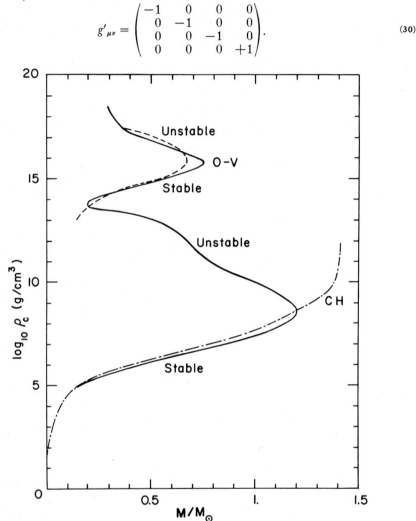

FIG. 6.—Mass versus central density curve for a cold degenerate star. Dotted curve CH is that by Chandrasekhar, that marked O-V is due to Oppenheimer and Volkoff. The solid curve is due to Wheeler. Chandrasekhar used the non-relativistic approximation for the stellar structure equation and a perfect Fermi gas for the equation of state. Oppenheimer and Volkoff used the same equation of state but a relativistic form for the stellar structural equations. Wheeler took into account the beta transition.

at a particular point $\{g_{ij}\}$ can be diagonalized by "rotating" the $\{x^i\}$ coordinate system at this point. An additional scale change in the rotated $\{x^i\}$ system reduces the line element to

$$d s^2 = {}_i\Sigma_j \pm \delta_{ij} d x^i d x^j$$

(ii)

where δ_{ij} is the Kronecker delta and the sign ($\pm$) is chosen so as to be consistent with the signature of eq. (ii). Since g_{ij} varies with position, obviously this transformation is valid only at the particular point chosen.

Unless the $g_{\mu\nu}$'s change considerably over the dimension of elementary particles ($\sim \hbar/mc \approx 10^{-13}$ cm), it is not necessary to consider quantum effects of gravitational fields. Even in the extreme case when the time metric g_{00} vanishes at the center of a neutron star, quantum effects may still not enter. According to Oppenheimer and Volkoff (1939), one can write generally, in the center of a neutron star:

$$g_{00} = \left(1 - \frac{2m}{Rc}\right)^{1/2} \exp\left[-\frac{1}{c^2}\int_0^{P_c} \frac{dP}{(P/c^2)+\rho}\right] \tag{31}$$

when the mass of a neutron star approaches the critical mass, $P_c \to \infty$ and the integral in the exponential diverges logarithmically as one approaches the center, and g_{00} vanishes as $1/P$ $(P \to \infty)$.

Unless $P \to \infty$ abruptly over a dimension of an elementary particle, g_{00} cannot change substantially. This would not occur since the pressure is itself a macroscopic concept. Hence the center of neutron stars is not likely to be the dwelling place of quantum gravitational field theory.

b) Relativistic Limits on the Equation of State

General relativity does set up certain limits for the equation of state on the basis of positive (or negative) definiteness of the stress energy tensor, and that signals cannot propagate at a speed faster than light speed. These limitations manifest themselves in the relation of pressure to energy. Since the speed of sound v_s for a given medium is given by

$$v_s = c\left(\frac{dP}{d\epsilon}\right)^{1/2} \lesssim c \tag{32}$$

(ϵ is the energy density), integrating equation (32) one obtains

$$p \lesssim \epsilon. \tag{33}$$

For a non-interacting gas, the trace of the energy momentum tensor must be positive (e.g., Landau and Lifshitz 1961). This sets up an upper limit for P:

$$P \leq \tfrac{1}{3}\epsilon.$$

Recently, Zel'dovich (1961) demonstrated that for a gas composed of classical point charges, interacting through a classical vector field *with a finite mass*, the relativistic limit of equation (33) can be reached.

In any case, the pressure cannot exceed the energy density. This excludes incompressible fluid as a physical equation of state.

c) Model for Neutron Stars: Limits on the Value of the Central Density and Their Implications

A very elementary theorem tells one that the self-gravitational energy of a body cannot exceed its proper mass or energy, otherwise energy can be "manufactured" by accumulating matter. This sets up a limit on the central density of an object if gravitational binding is required. Applying equation (26) to neutron matter, we have

$$\rho \approx 6 \times 10^{15} \left(\frac{p_F}{m_n c}\right)^3.$$

If $p_F \gg m_n c$, then the kinetic energy of the neutron gas will exceed the rest energy. Since the maximum self-gravitational energy is Mc^2, this can only mean that when the average density of a neutron star is much greater than 6×10^{15} gm/cm^3, there can be no gravitational binding.

Indeed, the binding energies of most neutron star models become positive when one crosses the mass maximum in Figure 6 (A. G. W. Cameron, private communication). Only for some pathological equation of state can one get gravitational binding at arbitrarily high density.

It thus seems that in practice it is impossible to accumulate matter until the central density becomes infinite. Hence the singularity $g_{00} = 0$ (obtained from eq. [31] by requiring $\rho \sim p \rightarrow \infty$) discussed by Wheeler, cannot take place *statically* by accumulating matter. The inclusion of strange particles may change the critical mass discussed above, but one still cannot build up a singularity $g_{00} = 0$ just by accumulating masses. This is true in all model neutron stars studied so far.

Unlike the Schwarzschild singularity, the singularity $g_{00} = 0$ cannot be removed by a mere coordinate transformation. This implication of the singularity $g_{00} = 0$ is discussed by J. A. Wheeler.

When one accumulates masses, one first comes to the so-called second crushing point (the mass maximum near $\rho_c \sim 10^{16}$ gm/cm^3 in Fig. 6). From then on, one has only a dynamical collapse. The value of the mass maximum, however, depends *sensitively* on the equation of state. It ranges from 0.3 $M\odot$ to 4 $M\odot$.

d) *Schwarzschild Singularity and the Ultimate Mass Limit*

For a point mass, the Schwarzschild solution for the metric has the form

$$ds^2 = g_{ij}dx^i dx^j = \frac{-dr^2}{1 - (2GM/rc^2)} - r^2 d\theta^2 - r^2 \sin^2\theta\, d\varphi^2 + \left(1 - \frac{2GM}{rc^2}\right) dt^2. \quad (34)$$

For a mass m, a singularity occurs at $r_s = 2GM/c^2$. That is, $ds^2 = \infty$. Consequently, no light signal can cross the boundary defined by $r = r_s$.[7] For massive objects like the Sun, the Schwarzschild radius is around 2.6 km, which is about the size of a neutron star of the same mass with a density of around 10^{16} gm cm^{-3}.

This singularity has been the subject of discussion among relativists ever since the solution was found. Is it a real singularity? Or is it just a singularity related to a particular coordinate system?

By a change of coordinates of $r \rightarrow r'$, $\theta \rightarrow \theta$, $\varphi \rightarrow \varphi$, $t \rightarrow t$, where r' is related to r by the following transformation[8]

$$r = \left(1 + \frac{GM}{2r'c^2}\right)^2 r', \quad (35)$$

equation (34) becomes

$$ds^2 = -\left(1 + \frac{m'}{2r'}\right)^4 (dr'^2 + r'^2 d\theta^2 + r'^2 \sin^2\theta\, d\varphi^2) + \frac{(1 - m'/2r')^2}{(1 + m'/2r')^2} dt^2, \quad (36)$$

where

$$m' = GM/c^2$$

---

[7] We might remark that such behavior was first predicted by Laplace on the basis of a corpuscular theory of light.

[8] This coordinate system is known as the isotropic coordinate system.

is the geometrized mass. In equation (36) the singularity in r' coordinates disappears. Hence it seems that the singularity at $r = r_s$ is a coordinate singularity.

Robertson (1928) has demonstrated that by a coordinate transformation one can eliminate this singularity in the following sense: An observer in flat space observes the free fall of a test particle toward the singularity. The time it takes the test particle to cross the boundary (which is at $r_s = 2GM/c^2$) is infinite; this is because $g_{00} = 0$ at the boundary, and the test particle suffers infinite time dilatation as it approaches the singularity. However, if the observer moves with the test particle, the time duration that he observes for the test particle (and himself) to cross the boundary is *finite*. Hence, in the opinion of many relativists, this singularity is a *coordinate* singularity since it can be removed by a proper choice of coordinate systems (transformation to a co-moving frame).

We regard the Schwarzschild singularity as a *physical singularity* in the following sense. Given a matter distribution such that initially nowhere within the matter distribution is $r_s \leq 2GM/c^2$. An observer observes this distribution of matter in a nearly flat space (since almost all points of the universe are locally nearly flat). Since it takes an infinite time for this distribution of matter to cross the Schwarzschild singularity, we may regard the Schwarzschild singularity as a real, physical singularity. Once matter is found in a non-singular state, within the finite lifetime of the universe it will remain in the non-singular state. Similarly, if a Schwarzschild singularity were found in nature, it would have been created with the universe.

Since all massive stars undergo supernova explosion, their core will inevitably collapse to extremely high densities. It might be worthwhile to investigate whether they collapse asymptotically to become Schwarzschild singularities or not.

e) Dynamical Collapse

To date, there is only one analysis of dynamical, relativistic collapse. This is the famous investigation of Oppenheimer and Snyder (1939). Although their analysis involves some unlikely physical assumptions (zero pressure), it will serve as a good example. In the absence of pressure, the collapse may be treated analytically. Oppenheimer and Snyder computed the world trajectories of material bodies falling toward a common center under the gravitational field produced by these material bodies. They obtained the following result: To an external observer, these particles fall toward the Schwarzschild singularity asymptotically, and the total time of fall is infinite. This is because of the infinite time dilatation effect mentioned earlier. To a local observer, the time is finite, and for the case of the Sun, it is of the order of 1 day. Since the star continues to fall indefinitely, the star is always in some dynamical motion, and this is consistent with the fact that no static structure for such star exists if its mass exceeds a certain limit.

f) Angular Momentum and Stellar Collapse

A rapidly rotating star need not preserve rotational symmetry, as the classical analysis of Jacobi showed. Modern versions of Jacobi's discussion have been extensively investigated by Chandrasekhar (1962) and Chandrasekhar and Lebovitz (1962a–e).

Angular momentum conservation sets a limit on stellar collapse. The angular momentum $I\omega$ is a conserved quantity (ω is the angular velocity). For a normal star, $R \approx 10^{11}$ cm and a period of rotation of 1 day,

$$I\omega \propto R^2\omega \approx 6 \times 10^{17} . \tag{37}$$

The centrifugal force f_c per unit mass at the equator of the star is

$$f_c = \frac{v_{eq}^2}{R} , \tag{38}$$

where $v_{eq} = R\omega$ is the speed at the equator. Since $f_c < MG/R^2$ (otherwise the star will be torn apart by rotation), we have the upper limit on R:

$$\frac{(R^2\omega)^2}{R^3} < \frac{MG}{R^2}$$

or

$$R > \frac{(R^2\omega)^2}{MG}. \tag{39}$$

This is the minimum radius a rotating star may collapse to, and this is the radius at which bifurcation of a spherical star to non-symmetrical shape takes place. Using $M = 20\ M_\odot$, and the value of $R^2\omega$ given by equation (37), we find

$$R > 10^8 \text{ cm} , \tag{40}$$

and at this limiting value of R the angular velocity ω is around 1 rad/sec, and the period is around 1/10 sec. It is highly dubious that such rapidly rotating stars can still preserve rotational symmetry. As an estimate, we apply to our rotating star the formula of gravitational wave radiating power computed for a spinning rod. The radiating power is

$$P = \frac{32GI^2\omega^6}{5\,c^5}. \tag{41}$$

The rotational energy is $\frac{1}{2}I\omega^2$. Hence the relaxation time τ for the star to lose its angular momentum is

$$\tau = \frac{5\,c^5}{64GI\omega^4}. \tag{42}$$

For the parameters we consider, we find $\tau \sim 50$ sec. Hence one need not consider angular momentum as a hindrance to stellar collapse.

V. OBSERVABLE FEATURES OF NEUTRON STARS

From our discussions, it is seen that during stellar collapse the density of a star will reach that of a neutron star. There is no assurance, however, as to what kind of object one may expect to find after the collapse. Indefinite collapse state as suggested by Oppenheimer and Snyder can certainly be one solution; on the other hand, stars in certain mass ranges can collapse to form neutron stars while ejecting mass. It seems that the critical mass for a neutron star is quite sensitive to the equation of state. In certain models, the critical mass even exceeds the Chandrasekhar mass limit. In such cases, it is conceivable that neutron stars exist in nature.

It has been suggested previously (Chiu 1964) that the surface temperature of a neutron star is around $10^{7\,\circ}$ K, and most radiation will be in the X-ray band. It is not possible to locate them by optical means. We now discuss the surface structure of neutron stars in more detail.

The internal structure of neutron stars has been widely studied. The general results (independent of the detailed form of any *covariant* equation of state) are as follows: the mass is between 0.2 $M_\odot$ to around 1.3 $M_\odot$; neutron stars with mass outside the above range cannot exist. The radius is around 10^6 cm. Hyperons as well as neutrons may exist if the density is greater than 10^{15} gm/cm^3. Since neutron matter is unstable against beta decay when the density is below 10^{12} gm/cm^3, the outer shell of a neutron star must be composed of ordinary matter. Most likely, elements are in an equilibrium state; at $\rho < 10^7$ gm/cm^3, Fe^{56} is mostly abundant. However, other elements may exist, and their presence may give clues to the history of formation of neutron stars.

We now estimate the energy content, the internal temperature, and the surface properties of neutron stars.

a) Internal Energy

There are no energy sources inside a neutron star: the radiated energy comes from the remaining thermal energy of the degenerate neutron gas. The heat capacity C_v is

$$C_v = \frac{\pi^2 k^2}{m_n c^2} \frac{(x_n^2 + 1)^{1/2}}{x_n^2} T = 0.75 \times 10^{-4} \frac{(x_n^2 + 1)^{1/2}}{x_n^2} T , \qquad (43)$$

where k is the Boltzmann constant, m_a the mass for particle a, T the temperature, c the speed of light; $x_a = p_F^{(a)}/m_a c$, and $p_F^{(a)}$ is the Fermi momentum for particle a. In

TABLE 3

NEUTRON STAR EMISSION CHARACTERISTICS*†

Internal Temperature (° K)	Total Thermal Energy (ergs)	Photon Luminosity (ergs/sec)	Surface Temperature (° K)	Lifetime (Photon) (years)	Lifetime (Neutrino) (years)	Wavelength of Maximum in Spectrum (Å)
5×10^9	10^{48}	5×10^{37}	1.7×10^7	7×10^3	1	1.9
2×10^9	1.6×10^{48}	2×10^{37}	1.3×10^7	3×10^3	10^2	2.5
10^9	4×10^{47}	8×10^{36}	1.1×10^7	1.7×10^3	10^3	3
5×10^8	10^{47}	2.8×10^{36}	0.8×10^7	10^3	$\gg 10^3$	4.1

* Model mass = 10^{33} gm; radius = 10^6 cm.

† When this paper was finished, the author learned that Dr. D. Morton (to be published) obtained results similar to those given in Table 1. However, Dr. Morton did not obtain the neutrino life time.

R. Stabler (Cornell thesis, 1960, unpublished) has first considered the observable features of neutron stars. However, he used a simplified form of bound-free opacity (Kramer's Law) all throughout the calculation, and he obtained a surface temperature ~3 times lower than that obtained in this paper. Kramer's Law is not applicable to the surface of neutron stars.

gravitationally bound neutron star models, x_n has a value in between 0.1 and 0.5. Taking a value 0.3 for x_n, the total energy E_t of a star is estimated to be

$$E_t = 3.8 \times 10^{47} T_9^2 M_{33} \text{ ergs} , \qquad (44)$$

where $T_n = T/10^n$, $M_{33} = M/10^{33}$.

b) Neutrino Production and Internal Temperature

The plasma neutrino process is the most important neutrino process (Adams, Ruderman, and Woo 1963). From the *equilibrium* electron density in a typical neutron star ($M = 10^{33}$ gm, radius $R = 10^6$ cm, mean density $\rho = 10^{14}$ gm/cm^3), an average neutrino emission rate can be estimated; the results are listed in Table 3. The lifetime against neutrino emission decreases strongly with increasing temperature. A maximum in the lifetime exists at $T \sim 10^9$ ° K is around 10^3 years. This we take to be the typical time scale.

The mean energy of plasma neutrinos at $T \sim 10^9$ ° K in the neutron core is around 10 MeV. Because of strong degeneracy, the mean free path of 10 MeV neutrino in neutron core is fairly long ($\geq 10^4$ cm). One does not need to consider corrections to the neutrino rate due to scattering.

c) Surface Composition and Structure[9]

As the density drops drastically from 10^{15} gm/cm³ in the center to 10^6 gm/cm³ on the surface, the temperature in these regions remains virtually unchanged. This is because of the high thermal conductivity of degenerate electrons. Hence we can take the temperature to be virtually constant up to $\rho \sim 10^6$ gm/cm³. A small amount of matter supports all temperature gradients.

Near the surface of a typical neutron star, the relativity parameter, $GM/Rc^2 \approx 0.1$ (R is the radius of the neutron star, G is the gravitational constant). As a good approximation, non-relativistic theory may be used. Neglecting the mass contained in the shell, the structure of the outer layer of the atmosphere is given by

$$\frac{dP}{dr} = -\rho \frac{GM}{r^2}. \tag{45}$$

The physical meaning of equation (3) is that the gravitational force is balanced by the hydrostatic pressure gradient. The pressure P for a degenerate electron gas is related to ρ through the following equations (Chiu 1961):

$$P = \frac{1}{24\pi^2} \frac{m_e^4 c^5}{\hbar^3} f(x), \tag{46}$$

$$\rho = \frac{1}{3\pi^2} \frac{m_e^3 c^2}{\hbar^3} x^3 \mu_e m_p, \tag{47}$$

$$f(x) = x(2x^2 - 3)(x^2 + 1)^{1/2} + 3 \sinh^{-1} x, \tag{48}$$

where $x = p_F^{(e)}/m_e c$; $\mu_e = \langle A \rangle / \langle Z \rangle$, where $\langle A \rangle$ and $\langle Z \rangle$ are the average mass number and atomic number for the outer layer ($\mu_e \sim 2$). Solving equation (45), one obtains

$$\rho = 4 \times 10^{13} \left(\frac{M_{33}}{R_6}\right)^3 \left(\frac{1}{\xi} - 1\right)^{3/2} \left[\left(\frac{1}{\xi} - 1\right) + 7.4 \times 10^{-3} \frac{R_6}{M_{33}}\right]^{3/2}, \tag{49}$$

where $\xi = r/R$, $R_6 = R/10^6$ cm. For $R_6 = M_{33} = 1$, and $\rho = 10^{12}$ gm/cm³, we find $1 - \xi \approx 0.1$. The mass contained in the outer layer (non-neutron matter) amounts only to about 10^{-3} of the star.

Matter is non-degenerate at low density; hence equation (49) will break down eventually. In the non-degenerate layer, two physical processes contribute to the opacity of matter to radiation: Compton scattering and photo-ionization of K-shell electrons of Fe^{56}. The cross-section of Compton scattering at $T = 10^9$ ° K is still quite close to its non-relativistic value, which is a

$$\text{constant} = \frac{8\pi}{3} \left(\frac{e^2}{mc^2}\right)^2 = 6.7 \times 10^{-25} \text{ cm}^2.$$

The photo-ionization process has a ν^{-3} dependence (ν is the frequency of the photon). At $T > 5 \times 10^7$ ° K, there are very few bound electrons, and only Compton scattering need be considered.

We may define the beginning of the non-degenerate layer by using one of the following three criteria: (i) when the perfect gas pressure, $P = k/m_p(1/\mu_e)\rho T$, is equal to that

[9] The surface of neutron stars resembles that of white dwarfs (see n. 1).

for a degenerate gas (eq. [46]), this gives $\rho \sim 10^6$ gm/cm^3 at $T = 10^9$ ° K; (ii) when the thermal conductivity of electron gas is the same as for that due to Compton scattering: this gives $\rho \approx 5 \times 10^5$ gm/cm^3. These two criteria give the same value of ρ to within a factor of 2.

The equation of radiative transfer is

$$\frac{a}{3} \frac{dT^4}{dr} = -\frac{\kappa L}{4\pi c r^2} \rho , \tag{50}$$

where L is the total energy flux of the star, κ, the so-called Rosseland mean of opacity, $= 0.2$ cm^2/gm for Compton scattering ($[\kappa\rho]^{-1}$ is roughly the mean free path of photons), a is the Stefan-Boltzmann constant. Combining equations (45) and (50), and using the perfect gas pressure for P, one obtains

$$\frac{3}{a} \frac{k}{\mu_e m_p} \frac{d(\rho T)}{d(T^4)} = \frac{4\pi cGM}{\kappa L}. \tag{51}$$

The solutions for equations (50) and (51) are

$$\rho = \frac{4\pi cGM}{\kappa L} \frac{a\mu_e m_p}{3k} T^3 = \frac{1.92 \times 10^{-18}}{(L/L_\odot)(\kappa/0.2)} M_{33} T^3 \tag{52}$$

and

$$T = \frac{m_p \mu_e}{3k} GM \left(\frac{1}{r} - \frac{1}{R}\right) = 5.4 \times 10^{11} \left(\frac{1}{\xi} - 1\right) M_{33}, \tag{53}$$

where $L_\odot$ = solar energy output rate = 4×10^{33} ergs/sec.

We notice that the thickness of the envelope is *independent* of L so long as κ is a constant (or nearly so). For photo-ionization process (bound-free transition)

$$\kappa \sim \frac{\rho}{T^{3.5}}. \tag{54}$$

Again, if $\rho \sim T^3$ (eq. [52]), κ cannot vary too much. Thus, equations (52) and (53) are approximately true throughout the star. One can fit ρ and T from equation (52) to those at the boundary of the degenerate layer (the boundary has been discussed before) using L as the fitting parameter. The density of the boundary at $T = 10^9$ ° K is 10^6 gm/cm^3. Hence we find $L \approx 2 \times 10^3$ $L_\odot$. This value of L may be further checked by noticing that

$$L = \frac{a}{4} c T^4 4\pi R^2 / n_s = 7 \times 10^{44} \frac{T_9^4}{n_s} \text{ erg/sec}, \tag{55}$$

where n_s is the total number of scatterings an average photon suffers before leaving the star, and T is the internal temperature of the star. The proof of equation (55) may be found in Chiu (1964). The term n_s is given by

$$n_s = \int \kappa \rho dr . \tag{56}$$

The integration terminates at roughly the surface of the star. Using equations (52), (53), and a more precise value of κ from a Los Alamos calculation (known as the Los Alamos

Code[10] and considered to be the best opacity calculation available today), one finds $n_s =$ 1.8×10^8, of which around 10 per cent is contributed by the photo-ionization process. From equation (54) we find $L = 10^3 \, L\odot$, which is only a factor of 2 different from the value we obtained from fitting boundary conditions. Further, one can integrate equations (50) and (51) numerically throughout the star and find a central temperature corresponding to a certain surface temperature. The integrated temperature at $\rho \sim 10^6$ gm/cm^3 at a surface temperature of $10^7 \, °$ K is $0.8 \times 10^9 \, °$ K, and at $\rho \sim 10^{12}$ gm/cm^3, it is $1.2 \times 10^9 \, °$ K. Both values are close to the value of $10^9 \, °$ K that we assumed.

Table 3 lists the photon luminosity as a function of the central temperature, surface temperature, and $\tau \approx T/(dT/dt)$ (lifetime). Our method of computation will not yield reliable results when $T < 5 \times 10^8 \, °$ K, because then the photo-ionization process will contribute considerably to the opacity. However, when the internal temperature drops to below $10^8 \, °$ K, the spectrum of surface emission shifts to the ultraviolet region, for which interstellar absorption is large and the chance for observation is small.

d) Spectrum of Surface Emission of Neutron Stars

Although the energy output of a neutron star is high, only a small fraction of it ($\sim 10^{-3}$) will be able to penetrate through our atmosphere (see Salpeter in this volume),[11] and most of the emission will be in the X-ray region. The mean surface density is around 0.1 gm/cm^3. With a value of $\kappa = 2.6$ at $T = 10^7 \, °$ K (photo-ionization process) most of the emission will come from a layer of thickness around 5 cm ($\sim$ the mean free path of photons). The spectrum will show absorption lines or discontinuities at the ionization energy of K or L electrons; the width of these lines and discontinuities is of the order of kT. From the location of more than one of these discontinuities (or lines) one can determine the redshift and the composition.

The redshift is of the order of GM/Rc^2 (~ 0.1) and is quite large compared with the Doppler shift caused by the motion of heavenly bodies ($v/c \sim 10^{-4}$). The redshift is proportional to M/R. On the other hand, if we can obtain a *good, reliable* equation of state from elementary particle theory, we can obtain a theoretical M–R relation. Combining this result with the redshift measurement, the mass of neutron stars can be measured. The surface temperature and the measured flux on the earth, combining with an information on R, will give us a distance, which can be checked against known distances of supernova remnants, if any. Presently, the measurable flux is around 10^{-8} ergs/sec cm^2. This means that neutron stars at a few thousand light-years can *now* be detected. In the future, when space observatories are available, it is not beyond the present technology to detect all neutron stars (age ≈ 1000 years) in our Galaxy. Since at 10 Å, interstellar absorption is negligible, one can even detect those behind dust clouds. Supernova explosions obscured by dust clouds may now be observable in the X-ray band, since during the first year of the formation of neutron stars, they have an X-ray luminosity equivalent to $10^4 \, L\odot$.

Moreover, because the lifetime of neutron stars against optical emission is short, one can even observe annual declines of the energy flux and the decrease in temperature. One can get great sensitivity by observing the tail of Planck distribution (e.g., observe 10-KeV photons for 1-KeV surface temperature).

The rate of occurrence of supernovae is around one per 50–300 years. Hence the maximum number of experimentally observed neutron stars X-ray sources anticipated cannot exceed, say, 50. At present, only three discrete sources have been resolved (Gursky, Giacconi, Paolini, and Rossi 1963; Friedman 1963).

[10] A. Cox, "Stellar Envelope Coefficients and Opacities," Los Alamos Laboratory preprint (unpublished).

[11] Salpeter reported that the visible part of the Planck spectrum at $T \sim 10^7 \, °$ K is around 10^{-8} of the total energy output, but a large fraction of ultraviolet light ($\sim 10^{-3}$) can be converted into visible light by interstellar gas surrounding the neutron star.

Further examination of these X-ray sources may tell us whether they are neutron stars, and give answers to a very important question.

VI. CONCLUSION

It is inevitable that massive stars will collapse at the end of their evolution. During the collapse stage, most of the gravitational energy released will be rapidly converted into neutrinos and dissipated from the core. A density $> 10^{14}$ gm/cm^3 will be reached at the center of massive stars during collapse.

It is not known if the remnant of such collapse will cut itself off gravitationally. If the remnants do not cut themselves off, they will be observable in the 10 Å X-ray band for around 1000 years. The present technology allows us to observe all neutron stars (≤ 1000 years old) in our Galaxy.

Since the Galaxy is transparent in the 10 Å X-ray band, "X-ray pictures" of the Galaxy may be taken with appropriate apparatus, revealing those supernova neutron star remnants which would otherwise be obscured by dust clouds.

Although there are indications from recent rocket observations that discrete X-ray sources exist which might be interpreted as neutron stars (Gursky *et al.* 1963; Friedman 1963), only future experiments will tell us if these X-ray sources are indeed neutron stars or not.

I would like to thank Drs. A. G. W. Cameron, C. W. Misner, and E. E. Salpeter for discussions and Miss Jane Keston for help in numerical integrations.

REFERENCES

Adams, B., Ruderman, M., and Woo, C. H. 1963, *Phys. Rev.*, **129**, 1383.
Chandrasekhar, S. 1951, *Introduction to Stellar Structure* (New York: Dover Publications), chap. 11.
———. 1962, *Ap. J.*, **136**, 1048.
Chandrasekhar, S., and Lebovitz, N. R. 1962a, *Ap. J.*, **136**, 1032.
———. 1962b, *ibid.*, p. 1037.
———. 1962c, *ibid.*, p. 1069.
———. 1962d, *ibid.*, p. 1082.
———. 1962e, *ibid.*, p. 1105.
Chiu, H.-Y. 1961, *Phys. Rev.*, **123**, 1040.
———. 1964, *Ann. Phys.*, **26**, 364.
Friedman, H. 1963, Paper presented at Astronomical Society Meeting, Washington, D.C., December, 1963.
Gursky, H., Giacconi, R., Paolini, F. R., and Rossi, B. 1963, *Phys. Rev. Letters*, **115**, 30.
Hoyle, F., and Fowler, W. A. 1960, *Ap. J.*, **123**, 565.
Landau, L., and Lifshitz, E. 1961, *The Classical Theory of Fields*, trans. from Russian by M. Hamermesh (Cambridge, Mass.: Addison-Wesley Publishing Co.), p. 89.
Oppenheimer, J. R., and Snyder, H. 1939, *Phys. Rev.*, **56**, 455.
Oppenheimer, J. R., and Volkoff, G. 1939, *Phys. Rev.*, **55**, 374.
Robertson, H. P. 1928, *Phil. Mag.*, **5**, 835.
Stabler, R. 1960, unpublished thesis, Cornell University.
Zel'dovich, Y. B. 1961, *Zhur. Eksp. i Teoret. Fiz.*, **41**, 1609 (trans.: *Soviet Phys. JETP*, **14**, 1143).

chapter 34 NEUTRON STARS

L. GRATTON

Concerning the equation of state for a zero-temperature neutron gas, I should like to mention that some work on this subject has been carried on in our laboratory at the University of Rome by Professor Szamosi and myself. A paper containing our results is being published in *Nuovo Cimento*.

Perhaps our most interesting result concerns the behavior of the neutron gas at very high densities ($>10^{38}$ neutrons/cm^3).

Because the De Broglie wavelengths at these densities are smaller than the radius of the hard core, we assumed that it was possible to take into account the hard-core repulsion simply by considering the equation of state of a Fermi gas with excluded volumes. Even when one considers the Lorentz contraction of the hard core, it is interesting to note that when the density goes to the limit of the reciprocal volume, the energy per particle remains finite, although, of course, the pressure goes to infinity.

L. GRATTON, Laboratorio di Astrofisica, Osservatorio Astronomico di Roma.

PART VII

SUMMARIES OF THE

TEXAS SYMPOSIUM

chapter 35 SUMMARY

Peter G. Bergmann

I shall confine my remarks to one major topic, the relevance of general relativity to a better understanding of the quasi-stellar objects that have been the topic of our conference, and the relevance of the information that is being developed concerning these objects to research in general relativity.

At the outset, let us remind ourselves that the general theory of relativity does not represent the ultimate truth, any more than does any other physical theory. As we all know, Einstein developed this theory in response to a fundamental symmetry property of nature, one that we call the principle of equivalence, or in the formal theory the principle of general covariance. There is no need here to analyze the precise logical contents of this principle; we all know that it has been subjected again to a searching critique quite recently. But even assuming that we understand the principle and its implications thoroughly, it is entirely conceivable that under extreme conditions, differing from those under which it has been put to the experimental test in the past, the principle of equivalence might be found to break down. If this should happen, the principal motivation for general relativity would evaporate. That the other experimental test results can be duplicated in theories having an entirely different conceptual basis has been shown, among others, by Belinfante in 1957. I am not trying to predict that the principle will be found to fail, I am merely pointing out that this eventuality is not inconceivable.

Even if the foundations of the theory remain valid, the mathematical difficulties besetting any attempt to interpret the theory in actual physical situations remain formidable. Only in very recent years, through the work of Bondi, Pirani, and Robinson, has the existence of plane waves within the framework of the theory been demonstrated; spherical gravitational radiation has been placed on a somewhat believable foundation, as a prediction of the theory, very recently, again on the basis of work originating with Bondi's school. There is as yet no such thing as a rigorous proof of the existence of spherical quadrupole radiation. Perhaps the most important contribution by the theory in the realm of gravitational radiation to date has been to give us a measure of confidence in the qualitative correctness of the linearized approximation, which simply states that gravitational waves propagate along light cones and have a spin 2.

Relativists are aware of the many pitfalls, of the many unsolved questions, and of the controversial nature of many of the answers offered in the literature. But we owe it to our colleagues, the astronomers and astrophysicists, to give them as unretouched a picture of the status of the theory as possible. I hope that my remarks will help them to

Peter G. Bergmann, Belfer Graduate School of Science, Yeshiva University.

431

treat theoretical "results" with a measure of skepticism before accepting them as revealed truth.

What, then, does the general theory of relativity have to offer to the astronomer? Frankly, the rate of energy production of a collapsing mass can be obtained quite reasonably by Newtonian mechanics, to which we add the special-relativistic relationship $E = mc^2$; this approach will not lead to results essentially different from those of a general-relativistic treatment, I believe, until most of the rest energy of the contracting matter has been converted to kinetic energy. According to the general theory any actual collapse, that is to say, the disappearance of matter behind an event horizon, will take an infinite time as measured by any observer who does not participate in the collapse himself. Hence, I tend to feel that the chief contribution of general relativity to an analysis of collapse of an actual object will be the quantitative rate at which collapse takes place at its penultimate stage. For such an analysis, I am afraid, our data will not be ripe for some time to come.

Qualitatively, general relativity may have some contributions to make, under extreme conditions (i.e., if collapse has advanced to the point where an appreciable fraction of the rest mass has been converted to kinetic energy), by enabling us to estimate the rate at which gravitational waves are capable of transporting energy away from the collapsing core, by reminding us that some of our Newtonian and Lorentzian concepts (such as that of a local inertial frame of reference) may be reaching the limits of their validity, and by permitting a more precise estimate of the amount of angular momentum that will prevent the collapse from becoming complete.

Perhaps I may interpolate at this point that on the basis of numerical estimates furnished by Professors Fowler and Hoyle frequencies of the gravitational waves emitted by rapidly revolving multiple cores, of the order of the inverse periods of revolution, apparently will be at most 10^{-4} sec^{-1}. The design of detecting equipment sensitive at these frequencies will not be a trivial matter. But once this estimate has been validated by careful analysis of reasonable models, the designer at least will have a target to shoot for.

Conversely, what does the relativist expect to get out of collapsing quasi-stars? At this stage I think he can reasonably hope for two things. If it really turns out that some of these objects approach the stage at which weak-field approximations lose their credibility, he can hope that parallel analyses of the data and of the theory will furnish him with an area in which the theory of general relativity can be tested against other model theories of the gravitational field. The other is that conditions may be found to exist under which gravitational waves, as distinct from electromagnetic and other waves, can be detected with cleverly designed equipment.

Both of these hopes, I think, point into the rather distant future; it is not probable that either kind of test can be performed in, say, the next five years. Nevertheless, the relativist has not in the past been spoiled by an overabundance of critical tests of his theory, and he will watch with great enthusiasm the story that is now unfolding. I think I have made it clear why I am not very optimistic that right now we relativists can make any major contribution to the astronomers who are attempting to unravel the data that they are obtaining with such great ingenuity; I should be extremely pleased if my skepticism should turn out to be unwarranted. Certainly we cannot complain that our colleagues in astronomy and astrophysics have bored us these past three days.

chapter 36 SUMMARY

R. Minkowski

First, a comment on radio positions seems appropriate. A positional accuracy of the order of $\pm 10''$ or higher in both right ascension and declination has been achieved with interferometers. Lunar occultations, whose use has been pioneered by Hazard, lead to positions with errors of $\pm 1''$ and permit, as Scheuer has shown, the investigation of detail of about $0.3''$. The validity of identifications, even with objects of stellar appearance, thus is no longer a matter of concern.

The over-all picture presented by Matthews shows a clear-cut difference between strong and weak sources, with a total power near 10^{40} erg/sec as the dividing point.

"Normal" spirals and irregular galaxies are weak sources. The Seyfert galaxy NGC 1068 is a source close to the dividing point and thus a somewhat more powerful source than most spirals; no other Seyfert galaxy has been found to be a source of observable strength. The bulk of "normal" spheroidal galaxies is unobserved as sources; they seem to be less powerful sources than spirals.

The great majority of strong sources—the "radio galaxies"—with powers in the range from 10^{40} to 10^{45} erg/sec are spheroidal without easily recognizable peculiar appearance. About 90 per cent of the radio galaxies are in this group. No highly flattened galaxy has been found among the radio galaxies. A large fraction are in clusters, 50 per cent in rich clusters with more than fifty members within a range of 2 mag. below the brightest galaxy. The radio galaxy tends to be the brightest galaxy in the cluster. About 10 per cent of the radio galaxies are peculiar objects. These are the—mostly well known—objects shown by E. M. Burbidge. Some of the peculiarities—e.g., weak or narrow absorption features—are not very conspicuous, and could well be found in galaxies that are not radio sources if they were subjected to the same painstaking investigation as the radio galaxies.

A high percentage of the radio galaxies shows emission lines. Only about 25 per cent of fifty-three observed objects do not show any emission lines, 25 per cent show [O II] λ 3727, and 50 per cent show other lines in addition. Spheroidal galaxies in general, and in particular those in rich clusters of galaxies, show emission lines much less frequently, and very rarely more lines than λ 3727. The question is not settled of whether the presence or absence of emission lines is determined by differences of gas content or of physical conditions responsible for the excitation. In all those spheroidal galaxies that show dust features, the presence of gas seems probable. Since mass loss of evolving stars must have furnished gas, it seems likely that all spheroidal galaxies contain gas, but the total amount of gas is still open to conjecture.

R. Minkowski, University of California, Berkeley.

A large fraction, more than 75 per cent of the sources, are double or multiple; some of the single sources show a core surrounded by a halo. The separation of the components and the diameters of the halos reach values of 250000 pc and more. It seems that the formation of a double source is going on in M82, an irregular galaxy in which gas streams out from the ends of the minor axis with a velocity of about 1000 km/sec relative to the center of the galaxy.

The quasi-stellar sources, the main concern of this volume, do not seem to be rare. Among the twenty-five strongest extragalactic sources in the 3C catalogue are four, or 16 per cent, quasi-stellar sources. It seems necessary to point out that not the small angular diameter of the source but the presence of a starlike object is the characteristic feature, and that only optical observations can decide which of the small sources, for instance those reported here by Hazard, actually are in this class.

How the quasi-stellar sources fit in the picture depends largely on their distances. The interpretation of their spectra, by Schmidt for 3C 273 and by Greenstein and Matthews for 3C 48, as showing large redshifts is beyond reasonable doubt. The question to be answered is that of the nature of the redshift, of whether it is gravitational or cosmological.

If the redshift is cosmological, one would expect these objects to be contained in galaxies. The absolute brightness of the stellar objects, for 3C 48 $M_v = -24.3$ with $z = 0.37$ and for 3C 273 $M_v = -25.6$ with $z = 0.16$, is so much higher than that of even the brightest galaxies with $M_v = -22$ that it must be exceedingly difficult to see the image of the galaxy which contains the overexposed, photographically spread image of the stellar object.

Three arguments favor the interpretation that the objects are distant and that the redshift is cosmological.

The presence in 3C 273 of the 21-cm line of hydrogen in absorption with a strength quite similar to that in neighboring sources known to be extragalactic and the presence of interstellar absorption lines of Ca II were reported by Williams. The object must be outside of the layer of dust that is close to the galactic plane, at a distance from the Sun that is larger than about 200 pc.

The proper motion of 3C 273 was found too small to be observable by Jefferys. The accuracy of the result, not the result itself, has been questioned by Luyten. Proper motion without knowledge of the transverse velocity does not permit a distance determination of an individual object. Any reasonable assumption on the transverse velocity puts the object at a considerable distance, near the border or outside of the Galaxy.

Considerations of the upper limit to the gas density set by the presence of forbidden lines and of a limit to gravitational perturbations on the solar system and on the Galaxy lead, as Schmidt has shown in discussions, to the conclusion that the quasi-stellar objects cannot be a collapsed body of low mass at a small distance, but must in any case be extragalactic.

If, then, the interpretation of the redshift as cosmological is accepted, the quasi-stellar objects are at large distances. The small angular diameters of the sources connected with these objects now correspond to linear sizes well in the range found for the radio galaxies. The source, with the smallest angular diameter, 3C 48, is still unresolved and only an upper limit of 2500 pc can be stated for the size. The two components of 3C 273 are separated by 20000 pc, although their individual size is much smaller, and 3C 47 with a source diameter near 300000 pc ranges with the largest sources known.

The light variations found by H. Smith pose interesting problems. The light-travel time across the emitting region cannot be much larger than the time scale of the variations. The slow fluctuations of intensities would be consistent with diameters of the order of 1 pc. There may be some doubt as to the reality of some of the rapid changes, but distinct variations in a time of the order of a week seem well established. It seems necessary to think of small structural details of the order of 0.01 pc.

The only information on the size of the object refers to the H II region in which the emission lines originate. With the aid of standard methods for the analysis of emission spectra, Greenstein and Schmidt find the following data for the electron density N_e, the mass $\mathfrak{M}/\mathfrak{M}_\odot$ and the radius r of the H II region:

Object	$N_e(\text{cm}^{-3})$	$\mathfrak{M}/\mathfrak{M}_\odot$	r (pc)
3C 48..........	$\leq 3\times10^4$	$\leq 5\times10^6$	≤ 10
3C 273.........	3×10^6	6×10^5	1

The size of the H II region in 3C 273 is not inconsistent with the observed slow light variations. As to the fast variations, it must be noted that the analysis is carried out with the assumption that the gas is homogeneous; the existence of much smaller condensations is not excluded; if they are present, the analysis has to be modified. Part of the light in the continuous spectrum may not be from the H II region, particularly if optical synchrotron radiation is involved. At this moment, the problem of the size and structure of the optical object is still open, but it does not seem necessary to believe that the interpretation of the time scale of the light variations involves fundamental problems.

The most important problem raised by the quasi-stellar objects is the enormous energy contained in the emission lines. As sources, these objects have total powers up to 10^{45} erg/sec, near, but not above, the largest powers emitted by radio galaxies. Their energy content, computed from equipartition synchrotron models, is not beyond the maximum at 10^{60} erg found for radio galaxies. To the unsolved problem of understanding these energies is now added the problem of understanding how luminosities in the Hβ line of 10^{44} erg/sec, almost equal to the total luminosity of an average galaxy, are generated in a gas mass which is equal to about 10^{-5} times the total mass of an average galaxy, and is contained in a volume of the size shown by galactic nuclei.

chapter 37 SUMMARY

P. Morrison

There is little doubt that the most striking feature of the events we discussed here is the over-all energy scale they attain. Improved knowledge of this point is fundamental to a physical understanding. It has been impressive to see how classical astronomical methods, such as proper motion, have been invoked to give strength to the more modern but less secure redshift determinations of distance. It seems to me that the distance measures must be accepted as at least roughly correct.

From the distance measures and received radio-optical fluxes, minimum luminosities of course follow. Lifetimes are more uncertain, and stored energy in fields and particles is still more uncertain. Balancing these uncertainties against the probabilities that many more frequencies are emitted with considerable power than those we happen to be able to see, it remains difficult to believe that the biggest events can have released energy less than that contained in 10^6 or even 10^8 solar rest masses, or 10^{60} to 10^{62} erg. Every effort to test this guess is, of course, to be applauded.

The push of this energy number against the total *nuclear* energy of a large galaxy mass of hydrogen is not decisive, but it strongly favors the general look of a gravitational event. Matthews, Morgan, and Schmidt, Hazard, and the Burbidges have given an over-all picture of a large and varied class of such events, always associated with highly excited and fast-moving gas in the centers of galaxies, by no means uncommon, and spread along an energy scale which culminates in events like 3C 273. It seems hard to doubt that the Seyfert phenomenon, M82, M87, and the strong radio galaxies like Cyg A are related to the quasi-stars. (In June, 1964, it appears possible that the Scorpio X-ray source might mark a similar event in our own Galaxy.)

The relativists have excited us with their discussion of collapse of a large mass into its Schwarzschild radius, and some participants, notably Hoyle and Wheeler, have been bold enough to speculate on completely new physics at the basis of these events. I remain interested but unpersuaded. The key point at which relativity enters is that where gravitational potential energies approach rest mass. But here a remark may be worth making. The differences between a naïve use of relativity and a deep one is not great if the potential remains, say, a half or a third of the rest energy. But then the experimental difference would be small compared to the uncertainties to be expected from quite other reasons. The one key point seems to be to take into account, in addition to merely Newtonian mechanics and gravity theory, the evident fact that the gravitational field energy of any assemblage itself contributes gravitational mass according to $E = Mc^2$—

P. Morrison, Department of Physics, Cornell University.

to be sure, the contribution is always negative. Thus the total energy of a uniform sphere assembled out of a diffuse rest mass M_0 is *not*

$$M c^2 = M_0 c^2 - \tfrac{3}{5}G \left(\frac{4\pi\rho}{3}\right)^{1/3} M_0^{5/3}$$

but

$$M c^2 \left[1 + \tfrac{3}{5}\frac{G}{c^2}\left(\frac{4\pi\rho}{3}\right)^{1/3} M^{2/3}\right] = M_0 c^2.$$

Then no paradoxes of energy remain. (Arnowitt, Deser, and Misner have justified this naïve approach in *Phys. Rev.*, **120** [1960], 313.) It still remains to be seen how relevant to these events is any fundamentally new physics. (In June, 1964, it appears plausible that a long-continued, sporadic asymmetrical draining of galactic gas clouds down an initially non-relativistic gravitational potential well, nucleated by some large but relatively non-explosive mass condensation such as a central cluster, might eventually explain the phenomena. The gravitational energy is converted to kinetic, and then to radiant and explosive form, by collision, shock, and magnetic compression. The nucleus might grow catastrophically under the right conditions.)

It is of great importance to find out what else is in these objects. Is there a full-grown galaxy unseen in the bright central light? Is there a growing one? Are there cosmic-ray protons as well as synchrotron electrons? What is the output in X- and gamma-rays? What is the geometry of the sources in all sorts of "light"? Do we see the full volume? Are there non-magnetic electron halos?

We are at the beginning of the study of these objects, a study which appears to me unmatched in excitement and importance in astronomy since the first exploitation of the radio channel itself. Once we have understood their physics, we can ask how these objects bear on the problems of cosmology, which managed somehow to rise in ignorance of such grand events.

APPENDICES

FURTHER

CONTRIBUTIONS

REPRINTS FROM

appendix i   *NATURE*

NATURE OF STRONG RADIO SOURCES

F. HOYLE AND WILLIAM A. FOWLER

IN a recent paper[1] we have considered the possibility that masses of gas, $10^5 \, M_\odot$ to $10^8 \, M_\odot$, may accumulate at the centres of galaxies, and may behave as stars. The existence of such objects is supported theoretically by the energy requirements of strong radio galaxies, $\sim 10^{60}$ ergs or more[2,3], which seem to demand large aggregations which either draw on, nuclear energy or on the very considerable gravitational energy that can arise in a massive body of stellar dimensions. The reason why gravitation can play a decisive part in the evolution of a very massive body is that the gravitational energy depends on $|\Omega| = GM^2/R$, where G is the gravitational constant, M the mass, and R a characteristic dimension. Since gravitational energy depends on the square of the mass, it can be of decisive importance for bodies in the range $10^5 \, M_\odot$–$10^8 \, M_\odot$, whereas it is in general unimportant in ordinary stars.

The view that such objects can exist is supported observationally by the Seyfert galaxies[4], which possess nuclei having dimensions of ~ 100 parsec containing gas in violent dynamical motion with velocities from $\sim 1{,}000$ km sec^{-1} to $\sim 5{,}000$ km sec^{-1}, the total dynamical energy of the gas being of order 10^{56} ergs. The energy in emission lines amounts to $\sim 10^{43}$ ergs sec^{-1}, corresponding to an astronomical magnitude of about -19. In ref. 1 our

F. HOYLE and WILLIAM A. FOWLER, California Institute of Technology.

Reprinted from *Nature*, **197**, 533–535, March 16, 1963.

consideration of the hydrogen-burning phase for a star of mass $\sim 10^5$ $M_\odot$ showed that the magnitude is in the region of -18. Moreover, the total energy output from the whole hydrogen-burning phase is $\sim 10^{57}$ ergs, which is of the order observed in the Seyfert galaxies.

We may add that although Seyfert galaxies appear at first sight to be uncommon objects, comprising perhaps 1 per cent of all major galaxies, their very short lifetimes, as galaxies with nuclei in eruption, imply that their number taken over a cosmological lifetime of $\sim 10^{10}$ years is high. To explain the observed frequency of Seyfert galaxies it is necessary that the average major galaxy (mass $> \sim 5 \times 10^{10}$ $M_\odot$) shall undergo an outburst 10–100 times during its lifetime.

Two or three of the Seyfert galaxies are radio sources of intensities intermediate between normal galaxies and the strong sources. Our suggestion is not therefore that the observed activity explains the strong sources, but rather that the observed activity in Seyfert galaxies is a weak example of the process that gives rise to the strong sources—explicitly that masses of $\sim 10^8$ $M_\odot$ are involved in the strong sources rather than 10^5–10^6 $M_\odot$.

In our former paper[1] we considered evolution beyond helium burning, up to temperatures of $T_9 = 1$ or 2 (T_9 is in units of 10^9 K). We were concerned with comparing the loss of energy due to neutrino emission and the energy released by the burning of oxygen-16. Our aim was to show that the latter was greater than the former, and that an explosion could ensue from catastrophic oxygen burning, in analogy to what we have found[5] for stars with masses of ~ 30 $M_\odot$. Our conclusion was that such explosions could occur, and we termed them super-supernovæ. However, it has appeared on further investigation that this conclusion, in the form in which we stated it, was erroneous. The energy required for the creation of electron-positron pairs, which we had found at $M \simeq 30$ $M_\odot$ to be less than the yield of energy from burning oxygen, turns out to play a dominant part at very large masses. It entirely overwhelms any form of nuclear energy generation, which therefore cannot lead to an explosive outburst of a really massive star. This is not to say that very massive stars cannot undergo violent disruption, but that the cause of disruption does not lie in a sudden nuclear energy generation at $T_9 \simeq 2$, as it probably does in ordinary supernovæ.

During burning of hydrogen and helium the star is entirely convective (it being assumed that convection is not inhibited by a magnetic field). During these phases the ratio β of gas pressure to total pressure is $\ll 1$, and the density is proportional to $M^{-1/2}T^3$, both for a particular element of material as the star evolves, and also from one element to another at any moment. The radius R of the star is proportional to $M^{1/2}$ and to the reciprocal of the central temperature T_c; in fact:

$$R \simeq \frac{5 \cdot 8 \times 10^9}{(T_9)_c} \left(\frac{M}{M_\odot} \right)^{1/2} \text{cm} \qquad (1)$$

where $(T'_9)_c$ is in units of 10^9 deg K. During burning of hydrogen $(T_9)_c \simeq 0 \cdot 07$, so that $R \simeq 8 \times 10^{10} (M/M_\odot)^{1/2}$ cm. The radius is about seven times smaller than this during burning of helium when $(T_9)_c \simeq 0 \cdot 5$.

After burning of helium to oxygen-16, which lasts for $\sim 10^4$ years or less, the central temperature rises. As $(T_9)_c$ approaches unity, neutrino losses shorten the evolution time to about a day. This, however, is the main physical effect of the neutrino losses, since pair creation then dominates energy considerations. With pair creation dominant we have the following formulæ, deduced on the basis that the star is still in approximate hydrostatic equilibrium as a polytrope of index $n = 3$:

$$\beta \simeq \frac{180}{\pi^4} \bar{K}_2 \left(1 + \frac{180}{\pi^4} \bar{K}_2 \right)^{-1} \qquad (2)$$

$$\mu \simeq \left(\frac{180}{\pi^2} \right)^{1/2} \left(\frac{M_\odot}{M} \right)^{1/2} \left(1 + \frac{180}{\pi^4} \bar{K}_2 \right)^{3/4} \left(\frac{180}{\pi^4} \bar{K}_2 \right)^{-1} \qquad (3)$$

$$\mu\beta \simeq \left(\frac{180}{\pi^2} \right)^{1/2} \left(\frac{M_\odot}{M} \right)^{1/2} \left(1 + \frac{180}{\pi^4} \bar{K}_2 \right)^{-1/4} \qquad (4)$$

$$\rho \simeq 1 \cdot 30 \times 10^5 \left(1 + \frac{180}{\pi^4} \bar{K}_2 \right)^{3/4} \left(\frac{M_\odot}{M} \right)^{1/2} T_9^3 \text{ g cm}^{-3} \qquad (5)$$

and equation (1) becomes:

$$R \simeq \frac{5 \cdot 8 \times 10^9}{(T_9)_c} \left(\frac{M}{M_\odot} \right)^{1/2} \left(1 + \frac{180}{\pi^4} \bar{K}_2 \right)_c^{-1/4} \qquad (1')$$

Here ρ = density, β = ratio of gas pressure to total pressure, μ = mean molecular weight, $\theta = m_e c^2 / kT$ and $\bar{K}_2(\theta) = \frac{1}{2}\theta^2 K_2(\theta)$, K_2 being the modified Hankel function of order two. Note that $\bar{K}_2(\theta)$ is normalized to unity as $\theta \to 0$, $T \to \infty$. At low temperatures $\bar{K}_2(\theta)$ approaches zero. In equation (1'), c designates centre. The foregoing expressions have been derived on the assumption that the electron–proton pairs are much more numerous than the electrons associated with nuclei but are still strictly non-degenerate. More accurate expressions for pairs dominant but not necessarily non-degenerate can be derived on the assumption that the chemical potential is zero for electrons and positrons in which case $\overline{K}_2(\theta)$ is replaced by various series expansions involving $\overline{K}_2(n\theta)$, $n = 1, 2, 3, \ldots$. At $T_9 \sim 1$ the foregoing expressions are sufficiently accurate for $M/M_\odot \gtrsim 5,000$ and at $T_9 \sim 2$ for $M/M_\odot \gtrsim 100$. The expression for β is independent of the assumption that the star is a polytrope of index $n = 3$. The numerical coefficients in the remaining expressions are not too sensitive to this assumption.

As T_9 approaches 2 the energy necessary for pair creation must be supplied by gravitation—it cannot be supplied by oxygen burning, as it is in stars with $M \simeq 30\ M_\odot$. This leads to a departure from hydrostatic equilibrium and the above formula relating ρ and T is no longer valid, the density rises without the temperature keeping step.

In this connexion we have derived the following curious result. For a normal star all equilibrium states possess negative total energy, that is, less energy than a dispersed state at infinity. But in the case of very massive stars, with T_9 high enough for pairs to play a critical part, the equilibrium state has positive total energy. We find the excess of energy, Q, compared with the dispersed state, is:

$$Q = \tfrac{1}{3}\ |\Omega|\ <\ \beta \mathrm{dln}\overline{K}_2/\mathrm{dln}T > \qquad (6)$$

where again $|\Omega|$ is the absolute magnitude of the total gravitational energy of the star. The average must be taken throughout the star. But, since β and $\mathrm{dln}\overline{K}_2/\mathrm{dln}T$ are everywhere positive, the average is positive. In deriving this result we included the rest mass of the pairs. If this had not been included we should have obtained a negative value, as in the normal case. However, since pairs annihilate on dispersal our procedure would seem to be correct. At $M = 10^8\ M_\odot$ the rest mass of the pairs is comparable with that of the original nuclei when high temperatures are reached.

It is emphasized that hydrostatic equilibrium was assumed in obtaining the above result. An actual star need not be in hydrostatic equilibrium—indeed, the obtaining of a positive value demands that an actual star cannot be in equilibrium once pairs dominate over the electrons that were originally present. For the total energy cannot become positive, except possibly in the case of an explosive release of nuclear energy—and for very massive stars this is not the case. Hence an actual star implodes.

Lack of mechanical equilibrium implies that dynamical velocities are generated. For the masses under consideration, these velocities are not greatly below the speed of light. Thus, the velocities are of the order of, but less than, $(GM/R)^{1/2}$. Using the equation (1') for R:

$$\frac{GM}{R} \simeq 2{\cdot}3 \times 10^{16} \left(\frac{M}{M_\odot}\right)^{1/2}\left[T_9\left(1 + \frac{180}{\pi^4}\ \overline{K}_2\right)^{1/4}\right]_c \qquad (7)$$

For $M/M_\odot = 10^6$, $(T_9)_c = 2$, $\theta \simeq 3$, $\overline{K}_2 \simeq 0\cdot28$, $(GM/R)^{1/2}$ $\simeq 7 \times 10^9$ cm sec^{-1}, while for $M/M_\odot = 10^8$ the velocity of light is approached closely.

Two possibilities now arise. First, an idealized case of spherically symmetric implosion to the relativity limit $2|\Omega| \to Mc^2$. As this limit is approached general relativity must be used, and the effect of radiation on the gravitational field must be considered.

A more likely practical situation is one in which the star is rotating or does not possess strict symmetry and in which portions of the star break away from a central mass. The simplest case is one in which two pieces break away, moving in opposite directions, leaving a central mass that ultimately condenses to the relativity limit. Such a central mass must always be present, since energy considerations demand that the energy of the dynamically ejected portions be compensated by the gravitational binding of the remaining mass.

We see that masses perhaps of order 10^7 $M_\odot$ can in this way be ejected at speeds comparable to c. The dynamical energy is less than, but comparable to c^2, say $\sim 10^{20}$ ergs g^{-1}. For $M = 10^7$ $M_\odot$ this implies an outburst of $\sim 10^{60}$ ergs. This we regard as the energy of outburst of a strong radio source. Our point of view is that the energies demanded by the strong sources are so enormous as to make it clear that the relativity limit must be involved. Normal dynamical motions within a galaxy give kinetic energies of no more than 10^{16} ergs g^{-1}, and this falls far short of the radio source requirement on any reasonable basis for the total mass involved. Even nuclear energy, yielding 6×10^{18} ergs g^{-1} in the case of hydrogen burning[6], requires an outburst involving 10^8 $M_\odot$. While this mass is not impossibly high, hydrogen burning is not an explosive process, as has formerly been pointed out[7]. The light elements, carbon and oxygen, are the best materials for providing a sudden outburst, but these materials yield only 5×10^{17} ergs g^{-1}, and the necessary mass is then increased to $\sim 10^9$ $M_\odot$. The situation is made worse by the circumstance that upwards of 10^{60} ergs is very likely required for the most powerful radio sources. On any reasonable basis as to the efficiency of production of radio waves, the energy required lies at maximum in the range 10^{61}–10^{62} ergs, and this seems too much to attribute to the burning of the light elements. Our present opinion is that only through the contraction of a mass of 10^7–10^8 $M_\odot$ to the relativity limit can the energies of the strongest sources be obtained.

Finally, the materials ejected have an important bearing on nucleosynthesis, particularly in their relation to what we have called the r-process[6]. There is strong evidence that the r-process nuclei were built from seed nuclei immersed in a sea of neutrons: to build the heaviest nuclei at least 200 neutrons per seed nucleus are needed. The temperature must have been about 10^9 deg. K, as was shown by Burbidge, Burbidge, Fowler and Hoyle[6]. At this temperature, light nuclei, magnesium in particular, are strong neutron absorbers, and hence there cannot have been large numbers of light nuclei present (as there can be in the case of the s-process, which operates at lower temperature). This led us to propose[7] that the r-process arises from a mixture of neutrons and α-particles, a mixture given by a phase change break-up of iron-group nuclei, the phase change occurring at $T_9 \simeq 5$. Such material on being ejected from a star cools due to adiabatic expansion, and as it does so the tendency is to rebuild heavy nuclei. However, the first step of the rebuilding process 3 helium-4 $\rightarrow$ carbon-12 is slow. We pointed out that for sufficiently low density only a very small fraction of the helium is able to build to carbon-12, and this small fraction we took as our seed nuclei. But we were not really able to keep the density low enough for the case $M \simeq 30\, M_\odot$, which we then considered. We wish now to point out that at much larger masses the density is significantly lower (see equation 5) and the process works without difficulty.

A further satisfactory feature is that a difficulty concerning the absolute amount of r-process material is also resolved. So long as we took supernovæ occurring at a frequency of 1 per 300 years as the seat of origin of the r-process, the amount was grossly too large, at least by two orders of magnitude[8]. We now estimate that the amount of r-process material produced per outburst is $\sim 10^2\, M_\odot$, approximately independent of M. With about 100 such occurrences in the lifetime of the Galaxy, the total production $\sim 10^4\, M_\odot$, in good agreement with the observed absolute abundances.

Our previous estimates of the age of the Galaxy are changed by these considerations. On the basis of the observed abundances of thorium-232, uranium-235 and uranium-238 in solar system material and the calculated production rates in r-process events, we showed[8] that nucleosynthesis occurred over an interval 7 to 8 $\times$ 10^9 years in duration prior to the formation of the Solar System 4 to 5 $\times$ 10^9 years ago. This sets a low limit on the age of the Galaxy equal to 12 $\times$ 10^9 years with an uncertainty of the order of 2–3 $\times$ 10^9 years. We placed the r-process in stars with masses just above 1·5 $M_\odot$ for which the evolution time is $\sim$ 3 $\times$ 10^9 years and thus arrived at a galactic age $\sim$ 15 $\times$ 10^9 years. In a later paper Fowler[9] placed the r-process in stars of somewhat lower mass and arrived at an age $\sim$ 20 $\times$ 10^9 years. For the reasons advanced in this work we now assign the r-process primarily to very massive stars with very short lifetimes which lie in the centre of the Galaxy and hence believe that the best present estimate for the age of the Galaxy, or more specifically the galactic nucleus, is:

$$t_{GN} = 12^{+3}_{-2} \times 10^9 \text{ years}$$

Small stars which formed early in the history of the Galaxy and which still exist because of long evolutionary lifetimes will contain heavy elements previously produced in the rapidly evolving very massive stars. The abundance distribution among the heavy elements and their isotopes in these old stars will differ considerably from that in young stars. Elements and isotopes produced in the r-process will be relatively over-abundant compared with those produced in the s-process[10,11]. The e-process elements near iron will be peculiar in that a short time scale e-process leads to abnormal ratios of chromium, manganese, iron, cobalt and nickel and especially among the isotopes of these elements. Comparisons of old-star spectra and young-star spectra should prove to be most significant in this respect.

This work was supported in part by the Joint Program of the Office of Naval Research and the U.S. Atomic Energy Commission, and in part by the National Aeronatics and Space Administration.

[1] Hoyle, F., and Fowler, W. A., *Mon. Not. Roy. Astro. Soc.*, **125**, No. 2 (January 1963).

[2] Burbidge, G. R., *Paris Symp. Radio Astronomy*, 1958, edit. by Bracewell, R. W. (Stanford Univ. Press, 1959).

[3] Maltby, P., Matthews, T. A., and Moffet, A. T., *Astrophys. J.* (in the press).

[4] Seyfert, C. K., *Astrophys. J.*, **97**, 28 (1943).

[5] Fowler, W. A., and Hoyle, F. (in preparation).

[6] Burbidge, G. R., Burbidge, E. M., Fowler, W. A., and Hoyle, F., *Rev. Mod. Phys.*, **29**, 547 (1957).

[7] Hoyle, F., and Fowler, W. A., *Astrophys. J.*, **132**, 565 (1960).

[8] Fowler, W. A., and Hoyle, F., *Ann. Phys.*, **10**, 280 (1960).

[9] Fowler, W. A., *Proc. Rutherford Jubilee Intern. Conf.*, edit. by Birks. J. B. (Heywood and Co., Ltd., London, 1961).

[10] Clayton, D. D., Fowler, W. A., Hull, T. S., and Zimmerman, B. A., *Ann. Phys.*, **12**, 331 (1961).

[11] Clayton, D. D., and Fowler, W. A., *Ann. Phys.*, **16**, 51 (1961).

INVESTIGATION OF THE RADIO SOURCE 3C 273 BY
THE METHOD OF LUNAR OCCULTATION

C. HAZARD, M. B. MACKEY, AND A. J. SHIMMINS

THE observation of lunar occultations provides the most accurate method of determining the positions of the localized radio sources, being capable of yielding a positional accuracy of the order of 1 sec of arc. It has been shown by Hazard[1] that the observations also provide diameter information down to a limit of the same order. For the sources of small angular size the diameter information is obtained from the observed diffraction effects at the Moon's limb which may be considered to act as a straight diffracting edge.

The method has so far been applied only to a study of the radio source 3C 212 the position of which was determined to an accuracy of about 3 sec of arc[1,2]. However, 3C 212 is a source of comparatively small flux density and although the diffraction effects at the Moon's limb were clearly visible the signal-to-noise ratio was inadequate to study the pattern in detail and hence to realize the full potentialities of the method. Here we describe the observation of a series of occultations of the intense radio source 3C 273 in which detailed diffraction effects have been recorded for the first time permitting the position to be determined to an accuracy of better than 1″ and enabling a detailed examination to be made of the brightness distribution across the source.

The observations were carried out using the 210-ft. steerable telescope at Parkes, the method of observation being to direct the telescope to the position of the source and then to record the received power with the telescope in automatic motion following the source. Three occultations of the source have been observed, on April 15, at 410 Mc/s, on August 5 at 136 Mc/s and 410 Mc/s, and on October 26 at 410 Mc/s and 1,420 Mc/s, although in October and April only the immersion and emersion respectively were visible using the Parkes instrument. The 410 Mc/s receiver was a double-sided band receiver, the two channels, each of width 10 Mc/s, being centred on 400 Mc/s and 420 Mc/s, while the 136 Mc/s and 1,420 Mc/s receivers each had a single pass band 1·5 Mc/s and 10 Mc/s wide respectively.

The record of April 15, although of interest as it represents the first observation of detailed diffraction fringes

C. HAZARD, M. B. MACKEY, and A. J. SHIMMINS, C.S.I.R.O. Division of Radiophysics, University Grounds, Sydney.

Reprinted from *Nature*, **197**, 1037–1039, March 16, 1963.

during a lunar occultation, is disturbed by a gradient in the received power and is not suitable for accurate position and diameter measurements. Therefore, attention will be confined to the occultation curves recorded in August and October and which are reproduced in Fig. 1. It is immediately obvious from these records that 3C 273 is a double source orientated in such a way that whereas the two components passed successively behind the Moon at both immersions, they reappeared almost simultaneously. The prominent diffraction fringes show that the angular sizes of these components must be considerably smaller than 10″, which is the order of size of a Fresnel zone at the Moon's limb.

The most interesting feature of Figs. 1(e) and 1(f) is the change in the ratio of the flux densities of the two components with frequency. The ratio of the flux density of the south preceding source (component A) to that of the north following source (component B) is 1 : 0·45 at 410 Mc/s and 1 : 1·4 at 1,420 Mc/s, indicating a striking difference in the spectra of the two components. If it be assumed that the flux densities[3] of 3C 273 at 410 Mc/s and 1,420 Mc/s are 60 and 35 Wm^{-2} (c/s)$^{-1}$ and that over this frequency-range the spectrum of each component may be represented by $S \alpha f^n$, then the above ratios correspond to spectral indices for components A and B of $-0·9$ and $0·0$ respectively. The spectral index of A is a representative value for a Class II radio source; but the flat spectrum of B is most unusual, no measurements of a comparable spectrum having yet been published. If the spectral indices were assumed constant down to 136 Mc/s then at this frequency component A must contribute almost 90 per cent of the total emission, a conclusion which is confirmed by a comparison of the times of immersion at 136 Mc/s and 410 Mc/s on August 5.

It has been shown by Scheuer[4] that it is possible to recover the true brightness distribution across the source from the observed diffraction pattern, the resolution being subject only to limitations imposed by the receiver bandwidth and the finite signal to noise ratio and being independent of the angular scale of the diffraction pattern. However, in this preliminary investigation we have not attempted such a detailed investigation but based the analysis on the calculated curves for uniform strip sources of different widths as published by Hazard[1]. As a first step in the investigation approximate diameters were estimated from the intensity of the first diffraction lobe and the results corresponding to the three position angles defined by the occultations and indicated in Fig. 2 are given in Table 1.

As already indicated here, the 136-Mc/s measurements refer only to component A and hence no diameter measurements are available for B at this frequency. The 410-Mc/s

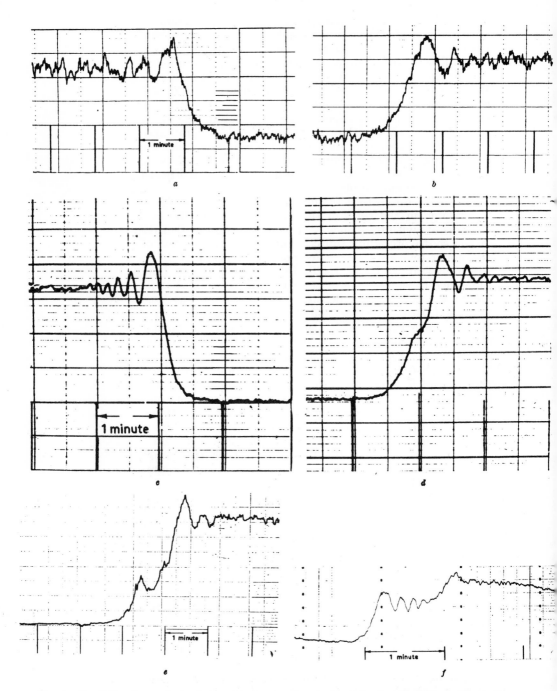

Fig. 1.—Facsimiles of records showing occultations on August 5 and October 26, 1962, at different frequencies. (a) Emersion of August 5, 1962, at 136 Mc/s; (b) immersion of August 5, 1962, at 136 Mc/s; (c) emersion of August 5, 1962, at 410 Mc/s; (d) immersion of August 5, 1962, at 410 Mc/s; (e) immersion of October 26, 1962, at 410 Mc/s; (f) immersion of October 26, 1962, at 1420 Mc/s. Abscissae, U.T.; ordinates, flux density.

Table 1. EFFECTIVE WIDTH OF EQUIVALENT STRIP SOURCE
(Sec. of arc)

Frequency Mc/s	Component A Position angle			Component B Position angle		
	106°	313°	84°	105°	314°	83°
136	6·4	6·4	—	—	—	—
410	3·1	4·2† 2 (6)*	4·2	3·1	3·0†	2·7
1,420	—	—	2·9	—	—	2·1 0·5 (7)*

* Estimated from an analysis of the whole diffraction pattern.
† Component B assumed to have width of 3″.

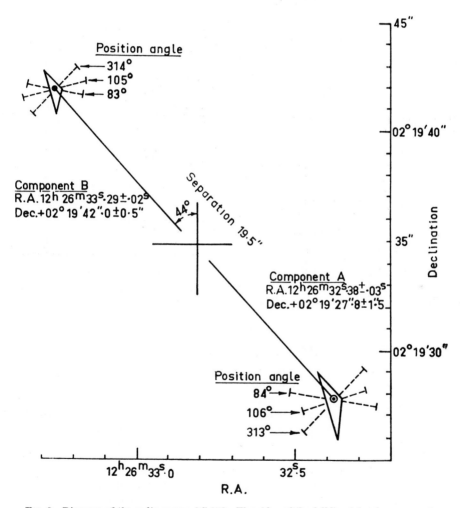

FIG. 2.—Diagram of the radio source 3C 273. The sides of the full line triangles represent the positions of the limb of the Moon at the times of occultation. The broken lines represent the widths of the equivalent strip source as measured at 410 Mc/s for each of three position angles indicated.

observations of the August occultation are the most difficult to interpret owing to the components having both comparable flux density and small separation relative to the angular size of the first Fresnel zone. At immersion the widths were estimated by using a process of curve fitting to reproduce Fig. 1(*d*); at emersion (position angle 313°) the diameter of component *B* was assumed to be 3″ as indicated by the estimates at position angles 105° and 83°. The individual measurements at each frequency are reasonably consistent but there is a striking variation of the angular size of component *A* with frequency and evidence of a similar variation for component *B*. As at the time of the August occultation the angular separation of the Sun and the source was about 50° and hence coronal scattering of the type observed by Slee[5] at 85 Mc/s is not likely to be significant, this variation in size suggests that the model of two uniform strip sources is inadequate.

Therefore, a more detailed analysis was made of the intensity distributions of the lobe patterns given in Figs. 1(*c*) and 1(*f*), and it was found that in neither case can the pattern be fitted to that for a uniform strip source or a source with a gaussian brightness distribution. The 1,420-Mc/s observations of component *B* can be explained, however, by assuming that this source consists of a central bright core about 0·5″ wide contributing about 80 per cent of the total flux embedded in a halo of equivalent width of about 7″. Fig. 1(*b*), where component *A* predominates, suggests that this source has a similar structure but with a core of effective width about 2″ at 410 Mc/s and a halo of width 6″. It therefore seems that the overall extent of both components are comparable but that the emission is more highly concentrated to the nucleus in *B* than in *A*. The close agreement between the halo size of *A* and its effective diameter at 136 Mc/s suggests that the observed variation of effective size with frequency may be due to a difference in the spectra of the halo and central regions. This would imply that the spectrum becomes steeper in the outer regions of the sources, that is, in the regions of lower emissivity. It is of interest that the integrated spectral indices of the two components show an analogous effect. Thus the spectrum of *B*, where most of the emission arises in a source about 0·5″ wide, is markedly flatter than that of *A*, where it arises in a source about 2″ wide.

The analysis is not sufficiently accurate to reach any reliable conclusions on the ellipticity of the individual components of 3*C* 273, but allowing for the uncertainty in the estimated widths and position angle 314°, the 410-Mc/s observations indicate that both components may be elliptical with *A* elongated approximately along the axis joining the two components and *B* elongated perpendicular to this axis.

The position of each source was calculated from the observed times of disappearance and reappearance, which were estimated from the calculated flux density at the edge of the geometrical shadow and, where possible, from the positions of the diffraction lobes; these times are given in Table 2. In estimating the values of $T_D{}^A$ and $T_R{}^A$ from the 136-Mc/s records a small correction was applied for the effects of component B, this correction being estimated by comparison with the 410-Mc/s records. The corresponding times for B were estimated from the 410-Mc/s observations using the estimated position of component A and the known flux density ratio of the two components. For each component the times and associated errors given in Table 2 define three strips in each of which the source should lie ; the centre lines of these strips represent the limb of the Moon at the time of observation and define in each case a triangular-shaped area. In principle, the position of the source lies in the area common to the three associated strips but it was found that for each component, and in particular for component A, that the size of the triangles defined by the Moon's limb was larger than would be expected from the estimated timing errors. This suggests that errors in the positions of the Moon's limb are more important than the estimated timing errors, and possibly that the effective position of the source varies slightly with frequency. The position of each source was therefore assumed to be given by the centre of the circle inscribed in the triangle defined by the Moon's limb at the relevant times. Dr. W. Nicholson of H.M. Nautical Almanac Office has kindly carried out these calculations and the estimated positions are as follows:

Component A	R.A.	12h 26m 32·38s ± 0·03s
(Epoch 1950)	Decl.	02° 19′ 27·8″ ± 1·5″
Component B	R.A.	12h 26m 33·29s ± 0·02s
(Epoch 1950)	Decl.	02° 19′ 42·0″ ± 0·5″

The average positions of the two sources given here represent the most accurate determination yet made of the position of a radio source. The quoted errors were estimated from the size of the triangles defined by the Moon's limb at the times of disappearance and reappearance, for the method is not subject to uncertainties intro-

Table 2. Observed Occultation Times of the Two Components of 3C 273

	Component A (U.T.)	Component B (U.T.)
Time of disappearance August 5, 1962	07h 46m 00s ± 1s	07h 46m 27·2s ± 0·5s
Time of reappearance August 5, 1962	09h 05m 45·5s ± 1s	09h 05m 45·7s ± 1·5s
Time of disappearance October 26, 1962	02h 55m 09·0s ± 1s	02h 56m 01·5s ± 0·4s

duced by refraction in the Earth's ionosphere or troposphere and is also free from the effects of confusion. A comparison of the times of disappearance and reappearance at different frequencies indicates that there is also no significant source of error due to refraction in either the solar corona or a possible lunar ionosphere; any refraction appears to be less than 0·3″ even at 136 Mc/s. This may be compared with the upper limit of 2″ at 237 Mc/s and 13″ at 81 Mc/s as estimated by Hazard[1] and Elsmore[6] respectively, and allows a new limit to be set to the density of the lunar ionosphere. Thus, from his observations at 81·5 Mc/s, Elsmore has set an upper limit to the electron density of 10^3 cm⁻³; and it follows that the present measurements set a limit of about 10^2 cm⁻³. Similarly, Buckingham[7] has estimated that at 50 Mc/s a ray passing at 50° to the Sun would be deviated by 1″ if the electron density in the solar corona at the Earth's distance from the Sun is 100 cm⁻³. The present observations at 136 Mc/s and 410 Mc/s on August 5 indicate that at 50 Mc/s the deviation is less than 2″ at this angle, setting an upper limit to the electron density of about 200 cm⁻³, which may be compared with an upper limit of 120 cm⁻³, set by Blackwell and Ingham[8] from observations of the zodiacal light.

In a preliminary examination of a print from a 200″ plate it was noted that the position of component B agreed closely with that of a thirteenth magnitude star. We understand that the investigations by Drs. A. Sandage and M. Schmidt of the Mount Wilson and Palomar Observatories have revealed that this star and an associated nebulosity is very probably the source of the radio emission.

We thank Mr. J. G. Bolton for his interest in this work, and his assistance, with that of the staff at Parkes, in ensuring the success of these observations. We also thank Dr. W. Nicholson, who calculated the positions of the sources, for his valuable co-operation and interest in the occultation programme. One of us (C. H.) thanks Dr. E. G. Bowen for his invitation to continue occultation work at Parkes as a guest observer from the Narrabri Observatory of the School of Physics of the University of Sydney.

[1] Hazard, C., *Mon. Not. Roy. Astro. Soc.*, **134**, 27 (1962).
[2] Hazard, C., *Nature*, **191**, 58 (1961).
[3] Bolton, J. G., Gardner, F. F., and Mackey, M. B. (unpublished results).
[4] Scheuer, P. A. G., *Austral J. Phys.*, **15**, 333 (1962).
[5] Slee, O. B., *Mon. Not. Roy. Astro. Soc.*, **123**, 223 (1961).
[6] Elsmore, B., *Phil. Mag.*, **2**, 1040 (1957).
[7] Buckingham, M. J., *Nature*, **193**, 538 (1962).
[8] Blackwell, D. E., and Ingham, M. F., *Mon. Not. Roy. Astro. Soc.*, **122**, 129 (1961).

3C 273: A STAR-LIKE OBJECT WITH LARGE RED-SHIFT

M. Schmidt

THE only objects seen on a 200-in. plate near the positions of the components of the radio source 3*C* 273 reported by Hazard, Mackey and Shimmins in the preceding article are a star of about thirteenth magnitude and a faint wisp or jet. The jet has a width of 1″–2″ and extends away from the star in position angle 43°. It is not visible within 11″ from the star and ends abruptly at 20″ from the star. The position of the star, kindly furnished by Dr. T. A. Matthews, is R.A. 12h 26m 33·35s ± 0·04s, Decl. + 2° 19′ 42·0″ ± 0·5″ (1950), or 1″ east of component *B* of the radio source. The end of the jet is 1″ east of component *A*. The close correlation between the radio structure and the star with the jet is suggestive and intriguing.

Spectra of the star were taken with the prime-focus spectrograph at the 200-in. telescope with dispersions of 400 and 190 Å per mm. They show a number of broad emission features on a rather blue continuum. The most prominent features, which have widths around 50 Å, are, in order of strength, at 5632, 3239, 5792, 5032 Å. These and other weaker emission bands are listed in the first column of Table 1. For three faint bands with widths of 100–200 Å the total range of wave-length is indicated.

The only explanation found for the spectrum involves a considerable red-shift. A red-shift $\Delta\lambda/\lambda_0$ of 0·158 allows identification of four emission bands as Balmer lines, as indicated in Table 1. Their relative strengths are in agreement with this explanation. Other identifications based on the above red-shift involve the Mg II lines around

M. Schmidt, Mount Wilson and Palomar Observatories, Carnegie Institution of Washington, California Institute of Technology.

Reprinted from *Nature*, **197**, 1040, March 16, 1963.

2798 Å, thus far only found in emission in the solar chromosphere, and a forbidden line of [O III] at 5007 Å. On this basis another [O III] line is expected at 4959 Å with a strength one-third of that of the line at 5007 Å. Its detectability in the spectrum would be marginal. A weak emission band suspected at 5705 Å, or 4927 Å reduced for red-shift, does not fit the wave-length. No explanation is offered for the three very wide emission bands.

It thus appears that six emission bands with widths around 50 Å can be explained with a red-shift of 0·158. The differences between the observed and the expected wave-lengths amount to 6 Å at the most and can be entirely understood in terms of the uncertainty of the measured wave-lengths. The present explanation is supported by observations of the infra-red spectrum communicated by

Table 1. WAVE-LENGTHS AND IDENTIFICATIONS

λ	$\lambda/1\cdot158$	λ_0	
3239	2797	2798	Mg II
4595	3968	3970	Hϵ
4753	4104	4102	Hδ
5032	4345	4340	Hγ
5200–5415	4490–4675		
5632	4864	4861	Hβ
5792	5002	5007	[O III]
6005–6190	5186–5345		
6400–6510	5527–5622		

Oke in a following article, and by the spectrum of another star-like object associated with the radio source 3C 48 discussed by Greenstein and Matthews in another communication.

The unprecedented identification of the spectrum of an apparently stellar object in terms of a large red-shift suggests either of the two following explanations.

(1) The stellar object is a star with a large gravitational red-shift. Its radius would then be of the order of 10 km. Preliminary considerations show that it would be extremely difficult, if not impossible, to account for the occurrence of permitted lines and a forbidden line with the same red-shift, and with widths of only 1 or 2 per cent of the wave-length.

(2) The stellar object is the nuclear region of a galaxy with a cosmological red-shift of 0·158, corresponding to an apparent velocity of 47,400 km/sec. The distance would be around 500 megaparsecs, and the diameter of the nuclear region would have to be less than 1 kiloparsec. This nuclear region would be about 100 times brighter optically than the luminous galaxies which have been identified with radio sources thus far. If the optical jet and component A of the radio source are associated with the galaxy, they would be at a distance of 50 kiloparsecs, implying a time-scale in excess of 10^5 years. The total energy radiated in the optical range at constant luminosity would be of the order of 10^{59} ergs.

Only the detection of an irrefutable proper motion or parallax would definitively establish 3C 273 as an object within our Galaxy. At the present time, however, the explanation in terms of an extragalactic origin seems most direct and least objectionable.

I thank Dr. T. A. Matthews, who directed my attention to the radio source, and Drs. Greenstein and Oke for valuable discussions.

ABSOLUTE ENERGY DISTRIBUTION IN THE OPTICAL SPECTRUM OF 3C 273

J. B. OKE

THE radio source 3C 273 has recently been identified with a thirteenth magnitude star-like object. The details are given by M. Schmidt in the preceding communication. Since 3C 273 is relatively bright, photoelectric spectrophotometric observations were made with the 100-in. telescope at Mount Wilson to determine the absolute distribution of energy in the optical region of the spectrum; such observations are useful for determining if synchrotron radiation is present. In the wave-length region between 3300 Å and 6000 Å measurements were made in 16 selected 50-Å bands. Continuous spectral scans with a resolution of 50 Å were also made. The measurements were placed on an absolute-energy system by also observing standard stars whose absolute energy distributions were known[1]. The accuracy of the 16 selected points is approximately 2 per cent. The strong emission features found by Schmidt were readily detected; other very faint features not apparent on Schmidt's spectra may be present.

The source 3C 273 is considerably bluer than the other known star-like objects 3C 48, 3C 196, and 3C 286 which have been studied in detail[2]. The absolute energy distribution of the apparent continuum can be accurately represented by the equation:

$$F_\nu \propto \nu^{+0.28}$$

where F_ν is the flux per unit frequency interval and ν is

J. B. OKE, Mount Wilson and Palomar Observatories, Carnegie Institution of Washington, California Institute of Technology.

Reprinted from *Nature*, **197**, 1040–1041, March 16, 1963.

the frequency. The apparent visual magnitude of 3C 273 is +12·6, which corresponds to an absolute flux at the Earth of $3·5 \times 10^{-28}$ W m^{-2} (c/s)$^{-1}$ at 5600 Å. At radio frequencies[3] the spectral index is $-0·25$ and the flux at 960 Mc/s is $5·0 \times 10^{-25}$ W m^{-2} (c/s)$^{-1}$.

Between 6000 Å and 10,250 Å, eleven 120-Å bands were measured with an accuracy of 10 per cent. These measures indicate that the relatively flat energy distribution given in the equation here applies as far as 8400 Å. Beyond 8400 Å the flux may increase significantly. Between 3300 Å and 8400 Å the energy distribution cannot be represented, even approximately, by the flux from a black-body or a normal star. At least part of the optical continuum radiation must be synchrotron radiation.

During the course of the infra-red observations a strong emission feature was found near 7600 Å. Further observations with a 50-Å band-width placed the emission line at 7590 Å with a possible error of about 10 Å. The emission profile was found to be similar to that of the emission line at 5632 Å. Using this line and others in the visual spectrum Schmidt has shown that the most prominent emission features are Balmer lines and that the line at 7590 Å is $H\alpha$. Using Schmidt's red-shift $\Delta\lambda/\lambda_0$ of 0·158, $H\alpha$ should appear at 7599 Å; this is in satisfactory agreement with observation, when it is recalled that the atmospheric A band absorbs strongly beyond 7594 Å. It is possible that the [NII] lines which have unshifted wave-lengths of 6548 Å and 6583 Å can contribute to the emission feature identified as $H\alpha$. A large contribution, however, would shift the line significantly towards the red. The relative positions of $H\alpha$, $H\beta$, $H\gamma$, and $H\delta$ cannot be produced by applying a red-shift to any other hydrogen-like ion spectrum.

Further observations, particularly in the infra-red, will be made in the near future.

[1] Oke, J. B., *Astrophys. J.*, **131**, 358 (1960).
[2] Matthews, T. A., and Sandage, Allan, *Astrophys. J.* (in the press).
[3] Harris, D. E., and Roberts, J. A., *Pub. Astro. Soc. Pacific*, **72**, 237 (1960).

RED-SHIFT OF THE UNUSUAL RADIO SOURCE: 3C 48

Jesse L. Greenstein and Thomas A. Matthews

THE radio source 3C 48 was announced to be a star[1] in our Galaxy on the basis of its extremely small radio diameter[2], stellar appearance on direct photographs and unusual spectrum. Detailed spectroscopic study at Palomar by Greenstein during the past year gave only partially successful identifications of its weak, broad emission lines; the possibility that they might be permitted transitions in high stages of ionization could not be proved or disproved. Hydrogen was absent but several approximate coincidences with He II and O VI were suggested.

The discovery by Schmidt (a preceding article) of much broader emission lines in the apparently stellar radio source, 3C 273, suggested a red-shift of 0·16 for 3C 273 if the lines were interpreted as the Balmer series. In 3C 48 no such series was apparent; measurable lines still do not coincide with the hydrogen series. However, the possibility of a very large red-shift, which had been considered many times, was re-explored successfully. 3C 48 has a spectrum containing one very strong emission feature near λ3832 which is 35 Å wide and about 10 other weaker features near 23 Å in width. The sharper lines are listed in Table 1 in order of decreasing intensity. Some broad lines or groups of lines between 50 and 100 Å width may be red-shifted hydrogen lines.

Table 1. IDENTIFICATIONS AND OBSERVED RED-SHIFTS

$\lambda*$	Wave-length λ lab.	Source	$\lambda*/\lambda$ lab.
3832·3	2796 ⎱ 2798 2803 ⎰	Mg II	1·3697:
4685·0	3426	[Ne V]	1·3676
5098	3729 ⎱ 3727 3726 ⎰	[O II]	1·3679
4575	3346	[Ne V]	1·3673
5289	3868	[Ne III]	1·3671
4065·7	2975 :	[Ne V]	1·3667:

The weighted mean red-shift $d\lambda/\lambda_0$ is $0·3675 \pm 0·0003$, an apparent velocity of $+110,200$ km/sec. The slightly discrepant value for λ2975 of [Ne V] is compatible with the uncertainty of ± 3 Å in the wave-length predicted by Bowen[3]. The Mg II permitted resonance doublet has a small additional displacement to longer wave-lengths,

Jesse L. Greenstein, Mount Wilson and Palomar Observatories, Carnegie Institution of Washington, California Institute of Technology. Thomas A. Matthews, Owens Valley Radio Observatory, California Institute of Technology.

Reprinted from *Nature*, **197**, 1041–1042, March 16, 1963.

possibly caused by self-absorption in an expanding shell; it is the strongest emission line in the rocket-ultra-violet spectrum of the Sun. The forbidden lines are similar to those in other intense extragalactic radio sources.

So large a red-shift, second only to that of the intense radio source $3C$ 295, will have important implications in cosmological speculation. A very interesting alternative, that the source is a nearby ultra-dense star of radius near 10 km containing neutrons, hyperons, etc., has been explored and seems to meet insuperable objections from the spectroscopic point of view. The small volume for the shell required by the observed small gradient of the gravitational potential is incompatible with the strength of the forbidden lines.

The distance of $3C$ 48, interpreted as the central core of an explosion in a very abnormal galaxy, may be estimated as $1 \cdot 10 \times 10^9$ parsecs; the visual absolute magnitude is then $-24 \cdot 0$, or $-24 \cdot 5$ corrected for interstellar absorption. The minimum correction for the effect of red-shift is of the order of 2 v/c and a value between 4 and 5 times v/c is probable for a normal galaxy. The absolute visual magnitude of $3C$ 48 is then brighter than $-25 \cdot 2$ and possibly as bright as $-26 \cdot 3$, 10–30 times greater than that of the brightest giant ellipticals[4] hitherto recognized, which are near $-22 \cdot 7$ and another factor of five brighter than our own Galaxy, near $-21 \cdot 0$.

As a radio source at a distance of $1 \cdot 1 \times 10^9$ parsecs $3C$ 48 is not markedly different from other known strong radio sources like $3C$ 295 or Cygnus A. The one feature in which it does differ from most sources is in its high surface brightness. This is partially due to its extremely small radio size of $\leqslant$ 1 sec of arc^2. The optical size is comparable, being also $\leqslant$ 1 sec of arc[5]. At the assumed distance such angular sizes indicate that both the optical and radio emission arise within a diameter of $\leqslant$ 5500 parsecs. The radio diameter might even be comparable with or less than that of $3C$ 71 (NGC 1068) the diameter of which is about 700 parsecs. However, $3C$ 71 has 5 orders of magnitude less radio emission.

If we determine the integrated radio emission of $3C$ 48 from the observed spectral index of the radio spectrum, and correct for the red-shift, we find that $3C$ 48 is comparable with $3C$ 295, emitting 4×10^{44} erg/sec of radio-frequency power. The cut-off frequencies were 7×10^7 c/s and 10^{11} c/s. The lower limit is indicated by the observed radio spectrum and the upper limit is an assumed one.

The absolute magnitudes of the galaxies connected with $3C$ 295 and Cygnus A, corrected for interstellar absorption, are $M_v = -21 \cdot 0$ and $-21 \cdot 6$ (using a red-shift correction of 2 v/c) or $M_v = -22 \cdot 4$ and $-21 \cdot 8$ (using a correction of 5 v/c) respectively. Thus 3C 48 radiates about 50 times more powerfully in the optical region than other more normal but intense radio galaxies. In contrast, the absolute radio luminosity of 3C 48 is the same as that of Cygnus A and 3C 295. The unusually strong optical radiation may be synchrotron radiation as suggested (for other reasons) by Matthews and Sandage[5].

[1] Matthews, T. A., Bolton, J. G., Greenstein, J. L., Münch, G., and Sandage, A. R., Amer. Astro. Soc. meeting, New York, 1960; *Sky and Telescope*, **21**, 148 (1961). Greenstein, J. L., and Münch, G., *Ann. Rep. Dir. Mt. Wilson and Palomar Obs.*, 80 (1961).

[2] Allen, L. R., *et al.*, *Mon. Not. Roy. Astro. Soc.*, **124**, 447 (1962). Rowson, B., *ibid.* (in the press).

[3] Bowen, I. S., *Astrophys. J.*, **132**, 1 (1960).

[4] Abell, G., *Problems of Extragalactic Research*, I.A.U. Symp. No. 15, edit. by McVittie, G. C., 213 (Macmillan, New York, 1962).

[5] Matthews, T. A., and Sandage, A. R., *Astrophys. J.* (in the press).

LIGHT VARIATIONS IN THE SUPERLUMINOUS RADIO GALAXY 3C273

HARLAN J. SMITH AND DORRIT HOFFLEIT

SEVERAL radio sources among those known to have small angular diameters[1] have recently been identified at the California Institute of Technology[2,3] with star-like objects. On closer examination at least two of the objects, 3C48[4] and 3C273[5-7], appear to be abnormally luminous nuclei of distant, highly redshifted galaxies. On this interpretation 3C273 with $M_v = -26\cdot5$ becomes the most luminous object now known in the universe.

With the kind permission of the Director of the Harvard Observatory, and with finder charts provided by Dr. Matthews, of the California Institute of Technology, we have investigated the photographic history of 3C48, 147, 196, 273 and 286 using Harvard's valuable historical plate file reaching back well into the nineteenth century. On each plate showing an image of one of the objects, the brightness was estimated by eye in the standard fashion in terms of suitable comparison stars. Being fainter than 17th magnitude, 3C 147, 196 and 286 each yielded detectable images on only about half a dozen of the nearly half-million plates in the collection, and no positive evidence for

HARLAN J. SMITH and DORRIT HOFFLEIT, Yale University Observatory, New Haven, Connecticut.

Reprinted from *Nature*, **198**, 650–651, May 18, 1963.

variation greater than several tenths of a magnitude was found. The earliest of these objects to be isolated, 3C48, is a magnitude brighter; hence in 1961 we were able to estimate it on 75 plates, again without finding significant variation greater than 0·3 mag.[8]. However, the most recently identified of the five, 3C273, at $m_{pg} = 12·5$ mag. is sufficiently bright to be visible on a significant fraction of the thousands of plates on its region. While work is continuing on the complete collection, we report results based on the 600 measures so far reduced. These suffice to give convincing proof of variability and to show provisionally its character. The earliest useful plates date from 1887; for the period 1893–1953, during which Harvard maintained regular patrols, only two years lack observations in the material reported here.

Conditions for photographic photometry are uncommonly favourable in the case of 3C273. For many of the available exposures its brightness falls in the linear portion of the characteristic curve; moreover, closely adjacent to this object are three field stars one of which has a brightness equal to the magnitude of 3C273, the other two are respectively 0·2 mag. brighter and fainter. Accordingly, despite the use of plates from 17 different telescopes, it has proved possible to make eye estimates of magnitude with mean errors of an individual estimate averaging less than ± 0·1 mag. Since the heavy dots in the light curve of Fig. 1 represent annual means of some 5–50 measures, the internal probable error of each annual mean is normally of the order of, or smaller than, the diameter of the dots (0·06 mag.) in Fig. 1. We concede the probability of a systematic error arising from the colour index of 3C273 which is bluer by 0·5 mag. than the

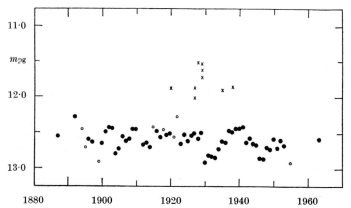

FIG. 1.—Mean light curve of 3C273 for the years 1887–1963. Circles are annual means; black circles, include five or more individual observations; white circles, four or less. The x's refer to strong individual observations more than 0·5 mag. brighter than the annual means (these apparent flashes were not included in the annual means).

mean of the comparison stars. This implies dependence of the results on the redward limit of sensitivity of the ordinary photographic plates. However, even under extreme assumptions it seems unlikely that such errors will reach 0·1 mag.; neither do the observed variations have the plateau-shift character which such errors should produce.

At least four observational conclusions are suggested by the provisional light curve of Fig. 1.

(1) The average photographic brightness appears to have declined at a rate of about 0·2 mag./century over the 76 years of observation. Even if real, however, such an apparent secular decline may of course represent only a sampling of some much longer variability.

(2) Over the 70 years of strong observations, there occurred one well-marked cycle and five or six less-distinct cycles indicating a time-scale for major fluctuations of the order of ten years.

(3) Rarely (on less than 2 per cent of the plates) the image of 3C273 is abnormally bright corresponding to pronounced enhancements of more than half a magnitude. The clearest such cases are indicated by ×'s in Fig. 1. To bring out the character of the apparent variation on an expanded time scale, Fig. 2 shows the individual readings from the large-scale plates for the 1929 observing season. We believe that most of these apparent flashes are not plate defects but are real images. This belief is based on their often complex character (agreeing with that of adjacent stars), on the accurate coincidence with the position of 3C273, and on the concentration of flashes during certain periods, notably 1927–29. The enhanced images usually have a subtly different character from those of the comparison stars or of 3C273 itself when more quiescent; we suggest that this difference arises from a strongly biased colour distribution of the light in the flash manifested by colour-dependent aberrations of the optical systems. The plate material thus far examined contains only one instance where more than one observation is available within a single outburst (Fig. 2). However, the normal magnitude of 3C273 seems to be recovered within one or two weeks after any flash.

(4) It is remarkable that the major group of flashes in 1927–29 was followed by the most precipitous drop of average brightness in the whole body of data. The individual points are consistent with decline over the interval September 1929–April 1930. The subsequent gradual rise up to 1941 suggests an exponential recovery with $\tau \sim 2 \times 10^8$ sec.

Such variations bear strongly on the size and nature of 3C273 and, by implication, of other similar objects. If the flashes are real, either the optical source itself is of

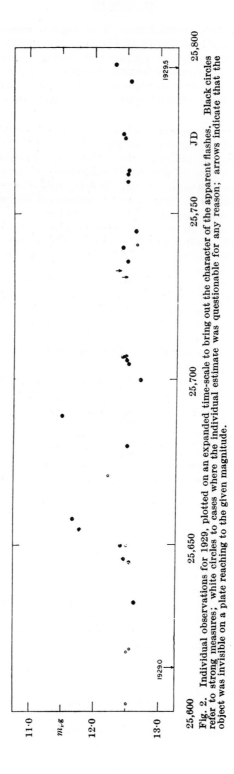

Fig. 2. Individual observations for 1929, plotted on an expanded time-scale to bring out the character of the apparent flashes. Black circles refer to strong measures; white circles to cases where the individual estimate was questionable for any reason; arrows indicate that the object was invisible on a plate reaching to the given magnitude.

the order of light-days in size, or at least it must contain substructures of this scale which are capable of reaching $M_{pg} \sim -27$ to $-27 \cdot 5$ for times of the order of 10^4–10^6 sec. In comparison with such hypernova-like activity, even very luminous supernovæ of conventional Type II probably do not exceed $M_{pg} \sim -19$. A more conservative estimate of the size of the principal luminous nucleus could be derived on the assumption that the major flashes of 1927–29 in some way induced the subsequent sharp decline. Since this time was 10^7–10^8 sec., the corresponding size would be several light years if the disturbing effect were propagated at the speed of light and proportionately less if propagated more slowly. These numbers suggest interesting energy requirements for 3C273.

Finally, it is now clear that similar behaviour of 3C 48, 147, 196 and 286 cannot be ruled out from existing material, since the total number of usable plates for all these together is less than 100. If flashes are no more frequent than with 3C273, statistically we might expect the present material on the other objects to contain not even a single clear case of striking activity. Search of other plate files and continued observation of all of these objects is in order.

[1] Allen, L. R., *et al.*, *Mon. Not. Roy. Astro. Soc.*, **124**, 477 (1962). Rowson, B., *ibid.* (in the press).

[2] Matthews, T. A., *et al.*, Amer. Astron. Soc. meeting, New York, 1960; *Sky and Telescope*, **21**, 148 (1961). Greenstein, J. L., and Munch, G., *Ann. Rep. Dir. Mt. Wilson and Palomar Obs.*, **80** (1961).

[3] Matthews, T. A., and Greenstein, J. L., Conf. Radio Sources, Nat. Aeronaut. Space Admin., Goddard Inst. Space Studies, New York, Dec. 1962 (unpublished).

[4] Greenstein, J. L., and Matthews, T. A., *Nature*, **197**, 1041 (1963).

[5] Hazard, C., Mackey, M. B., and Shimmins, A. J., *Nature*, **197**, 1037 (1963).

[6] Schmidt, M., *Nature*, **197**, 1040 (1963).

[7] Oke, J. B., *Nature*, **197**, 1040 (1963).

[8] Smith, Harlan J., and Hoffleit, Dorrit, *Pub. Astro. Soc. Pacific*, **73**, 292 (1961).

COSMIC RAYS AND PARTICLES
appendix ii OF NEGATIVE MASS

YAKOV P. TERLETSKY

Let us suppose that in the universe there exist not only particles of positive mass (plus-particles) but also particles of negative mass (minus-particles). If the law of conservation of energy and momentum and Einstein's equivalence principle are not to be violated, the minus-particles must not only possess a negative energy and non-positive rest mass, i.e.,

$$E < 0, \qquad M = \frac{1}{c}\sqrt{\left(\frac{E}{c}\right)^2 - p^2} \le 0, \tag{1}$$

but must also have a negative gravitational mass.

If the existence of minus-particles is admitted, it is necessary to radically revise the thermodynamic laws of the Universe. Indeed, if a heat reservoir consisting of minus-particles can be realized, a thermodynamic machine of the second kind is possible, i.e., a machine which produces unlimited work at the expense of some heat reservoir which is cooled indefinitely.

Such a change in the thermodynamic laws is not entirely unexpected. In contemporary thermodynamics, systems with negative temperatures are not unknown (e.g., spin systems in a magnetic field). Using such heat sources, devices such as the laser, which can be considered a thermodynamic machine of the second kind (after its population has been inverted), have been realized in practice. In any case, the proposed violation of the second law is not as radical as the non-conservation of energy proposed by Hoyle. According to Hoyle, the first law of thermodynamics, i.e., the most fundamental law of physics, can be violated. Our proposal is only a violation of the statistical law.[1]

Minus-particles must have some unusual physical properties.[2] They must repulse each other gravitationally and be attracted by large positive masses. Therefore, minus-

---

YAKOV P. TERLETSKY, on leave from the Physical Faculty of Moscow State University (U.S.S.R.) as visiting exchange professor in the United States, sponsored by the Inter-University Committee on Travel Grants, Bloomington, Indiana. Currently in the Department of Physics, New York University.

[1] A more detailed consideration of the possibility of macroscopic violations of thermodynamics was discussed at a theoretical seminar at New York University, which will be published elsewhere (Terletsky 1964).

[2] The possible physical properties of minus-particles have been considered (Terletsky 1962).

particles tend to fill the entire cosmic space with approximately homogeneous density. Higher densities of minus-particles can appear only in localities where there is a large accumulation of positive mass. Minus-particles can exist in thermodyamic equilibrium only at negative absolute temperatures, since the statistical integral (or the statistical sum) diverges at positive temperatures for systems of unlimited negative energy.

If the minus-particles are distributed throughout space in the above manner, they can act as heat reservoirs with negative temperature for plus-particles if there is an interaction between the two types of particles. However, according to classical thermodynamics, a thermodynamic machine can be realized that perpetually produces work at the expense of such reservoirs that can undergo infinite cooling. Consequently, the usual plus-particles will undergo an increase in mean kinetic energy as a result of collisions with minus-particles. Thus a new mechanism for the acceleration of cosmic ray particles is proposed. Let us consider this mechanism in greater detail.

Let $f(E, r, t)$ be the distribution function in terms of energy, space, and time coordinates; ρ_0^+ space density of non-relativistic plus-particles, i.e., the density of normal matter (the density of stars, planets, interstellar gas, etc.); ρ^- the space density of minus-particles. A relativistic particle with energy E will gain an amount of energy per unit time proportional to some fraction a of its own energy when it collides with minus-particles. Thus, the mean energy will increase according to the equation

$$\frac{dE}{dt} = a\bar{E}. \tag{2}$$

It is evident that the coefficient a is proportional to the density of minus-particles, the velocity of cosmic ray particles, and the effective elastic collision cross-section between plus-particles and minus-particles, i.e.,

$$a = c\rho^- \sigma_{+-}. \tag{3}$$

On the other hand, as a result of collisions of cosmic-ray particles with usual matter, their energy-space-density f function will decrease by a factor of $1/T$ per unit time, where T is the mean free path time of a cosmic-ray particle. It is evident that

$$T = \frac{1}{c\rho_0^+ \sigma_{+0}}, \tag{4}$$

where σ_{+0} is the full effective collisional cross-section of cosmic-ray particles with non-relativistic particles.

The space-energetic density function f may also change as a result of ordinary diffusion of cosmic-ray particles in interstellar magnetic fields.

If the three above interaction processes occur, the space-energetic diffusional equation of cosmic-ray particles can be written as:

$$\frac{\partial f}{\partial t} - D\nabla^2 f + \frac{\partial}{\partial E}(aEf) + \frac{f}{T} = Q, \tag{5}$$

where Q is the density of injection sources of cosmic rays and D is the coefficient of space diffusion of cosmic-ray particles.

In accordance with the work of Terletsky and Logunov (1951), Logunov and Terletsky (1953), Morrison, Olbert, and Rossi (1954), and Terletsky (1955), this equation is simplified, i.e., fluctuations in energies are neglected. However, it is sufficient to describe the acceleration mechanism which is similar to Fermi's (1949) mechanism.

The simplest solution of this equation is the steady-state solution, which is homogeneous in space. This solution must satisfy the equation

$$\frac{\partial}{\partial E}\,(\,aEf\,)+\frac{f}{T}=0\,,\tag{6}$$

which applies for energies higher than that of the injector. This solution has the form

$$f\sim E^{-\gamma}\,,\tag{7}$$

where

$$\gamma=1+\frac{1}{aT}=1+\frac{\sigma_{+0}\rho_0^{+}}{\sigma_{+-}\rho^{-}}\,.\tag{8}$$

It is apparent that minus-particles exist at a high mean negative temperature, since the negative kinetic energy increases continually as a result of their collisions with cosmic-ray particles and they cannot aggregate to form regions of high density as does usual matter. Therefore ρ^{-} can be considered as approximately constant for all metagalaxies.[3]

Thus, the coefficient γ must be minimal in intergalactic space and must increase inside nebulae and in the vicinity of stars.

The hypothesis of the metagalactic origin of cosmic radiation, which is probable because of their isotropy, agrees with the supposition

$$\frac{\sigma_{+0}}{\sigma_{+-}}\,\frac{\rho_0^{+}}{\rho^{-}}\cong 2\,,\tag{9}$$

since for the primary component of cosmic rays $\gamma\cong 3$. The relation (9) appears to be reasonable if it is assumed that the mean metagalactic density of plus-particles and minus-particles is about the same, and their effective cross-sections σ_{+0} and σ_{+-} are of the same order of magnitude.

If the electron and neutrino components of the primary cosmic rays have the same index γ as the proton components, then it is necessary to assume that minus-particles are capable of interacting with plus-particles with either strong or weak interaction. This indicates that either minus-baryons or minus-leptons exist.

In the vicinity of stars the density ρ_0^{+} increases and correspondingly (at a constant density ρ^{-}) the index γ increases. In this manner, cosmic rays must be formed in the vicinity of the Sun; however, their energy spectrum must decrease more rapidly than is the case for cosmic rays which are of metagalactic origin.

The intensity of energy emission, i.e., the energy obtained by cosmic-ray particles per unit time in unit volume, evidently is proportional to the density of cosmic-ray particles and the coefficient a multiplied by E, that is,

$$\frac{\partial W}{\partial t}+\mathrm{div}\,\mathbf{S}=\int aEf\,dE\,,\tag{10}$$

---

[3] The density of minus-particles can increase within stars, since at negative temperatures according to the Boltzmann distribution

$$\rho^{-}\sim\exp\left(-\frac{m\varphi}{kT}\right)=\exp\left(\frac{|m|}{k\,|T|}\,\varphi\right),$$

where φ is the Newtonian gravitational potential.

where W and S are the energy density and energy-flow density of cosmic-ray particles, respectively.

Thus, at an approximately constant a for all space regions, the intensity of energy emission is proportional to the density of cosmic-ray particles. Consequently, if in some region of space, e.g., near supernovae, an accumulation of relativistic particles occurred, an increased emission of energy from this region will take place. It may be even greater if minus-particles aggregate in the vicinity of high gravitational masses.

The general problem of the space distribution of cosmic-ray particles and intensity of energy emission can be investigated by means of solution of the general equation (5) of the diffusion of cosmic-ray particles. Magnetic fields, whose existence is necessary for the occurrence of mixing and space diffusion of cosmic-ray particles, can be considered to originate as a result of energy transfer between cosmic-ray particles and turbulent hydromagnetic plasma.

It is evident that the hypothesis of minus-particles also supposes the existence of additional energetic sources for non-relativistic particles; the intensity of energy emission from such sources must also increase with increasing density of the matter.

REFERENCES

Fermi, E. 1949, *Phys. Rev.*, **75**, 1169.
Morrison, P., Olbert, S., and Rossi, B. 1954, *Phys. Rev.*, **94**, 440.
Logunov, A. A., and Terletsky, Ya. P. 1953, *Izvest. Akad. Nauk SSSR* (Ser. Fiz.), **17**, 119.
Terletsky, Ya. P. 1955, *Doklady Akad. Nauk. SSSR*, **101**, 59.
———. 1962, *J. Phys. et Radium*, **23**, 910.
———. 1964, "On the Possibility of Macroscopic Violations of the Laws of Thermodynamics" (in press).
Terletsky, Ya. P., and Logunov, A. A. 1951, *J.E.T.P.* (USSR), **21**, 567.

SUMMARY OF AFTER-DINNER
appendix iii # SPEECH

T. Gold

It is my misfortune to have to make a speech to you and yours to have to listen. But many of you are in fact to blame—all those who the organizers in their wisdom had, in fact, asked before asking me.

First, let me use the occasion to thank our hosts; let us also thank the organizations that donated funds for the meeting. They all will get nothing in return other than a lot of papers and a chance to look at a bunch of confused and bewildered scientists.

This, of course, is a historic meeting. It will be remembered as the meeting where these great new astronomical discoveries were first discussed. It will also be remembered for the display there of strong men wrestling with even stronger facts.

It was, I believe, chiefly Hoyle's genius which produced the extremely attractive idea that here we have a case that allowed one to suggest that the relativists with their sophisticated work were not only magnificent cultural ornaments but might actually be useful to science! Everyone is pleased: the relativists who feel they are being appreciated, who are suddenly experts in a field they hardly knew existed; the astrophysicists for having enlarged their domain, their empire, by the annexation of another subject—general relativity. It is all very pleasing, so let us all hope that it is right. What a shame it would be if we had to go and dismiss all the relativists again.

Texans will wonder what it is that they have got themselves into here. These people who come here instead of concerning themselves with constructive aspects like "the impact of relativity on contemporary American thought" or "relativity and the American way of life" or perhaps even "gravitation and the search for oil." Instead these people concern themselves with so obviously negative a topic as "Collapse: The Morbid Pathology of Matter."

The critics can now fortunately be silenced—I don't mean in the grand manner of the West—but they will be silenced by the discovery made by Harlan Smith that finally the elusive origin of the stock-market fluctuations has been found. Stellar photometry will never have to worry again about financial support.

Now I must stop so the people can go in the local tradition to their favorite club with their little brown paper bags.

appendix iv QUASI-POETRY

QUASI-STELLAR RADIO SOURCES

At its far limits, the universe is daft.
Out edgeward nothing is itself no more:
Stars are no longer fat scuts of gas
But clots of stuff uncertain
As eccentric maiden aunts.

These lights called quasi-stellar,
Anarchic, observe not the curfew
Of thermodynamics: they run on
After they have run down, or
Shine with a brighter fire
Than they have fuel for.

This is not right.
For if I must pay for jot with tittle
And am not to be both big and little,
How is it they
Can play
According to neither Hoyle
Nor Boyle?

HOWARD McCORD

THE GHOST OF NEWTON REPLIES[1]

The reason, sir, is simply this;
Boyle and Hoyle we all dismiss:
One's dead,
One's Fred.

All is change, and that's in flux.
Nothing's sure but Lady Luck's
Encrypted program; and who'll compute her
Pressure, volume, vector, mass? What tutor
Taught her that lithe arbitrament
That rules our spacious firmament?

[1] To Howard McCord's "Quasi-Stellar Radio Sources" (*New York Times*, March 1, 1964). And see article of same title by Professor Jesse Greenstein in *Scientific American* a few months ago.

471

The field of force, the grand design,
Springs from the boundless mental mine
Of the Masters of the massless line:
From Sandage, Schmidt, and J. Greenstein!

W. T. GOLDEN

THE QUASAR[2]

Quasar, quasar shining bright
Both by radio and by light
Is it true that gravity
Is thy source of energy?

In your core, perhaps there lies
Schwarzschild's singularities
Does neutrino radiation
Damp your rapid fluctuation?

Quantum theory may break down
Under pressure like your own
Leaving theorists to say
Quasar, won't you go away?

G. FEINBERG

TWINKLE, TWINKLE, QUASI-STAR[3]

Twinkle, twinkle, quasi-star
Biggest puzzle from afar
How unlike the other ones
Brighter than a billion suns
Twinkle, twinkle, quasi-star
How I wonder what you are.

GEORGE GAMOW

[2] The following was found on the body of a particle physicist who committed suicide after hearing a talk on quasi-stellar objects last month (May 8, 1964).

[3] Newsweek, May 25, 1964.

appendix v LIST OF PARTICIPANTS

ABOUD, A., Ling-Temco-Vought, Inc.
AGINS, MAJ. B. R., AFOSR
ALBADA, G. B. VAN, Institute for Advanced Study
ALLEN, LT. COL. R. G., AFSOR
ALPHER, R. A., General Electric Research Laboratory
ANAND, S. P. S., Yale University
ANDERSON, J. L., Stevens Institute of Technology
ARNY, T., Steward Observatory, University of Arizona
BAGGERLY, L. L., Ling-Temco-Vought, Inc.
BARTLEY, W. C., Southwest Center for Advanced Studies
BEHR, C. G., University of Texas
BEL, L., Collège de France, Paris
BELINFANTE, F. J., Purdue University
BERGH, VAN DEN, S. University of Toronto
BERGMANN, P. G., Yeshiva University
BERKNER, L. V., Southwest Center for Advanced Studies
BÖHM, K. H., University of California, Berkeley
BÖHM, V. E., University of California, Berkeley
BOYD, R., Texas Instruments, Inc.
BOYER, R. H., University of Liverpool
BRAND, L., University of Houston
BRILL, D. R., Yale University
BROWN, R. L., Ling-Temco-Vought, Inc.
BROWNLEE, R. R., Los Alamos Scientific Laboratory
BRUECK, R. L., Southwest Center for Advanced Studies
BUDWINE, R. E., North Texas State University.
BURBIDGE, E. M., University of California, La Jolla
CAMERON, A. G. W., Goddard Institute for Space Studies (NASA)
CARTER, R. J., University of Texas
CHENEY, M. G., Arlington State College
CHIU, H. Y., Goddard Institute for Space Studies (NASA)
CHOQUET-BRUHAT, Y., Cornell University
CLARK, B., Southern Methodist University
CLAYTON, D. D., Rice University
COCKE, J., Cornell University
COLCHAGOFF, COL. G. D., AFOSR
COLEGROVE, D., Texas Instruments, Inc.
COLGATE, S., Lawrence Radiation Laboratory, Livermore, California

COLLINS, G. W., II, Perkins Observatory, Ohio State University
COOKE, J. H., University of North Carolina
CORRIGAN, K. E., William Beaumont Hospital, Wayne State University
COX, A. N., Los Alamos Scientific Laboratory
COX, J. P., University of Colorado
CROSBY, G. W., Atlantic Refining Co.
CUDABACK, D. D., University of California, Berkeley
DAM, H. VAN, University of North Carolina
DEBNEY, G. C., JR., University of Texas
DEEMING, T. J., University of Texas
DENT, W. A., University of Michigan
DESER, S., Brandeis University
DEWHIRST, D. W., The Observatories, Cambridge University
DEWITT, B. S., University of North Carolina
DEXTER, W., Planetarium Director, St. Marks School of Texas, Dallas
DINHOFER, A. D., Texas Instruments, Inc.
DYSON, F. J., Institute for Advanced Study
EDELEN, D., The RAND Corp.
EDMONDS, F. N., University of Texas
EDWARDS, G., Rice University
EHLERS, J., Hamburg University, Germany
ELLIS, J., Arlington State College
ESTABROOK, F. B., Jet Propulsion Laboratory, California Institute of Technology
FARMER, B. J., Ling-Temco-Vought, Inc.
FARNSWORTH, D. L., University of Texas
FEDERER, C. A., *Sky and Telescope*, Sky Publishing Corp.
FICKLER, S. I., Aerospace Research Laboratories
FITCH, J. L., Socony Mobil Oil Co.
FLETCHER, J. G., Lawrence Radiation Laboratory, Livermore, California
FLOWERDAY, T. W., Southwest Center for Advanced Studies
FOWLER, W. A., California Institute of Technology
FOSTER, W. R., Socony Mobil Oil Co.
FRIEDLANDER, M. W., Washington University
GAINES, MAJ. E. P., JR., AFOSR
GILBERT, C., University of Newcastle upon Tyne
GILES, R., Tulane University
GOLD, T., Cornell University
GOLDBERG, J. N., Syracuse University
GOLDSTEIN, J. S., Brandeis University

473

GOOD, W. B., New Mexico State University
GOURLEY, M. F., Austin College
GOURNAY, L. S., Socony Mobil Oil Co.
GREEN, C. H., Texas Instruments, Inc.
GREEN, L. C., Haverford College
GREENSTEIN, J. L., California Institute of Technology
GREYBER, H. D., Northeastern University
GRONSTAL, P. T., North Texas State University
GROSJEAN, P. V., University of Tunis
HADDOCK, F., University of Michigan
HALPERN, L. E., Institute of Theoretical Physics, University of Stockholm, Sweden
HAMBERGER, S. M., University of Oklahoma
HANSON, H. P., University of Texas
HANSON, W. B., Southwest Center for Advanced Studies
HARRINGTON, M. C., AFOSR
HARRISON, M., Texas Christian University
HARVEY, A. L., Queens College, New York
HAZARD, C., Sydney University, Sydney, Australia
HECKMANN, O., European Southern Observatories, Hamburg, Germany
HEIKKILA, W., Southwest Center for Advanced Studies
HELLER, J., Socony Mobil Oil Co.
HELSLEY, C. E., Southwest Center for Advanced Studies
HERCZEG, T. F., Hamburg Observatory, Germany
HINES, C. O., University of Chicago
HLAVATY, V., Indiana University
HOEHN, G. L., Socony Mobile Oil Co.
HOERNER, S. VON, National Radio Astronomy Observatory
HOFFMANN, B., Queens College, New York
HOGARTH, J. E., Queen's University, Kingston, Ontario, Canada
HOLMQUIST, F. N., Southwest Center for Advanced Studies
HOLT, O., Southwest Center for Advanced Studies
HOOD, J. D., University of Oklahoma
HOYLE, F., Cambridge University
HUBBARD, H., RAND Corp.
HUEBNER, W. F., Los Alamos Scientific Laboratory
HURT, J. T., Texas A. & M. University
IBEN, I., JR., California Institute of Technology
INGERSON, T. E., University of Colorado
INMAN, C. L., Institute for Space Studies
ISRAEL, W., University of Alberta, Edmonton, Canada
JACKSON, A., North Texas State University
JANIS, A. I., University of Pittsburgh
JÄRNEFELT, G., Astronomical Observatory, Helsinki
JEFFERYS, W., III, Yale University
JENNINGS, MAJ. C. S., AFOSR
JOHNSON, F. S., Southwest Center for Advanced Studies
JONAH, F. C., Ling-Temco-Vought, Inc.
JORDAN, P., Hamburg University, Germany
JOST, R., ETH, Zurich
JUST, K., University of Arizona
KANTOWSKI, R., University of Texas
KAUFMAN, M., Harvard College Observatory
KERNZ, G. S., Socony Mobil Oil Co.
KERR, R. P., University of Texas

KIEHN, R. M., University of Houston
KIPPENHAHN, R., Max-Planck Institute, Munich, Germany
KISSEL, K. E., Aerospace Research Laboratories
KLARMANN, J., Washington University
KOMAR, A., Yeshiva University
KRISTIAN, J., University of Texas
KUNDT, W., Hamburg University, Germany
KUNZ, K. S., New Mexico State University
LEIBACHER, J. W., Harvard College Observatory
LEQUEUX, J., Observatoire de Meudon, France
LIMBER, D. N., Yerkes Observatory
LINDQUIST, R. W., Adelphi University
LIVIO, G., University of Rome, Rome, Italy
LOCKENVITZ, A., University of Texas
LODHI, M. A. K., Texas Technological College
LUDAWECKI, S. M., Texas Woman's University
LUYTEN, W. J., University of Minnesota
LYNCH, R. H., University of Oklahoma
LYNDS, R., Kitt Peak National Observatory
LYTTLETON, R. A., St. John's College, Cambridge
McCREA, W. H., University of London
McDERMOTT, E., Southwest Center for Advanced Studies
McMILLEN, J. M., Socony Mobil Oil Co., Inc.
McNALLY, D., Yerkes Observatory
McVITTIE, G. C., University of Illinois Observatory
MALTBY, P., Institute of Theoretical Astrophysics, University of Oslo
MARSHALL, B. J., Arlington State College
MARSHALL, L. C., Southwest Center for Advanced Studies
MARX, G., Institute for Theoretical Physics, University of Budapest
MAST, C. B., University of Notre Dame
MATTHEWS, T. A., California Institute of Technology
MAVRIDES, S., Institute Henri Poincaré, Paris
MAXFIELD, J. R., JR., University of Texas Southwestern Medical School
MAXWELL, A., Harvard University, Fort Davis Station
MAYALL, N. U., Kitt Peak National Observatory
MEDLIN, W. L., Socony Mobil Oil Co.
MELVIN, M. A., Florida State University
MERCIER, A., University of Bern, Switzerland
METZNER, A. W. K., San Diego State College
MICHEL, F. C., Rice University
MICHIE, R. W., Kitt Peak National Observatory
MIELNIK, B., National Polytechnic Institute, Mexico, D.F.
MINKOWSKI, R., University of California, Berkeley
MISNER, C. W., University of Maryland
MISRA, M., University of Texas
MOFFAT, A. T., California Institute of Technology
MOFFAT, J. W., Research Institute for Advanced Studies
MOORE, E., University of Arizona
MORGAN, T., Syracuse University
MORGAN, W. W., Yerkes Observatory
MORRISON, P., Cornell University
MOSELEY, H. M., Texas Christian University
MURPHY, J. J., Department of Defense
NARLIKAR, J. V., King's College, Cambridge
NARUMI, H., University of Oklahoma
NE'EMAN, Y., California Institute of Technology

NEWMAN, E. T., University of Pittsburgh
NEY, E. P., University of Minnesota
NEYMAN, J., University of California, Berkeley
NOONAN, T. W., University of North Carolina
OETKING, P., Southwest Center for Advanced Studies
OLSEN, K. H., Los Alamos Scientific Laboratory
OPPENHEIMER, F., University of Colorado
OPPENHEIMER, J. R., Institute for Advanced Study
OZSVATH, I., Southwest Center for Advanced Studies
PAGE, T. L., Van Vleck Observatory, Wesleyan University
PANDRES, D., JR., Lockheed
PAPAPETROU, A., Institute Henri Poincaré, Paris
PEEBLES, P. J., Princeton University
PENROSE, R., University of Texas
PERES, A., Technion, Haifa, Israel
PISHMISH, P., Observatorio Astronómico Nacional, University of Mexico
PLASS, G., Southwest Center for Advanced Studies
PLEBANSKI, J., National Polytechnic Institute, Mexico, D.F.
PLILER, D. R., North Texas State University
PORTER, J. R., University of Texas
PRIESTER, W., Goddard Institute for Space Studies (NASA)
PROUSE, E. J., University of Texas
RAO, U. R., Southwest Center for Advanced Studies
RASTALL, P., University of Texas
RAYCHAUDHURI, A. K., Presidency College, Calcutta
REED, C. K., AFOSR
RESTER, D. H., Ling-Temco-Vought, Inc.
RICKER, N., University of Oklahoma
RINDLER, W., Southwest Center for Advanced Studies
ROBINSON, I., Southwest Center for Advanced Studies
ROBINSON, L. V., Wright-Patterson Air Force Base
ROEDER, R. C., Queen's University, Kingston, Ontario, Canada
ROGERS, H., University of Texas
ROSEN, N., Technion, Haifa, Israel
ROXBURGH, I. W., King's College, University of London
RUBIN, V. C., University of California, La Jolla
RUDERMAN, M. A., New York University
RUEHLE, N. H., Socony Mobil Oil Co.
SACHS, R. K., University of Texas
SADEH, D., Israel Atomic Energy Commission Laboratories, Yavne, Israel
SALPETER, E., Cornell University
SAMARAS, D. G., AFOSR
SCHEUER, P. A. G., Cavendish Laboratory, Cambridge
SCHIFF, L. I., Stanford University
SCHILD, A., University of Texas
SCHLOSSER, J. A., University of Texas
SCHLUTER, H. W., University of Texas
SCHMIDT, M., California Institute of Technology
SCHÜCKING, E. L., University of Texas
SCHWARTZ, M., Adelphi University
SCHWARTZ, R. A., Goddard Institute of Space Studies (NASA)

SCHWARZSCHILD, M. Princeton University Observatory
SCIAMA, D. W., Jet Propulsion Laboratory, California Institute of Technology
SCOTT, E. L., University of California, Berkeley
S. E. BAHH, L., University of Oklahoma
SERSIC, J. L., Cordoba Observatory, Argentina
SHAKESHAFT, J. R., University of Maryland
SHIVANANDAN, K., U.S. Naval Research Laboratory
SILBERBERG, R., U.S. Naval Resarch Laboratory
SIMKIN, S., Washburn Observatory, University of Wisconsin
SMITH, H. J., University of Texas
SPIEGEL, E. A., New York University
STACHEL, J., University of Pittsburgh
STETSON, R. F., AFOSR
STRECKER, J. L., General Dynamics Corp.
STRELZOFF, J. A., Michigan State University
SYBERT, J. R., North Texas State University
TAKENO, H., Hiroshima University
TANGHERLINI, F. R., Duke University and Army Research Office
TAUB, A. H., University of Illinois
TAUBER, G. E., Western Reserve University
TEAL, G. K., Texas Instruments, Inc.
TERLETSKY, YA. P., Moscow University
THOMAS, H. C., Texas Technological College
THOMAS, L. H., Watson Laboratory, Columbia University
THOMAS, P. D., North Texas State University
THOMPSON, A. H., University of Pittsburgh
THOMPSON, A. R., Stanford University
THORNE, K. S., Princeton University
TINSLEY, B. A., Southwest Center for Advanced Studies
TINSLEY, B. M., Southwest Center for Advanced Studies
TITTLE, C. W., Southern Methodist University
TRÜMPER, M., Yeshiva University
UREY, H. C., University of California, La Jolla
VALI, V., Boeing Scientific Research Laboratories
VANDEKERKHOVE, E., Royal Observatory, Uccle, Belgium
VAUCOULEURS, G. DE, DR. AND MRS., University of Texas
WADEL, L. B., Southwest Center for Advanced Studies
WAGONER, R., Stanford University
WAITE, J. M., Socony Mobil Oil Co.
WEBER, J., University of Maryland
WEIDEMANN, V., Federal Institute of Physics and Technology, Braunschweig
WEINBERG, J., Western Reserve University
WEINSTEIN, D. H., University of Houston
WHALEN, J. W., Socony Mobil Oil Co.
WHEELER, J., Princeton University
WHITNEY, B. S., University of Oklahoma
WILLIAMS, D. R., University of California, Berkeley
WILLIAMS, G., University of Florida
WINDHAM, P. M., North Texas State University
WOOD, L. A., AFOSR
WRIGHT, J. P., University of Wisconsin
ZUND, J., Southwest Center for Advanced Studies
ZUND, J. D., University of Texas